Y0-BST-123

RADICALISM IN ISLAM

Resurgence and Ramifications

Nirode Mohanty

WITHDRAWN
UTSA Libraries

University Press of America,® Inc.
Lanham · Boulder · New York · Toronto · Plymouth, UK

Copyright © 2012 by
University Press of America,® Inc.
4501 Forbes Boulevard
Suite 200
Lanham, Maryland 20706
UPA Acquisitions Department (301) 459-3366

Estover Road
Plymouth PL6 7PY
United Kingdom

All rights reserved
Printed in the United States of America
British Library Cataloging in Publication Information Available

Library of Congress Control Number: 2011938135
ISBN: 978-0-7618-5733-4 (paperback : alk. paper)
eISBN: 978-0-7618-5734-1

™
⊖∞ The paper used in this publication meets the minimum
requirements of American National Standard for Information
Sciences—Permanence of Paper for Printed Library Materials,
ANSI Z39.48-1992

Library
University of Texas
at San Antonio

In memory of

my mother Sabitri and father Chakradhar

* * * * *

May everyone enjoy happiness and joy,
May everyone enjoy good health,
May everyone see and realize goodness around them,
May no one suffer from pain and misery.

—Adi Shankara (788–820)

Contents

Figures

Tables

Preface

With the demise of the Soviet Union in 1991, the Cold War ended and the Communist threat was gone. Ten years later, a bigger, much more dangerous and deadly threat—terrorism—shook and shocked the world, when the World Trade Center in New York City and the Pentagon in Washington, D.C. were attacked. These attacks, carried out by 19 terrorists who hijacked 4 American planes on September 11, 2001, killed 2,974 people and marked the beginning of a string of deadly acts. On December 5, 2002, a nightclub frequented by tourists in Bali, Indonesia, was bombed, killing 202 people. On May 12, 2003, suicide bombings resulted in the deaths of 51 in Riyadh, 12 in the Marriot Hotel in Jakarta, and 25 in synagogues in Istanbul. The following year, on March 11, 2004, 202 people were killed in Madrid. In London on July 7, 2005, 3 bombs went off simultaneously in subway trains and a fourth on a bus, killing a total of 52 people. On February 22, 2006, the ancient, gold-domed Al Askari mosque in Samarra—situated 78 miles from Baghdad and one of the holiest shrine in Islam—was struck by suicide bombers using an improvised explosive device (IED). On December 20, 2007, the former prime minister of Pakistan, Mrs. Benazir Bhutto, was killed along with 20 others in a gun and bomb attack at Rawalpindi, a military garrison town. On November 26, 2008, 173 people were killed in more than 10 coordinated shooting and bombing attacks across Mumbai (Bombay), India's financial capital and its largest city. On March 27, 2009, at least 48 people were killed when a suicide bomber detonated explosives during Friday prayers at the Jamrud mosque in the Khyber region of northwest Pakistan. On March 30, 2009, in a chillingly methodical attack, gunmen in police uniforms stormed a police-training center in the eastern city of Lahore, Pakistan, reportedly killing up to two dozen recruits.

Every one of these attacks was carried out by Muslim radicals, militant warriors, and jihadists (holy warriors, wager of jihad, holy war) fighting for the worldwide establishment of Islamic rule. Additionally, almost all of the victims were Muslims, with the exception of those who perished in the

September 11th attacks in the United States, and the November 2008 attacks in Mumbai.

Is Islam a religion of peace, love, and tolerance or one of violence, hatred, intolerance, and barbarism? Is Islam unfairly blamed for terrorism? And who are these militants? This book answers these and other questions, and provides a much-needed perspective on the heated discussions of terrorism and Islam. It corrects biases, challenges the partisan analyses featured in several post-2001 books (including the practice of selectively quoting from the Quranic verses), and updates the discourse to include the evolving dynamics of our twenty-first century world and the diversity of terrorism's operational methods using digital technologies. This book is addressed to global jihadists who believe in paradise under the shadow of swords, and in waging terror to establish a worldwide Islamic caliphate around the world. More importantly, it is addressed to those who wish to understand regional jihadists such as the Islamic Jihad, Hamas, the Islamic Salvation Front, the Armed Islamic Group and their ilk in countries including Lebanon, Palestine, and Algeria.

The Quran (Koran) forbids a good Muslim to kill all unbelievers, be they *Kefirs* (infidels) or takfirs (Muslim apostate). Yet Islamic militants, who claim to be holy warriors, are defaming Islam by redefining the spiritual concept of holy war to align it with violent jihads and suicide attacks. They are destroying pluralism, secularism, and democracy as they seek to forcibly spread *Sharia* Islamic law. These hardened militants, trained in the Islamic schools known as *madrassa, dini madras,* or *madrasis*, are often well-educated young engineers and computer scientists who are indoctrinated in the madrassas. They are equipped with assault rifles, Global Positioning System (GPS) navigators, BlackBerry™ phones loaded with switchable SIM cards, Google Earth maps, Research in Motion(RIM), text messaging, and VoIP applications to pinpoint their targets. They constitute less than one percent of the one billion or more Muslims worldwide, but they have the ability to destabilize and destroy the world with their violent extremism. These new breeds of rabidly radical military terrorists are the product of several thousand radical religious schools, the *Quami madrassas*, which are located across Asia and financed by petrodollars. It is a pity that these misguided and mindless killers are willing to commit suicide to achieve the following goals: to counter perceived threats to Islam, to spread Islam, or to regain the Islamic empires of ages past.

President George W. Bush declared a War on Terror on October 7, 2001, and promised that the United States would show resolve against terrorists' threats just as it had against Communism. While some have called this a war on the global jihadist insurgency and some Muslim organizations in America and Britain have alleged that the "war on terror" was a war on Islam, a crusade exclusively directed against Muslims. Yet no one wants to declare Muslims are the enemy, not just for diplomatic reasons or by way of political correctness, but because the majority of Muslims view these terrorist attacks as un-Islamic. The real enemies are Islamic extremists, the militant jihadists, "Islamo-fascists," and holy warriors who engage in unholy wars. September 11, 2001 (9/11) changed many things in the United States. These changes included the creation of a new Department of Homeland Security, and an overhaul of intelligence, security and communication agencies, which were augmented with new systems of distributed communications and data mining as well as means of data fusion and signal processing that had never been used before. Airport and other travel security have become much more rigorous and complicated due to the threat of the holy militants potentially hiding bombs in shoes, baby bottles, bags, and cameras. Additionally, cyber terrorism now has the potential to paralyze information and intelligence infrastructures.

Some of the more liberal Muslim intellectuals believe that the surge in the number of militants is a result of the colonization of Islamic lands, forcible modernization, and prevailing underdevelopment and illiteracy. But nothing—neither religious oppression, economic compulsion, humiliation, loss of empire, ethics, nor religious beliefs—justifies the killing, kidnapping, and hijacking of innocent people. Jihadists are not fighting for the clash of cultures, and their movement is neither against imperialism nor against military dictators. They are merely fighting for violent ideas. "Not just the methods" of Islamism must be confronted, said former British Prime Minister Tony Blair, after the suicide bombing in London on July 7, 2005, "but the ideas" (BBC News). Radical militants are prisoners of ideological blindness and obscurantism. In the face of the resurgence of radical Islam, the world's anxiety is real.

This book expounds upon the sensitive and frightening topic of radical Islam and puts the problem in proper perspective by using analytical methods to derive empirical results. It will make an important contribution to the existing discourse on religious fundamentalism and terrorism. The causes of Islamic terrorism, the resurgence of radicalism, the global jihad of Osama bin Laden, and the synergy between terrorism and new technologies (including deadly threats to the environment, and the vulnerability of information systems and weapons of mass destruction) will be examined, while mitigation strategies will be proposed.

The subject of the resurgence and rejuvenation of holy militants and jihadists is vast and covers many disciplines, including economics, education, and international relations. Its modern-day surge touches on secularism and religion, international relations and law, science, and technology. Its scope is such that many universities now offer undergraduate and advanced degree programs in the study of terrorism. This book may be used as a text for these courses.

Chapter 1 reviews attacks by Islamic militants, also known as the Islamic insurgency, and discusses the present threats to world peace and stability, with views from Islamic scholars. Chapter 2 examines the causes of terrorism from various perspectives. Chapter 3 deals with radical Islam and its main organizations. Much of Asia, home to the majority of Muslims, is rife with tension, turmoil and insurgency, and as discussed in this chapter, radical Islam has found soft targets in Central, South, and Southeast Asia. Chapter 4 deals with radicalization and deradicalization as a non-violent component of counter-terrorism, and includes a discussion of the resurgence of radical Islam in Africa, Central Asia, South Asia, Southeast Asia, and Europe. Terrorists can cause colossal damage using chemical and biological weapons, which are now easy to obtain, and may take advantage of recent scientific and technical advancements in the manufacture of WMDs. This topic will be covered in Chapter 5. Chapter 6 discusses mitigation schemes for terrorism, including counter-terrorism, counterinsurgency, and other methods. Finally, in the Epilogue, we review the current status of terrorism and how the saga of holy to unholy war has unfolded. There are five appendices: Appendix 1 lists terrorist attacks and terrorist groups, Appendix 2 deals with the United Nations, Appendix 3 features a glossary, Appendix 4 outlines some Quranic verses and Islamic sects, and Appendix 5 provides a list of the abbreviations used throughout this book.

Sources including newspapers, journals, websites, and books have been used throughout; the author is not responsible for their veracity. Nonetheless, I apologize for any and all errors.

The world is facing severe economic recession, unemployment, and the widespread failure of banks. Unprecedented global warming is intensifying, the sea level is rising, and carbon dioxide is approaching life-threatening levels. HIV and other diseases are not yet controlled. Drug trafficking is still strong. Yet far greater than any of these threats is the peril of Islamic terrorism. It is time to dispel the myths and misconceptions about radical Islam. I thank Lindsay Macdonald of the University Press of America for her editorial assistance. Without the help of Julie Kirsch, Vice President of University Press of America, and Dorothy Albritton of Majestic Wordsmith, the book would not have been published. I appreciate the kind permission of Professor Marc Shaw of The School of Public Health, James Cook University, Townsville, Australia, and the Medical Director for WORLDWISE Travellers Health & Vaccination Centres—NZ for including the burqa figures inside and in the cover page and of Kartik Suri of Maps of World for figures of Asia and Africa.

Chapter 1

Worldwide Terrorism—An Introduction

We make war that we may live in peace.
—*Aristotle*

Seek peace, and pursue it.
—*Psalms 34:14*

Our world faces many threats, including but not limited to a deteriorating environment, killer diseases, poverty, illiteracy, and energy shortages. It is the threat posed by radical terrorists, however, that is perhaps the most dangerous and severe. Using conventional and unconventional weapons, these extremists are intent on spreading global jihad across the globe as retaliation for their perceived humiliation. The resurgence of radical Islamic movements driven by fundamentalists and holy militants, with their access to wealth and technology and support spanning the world, has led to a global network of terror. Underestimating or yielding to these extremists will result in formidable risks. This chapter will discuss the following:

1. The meaning of terrorism
2. Elementary definitions of jihad, and of fundamentalist, radical, and political Islam
3. The beginning of political Islam
4. Muslim intellectuals' views on radical Islam
5. The threat of weapons of mass destruction in the hands of jihadists
6. Multilateral and multinational approaches to combating terrorism

The resurgence of radical Islam, and the fear that Islamic terrorists and Islamic fundamentalism may trigger a third world war or nuclear annihilation has aroused worldwide anxiety. In 2005, the General Assembly of the United Nations adopted, by consensus, an International Convention for the Suppression of Acts of Nuclear Terrorism. This "Nuclear Terrorism Convention" addressed the unlawful possession or use of nuclear devices or materials by non-state actors.[1] Five years later, at a Nuclear Security Summit, U.S. President Barack Hussein Obama commented: "The single biggest threat to U.S. security, both short-term, medium-term and long-term, would be the possibility of a terrorist organization obtaining a nuclear weapon." Al Qaeda (AQ), he said, is "trying to secure a nuclear weapon—a weapon of mass destruction that they have no compunction about using."[2] His remarks underline the fact that the much-publicized War on Terror is a result of the very real threats posed by modern-day terrorism.

Back in the 1990s, Islamic terrorists were inspired by the success of the Islamic Revolution in Iran, which had embarrassed and humiliated America—a vaunted superpower—two decades earlier. Also heartening to them was the defeat in Afghanistan of another superpower, the Soviet Union, by Islamic *mujahedeen* (holy warriors). Since that time, the dynamics of international order have changed from multilateral to unilateral power. The demise of Communism has brought America, as the world's last superpower, to the forefront of the War on Terror. Another factor now in play is the explosion of technology and information now accessible via the Internet. Internet is an infrastructure of worldwide information systems via wired, wireless, microwave, cable communications systems. A worldwide seamless connected telephone, computer connection links to provide multiple access to billion users same time. The systems consists of millions of private, public, academic, business, and government networks, of local to global scope, that are linked by a broad array of electronic, satellite, and optical networking technologies. It is a brainchild of DARPA, Rand, and other agencies in 1960s for robust distributed communications.

With more than six billion people in disparate lands, the size and diversity of our globe is dwarfed by modern science, technology, and world organizations, as well as by universal communications and transportation systems. Instant access by anyone, including terrorists, to the means of receiving and transmitting information and imagery to any part of the world is available via satellite telephone, wireless technologies, BlackBerry[TM] phones loaded with switchable SIM (subscriber identity module) cards, Google Earth maps, VoIP (voice over Internet protocol) applications, satellite television, and navigational global positioning systems (GPS). Terrorists have covert access to these powerful technology systems, aided by hidden state and non-state funds. They regularly receive material support and training to pursue strategic goals, goals that include the ability to manufacture dirty bombs that can contaminate any city they choose. Whether its underlying ideology is political, environmental, ethical, or religious in nature, terrorism can occur in any place at any time: It is an international phenomenon.

While the majority of Muslims believe that the War on Terror is a war against Islam, most Muslims are not militants, terrorists or radicals. As former British Prime Minister Tony Blair has said,

> We know that these people act in the name of Islam but we also know that the vast and overwhelming majority of Muslims here and abroad are decent and law abiding people and abhor terrorism every bit as much we do.

So who are these terrorists, and why are they intent on inciting a holy war? Is the 1,400-year-old religion of Islam in and of itself the driving force? Many, including Muslims, may wonder why Christians, as a group, were not blamed when Timothy McVeigh bombed the Alfred P. Murrah Federal Building in Oklahoma City, killing 168 people? Why weren't Hindus blamed for the Tamil Tigers' assassination, by bombing, of the late Prime Minister Rajiv Gandhi of India, or Jews for the Yigal Amir assassination of Prime Minister Yitzhak Rabin? Why weren't Buddhists blamed for the Aum Shinrikyo killing of 12 people in the Tokyo subway systems using sarin nerve gas, or the white race for Ku Klux Klan attacks on Black churches in America?

The May 3, 2010 arrest of 30-year-old Faisal Shahzad, a naturalized U.S. citizen from Pakistan, for an alleged attempt to set off a bomb in Manhattan, has spurred debates about how he might be categorized. Was he a home-grown lone wolf, a member of the lesser jihad (*al-jihad al-ashgar*), or were his alleged actions a jihad of the sword (*jihad al-sayf*) that suggest terrorist links with al Qaeda (AQ), linking him to the greater jihad (*al-jihad al-akbar*)? Shahzad admitted that he attempted to detonate the bombs, which included weapons of mass destruction (WMD), and it is known that he was in Pakistan last year for several months to learn bomb making. There have been more than 20 Islamist terrorist attacks in America since 9/11, and more than 10, 000 terrorist attacks by various groups around the globe. Theodore Kaczynski, the "Unabomber," who killed 3 people and wounded 23 others; Eric Rudolph, who set off bombs at several abortion clinics; and Timothy McVeigh, the Oklahoma City bomber, are not linked to any terrorist organizations. In light of all this, is it fair for Muslims to claim that Islam is unfairly treated, while such offenses are ignored in people of other religions?

Definitions and Development

Terrorism: Title 18 of the U.S. Code, the statuary law of the United States, Section 2331, defines international terrorism as constituted by activities that:

1. are dangerous to human life, as a violation of criminal laws of the United States,
2. are intended to intimidate or coerce a civilian population and to affect the conduct of a government by mass destruction or kidnapping, and
3. occur outside the United States (are committed by non-state actors). (U.S. Code 18 (1992) § 2331)[3]

(a) The Federal Bureau of Investigation (FBI) defines terrorism as, "the unlawful use of force or violence against persons or property to intimidate or coerce a government, the civilian population, or any segment thereof, in furtherance of political or social objectives." The FBI further describes terrorism as either domestic or international, depending on the origin, base, and objectives of the terrorist organization. Per their definition:

- Domestic terrorism involves groups or individuals who are based and operate entirely within the United States and Puerto Rico without foreign direction and whose acts are directed at elements of the U.S. government or population.
- International terrorism is the unlawful use of force or violence committed by a group or individual, who has some connection to a foreign power or whose activities transcend national boundaries, against persons or property, to intimidate or coerce a government, the civilian population, or any segment thereof, in furtherance of political or social objectives.[4]

(b) The United States Department of State, in April 2004, provided the definition of terrorism as contained in Title 22 of the United States Code, Section 2656f(d). That statute contains the following definitions: The term terrorism means premeditated, politically motivated violence perpetrated against noncombatant targets by sub-national groups or clandestine agents, usually intended to influence an audience. The term international terrorism means terrorism involving citizens of more than one country. The term terrorist group means any group practicing, or that has significant sub-groups that practice, international terrorism. The U.S. Government has employed this definition of terrorism for statistical and analytical purposes since 1983.[5]

(c) The National Counterterrorism Center (NCTC) applies the definition of "terrorism" that appears in the 22 U.S.C., § 2656f (d) (2): "premeditated, politically motivated violence, perpetrated against non-combatant targets by sub-national groups or clandestine agents."[6]

It seems that the U.S. State Department has extended the scope of terrorism to include combatant targets including military personnel, organizations, installments, and bases.

(d) The UN Security Council Resolution 1566 on October 8, 2004, defined terrorism as follows below. The definition of terror was remarkable in that, for the first time, it seemed to provide an inclusive ban on all forms of violence that intentionally targets civilians, regardless of the motive. Paragraph 3 states:

> Recalls that criminal acts, including against civilians, committed with the intent to cause death or serious bodily injury, or taking of hostages, with the purpose to provoke a state of terror in the general public or in a group of persons or particular persons, intimidate a population or compel a government or an international organization to do or to abstain from doing any act, and all other acts which constitute offences within the scope of and as defined in the international conventions and protocols relating to terrorism, are under no circumstances justifiable by considerations of a political, philosophical, ideological, racial, ethnic, religious or other similar nature, and calls upon all States to prevent such acts and, if not prevented, to ensure that such acts are punished by penalties consistent with their grave nature.

These definitions illustrate that there is no unanimity regarding the meaning of terrorism. In fact, some countries might call terrorists freedom fighters, because at times, their violent acts have been committed in order to liberate occupied regions. Yet there are more than one hundred countries that were established without violent means. There are democratic, diplomatic, and constitutional methods, including United Nations arbitration, to liberate regions that are illegally occupied by another state. The UN Forum on Crime and Society (Volume 4, Numbers 1 and 2, December 2004) reports:

> Without attempting a comprehensive definition of terrorism, it would be useful to delineate some broad characteristics of the phenomenon. Terrorism is, in most cases, essentially a political act. It is meant to inflict dra-

matic and deadly injury on civilians and to create an atmosphere of fear, generally for a political or ideological (whether secular or religious) purpose. Terrorism is a criminal act, but it is more than mere criminality.[7]

Terrorism may be defined as the use of violence, threats, intimidation, or coercion, including hostage taking, hijacking, killing or torturing civilians, bombing public and civilian facilities such as places of worship, air, bus, and rail terminals, and utilities, destroying and burning public institutions, sabotage, or subversion. It may be done to achieve political, religious, military, or ideological objectives, or to settle grievances or injustices, as well to retaliate on grounds of race, religion, ethnicity, or nationality, or as a means of revolting against oppression by despotic rulers.

Islam means "submission to God." According to *The Encyclopedia Britannica*, Islam is:

> [A] major world religion belonging to the Semitic family; it was promulgated by the Prophet Muhammad in the 7th century AD. The Arabic term *Islam*, literally "surrender," illuminates the fundamental religious idea of Islam—that the believer (called a Muslim) accepts "surrender to the will of Allah (in Arabic: God)." Allah is viewed as the sole God—creator, sustainer, and restorer of the world. The will of Allah, to which man must submit, is made known through the sacred scriptures, the Quran (Qur'an, Koran), which Allah revealed to his messenger, Muhammad. In Islam, Muhammad is considered the last of a series of prophets (including Adam, Noah, Abraham, Moses, Jesus, and others), and his message simultaneously consummates and completes the "revelations" attributed to the earlier prophets.

Islamism is a radical political ideology that promotes Islam in all of society. Radical Islamists, supporter of Islamic fundamentalism, want to establish Islamic society by violence, and by killing all those who are against their cause though some are non-violent. *Dar al-Harb*, "house of war," is the Islamic term for that part of the world not yet subject to Islam. Islamists want to forcibly convert and capture *Dar al-Harb*, turning it into *Dar al-Islam*, the "house of Islam." Islamism is an Islamic revivalist movement, often characterized by moral conservatism, literalism, and the attempt to implement Islamic values in all spheres of life. Terrorists are practitioners of Islamism, modeled on the attempt to recapture Muhammad's early role of rebel in Mecca. Radical Islamists can be society-centered or state-centered in the pursuit of Islamic justice. Radical Islamists' approach is violent, and they believe that waging armed struggle against unbelievers (*jihad bi-al-sayf*, i.e., "jihad of the sword") is the only path to victory over the forces of *kuffars* and *takfirs* (infidels and Muslim apostates), as well as *dhimmis* (non-Moslems living under Islamic sovereignty). Often, they are called Islamist militants. These violent acts are not a mode of struggle, but a social, moral, and political aberration. The causes, conditions or circumstances of these violent approaches to the struggle for freedom, the avenging of injustices, or proselytizing through suicide attacks, are not self-sacrifice, scripture sanctioned, or holy.

Islamophobia is an exaggerated, usually inexplicable and illogical fear of Islam.

Islamofascism is fascism with an Islamic face. Understandably, most Muslims consider it an insult when their religion is labeled as fascist.

Political Islam is the propagation of and reform of Islam by political means, not necessarily by violence.[8]

Radical Islam is promoted by those who follow radical versions of the Quran, and who want to implement orthodox Islam by violence and bloodshed, not by any political, constitutional, or democratic processes.

Militants are those who, while espousing radical Islam, have not joined terrorist organizations or radical groups and are not involved in terrorism. For example, Germany now has 29 militant Islamist organizations, with an estimated 36,000 members in 2009. Terrorists (some prefer to be called militants) and militants have the support of the community and organizational networks.

Jihad is holy war. The central meaning of greater jihad (*jihad akbar*) was originally the inner struggle to live a spiritual life according to the Quran, the *sunna* (habits), and *Hadith* (sayings of the Prophet, holy teachings). Military conflict was considered a lesser *jihad* (*jihad asqar*, or violent jihad). Jihad can be either spiritual or violent. According to Douglas Streusand, "in hadith collections, jihad means armed action; for example, the 199 references to jihad in the most standard collection of hadith, Sahih al-Bukhari, all assume that jihad means warfare."[9] Jihadists are following the doctrine *"al-wala wal Bara* ('of *Love and Hate for Allah's Sake'*), one of the most important beliefs of Islam after *Tawhid*, unity, as a part of their holy duty and as a part of 'social movement' to destroy the world of Allah's enemy."

A *jihadist* or *jihadi* is a person involved in jihad. An alternate word is *mujahid*; the plural is *mujahideen*. Most Muslims see the spiritual jihad, jihad bil-nafs, as the greater jihad. On the other hand, there also is the concept of *jihad bil sayf*, literally "jihad by the sword," or violent jihad: which was traditionally viewed as a lesser jihad. Violent jihad, whether by war, insurgency, or terrorism, has become an increasingly popular tool for extremist organizations that maintain violent jihad is the only jihad.[10]

Insurgency is an armed rebellion against a constituted government recognized by the United Nations, through the use of sabotage, subversion, and armed conflict. An insurgent is a participant in the insurgency. Guerrillas are the overt military aspect of the insurgency. Guerrillas are part of the insurgency and overlap with terrorists and militants, while terrorists and insurgents also overlap in their mission. Militant may refer to members of armed militias, which have a variety of agendas. For example, in Afghanistan, the United States is fighting militants. But in Iraq, America is fighting insurgents. The relationship is shown in Figure 1.1.

Figure 1.1. Relationships among Terrorists, Insurgents, Militants, and Guerrillas

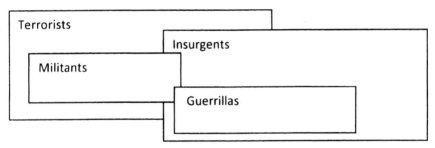

They are all violent. Terrorists pursue theological–religious goals and target both combatants and noncombatants, while insurgents seek political agendas and do not target noncombatants. War is the widespread use of physical power and resources, between two sovereign states, by means of their military. Because non-state agencies or individuals instigate terrorism, terrorism cannot be classified as war.

Three weeks after hijacked planes plowed into the World Trade Center and the Pentagon, a car bomb exploded outside the state legislature in Srinagar, Kashmir. The attacks on American soil, which killed thousands, were almost universally blamed on *terrorists*. The attack in Kashmir, which left more than two dozen dead, was widely reported as a strike by *Muslim militants*. On September 1, 2004, thirty armed men and two women wearing explosive belts seized the Russian schoolhouse at Beslan, taking children hostage as they demanded the withdrawal of Russian troops from Chechnya. More than 350 adults and children were killed in a gun battle between these armed men and Russian troops. The siege was widely blamed on separatist Chechen rebels.

However violent or atrocious it may be, terrorism remains a matter of perspective: one man's terrorist is another man's freedom fighter. For example, Pakistan's President Asif Ali Zardari calls the Muslim insurgents in the Kashmir Valley terrorists while former President Pervez Musharraf calls them freedom fighters. And terrorist attacks in South Asia get little attention in the Western media. Terrorism provokes hatred, spreads fear, and causes death and destruction. If terrorism is considered a politico–religious system in terms of System Engineering Modeling, then the inputs are illiteracy, poverty, prejudice, religious fundamentalism, politics, and grievances (see Chapter 2). The output or responses consist of some measurable parameters and some non-measurable parameters (see Figure 1.2). The output, on the right from the Target/ Environment box, is OMNP—output measurable and non-measurable parameters. In the input box, on the left, * denotes factors that can be political, economic, unemployment and poverty, social, religious education, mosques' teaching of hatred, and lack of education, cultural, or historical. Some of the input parameters can be psychological. The arrow in the right facing down, just crossing the output on the right, is a possible disturbance in the output. The feedback from the output is subtracted (-) from the input, in the left, to the Target/Environment box.

Figure 1.2. Terrorism Systems

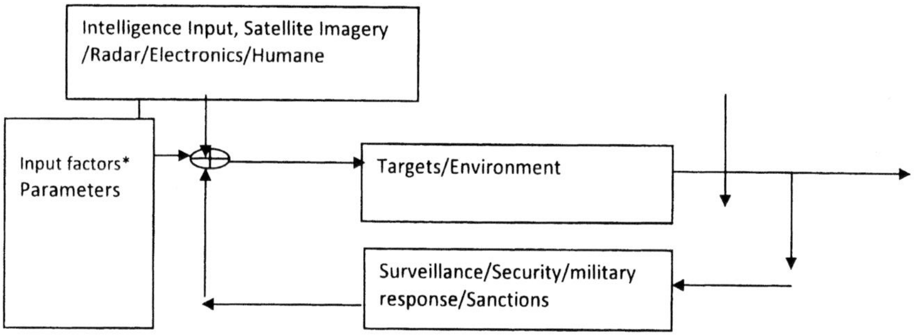

Some of these measurable parameters (consequences) are material damage, destruction, death, economic insecurity, loss of freedom, threats to internal security, and erosion of civil liberties. Some non-measurable parameters are fear, unrest, underground financing, militancy, political turmoil, episodic violence, abnormal psychological behavior, and inter-state relations. One of the intentions of terrorists is to influence a wide audience and to have a major impact on economic and political changes. With this in mind, some feedback elements could include surveillance with smart sensors, increased security, public relations, possible mitigation techniques, and punishment. An intelligence input from satellites or human intelligence could be seen as a preemptive strike. The war on terror, military actions, and economic sanctions are a feedback input to thwart the terrorists' goals.

Western targets may be seen as dynamic (i.e., changeable over time) systems. After 9/11, the measurable parameters were 11.3 billion dollars in damages and cleanup costs, and a death toll of approximately 3,650, including emergency workers and the passengers of United Airlines Flight 93. Nonetheless, the stock market remained resilient. The non-measurable psychological impact was negligible, except for a temporary increase in alcohol consumption of 25 per cent.

In Israel, where a large number of terrorist attacks occur, bus ridership and frequenting of coffee shops remains unchanged. This was also true in New York after 9/11 and in Mumbai, India after the November 2008 terrorist attacks. The political effects are measurable, but the correlation can go either way. It is premature to conclude that aid, development, and education can mitigate terrorism, that is, to control the output or produce the desired solution, because other input variables are complicated and difficult. Terrorism breeds hate crimes and more extremism, and these are a major concern to many countries. Terrorism has even impacted Muslim countries. The Pew Survey of 2006 found that 72 per cent of Americans are concerned about Islamic extremism, as are 74 per cent of Pakistanis and 82 per cent of Indians. Among European countries, the country most concerned about Islamic terrorism is Germany, with 82 per cent expressing this sentiment (see Figure 1.3). In 2008, the population of Germany was 82 million of which 5 per cent were Muslims.

Islamic Fundamentalists

Islamic fundamentalists believe that Muslims must return to the ways of the Prophet and his companions as they follow the Holy Quran, God's final message to mankind. They strictly adhere to the Quran, Sunnah, Sharia, and Hadith.[11] Radical Islamism (also known as militant Islam, political Islam, or Islamist movements),[12] is a political manifestation of Islamic fundamentalism and is associated with Muslim governments in various countries, including Saudi Arabia, Iran, and Sudan. But it has taken a violent course and a path of intolerance in some places.[13] According to Bassam Tibi,[14] author of *The Challenge of Fundamentalism: Political Islam and the New World Disorder* and a participant in the famous Fundamentalism Project at the University of Chicago, Islamic fundamentalism "strongly rejects (the) spirit of religious pluralism, dismissing it as a heresy threatening the neo-absolutist claim for the dominance of political Islam throughout the world. The Egyptian scholar Syed Qutb (see Chapter 3), the intellectual father of Islamic fundamentalism who inspired Osama bin Laden,[15] advocated an Islamic world order to replace the present one. He wrote:

Figure 1.3. Concern About Islamic Extremism

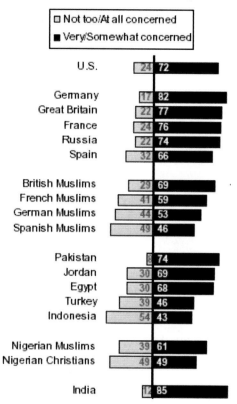

Concern About the Rise of Islamic Extremism in Your Country?

Legend:
- ☐ Not too/At all concerned
- ■ Very/Somewhat concerned

Country	Not too/At all concerned	Very/Somewhat concerned
U.S.	24	72
Germany	17	82
Great Britain	22	77
France	24	76
Russia	22	74
Spain	32	66
British Muslims	29	69
French Muslims	41	59
German Muslims	44	53
Spanish Muslims	49	46
Pakistan	8	74
Jordan	30	69
Egypt	30	68
Turkey	39	46
Indonesia	54	43
Nigerian Muslims	39	61
Nigerian Christians	49	49
India	12	85

* Source: 07.06.06: The Pew Global Attitudes Project

> Fundamentalism is not only an intellectual challenge; it is a challenge to security inasmuch as it proposes to topple the existing order. . . . The challenge [is] a very concrete one posed and practiced by . . . *jihad*-fighters willing to sacrifice their lives.

Tibi further asserts,

> There is a real challenge of fundamentalism as a threat that results in creating disorder. This challenge is not only posed to the West and to its civilization, but also to decent Muslims—men and women—who suffer the intolerance and totalitarian views and practices of the Islamists.[16]

The resurgence of holy militants and fundamentalist Islamists who engage in terrorism has been occurring at a formidable rate for the last three decades, and it is an inverted phenomenon. Their holy zeal to avenge themselves upon their enemies and to restore the glory of their lost golden age is escalating unbounded. They are determined to dump the democratic and secular world into the dustbin of history and to annihilate their foes. This is a real risk to mankind.

Modern Islamic fundamentalism was fathered by the Ayatollah Khomeini (1902–1989), a Shiite leader in Iran whose principles were based on the seventh century sacred book, the Quran, and on the life of the Prophet Muhammad. Shiites are known for their martyrdom, self-sacrifice, revolutionary drive, and insurrectionary movements. Khomeini was able to overthrow the pro-Western regime of Mohammad Reza Pahlavi who had ruled Iran for many years. Khomeini called it an "Iranian Revolution" and said that "we must strive to export our Revolution throughout the world." Revolutionary Guards took 66 American hostages at the U.S. Embassy at Teheran for several months. President Carter failed to rescue them. It is reported that Khomeini killed more dissidents during his first year of rule, in 1979, than the Shah had during his entire 25 years of repressive rule. Following the Ayatollah's declaration of revolution, various terrorist organizations sprang up. They included: the Hezbollah (Army of God) in Lebanon, which was involved in a suicide truck bombing of the U.S. Embassy and Marine barracks in Beirut, forcing the U.S. to pull out of Lebanon; the Islamic Jihad in Egypt, known as the Al-Gama'a Islamiya, which was responsible for bombing the World Trade Center in New York in 1993; several militants' organizations in Palestine, including the Abu Nidal Organization (ANO), the Palestine Liberal Front (PLF); and in Pakistan, Harakat ul Ansar, Harakat ul Mujahidin (HuM) and Lashkar-e-Taiba (LeT), and Jaish-e-Mohammed (JeM). Along with the nation of Iran, Muhammar al-Qaddafi of Libya has allegedly funded these terrorist organizations.

The resurgence of Islamists started in 1979, when the Soviets were defeated in Afghanistan with the help of the Taliban mujahedeen and was fomented by Osama Bin Laden in 1990s. This was done in cooperation with Saudi Arabia, organized by Pakistan's Inter Service Intelligence (ISI), and funded and equipped by the United States. (See Chapter 3 for further discussion of the Taliban and its Deobandi followers.) The success of these terrorist movements and their anti-Western ideologies germinated in the mind of Osama bin Laden, who belonged to the Wahhabi, a radical Islamic group. He issued a *fatwa* to commit terrorist acts against Jews and "Crusaders" on 9/11. OBL is now the most wanted man in the world, for originating the world's foremost terrorist organization, Al Qaeda (AQ), who are followers of Wahhabi, for creating a network of Islamic terrorists, and for setting up Islamic militant camps in Yemen, Sudan, Kenya, Pakistan, and Afghanistan.

The word terrorist is associated with the French phrase "*de la terreur,*" referring to the eighteenth-century French Revolution in which forty thousand people were executed as part of a political process of revolutionary change. Religious terrorism began in the Middle East with a tribe of religious fundamentalists called the Kharijites tribes whose goal it was to restore pristine Islam. Terrorists kidnap, take hostages, hijack, bomb, and loot. They kill civilians, noncombatants, and military personnel without discriminating among them. They rape non-Muslim girls and women. They burn houses, temples, institutions, and anything else they consider *haram* (prohibited by the faith), or un-Islamic. In short, they will harm anyone because of their religion, race, ethnicity, sectarian belief, or culture. For example, Christians, Buddhists, Jews, and Hindus are killed because of Islam's animosity towards unbelievers (*kuffar*), or against certain ethnic groups, as evidenced in the Philippines, Thailand, Chechnya, Germany, Israel, Palestine, Kashmir, and Sudan. Three million or more Bangladeshi Muslims were killed on the basis of their ethnicity by the Punjabi-Muslim-dominated Pakistani Army.

Shiite Muslims and Ahmadiyya Muslims are not considered true Muslims by Sunni Muslims. Sunnis and Shi'as kill each other in Pakistan, Iraq, and Lebanon because of sectarian differences. Muslim terrorists kill for the sake of religion, or as warriors of God. They chant "*Allahu Akbar,*" "God is great," before undertaking any such violence and belligerence. They do not believe in democracy, including the right to vote. Holy militants are also known as Muslim fundamentalists, Islamic radicals, Islamic fundamentalists, or political Islamists. When a holy militant becomes violent, then his goal is to become a *shaheed*, or martyr, by killing unbelievers. Jihadists have no place among nonviolent Islamists. Mahmood Mamdani, a former professor at Columbia University, describes political Islam and jihad:

> To be sure, one can trace several practices in political Islam—opium production, *madrassa* education, and the very notion of jihad—to the era before modern colonization. In fact, opium, *madrassa* education, and *al-jihad al-akbar* (the greater jihad) were all reshaped and remade within modern institutions as they were put in the service of a global American campaign against the "evil empire."[17]

Although the Muslim Brotherhood (MB, or *Ikhwanis*) of Egypt presents itself as a political party, and part of Political Islam, to gain the governance of Egypt by constitutional means, it has used violence and murders to spread radical Islam (see Chapter 3). Political Islam bears a close similarity with Islamism. The founder of Pakistan's *Jamaat-e-Islam (JI)*, Syed Maududi (aka Mawlana Mawdudi), has commented: "The belief in the unity (*tawhid*) and the sovereignty of Allah is the foundation of the social and moral system propounded by the Prophet. It is the very starting point of the Islamic political philosophy." Iran and Sudan exemplify Islamic radicalization in the guise of political Islam. Both these countries have been declared terrorist states by the United States. While Professor Mohammed Ayoob defines Islam as a political ideology rather than as a religious or theological construct. He writes:

> Most Islamists believe that if Muslims could return to the model of the imagined golden age of the early years of Islam they would be able to transform their relationship with the West into one of equality rather than subordination. The common denominator among Islamists, therefore, is the quest for dignity. Extremist groups, which arrogate to them the right to speak in the name of Islam, justify terrorism as the only way to overcome the asymmetry in power between "Muslims" and the "West." By promoting terrorism under a perverted definition of "jihad," extremists succeed in making political Islam appear monolithic and supremely dangerous in the eyes of the West.[18]

They do not seem to realize that the quest for dignity comes through a civilized, peaceful, humanistic, and enlightened approach. Dignity does not go hand in hand with demolishing other religions or another country's heritage. And Islamists' model of the imagined golden age would return to Sharia by military force, not by political force. This has not succeeded in the past, even in Muslim countries. Iran and Sudan exemplify Islamic radicalization in the guise of political Islam. Both these countries have been declared terrorist states by the United States.

Professor Khaled Abou El Fadl writes: "Islamic tradition does not have a notion of holy war. Jihad simply means to strive hard or struggle in the pursuit of a just cause."[19] The respected Pakistani journalist Ahmed Rashid writes:

> The greater jihadi explained by the Prophet Muhammad is first inward-seeking: it involves the effort of each Muslim to become a better human being, to struggle to improve him or herself. . . . Today's global jihadi movements, from the Taliban in Afghanistan to Osama Bin Laden's worldwide Al Qaeda to the Islamic Movement of Uzbekistan (IMU), ignore the greater jihad advocated by the Prophet and adopt the lesser jihad as a complete political and social philosophy.[20]

But the Quran in chapter 9 says that jihad is a holy war against the kafir and the infidel that must continue until they are wiped out (see Appendix 4).[21] Walter Laqeuer writes:

> Jihad is the sacred duty of every Muslim believer, that Jews and Christian should be killed, and this fight should continue until only Muslim religion is left. Adherents of all other major religions strive to improve themselves, for a just cause and for purification of body and soul by spiritual means, meditation, and prayers, not by violence. *Jihad* has been an institutional struggle to conquer, plunder, and loot from the early days of Islam.[22]

Suicide Terrorism

Terrorism is motivated by religious or political objectives. It is perpetrated by an individual or groups to inflict the maximum number of deaths and massive destruction on noncombatants, combatants, and on civilian or military targets. When terrorists commit these acts while taking their own lives, often using guns or explosives, this is known as suicide terrorism: the most virulent and horrible form of terrorism. From 2000 to 2004, there were 472 suicide attacks in 22 countries with more than 7000 deaths.[23] Their lethality is much higher than that of conventional terrorist attacks. Most of these attacks have been carried out by Muslim extremists. Suicide bombers are mujahedeen while alive and become martyrs after their deaths. These types of attacks have a long history: Suicide attacks were carried out by a twelfth-century Muslim sect that came to be known as Assassins.[24]

Suicide killings have taken place in almost all parts of the world, in every era, and have been perpetrated by almost all religious groups, age groups, cultures, and ethnicities, by males and females, in times of peace and war, and against combatants and noncombatants. On September 9, 2001, two days before the September 11 attacks in the United States, a Tajik Muslim, Ahmed Shah Massoud, the Opposition Leader in Afghanistan, was assassinated in Takhar Province of Afghanistan by a suspected AQ Pashtun, who posed as a journalist. It is believed by some Muslim fundamentalists that suicide deaths in the cause of Islam earn a place in Paradise.

In 1999, the Organization of Islamic Countries (OIC), a Jeddah, Saudi Arabia, -based group of 57 Muslim member states, from Africa, Central Asia, the Caucasus, the Balkans, Southeast Asia, South Asia and South America, adopted the OIC Convention on Combating International Terrorism. According to the Convention,

> Terrorism means any act of violence or threat thereof notwithstanding its motives or intentions perpetrated to carry out an individual or collective criminal plan with the aim of terrorizing people or threatening to harm them or imperiling their lives, honor, freedoms, security or rights or exposing the environment or any facility or public or private property to hazards or occupying or seizing them, or endangering a national resource, or international facilities, or threatening the stability, territorial integrity, political unity or sovereignty of independent States.[25]

President George W. Bush declared a war on terror in 2001. He faced a situation in which there are no enemy armies, and no negotiations, but hundreds of state or non-state actors who are conducting a proxy war on terror. The enemy consists of invisible brigades of would-be martyrs whose weapons are handguns, hand grenades, suicide jackets, gas masks, Kalashnikov automatic rifles, improvised explosive devices (IED), and even box cutters, shoes that conceal explosives, and bottles filled with hazardous liquids. They do not use, nor do they need, fighter jets, tanks, or missiles. However, the modern Islamic terrorists, aided by information and communications technology and driven toward at the desire of becoming a martyr, are winning the war or terror, defeating the American dream of human progress. But, according to the Pulitzer Prize winning American journalist Ron Suskind:

> Thomas Jefferson, in calling his newly founded country "the last hope of human liberty in this world," would say that the solution itself is America— the place where certain immutable principles will allow citizens to try to arrive at a common definition of human progress.[26]

Addressing a joint session of Congress on September 20, 2001, President Bush said:

They [terrorists] hate our freedoms: our freedom of religion, our freedom of speech, our freedom to vote and assemble and disagree with each other. . . . These terrorists kill not merely to end lives, but to disrupt and end a way of life. With every atrocity, they hope that America grows fearful, retreating from the world and forsaking our friends. They stand against us, because we stand in their way. We are not deceived by their pretenses to piety. We have seen that kind before. They are the heirs of all murderous ideologies of the twentieth century. By sacrificing human life to serve their radical visions—by abandoning every value except the will to power—they follow in the path of fascism, Nazism, and totalitarianism. . . . The enemy of America is not our many Muslim friends. It is not our many Arab friends. Our enemy is a radical network of terrorists. . . . Our war on terror begins with al Qaeda, but it does not end there. It will not end until every terrorist group of global reach has been found, stopped, and defeated.[27]

His successor, President Obama, echoed the idea that the enemy of America is not Islam. On April 6, 2009, in a speech before the Turkish Parliament in that nation's capital, Ankara, President Obama said,

The United States is not, and will never be, at war with Islam. In fact, our partnership with the Muslim world is critical not just in rolling back the violent ideologies that people of all faiths reject, but also to strengthen opportunity for its entire people. I also want to be clear that America's relationship with the Muslim community, the Muslim world, cannot, and will not, just be based upon opposition to terrorism.

Echoing his sentiments, Senator Joseph Lieberman believes that the United States is at war with violent Islamist extremism, and that the Obama administration does moderate Muslims no favor by refusing to recognize this.[28]

America has offered its support to Muslim countries for decades. American involvement and intervention in Bosnia and Kosovo has prevented the massacre of thousands of Muslims in Yugoslavia. Furthermore, America's second and third largest aid packages go to Turkey and Pakistan. Pakistan, moreover, will soon be the recipient of the highest amount of American aid, displacing Israel.

President Bush appointed the bipartisan 9/11 Commission to investigate terrorism in America, with Governor Thomas H. Kean and Congressman Lee H. Hamilton as the chairman and vice chairman, respectively. The commission's report addresses many topics, including intelligence gathering, counter-terrorism, and airport security. Kean and Hamilton wrote:

We face a rising tide of radicalization and rage in the Muslim world—a trend to which our own actions have contributed. The enduring threat is not Osama Bin Laden but young Muslims with no jobs and no hope, who are angry with their own governments and increasingly, see the United States as an enemy of Islam.[29]

On September 9, 2007, then-Defense Secretary Donald H. Rumsfeld famously asked his advisers: "Are we capturing, killing or deterring and dissuading more terrorists every day than the madrassas (madrasi) and the radical clerics are recruiting, training and deploying against us?" The answer is no. U.S. foreign policy has not stemmed the rising tide of extremism in the Muslim world. In July 2004, the 9/11 commission recommended putting foreign policy at the center of counter-terrorism efforts and warned that it was imperative to eliminate terrorist sanctuaries in Afghanistan and Pakistan. The Obama Administration has been using armed drone aircraft to eliminate the terrorists' sanctuaries in Pakistan.[30] It can be observed that the 9/11 attacks showed a massive failure of communications, command, control, computers and intelligence (C[4]I) and surveillance, particularly intelligence gathering and data fusion from several sources and implementations. A report led by former Commissioners Kean and Hamilton released on September 10, 2010, found that terrorism is increasingly taking on an American cast, reflected in the growth of homegrown threats and the movement of terrorists recruited from the United States to areas like the Horn of Africa and Yemen. In 2009 there were 10 U.S.-linked jihadi attacks, plots, or incidents involving individuals traveling outside the country to receive terrorist training, and at least 43 American citizens or legal residents were charged or convicted in terrorism cases in the United States and elsewhere.[31]

In examining the backgrounds of terrorists involved in the September 11, 2001 attacks on America, or in London on July 7, 2005, it becomes evident that these jihadist holy warriors are neither poor nor uneducated. "Terrorism is not caused by poverty. . . . Indeed, many terrorists come from relatively well-off families."[32] The mentors of these terrorists include the multimillionaire OBL and his deputy Ayman al-Zawahiri (AAZ), a well-established Egyptian physician.

Terrorists, Guerrillas, and Freedom Fighters

According to the Executive Dean of the Radcliffe Institute for Advanced Study at Harvard, Louise Richardson, there are some subtle differences in the definition of terrorists, guerillas, and freedom fighters.

It goes without saying that in the very messy worlds of violence and politics, actions don't always fit neatly into categories. Guerrillas occasionally target civilians, and terrorists occasionally target security forces. But if the primary tactic of an organization is deliberately to target civilians, it deserves to be called a terrorist group, irrespective of the political context in which it operates or the legitimacy of the goals it seeks to achieve. There are, of course, other differences between guerillas and terrorists. Guerrillas are an irregular army fighting the regular forces of the state. They conduct themselves along military lines and generally have large numbers of adherents, which permit them to launch quasi-military operations. Their goal is the military defeat of the enemy. Terrorists, by contrast, rarely have illusions about their ability to inflict military defeat on the enemy. Rather, they seek either to cause the enemy to overreact and thereby permit them to recruit large numbers of followers so that they can launch a guerrilla campaign, or to have such a psychological or economic impact on the enemy that it will withdraw of its own accord. Osama Bin Laden called this the "bleed-until-bankruptcy" plan.[33]

According to Professor John Esposito,

During much of the 1980s, for example, for many Western observers, someone who placed a bomb in a market in Kabul (against Soviets) was a legitimate freedom fighter or opponent of aggression, while someone who placed a bomb in a market in Algiers, Beirut, or Cairo was a fanatic terrorist.[34]

AQ and the Taliban jihadists believed that the Afghan war (1979–1990) was won by the mujahedeen, and that having crushed the Soviet power, they would try to win against the remaining power: the West. In doing so, they would convert the non-Muslim world to Islam. OBL considers jihad a holy war, and feels it is a Muslim's duty to fight against the Crusaders, as the Quran 5:33 commands: "Those that make war against God and His apostle and spread disorder in the land shall be put to death or crucified or have their hands and feet cut off on alternate sides, or be banished from the country." The Crusades (1096–1270) have been over for more than 700 years, while the 1400-year-old jihad, dating from 638 A.D., is still going strong. Domination by Quranic law, from one end of the earth to the other, is the goal of this war of conquest, in direct opposition to the values and goals of the Christian world. Prophet Muhammad is quoted as saying that the sword is the key to Heaven and Hell,[35] while six hundred years earlier, Jesus said that "Those who live by the sword shall perish by the sword."

Since 1998, suicide attacks have been significant. There have been more than 7800 deaths in 894 attacks in more than 25 locations, including Afghanistan, Iraq, Sinai, Jordan, Bali, Indonesia, and London. These attacks cannot be blamed on foreign occupation of Muslim lands or deprivation and destitute conditions in these places. Yet Muslims claim that suicide bombings, kidnappings, blowing up airplanes and buses, killing by stoning, or any other terrorist acts by these modern jihadists are un-Islamic. A pernicious state of denial exists through the traditional Islamic claim of rejecting categorically any truck with terrorism and proclaiming that it is a religion of peace, plurality, and tolerance. It is claimed that Islam also rejects suicide bombing unless there is a threat to Islam. However, most suicide bombings have been carried out by Islamist jihadists.[36] World history and current events illustrate how Islam has polarized humanity, cultivated a culture of violence and atrocities, and has remained a bastion of intolerance. In September 2006, Pope Benedict XVI delivered a scholarly lecture at the University of Regensburg in Germany. He said:

> In the seventh conversation . . . the emperor touches on the theme of the holy war. . . . He addresses his interlocutor with a startling brusqueness on the central question about the relationship between religion and violence in general, saying: "Show me just what Muhammad brought that was new, and there you will find things only evil and inhuman, such as his command to spread by the sword the faith he preached."[37]

Pope Benedict's call for inter-religious dialogues, interfaith harmony, the abolition of religious schisms, and for the spread of universality in humanity was misunderstood. His comments caused an uproar in Europe and in the Muslim world. There were violent protests, and the nation of Morocco recalled its ambassador from the Vatican. Several churches were burned around the world and in Somalia an Italian nurse was killed. On the other hand, many church personalities and Western politicians want to infuse into their own societies the Islamic values of respecting elders, caring for family, refraining from promiscuity, oneness with God, and emphasizing spirituality over materialistic life, which were prevalent in Eastern religions and societies before the advent of Islam. The infusion of Islam into Christianity has yielded strange, unholy results, though there are several thousand converts to Islam in Germany, Italy, and elsewhere in Europe, and in America every year. These converts have included the Belgian Catholic Lionel Dumont, another Belgian, Muriel Degauque, and Britain's Germaine Lindsay, all of whom became violent terrorists, ending their own lives and killing others. Additionally, many other Muslim converts have been involved in terrorist attacks throughout the past decade.

The French scholar Olivier Roy states,

Islamism is the brand of modern political Islamic fundamentalism which claims to recreate a true Islamic society, not simply by imposing Sharia, or Islamic law, but by first establishing an Islamic state through political action. Islamists see Islam not as a mere religion, but as a political ideology, which should be integrated into all aspects of society (politics, law, economy, social justice, foreign policy, etc.). The traditional idea of Islam as an all-encompassing religion is extended to the complexity of modern society.[38]

The distinguished historian Niall Ferguson wrote:

But "Islamism" was a militantly political movement with an anti-Western political ideology that had the potential to spread throughout the Islamic world, and even beyond it. Ironically, the United States had a hand in its spread. . . . The greatest of all the strengths of radical Islam, however, is that it has demography on its side.[39]

The European Union is ignoring a demographic time bomb: its Muslim population has more than doubled in the past 30 years and is likely to be doubled again by 2015. It is projected that in 2025, the world will be 25% Christian and 30% Muslim.

Deaths due to Islamic fundamentalists have been reported in the NCTC Report on Terrorist Incidents, 2006–2008.[40] Methods of fatality incidents, fatalities by region, primary methods, and injuries by weapons in attacks in 2006–2008 are listed in Tables 1.1, 1.2, and 1.3. Table 1.4 shows deaths due to terrorists, with Islamic terrorists heading the list. Table 1.5 shows deaths in Iraq and deaths excluding those in Iraq from 2005 to 2008. Table 1.6 shows a comparison of attacks and victims by region.

In Iraq, deaths have gone down significantly but they have gone up in other parts of the world. In terms of total terrorist attacks, deaths have decreased, but they are still higher than in 2005. Total deaths due to terrorists from 1995 to 2008 number 80,094. It can be noted that there are more civilian deaths than deaths in other categories. This is the terrorists' intent, as a way to establish their political objective and wreak revenge. The large number of deaths in Iraq is caused by the war, while India is the biggest victim of terrorism. India is one of the most terrorism-afflicted countries in the world. The U.S. State Department's 2007 *Country Report on Terrorism*, released in April 2008, states that terrorists, separatists, and extremists killed more than 2,300 people in India in 2007. As one of the world's most ethnically, linguistically, and religiously diverse countries, India has dealt with numerous separatist and insurgent movements over the past 30 years, including a Sikh uprising in the state of Punjab in the 1980s, a Muslim

Table 1.1
Terrorist Attack Statistics in 2006/2008:
Methods Used in Fatality Incident

Armed attacks	46%
Bombing	31%
Suicide	10%
Kidnapping	4%
Arson	3%
Others	6%

Table 1.2
Terrorist Attack Statistics in 2006/2008:
Fatalities by Region

Total Death	15,756
Africa	2987
East Asia and Pacific	762
Europe and Eurasia	292
Near East	5528
South Asia	5826
Western Hemisphere	370

Table 1.3
Terrorist Attack Statistics in 2006/2008:
Injuries by Weapons (per cent)

Improvised Explosive Device, IED	33
Explosive	20
Vehicle	17
Firearm	10
Mortar	7
Rocket	4
Grenade	3
Primitive	1
Land Mines	1
Others	4

Table 1.4
Terrorist Attack Statistics in 2006/2008:
Death by Perpetrator Categories

Total Deaths	15765
Islamist	8284
Unknown	3721
Secular/Political	2513
Christian Extremist	932
Others	906

Table 1.5
Terrorist Attack Statistics in 2006/2008: Deaths from 2005 to 2008

	Excluding Iraq	**In Iraq only**	**Total**
2005	6138	8242	14380
2006	7123	13345	20468
2007	8902	13606	22508
2008	10749	5016	15765

Total death in 2005-2008	73121
Death from 1995-2003 (3547 in 2001)	6973
Total from1995-2008	80094

Table 1.6
Comparison of Attacks and Victims by Region

Region	Dead	Wounded	Hostage	Attacks
Africa	2987	3918	1002	718
Europe +				
Eurasia +				
Western Hemisphere	662	1586	259	1126
Near East	5526	15820	849	4594
East Asia	762	1573	277	978
South Asia	5828	11227	2477	4354
Total	15765	—	—	11770

separatist movement in the state of Jammu and Kashmir from 1979 to the present, and various ethnic separatist movements in the northeastern states. Another challenge facing the Indian government is a leftist extremist movement (Maoist and Naxalite) that is spreading in the rural areas of eastern and central India.[41] It is alleged that the Sikh uprising in Punjab and the Leftist extremist movement in North East India were instigated and abetted by neighboring countries to destabilize India.

The mastermind of the 9/11 terrorists attacks was Osama bin Laden (OBL), a multimillionaire businessman from Saudi Arabia. He has had several businesses in Saudi Arabia and is related to the Saudi Royal family. This fundamentalist rebel was the seventeenth son of his wealthy father's fifty-two sons and daughters. He is opposed to the American presence in his state, home to the two great holy sites of Mecca and Medina (Yathrib), Jerusalem being the third. OBL hates America because with American help, Israel defeated Arab countries in 1948, 1967, and 1972. He waged *jihad,* or holy war, against the Soviet Union in Afghanistan during the 1980s, and to date, he has assembled thousands of mujahedeen, or holy warriors, from more than 35 countries around the world. With the help of Saudi Arabia, Pakistan, and the United States, OBL led his holy warriors in defeating the Communist superpower in Afghanistan.

Three decades earlier, in 1952, Syed Qutb—the leading intellectual of Egypt—had used jihad to unite Arabs in establishing a nation based on Islam, overthrowing the pro-Western government in Egypt.[42] With this in mind, OBL financed his own organization, AQ, along with several militant organizations in the Middle East. These included the Algerian terrorist group, Armed Islamic Group (Algeria Islamists, a.k.a. *Groupe Islamique Armé,* or *al-Jama'ah al-Islamiyah al-Musallaha*, GIA), which was involved in several bombings in Paris in 1995. The U.S. military housing complex in Dharan, Saudi Arabia, was bombed in 1996 by OBL's associates. In 1998, he was involved in terrorist killings in Kenya and Tanzania, and also had a hand in the attack on the USS Cole in Aden, Yemen in 2000. Finally in 2001, he directed several jihadists to hijack four American planes and commit terrorist attacks in America. Leaving behind his multimillion-dollar wealth, he has gone into hiding, mostly likely in the caves of the hinterlands of Afghanistan or Pakistan. It is reported that he is suffering from severe liver disease without any proper medical care. Still, he is the most popular leader of the world's one billion Muslims, having defeated the Soviet Empire and humbled the mighty American power. OBL's goal is establishing *Sharia* all over the world by way of *jihad, to* defeat Western culture and values. Some people say he is dead, but his death could be the catalyst for thousands more OBLs. His threats in the name of God cannot be brushed aside. Whether or not there is a God, whether or not Crusaders enacted similar violence in the name of religion, or were responsible for worse massacres, plunders and looting, the present dangers of *jihad* require serious deliberation. The solution is neither a preemptive strike on terrorist bases nor unilateral diplomatic action, since those have been proven counterproductive. Since a militant *jihad* is a global phenomenon, a global strategy is prudent. This is a religious war, causing destabilization and destruction of world peace and prosperity; it requires a concerted effort on the part of all countries, with the involvement of the United Nations (UN). The UN has done a great deal of peacekeeping and sheltering of political and religious refugees, and is also engaged in economic deployment and democratic order while preserving universal human rights (see Appendix 2). No organization or state is allowed to impede UN efforts on the pretext of defending religion. It is essential that China and Russia cooperate in this effort for their national interest.

The noted security experts Daniel Benjamin and Gabriel Weimann believe that

> the radicals see themselves as gaining ground in their effort to convince other Muslims around the world that jihad is a religiously required military obligation. And the American presence in the region is making the case for fulfilling this obligation all the more powerful.[43]

OBL's AQ movement was aligned with the terrorist organizations of al-Tawhid w'al Jihad, which were founded by the late Abu Musab Zarqawi of Jordan (1966–2006). OBL has said that he wants to spread their version of Islam from the two rivers in Iraq, the Euphrates and the Tigris, to all the river basins of the world—to the Mississippi (America), to the Volga (Russia), to the Ganges (India), and to the Amazon in South America and beyond.

Two formerly secular Muslim countries, Lebanon and Iraq, are now led by non-secular governments, while Turkey is governed by a religious party. The Taliban, a radical Islamic organization affiliated with AQ, is residing in the borders of Afghanistan and Pakistan. Its top leaders are also hiding with AQ leaders in this remote and desolate terrain. The region provides a sanctuary for Islamist terrorists, and as such it is an imminent threat to the world. The Taliban are against women's education and employment in the region; in the past, they have even burned down girls' schools. In 1980–1989, America worked closely with Pakistan's General Zia-ul Haq against the Soviet occupation of Afghanistan. This was followed by nine years (1990–1998) of punishing Pakistan with all manner of sanctions for its secret nuclear weapons development. Next came twelve years (1999–2010) spent working with General Pervez Musharraf and others to position Pakistan as "a major non-NATO ally" and enlist its support against al Qaeda and the Taliban. While America went to war to oust the Taliban in 2001, the Obama Administration is negotiating with less extreme members of the Taliban to form a stable government in Afghanistan.

According to a National Intelligence Estimate (NIE) report:

> Al Qaeda is and will remain the most serious terrorist threat to the (U.S.) Homeland, as its central leadership continues to plan high-impact plots, while pushing others in extremist Sunni communities to mimic its efforts and to supplement its capabilities. We assess the group has protected or regenerated key elements of its Homeland attack capability, including: a safe haven in the Pakistan Federally Administered Tribal Areas (FATA), operational lieutenants and its top leadership. . . . We assess that Al Qaeda will continue to enhance its capabilities to attack the Homeland through greater cooperation with regional terrorist groups. Of note, we assess that AQ will probably seek to leverage the contacts and capabilities of Al Qaeda in Iraq (AQI), its most visible and capable affiliate and the only one known to have expressed a desire to attack the Homeland. In addition, we assess that its association with the AQI helps AQ to energize the broader Sunni extremist community, raise resources, and to recruit and indoctrinate operatives, including for Homeland attacks. We assess that Al Qaeda's Homeland plotting is likely to continue to focus on prominent political, economic, and infrastructure targets with the goal of producing mass casualties, visually dramatic destruction, significant economic aftershocks, and/or fear among the U.S. population. The group is proficient with conventional small arms and improvised explosive devices, and is innovative in creating new capabilities and overcoming security obstacles. We assess that Al Qaeda will continue to try to acquire and employ chemical, biological, radiological, or nuclear material in attacks and would not hesitate to use them if it develops what it deems are sufficient capability.[44]

These views are shared by other security experts, including Eliza Manningham-Buller, Director General of the British Security Service. Professor Bruce Hoffman, Director of the Security Studies Program at Georgetown University's Edmund A. Walsh School of Foreign Service in Washington, D.C., says,

> Al Qaeda is much like a shark, which must keep moving forward, no matter how slowly or incrementally, or die. Al Qaeda must constantly adapt and adjust to its enemies' efforts to stymie its plans while simultaneously identifying new targets.

Al Qaeda has become a great danger with or without its central leadership. It has spread worldwide, but terrorism is a double-edged sword that also destroys its protector and patron, as it is hurting Pakistan in FATA.

Moderate Muslims, *Takfir* (apostate Muslims), *Dhimmis (Zimmis)*, and *kafir* (infidels) are threatened by these holy warriors, who derive inspiration from this verse: "God revealed His will to the angels, saying: 'I shall be with you. Give courage to the believers. I shall cast terror into the hearts of the infidels. Strike off their heads, strike off the very tips of their fingers."[46] (Quran 8:12, Appendix 4). There are a total of 164 verses on jihad or military expedition in the Quran.[47] Dr. Syed al Sharif Fadl of AQ's Jihad Council has reportedly cautioned Muslims that: "I say to Muslims in all candor that secular, nationalist democracy opposes your religion and your doctrine, and in submitting to it you leave God's book behind."[48] The noted journalist Lawrence Wright believes that

> When one looks for hopeful parallels for the end of Al Qaeda, it is discouraging to realize that its leadership is intact, its sanctuaries are unthreatened, and the social conditions that gave rise to the movement are largely unchanged. On the other hand, Al-Qaeda has nothing to show for its efforts except blood and grief. The organization was constructed from rotten intellectual bits and pieces—false readings of religion and history— cleverly and deviously fitted together to give the appearance of reason. Even if (Dr) Fadl's rhetoric strikes some readers as questionable, Al-Qaeda's sophistry is rudely displayed for everyone to see. Although it will likely continue as a terrorist group, who could still take it seriously as a philosophy?[49]

Terrorism is a mode of virulent violence that obtains political objectives by employing murder, extortionist kidnapping, arson, remotely detonated explosions, suicide bombings, aerial bombing of civilians, and premeditated, belligerent subversion. It is always a blatant, brutal criminal act. In the recent history of the independence movement of Algeria (1954–1962), the *Front de Liberation Nationale* (FLN) murdered over 28,000 Muslims and kidnapped over 50,000 non-Muslims. Even if it was an anti-colonialist movement against the French, it was terrorism. When citizens are revolting against a state, some analysts call it a guerilla war. However, the freedom movement by Mahatma Gandhi in India, the civil rights movement by Martin Luther King in the United States, and the anti-apartheid movement of Nelson Mandela, *inter alia,* were nonviolent. The insane mass killing of civilians by Bolsheviks in Russia's Leninist revolution, and by the Maoist marauders in China or India to dominate a territory and change its laws is terrorism. States use aggressive insurgency against other states as a strategy, and this is terrorism, not holy war. Terrorism is both totalitarian and immoral. If freedom fighters use destructive actions such as sabotage or killing, they are terrorists. Ariel Merari lists the differences between guerrilla war and terrorism in Table 1.7.[50]

Table 1.7
Guerrilla War and Terrorism (Partial and Modified)

Features	**Guerrilla war**	**Terrorism**
Size	Medium-platoons, companies, battalions	Small
Weapons	Light weapons, artillery	Guns, grenades, car bombs, remote control bombs, Barometric pressure bombs, etc.
Tactics	Commando-type	Kidnapping, assassination, car bombing, hijacking, Hostage taking, robbery, fake currency, etc.
Targets	Military and civilian infrastructure	political opponents, state apparatus
Uniform	often wear	none
Control of territory	Yes	Sometime
War zones	Limited to the country in strife	none, carried out worldwide
Support	Unauthorized State Parties	State and non-State actors

Provocations by terrorists are designed to elicit state response and international condemnation, as well as recognition and aid. The Palestinians received such recognition, with the Palestine Liberation Organization (PLO) opening offices in Europe and elsewhere; in addition, the PLO was given UN Observer status. Other separatists' organizations are struggling to achieve a similar status. The Kurdistan Workers' Party (aka Parti Karkerani Kurdistan, PKK) is a Kurdish separatist organization that engages in armed struggle against Turkey, Syria, Iraq, and Iran for the goal of creating an independent Kurdistan. The Baluchistan Liberation army (also Baloch Liberation Army, BLA) is a Baloch nationalist militant secessionist organization that wishes to establish an independent state of Baluchistan. They are reportedly discriminated against in Pakistan and Iran.

Intellectuals with Sympathetic Views

Reform in Islam started 120 years ago with Egypt's grand mufti, Muhammad Abduh, and his student, Ali Abdul Raziq. It was followed by Morocco's Abdou Filali-Ansary and Iran's Abdul Karim Soroush, among others, who infused Islam's spirituality with the importance of the individual, rather than the state. The Georgetown University Professor Daniel Brumberg noted:

> The Islamic modernists' approach pivots around the basic idea that it is both possible and vital to distinguish between the timeless, core values of Islam and the way such norms are interpreted to address the evolving political, legal, social, and economic needs of each generation. Values such as tolerance, justice, equality, and moderation are identified from a comprehensive or holistic reading of the Quran, rather than from any particular line or paragraph. Islamic modernists argue that a literalist reading of any injunction in the Quran can be deeply antagonistic to Islam because that interpretation conflates the Quran's ageless ideals with the time-specific tasks that Muhammad faced.[51]

In this wise, it became a problem for liberal thinkers to endure the wrath of the autocratic regimes. There are a few liberal Islamic scholars in this category, including Kuwait's Khaled Abou El-Fadl, professor of jurisprudence at the University of California, Los Angeles, Egypt's Nasr Abu Zaid, who currently resides in Amsterdam, and Sudan's Abdullahi An-Naim, professor of law at Emory University. The late Professor Fazlur Rahman of Pakistan, who taught at the University of Chicago, also fit into this category.

The Emory University Professor Abdullahi An-Naim defines a secular state as "one that is neutral regarding religious doctrine," and endorses the fact that Sharia cannot be codified as state law. His premise is as follows:

Muslims everywhere, whether minorities or majorities, are bound to observe Sharia as a matter of religious obligation, and this can be best achieved
when the state is neutral regarding all religious doctrines and does not
claim to enforce Sharia principles as a state policy or legislation.[52]

This implies that the state cannot interfere in Muslim inheritance, or in
Sharia-sanctioned punishments such as stoning, or in divorce laws. It means
that Muslims will have separate Sharia law in secular countries. Abdullahi
An-Naim claims that Sharia is necessary for legitimizing and implementing
the principles and institutions of constitutionalism, human rights, and citizenship in Islamic societies. But this rule cannot be enforced by Muslims
who live by the state laws wherever they live. His suggestion is an infringe-
ment of the secular laws of a country, including its judiciary and administration. It is the author's opinion that citizens should be governed by one law
irrespective of their religion. Recently, the Bangladesh High Court rejected
the Sharia law of stoning, among other Sharia practices.

Many Muslim intellectuals are critical of the media coverage of Islam,
which they perceive to be unfair, and do not see radical Islam as posing a
threat. The Muslim scholar Tariq Ali, author of fifty books, is against imperialism, capitalism and Communism. He opined that the decline of Islamic
civilization is due to a combination of capitalism, imperialism, its defeat in
World War I, and failure to assimilate to modern development. He blames
9/11 on American imperialism and its occupation of the environs of Saudi
Arabia. He excoriated the cartoons of the Prophet Muhammad that were
published in the Danish newspaper *Jyllands-Posten* in September of 2005.
These twelve editorial cartoons of the Prophet Muhammad were reprinted
in several newspapers in more than fifty countries. They prompted severe,
violent protests by Muslims worldwide, resulting in more than 100 deaths,
fires being set in the Danish Embassies in Syria, Lebanon, and Iran, and the
storming of European-owned buildings in several places. Tariq Ali writes:

> *Jyllands-Posten* published the cartoons in bad faith. Their aim was not to
> engage in debate but to provoke, and they succeeded. The same newspa-
> per declined to print caricatures of Jesus. I am an atheist and do not know
> the meaning of the "religious pain" that is felt by believers of every cast
> when what they believe in is insulted. . . . But the cartoon depicting
> Muhammad as a terrorist is a crude racist stereotype.[53]

Biology is not taught in most Muslim countries, because of Islamic
inhibitions of un-Islamic creations. The separation of the state and religion,
as it pertains to state-run schools, is a major issue in Islam. Ali comments:

Biology can't be taught in many Muslim countries, because to teach it means you give people other ideas. When I was growing up, the one subject we were not taught, even in those missionary schools, was biology. So in the end, is it really this inability to separate religion from the state in the Islamic world that is the key problem? Or is the problem of the Muslim world's relation to the Western empire more important? It's a combination of both. The critique, therefore, has to be a dual critique, both of the empire, but also of the failure of these regimes in [the Islamic] world to sort out their own problems. You can't blame everything, after all, on Western intervention.

Ali calls the abuses at Abu Ghraib the result of a misplaced clash of civilizations and cultures:

Cultures and civilizations are now, and have always been, hybrids. To suggest otherwise is to fall prey to the twin devils of ideology and chauvinism. The tragedy of the abuses at Abu Ghraib is that they created a clash of civilizations where no such clash had existed. Through its own myopia, the West has given radical Islam the ammunition it was thirsting for.[54]

Ali appears uncritical of intolerance or harsh punishment in Islam, but Abu Ghraib happened after 9/11, and has nothing to do with religion, except the fact that the prisoners are Muslims. Ali was also appreciative of the Taliban in his several lectures, and differed with the views expressed in Huntington's (1997) *The Clash of Civilizations*.

The great scholar of Islam, Tariq Ramadan, is a second generation Egyptian and author of several books, including *Footsteps of the Prophet: Lessons from the Life of Muhammad*. He comments on multiculturalism as follows:

The growing Muslim presence in Europe has become a central issue for all European countries, east and west. The numerous debates that have been breaking out across the continent about "multiculturalism," "secularity," or even "identity" are almost always connected to this "Islamic" factor. This link is not necessarily bigoted, because there is a fundamental relationship between "values" and "laws" on the one hand, and "culture" and "diversity" on the other. Indeed, more than a debate over "Islam" and the "Muslims," Europe needs a serious dialogue with itself over this relationship, for it is facing a crisis. The right question to ask is this: can Europe remain consistent with its own values (democracy, equality, justice, respect) and at the same time tolerate and accommodate new citizens from different backgrounds and religions? Or, to put it differently, are Europeans intellectually, linguistically, and culturally equipped to face the challenge of marrying equality with an ever more diverse European citizenry? The starting point here is actually clear: governments should not confuse socioeconomic problems (unemployment, violence, marginalization and so on) with questions about culture and religion.[55]

Swiss-born Professor Tariq Ramadan asserts that in Europe, he favors multiculturalism and secularity to protect ethnic identity. He believes in pluralistic, democratic societies and regards pluralism and diversity as unavoidable facts.[56] Yet he supports Sharia law, which overrides secularism, democracy, and pluralism, and cannot condemn stoning adulterers. He cites the fact that the Prophet Muhammad commanded his followers to jihad and qital (armed resistance), in view of the Quraysh tribes' imminent threat to Medina and their polytheism. His new interpretation of the Quran emphasizes resistance and reform: "All the forms of jihad are, as can be seen, linked to the notion of resistance. On the level of qital (armed fighting), it is so as well."[57] When returning from the Hunayn expedition (a battle in 630), the Prophet had declared, "We are back from the lesser jihad—effort, resistance, and struggle for reform—to greater jihad." A companion asked: "What is greater jihad, Messenger of God?" He answered: "It is fighting the self (the ego)." Ramadan publicly rejects violence, and urges change through the democratic process, but even as he denounces terrorism he reiterates its basic logic. His condemnation of intentional attacks on civilians is tempered by an innocuous-seeming suggestion: that they will cease when European, American, and Israeli foreign policies bend to the terrorists' underlying demands. He draws a connection between what he considers to be the errant ways of Western foreign policy and the terrorist acts it supposedly engenders. Could enthusiastic young crowds drawn to Ramadan's charismatic public lectures understand this as the tacit approbation of these acts? By "explaining" the attacks, he declines to denounce them as incomprehensible; he keeps the door open to future justifications of violence against civilians on religious and political grounds. He says this about the London train bombings:

> You cannot accept that people disagree and then they kill, you must condemn this. But in the discussion afterwards, you cannot say there is no connection. On ethical grounds, it's wrong. On political grounds, there is a connection.[58]

The noted journalist Christopher Caldwell observes that resistance is the key to Ramadan's writing.

Resistance is what one offers against a system that has no legitimacy whatsoever behind it. The French *reformed* their constitutional order in 1958; they *resisted* the Nazis after 1942. . . . Contemporary Europeans, unable to conceive of themselves as thoroughly without legitimacy in anyone's eyes, have chosen to believe that when Ramadan speaks of "resistance," he calls on Muslims everywhere to wage it, he really means "reform." He does not. He means jihad.[59]

Ramadan believes in both the inner and outer views of jihad—moral, spiritual struggle and Islamic holy war. He is a grandson of Hassan al Banna—founder of the Muslim Brotherhood (MB) of Egypt, who was considered to be one of the most radical Islamic thinkers. The *Wall Street Journal* of August 19, 2009, in an opinion piece, described him as follows:

Mr. Ramadan, who has managed to impress a predominantly leftist audience with his eloquent talk of a "European Islam," likes to talk about democracy and following the rule of law—but only as long as the law doesn't contradict an Islamic principle. He rejects terrorism and violence but thinks that blowing up eight-year-old Israeli children is "contextually explicable." Ramadan is not a literalist, not a Wahhabi traditionalist, but a non-violent Islamist. Though not a reformist, he considers Sharia as a personal moral code for Islamic faith, not the law of the land.[60]

The late Edward Said, a Palestine-born professor at Columbia University and the author of *Orientalism*, wrote a piece about the War on Terror for the *Observer* special edition in 2001. In the *Observer* Said (an Arab Christian), wrote:

What is bad about all terror is when it is attached to religious and political abstractions and reductive myths that keep veering away from history and sense. This is where the secular consciousness has to try to make itself felt, whether in the U.S. or in the Middle East. No cause, no God, no abstract idea can justify the mass slaughter of innocents, most particularly when only a small group of people are in charge of such actions and feel themselves to represent the cause without having a real mandate to do so. . . . The trouble with religious or moral fundamentalists is that today their primitive ideas of revolution and resistance, including a willingness to kill and be killed, seem all too easily attached to technological sophistication and what appear to be gratifying acts of horrifying retaliation. The New York and Washington suicide bombers seem to have been middle-class, educated men, and not poor refugees. Instead of getting a wise leadership that stresses education, mass mobilization and patient organization in the service of a cause, the poor and the desperate are often conned into the magical thinking and quick bloody solutions that such appalling models provide, wrapped in lying religious claptrap. . . . Demonization of the other is not a sufficient basis for any kind of decent politics, certainly not now when the roots of terror in injustice can be addressed, and the terrorists isolated, deterred or put out of business. It takes patience and education, but is more worth the investment than still greater levels of large-scale violence and suffering.

As to the clash of civilizations, Said remarked:

> The sense of Islam as a threatening other—with Muslims depicted as fanatical, violent, lustful, irrational—develops during the colonial period in what I called Orientalism. The study of the other has a lot to do with the control and dominance of Europe and the West generally in the Islamic world and it has persisted because it's based very, very deeply in religious roots, where Islam is seen as a kind of competitor of Christianity.[61]

Said, who is not only a moderate but a pacifist intellectual, believes that Islamic religious intolerance has its roots in injustices, and has emerged from a long dialectic of U.S. involvement in the affairs of the Islamic world, the oil-producing world, the Arab world, and the Middle East, areas that are considered to be essential to U.S. interests and security. He ponders: "How many of us, for example, have openly and honestly stood for secular politics and have condemned the use of religion in the Islamic world as we have denounced Judaism, Christianity and the West?"[62]

The UCLA Professor Khalid Abu El-Fadl, a Kuwait born scholar, says of Sharia:

> Shari'ah law, according to Muslim jurists, fulfills the criteria of justice and legitimacy and binds governed and governor alike . . . the caliphate system was considered superior to any other . . . [and] that Shari'ah is a complete moral code that prescribes for every eventuality. In asserting the supremacy of Sharia, Muslim scholars typically were arguing that its positive commandments, such as punishment for adultery or the drinking of alcohol, ought to be honored by the government. Sharia, as a whole, with all its schools and variant points of view, remains the Way and Law of God.

On prohibitions, El-Fadl writes:

> Muslim jurists contended that the prohibition of murder in Islamic law served the basic value of life, the law of apostasy protected religion, the prohibition of intoxicants protected the intellect, the prohibition of fornication and adultery protected lineage, and the right of compensation protected the right to property.[63]

The Quran states: "As to the thief, male or female, cut off *(faqta'u)* their hands as a recompense for that which they committed, a punishment from God and God is all-powerful and all-wise" (Quran 5:38). Although the legal import of the verse seems to be clear, it requires at minimum that human agents struggle with the meaning of "thief," "cut off," "hands," and "recompense."

El-Fadl says of democracy:

> A case for democracy presented from within Islam must accept the idea of God's sovereignty: it cannot substitute popular sovereignty for divine sovereignty, but must instead show how popular sovereignty—with its idea that citizens have rights and a correlative responsibility to pursue justice with mercy—expresses God's authority, properly understood. Similarly, it cannot reject the idea that God's law is given prior to human action, but must show how democratic lawmaking respects that priority.[64]

El-Fadl is of the opinion that Sharia is a complete divine law, that its sovereignty should override that of the democratic government's sovereignty, and that Sharia's prohibitions should also be regarded as sacrosanct. Modern jihadists have combined the goals of revenge, restoration, and revival of Islam, as noted by El-Fadl:

> The September 11 attacks aimed to strike at the symbols of Western civilization and to challenge its perceived hegemony, in the hope of empowering and reinvigorating Islamic civilization. . . . While national liberation movements—such as the Palestinian or Algerian resistance—resorted to guerrilla or non-conventional warfare, modern-day terrorism of the variety promoted by Osama Bin Laden is rooted in a different ideological paradigm. There is little doubt that organizations such as the Jihad, Al-Qaeda, Hizb al-Tahrir and Jama'at al-Muslim were influenced by national liberation and anti-colonialist ideologies, but they have anchored themselves in a theology that can be described as puritan, supremacist and thoroughly opportunistic. This theology is the byproduct of the emergence and eventual dominance of Wahhabism, Salafism and apologetic discourses in modern Islam. The predominant intellectual response to the challenge of modernity in Islam has been apologetics. But one must also come to terms with the fact that supremacist Puritanism in contemporary Islam is dismissive of all moral norms or ethical values, regardless of the identity of their origins or foundations.[65]

The veteran journalist Franklin Foer gave a detailed account of El-Fadl's trouble in Los Angeles for his writings, his torture at Cairo, harassment in Austin, Texas, and his dealings with Saudi Arabian agents. El-Fadl comes from a Usuli school of conservative tradition. He is a part of an international movement of Moslem intellectuals who oppose the extremism of the Wahhabis, and has refused many enticements by Saudis: "Even within the confines of Western academia, the Saudis have attempted to impose their Wahhabi interpretation of Islam, to re-create their takeover of Al Azhar (the famous university in Cairo). . . . And, just as with the Azharis, their primary inducement has been monetary. There is no better way to gauge the Saudi effort than reading off the names of prominent Middle East studies departments and the gifts they have received from the Saudi royal family. Five years ago, King Fahd gave Oxford University more than $30 million to its Islamic studies center. In 1994, the University of Arkansas received a $20 million grant to begin the King Fahd Program in Middle East Studies. Thanks to a $5 million gift, U.C. Berkley now houses the Sultan Bin Abdel Aziz Program in Arab Studies. Even Harvard University has a chair, currently occupied by legal scholar Frank Vogel, and is subsidized by at least $5 million from the Saudis.[66] It seems the Saudis are winning in the intellectual battlefield against the secularization of Islam.

In February of 2006, the famous journalist Fareed Zakaria, a *Washington Post* columnist, expressed his views on the Danish cartoon of the Prophet Muhammad:

> There is a tension in the Islamic world between the desire for democracy and a respect for liberty. (It is a tension that once raged in the West and still exists in pockets today.) This is most apparent in the ongoing fury over the publication of cartoons of the Prophet Muhammad in a small Danish newspaper. The cartoons were offensive and needlessly provocative. Had the paper published racist caricatures of other peoples or religions, it would also have been roundly condemned and perhaps boycotted. But the cartoonist and editors would not have feared for their lives. It is the violence of the response in some parts of the Muslim world that suggests a rejection of the ideas of tolerance and freedom of expression that are at the heart of modern Western societies. There were extremist elements, of course, still holding true to the cause of the caliphate, and they broke off to create separate groups like Al Qaeda. This coming to terms with democracy, however, should not be mistaken for a coming to terms with Western values such as liberalism, tolerance and freedom. The program that most of these groups espouse is deeply illiberal, involving the reversal of women's rights, second-class citizenship for minorities and confrontation with the West and Israel. . . . In much of the Muslim world Islam became the language of political opposition because it was the only language that could not be censored.[67]

Zakaria writes,

How would you describe Faisal Ahmad Shinwari, a judge in Afghanistan? He has banned women from singing on television and called for an end to cable television altogether. He has spoken out against women and men being educated in the same schools at any age. He has upheld the death penalty for two journalists who were convicted of blasphemy. (Their crime: writing that Afghanistan's turn toward Islam was "reactionary.") Shinwari sounds like an Islamic militant, right? Actually, he was appointed chief justice of the Afghan Supreme Court after the American invasion, administered Hamid Karzai's oath of office and remained in his position until three years ago.[68]

The violence following the cartoon is unwarranted and gratuitous in view of the Quranic verse 41:34: "The good deed and the evil deed are not alike. Repel the evil deed with one which is better, then lo! he, between whom and thee there was enmity (will become) as though he was a bosom friend."

The confrontation between the West and Islam is not just about the adoption of secularism or Sharia, but the rise of jihadism and its threat to the world. Yusuf al-Qaradawi, a prominent Egyptian Muslim scholar and preacher, endorse jihads, and has been barred from the United States and the United Kingdom for his provocative speeches and writings. The Palestinian al-Maqdisi, mentor of Jordanian terrorist Abu Musab al-Zarqawi, is a radical jihadi intellectual. The Center for Combating Terrorism of the United States Military Academy (USMA) has characterized him (al-Maqdisi) as the most influential living "Jihadi Theorist." "By all measures, Maqdisi is the key contemporary ideologue in the Jihadi intellectual universe."[69] Maqdisi believes that democracy originates with depraved, morally bankrupt societies, and denounces secular Arab countries that have forbidding polygamy. He condemns those who are tolerant of other religions, and those who believe that faith is a personal matter between an individual and their God.

The Muslim scholar Ali Allawi has this to say about such conflict:

In the past three decades, the issues of secularism and Islam have moved to center stage as the world seeks to "uncover" the religious basis of Islam's violent fringe. The thesis of previous time, that Islam will inevitably bow to the winds of secular change—a discussion which was carried in polite terms in the West—has now been superseded by the urgency to find a solution to the supposed proneness of Islamic religious culture to extreme violence. It is all reminiscent of John Buchan's classic novel, *Greenmantle,* where the foreign office mandarin tells the hero: "Islam is a fighting creed, and the Mullah still stands in the pulpit with the Quran in one hand and a drawn sword on the other."[70]

The intellectual Atiyat-Ollah (a pseudonym) feels that Al-Qaeda shattered America's self-confidence. He also believes that OBL has forced America to reduce its support for Israel, to start the Middle East peace process, to initiate a plan to withdraw troops from Iraq, and to minimize its presence in Saudi Arabia and other 'godless' Muslim countries. He believes that America pulled out of Lebanon and Somalia because of the success of the jihadists' war in Afghanistan and Bosnia. He believes that 9/11 has proved that America's two great intellectuals, Francis Fukuyama (author of *End of History* and *the Last Man*) and Samuel Huntington (author of *Clash of Civilizations*) are wrong, and that a new civilization, Islam, is reviving.

> According to Atiyat Ollah, Al Qaeda changed the mental situation of Muslims, who can now envisage the destruction of America as a realistic project, whereas before September 11 it was an unrealizable dream. . . . September 11 has infused a new hope into the Jihadists' souls. It is more than revenge; it is the dawn of a new world in which Islam takes its revenge against an arrogant West.[71]

In Islam's 1400-year history, there were rare occasions for peace and harmony as a respite from the merciless wars among themselves, or from military conquests and conflicts with other religions.

Intellectuals and Reformists Against Radical Islam

There are probably countless Muslims who believe violence by radicals has harmed their religion, and that some passages of the Quran suggest unduly harsh and oppressive treatment of women. They see its violent statements about non-Muslims in a negative light. Several female Muslim authors, including Ayaan Hirsi Ali, Irshad Manji, and Taslima Nasrin, have advocated the removal of some discriminatory passages from the Quran. Most of them are now victims of *fatwa* (legal sanction for a death sentence).

Ayaan Hirsi Ali was named one of the one hundred most influential people of the world in 2005 by *Time* magazine. The number of death threats she has received, however, far outnumber her awards. In expressing her views on Islam, she has said that

> violence is inherent in Islam—it is a destructive cult of death. It legitimates murder. . . . Sharia law is as inimical to liberal democracy as Nazism. . . . We have to persuade young Muslims that liberal democracy is superior, that what the Prophet Mohammed said is not right, that the Quran is a man-made brutal doctrine of death whose time has long passed."[72]

Hirsi Ali, a Somalian-born Muslim scholar, is a former Dutch Parliamentarian and now a scholar in America. Her 2006 book, *Infidel,* a *New York Times* bestseller, is her autobiography, a translation of the Dutch book *Mijn Vrijheid* ("My Freedom"). The book has caused worldwide Muslim protests as well as threats to her life. She is against the *hijab* and the *burqa,* or head-to-toe veiling, a mandatory tradition for Muslim women. She has been denied entry to many Muslim countries for questioning the Quran. The following passage illustrates her viewpoint:

> Surely, no Muslim could continue to ignore the clash between reason and our religion? For centuries, we had been behaving as though all knowledge was in the Quran, refusing to question anything, refusing to progress. We had been hiding from reason for so long because we were incapable of facing up to the need to integrate it into our beliefs. And this was not working; it was leading to hideous pain and monstrous behavior.[73]

Ian Buruma comments:

> Ayaan Hirsi Ali believes that Cohen (Job Cohen in his Clevering Lecture of 2002) is fighting demons from the past, that "true Islam" is irreconcilable with a secular, liberal state, that Muslims, unlike Jews in the 1930s, are not hated in Europe today, but they, the Muslims, hate secular, liberal Europe. The idea that true Muslims can be integrated through the mosque, she says, is to make the same naïve mistake as the U.S. government, which supported the Taliban against the Soviet Union, only to see the believers bite back and destroy the Twin Towers. A True Muslim, she argues, believes that a conspiracy of Jews is running the world; a true Muslim thinks democracy is sinful, and that God's laws must be obeyed; a true Muslim, in short, is the enemy of all freedom-loving heirs of the Enlightenment.

She deplores that "I wanted secular, non-Muslim people to stop kidding themselves that "Islam is peace and tolerance."[74]

Irshad Manji, a Ugandan-born Canadian, is currently Director of the Moral Courage Project at New York University and author of the bestselling book *The Trouble with Islam.* She is a popular speaker and TV commentator whom *NYT* described as OBL's worst nightmare, due to her views on Islam. *The Trouble with Islam* has been translated into 30 languages. Despite several death threats, in her successful PBS documentary *Faith without Fear,* she says that far from being a relic of the past, *ijtihad,* Islam's own tradition of independent thinking, is key to curbing atrocities in the name of Islam. She quotes Dr. Eyad Sarraj, a psychologist from the Gaza Community Mental Health Program:

I know we have a lot of psychopathology. It's a male dominated society, there is no role for women, there is no freedom of expression, there is a heavy atmosphere of intimidation. . . . This is a tribal structure in which dissent is seen as treason. We have not yet developed a state of citizenry, within all the Arab countries, in which people are equal before law. This is very serious.[75]

Manji criticizes Arabs for imposing tribalism on non-Arab Muslims, in the guise of Islam, and for being against any reforms. She writes,

In the mid-nineteenth century, desert mullahs bullied the Ottoman Empire to drop three seminal issues of religious reform: ending the Muslim role in the African slave trade, freeing women from the yoke of the veil, and letting unbelievers live in the land of the Prophet. Mecca's chief cleric leveled a handy-dandy fatwa against these rumored changes emanating from Istanbul. "The ban on slaves is contrary to the Holy Sharia," he inveighed. "Furthermore . . . permitting women to walk unveiled, placing divorce in the hands of women and such like are contrary to the pure Holy Law. . . . With such proposals the Turks have become infidels and it is lawful to make their children slaves."[76]

While criticizing, with reservations, the fact that the proposed Muslim Center at Ground Zero will not permit the equal treatment of women, she has endorsed the fact that it is being built.

Taslima Nasrin, a writer and doctor exiled from Bangladesh, has won the Sakharov Award, the UNESCO Prize for Tolerance, and France's Simone de Beauvoir Feminist Award. She objects to praying in Arabic and adhering to Arab culture. A Bengali Muslim and author of the novel *Lajja* ("Shame"), Nasrin has described the inhumane treatment of Hindus in Bangladesh. She is against the inhumane, cruel, and barbaric nature of Islam, and is in favor of revising the Quran. Currently, Nasrim is traveling from country to country, seeking asylum. Ironically, she has been denied asylum by the province of West Bengal in neighboring India, a secular country. In a speech to Commission V of the UNESCO General Assembly on November 12, 1999, Nasrin said that she was

surprised that some Western states have declared the protection of human rights to be one of their supreme objectives, but they have patronized fundamentalists both overtly and covertly. They [secular states] tolerate even the completely inhuman behavior of their own fundamentalists. . . . Such double standards practiced by the so-called democratic and secular states at home and abroad give fundamentalists a sort of legitimacy. If (the) veil is bad for Western women, then it is bad for their Oriental sisters as well. . . . Religious education and politics based on religion should be banned to save the humanity.[77]

Regarding the veil, we note that Soheib Bencheikh, the Grand Mufti of Marseilles, France, publicly supports not only the French headscarf ban, but more broadly, the principles of secularism and laicism (terms he uses interchangeably). Bencheikh defines secularism as "administrative neutrality," by which he means that the state should perform the tasks of governance as separate from religion. In an interview, he stated that "the separation between religion and politics will clarify Islam as a divine spiritual doctrine, not as an instrument which can be misused to gain the power." This, he argues, was the original nature of Islam. "Assimilation between religion and politics in Islam is a new phenomenon," he says, and one which is "hazardous to Islam."[78]

On a related note, Indian-born novelist Salman Rushdie's book *The Satanic Verses* was banned in India, burned in Bradford, England, among other places. Iran's Khomeini issued a fatwa against the novelist on February 14, 1989 for his allegedly blasphemous portrait of the Prophet Muhammad in this novel. Some translators of *The Satanic Verses* were murdered. Khomeini offered several million dollars to his killer, and Rushdie is still hiding in order to avoid assassination by terrorists. All of these noted intellectuals and Muslim scholars do not want to destroy Islam, but are interested in reforms to enforce gender equality, plurality and freedom of speech, writing, and criticism, as other religion do, with no stoning, no honor killing, no Sharia-Islamic law, and no "outer jihad." As Rushdie writes:

> If tomorrow the Israel/Palestine issue was resolved to the total happiness of all parties, it would not diminish the amount of terrorism coming out of Al Qaeda by one jot . . . What they want is to change the nature of human life into the image of the Taliban.[79]

On culture and terrorism, former Michigan State University Professor Sami Alrabaa writes:

> To defeat terrorism, first uproot the hate culture. The majority of Westerners, mostly Europeans, the mainstream media, and think-tanks, on the one hand, and Islamists, a minority of radical Muslims, on the other, are exaggerating the impact and clout of Islam and Muslims. The "Westerners" are convinced that they are waging a great "war on terror" in self-defense, and the Islamists accuse their enemies of suffering from Islamophobia.[80]

Islamists are also convinced that the "only true religion on earth"—their version of it, of course—will ultimately prevail. They also believe that there is no room for compromise or new interpretations of Islam. They feel that they are "commissioned" by Allah to spread His word and remove everything that is "un-Islamic." Their reward is clear to them: to enjoy Paradise in Heaven.

The most radical Muslims value death much more than life. Becoming a Shaheed (see Appendix 4) is a worthy and justifiable means to establish a "Muslim society." Dying, along with killing the "infidels" and their Muslim accomplices is the best a devout Muslim can do in the name of Allah—it is the epitome of obedience to Allah. In their own minds, the suicide bombers are fomenting Islamism. In most Arab and Muslim regimes, the Islamists—radical Muslims who are struggling, by force if necessary, to impose a rigid, dogmatic fundamentalist version of Islam on the whole world—are in control of some religious institutions, the media, and religious schools.

Several Islamic scholars who are against radical Islam and Sharia, including Ayaan Hirsi Ali, Chahla Chafiq, Caroline Fourest, Bernard-Henri Lévy, Irshad Manji, Mehdi Mozaffari, Maryam Namazie, Taslima Nasreen, Salman Rushdie, Antoine Sfeir, Philippe Val, and Ibn Warraq, have made appeals for a democratic Islam: "We appeal to democrats and free spirits of all countries that our century should be one of Enlightenment, not of obscurantism." Most of these intellectuals are facing fatwa-of-death threats and are provided with police protection. Several of them are hiding or afraid to speak against Islamists. Some Muslim intellectuals have been killed by Islamists who allegedly include Seikh Omar Rahman of Egypt, a blind Muslim scholar and mosque preacher in Jersey City, New Jersey. The murdered Muslim intellectuals include Egyptian novelist Naguib Mahfouz, Egyptian author Farag Foda (shot to death), Algerian scholar Boualem Sansal, Egyptian-born Italian journalist Magdi Allam, Italian journalist Fiamma Nirenstein, the French intellectuals Caroline Fourest, Robert Redeker, and Pascal Bruckner, Turkish novelist Orhan Pamuk, Danish cartoonist Kurt Westergaard, Danish journalist Flemming Rose, and German scholar Bassam Tibi.[81] The author of *From Fatwa to Jihad,* Indian-born British author Kenan Malik argues that Western intellectuals have lacked the political and moral resources to respond to the jihadist's threats. He categorizes terror as an expression of the impotence of Islamism, and writes that "nothing reveals the moral squalor of radical Islam better than its celebration of suicide bomber."[82]

It is not a lack of resources that is to blame; it is possibly a lack of interest in religion. To most people, intellectuals and others, religion is not even a secondary matter. School and university textbooks carry the hate-culture, particularly in Palestine, Pakistan, and Saudi Arabia. Curbing this hate-culture is both possible and of dire necessity. All that is needed is for America to put pressure on its "friends" in the Arab capital cities to do so, since these regimes depend totally upon America for their existence.

Sami Alrabaa writes:

> The war on terror will never be won unless the West forces Saudi Arabia to STOP funding Islamic fundamentalism and exporting jihad. Wahhabism must be banned, and all those atrocious passages that incite hatred, violence, and discrimination must be removed from the Qur'an and Hadith. . . . Increasingly, the West loses credibility because it keeps placing economic and geostrategic interests in the front row, at the expense of human rights and moral principles.

South Asian Muslim workers in the Gulf states are allegedly physically abused, tortured, imprisoned, and denied their wages. Alrabaa writes that

> the so-called morality police—*Mutawas*—the civilian police terrorize the population, in particular foreign workers, and who are subject day in and day out, to cruel, arbitrary victimization. They are picked up and arrested, jailed without trial, and barbarically tortured. Some are publicly and inhumanly slain after Friday prayer services.[83]

This is not condemned or even widely publicized in the West.

Syrian-born Muslim psychiatrist Wafa Sultan is extremely critical of Islam and the Prophet Muhammad, and is urging the world to press for the reform of Islam. Dr. Sultan believes that the world is not witnessing a clash of religions or cultures, but a battle between modernity and barbarism, "a clash between freedom and oppression," a battle that the forces of violent reactionary Islam are destined to lose. In an interview by Al Jazeera TV in her home in a Los Angeles suburb, she said: "The clash we are witnessing around the world is . . . a clash between a mentality that belongs to the Middle Ages and another that belongs to the 21st century." The *New York Times* quotes her as saying: "I believe our people are hostages to our own beliefs and teachings. . . . Knowledge has released me from this backward thinking. Somebody has to help free the Muslim people from these wrong beliefs."[84] Sultan is concerned that some important American leaders are ignorant of the Islamic history and injustices that she has known since she was in third grade. "My fear for America was that a victory for Obama could breathe fresh life into Islamic terrorism because of what his middle name might suggest to those watching in Islamic countries."[85] She believes that the trouble with Islam is deeply rooted in its teachings. Islam is not only a religion, Islam is also a political ideology that preaches violence and applies its agenda by force. Dr. Sultan was shocked into secularism by the 1979 atrocities committed by the Islamic extremists Muslim Brotherhood against innocent Syrian people. This included the machine-gun assassination of her professor, Yusef al Yusef, a world-renowned ophthalmologist, in her classroom in front of her eyes. The radical Islamists shot hundreds of bullets into him, shouting, "*Allahu Akbar*"—God is great. At that point, she lost her trust in Allah and began to question all Islamic teachings.

> The sound of the killer's voice glorifying God mingled with the sounds of the shots. Ever since that moment, Allah has been equated in my mind with the sounds of a bullet and became a God who has no respect for human life. From that time on I embarked upon a new journey in a quest for another God—a God who respects human life and the values of every human being.[86]

Any civilization that lacks culture, ethics, spirituality, equality, tolerance, and compassion for all, and advances warfare, belligerence, violence, tyranny, killing, subversion, sectarianism, coercion, deceit, deception, and hypocrisy, and "where the mind is without fear and the head is held high" is destined to decline in time.[87]

The Muslim physician Halima Bashir, from Sudan, narrates the religious killing and raping of women in her book, *Tears of the Desert*, by Janjaweed Arab terrorists with the backing of the Sudan military. These terrorists attacked Bashir's village, raping forty-two schoolgirls and their teachers. Her university became the recruiting center for jihadis, and began to teach that jihad is superior to academic study. Dr. Bashir fumes that "if it was not for us black Africans the Arabs could not feel so superior."[88]

Iranian-born Islamic reformer Ali Shari'ati (1933–1977) declared his belief that: "All men are not simply equal. Man and woman are equal. In Islam man is not humbled before God, for he is the 'helper' of God, His friend, the bearer of His trust upon earth."[89] *The New Republic*, February 17, 2010, notes that Shari'ati had a gift for ideological alchemy, which perhaps explains his outsize influence. While studying in Paris, he absorbed all the revolutionary doctrines of the era. His lectures in Tehran attempted to synthesize Marx and Muhammad, Imam Hussein (the quintessence of the Shia cult of martyrdom) and Che Guevara, adding up to a new kind of liberation theology. His eclectic brand of Shiism promised to usher in revolution in this world and salvation in the next.

Iranian scholar Abdul Karim Soroush (Hosein Dabbagh) is of the opinion that: "Islam and democracy are not only compatible, their association is inevitable. In a Muslim society, one without the other is not perfect."[90] His advocacy of democracy for the Islamic world rests on two pillars. First, to be a true believer, one must be free. Belief attested to under threat or coercion is not true belief. And if a believer freely submits, this does not mean that he has sacrificed freedom. He must also remain free to leave his faith. The only real contradiction is to be free in order to believe, and then afterward to abolish that freedom. This freedom is the basis of democracy. Soroush goes further:

> The beliefs and will of the majority must shape the ideal Islamic state. An Islamic democracy cannot be imposed from the top; it is only legitimate if it has been chosen by the majority, including nonbelievers as well as believers.[91]

Second, says Soroush, our understanding of religion is evolving. The next broad subject that Soroush addresses is the clergy. The rights of the clergy are no greater than the privileges of anyone else, he argues. Thus, in the ideal Islamic democracy, the clergy also have no *a priori* right to rule. The state should be run by whoever is popularly elected on the basis of equal rights under law. When you read the Quran, it is full of passages that incite hatred, killing, and discrimination against women.[92] Some quotations from the Quran that illustrate this point are listed in Appendix 4. For many Muslims who believe the Quran, Christians and Jews have left the true path of their religion. Therefore, they are infidels (unbelievers), as are Buddhists and Hindus. In other words, according to the Quran, only Muslims (i.e., 20 per cent of the world population) are true believers.

Several Muslim women scholars, including Fatima Mernissi, Asma Barlas, Amina Wadud, Aisha Rahman, Asma Jahangir, Mona Eltahawy, Zuhdi Jasser, and Bilal Kaleem are in favor of reinterpreting the Quran to usher in justice, equality, and dignity for women—equality in inheritance, equality in society and government, freedom in choosing their husbands, equality in divorce, and abolishing verbal divorce. Women in Morocco have fostered a new form of Sharia there.

Young Muslims and students in the madrassas are guided by the following verse, which isolates them from non-Muslims. These students recite the Quranic verses and take the contents to heart:

> O you who believe! Do not take the Jews and the Christians for friends; they are friends of each other; and whoever amongst you takes them for a friend, then surely he is one of them; surely Allah does not guide the unjust people. (Quran 5.51)

Two non-Muslim intellectuals, Professor Francis Fukuyama of John Hopkins University and Professor Ira Lapidus of the University of California, Berkley, have some thoughts on radical Islam: Commenting on home grown-radical Islamists in Europe, Fukuyama says:

> One year ago today, the Dutch filmmaker Theo van Gogh had his throat ritually slit (allegedly) by Mohamed Bouyeri, a Muslim born in Holland who spoke fluent Dutch. This event has totally transformed Dutch politics, leading to stepped-up police controls that have now virtually shut off new immigration there. Together with the July 7 bombings in London (also perpetrated by second generation Muslims who were British citizens), this event should also change dramatically our view of the nature of the threat from radical Islamism. We have tended to see militant jihadist terrorism as something produced in dysfunctional parts of the world, such as Afghanistan, Pakistan or the Middle East, and exported to Western countries. Protecting ourselves is a matter either of walling ourselves off, or, for the Bush administration, going "over there" or trying to fix the problem at its source by promoting democracy. There is good reason for thinking, however, that a critical source of contemporary radical Islamism lies not in the Middle East, but in Western Europe. In addition to Bouyeri and the London bombers, the March 11 Madrid bombers and ringleaders of the September 11 attacks such as Mohamed Atta were radicalized in Europe. In the Netherlands, where upwards of 6 per cent of the population is Muslim, there is plenty of radicalism despite the fact that Holland is both modern and democratic. It is critical to examine if America's unilateralism and preemption of terrorism can prevent Islamic terrorists from destroying the pillars of modern civilization that have been built over the last centuries, the great institutions of the United Nations, the Bretton Woods institutions, the GATT/WTO, and myriads of world bodies to protect human values and dignity based on liberty, freedom, and equality.[93]

Professor Ira Lapidus remarked in an interview[94] that radical Islamists think their culture is threatened by Western traditions:

> On a cultural level, the U.S. in particular, but also Europe, is extraordinarily forceful in promoting a consumer culture. All over the world, what people want in everyday life is Coca-Cola, jeans, movies—those must be the principal American mass products sold everywhere. They are very important to people all over the world because they symbolize liberation from tradition—liberation from traditional restraints on behavior, liberation from family control, liberation from political control. That has enormous appeal. However shallow we might think it, it's a symbol of something really potent. And so it's an enormous threat to conservative milieus, to societies which still live in small family and village communities. It's an

enormous threat. It dissolves the family. People want to go out and make money rather than remain at home and live under the authority of papa and mama. So that is a huge threat. Conservative Muslims all over the world see it as a threat rather than as an opportunity. Many do. That's one dimension of it that makes the unease and the hostility with the West very widespread in the Muslim countries. Then there are reasons, politically, why the strength of the West provokes antagonism. And that is, essentially, because the United States backs the existing governments in most countries. And backing those governments, we help those governments in Muslim countries to refuse reforms and to put down the opposition. So the Muslim radicals see local governments, and the U.S. behind them, as their dual enemy. In that sense, globalization, the ever-greater influence of America around the world, is provoking resistance and a reaction.[95]

Terror Trail

Congressman Peter Hoekstra, as Chairman of the House Permanent Select Committee on Intelligence, made these remarks on the floor of the House:

> When we considered—and decisively approved—the Global War on *Terror Resolution* in June, the war we find ourselves in with radical Islamists was not of our choosing, but it is the central struggle of our time, the first major conflict of the Information Age. . . . While terrorist forays carried overseas datelines, it is vital to recognize the threat of home grown terrorism—a strain of the terror virus that has been already experienced in Spain, the United Kingdom, Australia, the Netherlands, and most recently, Canada—that is unquestionably in the planning stages in our own country as well.[96]

The 2005 bombings in the London transportation systems, the murder of the Dutch filmmaker Theo Van Gogh in 2004, the French riots in 2005, and the terrorist killings in Spain, Belgium, Sweden, and Australia, have caused cultural convulsion across mainland Europe and Britain. The British journalist Melanie Phillips writes that

> the attacks had been carried out by home-grown Muslim terrorists, suburban boys who had been educated at British schools and had degrees, jobs, and comfortable families. . . . These British terrorists and their sympathizers were not radicalized by their experience in refugee camps in faraway lands, or by living under despotic regimes, or by coming from countries whose national project was hatred of the West. They are born and brought up in one of the freest, most prosperous and most humane countries in the world.[97]

Radical Islamists are concerned about strategic, separatist, seditious, and military agendas and advantages, not with addressing poverty, illiteracy, centuries of intolerance, injustice to women, and hatred of other communities (see Chapter 2). Some Islamists are Muslim converts who are misguided and are used by radicals to spread Islam by any means. But there is no specific profile for Islamic terrorists. They can be black, brown, or white, and speak English, Arabic, Persian, or Urdu. They have no specific dress codes and can be of either gender. They may come from any country, and from any family or social background. An Afghan pathologist has identified one similarity among them: He found that 94 out of 110 attackers had some kind of physical or mental disability, according to a 2007 study of 110 suicide bombers in Afghanistan.

Humanity has suffered at the hands of radical people for decades. The brutal killing of people because of religion, race, ideology, or any ethnic criterion is a heinous crime against humanity. These crimes have been committed by Adolf Hitler (1889–1945) of Germany, Leopold II (1906–1984) of Belgium, Benito Mussolini (1883–1945) of Italy, Vladimir Lenin (1870–1924) and Joseph Stalin (1878–1953) of Russia, Mao Zedong (1893–1976) of China, Pol Pot (1928–1998) of Cambodia, Yahya Khan (1917–1980) of Pakistan, and Kusno Sukarno (1901–1970) of Indonesia, causing the deaths of 6, 15, 0.5, 20, 30, 1.7, 0.3–3, and 0.5 million, respectively. The ten months of killing (in Bangladesh) resulted in the deaths of an estimated 500,000 to 3 million people, mostly Hindus. "Kill three million of them," then-Pakistani President Yahya Khan reportedly said at the time, "and the rest will eat out of our hands." None of the Pakistani generals involved in the genocide has ever been brought to trial, and they remain at large.[98] (*Genocide Since 1945, Never Again?* Scott Lamb, Spiegel Online International, January 26, 2005; as this article reports: 0.2 million people were killed in Guatemala, 0.2 million in Bosnia, 0.8 million in Rwanda, and 0.07 million in Sudan). These brutal killers are gone but are never forgotten. Anti-Semitism, the prejudice against and hostility toward Jews and Zionism, and the religious and political movements of Jewish people, and other fundamentalism, are all causes of terror.[99]

Even today, in 2010, unthinkable events are taking place in secular India. For example, Shah Rukh Khan, a Muslim and the top Indian movie actor, may go to jail for three years if proven guilty of making a disparaging comment about the Prophet Mohammed. The Mumbai Aman Committee, a religious organization, has filed a case in the Mumbai court in objection to this remark, which he made during a recent interview in *Time* and *Style* magazine. In this interview, Khan listed "Prophet Mohammed as one of the most unimpressive personalities in history." Zarar Qureshi, secretary of the committee, claimed: "Shah Rukh Khan bracketed the Prophet along with Adolf Hitler and Winston Churchill." Farid Sheikh, president of the committee, said they would not allow Khan's body to be buried anywhere in Maharashtra (India) when he dies.[100]

There is genuine concern that the worldwide terror threat is increasing. Richard Clarke, who was chief counter-terrorism adviser on the U.S. National Security Council in the Clinton Administration, has commented:

> Some believe that the jihadi movement has lost its fervor. Others believe that with Islamic governments holding power in the former Saudi Arabia and in Pakistan, as well as in large parts of Iraq and Afghanistan, the terrorists are now too busy governing to be planning further assaults. . . . As early as 2004, our nation's leaders were admitting that the war on terror would probably last a generation or more, even as they continued to argue among themselves about whether it could ever truly be won.[101]

The Brookings Institution scholar Bruce Riedel, who served as the co-author of President Obama's review of the U.S. Afghanistan–Pakistan strategy, reflected the administration's concern in a recent interview. He said that Pakistan "has more terrorists per square mile than any place else on earth, and it has a nuclear weapons program that is growing faster than anyplace else on earth."[102]

Terrorism should be treated essentially as a criminal problem, to be addressed by policing methods. Terrorists are not after money, or killing for personal problems. Terrorists have radical ideological, theological, and political goals, most often supported by states, and sometimes from wealthy families with criminals in their employ. According to most experts, chemical and radiological weapons as well as most biological ones as well are capable of mass destruction. The likelihood that terrorists will be able to master nuclear weapons any time is extremely small.[103]

The terrorist group AQ has had contact with the nuclear weapons authorities in Pakistan. The nuclear weapons expert David Singer writes:

> Gary Samore, a senior fellow at the International Institute for Strategic Studies in London and a former senior nonproliferation specialist in the Clinton White House, returned from Pakistan last week with a similar report. "Pakistani officials claim that no sensitive nuclear materials or information was provided by these retired scientists to Al Qaeda, although they acknowledged that there were discussions that were ongoing," he said. The critical question is whether that is accurate, and whether there are other cases of individual Pakistani scientists willing to sell nuclear or missile information.[104]

AQ has become the world's "first terrorist nuclear power without demonstrating possession of a single nuclear weapon," according to U.S. security analyst Brian Jenkins, author of the book *Will Terrorists Go Nuclear?* A senior advisor at an American think-tank, the Rand Corporation, Jenkins was commenting on remarks made by U.S. Central Intelligence Agency (CIA) chief Michael Hayden. Hayden believes that AQ is "the CIA's top nuclear concern." "The CIA director based his assessment on intentions rather than capabilities," Jenkins, said in an interview with Rome-based news agency Adnkronos International (AKI), in October of 2008. The likelihood that any individual American will be killed in terrorist attacks is microscopic. This contradicts a Harris Interactive survey conducted in October of 2001 that asked respondents about several types of terror attacks and asked whether they were "likely or not likely to occur in the United States in the next 12 months."[105]

The list was deemed to be likely by a majority, expressed in percentages:

- A bomb carried in a car or truck—83%
- A chemical or biological weapon other than anthrax—70%
- At a major public event, like a concert or athletic event—67%
- On some part of the nation's water supply—64%
- Against a nuclear power plant—58%
- Against the Internet—59%.[106]

Freedoms of speech and writing have provoked several *fatwa* and edicts, with the result that authors have gone into hiding. Tolerance in the guise of secularity that imposes restrictions on writing is not the answer to containing terrorism. Bernard-Henry Levy deplores the fact

> that European progressiveness has, for the last ten or twenty years, developed the worst possible reflexes: tolerating the discomfort of the Moroccan who killed Theo van Gogh in Amsterdam; tolerating the pain of the Muslims offended by Redeker's article (Robert Redeker is hiding for writing in *Le Figaro*)[107] and demanding laws or guidelines that would have prevented *Le Figaro* from publishing it; tolerating, from Damascus to Gaza, and from Teheran to Lagos, protests involving burning flags, sacking embassies, killing Christians, and marching behind banners reading "Get ready for the real Holocaust," to object to the caricatures in a newspaper; tolerating the anger against Benedict XVI, the hatred aimed at Ayaan Hirsi Ali, the effigies of Salman Rushdie burned in the middle of London; the field of tolerance is infinite, and it's once again in the name of tolerance, in the name of our comprehension of the humiliation of Muslims and their suffering.[108]

Reformists

The holy militants, the violent jihadists, have metamorphosed the culture of violence into a culture of death and suicide, disgracing, diminishing, and demonizing the dignity of Islam. They are opposed to secularity, democracy, political pluralism, and modernity, and are desperate to rewrite history, restore lost empires, and redress perceived injustices to Islam (see Chapter 2). They have assimilated the worst of Marxism, the worst of fascism, the worst of the Kharijites and Qaramatis (see Appendix 4), and the philosophy of the Assassins, based on apocalyptic visions of murder, annihilation, invasion, and supremacy. They have incorporated the worst of Nazism and totalitarianism, and have become self-appointed *fidayeen* (suicide squads) of political Islam to impose Sharia around the world. They wish to ensure strict laws against blasphemy, and have taken the law into their own hands: Nine Christians in Pakistan were killed and 50 houses burned for allegedly tearing a page from the Quran on Saturday August 1, 2009). This movement of Islamism has been nurtured by the Saudis. Francis Fukuyama and Nadav Samin comment:

> Though many Muslims continue to favor Islamism in the abstract, the movement has left a disastrous record everywhere it has come to power. Saudi Arabia, home of the extremist Wahhabi (see Chapter 3) strain of fundamentalist Islam, is one of the most corrupt and mismanaged regimes in the contemporary world. . . . It is important not to overestimate the strength of Islamism as it is fatal to underestimate it. It has little to offer Arabs, much less the rest of the Muslim world. Its glorification of violence has already produced a sharp counter-reaction, and—provided it is defeated—its 'success' may yet help pave the way for long-overdue reform. If so, this would certainly not be the first time that the cunning of history has produced so astounding a result.[109]

The doctrine of jihad is to urge Muslims to wage war against unbelievers, as a part of their religious obligation. If killed, they become martyrs (*shaheed*) and go to Paradise.[110] Professor Reuven Firestone writes:

> In conclusion, the traditions in the canonical collections tend to confirm the victory of militant Islam over the non-or less militant factions of the earlier period reflected in the verses we have examined from the Quran.[111]

With this in mind, it may be said that Islam an imperialist religion, more so than Western culture is imperialist. As the Quran 9:5 states (see Appendix 4): "Then fight and slay the pagans wherever you find them. And seize

them, beleaguer them and lie in wait for them, in every stratagem (of war)."
The Ottoman Empire—the most famous of the Muslim empires—rose to become the greatest jihadist power in its campaign against non-Muslim rulers.[112]

The Muslim scholar Farhad Khorsrokhavar writes:

> In many respects, Jihadism is a regressive, repressive, and dangerous trend within the Muslim world. Its enemies are not only Western societies but also Muslims themselves, besides a tiny minority of Islamic radicals. Jihadism is also overwhelmingly a modernization vis-à-vis traditional Islam, but a perverse one. It puts into question the traditional distinctions within Islam in the name of a rigid, and intolerant, universalism that transcends all ethnic, regional, and political bonds among nations and races. It revitalizes the utopia of a "pure" society, devoid of the double dealings of traditional Muslims. But it is a dangerous holistic ideology, akin to totalitarian ones, while it is the only one that challenges democracy in the post-Soviet era.[113]

It was Mustafa Kemal Atatürk [1881-1938] who changed Turkey, abolishing the caliphate and introducing modernity. Atatürk created the Turkish nation-state by imposing a secularist constitution, adopting a secular legal system, banning Islamic dress, expelling *ulema* (*ulama,* Muslim priests, scholars) from public office, forbidding polygamy, and by purging Arabic words from Turkish and adopting the Latin alphabet, thus cutting the language off from its cultural antecedents. In today's Turkey, there is an attempt to revisit and revive Sharia despite the nation's legitimate move to get into the European Union. It is believed that there will be a wind for *tajdid,* or renewal, in Islam. Hans Kung has listed several intellectuals who favor *tajdid,* from Africa to Asia. These include the Algerian philosopher Mohammad Akourn (1928–2010) who taught at the Sorbonne in Paris, Egyptian philosopher Professor Hasan Hanafi, Iranian theologian Abdol karim Soroush, Iranian Professor Hashem Aghajari, Indonesians Abdurrahman Wahid and Ulil Abshar-Abdall, Malaysians Anwar Ibrahim and Islamic reformist Chandra Muzaffar, Prince Hasan bin Talal of Jordan, Pakistan's Riffat Hasan and Pervez Hoodbhoy, Afghani physician Sima Samar, Sari Nusseibeh of the East Jerusalem University of Al-Quds, the journalist Jamal Khashoggi of Saudi Arabia, Tunisian scholar Mohamed Talbi (winner of the Tubingen Lucas Prize in 1985) and Tunisian Rashid Ghannouchi. Talibi has stated his belief that "God is with me in the sense of the Qur'an, which says that there is a part of the divine in every human being," similar to the tenets of Hinduism. Iran's Soroush is a leading advocate of secular democracy and pluralism, for which he is being troubled by Iran's conservatives.

In 2005, *Time* magazine named him one of the world's 100 most influential people, and in 2008 *Prospect* magazine named him the seventh most influential intellectual in the world. One leading Islamic reformist is Dr. M. Zuhdi Jasser. Dr. Jasser's liberal views have appeared in the *Washington Times, Beliefnet, Middle East Quarterly*, and *National Review*. In Pakistan, lawyer and human right activist Asma Jilani Jahangir has been defending women as well as minorities, working as a dedicated, low-profile peace activist in the Indian subcontinent.

Saying No to Terrorists

The jihadi movement, by holy militants, is seen as a just war of retaliation against all injustices (see Chapter 2), one that has been endorsed by religious scholars including Egypt's Muhammad Abduh (1849–1905), Syria-Egyptian thinker Muhammad Rashid Rida (1865–1935), Iran's Ruhollah Khomeini (1902–1989), Egypt's Hassan al-Banna (1906–1949) and Syed Qutb (1906-1966), Pakistan's Syed Maududi (1903-1979), al-Banna's descendent Tariq Ramadan and others, and partly by Iran President Mahmoud Ahmadinejad. John Kelsay asked, in response to President Ahmadinejad's litany of questions to President Bush regarding the War on Terror:

> How can one be committed to Islamic values, a follower of Muhammad, "peace and justice" one's slogan, and say that war is authorized only for defensive purposes while at the same time sending material support to Shi'i militia in Iraq and Lebanon, associating oneself with kidnapping and hostage-taking, and declaring that other states should be wiped off the map or vanish in the pages of time? How can one say that Islamic government is good for all humanity, yet oversee policies that discriminate against Jews and Baha'is on the basis of religion? How can one urge that Islam regards all people are equal, yet enforce restrictions on women, dissidents, and minorities that suggest they are not?[114]

A strategy is required to defeat militants who want to spread Islam worldwide by violent jihad (holy war) and *tawhid* (self-sacrifice). There is a need for all nations to develop strategies of counter-terrorism and counter-insurgency (see Chapter 6), to thwart retrogressive terrorists by disrupting, dismantling and destroying terrorist groups and networks. These strategies could be similar to several alliances that existed during the Cold War (1917–1992), which were employed to contain repressive Communist regimes. These terrorists want to coerce negotiations, change territories, and impose their ideologies by savage and barbaric methods. The basic principles needed to resist them are: (a) no concession, yielding, appeasement of terrorists, or acquiescence to radical Islamists (see Chapter 2); (b) terrorists are to be treated as radical criminals motivated by compelling beliefs, such as the Islamic notion that suicide bombers are rewarded with virgins in heaven (see Chapter 3); and (c) to punish, with economic sanctions, states that breed, harbor, and use terrorists and their networks in Asia, Africa, and Europe (see Chapter 4). There is evidence that OBL has tried to acquire weapons of mass destruction (WMDs) (see Chapter 5) and has been in touch with several terrorist states. Speaking at the World Economic Forum in Davos, Switzerland, on January 27, 2005, U.S. Senate Majority Leader William Frist stated that "The greatest threat we have in the world today is biological." He added the prediction that "an inevitable bio-terror attack would come at some time in the next 10 years."[115]

The three most dire threats faced by nations today are:

- Nuclear terrorism
- 640 million small arms and light weapons around the world, which are responsible for an estimated 300,000 deaths per year
- a terrorist attack using high explosives aimed at the cooling ponds that store irradiated nuclear reactor rods at civil nuclear power plants, leading to a reactor core meltdown and radiation release like the Chernobyl reactor disaster

Rogelio Pfirter, Director General of the UNO for the Prohibition of Chemical Weapons, has stated that "chemical terrorism has been identified in different regions of the world as the number one potential threat."[116] He has also said:

The spread of weapons of mass destruction (WMD)—chemical, biological, nuclear and radiological—poses one of the most serious threats to international security. No country in the world today can remain indifferent to the catastrophic possibility that terrorists may acquire these deadly weapons and use them against innocent civilians. It is critically important to counter this threat by ensuring that all governments have the means to prevent the illicit production or trafficking of WMDs and the materials to produce them.[17]

Because terrorism and technology are inherently dynamic phenomena—in other words, they are ever-changing—jihadist terrorism and the technologies underlying WMD have proven to be not only dangerous, but diabolic.

Terrorists must be denied any access to biological, chemical, and nuclear weapons that may cause thousands of deaths (based on the estimates published by the Department of Homeland Security). The imminent danger of the WMD arsenal in Pakistan is real. The Pakistani Army is currently fighting with the Taliban in Pakistan's Northwest Frontier Province (also known as Khyber Pakhtoonkhwa), and there are several AQ sympathizers in the Army who are surreptitiously supporting the Taliban. Ilyas Kashmiri has emerged as AQ's most dangerous field commander in charge of a network of deep-cover agents in Europe. He lost an eye while fighting the Soviets in Afghanistan, and became a member of Pakistan's elite Special Services Group. Kashmiri sealed his reputation when he allegedly escaped from an Indian jail in 1998. In August 2010, the U.S. government added him to its official list of terrorists, who include top AQ leaders such as Osama bin Laden and Ayman al-Zawahri. The Taliban leader Mohammed Omar and as well as AQ leaders are hiding in Quetta, Pakistan, and are eager to capture nuclear weapons.

Terrorism is forbidden in Islam and such acts should not be reciprocated at any cost, Grand Mufti Sheikh Abdul Aziz bin Abdullah said in his Haj sermon at Mount Arafat on November 15, 2010. He said: "Once Muslims start following the sharia in their collective lives, the end of trial and tribulation will be nigh."[118]

The former diplomat Bruce Reidel, an expert on terror, commented:

> Today the arsenal is under the control of its military leaders; it is well protected, concealed and dispersed. But if the country fell into the wrong hands—those of the militant Islamic jihadists and Al Qaeda—so would the arsenal. The U.S. and the rest of the world would face the worst security threat since the end of the Cold War.[119]

Nuclear proliferation remains the biggest threat if the WMD are seized by AQ through rogue elements in Pakistan's Army. Insider threats have repeatedly been exposed—the same weapons ring that sold centrifuge technology and bomb designs to the jihadist charity set up by two senior nuclear scientists, Sultan Bashiruddin Mahmood and Abdul Majeed. Mahmood, along with A.Q. Khan, designed the first Khushab reactor, and advocated that Pakistan had a duty to share nuclear technology with other Muslim states. Weeks before 9/11, "Mahmood and Majeed met with Osama Bin Laden and Ayman al Zawahiri in Afghanistan," then-CIA chief George Tenet wrote in his memoir, *At the Center of the Storm: My Years at the CIA*.[120] Professor Brahma Chellany remarks: "There, around a campfire, they discussed how Al-Qaeda should go about building a nuclear device."[121]

Nuclear weapons and some military installations may not be physically connected to the territories where terrorists reside, but even with the best computer security, encryption, decryption, and firewalls, computers and the Internet are vulnerable to cybercrimes and hacking. Any battlefield, business, and financial systems, plus traffic control, airport security, power generation and distribution or any other devices that are controlled by computers can be infested with a virus, or undesired, disruptive commands. They are subject to hacking as part of information warfare. Computer networks connected via landlines, satellites, undersea cables, and optic fiber wires can be infiltrated, disintegrated, and subverted, without its being detected. Computer networking technology has also blurred the boundaries between cyberwarfare, cybercrime, and cyberterrorism. Terrorists only need a computer (as their weapon), programming software skills (a violent act to coerce) and access to the Internet to disrupt and damage the information infrastructures worldwide (their innocent victims). Cyberterrorism that compromised sensors, signals, connections, information transmissions, processors, and controllers paralyzed the Baltic nation of Estonia in 2007. There is no need for terrorists to physically carry a bomb.

The cyber security experts Sean Costigan and David Gold write:

> With regard to cyber-crime and cyber terrorism, furthering international cooperation is a key step in preventing the next generation of terrorists from using information technologies both as weapons and force multipliers, since insufficient mutual aid and limited enforcement regimes in many regions of the world currently allow criminals the space to work with relative impunity and at little risks to themselves.[122]

The perpetrators of horrendous crimes of colossal destruction must be brought to justice. This justice can be conducted by individually affected country's legal systems, or by an international body, the UN, which can serve as judge, jury, and executioners of these perpetrators, while preserving their human rights (see Appendix 2). It is crucial to isolate militant criminals and their sponsors, the merchants of death and destruction, from the civilized world. The late Milton Friedman, Nobel laureate in Economics, has remarked that the biggest risk to the world economy is Islamofascism, with terrorism as its weapon.[123]

Terrorist weapons range from sword to gun to grenade to IED to WMD, and their targets include non-Muslims. They know that they sometimes cannot be identified, that they have places to hide, and have many state as well as non-state supporters. Western strategists sometimes use them as a strategic asset against enemies, and they are groomed underground to this end, receiving coveted money and arms. They have an additional supply of petro dollars from regressive regimes that are the custodians of jihadism. It is not just non-Muslims, but modern, progressive women who are their targets.

They want to deny equality to women, keep them as slaves, and administer draconian punishment for any deviation from Sharia law. Pakistan and Afghanistan have become their playing fields, while the people of those nations have become their religious guinea pigs.

Despite the rise of jihadism worldwide, the oil kingdoms and Islamists have the unflinching support of the West. We must consider mitigation techniques and strategies to combat terrorism, to detect the threat and to apply all resources to destroy it immediately (see Chapter 6). Mathematical modeling on counter-terrorism is one option currently in progress. Such counter-measures have already prevented terrorist attacks, notably foiling the Millennium Plot by Canadian based jihadi terrorists, which was a plan to attack Los Angeles International Airport. Following the 9/11 attacks, Canada has spent $7.7 billion in new counter-terrorism efforts. The United States has established a new cabinet-level organization, the Department of Homeland Security (DHS), and has created the Office of the Director of National Intelligence Estimate (NIE) to enhance its counter-terrorism efforts. It is estimated that worldwide annual counter-terrorism spending reached $350 billion in 2010.

Professor Bruce Hoffman observes,

> For religious terrorists, violence is first and foremost a sacramental act or divine duty executed in direct response to some theological demand or imperative. Terrorism thus assumes a transcendental dimension, and its perpetrators are consequently unconstrained by the political, moral or practical constraints that may affect other terrorists. . . . [T]he rhetoric common to "holy terror" manifestos describing persons outside the terrorists' religious community in denigrating and dehumanizing terms as, for example, "infidels," dogs, children of Satan, and "mud people." The deliberate use of such terminology to condone and justify terrorism is significant, in that it further erodes constraints on violence and bloodshed by portraying terrorists' victims as either subhuman or unworthy of living.[124]

Several authors, organizations, and institutions consider deaths due to terrorism negligible compared to the large number of deaths from road accidents, hunger, diseases, and political and economic unrest. Whether terrorists belong to a religion which is the largest, or the second largest and growing, or have had a glorious past, or are part of Abraham's family, there is no justification, rationale, or defense for cutting off someone's head. These brutal terrorists, misguided and deluded, are receiving undue compassion from Islamic cultural centers, public relations organizations, and intellectuals, because the root causes of terrorism have remained unaddressed, or are viewed as a result of injustices brought on by the West. The global resurgence of evangelical religion, right wing nationalism, and primal ethnicity should not be a breeding ground for suicide bombers. Religion or no religion, God or no God, rich heritage or unknown civilization, democracy and secularism or Sharia, everyone has a right to live freely with dignity, equality, and tranquility. Neither is there justification to occupy others' territory, to exploit cheap labor, ignorance, or resources, nor to discriminate on the basis of religion, race, and gender, nor to deny people's freedom of non-violent expression. The idea of individualism, liberalism, constitutionalism, human rights, equality, liberty, the rule of law, democracy, a free market, and the separation of church and state is more resonant than ever in the hearts of the majority of mankind. Violence in any form and in any context has to be condemned categorically to deny terrorists' their passport to kill. No state can provide sanctuaries to these terrorists on the basis of sovereignty, or as "freedom fighters."

It is evident that unilateralism is not the answer to defeat radicalism and terrorism. There is a need for multilateralism, a need to forge a joint effort in counter-terrorism and counter-insurgency. We need international cooperation to build an anti-terrorist organization that will neither shelter nor provide material and military support to terrorists. The Diplomat Richard Haass writes:

> Multilateralism is more and more essential, not simply as a way to get others to share burdens, but also as a way to forge global arrangements that are essential to address global challenges such as the spread of nuclear weapons, terrorism, protectionism, disease and climate change-challenges that have emerged as the hallmark of this era of international relations.[125]

All multilateral actions by several countries, or any action by a single affected country, need the approval of the UN Security Council. This council has 15 members, five of which are permanent members with veto power: China, France, Russia, the United Kingdom, and the United States. Any of these can veto a proposal if it is not in interest of that country or its client state(s). Yet as Professor Alan Dershowitz admonishes:

> A rule that authorizes any country to act unilaterally in cases of no imminent danger, even nuclear danger, would indeed invite self-serving decisions, if not anarchy. But a rule that requires nations to put their own survival in the hands of a potentially hostile international organization will simply not be followed. The concern is not so much with the rule in theory as with the failure to take into account the reality of how the Security Council is constituted and how it makes its decisions.[126]

In the past, UN Security Council resolutions have been manipulated by the superpowers to punish certain countries that do not have veto powers. But because terrorism affects all five permanent members, and a large number of other countries, a unanimous resolution was in order. In 2001, the UN Security Council, which requires all states to criminalize terrorist acts, unanimously established Resolution 1373 (see Appendix 2), to prevent and prohibit the financing of terrorists and terrorists organizations (see Appendix 1) and freeze the financial assets of those who do so. It has also established a Counterterrorism Committee (CTC) to monitor the implementation of this Resolution. The implementation of terrorism prevention measures in the United States and Europe has almost successfully eliminated any new attacks in America. These measures have curbed terrorism without creating fear or panic. As most terrorists come from, or are trained by, another country, the threats are transnational. Two leading constitutional law experts, David Cole and Jules Lobel plead for multilateralism to this transnational problem:

> As examples of how a multilateral approach might help to prevent terrorism, we will discuss, in turn, the proliferation of nuclear weapons, the use of the international tribunals to hold terrorists accountable, the role of the United Nations in regulating preventive war, and the importance of making a meaningful commitment to human rights and humanitarian law.[127]

Are jihadi attacks diminishing as a result of the War on Terror? Rand's security specialist Brian Jenkins testifies:

> According to research at RAND, except in Afghanistan and Iraq, the number and geographic range of Al Qaeda-inspired attacks has been growing each year, although there has clearly been a decline in the quality of these operations. Some analysts say that Al Qaeda is currently following a strategy of "leaderless resistance." Eight years of unrelenting pressure worldwide have greatly reduced Al Qaeda's operational capabilities. Outside of Pakistan and Afghanistan, its leaders can do little other than exhort others to violence. . . . Authorities uncovered eight of these terrorist plots in 2009; adding two actual attacks (the shooting in Arkansas and the Fort Hood case) puts the level of activity in 2009 much higher than that of previous years.[128]

Even in Afghanistan and Iraq, AQ has inflicted several deadly attacks. Michael Leiter, Director of the National Counterterrorism Center, reported on September 22, 2010 that during the past year, America has dealt with the most significant developments in the terrorist threat to the homeland since

9/11. The war in Iraq, particularly the occupation of Baghdad, the former seat of the Islamic caliphate and the citadel of Islamic civilization and culture, has brought together Western radical Islamists to wage a global jihad, aided and abetted by Abou al-Zaraqwi, Abu Muhammad al-Maqdisi, Ayman al-Zawahir, and Osama bin Laden. Muslims from France, Britain and Germany, among others are fighting in Iraq against the Western forces. Most Arabs, Iranians, their diasporas and Palestinians consider jihad in Iraq and Palestine is their religious duty and an opportunity to their martyrdom. Their puritanical Wahhabi-Salafism is intensified by unemployment, living in alienated, ghettoized neighborhoods in London, Paris, Lyons, Hamburg, and Madrid, and indoctrinated by radical Imams. These are conducted from overseas-based groups, and include the Pakistan-based AQ plan to attack the New York City subway one year ago, the attempt by its regional affiliate in the Arabian Peninsula to blow up an airliner over Detroit last Christmas, and the foiled plot by AQ's closest ally, Tehrik-e-Taliban in Pakistan, to bomb Times Square in May 2010. In addition to these, there were two lone-actor attacks conducted by homegrown extremists Carlos Bledsoe and Nidal Hassan. The range of threats posed by AQ's core, affiliated, allied, and inspired U.S. citizens and residents during the past year has become more complex and underscores the challenges of identifying and countering a more diverse array of Homeland plotting.[129] While the jihadi war in Afghanistan and the insurgence in Kashmir is being waged by mostly Taliban, al Qaeda, Laskar-e-Taiba, and Pakistani diasporas. Radical Islamists, compassing Wahhabis-Salafists, Deobandis, the Khomeinists, al Qaeda, and the Taliban terrorists, are seeking to establish Sharia worldwide through global jihad, financed, sponsored, and operated by some Islamic governments (see Chapters 2, 3, and 4).

The resurgence of Islamist terrorists, the holy warriors, is not just because of the Soviet Army's defeat in Afghanistan in the 1980s by the mujahedeen, or the Americans pulling out of Somalia and Lebanon in the face of deadly attacks, or Russia's inability to deal with Islamic mujahedeen in Chechnya. Many other complex factors must be studied in order to thwart the violence. Professor Olivier Roy writes: "Interracial Islamic terrorism is a pathological consequence of the globalization of the Muslim world rather than a spillover of the Middle Eastern conflicts." In the case of Faisal Shazad and others who have obtained American citizenship, Professor Fouad Ajami remarks:

> The Islamists are now within the gates. They fled the fires and the failures of the Islamic world but brought the ruin with them. They mock national borders and identities. A parliamentary report issued by Britain's House

of Commons on the London Underground bombings of July 7, 2005 lays bare this menace and the challenge it poses to a system of open borders and modern citizenship. Nowadays the Islamic faith is portable. It is carried by itinerant preachers and imams who transmit its teachings to all corners of the world, and from the safety and plenty of the West they often agitate against the very economic and moral order that sustains them. . . . This is a long twilight war, the struggle against radical Islamism. We can't wish it away. No strategy of winning "hearts and minds," no great outreach, will bring this struggle to an end. America can't conciliate these furies. These men of nowhere—Faisal Shahzad, Nidal Malik Hasan, the American-born renegade cleric Anwar Awlaki now holed up in Yemen and their likes—are a deadly breed of combatants in this new kind of war. Modernity both attracts and unsettles them. America is at once the object of their dreams and the scapegoat onto which they project their deepest malignancies.[130]

Jihad is not caused by poverty, illiteracy or hostile environment (see Chapter 2). The famous columnist Fareed Zakaria comments:

Faisal Shahzad, the would-be terrorist of Times Square, seems to have followed a familiar path. Like many recruits to jihad, he was middle-class, educated, seemingly assimilated—and then something happened that radicalized him. . . . The British government has estimated that 70 per cent of the terror plots it has uncovered in the past decade can be traced to Pakistan. . . . For a wannabe terrorist shopping for help, Pakistan is a supermarket. There are dozens of jihadi organizations: Jaish-e-Muhammad, Lashkar-e-Taiba, Al-Qaeda, Jalaluddin, Siraj Haqqani's network and Tehrik-e-Taliban. Over the past four decades, much Islamic terrorism has been traced to two countries: Saudi Arabia and Pakistan. Both were founded as ideological, Islamic states; the governments sought legitimacy by reinforcing that religious ideology, and that made the countries hothouses of militancy, fundamentalism and jihad.[131]

Since 2001, there have been 11 foiled plans to blow up landmarks in New York City, including the Brooklyn Bridge and the New York Stock Exchange. Last autumn, the Afghani Najibullah Zazi, who grew up in New York, was alleged to be involved in a plot to blow up the New York subway.[132]

The twentieth century saw the marginalization of religion, with a burgeoning number of atheists, making atheism the fourth largest religion after Christianity, Islam, and Hinduism. The significant atheism literature has included Sam Harris's best-selling book, *The End of Faith*, Richard Dawkin's *The God Delusion*, Christopher Hitchens's *God is not Great—How Religion*

Poisons Everything, and Stephen Hawking and Leonard Mlodinow's *The Grand Design.* The last two authors believe that God was not needed to create the Universe, stating that: "There is a fundamental difference between religion, which is based on authority, and science, which is based on observation and reason. Science will win because it works." Sam Harris wrote in *The Daily Beast* of August 10, 2010:

> The first thing that all honest students of Islam must admit is that it is not *absolutely* clear where members of al Qaeda, the Taliban, al-Shabab, Lashkar-e-Taiba, Hamas, and other Muslim terrorist groups have misconstrued their religious obligations. If they are "extremists" who have deformed an ancient faith into a death cult, they haven't deformed it by much. When one reads the Koran and the *hadith*, and consults the opinions of Muslim jurists over the centuries, one discovers that killing apostates, treating women like livestock, and waging jihad—not merely as an inner, spiritual struggle but as holy war against infidels—are practices that are central to the faith. Granted, one path out of this madness might be for mainstream Muslims to simply *pretend* that this isn't so—and by this pretense persuade the next generation that the "true" Islam is peaceful, tolerant of difference, egalitarian, and fully compatible with a global civil society. But the holy books remain forever to be consulted, and no one will dare to edit them. Consequently, the most barbarous and divisive passages in these texts will remain forever open to being given their most plausible interpretations. Thus, when Allah commands his followers to slay infidels wherever they find them, until Islam reigns supreme (2:191-193; 4:76; 8:39; 9:123; 47:4; 66:9)—only to emphasize that such violent conquest is obligatory, as unpleasant as that might seem (2:216), and that death in jihad is actually the best thing that can happen to a person, given the rewards that martyrs receive in Paradise (3:140-171; 4:74; 47:5-6)—He means just that. And, being the creator of the universe, his words were meant to guide Muslims for all time. Yes, it is true that the Old Testament contains even greater barbarism—but there are obvious historical and theological reasons why it inspires far less Jewish and Christian violence today. Anyone who elides these distinctions, or who acknowledges the problem of jihad and Muslim terrorism only to swiftly mention the Crusades, Israel's treatment of the Palestinians, the Tamil Tigers, and the bombing of the federal building in Oklahoma, is simply not thinking honestly about the problem of Islam.

But the last hundred years have brought a resurgence of religious fundamentalism, with the advent of Islamist parties and pro-Islamic governments in Asia and Africa (see Chapter 4). There has also been an effort to erase the stigma associated with terrorism, and to mitigate the barring of militant Islam or Islamic terrorists from state policy. Though democracy has been established in moderate Muslim countries such as Malaysia and Indonesia, there are movements in both countries to revert to Sharia. On May 12, 2010, the Indonesian police foiled a plot to assassinate President Susilo Bambang Yudhoyono and other top officials to declare an Islamic state. The group is allied with AQ in Aceh. The wearing of the burqa is also becoming a political issue in Europe. First and second-generation immigrant Muslim women are wearing more than their mothers and grandmothers to establish their Muslim identity. In 2010, support for banning the burqa in France culminated with the passage of a law that prohibited the wearing of this garment in public. Some women have been wearing burqa against their will, with France at 70 per cent, Spain at 65 per cent, Britain 57 per cent, Italy 63 per cent, and America 33 per cent. U.S. President Obama has said that Western countries should not be "dictating which clothes a Muslim woman should wear," while Mohammed Moussaoui, head of the French Council of the Muslim Faith (CFCM), comments: "[N]o Koranic text prescribes the wearing of the burqa or niqab, a very small opening in the shape of eye in front of the eyes."[133] Egyptian-born Muslim writer Mona Eltahawy says:

> The pioneering Egyptian feminist Hoda Shaarawi famously removed her veil in 1923, declaring it a thing of the past. Almost a century later, we are foundering. The best way to support Muslim women would be to oppose both the racist political right wing and the niqabs and burqas of the Muslim right wing. Women should not be sacrificed to either. . . . The French were right to ban the veil in public. Those of us who really care about women's rights should talk about the dangers in equating piety with the disappearance of women.[134]

The distinguished philosopher Roger Scruton, author of *The West and the Rest: Globalization and the Terrorist Threats*, observes:

> The West today is involved in a protracted and violent struggle with the forces of radical Islam. . . . They (The citizens of Western States) have been confronted with a new opponent, one who believes that the Western way of life is profoundly flawed, and perhaps even an offense against God. In a "fit of absence of mind," Western societies have allowed this opponent to gather in their midst; sometimes, as in France, Britain, and the Netherlands, in ghettos which bear only tenuous and largely antagonistic relations to the surrounding political order. And in both America and Europe there has been a growing desire for appeasement: a habit of public contrition; an acceptance, though with heavy heart, of the censorious edicts of the mullahs; and a further escalation in the official repudiation of our cultural and religious inheritance. Twenty years ago, it would

have been inconceivable that the archbishop of Canterbury would give a public lecture advocating the incorporation of Islamic religious law (*shari'ah*) into the English legal system. . . . All this suggests that we in the West stand on the edge of a dangerous period of concession, in which the legitimate claims of our own culture and inheritance will be ignored or downplayed in an attempt to prove our peaceful intentions.[135]

The British historian Paul Johnson remarks:

International terrorism, in its Muslim-extremist variety, is a world phenomenon. In my view it will eventually blow itself out, probably by the collapse of the Muslim world into secularism. But in the meantime it constitutes the biggest threat that Western civilization faces.[136]

Suicide bombers are capable of killing thousands in an instant, to achieve strategic goals and gain more concessions. Three recent incidents of radical Islamic terror—the Fort Hood massacre, the Christmas Day 2009 airline bombing attempt, and the Times Square bomb plot—indicate that there has been no diminution of terrorism. Denying the existence of radical Islam will not make it go away. The attempt to disassociate Islam from terrorism in public comments, using the phrase "violent extremism" in place of words like "jihad" and "Islamic terrorism," will not yield the intended result of not alienating the Islamist groups engaged in terrorism; as the AQ manual narrates, there shall be no compromise with unbelievers. Rigorous screening and surveillance as well as counter-terrorism efforts are needed.[137]

Another approach to counter-terrorism has been put forth by Professors Joseph Nye and Peter Scott, who believe that America can defeat Islamic terrorism by its soft power—in other words, by its ability to influence the rest of the world culturally and by example, and by strengthening America's civil society and its strongest resource, its people. This strategy is multinational and multilateral, diplomatic and economical. Their personal impression is that the roots of jihadism are more situational than endemic to Islam itself. But is this true?

Jihad is an Arabic word, terrorism a coined French word. Jihad terror has been suffused with fascism, Bolshevism, and Nazism, and is now a monster. Several religions claim ownership of God and some intellectuals and others disown God. But if God is homeless, so are monsters. In the June 2010 PEW Global Attitude Surveys, views of extremism are recorded in Table 1.8. This survey gauged attitudes in seven Muslim countries on suicide attacks, confidence in OBL, and confidence in AQ. Each category is lowest in Turkey, while confidence in suicide attacks is high in Lebanon (39 per cent). The highest level of confidence in OBL (48 per cent) and for AQ

Table 1.8
Views of Extremism in Seven Muslim Countries (given in percentages)

	Suicide attacks Oft/sometimes Justified	Confidence in bin Laden	Favorable view of al Qaeda
	%	%	%
Lebanon	39	0	3
Nigeria	34	48	49
Egypt	20	19	20
Jordan	21	14	34
Indonesia	15	25	23
Pakistan	8	18	—
Turkey	5	3	4

Based on Muslim respondents.
Pew Research Center Q7p, Q34e, & Q96.

* Courtesy of the PEW 2010 Global Attitude Surveys

(49 per cent) are found in Nigeria. Concern about Islamic extremism in Egypt (the most powerful and prestigious Muslim country) is 61 per cent, and in Indonesia (the largest Muslim country) 59 per cent, Jordan 44 per cent, and Turkey 43 per cent.

The spread of jihad in Pakistan, carried out by AQ in their training camps, causing terrorism in Britain, and elsewhere and escalating the insurgency in Afghanistan, has worried British authorities. British Prime Minister David Cameron remarked:

> We cannot tolerate in any sense the idea that (Pakistan) is allowed to look both ways and is able in any way to promote the export of terror, whether to India or whether to Afghanistan, or anywhere else in the world.

Cameron's predecessor Gordon Brown once described Pakistan as the "Crucible of Terrorism." Common to all of these plots was al Qaeda's recruitment of British citizens, most of whom were of Pakistani origin. Some had traveled to Pakistan for operational training and ideological guidance. With some 400, 000 yearly visits to Pakistan by Britons of Pakistani origin, it is becoming increasingly difficult for British authorities to identify potential radicals.[138]

Suicide attacks (*istishhad*), an offshoot of twentieth-century Islamic fundamentalism, have been the scourge of the last quarter century. With suicide attacks, there is no separation between the political and the religious domains. Suicide killing, a jihad as physical warfare, is urged by several Muslim scholars, including Abdallah Ibn al-Mubarak, Muhammad ibn Isma'il al-Bukhari, and Muhammad Jarir al-Tabari. Ibn Taymiyah and the Muslim Brotherhood have been the driving force for OBL and others. Al-Tabari was among the first to use *takiyya,* concealing the real feeling (deception) against *kafirs* (unbelievers) as religiously sanctioned to protect or promote Islam.[139] All of them, including modern Islamists, endorse *al-wala' walbara'* (love and hate for Allah's sake), and were vehemently opposed to *shirk* (idolatry), secularism, and democracy. Radical Islam, it is believed, was born of the Israeli–Arab conflict, resentment against Western cultural colonialism, alienation, poverty, oppression, and loss of former Muslim territories. Many societies have similar grievances, but have not given birth to religious terrorism. Religious innovations, philosophical relativism, and intellectual or political pluralism are anathema to Islam. It seems that "the radical ideology does not represent a marginal and extremist perversion of Islam but rather a genuine and increasingly mainstream interpretation."[140] Even after 9/11, the sermons broadcast from Mecca are not much different from those of al Qaeda.

It is evident that the vast majority of Muslims see themselves as part of a civilization that is heir to a noble tradition of science, philosophy, and spirituality, one that places paramount importance on the sanctity of human life. They fervently reject fanaticism in all its varied guises. They believe the Prophet Muhammad's statement that "difference within my community is part of God's mercy," and reject the harsh laws of Sharia that permit killing apostates, and violence against women and infidels. Radical Islamists should understand that the imposition of Sharia law worldwide is an impossibility and the recovering lost lands from infidels is unrealizable. Nothing can be achieved, even in Muslim countries, if Sharia cannot treat its own Muslims—including Shiites, Ahmadias (see Appendix 4), and women—with dignity, and above all, if those who follow it distrust and loathe four-fifths of the world. It is reported recently[141] by Richard Mitiner and Anatol Liven that radical Islam is a great threat to the West and South Asia. The distinguished author Mitiner describes:

Since the 1970s, the Western world has been plagued by hijackings, assassinations, kidnappings, and mass murders of civilians. What unites all these atrocities is an ideology that goes by many names, including "radical Islam." (Perhaps the best name for a global terrorist movement, borrowing from intelligence reports on the Indian subcontinent, is "jihadi," someone who uses mass murder to terrify civilians into submission to bring about their dark, coercive utopia.)

The veteran journalist Lieven finds:

> All the groups (Laskar-e-Taiba), Al Qaeda, Jamat-ud-Dawa, among others) and individuals within this net hate the U.S., Israel, India and indeed Russia alike, though they have different targets at different times. Despite Laskar e-Taiba's strategic decision to concentrate on India, there is no ideological barrier to its members taking part in actions against the West. The jihadi world could even be called a kind of cloud of interplanetary gas in which individuals join some clump for one.

Former UK Prime Minister Tony Blair has described radical Islam as the greatest threat facing the world today. He made the remark in a BBC interview marking the publication of his memoirs:

> Mr. Blair said radical Islamists believed that whatever was done in the name of their cause was justified—including the use of chemical, biological or nuclear weapons. Mr. Blair, who led Britain into war in Afghanistan and Iraq, denied that his own policies had fuelled radicalism. Asked about the argument that Chechens, Kashmiris, Palestinians, Iraqis and Afghans were resisting foreign occupation, he said Western polices were designed to confront radical Islamists because they were "regressive, wicked and backward-looking." The aim of al-Qaeda in Iraq was "not to get American troops out of Baghdad [but] to destabilize a government the people of Iraq have voted for," he told the BBC's Owen Bennett Jones in a World Service interview.[142]

How does radical Islam differ from moderate Islam? In a symposium, six distinguished intellectuals[143] have discussed, 'what is moderate Islam.' The participants are: Anwar Ibrahim: *The Ball Is in Our Court*, Bernard Lewis: *A History of Tolerance*, Ed Husain: *Don't Call Me Moderate, Call Me Normal*, Reuel Marc Gerecht: *Putting Up With Infidels Like Me*, Tawfik Hamid: *Don't Gloss Over The Violent Texts* and, Akbar Ahmed: *Mystics, Modernists and Literalists*.

Moderate Muslims are far less in number than radical Muslims. The moderates fear for their lives, like all other nonbelievers. In the following chapters, we will study the resurgence and ramifications of radical Islam.

Notes

1. Nuclear Terrorism Convention: International Convention for the Suppression of Acts of Nuclear Terrorism, Steven C. Welsh, swelsh@cdi.org, May 17, 2005. The text of the treaty may be viewed in PDF form at www.un.int/usa/a-59-766.pdf. www.cdi.org/news/law/ntc.cfm.

2. David E. Sanger. "Obama Meets With a Parade of Leaders." *New York Times,* April 11, 2010; *Obama's Challenge in the Muslim World: Arab Spring Fails to Improve U.S. Image,* May 17, 2011, http://pewglobal.org/2011/05/17/arab-spring-fails-to-improve-us-image/.

3. www.law.cornell.edu/uscode/uscode18/usc_sec_18_00002331——000-.html.

4. http://denver.fbi.gov/nfip.htm, McCarthy 2010, 198. Springer, Regens, and Edger 2009, 142.

5. www.state.gov/documents/organization/31932.pdf.

6. *NCTC Report on Incidents of Terrorism,* 11 April 2006, http://wits.nctc.gov/reports/crot2005nctcannexfinal.pdf.

7. www.unodoc.org/documents/data-and-analysis/Forum/V0581059_EBOOK.pdf.

8. http://denver.fbi.gov/nfip.htm, McCarthy, 2010, 19-41, 153, 155. Springer, Regens, and Edger, 2009, 5-6, 8-9, 212-214; David Bukay. "The Religious Foundations of Suicide Bombings, Islamist Ideology." *Middle East Quarterly,* Fall 2006, pp. 27–36; "Peace or Jihad? Abrogation in Islam." David Bukay. *Middle East Quarterly,* Fall 2007, pp. 3-11; Bernard Lewis, *The Political Language of Islam,* Chicago: University of Chicago Press, 1988, 72.

9. Selbourne, *The Losing Battle with Islam* 86, 342-343, 404-407, 430; Douglas E. Streusand. "What Does Jihad Mean?" *Middle East Quarterly,* September 1997, pp. 9-17, http://www.meforum.org/357/what-does-jihad-mean; Haugen, *Islam,* 71-73; Margulies, *The Rise of Islamic Fundamentalism,* 2006, 8, 9, 10; *Islamic Organizations,* 45-55; *Islamic Fundamentalism in Pakistan,* 121-131; Ibn Warraq. *Islamic Societies Must be Reformed,* 172-180; Ruthven, 1984, 27, 45, 56, 100, 105-107, 129, 137, 149-172.

10. Springer, Regens, and Edger. *Islamic Radicalism and Global Jihad,* 18. Lousi Richardson. *What Terrorists Want,* 6.

11. Ruthven, 1984, 27, 45, 56, 100, 161, 177.

12. Martin Kramer, Coming to Terms: Fundamentalists or Islamists, *Middle East Quarterly,* Spring 2003; Shmuel Bar, *The Religious Sources of Islamic Terrorism, Policy Review,* Hoover Institute, no 125, 2010, www.hoover.org/publications/policy-review/article/6475.

13. "The Most Dangerous Place." *The Economist,* January 3, 2008. "Pakistan, The Most Dangerous Country." *The Nation,* March 20, 2009.

14. Tibi. 2008, 65.

15. Osama Bin Laden was killed on May 2, 2011 in Pakistan.

16. Tibi. *The Challenge of Fundamentalism,* 2008, 138-148.

17. Mamdani. *Good Muslim, Bad Muslim, America, Cold War, and the Roots of Terror,* 175.

18. Yvonne Yazbeck Haddad, John Obert Voll, John L. Esposito. *The contemporary Islamic revival: a critical survey and bibliography,* Westport, CT: Greenwood Press, 1991, 37-57; Mohamed Ayoob. "Political Islam: Image and Reality." *World Policy Journal,* Vol. XXI, No. 3, 2004.

19. El-Fadl. *The Place of Tolerance,* 19.

20. Rashid. *Jihad, The Rise of Militant Islam,* 2002, 2.

21. Albert L. Weeks. *The choice of war: the Iraq War and the just war tradition,* Santa Barbara, CA: ABC-CLIO, 2009, 34.

22. Walter Laqeuer. 2006, 192. Walter Laqueur. 2003, 78-194, 223-229, 233.

23. Scott Aran. *Risk in the Wild: Reassessing Terrorist Threats from the Field,* Centre National de la Recherche Scientifique, Paris, and University of Michigan http://sitemaker.umich.edu/satran/files/ratranaaas0206.pdf.

24. Chaliand and Blin. 2007, 12-15, 59-60.

25. OIC Convention to Combat Terrorism (1999-1420H) Convention of the Organization of the Islamic Conference on Cambating International Terrorism, Article 1. www.oicun.org/articles/55/1/OIC-Convention-on-Combating-International-Terrorism/1.html.

26. Suskind. 2008, 395.

27. President Bush Declares "War on Terror." Speech to a Joint Session of Congress, Sept. 20, 2001, *Washington Post,* September 20, 2001; http://www.washingtonpost.com/wp-srv/nation/specials/attacked/transcripts/bushaddress_092001.html.

28. Lieberman, Joseph. "Who's the Enemy in the War on Terror?" *Wall Street Journal,* June 15, 2010; Michael B. Mukasey. "Shahzad and the Pre-9/11 Paradigm." *Wall Street Journal,* May 12, 2010; "Obama's Invisible Islam." *Washington Times,* May 17, 2010.

29. Tomas Kean and Lee Hamilton. "Are We Safer Today?" *Washington Post,* September 9, 2007.

30. Woodward. *Obama's Wars,* 2010, 44, 63, 121, 122, 215, 216, 224, 288-289, 297, 302-303, 328, 356, 363-369, 379.

31. "Nine Years Later, the Attacks Continue: Bin Laden's mission lives through new extremist figureheads and inspired lackeys." Opinion, *Wall Street Journal,* September 9, 2010; Jerome P. Bjelopera and Mark A. Randol. *American Jihadist Terrorism: Combating a Complex Threat,* December 7, 2010, http://www.fas.org/sgp/crs/terror/R41416.pdf.

32. National Commission on Terrorists Attacks upon the United States, *The 9/11 Commission Report,* 2004 www.9-11commission.gov/report/911Report.pdf, 378.

33. Richardson. *What Terrorists Wants,* 2006, 3, 7-9, 30, 35, 434-47, 54, 99-100, 141, 176, 179, 194-198, 200, 219, 229; Chaliand and Blin. 2007, 21-27.

34. Esposito. 1997, 241.

35. There is a clear and irrefutable link between the today's terrorism, known as *jihad,* and the past wars of Muslim expansion which were begun by the 'prophet' Muhammad as a clear and instructed path for the creation of Allah's 'kingdom on

earth.' Muslims make the same claim for 'the crusades' as Professor John Casey attempts in the biased account printed in the *Daily Mail*, "The History of Jihad and the Return of Islamic Terrorism," 22nd September, 2001, http://www.thechristian expositor.org/page120.html.

36. Scott Atran. "The Moral Logic and Growth of Suicide Terrorism." *The Washington Quarterly* 29:2, pp. 127–147; Justin Marozzi. *Tamerlane: Sword of Islam, Conqueror of the World*, Da Capo Press/Perseus Publishing Group, February 2006, 55; Berg. *Al-Qaida's Jihad in Europe: The Afghan-Bosnian Network*. Oxford University Press, 2002; Evan Kohlmann. "Breeding Ground: A home for al Qaeda in Iraq." *National Review*. May 14, 2004; Evan Kohlmann. "The Real Online Terrorist Threat." *Foreign Affairs*, September/October 2006; Evan F. Kohlmann. "'Homegrown' Terrorists: Theory and Cases in the War on Terror's Newest Front." *The ANNALS of the American Academy of Political and Social Science* 618 (1): 95–109; Steven Emerson. 2006, 11, 187, 218, 346, 389.

37. *Lecture of the Holy Father, Aula Magna of the University of Regensburg*, 12 September 2006 www.vatican.va/holy_father/benedict_xvi/speeches/2006/september/documents/hf_ben-xvi_spe_20060912_university-regensburg_en.html.

38. Olivier Roy. UNHCR Emergency and Security Service Write Net Paper No. 06/2001: *Islamic Radicalism In Afghanistan and Pakistan*, (Paris: CNRS, 2002); and Olivier Roy, *The Failure of Political Islam*, Cambridge, MA: Harvard University Press, 1994, 5-19.

39. Ferguson. 2006, 639.

40. http://wits.nctc.gov/reports/crot2006/2008nctcannexfinal.PDF; *2008 Report on Terrorism*, 30 April 2009. *2009 NCTC Report on Terrorism*, 30 April 2010, Charts 1-15.

41. Lisa Curtis. "After Mumbai: Time to Strengthen U.S.-India Counterterrorism Cooperation." Heritage Foundation *Backgrounder # 2217*, December 9, 2008; Chapter 2. "Country Reports: South and Central Asia Overview." *Office of the Coordinator for Counterterrorism Country Reports on Terrorism 2009*, August 5, 2010, http://www.state.gov/s/ct/rls/crt/2009/140887.htm.

42. Syed Qutb, J. Calvert, and W. Shepard, Eds. *A Child From the Village*, Syracuse, NY: Syracuse University Press, 2003, 45-47.

43. "What the Terrorists Have in Mind." Daniel Benjamin and Gabriel Weimann. *New York Times*, October 27, 2004.

44. *The Terrorist Threat to the U.S. Homeland*, July 2007, www.dni.gov/press_releases/20070717_release.pdf, The National Intelligence Council: Issues and Options for Congress by Richard A. Best Jr., Congressional Research Service 7-5700, January 10, 2011, www.crs.gov, R40505.

45. "The Myths of Grass-Root Terrorism." Bruce Hoffman. *Foreign Affairs*, Vol. 87, No. 3, 2008.

46. Quran 8:12, Appendix 4.

47. 164 *Jihad* Verses in the *Quran*, Compiled by Yoel Natan, www.answering-islam.org/Quran/Themes/jihad_passages.html.

48. "Islam and the Power of Theology." Khaled Abou El Fadl. *Middle East Report 221,* Winter 2001, 28-33; Franklin Foer. "Moral Hazard: The Life of a Liberal Muslim." *The New Republic,* November 18, 2002.

49. Lawrence Wright. "The Rebellion Within." *The New Yorker,* June 2, 2008.

50. Chaliand and Blin (Eds.). 2007, 21-27, 221-420.

51. Daniel Brumberg. "Islam is not the Solution (or the Problem)." *The Washington Quarterly,* 29:1, pp 97-116.

52. An-Na'im. *Islam and the Secular State,* 98.

53. Tariq Ali. "This is the real outrage: Amid the cartoon furor, Danish imams ignore the tragedies suffered by Muslims across the world." *The Guardian,* 13 February 2006.

54. Tariq Ali. "Tortured Civilization: Islam and the West." *The Walrus,* September, 2004,1-5, http://www.walrusmagazine.ca/articles/2004.09-world-affairs-U.S.-intervention-in-Iraq/.

55. Tariq Ramadan. "Islam's Role in an Ethical Society." *Guardian,* February 23, 2010.

56. Tariq Ramadan. "The problems of being called a 'Muslim intellectual'." *Guardian,* September 14, 2010.

57. Ramadan. 2007, 98, 194.

58. Jonathan Laurence. "The Prophet of Moderation: Tariq Ramadan's Quest to Reclaim Islam." *Foreign Affairs,* May/June 2007.

59. Caldwell. 2009, 295.

60. "The Dismissal of Tariq Ramadan." Opinion Europe, *Wall Street Journal,* August 19, 2009, http://online.wsj.com/article/SB100014240529702035506 04574360193435076088.html; Marc Lynch. "Veiled Truths." *Foreign Affairs,* July/August 2010.

61. David Barsimanian, Interview with Edward Said, Observer, *The Progressive,* November 2001, http://www.progressive.org/0901/intv1101.html (In introduction to the updated version of Covering Islam).

62. David Barsimanian, Interview with Edward Said, Observer, *The Progressive,* November 2001. *Dialectical Confusions,* September 26, 2007, http://dialecticalconfusions.blogspot.com/.

63. Khaled Abou El-Fadl. "Theology of Power." *Middle East Report 221,* Winter 2001. 28-33, http://www.scholarofthehouse.org/thetmerwin20.html.

64. Khaled Abou El Fadl. "Islam and the Challenge of Democracy :Can individual rights and popular sovereignty take root in faith?" *The Boston Review,* April/May 2003.

65. Khaled Abou El-Fadl. "Theology of Power." *Middle East Report 221,* Winter 2001, 28-33, http://www.scholarofthehouse.org/thetmerwin20.html.

66. Franklin Foer. "Moral Hazard: The Life of a Liberal Muslim." *The New Republic,* November 18, 2002.

67. Ruth Conniff. "Fundamentalism's Bait-and-Switch." *Newsweek,* February 13, 2006.

68. "As Death Toll Rises, Media Should Look at Role in Quran-Burning Flap." Joel Schectman. *Newsweek*, September 13, 2010.

69. "Abu Muhammad al-Maqdisi." Robert F. Worth. *New York Times*, April 30, 2009.

70. John Buchan. *Greenmantle*, Oxford, UK: Oxford University Press, 1999, 92-94.

71. Khosrokhavar. 2009, 280–281.

72. "Violence is inherent in Islam—it is a cult of death." David Cohen. *Evening Standard*, 7 February 2007.

73. Hirsi Ali. *The Trouble with Islam*, New York, St. Martin Press, 2004, 271; Hirsi Ali. *Infidel,* New York: Free Press, 2007, 307.

74. Buruma. 2007, 245.

75. Manji. 2003, 137.

76. Manji. 2003, 146.

77. Nasreen. *For Freedom of Expression*, UNESCO General Conference: Commission V, November 12, 1999, http://www.unesco.org/webworld/points_of_views/nasreen_121199.shtml.

78. Rabasa, Benard, and Schwartz. *Building Moderate Muslim Networks* (RAND Corporation, 2007), www.rand.org/www.rand.org/pubs/monographs/2007/RAND_MG574.pdf.

79. Rushdie. "We're living under a Fatwa now." *The Independent*, UK, October 13, 2006.

80. Alrabaa. *World Tribune,* June 12, 2007, www.worldtribune.com/worldtribune/WTARC/2007/ss_terror_06_12.asp; *Is Islam a Violent Faith?* January 16, 2009; *Is Islam a Violent Faith? Violence, Hatred and Discrimination in the Koran* By Dr. Sami Alrabaa; www.familysecuritymatters.org/publications/id.2287/pub_detail.asp. *Women in Hadith*; www.familysecuritymatters.org/publications/id2752/pub_detail.asp; *Europe News*, Sept 7, 2008; Alrabaa, *Veiled Atrocities*, Amherst, NY: Prometheus Books, 2010, 273-274.

81. Kenan Malik. "The Fatwa." *Foreign Policy,* July 15, 2010.

82. "'From Fatwa to Jihad' by Kenan Malik: A review." Nicholas Blincoe. *The Telegraph*, May 2009.

83. Alrabaa. *World Tribune,* June 12, 2007, www.worldtribune.com/worldtribune/WTARC/2007/ss_terror_06_12.asp; *Is Islam a Violent Faith?* www.familysecuritymatters.org/publications/id.2287/pub_detail.asp. *Women in Hadith*; www.familysecuritymatters.org/publications/id2752/pub_detail.asp. See also *Europe News*, Sept 7, 2008.

84. John N. Broder. "For Muslim Who Says Violence Destroys Islam, Violent Threats." *New York Times,* March 11, 2006.

85. Sultan. *A God Who Hates*, New York: St. Martin's Press, 2009, 239.

86. Sultan. *A God Who Hates,* New York: St. Martin's Press, 2009, 45, 208, 211, 241, 242.

87. Tagore. *Gitanjali-Song Offerings*, Madras, India: Macmillan Books, 1992, 35, 36, 40, 44.

88. Bashir. 2008, 159.

89. Stark. "Subverting the Sacred: The Politics of Script and Ritual in the Thought of Ali Shari'ati, with Reference to James C. Scott and Victor Turner" (compressed version), presented at the American Academy of Religion Division, Southeastern Commission for the Study of Religion Conference, Louisville, KY, March 6, 2011, http://esr.academia.edu/thomstark/Papers/171991; Altran Scott. "The Moral Logic and Growth of Suicide Terrorism." *The Washington Quarterly.* 29-2, 127-147, Spring 2006.

90. Robin Wright. "Islam and Liberal Democracy: Two Visions of Reformation." *Journal of Democracy* 7.2 (1996), pp. 64–75.

91. Wafa Sultan. *A God Who Hates*, NY: St. Martin's Press, 2009, 45, 81.

92. *Europe News*, Sept 7, 2008; Sami Alrabaa, *Veiled Atrocities*, Amherst, NY: Prometheus Books, 2010, 468.

93. Fukuyama. "A Year of Living Dangerously." *Wall Street Journal,* November 2, 2005.

94. *Conversations with History: Islamic Societies*, with Ira Lapidus.

95. Lapidus. "Conversation with Ira Lapidus." *Islamic Societies,* January 14, 2003. http://wn.com/lapidus.

96. Emerson. 2006, 11-12.

97. Phillips. 2006, viii, xi, xviii-xxv, 58, 62, 68-76, 174-175.

98. Lamb. "Genocide Since 1945, Never Again?" *Spiegel Online International,* January 26, 2005. As this article reports: 0.2 million people were killed in Guatemala, 0.2 million in Bosnia, 0.8 million in Rwanda, and 0.07 million in Sudan. http://www.spiegel.de/international/0, 1518, 338612, 00.html.

99. Dershowitz, Alan M. *Chutzpah*. Touchstone Books, Clearwater, Florida, 1992, 35, 41; Dershowitz, Alan. *Blasphemy*, John Wiley & Sons, Hoboken, New Jersey, 2007, 157-167.

100. "FIR against Shah Rukh for comment on Prophet." *Hindustan Times*, June 18, 2009.

101. Richard Clarke. "Ten Years Later." *Atlantic Monthly*, Jan/Feb. 2009.

102. "Pakistan Is Rapidly Adding Nuclear Arms, U.S. Says." T. Shanker and D. Sanger, *New York Times*, May 17, 2009.

103. Ibn Warraq (Ed.). 2000, 99-101. John Mueller. "Is There Still a Terrorist Threat? The Myth of the Omnipresent Enemy." *Foreign Affairs,* Sept./Oct.2006; David E. Sanger. "A Nation Challenged: Intelligence and Nuclear Experts in Pakistan May Have Links to Al Qaeda." reported by Douglas Frantz, James Risen, and David E. Sanger. *New York Times,* December 9, 2001, http://www.nytimes.com/2001/12/09/world/nation-challenged-intelligence-nuclear-experts-pakistan-may-have-links-al-qaeda.html?src=pm. Public opinion on the problems of terrorism (in USA).

104. David E. Sanger. "A Nation Challenged: Intelligence and Nuclear Experts in Pakistan May Have Links to Al Qaeda." reported by Douglas Frantz, James Risen, and David E. Sanger, *New York Times,* December 9, 2001, http://www.nytimes.com/2001/12/09/world/nation-challenged-intelligence-nuclear-experts-pakistan-may-have-links-al-qaeda.html?src=pm. Public opinion on the problems of terrorism (in USA).

105. "U.S. Public Opinion and the Terrorist Threat." Karlyn Bowman. *One Issue, Two Voices*, Tuesday, November 1, 2005, American Enterprise Institute for Public Policy Research, http://www.aei.org/article/24492.

106. *Terrorism, Perception of Risk of Terrorist Attacks*, www.americans world.org/digest/global_issues/terrorism/terrorism_perception.cfm.

107. Angelique Chirsafis. "Death threats provoke freedom of speech debate." *The Guardian*, 4 October 2006, Buzz up!Digg itwww.guardian.co.uk/world/2006/oct/04/france.schoolsworldwide/print.

108. Bernard-Henry Levy. *Left in Dark Times*, 2008, 178–179.

109. Orens (Ed.). 2003, 68.

110. Rudolph Peters. 2005, 5.

111. Reuven Firestone. 1999, 103.

112. Stephen Schwartz. 2002, 62, 135.

113. Khosrokhavar. 2009, 297.

114. Kelsay. *Arguing the Just War in Islam*, Cambridge, MA, HUP, 2007, 220–221; Milton Leitenberg. *Assessing the Biological Weapons and Bioterrorism Threat*, U.S. Army War College Strategic Studies Institute, December, 2005, http://drum.lib.umd.edu/bitstream/1903/7879/1/assessing_bw_threat.pdf.

115. Milton Leitenberg. *Assessing the Biological Weapons and Bioterrorism Threat*, U.S. Army War College Strategic Studies Institute, December, 2005, http://drum.lib.umd.edu/bitstream/1903/7879/1/assessing_bw_threat.pdf.

116. Langwith. 2008, 33, 35–36.

117. Organisation for the Prohibition of Chemical Weapons (OPCW). *Keeping Weapons of Mass Destruction Out of Terrorist Hands. Future Foreign Perceptions of Chemical Weapons Utility*, October 2010, By John P. Caves, Jr. Workshop for CARICOM Members on Implementation of the Chemical Weapons Convention Held in the Bahamas, 29 June 2011. The workshop, organized by the OPCW in collaboration with the CARICOM Secretariat and Government of the Bahamas, was held in Nassau on 23-24 June 2011 and attracted participants from 14 CARICOM Member States, www.opcw.org/.

118. "Terrorism Forbidden in Islam." Grand Mufti. *The Dawn*, November 16, 2010, http://www.dawn.com/2010/11/16/terrorism-forbidden-in-islam-grand-mufti.html.

119. Bruce Riedel. "Pakistan and the Bomb." *Wall Street Journal*, May 30, 2009.

120. Tenet. 2007, 264.

121. Chellaney. "Insider threat to Pakistan's 'crown jewels'." *The Hindu*, May 25, 2009.

122. Costigan and Gold (Ed.). 2007, 91-98.

123. Opinion Archives. *Wall Street Journal*, January 22, 2007. WSJ interview with Milton Friedman, January 22, 2007 by James W. Fogal. http://blog.mises.org/6170/wsj-interview-with-milton-friedman/.

124. Hoffman. *Inside Terrorism*, 2006, 94–95.

125. Haass. 2009, 182.

126. Dershowitz. 2006, 208–209.

127. Cole and Lobel. 2007, 225.

128. Jenkins. *Going Jihad, The Fort Hood Slayings and Home-Grown Terrorism*, CT-336: Testimony presented before the Senate Homeland Security and Governmental Affairs Committee, November 19, 2009; Bassam Tibi, "War and Peace in Islam." 326–342; Sayyid Qutb, "Jihad in The Cause of God." 230-248; "Jihad in the Qura'n and Hadith." 125-141, Andrew Bostom. "A Modern Jihad Genocide." 518-525 in *The Legacy of Jihad*, Edited by Andrew G. Bostom, Prometheus Books, Amherst, New York, 2008; Fawaz Gerges. *Journey of the Jihadist*, New York, Harcourt, Inc, 2006, 268-271.

129. "Nine Years after 9/11: Confronting the Terrorist Threat to the Homeland," Statement for Record, Senate Homeland Security and Government Affairs Committee, 22 September 2010, by Michael Leiter, Director of the National Counterterrorism Center, http://dodreports.com/pdf/ada530466.pdf; Fawaz Gerges. *Journey of Jihadists*, New York: Harcourt, Inc, 2006, 271-273.

130. Fouad Ajami. "Islam's No where Men." *Wall Street Journal,* May 10, 2010.

131. Fareed Zakaria. "Why Pakistan keeps exporting jihad." *Washington Post,* May 10, 2010.

132. "The Times Square Scare: A failed bomb attempt reveals both strengths and weaknesses." *The Economist,* May 6, 2010.

133. "Running for Cover, Paris." *The Economist,* May 15, 2010.

134. Mona Eltahawy. "From liberals and feminists, unsettling silence on rending the Muslim veil." *Washington Post*, July 17, 2010.

135. Roger Scruton. "Islam and the West: Lines of Demarcation." *The Brussels Journal*, March 16, 2009.

136. Paul Johnson. "Relentlessly and Thoroughly." *National Review*, October 15, 2001; Paul Johnson, "The Biggest Threat We Face." *National Review*, December 6, 2005.

137. Rias Hassan. *What Motivates the Suicide Bombers? Study of a comprehensive database gives a surprising answer, Yale Global*, 3 September 2009, http://yaleglobal.yale.edu/content/what-motivates-suicide-bombers-0.

138. Sajjan Gohel. *Why Pakistan is crucial in fight against Taliban*, CNN, August 8, 2010; Lisa Curtis. *Pakistan Must Act Against Network That Shielded bin Laden*, June 25, 2011, The Heritage Foundation, http://www.heritage.org/Research/Reports/2011/06/Pakistan-Must-Act-Against-Network-That-Shielded-bin-Laden.

139. David Bukay. "The Religious Foundations of Suicide Bombings, Islamist Ideology." *Middle East Quarterly,* Fall 2006, pp. 27–36; David Bukay, "Peace or Jihad? Abrogation in Islam," *Middle East Quarterly,* Fall 2007, pp. 3-11.

140. Martin Kramer. "Coming to Terms: Fundamentalists or Islamists." *Middle East Quarterly,* Spring 2003; Shmuel Bar. "The Religious Sources of Islamic Terrorism." *Policy Review,* Hoover Institute, no 125, 2010, www.hoover.org/publications/policy-review/article/6475.

141. Richard Miniter. *Mastermind*, New York, N.Y.Sentinel, 2011, 7; Anatol Lieven. "Pakistan: A Hard Country." New York: *Public Affairs*, 2011, 196.

142. *Tony Blair on BBC: Radical Islam is world's greatest threat*, BBC News, September 3, 2010. http://www.hyscience.com/archives/2010/09/tony_blair_on_b.php.

143. "A Symposium: What Is Moderate Islam?" *Wall Street Journal*, September 1, 2010.

Chapter 2

Terrorism—Causes, Past and Present

Force is all-conquering, but its victories are short-lived.
—*Abraham Lincoln*

Truth being that which it can never be destroyed.
—*Mahatma Gandhi*

Terrorism is not simply caused by poverty, illiteracy, disparity, life in restive and repressive regions, disaffected citizens, or hostile environments, but by perceived injustices and religious and cultural prejudices, most of which are propagated through radical *madrassas* and mosques.[1] This chapter discusses several aspects of terrorists' real or imagined injustices, as well as what rewards and motivations lead these people to indulge in violence. These multifaceted, multidimensional problems are rooted in, and related to, U.S. foreign policy, economic issues, oil and gas, religion, multiculturalism, secularism, democracy, trade, globalization, illiteracy, poverty, clashes of religions and cultures, loss of the Muslim Empires, the use of the Internet to spread radical messages, and to the Afghanistan and Iraq wars. Militants are also encouraged by state-sponsored terrorism.

America's decision in October 2001 to attack Afghanistan in the aftermath of the 9/11 attacks unleashed a maelstrom of violent protests by Islamic activists, holy militants, and jihadists, to support Muslim causes, interest, and dignity. Publication of cartoons of the prophet in Denmark elicited a similar response. Most of the time, the protests have started after Friday prayers in the mosques, services that also included fiery speeches by radical Islamic preachers. The unrest was further aided by a rabid vernacular press, the new power of petrodollars, and most importantly, access to new communication-enabling technology—including satellite television and the Internet. As Quintan Wiktorowicz noted:

Islamic activism is rooted in the symbolism, language, and cultural history of Muslim society and as a result has successfully resonated with increasingly disillusioned populations suffering from political exclusion, economic deprivation, and a sense of growing impotence at the expense of outside powers and a faceless process of globalization. Much of the work of Islamic activism is devoted to creating frames that motivate, inspire, and demand loyalty.[2]

In the past, social movement theory was attributed to Islamic activism in violence and contention, networks and alliances, and cultural framing. In Islamic society, social movement dynamics, particularly violent mass movements, are regulated by *Ulema* (religious scholars), *Muftis* (Islamic legal experts), and *Imams* (prayer leaders). Their methods vary, depending on whether they are in Turkey, Iran, Egypt, Yemen, Algeria, Lebanon, or Bahrain. But many other factors have fed the unrest, including new generations who reside in urban environments, cut off from the mobility and hospitality of Muslim homes and alienated by foreign culture, perceived threats of Western cultural imperialism, and Western power. With money pouring from Saudi Arabia and other rich gulf countries, thousands of mosques worldwide have been importing radical Imams. They have been preaching the virulent venom of hatred, and they have managed to turn American citizens, even some born and raised in America, into terrorists who are willing to perpetrate massive killings. These radical Islamists espouse Muslim identity. Yet there is no consensus on defining a universal Muslim identity—customs and cultures vary widely, from Lebanon with its multiple faiths of Sunnis, Shias, Druze, Orthodox Christians, and Roman Catholic, to more uniformly Muslim countries such as Egypt, Morocco, Iraq, Algeria, Yemen, Turkey, Iran, South Asia, and Indonesia. Communism having been buried, many disconcerted individuals are attracted to hostile views of the West that allow for redressing grievances against the United States and Israel, as well as an outlet for resentment of authoritarian rulers.

Is Islam the solution or the problem? The solution lies in democracy as well as with the core values of Islam. Democracy fosters nationalism, guarantees religious freedom, and preserves national identity. Each Islamic country has its own agenda. For Egypt, it is to achieve the Muslim Brotherhood's goal of throwing away despotism, for Saudi Arabia it is the spread of Wahhabism worldwide, for Iran it is regional power and the spread of Shiaism, for Yemen it is tribal Sharia, and for Pakistan it is nationalism and regaining the Mogul Empire. Najam Sethi, editor in chief of *The Friday Times*, a Pakistani weekly, argues that the nationalist upwelling is part of a more general expression of angst. "The state-supported Islamist-jihadi politics of the last 30 years has had a profound impact on the mindset of the new urban middle classes," Sethi said. "This mind-set is anti-U.S., anti-India. It's a jihadi-nationalist mind-set."[3]

The following section will examine the prime factors that are driving terrorism, and explore why there has been resurgence and who is responsible. The rise and spread of radical Islam is a symptom of several factors including, (a) the West's quest for an unremitting oil supply from the Middle East; (b) the West's strategic interest in the Middle East, Asia, and Europe; (c) the West's primal goal of containing Communists using Muslim terrorists; (d) the instability of Muslim states in the former Soviet Union; and (f) the West's flawed domestic and international policies of politically correct public diplomacy. Fifty years back, Saudi Arabia, Iran, and Libya, among others, did not fund radical Islam or aid terrorist organizations abroad. They were fighting with despots or colonialists, and America was their hope. In the wake of seemingly unlimited petrodollars and Western approbation, several thousand orthodox Wahhabi mosques and madrassas sponsored by Saudi Arabia have sprung up in cities around the world. Pakistan did not have thousands of radical madrassas or an Islamic bomb and was relying on American aid. Two important American allies, Saudi Arabia and Pakistan are also states that serve as twin pillars of radical Islam worldwide. The freedom fighters of the 1980s are the terrorists of the twenty-first century.

Noam Chomsky wrote:

> The most extreme Islamic fundamentalist state, apart from the Taliban, is Saudi Arabia, a U.S. client since its founding. In the 1980s, the U.S. along with Pakistan intelligence (helped and trained by Saudi Arabia, Britain, and others), recruited, armed, and trained the most extreme Islamic fundamentalists they could find to cause maximal harm to the Soviets in Afghanistan. As Simon Jenkins observes in the *London Times*, those efforts "destroyed a moderate regime and created a fanatical one; from groups recklessly financed by the Americans" (most of the funding was probably Saudi). One of the indirect beneficiaries was Osama Bin Laden.[4]

First and foremost, terrorists believe that they will be rewarded with passage to Heaven in the cause of Allah because they are retaliating against injustices. In addition to this, they have many state supporters, and their violent acts will garner recognition. A PLO leader said, at the UN forum, that a few hijackings have more of an effect than several decades of pleading at the UN Assembly. Muslim grievances, as discussed below, have prevailed in influencing Muslim behavior for centuries. While even deeper grievances exist among other communities and religions, none has resorted to their level violence, killing, and destruction. Although the old post-Cold War rivalries between communists and Western democracies vanished along with the old Soviet Union, new tensions have arisen to take their place. A scarcity of energy in the West and China, coupled with the huge amount of petrodollars of the Middle East, have been an impetus for terrorist causes in the twentieth century and onwards. Any inducement to terrorists, politically, diplomatically, or morally, will yield more terrorism. Terrorists' violence, as a means to resolve injustice, has to be rejected categorically and substantially. According to the Harvard Professor Alan Dershowitz:

> The unequivocal message to all terrorists should be that the only response to acts of terrorism will be to make certain that it never succeeds, to inflict severe punishment on the terrorists, and to interdict their future terrorists act by incapacitating them and undertake effective protective measures.[5]

In reviewing some of the grievances, root causes, and consequences of terrorism, it becomes clear that Islam has had glorious periods, and has contributed to world civilizations through its Safavid, Mogul, and Ottoman Empires.[6] For example, as the French scholar Gilles Kepel observes: "Just as the early Muslim horsemen annihilated the Sassanid Empire, so the jihadists, as they saw it, have brought down the Soviet empire by defeating the Red Army in Afghanistan. Likewise, just the first caliphs hurled back the Byzantine Empire, conquering all its southern and eastern provinces from Syria to North Africa, so today's activists have set off an earthquake that they expect will rock the foundations of the empire of America." His thoughts are revealing:

> Instead of throttling jihadism, the American occupation of Iraq recruited an army of new martyrs to the cause. But far from rallying the Muslim world at large to its banner, the murderous *jihad* in Iraq—and al-Qaeda's killing of many Muslims in other Muslim lands—ended up repelling the very audience this epic struggle was intended to attract. Indeed, to the extent that radical Islam grew stronger during this encounter, it was not the Sunni zealots of al-Qaeda who benefited but their rival pretenders to leadership of the Muslim world: notably the Shia leaders of Iran and, after the 33-day war with Israel in 2006, Iran's Hizbullah co-religionists in Lebanon.

It is an unintended, great loss for America in the Middle East.[7]

Islam now has more than one billion followers living in every continent, enriching each region and each culture. Religion, culture, people, language, literature, art, architecture, music, cuisine, sculpture, astronomy, science, medicine, and mathematics all come together to constitute a civilization. Roman, Hellenic, Chinese, Mesopotamian, Aztec, Mayan, and Indus Valley civilizations have flourished because of advanced political thought, universality of ideas, agriculture, governance, harnessing and adoring nature, equality and justice for all, respect for women, and the creation of a healthy environment. Cultural differences are appreciated in these civilizations. Civilizations cannot sustain a prolonged period of death and destruction, but must be marked by respect, justice, sound economic development, and prosperity for everyone. Recent development and advancement in many countries, including Malaysia, Turkey, Dubai, Singapore, Taiwan, and Hong Kong are not rooted in religion.

The Causes of Terrorism

U.S. Foreign Policy: From the early days of the Cold War to the balkanization of Yugoslavia, America and its allies have sought the support of Muslim countries, whether secular or radical, headed by dictators, kings, sultanates, elected Prime Ministers or Presidents, to fight Communists everywhere, as Muslims believe Communists to be against God and religion. To combat Soviet Communism, America formed military pacts with Muslim countries including the Central Treaty Organization (CENTO) and the South East Asia Treaty Organization (SEATO), built military bases in these allied Muslim countries, modernized their armies, and provided them with cash, weapons, and training. The American-trained Muslim guerrilla army in Pakistan and Afghanistan was instrumental in overthrowing the Communist-led regime in Afghanistan during the 1980s, resulting in the emergence of OBL's AQ and its offshoot the Taliban (Chapter 3). These groups in turn have benefited from American money and equipment. The veteran journalist Mary Anne Weaver writes:

> With the Soviet defeat in 1989, the CIA closed down its arms pipeline to Afghanistan mujahedeen. Left behind were tens of thousands of well-trained and well-armed Arabs, and Afghan fighters available for new jihad. . . . Mohammed Atta (the 9/11 attacker), thirty-year-old Egyptian, was one of those men. . . . One of the legacies of that war had been the Children of the Jihad who came of jihad (bin Laden/ Taliban) on the battlefields. Zia, the CIA, and Saudi Arabia had created them.[8]

During the liberation of Kosovo and Bosnia from Yugoslavia, America acquiesced with the Kosovo Liberation Army (KLA) and OBL, which had supplied arms and training to terrorists to fight in the liberation movement. Some members of the KLA, which has financed its war efforts through the sale of heroin, were trained in terrorist camps run by OBL—an international fugitive who is wanted in the bombings of two U.S. embassies in Africa that killed 224 persons, including 12 Americans. The KLA members, embraced by the Clinton administration in the NATO (North Atlantic Treaty Organization) bombing campaign to bring Yugoslavian President Slobodan Milosevic to the bargaining table, were trained in secret camps in Afghanistan, Bosnia-Herzegovina and elsewhere, according to intelligence reports.[9] In 1953, Iranian leader Mohammed Mossadeg had been overthrown by the United States and replaced by a repressive ruler, Shah Mohammed Reza Pahlavi. In 1979, the Shah was shown the door by the Iranian Revolution, and the anti-American Ayatollah Ruholah Khomeini came into power in Iran. That event marked the birth of the Iranian radical movement. Iran is a prime supporter of Hezbollah and Hamas in Palestine, and of Shia Muslims in Iraq.

In addition, and most importantly, American foreign policy in Israel and Palestine has also created many Muslim terrorists. As a result, there are many critics of America's foreign policy towards Muslim countries in the last five decades. Critical of America's willingness to bargain with terrorists, Norman Podhoretz wrote:

> For this an American Navy Officer was shot and thrown into the sea, and hijackers (TWA Flight 847) were rewarded with the freeing of hundreds of terrorists held by Israel in exchange for the release of other passengers. Both the United States and Israel denied they were violating their own policy of never bargaining with terrorists but as with arms-for-hostages deals, no one believed them. And it was almost universally assumed that Israel had acted under pressure from Washington.[10]

The leading intellectual critic of American foreign policy in the Middle East, Noam Chomsky, believes:

> The present campaign of hatred in the Arab world is, of course, also fueled by U.S. policies toward Israel–Palestine. . . . The U.S. has provided the crucial support for Israel's harsh military occupation, now in its thirty-fifth year.[11]

Additional criticism of U.S. foreign policy is offered by Laura Egendorf:

> William Norman Grigg, a senior editor for *New America*, contends that U.S. support of the governments in Bosnia and Kosovo helped provide havens for terrorist leader Osama Bin Laden 's Muslim terrorist network, Al Qaeda (the group behind the September 11 tragedy). The United States

supported Bosnia when the mostly Muslim country declared independence from Yugoslavia in 1992, resulting in a war against Bosnian Serbs, who opposed independence. According to Grigg, U.S. support of the Muslim government in Bosnia, via American efforts to transport Iranian arms to the Bosnian capital, Sarajevo, led to the rise of Iranian terrorist groups in the war-torn nation. These groups were allied with Osama Bin Laden. Grigg also claims that the KLA, a national police force that the United States has provided with weapons and training to aid their efforts to gain Kosovo's independence from Serbia, is in reality a terrorist group that aids Osama Bin Laden and his operatives. Grigg concludes, What kind of 'war on terrorism' must we fight when we have found ourselves consistently lending material, *military, and* political support to Osama Bin Laden's allies?[12]

Indeed, the Bosnia war was responsible for the proliferation of several jihad organizations who were involved in terrorist attacks, including: Abu al-Malik, implicated in September 11, 2001 in the United States; Abu al-Haili, involved in the 2002 terrorist attack on U.S. ships in Gibraltar; Ali al-Shamrani, involved in terrorism in 1995 against the U.S. military in Saudi Arabia and Pakistan; Khlil Deek, a Millennium Plot cell in Canada; and Abu Hajir, involved in the 1998 U.S. embassy attack in Tirana. These terrorists received funds from Finsbury Park Mosque, London, the Islamic Cultural Center, Milan, the Benevolence International Foundation, Chicago, and the International Islamic Relief Organization, Saudi Arabia. These individuals and organizations all have connections with the terrorist group Muj, an AQ organization in Bosnia, and with the Sudanese National Islamic Front (NIF). The grievances in the Muslim world, whether they are real or perceived, historical or recent, need to be addressed. The primary concerns revolve around America's support of Israel and the wars in Iraq and in Afghanistan, the patronizing of dictators in Muslim countries by American officials, and the West's cultural colonization. Among their specific areas of interest are industries, including television, film, and commercial products; the location of America's military bases in Gulf countries, for the purpose of securing oil and gas; the spreading of secularism and democracy by the West, which is viewed as a threat to Muslim religion; Israel's occupation of the West Bank since the 1967 war; and the West's strategic and economic interest in the Middle East. Other resentments lie with Muslim kings, sheikhs, sultans, presidents, and prime ministers, who are seen as being responsible for the lack of development, education, employment, infrastructures, and access to healthcare, causing economic deprivation. Lawrence Wright comments:

From Iraq to Morocco, Arab governments had stifled freedom and sig-
nally failed to create wealth at the very time when democracy and personal
income were sharply climbing in virtually all other parts of the globe.
Saudi Arabia, the richest of the lot, was such a notoriously unproductive
country that the extraordinary abundance of petroleum had failed to generate any other significant income, indeed, if one subtracted the oil revenue
of the Gulf countries, 260 million Arabs exported less than the 5 million
Finns (people of Finland). Anger, resentment, and humiliation spurred
young Arabs to search for dramatic remedies.[13]

Palestinian scholar Azzam, the mentor of OBL, thought Islam was returning to world domination with the liberation of Afghanistan. He formulated
the idea of global jihad, and stressed that jihad and the rifle alone, not
negotiation or dialogues, serve the goal.

Radicals believe that the revival of Islam through the Quran, an uncreated,
eternal, divine and immutable doctrine, is a panacea for solving the crisis in
Islamic civilization. However, Iraqi Sunni intellectual Ali Allawi observed:

It was assumed that Muslims were alienated from the very countries in
which they lived because their consciousness as Muslims did not square
with the demands of loyalty to nation-state. This was an issue for Muslims
diasporas in the West as well as for a disaffected, radicalized youth in a
number of predominantly Muslim countries.[14]

OBL's main grievances include America's support of the Saudi Arabia
monarchy, American military bases in the Arabian Peninsula Gulf areas,
and American support of Israel in defiance of the UN Security Council
Resolutions on Palestine (see Appendix 2). America's strategic interest has
been paramount in foreign policy, and its commitment to democracy and
human rights has been questioned by Muslims due to its support of dictators
and repressive rulers in the Muslim world and elsewhere. These have included Manuel Noriega and Omar Torrijos of Panama, Anastasio Somoza
of Nicaragua, Leopoldo Galtieri of Argentina, Hector Gramajo and Manuel
Antonio Callejas of Guatemala, Hugo Banzar Suarez of Bolivia, and Generals Zia al-Haq and Pervez Musharraf of Pakistan. Even after 9/11, America
has not been critical of Saudi Arabia, despite the fact that fifteen out of the
eighteen 9/11 terrorists hailed from that nation, and that Saudi Arabia and is
aware of terrorists' camps and their operations in Pakistan. On December
13, 2001, the Indian Parliament House in Delhi was attacked by five gunmen armed with grenades, Kalashnikov rifles and explosives, who killed
themselves along with several military guards. It was discovered that
Pakistan's Lashkar-e-Taiba (Army of the Pious, LeT, founded in 1986) and

Jaish-e Muhammad (JEM) were involved with the mastermind Hafiz Muhammad Saeed. He is also reported to have been involved in the November 26, 2008 attack in Mumbai, India in which 173 people were killed. The LeT is the military wing of the Markaz al Daawa (Center for Islamic Call), which runs charities and an Islamic University at Mureedke in Lahore, Pakistan.

> Its curriculum included science, English, Arabic, Quranic studies and Jihad, and it urged its students to wage jihad wherever Muslims were oppressed, from Xingjian in western China to Chechnya to Bosnia to Afghanistan and Indian-administered Kashmir, thus subscribing to the pan-Islamic thesis, which Osama Bin Laden would later adopt, albeit independently. In Mureedke and elsewhere, mosques and bazaars displayed posters urging jihad under the LeT and other radical groups, a call that appealed to many poor, devout Muslims.[15]

Pakistan has been an incubator and a sanctuary for terrorists, and Pakistan's military agency, ISI, has been protecting and funding the Taliban and AQ leaders. Following 2001, the Bush Administration poured 10 billion dollars or more in aid to Pakistan to combat terrorists. In 2009, the Obama Administration increased the number to 1.5 billion dollars per year for the next five years for the counterinsurgency.

Through several cultural, social, political and educational Islamic organizations, at both the state and federal levels in America and the United Kingdom, Islamic militants are working with legislators, congressmen, community leaders, senators, parliamentarians, university academicians, and think tanks, to enhance and propagate radical Islam under the guise of multiculturalism, secularism, human rights, and religious freedom. In fact, they are abusing America's civil liberties, in order to change America's foreign policy to accommodate radical Islamism and redefine terrorism. Unfortunately, some ambiguous passages in sacred texts feed radicalism and violence.

"Let there be no compulsion in religion" (Quran 2:256). But there is no freedom for Muslims to convert to other religions (kefir, apostasy) and no freedom to criticize Islam (kufr, blasphemy). In both cases, these acts are considered crimes punishable by death. There is coercion on 'commanding right and forbidding wrong.' In early Islam, Mutazilites defended free will and emphasized the legitimate role of reason as well as revelation in the pursuit of truth. Notwithstanding, rejecting them, al-Mutawakkil in 847 declared "every discussion about a thing that the Prophet did not discuss is an error." Statements that there is no compulsion in religion and that jihad is primarily about internal struggle and not about holy war may receive applause in university lecture halls and diplomatic boardrooms, but they misunderstand the importance of abrogation in Islamic theology. It is important to acknowledge that what university scholars believe, and what most Muslims—or more extreme Muslims—believe are two different things. For many Islamists and radical Muslims, abrogation is real and what the West calls terror is, indeed, just.[16] However, in the last six years of Muhammad's life (626-32), God permitted Muslims to fight an aggressive war first against polytheists, and later against monotheists like the Jews of Khaybar. Once Muhammad was given permission to kill in the name of God, he instigated battle (see Chapter 3).

Suicide bombings have become more powerful than the Islamic sword, the Internet is more pervasive than the mosque's prayer calls, and Cultural Councils are defending radical Islam through diplomacy and public relations more than the *mullahs*. The Middle East-based Al Jazeera Broadcasting network has been serving as the main media outlet for both the Muslim world in the Middle East, and the Muslim diaspora throughout the world. The Muslim world asserts that peace can come only after the resolution of the situation in Palestine (see Figure 2.1). At the time of the establishment of Israel, Jews were expelled from Arab countries and their property confiscated. Christians from Arab countries sought refuge in Australia, Canada, Europe and the United States. The Arabs in Israel and adjacent areas are fighting for a Palestinian State, which has aroused turmoil in the Muslim world and resentment for America. While the Palestine problem has united Arab and Muslim countries in their enmity towards Israel and America, these same countries have not paid much attention to Palestinian suffering and grief in terms of economic aid and development. The richest Muslim country, Saudi Arabia, only donated 20 million dollars to Palestine in 2001, while America sanctioned 441 million dollars in 2008 alone. However, only Jordan grants citizenship to Palestinians. There have been several territorial adjustments in the world in the twentieth century, but Arabs never accepted the exiled Palestinians. The strategic experts David Frum and Richard Perle believe that this is not a territorial issue: "The Arab-Israel quarrel is not a cause of Islamic extremism; the unwillingness of the Arabs to end the quarrel is a manifestation of the underlying cultural malaise from which Islamic extremism emerges."[17]

For Pakistani Muslims, Jammu and Kashmir (J&K, Figure 2.2) is a major source of grievance adjoined to the cause of Palestine, even though the two situations are not comparable The Kashmir issue is raised solely by Pakistan along with the Palestine movement in all Muslim forums, and at meetings of the Organizations of Islamic Countries (OIC) to obtain support for the Arab cause. The inclusion is unfair and malicious, as Kashmir is

Figure 2.1. Israel and Palestine

* The map is adapted from originals at Atlas of the Oriental made by Tore Kjeilen.

ruled by an elected government by free and fair elections, while the separatist and Pakistani armed insurgents have been abetting terrorism in the state
of Jammu and Kashmir since 1989, boycotting the election and democratic
process. As one former British diplomat wrote:

> During the first half of February 1948, I made repeated efforts to persuade
> Pundit Nehru and Sardar Patel that it was not true that power politics and
> not ethics were ruling the attitude of most members of the Security Coun-
> cil to the Kashmir issue. But in this I was not successful. The belief spread
> during the first part of February (1948), being founded on the assumption,
> that the United Kingdom wished to appease the cause of Muslim solidarity
> in the Middle East, and that the United States wished to rehabilitate their
> position vis-à-vis the Arabs after their advocacy of partition in Palestine.

Kashmir has remained a disputed territory since the partition of India.[18]
With their success in pushing out the Soviet Union from Afghanistan, jihadist
opted for pursuing a similar insurgency in Indian part of Kashmir. "The
unfinished agenda of partition, they maintained, could also be finished in
Kashmir by waging a jihad."[19]

Like Palestine for Arabs and other Muslims, the Kashmir issue unites
Pakistan. Since the 1990s, Pakistan has been employing the Taliban, AQ,
and other state-sponsored separatists through its Interstate Intelligence Agency
(ISI) to send insurgents to Kashmir. There is no foreign occupation in Kashmir; while it has a duly elected government, it also has a Muslim majority
with a population of five million in the Kashmir Valley, while more than
150 million Muslims live elsewhere in secular India. Once a beautiful and
spiritual place, it is now one of the most dangerous places in the world to
visit (Figure 2.2).

Yielding to Violence and Appeasement

"You may gain temporary appeasement by a policy of concession to
violence, but you do not gain lasting peace that way."

—Sir Anthony Eden,
Prime Minister of Great Britain, 1955–1957

Terrorism and violence have triumphed over non-violence, truth, peace,
and the power of the pen. Some examples of triumphs and tragedies, intolerance and inaction are worth mentioning. All great powers have either
patronized or yielded to terrorism in the nineteenth century to promote their
national interest. Yassir Arafat (1929–2004), Chairman of the Palestine Liberation Organization (PLO), established the first terrorist training camps

and launched the first international campaign of airline hijacking and hostage taking. Commenting on the unholy alliance of Western radicals and Islamic jihadists, David Horowitz remarks:

> The attack of 9/11—whose weapon of choice was hijacked airliners loaded with hostages and whose targets were Wall Street and the Pentagon, the very symbols of American empire—was thus the juncture at which the two jihads finally met.[20]

Arafat was alleged to be linked to several terrorist attacks and yet was awarded the Nobel Prize for Peace, whereas Mohandas Gandhi (1869–1948), a pioneer in non-violence, toleration, harmony, and peace, was not even considered, apparently because he was a "half naked fakir" and philosopher living an austere, simple life. Even those alleged to be connected to genocide in Vietnam and Cambodia have been awarded Nobel Peace Prizes. Violence is preponderant over peace.

There are numerous examples of countries yielding to terrorist violence throughout the twentieth century. These include the 2004 Madrid bombing in Spain, in which AQ-inspired terrorist cells killed 191 people and wounded 1800. As a result, Spain withdrew 1300 troops from Iraq, Italy withdrew 3200, and the Netherlands withdrew 1345. In 1943, prior to the Partition of India, there was a famine in Bengal in which three million people died, thanks to inhumane callousness and abysmal mismanagement on the part of the British Raj. The United States came to their aid, but not Britain. In February 1945, British Prime Minister Sir Winston Churchill (1874–1965, Prime Minister in 1940–1945, and in 1951–1955) wished (as recorded by his private secretary Jock Colville) that Air Marshall Bert Harris could send some of his surplus bombers to destroy the Indians. Churchill was extremely upset by the liberation movement let by Indian Congress leaders Jawaharlal Nehru and Mahatma Gandhi's liberation movement. Gandhi adopted the *Satyagraha,* a non-violent non-cooperation movement, and went on a hunger strike to demand India's independence. His health condition became precarious. The incensed (Winston) Churchill sent the Viceroy 'a peevish telegram to ask why Gandhi hadn't died yet.' The loss of India from the British Empire plagued Churchill. While M.A. Jinnah of the AIML (All India Muslim Leagues) was cooperative with the British Raj, continuing the AIML governments in Bengal, Punjab, and Sindh, a furious Pundit Jawaharlal Nehru (1889–1964) asked the Congress governments in all states to resign in protest of the British Raj. Just as Jinnah regarded Nehru as a socialist atheist, Nehru regarded Jinnah as the leader of feudal landlords and obscurantist mullah. President Roosevelt supported giving "Indians the right of

self-determination," which infuriated Churchill. In 1946, Indian independence movement the British Raj reached a pivotal stage when Prime Minister Clement Attlee (1883–1967, British Prime Minister in 1945–1951) sent
a three member Cabinet Mission to India to discuss and finalize plans for
the transfer of power from the British Raj to the Indian leadership. This
would provide India with independence under Dominion status in the Commonwealth of Nations. While Indian Congress leaders Gandhi and Nehru
were reluctant to accept the mission's mandate, Jinnah accepted it as the
leader of the Muslim League. He declared: "We shall have India divided or
we shall have India destroyed." During the Muslim League Council Meeting held on July 27–29, 1946, a resolution was passed declaring a Direct
Action Day (DAD) that was intended to unfold "direct action for the achievement of Pakistan."21

India had been wrecked by the violence of partition, during which at
least one million people were slaughtered, and on the DAD in August of
1946, India was further damaged by mass killings in Calcutta. Jinnah's
DAD was meant to show the Congress Party the futility of opposing the new
nation. When asked about the implicit threat of violence behind the Direct
Action Day, which left the streets running with blood, Jinnah said: "I am
not prepared to discuss ethics." Jinnah had arguably already won the fight
for Pakistan in 1939 when Lord Linlithgow, the British Viceroy, effectively
recognized Jinnah's Muslim League as the sole spokesman of all Muslims
in British India in return for Jinnah's support of India's participation in the
Second World War.22

More than 5000 people were slaughtered on the DAD, 15,000 were
injured, and 100,000 were left without homes. This represented a direct
failure of the State and Federal British Government to prevent the massacre
that was planned by the Muslim League. It was a terrible defeat for Gandhi,
one which smashed his lifelong dream of peace, unity, and non-violence.
The British Empire was the first to yield to terrorist violence and brutality
before they left the Indian Subcontinent. By their divide-and-rule policy,
the British favored the Muslim martial races, and exacerbated religious hatred and animosity. They were silent witnesses to mayhem and massacres in
Bengal. Piers Brendon writes: "In Bengal, especially, Muslims embarked
on a pogrom, shouting 'jihad' and slaughtering thousands."23 It was the call
for holy war:

> Muslims must remember that it was in Ramazan (Ramadan) that the Quran
> was revealed. It was in Ramazan that the permission for Jihad was granted
> by Allah. It was in Ramazan that the Battle of Badr, the first open conflict
> between Islam and Heathenism, was fought and won by 313 Muslims and

again it was in Ramazan that 10,000 Muslims under the Holy Prophet conquered Mecca and established the kingdom of Heaven and the commonwealth of Islam in Arabia.[24]

Herman Arthur wrote: "It was violence, not nonviolence, that forced the British first to change course, then to seek Gandhi's approval, and then finally to leave." Still, Churchill had one more card to play. He had mentioned it in his letter to Clementine (spouse of Churchill) back in January 1945: Pakistan.

Through his secret support for Jinnah and India's Muslims, Churchill still hoped he could deny Gandhi his ultimate victory. Churchill revealed his bond with Jinnah in a crucial meeting with Mountbatten in May 1947.[25]

The Indian National Congress leaders Gandhi and Nehru were shocked by the violence. They, and the British Empire, agreed to the creation of Pakistan. The deadly day illustrated the victory of violence over non-violence or Constitutional methods.[26] An article appearing in *Time Magazine* on Monday, August 26, 1946, contained the following statement:

India suffered the biggest Moslem-Hindu riot in its history. Moslem League Boss Mohamed Ali Jinnah had picked the 18th day of Ramadan for 'Direct Action Day' against Britain's plan for Indian independence[27] (see Chapter 4).

As Hodson recounted:

The working committee followed up by calling on Muslims throughout India to observe 16th August as 'Direct Action Day.' On that day meetings would be held all over the country to explain the (Muslim) League's resolution. These meetings and processions passed off—as was manifestly the Central (Muslim) league leaders' intention without more than commonplace and limited disturbance with one vast and tragic exception. . . . What happened was more than anyone could have foreseen. In the next three days some 20,000 people were killed or seriously injured in Calcutta.[28]

The Middle East has been the scene of still more examples of yielding to terrorist violence: From the end of the Second World War to the end of the Cold War, the seeds of radical Islam were germinating, and the terrorist violence they engendered was not confronted. In 1979, Ayatollah Khomeini, a Shi'a religious leader, replaced pro-western Mohammed Reza Pahlavi as leader of Iran. Americans were taken hostage for 444 days, during which

President Carter failed to have them released. It was the first major victory of for the Islamists. In 1982–1983, the radical Islamist group Hezbollah forced the United States to withdraw its troops from Lebanon, President Reagan having yielded to their violent attacks. From 1979 to 1989, Islamic fighters from several Muslim countries, led by OBL and with the support of Saudi Arabia, Pakistan, the United States and others, were assembled to fight with the Soviet Union to drive out the Communist regime from Afghanistan. President Reagan was very appreciative of the Muslim fighters' role and radical methods in this effort. The American political scientist Robert Pape writes that there were 315 suicide bombings from 1980 to 2003, of which 239 (75 per cent) were committed by Islamic groups.[29] On October 23, 1983, a Hezbollah suicide bomber killed 241 American soldiers in the Marine barracks in Lebanon, demolishing the building. This coincided with a near-simultaneous second attack that killed 58 French troops. Hezbollah would chalk up a total of 36 suicide attacks against American, French, and Israeli targets during the 1980s. In Pakistan over a period of three weeks in September to October, 2009, nine suicide attacks killed more than 160 people. In all these events, the respective governments of the targeted countries yielded to terrorist organizations, including Hezbollah, Hamas, AQ, and the Taliban. America's attack against AQ and the Taliban in Afghanistan in 2001 was one instance of fighting back against terrorism amidst many other situations in which victim countries yielded to terrorist violence.

But in Sri Lanka, despite several suicide and other attacks by the Liberation Tigers of Tamil Eelam (LTTE), the government of Sri Lanka did not give in. After thirty years of violence, government forces finally routed the LTTE militants in May 2009. The Iran–Contra Deal is another situation that requires examination in this context. These operations provided assistance to the military activities of the Nicaraguan contra rebels and allowed for the sale of U.S. arms to Iran in contravention of stated U.S. policy, and in possible violation of arms-export controls (violating the Boland Amendment ban). When several Americans were kidnapped in Lebanon on July 26, 1987, one of them, Father Jenco, was freed with the help of Iranians. On August 4, 1987, the United States sent Iran spare missile parts. Later, the Lebanese terrorists seized more Americans: Frank Reed on September 9, Joseph Cicippio on September 12, and Edward Tracy on October 21. Yielding to terrorists did not work.

Another terroristic event occurred in 1993: More than five U.S. soldiers were killed and two Blackhawk helicopters shot down in a heavy firefight in Mogadishu, the capital of Somalia, on October 4, 1993. The death total for the Somali operation since 1992 had been 16. The helicopters were shot down in an operation to take members of a faction led by General Muhammad Aideed into UN custody. The United States was involved in Somalia as part of the UN humanitarian mission in place there since 1992. After the battle, the bodies of several U.S. casualties in the fight were dragged through the streets of Mogadishu by crowds of local civilians. On October 6, 1993, U.S. President Bill Clinton directed the acting chairman of the Joint Chiefs of Staff, Admiral David E. Jeremiah, to stop all actions by U.S. forces against Aideed except those required in self-defense, and announced that all U.S. forces would withdraw from Somalia no later than March 31, 1994. It is reported that OBL's al Qaeda (AQ) group was involved in killing American troops in Somalia in 1993. The American withdrawal was a victory for OBL, after which he took the jihad to Afghanistan. Besides yielding to the violence, there was a genuine desire by America not to damage its relationship with strategically important Muslim countries: yet this in turn has yielded counterproductive incidents. OBL declared in 1996 and again in 1998 that militant Islamists were at war with the United States. In 1998, his organization, AQ, arranged the near-simultaneous bombing of the American Embassies in Kenya and Tanzania. In 2000, OBL unleashed the attack in Yemen on the destroyer U.S.S. Cole, killing 17. There have been more than 20 Islamist terrorist plots aimed at America since 9/11, including the deadly shooting by U.S. Army Maj. Nidal Hasan, those of Umar Faruk Abdulmutallab and Faisal Shahzad, arrested on May 1, 2010, and those of Najibullah Zazi and his cohorts; Bryant Neal Vinas in a plot to sabotage commuter railroads and subways in New York. There have been plotters who targeted military personnel at Fort Dix, New Jersey, Quantico, Virginia, and Goose Creek, South Carolina; those who murdered an Army recruiter in Little Rock, Arkansas; and those who planned to blow up synagogues in New York, an office building in Dallas, Texas, and a courthouse in Illinois, among others. To this list can be added Ramzi Yusuf's first attempt to blow up the World Trade Center, and the later attempt by Khalid Sheikh Mohammed.[30]

Under Pakistani President General Zia-ul Haq, a coordination effort was formed with the Pakistani Inter Service Intelligence Agency (ISI) which allowed Pakistan's Army to receive money, training, and military equipment including missiles from the United States through the CIA. The stinger missile was key to destroying Soviet military fighter jets. The Soviet Army was finally defeated by the radical Muslim forces with the birth of AQ. Under General Haq, the ISI has become the most powerful institution in Pakistan with ties to the Taliban, which came to power in Afghanistan after the departure of the Soviet Union. The radical Islamists, the Taliban and AQ, grew strong in the interior of Afghanistan and Pakistan. During this period and onwards, Pakistan acquired nuclear weapons and delivery systems, in defiance of American strategic goals. Their development of nuclear weapons continued between 2001 and 2008, despite several reports that U.S. aid money was being diverted to the Pakistan Army to purchase arms and military aircraft for its strategic depth and defense, without combating terrorists. Terrorist organizations including AQ and the Taliban found shelter near the Afghanistan border. Terrorists trained and funded by these organizations went to Asia, America, and Europe, serving as Pakistan's second line of defense. UPI/Washington reported on June 6, 2009, that the Pentagon documents also revealed a major post-9/11 American defense payment of USD 5 billion to Pakistan under FMF (Foreign Military Financing), exclusive of Pakistan's fight against terrorism. While the Taliban and AQ gained ground in the tribal areas of Pakistan bordering Afghanistan, Islamabad bought eight P-3C Orion maritime patrol aircraft and their refurbishments, worth USD 474 million. It also placed orders for 5,250 TOW anti-armor missiles worth USD 186 million. As of this writing, 2,007 of these have been delivered, and the rest are in the process of being supplied.

During his administration, General Zia-ul Haq (1924–1988), with the generous assistance of Saudi Arabia and America, radicalized schools, universities, mosques, civil institutions, the military, and all aspects of Pakistan as per extreme Islamic doctrine. The outside world was a silent spectator in this metamorphosis of Pakistani secular society into a radical Islamic state, due to Zia's support for forming a mujahedeen army to fight against the Soviets. Pakistan became the mother of every kind of religious extremism, sectarianism, and the proliferation of religious monasteries and militias, as well as a breeding ground for terrorists. General Haq started sending terrorist insurgents into Jammu and Kashmir (see Figure 2.2) to seize Kashmir, a Muslim dominated area, and to foment unrest the state of J&K while initiating peace dialogue with India. Nobel Laureate V.S. Naipaul writes:

> Always in the background were the fundamentalists who—fed by the ecstasy of the creation of Pakistan and further fed by the partial Islamization of the laws—wanted to take the country back and back, to the seventh century, to the time of Prophet.[31]

From 1993 to 2001, terrorists from Pakistan, Somalia, Afghanistan, and other restive nations committed many major terrorist attacks. For a complete list of these terrorist attacks and the organizations responsible for them, see Appendix 1.

Several terrorists were assembled by AQ leader OBL to initiate rebellion, and to foment unrest in Asia and Africa. The Taliban leadership or their agents were alleged to have killed Prime Minister Benazir Bhutto. They were also implicated in the bombing of the Marriot Hotel in Islamabad, Pakistan. The Islamization initiated by Zia-ul Haq in 1978–1988 is causing havoc in Pakistan itself. After a request from the Government of Pakistan, headed by Asif Ali Zardari (Ms. Bhutto's husband), and extensive consultations with Pakistani officials as well as with members of the United Nations Security Council, UN Secretary-General Ban Ki-moon appointed a three-member Commission of Inquiry, with Ambassador Heraldo Muñoz, the Permanent Representative of Chile to the United Nations at its head. Also on the commission were Marzuki Darusman, a former Attorney-General of Indonesia, and Peter FitzGerald, a former Deputy Commissioner of the Irish Police, the Garda Siochána. The Commission provided its report (70 pages) to the Secretary-General in March, 2010. The report says:

> [T]he Pakistani Taliban now constitutes a significant threat to Pakistan's internal stability. The jihadi organizations . . . are Sunni groups based largely in Punjab. Members of these groups aided the Taliban's effort in Afghanistan at the behest of the Inter Service Intelligence (ISI) of Pakistan and later cultivated ties with Al-Qaida and Pakistani Taliban groups. The Pakistani military and ISI also used and supported some of these groups in the Kashmir insurgency after 1989. The bulk of the anti-Indian activity was and still remains the work of groups such as Lashkar-e-Taiba, which has close ties with the ISI. A common characteristic of these jihadi groups was their adherence to the Deobandi Sunni sect of Islam, their strong anti-Shia bias, and their use by the Pakistani military and intelligence agencies in Afghanistan and Kashmir.[32]

It is alleged that Faisal Shahzad's attempt on May 1, 2010, to bomb New York City was aided by Pakistani-Taliban terrorist groups, and that Shahzad reportedly took terror lessons from the TTP. The Taliban, under spiritual leader Mullah Mohammad Omar, have had links with, and have shown support for, AQ and its leader, OBL. Mullah Omar left Afghanistan for Pakistan along with several followers, instead of surrendering to NATO forces. The Taliban and AQ have started a global *jihad* movement, and as a result, there are now many terrorist organizations including Lashkar-e Taiba, LeT, Hizb ul-Mujahideen (HuM), al-Badr, the Harkat ul-Mujahideen (HuM), and the Jaish e-Muhammad (JeM). All of them have the same mission: the execution of global terrorist attacks. The rugged tribal area straddling Pakistan and Afghanistan (see Figure 2.2) has become a sanctuary for terrorists. American withdrawal from this area may lead to graver problems of accom-

modation and appeasement of terrorists elsewhere, without accomplishing
the objective of disrupting, dismantling, and defeating terrorist sanctuaries.
Barnett Rubin and Ahmed Rashid comment:

> [The] Pakistan military command, which makes and implements the
> country's national security policies, shares a commitment to a vision of
> Pakistan as the homeland for South Asian Muslims and therefore to the
> incorporation of Kashmir into Pakistan. It considers Afghanistan as within
> Pakistan's security perimeter. Add to this that Pakistan does not have bor-
> der agreements with either India, into which Islamabad contests the incor-
> poration of Kashmir, or Afghanistan, which has never explicitly recog-
> nized the Durand Line, which separates the two countries, as an interstate
> border.[33]

The interpretation is an open invitation to jihadis to incorporate India
and Afghanistan into Pakistan's writ and suzerainty. Surrendering to radicalism and territorial hegemony will have a catastrophic impact on the regions of Central Asia, including Uzbekistan, Tajikistan, Kazakhstan, and
beyond (see Figures 3 and 4). Several terrorist organizations like the Islamic Movement of Uzbekistan (IMU) and the East Turkestan Islamic Movement (ETIM) were blamed for what took place in Kyrgyzstan in late 2002
and in 2003. Hizb-ut-Tahrir (HuT), a London-based radical Islamic movement, is operating in the southern regions of Kyrgyzstan. Like the IMU, the
HuT is engaged in the creation of a region-wide Islamic form of governance. There are several religious separatists who can destabilize the region, including: Euskadi Ta Askatasuna (ETA), Kurdish Separatists, the
PKK in Turkey, All Parties Hurriyat Conference (APHC) in India, Abu
Sayyaf Group (ASG) in the Philippines, Pattani United Liberation Organization (PULO) in Thailand, Uighur Autonomous Region Separatists of
Xinjiang (Chinese Turkistan) in China,[34] and the Chechen Separatist Party
in Russia.[35]

There are some secular separatist organizations, such as the Baluchistan
Liberation Army (BLA), which is fighting to establish a separate sovereign
state of Baluchistan, as agreed upon in the 1940 Lahore Agreement. The
BLA considers Pakistan to be a terrorist state.

While Islamic terrorists target Christians, Jews, Hindus, and even Muslims, some commentators and authors ignore the severity of terrorism, pointing out that the casualties from earthquakes, tsunamis, road accidents, cigarette smoking, and crime far outnumber deaths due to terrorism. Some authors
compare the terrorists' assault of 9/11 to the Oklahoma City bombing, as a
justification for Islamic terrorism. They mention the Thugs of India of the
nineteenth century as the earliest religious terrorists (forgetting the Islamic

Assassins hundreds of years earlier). Thugs were bandits who looted travelers to get money and belongings. The thugs were Hindus, Sikhs, and Muslims, and had nothing to do with the Hindu goddess Kali, even if they prayed to her. The word thug comes from the Hindi word *thag,* meaning a swindler. Thugs terrorized travelers only to get money and goods, rarely killing people[36] (Chapter 3 on Hinduism).

Terrorists strike for political, ideological, and religious reasons and can get away with it, particularly in states that do not retaliate against them. Indian Airlines Flight 814 Airbus A 300 was hijacked on December 24, 1999, by five Pakistan nationals belonging to HuM, a Pakistan-based militant group. The hijacking lasted for seven days and ended after India released the following Islamic militants: Mushtaq Ahmed Zargar, Ahmed Omar Saeed Sheikh, and Masood Azhar (who later founded Jaish-e-Mohammed). The released Muslim criminals were Maulana Masood Azhar of LeT, JeM, Mushtaq Ahmed Zargar HuM, and al-Badr. Ahmed Omar Saeed Sheikh, who had been imprisoned in connection with the 1994 kidnappings of Western tourists in India, was later arrested for the murder of American reporter Daniel Pearl. These released extremists were later involved in various terror attacks in India and in the September 11, 2001 World Trade Center attack in the United States. Even in the wake of the LeT terrorist attacks in Mumbai (Bombay), India, which left 170 people dead, India has not been able to bomb terrorist sanctuaries, as America did in Afghanistan in 2001. As of 2000, the United States does not negotiate with terrorists under any circumstances. Under current international law, the government in each of the Middle East, South Asia, Somalia, among others, remains accountable for all actions, including mezzanine rulers, like Hezbollah, Hamas, Lashkar-e-Taiba, the Taliban,al Qaeda, within the territory over which it has sovereignty.

> This responsibility is grounded in the traditional Westphalia principle of territorial sovereignty and was reaffirmed in the resolution that the UN Security Council passed in response to 9/11, in which it directed all UN members to prevent and suppress, in their territories through all lawful means, the financing and preparation of any acts of terrorism. But the attacks of September 11, 2001, have exposed the flaws in the long-standing principles of territorial integrity and non-intervention in the internal affairs of another state without its consent.[37]

Terrorist attacks cause loss of tourism, economic hardship, and destruction of buildings and infrastructure. They damage communal harmony and cause traumatic disorders, including post-traumatic stress disorder (PTSD). Millions of Kashmir Pundits residing in refugee camps as a result of ethnic cleansing, driven by Islamic terrorists from Jammu and Kashmir, are suffering from PTSD. Terrorists have also caused havoc in Thailand and the Philippines, where ethnic cleansing has driven Buddhists and Christians from their homes in search of a safe haven. Even Pakistan, an Islamic state, has yielded to extremist fundamentalists in the SWAT Valley, allowing Sharia law in an attempt to appease the Taliban. But the Taliban interpreted this as a weakness, and started to exert control in Buner, closer to the Pakistani capital of Islamabad. As Fouad Ajami comments:

> The drama of the Swat Valley—its cynical abandonment to the mercy of the Taliban, the terror unleashed on it by the militants, then the recognition that the concession to the forces of darkness had not worked—is of a piece with the larger history of religious extremism in the world of Islam.[38]

Attempting to win the hearts and minds of terrorists through negotiations, complying with long lists of demands by AQ and others, and providing more aid to countries that support terror all fall into the category of yielding to violence, and represent symbolic weakness. Terrorists in Central Asia, the Northern Caucasus, and Xinjiang Province; Palestine's several groups, including Hamas; the Southern Thailand Groups; the Philippines' Abu Sayyaf Groups, and Kashmir's AHPC separatists are products of a culture of violence, brutality, and mayhem. After the American withdrawal of forces from Lebanon, Somalia, and other places in the face of terrorist attacks, terrorists and their patrons concluded that America was a paper tiger. But in the aftermath of 9/11, America responded correctly in Afghanistan. The response was appropriate and no additional major terrorist attacks followed, except a few by home-grown terrorists. These alienated domestic terrorists may be driven by "jihadi intent," by the failure to find "a sense of belonging, a sense of purpose," and sometimes by radical imams.[39] Such alienation in liberal, secular, democratic countries like France, Britain, and America is not due to financial difficulties or joblessness. After America's response in Iraq to the possible presence of WMDs, Libya immediately announced its abandonment of a nuclear weapon program. Britain and Spain, however, have experienced several terrorist attacks and have unearthed terrorist cells since 2001. India also has faced many terrorist attacks, partly because they have not retaliated.

Oil and Gas

There are numerous oil and gas reserves in Muslim countries including Iran, Iraq, and Indonesia. The western countries as well as Japan, China, and India depend on this supply. Energy dependency varies: the United States takes only 10 per cent of its oil and gas from this resource, while Japan takes 80 per cent, Europe 30 per cent, and China and India more than 25 per cent each. Radical Islamists want to destroy the energy supply routes to these countries, although most of the funding for militant religious schools that breed terror comes from petrodollars in the Gulf region. Table 2.1 shows oil and gas reserves, while Table 2.2 shows oil consumption by the top twenty-two energy-using countries.

Table 2.1
Oil and Gas Reserves

Countries	Oil Billion Barrel (bbl)	Natural Gas (Cubic Feet)
North America	209,910	308,794
Central and South America	122,689	266,541
Europe	13,651	169,086
Eurasia	98,886	1,993,800
Middle East	745,998	2,591,653
Africa	117,064	494,078
Asia and Oceania	34,006	430, 412
World Total	1,342,207	6,254,364

* *Oil and Gas Journal Estimate*, December 22, 2008, for January 1, 2009.

The Middle East has more energy reserves than any other region of the world; its reservoirs contain 60.4 per cent of the world's oil. Yet the Arab countries have the highest unemployment rates in the world. According to the IMF Estimates, the affluent Arab countries are listed in Table 2.3 lists the Arab countries by level of affluence, according to estimates by the International Money Fund.

Most of the Arab countries are headed by repressive leaders, and lag behind in investment, trade, productivity, education, and social development. The total manufacturing exports of the entire Arab world is less than that of the Philippines, even though the Philippines have less than one third the population of the Arab world. Unemployment among Arab youth is the highest in the world. In light of all this, some changes have taken place in the last five years, with the Gulf Countries Council (GCC) spending $50 billion on higher education. Qatar has persuaded some famous American

Table 2.2

Oil Consumption by Top Twenty-Two Countries

	Countries	Amount	Year
1	United States	20,680,000 bbl/day	2007
2	European Union	14,390,000 bbl/day	2007
3	China	7,578,000 bbl/day	2007
4	Japan	5,007,000 bbl/day	2007
5	Russia	2,858,000 bbl/day	2007
6	India	2,722,000 bbl/day	2007
7	Germany	2,456,000 bbl/day	2007
8	Brazil	2,372,000 bbl/day	2007
9	Canada	2,371,000 bbl/day	2007
10	Saudi Arabia	2,311,000 bbl/day	2007
11	Korea, South	2,214,000 bbl/day	2007
12	MexicoMexico	2,119,000 bbl/day	2007
13	France	1,950,000 bbl/day	2007
14	United Kingdom	1,763,000 bbl/day	2007
15	Italy	1,702,000 bbl/day	2007
16	Iran	1,679,000 bbl/day	2006
17	Spain	1,611,000 bbl/day	2007
18	Indonesia	1,219,000 bbl/day	2006
19	Netherlands	984,200 bbl/day	2007
20	Australia	966,200 bbl/day	2007
21	Taiwan	950,500 bbl/day	2006
22	Thailand	928,600 bbl/day	2006
	Total	**85,085,664 bbl/day**	
	Weighted average	**399,463.2 bbl/day**	

* *Oil and Gas Journal Estimate*, for January 2009

Notes: This entry is the total oil consumed in barrels per day (bbl/day). The discrepancy between the amount of oil produced and/or imported and the amount consumed and/ or exported is due to the omission of stock changes, refinery gains, and other complicating factors. The United States, the European Union, China, and Japan are top users with 24.3 per cent, 16.9 per cent, 8.9 per cent and 5.9 per cent of the total consumptions.

Source: All CIA World Fact books 18 December 2003 to 18 December 2008. This list was last updated on April 2, 2009.

Table 2.3
Affluent Arab Countries

Country	Population (million)	GDP (billion)	GDP (billion)/person
Saudi Arabia	25	370	14.7
United Arab Emirate	4.9	215	43.9
Kuwait	3.5	106	30.0
Qatar	1.2	100	81.9
Bahreïn	2.8	43	15.0
Oman	2.8	43	15.0
Libya	6.3	63	9.9
Lebanon	3.8	31	8.1
Tunisia	10.4	40	3.8
Algeria	35.3	129	3.6
Egypt	76.5	188	2.5

* See also: *The Economist*, July 25, 2009.

universities to open campuses in Doha. Dubai has 32 American university campuses, and Saudi Arabia will spend $10 billion on the King Abdullah University of Science and Technology.[40]

The huge wealth in the Arab world accompanies high unemployment rates as a result of the autocratic, theocratic, and despotic rulers' ineptitude. As Fouad Ajami observes:

> It is no mystery, this sorrowful decline of the Arabs. They have invested their hopes in states, and the states have failed. According to the UNDP's (United Nation Development Program) report, government revenues as percentage of GDP are 13 per cent in Third World Countries, but they are 25 per cent in the Middle East and North Africa. The oil states are a world apart in that regard: the comparable figures are 68 per cent in Libya, 45 per cent in Saudi Arabia, and 40 per cent in Algeria, Kuwait and Qatar. Oil is no panacea for these lands. The unemployment rates for the Arab world as a whole are the highest in the world, and no prophecy could foresee these societies providing the 51 million jobs the UNDP report says are needed by 2020 to absorb young entrants to the labor force who would otherwise face an empty future. . . . The simple truth is that the Arab world has terrible rulers and worse oppositionists. There are autocrats on one side and theocrats on the other. A timid and fragile middle class is caught in the middle between regimes it abhors and Islamists it fears.[41]

Poverty in the Arab countries is detailed in the Arab Human Development Report 2009, *Challenges to Human Security in the Arab Countries*, which projects that 65 million Arabs live in poverty:

> Arab countries are generally regarded as having a relatively low incidence of income poverty. In 2005, about 20.3 per cent of the Arab population was living below the two-dollars-a-day international poverty line. This estimate is based on seven Arab middle and low-income groups, whose population represents about 63 per cent of the total population of the Arab countries not in conflict. Using the international line indicates that, in 2005, about 34.6 million Arabs were living in extreme poverty. However, the two-dollars-a-day threshold may not be the most illuminating metric for looking at poverty in the Arab countries. The upper national poverty line shows that the overall poverty rate ranges from a low of 28.6–30 per cent in Lebanon and Syria to a high of 59.5 per cent in Yemen, with that for Egypt being about 41 per cent. Extrapolating from a sample of countries representing 65 per cent of the region's population, the Report projects that the overall headcount poverty ratio at the upper poverty line is 39.9 per cent and that the estimated number of Arabs living in poverty could be as high as 65 million.[42]

Radical Islamists believe that American forces are stationed in the Middle East and Gulf areas to have access to cheap oil and to protect Israel.

International Islamization and radicalization started in 1960s with the discovery that the Middle East had substantial oil resources, and the rise of fundamentalist schools in Asia and Africa and with proliferation radical madrassas and mosques. In 2007, there were 14,072 registered madrassas in Pakistan and the actual number of all kinds of madrassas is likely to be around 20,000.

> In Punjab, two militant groups fighting in Kashmir sponsored madrassas with the funding they partly received from Pakistani intelligence agencies.

> During the Taliban years, a good number of Deobandi and Ahle-Hadees madrassas in the NWFP, Punjab and Karachi used to send their students to Afghanistan to fight alongside the Taliban. On their return, they could be recruited for Pakistan-based militant groups.[43]

People from the Asian and African Muslim countries adopted Arabic culture. They and their children wanted to be Saudi. When they migrated to Western countries, they carried the baggage of Arabic culture and customs with them. Their children had lived in cross-cultural environments. Madrassas and mosques became the breeding ground for Islamic terrorism with the establishment of Wahhabi mosques featuring fiery, radical imams like Omar Abdel Rahman and Anwar al-Awlaki and others. These mosques were funded by Gulf countries to establish Islamic rule—no democracy, no secularism, no separation of church and state, no equality for women, and no criticism of Islam and the Prophet. Besides personal law, Sharia includes the five pillars of Islam: faith, prayer, fasting alms, and pilgrimage. To justify the spread of Sharia around the world by means of jihad, some Imams and AQ leaders cite this verse from the Quran (45:18): "And now. We have set you on the right path (Sharia). Follow it, and do not yield to the desires of ignorant men; for they can in no way protect you from the wrath of God."

Ulemas are legal scholars at the frontlines of totalitarian Islam who control and decide all aspects of Sharia law. They are quite closed-minded, despite the Quranic path of increasing personal knowledge. They have the authority to make Islamic laws, and do not represent a parliamentary body. Despite the power of the *ulemas,* these laws have been broken by many Muslim jurists. Damascus-born Izz al-Din Ibn Abd al Salam of the thirteenth century rejected the ban on interest, as well as stoning to death as punishment for adultery. For the vast majority of Muslim students and mosque goers, Islam means submission and a Muslim is one who has submitted to Allah. The Islamic obligation is to fight and overthrow any leader who does not govern according to Sharia. Any form of government (democratic, secular, or Communist) other than Sharia is considered a blasphemy.[44] It is reported that another Christmas tradition in Indonesia—which Mr. Obama neglected to mention (in his visit to Indonesia in November 2010)—is the annual round of threats and violence against Christians from the Islamic Defenders Front and other radical groups. In January, a mob of 1,000 Muslims burned down two churches in Sumatra because there were "too many faithful and too many prayers" going on. Between 2004 and 2007, Muslim radicals and local governments forced 110 Christian churches to close. If shared parking lots are the best example of tolerance in Indonesia, it has a long way to go. In Pakistan, Asia Bibi, a 45-year-old Christian mother of five, was sentenced to death for alleged blasphemy against Muhammad. She had been working on a farm with other women when she was asked to fetch some drinking water. Her Muslim co-workers refused to drink it because it was "unclean" after being touched by a Christian. An argument broke out, and later Ms. Bibi was attacked by a mob.

The oil revenue from Gulf countries has been a consistent source of funding for terrorist organizations. It also served as a weapon of leverage vis-à-vis the Western policy toward Muslim countries. Western countries have had to adopt a policy that is not hostile to Muslim countries or Islam. Violence, a marching order for jihad, flourishes with terrorism abroad and brutality at home. With the discovery of oil and gas in Islamic countries, there has been a resurgence of Islam in Muslim areas including Indonesia, Malaysia, and South Asia. The collapse of the Soviet Union added more fuel to the rise of Islam in Northern Caucasus and Central Asia, along with the separatist movements in these areas that have been responsible for savage killings. Muslims, constituting one fifth of humanity, are commanding respect and dignity. Other religious groups do not consider their size to be their strength. For radical Islamists, Islam was spread by the sultanic sword in the past, and could be spread again by violent jihad methods and by its non-violent weapon: oil wealth. Another non-violent weapon is religious conversion by non-Muslims. Among Muslim women, 80 per cent are converts. The distinguished historian Juan Cole notes: "Among the major drivers of Islam anxiety is the dependence of the United States and its major allies on petroleum and gas produced in the Gulf."[45] The American military presence in the Gulf area, which is perceived as being to secure energy, has been a major cause of suicide attacks on America. Robert Pape writes:

> First, Al Qaeda's suicide terrorists have not come from the most Islamic fundamentalist populations in the world, but mainly from the Muslim countries with heavy American combat presence. From 1995 through 2003, there have been a total of seventy-one Al Qaeda suicide terrorists. Only six per cent (4 out of 71) have come from the five countries with the largest Islamic fundamentalist populations—Pakistan (149 million), Bangladesh (114 million), Iran (63 million), Egypt (62 million), and Nigeria (37 million). By contrast, 55 per cent of al-Qaeda terrorists (39 of 71) have come from Saudi Arabia and other Persian Gulf countries, a region whose population totals less than 30 million, but where the United States has stationed heavy combat troops more or less continuously since 1990.[46]

Saudi Arabia has less population than Pakistan, Bangladesh, or Indonesia, but as home to Mecca, Medina, and Salafism/Wahhabism, it pours money into countries throughout the world to maintain radical mosques and madrassas. Recipients of Arab petrodollars including the state of Jammu and Kashmir in India, the South Asian and South East Asian countries, the Central Asian countries neighboring Afghanistan, and the Central Asian countries adjacent to Afghanistan, India and Pakistan are shown in Figures 2.2, 2.3, 2.4 and 2.5.

Figure 2.2. Jammu and Kashmir (J&K)

* Courtesy of Kashmir Newz

Figure 2.3. South Asia (Afghanistan, Pakistan, and India), and Southeast Asia (Bangladesh, Indonesia, Thailand, and the Philippines)

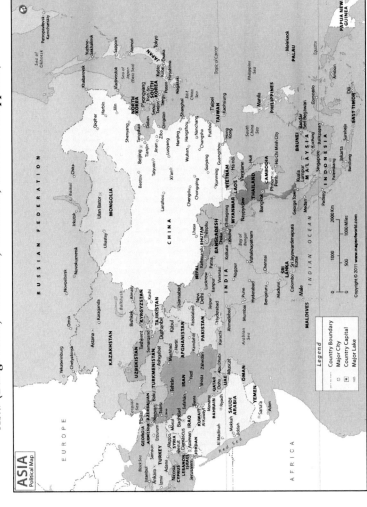

Courtesy of Kartik Suri, www.mapofworld.com.

Figure 2.4. Central Asia, Showing the Countries Neighboring Afghanistan, Tajikistan, Uzbekistan, Turkmenistan, Kazakhstan, and Pakistan

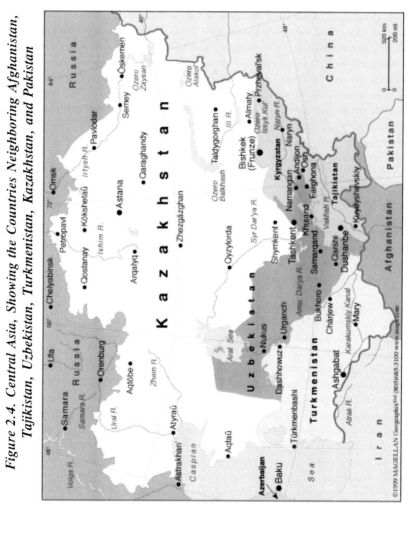

Courtesy of Indiana University Research Center, Bloomington, Indiana.

Figure 2.5. Central Asia, Showing the Countries Adjacent to Afghanistan, India and Pakistan, with Iraq and Turkey to the West

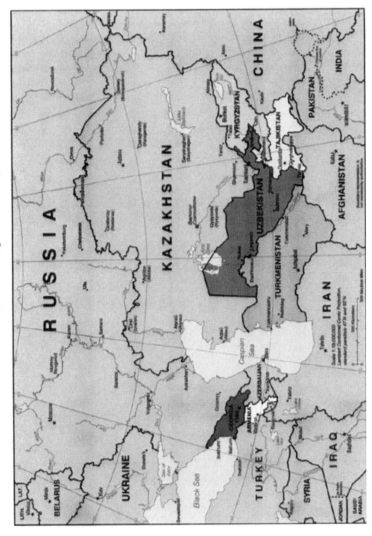

Courtesy of Indiana University Research Center. Bloomington. Indiana.

Multiculturalism and Muslim Identity

In the eighteenth century, a French immigrant, J. Hector St. John de Crevecoeur, wrote about multiculturalism in America in a series of letters now known as *Letters from an American Farmer.* He wrote:

> What then is the American, this new man? He is an American, who, leaving behind him all of his ancient prejudices and manners, receives new ones from the new mode of life he has embraced, the new government he obeys, and the new rank he holds. He has become an American by being received in the broad lap of our great Alma Mater. Here individuals of all races are melted into a new race of man, whose labors and posterity will one day cause great changes in the world.[47]

This has been echoed over generations by several authors, including Thomas Paine, Herman Melville, Ralph Waldo Emerson, George Washington, John Quincy Adams, Alexis de Tocqueville, James Bryce, and Gunnar Myrdal, who have observed the dissolution of individuals' nationality and ethnic identity. It has culminated with the election of America's first African-American President, Barack Hussein Obama. In 2009, African-Americans accounted for 13 per cent of the total of the U.S. population, but 35 per cent of the American Muslim population. A total of 2.5 million Muslims live in the United States, comprising approximately 0.8 per cent of the U.S. population.

Multiculturalism is a culture of many interwoven ethnicities, races, and civilizations, each one contributing and integrating into a magnificent cultural mosaic that allows understanding and appreciation of cultural differences in a friendly atmosphere devoid of hatred and prejudice. Multi-ethnicity and religiosity are brought about by immigrants and their children, who may be asylum and employment seekers, refugees, political dissidents, invaders, settlers, and laborers from colonial days, and people who have escaped from oppression, prosecution, or poverty in other countries with various religious and ethnic affiliations. There are some communities and people, however, who are attached to their roots and are striving to maintain a separate territory with only their own culture, heritage, and customs. They want separate schools, legal systems, and local governments. Islamists want to have Sharia wherever they reside, as well as separate Muslim schools: in fact, a mini-state of their own within the adopted country. They wish to use Sharia to support the abuse of women, forcing them into subservient roles; punish adultery and apostasy with death; and establish other rigid tenets of Islam. Multiculturalism allows citizens to make others understand their ethnic identity, culture, cuisine, customs, and even clothing as another color in the cultural mosaic. But homogeneous communities with only the culture of origin, in which the culture of their adopted country is forced out, can lead to segregated communities, diluted allegiances, and fractured national unity. The concept of multiple identities prevents Muslim immigrants from adopting the culture and heritage of their adopted country. But other ethnic and religious groups have integrated with their adopted country and merged with the mainstream. On the other hand, Muslims take advantage of multiculturalism to live and practice Sharia, adopting the seventh-century version of Islam just as they would in a Muslim country. Their keeping this separate identity leads to a threat of Islamic expansion and totalitarianism. Most of U.K.'s 1.6 million Muslims (in 2005) live in segregated Muslim neighborhoods, and there are 1500 plus mosques in the United Kingdom. Non-Muslims living in Muslim countries do not enjoy the benefits of multiculturalism.

The great thinker Paul Johnson wrote:

> The West is not alone in being under threat from Islamic expansion. While the Ottomans moved into South-East Europe, the Mogul invasion of India destroyed much of Hindu and Buddhist civilization there. The recent destruction by Moslems in Afghanistan of colossal Buddhist statues is a reminder of what happened to temples and shrines, on an enormous scale, when Islam took over. The distinguished writer V. S. Naipaul has recently pointed out that the destructiveness of the Moslem Conquest is at the root of India's appalling poverty today. Indeed, looked at historically, the record shows that Moslem rule has tended both to promote and to perpetuate poverty.[48]

Such lack of respect for other cultures, religions, and ethnicities leads to misunderstanding, misinformation, and the manufacture of bigots and zealots. The Saudi education systems has over 5 million students, all of whom are required to read *The Protocols of the Elders Zion,* a notorious anti-Semitic forgery that preaches deep hatred of Shiite Muslims, Christians, Jews, Hindus, Buddhists, and others. If one student per thousand in Saudi Arabia becomes radical as a result of reading this book, that will produce 5000 radical Islamists.

The great historian Arthur Schlesinger, Jr. wrote:

> History is littered with the wreck of states that tried to combine diverse ethnic or linguistic or religious groups with a single sovereignty. . . . The purpose of history is to promote not group-self esteem, but understanding of the world and the past, dispassionate analysis, judgment, and perspective, respect for the divergent cultures and traditions, and unflinching pro-

tection for those unifying ideas of tolerance, democracy, sand human rights that make free historical inquiry possible.[49]

Multiculturalism has failed or is failing in India, Canada, and the United Kingdom, among other countries. Religions or cultures that teach prejudice, hatred, and inequality and prohibits freedom and plurality must not be a part of multiculturalism. Tolerance has to represent strength, not weakness. Gustavo de Arstegui, the author of *The Jihad in Spain,* notes:

> *The Obsession to Reconquer al-Andalus* (2005), dispels the myth that medieval Spain was a perfect example of peaceful and prosperous existence of all three monotheistic religions and blames the University of al-Azzhar in Egypt for obsessing over the concept of conquering land that was once under the domain of Islam.

For Arstegui, the coexistence of multiculturalism and political correctness has failed miserably.[50] For Muslims, multiculturalism means that they will be under the rule of law as administered by Muslim legal systems in non-Muslim lands, not by Western legal systems. They also believe that their religion in a multicultural society is not just morally equal, but superior to any others practiced, as it is governed only by Allah. Muslim immigration has brought with it an upsurge in religious chauvinism. Although European immigrants blended with mainstream America, enhancing the American mosaic and galvanizing the melting pot, Muslim *hijras,* or immigrants, in Europe, remain in religious ghettos in order to be secluded from Western cultures and modernism. Multiculturalism is an appeasement policy or another form of segregation. This has sowed the seeds of Muslim separatism. As Francis Fukuyama observes:

> The real challenge for democracy lies in Europe, where the problem is an internal one of integrating large numbers of angry young Muslims and doing so in a way that does not provoke an even angrier backlash from right-wing populists. Two things need to happen: First, countries like Holland and Britain need to reverse the counterproductive multiculturalists' policies that sheltered radicalism, and crack down on extremists. But second, they also need to reformulate their definitions of national identity to be more accepting of people from non-Western backgrounds.[51]

During 2010, both the Dutch and British recognized that the old version of multiculturalism they formerly practiced was dangerous and counterproductive. Liberal tolerance was respected not for the rights of individuals, but of groups, some of whom were themselves intolerant (for example, dictating whom their daughters could befriend or marry). Muslim minorities were allowed to regulate their own behavior, an attitude which dovetailed with a traditional European corporatist approach to social organization. In Holland, it was easy enough to add a Muslim "pillar" that quickly turned into a ghetto disconnected from the surrounding society of other religions. New policies to reduce the separateness of the Muslim community, such as laws discouraging the importation of brides from the Middle East, have been accepted in the Netherlands. The Dutch and British police have new powers to monitor, detain, and expel inflammatory clerics. But the much more difficult problem is fashioning a national identity that connects citizens of all religions and ethnicities in a common culture, as the American society has served to unite new immigrants to the United States.

On the other hand, to promote multiculturalism and cultural diversity, the BBC network provides news and entertainment to religious minorities and ethnic groups. In the United Kingdom, apartments are built so that toilets do not face the direction of Mecca. Muslim students in the public schools are not allowed to watch Christian festivals or take part in Christian cultural traditions. Such students are not taught British history, civilization, customs, culture, heritage, and literature. As if this is not enough to prompt a resurgence of Islam extremism, students are sent to Pakistan to obtain the necessary background. It will be hard for these students to be assimilated and to feel British. Christopher Marlowe's play *Tamburlaine the Great* was banned in Britain in 2005 because Tamburlaine burned the Quran and criticized the Prophet Mohammed. These separatist trends have been supported by politicians in order to obtain Muslim votes. Democratic values have been abused; Dr. Yaqub Zaki, deputy leader of the Muslim Parliament was not charged after he said that he would be "very happy" if there was a terrorist attack on Downing Street and would not mind what happened to the inhabitants of No. 10, the residence of the Prime Minister of the United Kingdom.[52] France has banned Muslim head coverings at public schools to support integration. See Figure 2.6 for examples of the head coverings worn by Muslim women.

The *hijab* is a scarf used to cover the hair and neck, but not the face. The *burqa* is a garment that covers the head, neck, shoulders, and upper torso along with the face. It is also known as a *chador* or *chadri,* and is associated with Afghanistan and with the Indian subcontinent. *Niqab* refers to a slip of cloth that covers the face, and is worn with the *hijab.*[53] There are several variants of the *burqa* in Muslim countries. Banning the wearing of burqas and hijabs in public schools is meant to promote secular education, safety, and security, and to foster harmony among students. Critics say that banning headscarves is thus a Band-Aid, a conservative effort to halt the

Figure 2.6a. Head Coverings for Muslim Women: Burqa

Courtesy of Professor Marc Shaw of Australia

Radicalism in Islam

Figure 2.6b. Head Coverings for Muslim Women: Niqab

Courtesy of Professor Marc Shaw of Australia

Figure 2.6c. Head Coverings for Muslim Women: Burqa and Niqab

Courtesy of Professor Marc Shaw of Australia

ripping of the school's fabric. But it stops France's social unraveling on at least one front, and with luck and political leadership could initiate the process by which France finds its way to a new secularist covenant between all children of the country.[54] In 2009, French President Nicolas Sarkozy addressed Parliament on the religious identity of Muslim women who wear burqas. In doing so, he laid out a vision of France that included a withering critique of burqas as an unacceptable symbol of "enslavement." Speaking at the Palace of Versailles, Mr. Sarkozy confronted one of the most hotly debated social issues in France, saying there was no room in the republic for burqas, the garments that some Muslim women wear to cloak their bodies and faces. "The issue of the burqa is not a religious issue. It is a question of freedom and of women's dignity," Mr. Sarkozy said. "The burqa is not a religious sign. It is a sign of the subjugation, of the submission, of women." To enthusiastic applause, he continued, "I want to say solemnly that it will not be welcome on our territory. In our country, we cannot accept that women be prisoners behind a screen, cut off from all social life, deprived of all identity."[55] In 2008, 51.45 million of Europe's 735.2 million people were Muslims, with 10 per cent of those residing in France. According to a poll, 70 per cent of French respondents favor banning the burqa in public, followed by Spain and Italy with 65 per cent and 63 per cent, respectively. About 57 per cent of Britons and 50 per cent of Germans support such a ban, as do 33 per cent of Americans, according to the poll.[56]

The distinguished journalist Christopher Caldwell described Europe's basic problem with Islam:

> This problem exists in all European countries, despite a broad variety of measures taken to solve it—multiculturalism in Holland, *laicite* (secular society) in France, benign neglect in Britain, constitutional punctiliousness in Germany. . . . Islam is a magnificent religion that has also been, at times over the centuries, a glorious and generous culture. But, all cant to the contrary, it is in no sense Europe's religion and it is in no sense Europe's culture.[57]

In Europe and Canada, multiculturalism has secluded and segregated Muslim youth from Western values and liberalism. Unfortunately, unemployed Muslim youth who are being helped by the European and Canadian welfare systems have become radicalized. They believe the money has been effectively stolen from families like their own. In their view, the state takes away 50 per cent of the funds the United Nations sends for distribution. Following is a list of young men in this category who have attempted terrorist acts.[58] Mohammed Metin Kaplan of Germany, founder of Caliphate State, was extradited to Turkey for planning to fly a plane into the mausoleum of Kemal Ataturk. Ahmed Ressam of Montreal, Canada was arrested in Washington State en route to blow up Los Angeles Airport. Abdul Nacer Benbrika of Melbourne, Australia has been jailed for terrorism and related activities. Abu Hamza, a radical Imam of London, was charged for incitement and sent to jail. He sued the government for extra benefits on top of the 1,000 pounds a week his family already received. Abu Qatada of Britain, a leading AQ recruiter, has a bank account of 150,000 pounds. "Police are investigating allegations that the four suspected July 21 bombers collected more than 500,000 pounds in benefits payments in Britain," as reported in *The Times* of London.[59]

In Europe, Asia, and America, affirmative action, diversity, and multiculturalism are designed to foster equal opportunity for all races, cultures, religions, and ethnicities, while favoring minorities in education, and employment, and ensuring proportionate representation in police and law enforcement to reverse bias, and racism of past decades. Yet disaffected people still feel they are discriminated against, and believe that they should have the freedom, as well as state money, to re-establish (for example) Andalusia, the center of power in medieval, Muslim-dominated Spain, wherever they live. The welfare money they receive to alleviate their financial burden is used for the Islamization of their neighborhood. Riots in France and Denmark have forced the government to ensure diversity in jobs, education, entertainment, broadcast media, and even in cabinet positions. Some of the Cabinet appointees even suggested including diversity in the preamble to the French constitution.[60] There has been significant advancement and progress for minorities, who have become presidents, chief justices, and governors, among other high-profile occupations.

In Denmark, thousands of Tamils and several thousand Vietnamese assimilated without causing any problem. According to Danish People's Party's parliamentarian Jesper Langballe, "they are no problem—totally integrated." Mexican immigrants blend well in America, as Mexicans do not have jihad, honor killing, or polygamy, nor do they require halal meat, special schools, and dress code requirements. It is a family dishonor if a Muslim girl is in love with a non-Muslim boy and wants to marry him, and because of this, several Muslim girls have committed suicide to save their family's honor. A teenage girl in Canada was beaten to death by her parents for wearing non-Muslim dress in school, which she hid in her school locker. She simply wanted to be like any other girl in school, and to spared the embarrassment of curious looks from others. Italian journalist Oriana Fallaci wrote:

[T]en years ago a French–Turkish girl of Colmar was stoned by her mother and father and brother and uncles because she had fallen in love with a Catholic and wanted to marry him. ("Better dead than dishonored" was that family's comment). Where in November 2001, just two months after September 11, a French–Moroccan girl of Galleria, Corsica, was stabbed to death with twenty-four knife wounds by her father because she was about to marry a Corsican who was also Catholic ("Better a life sentence than dishonor" was the father's comment at the arrest).[61]

Rifqa Bary, a 17-year-old Christian convert from Columbus, Ohio who ran away to an Evangelical church in Orlando, Florida, claims that her Sri Lankan Muslim family has threatened to kill her.[62]

Another minority community, variously known as the Gypsies, Roma, or Romany, migrated out of India in the twelfth century, and went to Iran, then to Egypt, subsequently to Anatolia and then to Europe, including the former Communist countries. There are 6 million or more Gypsies in various countries, including Romania, Czechoslovakia, Germany, Kosovo, and Italy. Half a million Gypsies were massacred during the holocaust by Hitler because they were not pure Aryans. They are very docile, not rebellious, and they have not created problems. They have been absorbed into various countries in Europe, which have accepted their religion, language, and culture. American pop singer Madonna remarked while on stage during a music tour of Romania that she was "compelled" to comment on the discrimination against Romany Gypsies in Romania, despite being booed by fans. The 51-year-old was jeered by the audience in Bucharest after saying the discrimination "made me feel very sad." Publicist Liz Rosenberg said Madonna made the comments after being made aware of the prejudice towards Romany people in Eastern Europe. Madonna used a group of Roma musicians on her Sticky and Sweet tour. She paused during her two-hour show to say:

> It has been brought to my attention that there is a lot of discrimination against Romanies and Gypsies in general in Eastern Europe. We [Americans] don't believe in discrimination, we believe in freedom and equal rights for everyone.[63]

Muslims living in Europe and other places feel their religious identity more strongly than their national identity. This is because religiosity is high in the Muslim countries of origin. Christians respond differently. Table 2.4 charts terrorists attacks per million by the country of origin of the perpetrators and the target country of the victims.

Table 2.4
Terrorists Attacks per Million

Predominant Religion	Origin Country	Target Country
Muslim	0.44	0.14
Christian	0.21	0.28
Buddhist	0.09	0.05
Hindu	0.06	0.06
Mixed/Other	0.31	0.32

* Source: The 2006 PEW Attitude Project

As could be seen in Table 2.3, the occurrence of terrorism is mostly unrelated to GDP in the country of origin, but is almost always related to the GDP in the target country. Rich countries with high GDP are vulnerable to terrorist attacks, but terrorists do not always originate from poor GDP countries. In other words, poverty is not a major determinant of terrorism. Figure 2.7 looks at religious and nationality identity.

Muslims who have settled in the West have seldom adopted Western values, which include democracy, secularism, and respect and equality for women. Instead of assimilation and adoption, they demand Sharia, and to this end, they have established religious schools, the *madrassas,* where their children can be educated. They have been very successful at this in Canada. Teaching prejudice, racial and gender inequality, and religious brutality should not be a part of education. Values of democracy, freedom of speech, and nationalism should be emphasized rather than religious and ethnic bias and supremacy. Obscurantism and fanaticism should be excluded. In the words of Bruce Bawer,

> No aspect of Western democracy is more anathema to the multicultural mentality than free speech. For multiculturalism encourages self-censorship and condemnation of insensitive utterances that are perceived as potentially offensive to some protected group (Muslim). They know what they believe and stand for. And they are determined not to compromise.[64]

Whether in Tunisia or Indonesia, and despite a wide range of diversity in cultures, geographic locations, and historical heritage, people in Islamic generally adopt an Arab identity. They learn and live by the Arabic language and culture more than their present country's language and ethnicity. Interestingly, non-Arab Muslims constitute a major part of the Muslim world

Figure 2.7. What Do You Consider Yourself First?

What Do You Consider Yourself First?

| ☐ A citizen of your country |
| ■ A Muslim / A Christian |

Muslims in...

	A citizen	A Muslim/Christian
Great Britain	7	81
Spain	3	69
Germany	13	66
France	42	46
Pakistan	5	87
Jordan	21	67
Egypt	23	59
Turkey	19	51
Indonesia	39	36
Nigeria	25	71

Christians in...

	A citizen	A Muslim/Christian
United States	48	42
Germany	59	33
Great Britain	59	24
Russia	63	16
France	83	14
Spain	60	14
Nigeria	43	53

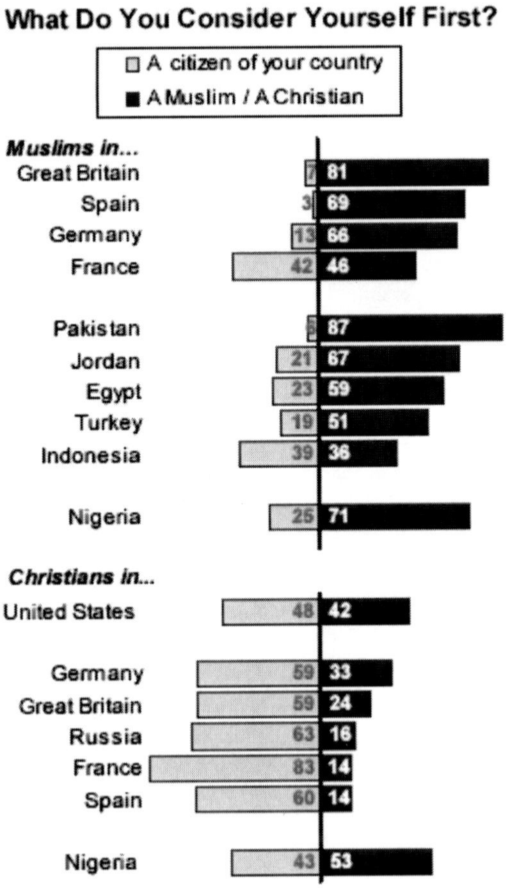

(75 per cent). They have enriched Islamic civilization and culture for centuries. But Arabic hegemony remains powerful, shadowing regional cultures. For example, Pakistani fundamentalists feel that the past history of Pakistan prior to Muslim invasion was barren and banal. The Nobel laureate V.S. Naipaul writes:

> The time before Islam is a time of blackness: that is part of Muslim theology. . . . The excavated city of Mohenjo Daro in the Indus Valley— overrun by the Aryans in 1500 B.C.—is one of the archaeological glories of Pakistan and the world. . . . The current fundamentalists wish in Pakistan to go back to that pure Islamic time has nothing to do with a historical

understanding of the Arab expansion. . . . It was the poet (Allama Muhammad) Iqbal's hope that an Indian Muslim state might rid Islam of "the stamp that Arab imperialism was forced to give it." It turns out now that the Arabs were the most successful imperialists of all time, since to be conquered by them (and then to be like them) is still, in the minds of the faithful, to be saved.[65]

Yet multiculturalism has never found a place in Islamic lands, in the face of Islamic. After the departure of French colonialists from Algeria and Tunisia in 1960s, several churches were burnt and destroyed, while Roman Catholic priests in Algeria were murdered. About 280,000 Christians living in Tunisia were reduced to only 28,000. In Pakistan, Hindus were reduced from 20 per cent to 2 per cent of the population, and there was a similar pattern in Bangladesh. Coptic Christians in Egypt, who constitute 6 per cent of the population, are facing major discrimination, and there are flagrant violations of Christian rights in Sudan. Christians in Pakistan and Bangladesh are often accused of blasphemy. Hindu and Christian girls are kidnapped and raped in Pakistan. Iranian Baha'is are routinely prosecuted. Over the years, a large number of Christians have been killed in, or driven out from, Libya, Turkey, and Iraq. Muslim apostates, converts to Christianity, are condemned to death in Sudan, Egypt, Kuwait, and Morocco.[66]

Secularism, Capitalism, and Globalization

The Middle East scholar Professor Bernard Lewis wrote:

> Secularism in the Christian world was an attempt to resolve the long and destructive struggle of church and state. Separation, adopted in the American and French revolutions and elsewhere after that, was designated to prevent two things: the use of religion by the state to reinforce and extend its authority and the use of state power by the clergy to impose their doctrines and rules on others.[67]

Religion is a private matter for an individual or community, while state affairs, government, and administration are a public matter. There are some overlapping areas, however, including marriage, divorce, inheritance, and abortion. Secular countries have single civil codes for all citizens. But India, a secular country, has three civil codes for each of its major religions, unlike Western countries. Secular governments are based on separation of religion and state affairs. In America, the State does not discriminate on the basis of religion, and religious freedom is pursued with the protection of diversity and pluralism guaranteed by the U.S. Constitution. The term *secu-*

larism was coined by a British scholar, George Jacob Holyoake (1817-1906).
His 1896 publication, *English Secularism,* states:

> Secularism is that which seeks the development of the physical, moral,
> and intellectual nature of man to the highest possible point, as the immedi-
> ate duty of life—which inculcates the practical sufficiency of natural mo-
> rality apart from Atheism, Theism, or the Bible—which selects as its meth-
> ods the promotion of procedure, the promotion of human improvement by
> material means, and proposes these positive agreements as the common
> bond of union, to all who would regulate by reason and ennoble by its
> service. Secularism is a code of duty pertaining to this life, founded on
> considerations purely human, and intended mainly for those who find the-
> ology indefinite or inadequate, unreliable or unbelievable. Its essential
> principles are three: (1) The improvement of this life by material means,
> (2) That science is the available Providence of man, and (3) That it is good
> to do well. Whether there be other good or not, the good of the present life
> is good, and it is good to seek that good.[68]

In the last hundred years, secularism has become established and has
spread on every continent—and it continues to grow. In his Templeton Prize-
winning book, *A Secular Age*, Charles Taylor observed that while function-
ing and following the norms and principles of maximum gain within the
economy, and the greatest benefit to the greatest number in the political
area, we do not mention God.[69] Additionally, as part of rationality in various spheres of activity, including education, the economy, politics, culture,
the professional and recreational spheres, or in any deliberations, we do not
refer to God or to religious beliefs. The earlier authoritative prescriptions of
Christianity and the obligation to enforce orthodoxy are ignored. Christians
and Jews have accepted the concept of the separation of church and state,
using the Bible and Torah to govern social and religious matters. Hindus
have historically viewed sacred matters as outside the realm of the state,
from the days of Vedic civilization.[70] Buddhists, who represent one fifth of
the world's population, keep strictly religious matters beyond the span of
government perimeters. However, in Islam, Sharia regulates Muslims in all
state and family matters.

Muslim scholars are of split opinions on the subject of secularism. For
Muslim societies, the acceptance of secularism means the denial of Islamic
values. In failing to follow a comprehensive system of worship (*'ibadah*)
and legislation (*Shari'ah*), the acceptance of secularism means the abandonment of *Shari'ah*, a denial of divine guidance, and a rejection of Allah's
injunctions. For these scholars, it is indeed a false claim that Shariah is not
appropriate for the present age. They feel that the acceptance of legislation

formulated by humans means a preference for humans' limited knowledge and experiences over divine guidance. In the words of Egyptian Sunni Muslim scholar Dr. Yusuf al-Qaradawi: "Say! Do you know better than Allah?" (The Quran 2:140).[71] The French scholar Professor Olivier Roy deals with the denunciation of fundamentalism in France. It is embodied in the law against the veil and the deportation of imams. This hostility is rooted in the belief that Islam cannot be integrated into French—and, consequently, secular and liberal—society. Muslim intellectuals have made it possible for Muslims to live concretely in a secularized world while maintaining the identity of a 'true believer.' They have formulated a language that recognizes two spaces: that of religion and that of secular society. There have been debates over whether Islam is compatible with Europe's increasingly secular society. Many scholars, politicians, and polemicists find it not compatible because Islam makes no distinction between religion and politics and that it is not just a religion but also a culture, which makes it hard for Muslims to assimilate and to accept secularism.[72]

The Saudi scholar Sheikh Salman argues that secularism violates the principle of monotheism. He believes that secularism has no place in the lands of Islam for two reasons:

> The first of these is that Islam is the religion that Allah sent down to replace the previous manifestations of the faith and to govern all aspects of life. The simplest Muslim can see how Islam explains all matters in detail. It is impossible for a Muslim to feel that the religion that regulates his marital affairs, his business, his eating habits, his manner of sleeping, and even how he goes to the bathroom, could ever leave managing the political and economic affairs of society to other than Allah. For Allah says:

> *"We have neglected nothing in the Book."* (Sûrah al-An`âm: 38)
> *"We have sent down to you the Book explaining all things."* (Sûrah al-Nahl: 89)

> This issue is not open for debate. Islam, as the final religion, has supremacy over all faiths and over every aspect of life. There is no place for secularism in the lands of Islam or among the Muslims. Secularism has served a measurable procedure of disintegration and segregation for Muslim diasporas and Muslim minorities in secular countries. The second reason is that throughout the history of Islam, it never experienced the troubles that were faced by Europe on account of its corrupted faith. Among the most important of these was the horrific breach that took place between religion and science.[73]

Turkey, a Muslim country, has been a secular state since 1937 under the Kemalist ideology and reforms of Mustafa Kemal Ataturk (1881–1938). Although the overwhelming majority of its population adheres to Islam, the state neither has an official religion nor promotes any. As a secular, democratic state, it is eager to become a member of the European Union, and has embraced secularism, democracy, and equality, while retaining Muslim values. Turkey rejects jihadi culture and sternly suppresses separatist Kurds. The following Muslim countries are secular: Chad, Guinea, Mali, Senegal, Somalia (Africa); Kazakhstan, Kyrgyzstan, Tajikistan, Turkmenistan, Uzbekistan (Asia); and, Albania, Azerbaijan, Bosnia and Herzegovina, and Kosovo (Europe). India, which has a very large number of Muslims and is home to the Deobandi, Islamic sect, has had a separate law code for Muslims since 1947. Yet Islamic terrorist organizations including Lashkar-e-Jhangvi (LeJ), the Indian Mujahedeen (IM), and the Students' Islamic Movement of India (SIMI) wish to overthrow the secular government and impose Sharia. This is because many Muslims believe that the state is God's state, and that religion and state are inseparable.

According to Middle East scholar Ali Allawi, secularism has been a precondition for the whole range of human and civil rights that western society is proud of—including freedom of expression and the rights of women. They flourish on the existence of a secular culture and society. They cannot flower if society is overly concerned with the rights of religious believers. Western society has given freedom of religion to everyone in their lands, even at the risk of spreading hatred, false beliefs, and obscurantism. However, the coexistence of secularist and Muslim laws depends on tolerance. Professor Bernard Lewis distinguishes between tolerance and coexistence:

> Tolerance means that a dominant group, whether defined by faith or race or other criteria, allows to members of other groups some—but rarely ever all—of the rights and privileges enjoyed by its own members. Coexistence means equality between the different groups composing a political society as an inherent natural right of all of them—to grant it is no merit, to withhold or limit it is an offense.[74]

Lewis elaborates:

> The declaration begins with an exordium quoting the more militant passages in the Quran and the sayings of the Prophet Muhammad, then continues: 'Since God laid down the Arabian peninsula, created its desert, and surrounded it with its seas, no calamity has ever befallen it like these Crusader hosts that have spread in it like locusts, crowding its soil, eating

its fruits, and destroying its verdure; and this at a time when the nations contend against the Muslims like diners jostling around a bowl of food.[75]

Lewis's statement goes on to discuss the need to understand the situation and act to rectify it. The facts, he says, are known to everyone and fall under three main headings:

First—For more than seven years the United States is occupying the lands of Islam in the holiest of its territories, Arabia, plundering its riches, overwhelming its rulers, humiliating its people, threatening its neighbors, and using its bases in the peninsula as a spearhead to fight against the neighboring Islamic peoples.

The World Islamic Front Statement, February 23, 1998 has listed the following scholars: Shaykh Usamah Bin-Muhammad Bin-Ladin, Ayman al-Zawahiri, Amir of the Jihad Group in Egypt; Abu-Yasir Rifa'i Ahmad Taha, Egyptian Islamic Group; Shaykh Mir Hamzah, Secretary of the Jamiat-ul-Ulema-e-Pakistan; Fazlur Rahman, Amir of the Jihad Movement in Bangladesh with the message: Praise be to Allah, who revealed the Book, controls the clouds, defeats factionalism, and says in His Book: "But when the forbidden months are past, then fight and slay the pagans wherever ye find them, seize them, beleaguer them, and lie in wait for them in every stratagem (of war)"; and peace be upon our Prophet, Muhammad Bin-'Abdallah, who said: I have been sent with the sword between my hands to ensure that no one but Allah is worshipped, Allah who put my livelihood under the shadow of my spear and who inflicts humiliation and scorn on those who disobey my orders.[76]

Christian fundamentalists did not indulge in any violence when a five-foot-tall, six-ton black granite monument bearing the Ten Commandants, with its religious message and inscription, reading, *"Love God and Keep His Commandments"* was removed from the front lawn of a courthouse in Alabama. Conversely, radical Islamic fundamentalists were responsible for several deaths in the course of their reaction to a Danish artist's cartoon of the Prophet.

With the demise of Communism, capitalism and globalization flourished, ushering in unlimited opportunities in trade, consumerism, and commerce worldwide. Even a Communist country like China has benefited significantly from globalization. Capitalism and globalization are seen as twin wings of Western culture, which provide equal opportunity and advancement for women, democracy, liberty, modernity in dress, and the development of banking, investment, and technology. Yet Muslims perceive two of the world's largest financial institutions, the International Monetary Fund (IMF) and the World Bank (WB) as agents of capitalism and imperialism and as exploiting impoverished Muslim countries.

The noted journalist Jessica Stern, who has interviewed several terrorists, outlines one of the reasons why terrorists feel humiliated:

> Terrorist leaders tell young men that the reason they feel humiliated— personally or culturally—is that international institutions like the IMF, the World Bank, and the United Nations are imposing capitalism and secular ideas on them with the aim of exterminating traditional values.[77]

While globalization has produced jobs, opportunity, and development in Muslim countries, ordinary Muslims see it as only enriching elites. Militant fundamentalists feel Sharia will be damaged with modernization and the advancement of globalization. The number of people in various countries who responded that "globalization is good," as shown in Table 2.5, reveals that the Islamic world is far behind North America and Western Europe in terms of positive perceptions of globalization.

Table 2.5
Globalization Rating (per cent)

North America	68
Western Europe	62
Asia	69
Latin America	58
Lebanon	42
Egypt	38
Jordan	28

These are approximations based on data supplied by: Pew Research Center for the People and the Press, *Pew Global Attitudes Project*, 2002 and 2003.

Figure 2.8 shows the relation between religion and wealth. The United States and Europe rank low on the religiosity scale, although their income is high. Muslim countries constitute 20 per cent of the world population, but are responsible for only 4 per cent of world trade.

The Pew survey found a strong relationship between a country's religiosity and its economic status. In poorer nations, religion remains central to the lives of individuals, while secular perspectives are more common in

**Figure 2.8. Wealth and Religiosity in Relation
to Gross Domestic Product (GDP)**

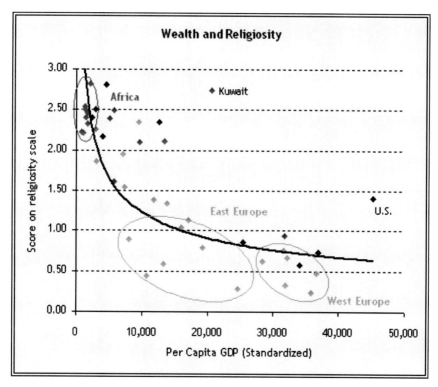

richer nations. This relationship generally is consistent across regions and countries, although there are some exceptions: most notably the United States, which is a much more religious country than its level of prosperity would indicate. Other nations deviate from the pattern as well, including the oil-rich, predominantly Muslim—and very religious—kingdom of Kuwait.[78] With only 25 per cent of Muslims against globalization, the overwhelming majority are in favor of it, as shown in Figure 2.9.

A poll of 5216 respondents was conducted January 12 through February 23, 2008 by WorldPublicOpinion.org, a collaborative research project involving research centers from around the world, and managed by the Program on International Policy Attitudes (PIPA) at the University of Maryland. Not all questions were asked in every country. Margins of error range from +/-3.2 to 4.1 per cent.

In addition to Gulf countries, various charitable organizations and private businesses have funded terrorist organizations. After 9/11, there was

Figure 2.9. Perception of Globalization in Muslim Countries

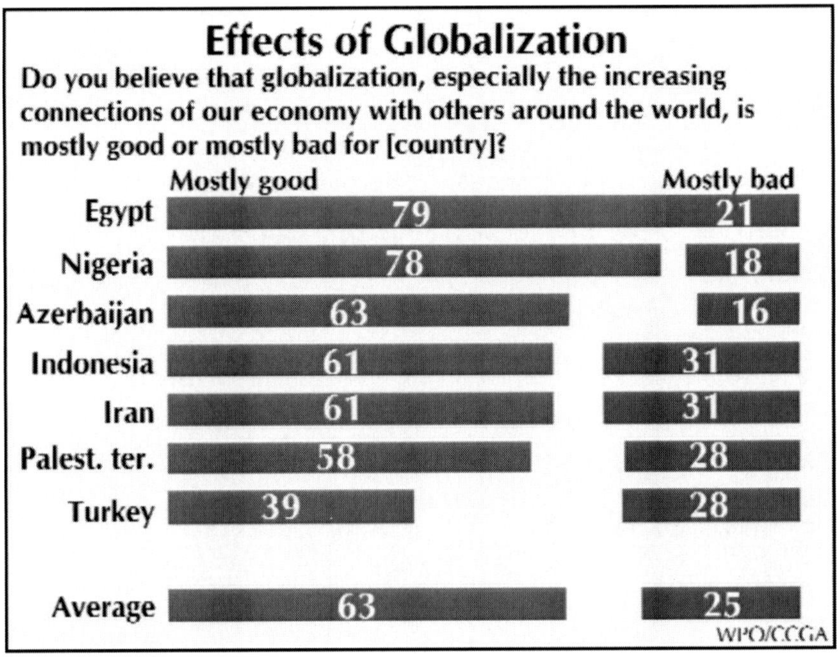

Effects of Globalization

Do you believe that globalization, especially the increasing connections of our economy with others around the world, is mostly good or mostly bad for [country]?

	Mostly good	Mostly bad
Egypt	79	21
Nigeria	78	18
Azerbaijan	63	16
Indonesia	61	31
Iran	61	31
Palest. ter.	58	28
Turkey	39	28
Average	63	25

WPO/CCGA

an effort to clamp down on these fake charitable institutions who serve as fronts for financing terrorists, from locations in disparate places. In the name of capitalism and globalization, these financiers open businesses in America, Europe, Africa, and elsewhere, and are very successful entrepreneurs. They then go on to fund terrorists. For example, seventy-year-old Youssaf Nada and seventy-six-year old Ahmed Nasreddin live like kings in Swiss territory, and have business empires across the world. They are reported to be providing funds to terrorist organizations. The Harvard Professor Lorenzo Vidino writes:

> But according to the intelligence agencies of a dozen countries, Nada and Nasreddin have also been the masterminds of a supplicated terrorism financing network that spanned four continents and funneled millions of dollars to various Islamic groups.[79]

It is surprising to think that the following stellar intellectuals buried secularism, multiculturalism, pluralism, diversity, and communal harmony to establish a theocratic state based on Islamic rule, with the patronage of secularist, multiculturalist British colonialists, to thwart India's independence. They were: British-educated Pakistani poet Allama Iqbal (1877–1938), whose ancestry was tied to the Sapru Kashmir Brahmin; the journalist and pioneer of radical politics Islam Syed Maududi; British-trained lawyer Muhammad Ali Jinnah (1876-1948), and a former British East India Company employee, educator Sir Syed Ahmed Khan (1817–1898), cofounder of political Islam. All of them were ardent liberals prior to the onset of India's independence movement. The world has had to pay a steep price for abolishing secularism in Pakistan. It is also strange that radical Islamists wanted to establish a caliphate, while political Islamists Iqbal and Jinnah were opposed to the Khilafat movement restoring the relationship between state and religion.

At an October 16, 2010 meeting of young members of her political party, the Christian Democratic Union, German Chancellor Angela Merkel declared that multiculturalism, "has failed totally." Small wonder, when political or religious violence is so prominent in certain religious texts. Islam has three such texts: the *Quran*, the *Sira* (The Prophet's biography) and *Hadith* (his tradition), making up the Islamic Trilogy. The trilogy has 327,547 words devoted to political violence. There are 34,039 words of political violence in the Hebrew Bible, and the New Testament—the major text of the Christian religion—has zero words of political violence.[80]

Illiteracy, Poverty, and Social Roots

Poverty and illiteracy are rampant in the Third World, including the Muslim countries. Indonesia, Bangladesh, Pakistan, Afghanistan, and India are stricken with poverty, unemployment, and illiteracy. Islamic schools, funded by rich Middle Eastern countries to propagate their extreme ideology of Salafi–Wahhabism, provide free education and lodging to the children of families who cannot afford schools and food. These religious schools, the *madrassas,* have existed from colonial days to provide education to poor Muslim students. They follow a curriculum that is probably several hundred years old, to impart the teachings of the Quran. There are no courses in science, mathematics or the humanities. Most of the holy militants of the world today are trained by these madrassas. Pakistani dictators and military leaders have supported these schools for their political survival, and for their strategic depth beyond Pakistan. During the tenure of Generals Zia ul Haq and Pervez Musharraf, the number of these *madrassas* has grown to more than 40,000, to train student fighters from the Middle East, Central Asia, Afghanistan, Indonesia and the West.

The popularity of traditional madrassas has had an unintended effect on Muslim mobility in India. Many Muslims send their children to madrassas rather than public schools, thus hindering their ability to adopt the knowledge necessary to integrate into modern Indian higher education and society. The result have been a gradual segregation of Muslims away from the mainstream and a sense of isolation and backwardness in the Muslim community.[81]

Students are required to learn Arabic and Persian, not Urdu, Sanskrit or computers. Terrorist organizations use these schools to recruit young people from poor backgrounds who need employment in Pakistan. The poverty rate is 34 per cent and illiteracy 45.8 per cent, the age group of 15 and above.[82] Its population is more than 170 million in 2010. Writing in the *Washington Post,* Thomas Kean and Lee Hamilton stated:

> Our report warned that it was imperative to eliminate terrorist sanctuaries. But inside Pakistan, al-Qaeda "has protected or regenerated key elements of its homeland attack capability," according to the National Intelligence Estimate. The chief threat to Afghanistan's young democracy comes from across the Pakistani border, from the resurgent Taliban. Pakistan should take the lead in closing Taliban camps and rooting out al-Qaeda. But the United States must act if Pakistan will not. . . . We must use all the tools of U.S. power—including foreign aid, educational assistance and vigorous public diplomacy that emphasizes scholarship, libraries and exchange programs—to shape a Middle East and a Muslim world that are less hostile to our interests and values. America's long term security relies on being viewed not as a threat but as a source of opportunity and hope.[83]

But there has been no change in the structure of the *madrassas,* despite American aid to modernize the curriculum.

Very often, no one considers the fact that the vast majority of non-Muslims, illiterate and poor, in other parts of South Asia, Africa, and South America, dwell in even worse and more repressive economic and political conditions, and yet do not engage in terrorist activities. Some analysts are attributing terrorism to socially repressive environments, lack of freedom, and economic conditions in Chechen, the Basque region of Spain, and in Palestine, but they do not explain why so many non-Muslim people living in these countries do not engage in terrorist activities.

Alberto Abadie of Harvard University, in an October 2004 report, shows that terrorist risk is not significantly higher for poorer countries, once the effects of other country-specific characteristics such as the level of political freedom are taken into account. Political freedom is shown to explain terrorism, but it does so in a non-monolithic way: countries with some intermediate range of political freedom are shown to be more prone to terrorism than countries with high levels of political freedom or countries with highly authoritarian regimes. This result suggests that, as experienced recently in Iraq and previously in Spain and Russia, transitions from an authoritarian regime to a democracy may be accompanied by temporary increases in terrorism. Finally, the results suggest that geographic factors are important to sustain terrorist activities.[84]

It is clear that the *madrassas* should provide modern education, beyond the traditional Quran, devoid of prejudice, with emphasis on science, computers, and the humanities. As the 9/11 Commission Report (completed in 2004) recommended: Education that teaches tolerance, the dignity and value of each individual, and respect for different beliefs is a key element in any global strategy to eliminate Muslim terrorism. There are also some societal and social factors. Terrorists are very emotional and are easily irritated and eager to take revenge for any injustice. It has shocked the world when they appear on TV, calling themselves jihadist mothers, dressing their young children with suicide bombs with the hope that they are going to be *saheeds*, or martyrs, for the cause of Islam. These jihadist moms are sometimes widows, and sometimes are competing with their husband's other wives to show their commitment to the faith. At the risk of repetition, it can be noted that Saudi Arabia, the richest Muslim country, has produced far more terrorists than Bangladesh, one of the poorest Muslim countries.

Clash of Religions, Cultures, and Societies

From the 600s A.D. all the way up to the early twentieth century, with the killing of 2 million Armenians in Turkey, Islam is responsible for the murder of 270 million people across the world—more than any other religion on earth. Brigitte Gabriel writes:

> Just look at Islam's history of 1,400 years of violence and bloodshed around the world. The Muslims did expand throughout the Mediterranean basin before faster advancing civilization and technology pushed them back. Today they are using the petrodollars these civilizations provided to give it another try on a worldwide scale. . . . The prophet Muhammad, founder of Islam, was a warrior who preached violence and the slaughter of thousands in establishing and spreading Islam. He participated in seventy-eight battles and approved the beheading of prisoners taken in the battle.

She is astonished that Siraj Wahaj (a first Muslim to deliver a daily prayer before the U.S. House of Representative) was singing a different tune to a different audience, and his words are were far from his moderate ones in front of U.S. House of Representatives when Wahaj said: "If Muslims were cleverer politically" he told his New Jersey listeners, they could take over the United States and replace its constitutional government with a Caliphate." Further she finds:

> What's more frightening is that, after all this (the 1995 World Trade Center bombing trial of Omar Abdul Rahman), our mindless, ignorant, oh-so-politically-correct elected leaders still insist that Islam is a religion of peace and the majority of Muslims are moderate.[85]

The questions that haunt many people are: Does Islam mean peace? Is it a religion of tolerance? Does it reject violence and promote religious and racial harmony? Is the enemy fanaticism, not Islam? Or is Islam intolerant, militant, and barbaric, and is stoning a relic of the Stone Age? A 2003 ABC News poll revealed that "fewer than half of Americans now call it peaceful, and one in three believes it encourages violence against non-Muslims—double what it was 20 months ago" (see Table 2.6).

Table 2.6
Views of Islamic Teachings (given in percentages)

	2006	2002
More Violent Extremists in Islam	58	38
Teaches Intolerance	48	22
Encourages violence	33	14

* Source: ABC News, John Cohen, March 8, 2006, Americans skeptical about Islam and Arabs

    Islam's history, influenced by the modern religions in the west and the Oriental religions in the east, goes back to the seventh century. It has become a religion of one billion people or more, from Morocco to Indonesia. It has fought brutally with Judaism, Christianity, Hinduism, Buddhism and Confucianism, while conquering lands and forcefully converting infidels to Islam throughout the ages. It has become a Kalashnikov culture employing thousands of mujahedeen to wage holy war, indulge in kidnapping, assassinate enemies, take hostages, hijack planes, and execute suicide bombings in various settings. It is neither peaceful and ethical, nor tolerant and harmonious toward other religions and cultures.

A clash amongst views of Islam was magnified by OBL's 1998 declaration in *Al-Quds al-Arabi*, an Arabic newspaper published in London, and signed by the leaders of Jihad in Egypt, Pakistan, and Bangladesh. The ruling commanded all Muslims to kill Americans and their allies—civilians and military—as an individual duty for every Muslim who can do it in any country in which it is possible to do it, in order to liberate the al-Aqsa Mosque and the holy mosque at Mecca from their grip, and in order for their armies to move out of all the lands of Islam, defeated and unable to threaten any Muslim. This is in accordance with the words of Almighty Allah, "and fight the pagans all together as they fight you all together," and "fight them until there is no more tumult or oppression, and there prevails justice and faith in Allah." This is similar to the Quran 8:39: "And fight them until persecution is no more, religion is all for Allah, But if they cease, then lo! Allah is Seer of what they do."

In a multicultural society, the social and cultural distinctions created by religion usually vanish. But Muslims reject a multicultural society. Many governments implement multiculturalism as an appeasement policy for minorities. The British author Michael Burleigh writes,

> Nor did liberal multiculturalists, who imagined a Herderian riot of diverse flowers living gaily in a huge garden, take adequate notice of the fact that one aggressive minority would seek to create cultural no-go areas, in which mosques and madrassas in what amount to ghettos of the mind, would be followed by calls for a separate Islamic banking system, Sharia law or, more outrageously, an Islamic parliament. . . . Western societies have tolerated various devils and pests in their midst, providing them with 'people carriers' as part of their welfare package, despite their vocal calls for our destruction. When Trevor Phillips, the black British and Labor-supporting chairman of the British Commission for Racial Equality pronounced that multiculturalism is inherently divisive, people became alert, even if others have been saying the same thing for several decades.[86]

In 2025, Europe may become Arabistan, with more Arabs than Europeans. Britain would be North Pakistan, with France as New Algeria, Germany as New Turkey, Belgium as Moroccostan, Sweden as Somsalistan, and Spain as the Moorish Emirate of Iberia.[87] By the collusion of the British colonialists, the Indian Subcontinent gave rise to Pakistan, incorporating the lands and descendants of brutal, savage Muslim invaders, converts, and immigrants who forcefully occupied the ancestral lands of Hindus. In 1935, Will Durant wrote:

Aurangzeb cared nothing for art, destroyed as heathen monuments with coarse bigotry, and fought, through a reign of half a century, to eradicate from India almost all religions (Hinduism, Buddhists, and Jain) but his own. He issued orders to the provincial governors, and to his other subordinates, to raze to the ground all temples of either Hindus or Christians, to smash every idol, and to close every Hindu school. In one year (1679-80) sixty-six temples were broken to pieces in Amber alone, sixty-three in Chitor, one hundred and twenty-three in Udaipur (all three cities in Rajasthan); over the site of a Benares temple especially sacred to the Hindus he built, in deliberate insult, a Mohammedan mosque. He forbade all public worship of the Hindu faiths, and laid upon every unconverted Hindu a heavy capitation tax.[88]

The clash of two cultures was very visible, says the BBC correspondent and journalist Malise Ruthven,

Here, as in Africa, the gradual proselytizing undertaken by Sufi orders had led to the development of forms of religious syncretism in which Islamic practices had become intermixed with local Hindu and Vedanta cults and beliefs. Hinduism, however, is far removed from African paganism. Though polytheistic in the sense of recognizing a multiplicity of forms through which the divine may manifest itself, it belongs to the tradition of an advanced and ancient civilization upheld by a literate and highly cultivated caste of Brahmins whose knowledge of the world and its arts was in no manner inferior to that part of their Muslim conquerors. In terms of prevailing values underpinning the two systems, a clash was inevitable. Whereas the thrust of Islam is towards social equality and religious conformity, that of Hinduism is towards social hierarchy and spiritual anarchism. Whereas the logic of Islam, as of other western monotheism, propels towards an intolerant rejection of alternative formulation of religious truth, the trend in Hinduism has been towards a universal acceptance of other faiths within a hierarchical order which links, however tenuously, the rarified speculations of the intellectuals with the superstitious fetishism of the masses.[89]

There are several madrassas, Islamic seminaries, in Pakistan. The number of secondary and higher madrassas are 6,000, Senior and graduate level madrassas 4,335, Deobandi madrassas 2,333, Barelvi madrassas 1,625, Ahl-i-Hadith madrassas 224, Shia madrassas 163, and number of all students 604,421. In 1960, there were 472 madrassas with 40,239 students, and in 2001 there were 4,345 madrassas with 604,421 students. The graduates are called *maulvi*, *maulana* or *mulla*. There are over 12,000 madrassas with 1700 foreign students. Most of the madrassas are radicalized. (However, the Deobandi movement is at Darul Uloom, one of the largest madrassas in the world, in Uttar Pradesh, India.)

> Throughout the 1980s and 1990s, madrassas sent many fighters first to the Mujahidin in Afghanistan, then to jihad in Kashmir; so groups like Lashkar-e-Taiba and Jaish-e-Mohammed, formerly backed by the Pakistani military to fight in Kashmir, have a strong presence in southern Punjab.[90]

The jihadists control media, newspapers, and television. They prescribe separate dress for men, women, boys, and girls—even hair and beard length for men. They keep their congregants unassimilated and segregated. Even third-generation Muslims in the United States and Great Britain feel that they do not fully belong in the land of their birth and residency, and are alienated from Western values. Imams' sermons based on seventh-century ideologies shape their congregants' thoughts and deeds. They ask Muslims to think in terms of *Umma,* a community of all Muslims. If any Muslim is attacked or is facing ill treatment anywhere in the world, or Islamic law is not being followed, it is the duty of all Muslims to revolt against this. They preach that it is the religious duty of a good Muslim to commit jihad for the cause of Islam. (Some Quran verses in support of these tenets appear in Appendix 4.)

Pakistan's blasphemy law has been criticized as being too severe, and many legal experts say it has been badly misused since its introduction in the 1980s by the military dictator General Zia-ul Haq. Pakistan's blasphemy law, 295-C, punishes derogatory remarks about Muhammad with execution. Anyone can file a charge of blasphemy, which may then be used to stir up hatred and justify sectarian violence. In one such incident, more than 100 Christian homes were burned and looted in a riot lasting approximately eight hours, at the hands of a crowd that authorities estimate at 20,000 strong. In addition to the seven members of the Hameed family who were killed, about 20 people were wounded. In the pretext of defending the Quran from desecration, Pakistani minorities are often burned, killed and raped and their homes, which are then looted and burned.

Religious prosecution continues throughout the Muslim world. In January of 2010, the *Wall Street Journal* reported that in Egypt, seven Coptic Christians were murdered by a Muslim gunman as they filed out of a midnight mass in the southern town of Nag Hamadi. In Pakistan, a Muslim mob ransacked more than 100 Christian homes in July 2009 in the village of Bahmaniwala. In Iraq that same month, seven Christian churches were bombed in Baghdad and Mosul in the space of three days.

As Samuel Huntington has warned, while a Marxist–Leninist Soviet Union no longer poses a threat to the free world, and the United States does not pose a countering threat to the Communist world, both worlds increasingly see threats coming from another civilization. The fault line between Islamic and non-Islamic civilizations, *Dar al-Islam and Dar al-Harb*, is becoming the central line of conflict in global politics. The political scientist Professor Ted Gurr reported that in 1993–1995, out of the twenty-six ethno-political conflicts taking place during that time, fifteen were between Muslims and non-Muslims. Of the six wars, three (Sudan, Bosnia, and East Timor) were between Muslims and non-Muslims, two (Somalia and Iraq) between Muslims and one (Angola) involved only non-Muslims. Over the last two decades, three million people have been killed due to communal wars in the Philippines, Sri Lanka, Kashmir, Sudan, Tajikistan, Croatia, Bosnia, Chechnya, Tibet, and East Timor. Chinese minorities have assimilated in Buddhist Thailand and the Catholic Philippines, but are facing anti-Chinese riots in Muslim Indonesia and Muslim Malaysia. Like India, China has border problems with Korea, Vietnam, the Philippines, Taiwan, Tibet, Singapore, Indonesia, Australia, Russia, India, and provinces in Central Asia in addition to its restive province Xinjiang. The Chinese are aligned with many Muslim countries, and are supplying armaments to Pakistan, Iran, and Iraq. They invest in Muslim courtiers, and support them in international forums. It would seem that there is no civilizational clash between Muslims and Chinese. Huntington writes: "Some Westerners, including President Clinton, have argued that the West does not have any problems with Islam but only with violent Islamist extremists. Fourteen hundred years of history demonstrates otherwise."[91] The veteran journalist Peter Bergen responds,

> In Huntington's view, the tectonic plates of Islam would grind up against the plates of Christianity and Hinduism, while in Christendom the Orthodox would war with Catholics. Such clashes, he predicted, would be the future ruptures of history.[92]

The public's views on religion in various countries are given in Table 2.7. Europeans are shown to be 23 per cent positive and 66 per cent negative on Islam, while they are 52 per cent positive and 13 per cent negative on Christianity.

Table 2.7
Perception and Acceptance of Religious Diversity

Religion	Positive (%)	Negative (%)
Christianity	52	13
Judaism	30	20
Islam	23	66

* France's National Consulting Committee on Human Rights conducted a survey in 2004 (Caldwell, 161) about religions.

The survey, titled "Perception and Acceptance of Religious Diversity," was conducted by the sociology department of the University of Münster in northwestern Germany, in partnership with the prestigious TNS Emnid political polling firm. Researchers surveyed 1,000 people each in the former West and East Germany, Denmark, France, the Netherlands and Portugal; the survey's margin of error is plus or minus 3 per cent.

The study, officially released in Berlin on December 2, shows that only 34 per cent of West Germans and 26 per cent of East Germans have a positive view of Muslims, compared to 55 per cent of those surveyed in Denmark, 56 per cent in the Netherlands and 62 per cent in France.

Fewer than 5 per cent of Germans think Islam is a tolerant religion, compared to roughly 20 per cent for the Danes, the Dutch and the French. Only 30 per cent of Germans say they approve of the building of mosques, while 50 per cent of Danes and two-thirds of the French and Dutch respondents say they do. The number of Germans who approve of the building of minarets or of the introduction of Muslim holidays is even lower.

Only 8 per cent of West Germans and 5 per cent of East Germans say that Islam is peaceful. When asked what they associate with Islam, more than 80 per cent of those surveyed in all five countries say discrimination of women, 70 per cent say fanaticism, 60 per cent say violence, and 50 per cent say bigotry.

According to the survey, only 49 per cent of respondents in West Germany and 53 per cent in East Germany think that all religious groups should have equal rights, in contrast to 72 per cent in Denmark, 82 per cent in the Netherlands, 86 per cent in France and 89 per cent in Portugal. More than 40 per cent of Germans believe that the practice of Islam should be vigorously restricted.

Only 20 per cent of Germans, and 30 per cent of French, believe that Islam is suitable for the Western world. Significantly, more than 80 per cent of those surveyed in all five countries agree with the statement "that Muslims must adapt to our culture."

"The study also reveals a more prevalent anti-Jewish undercurrent in Germany than in other western European countries. A little more than 28 per cent of West Germans and 29 per cent of East Germans have negative attitudes about Jews, the survey says. This compares to about 10 per cent in the Netherlands, 12 per cent in Denmark, and nearly 21 per cent in France."

In a 2007 survey, in Germany, people were asked the following question: When you hear the word "Islam," what do you think of? The responses included the following: 93 per cent said "oppression of women," 83 per cent said "terrorism," and 82 per cent said "radicalism."

Currently there are many clashes between Muslims and non-Muslims throughout the world. Ongoing conflicts include: those between the Islamist regime and Christian rebels in Sudan; between Muslims and Christians in the Philippines; between Muslims and Buddhists in Thailand: between Jews and Arab Muslims in Israel; between Orthodox Christians and Muslims in Russia, Bosnia, Kosovo, and Macedonia; between Muslims and Hindus in India; and between Xinjiang Muslims and Confucians in China. There is also plenty of intra-Muslim conflict around the world. For example, in Pakistan between Shiites and Sunnis, Sindhis and Pathans, Baluchis and Punjabis; in Afghanistan, between Tajiks and Pashtuns; in Iraq, between Shia and Sunnis; and in Turkey between Turks and Kurds. It is alleged that in all the above cases, clashes and killings are mostly carried out by violent Islamic extremists. In France, race riots were instigated by radical Muslims known as *Arabs-beurs* (French Muslims of North African descent). The wave of attacks on Jews that began in France in 2002 was instigated by the *beurs*. The Muslim-led gang of two-dozen self-described "barbarians," who used acid, knives, and lighter fluid in the three-week-long torture killing of Jewish victims in 2006, was a multicultural mix of recent immigrants from Africa and Asia, as well as several French-born minorities.[93]

There are differences in cultural attitudes between the West and the terrorists. It is not just a clash of religions. The terrorists consider suicide bombing in terms of gain, since they lose nothing by death, while the West considers death by terrorist attack a loss. OBL banks on the fear of Islam that prevails in Western societies. He watches the anxieties that are constantly conveyed through popular culture and the media, which portrays jihadists as the personification of unrestrained violence. Videos celebrating the beheading of hostages, and carefully orchestrated invasions of theaters and schools (i.e., the Beslan School in Russia) are designed to convey the message that jihadists will stop at nothing. When America pulled its forces out of Somalia, OBL rejoiced in the fear that terrorists had inflicted on

Americans. When American soldiers were killed and dragged through the streets of Mogadishu, OBL announced that Americans had left the area carrying with them disappointment, humiliation, and defeat. In 2001 and 2005, President George W. Bush said,

> I do believe there is an image of America out that we are so materialistic . . . almost hedonistic . . . that when struck, we wouldn't fight back . . . it was clear that OBL felt emboldened and didn't feel threatened by the United States. . . . The terrorists believe that free societies are essentially corrupt and decadent, and with a few blows they can force us to retreat.[94]

Lost Muslim Empires and Imperialism

The sword of Islam is subject to karmic fate, according to historian Arnold Toynbee:

> Time is, indeed, working against these unhappy empire builders from the outset; for sword-blades are foundations that never settle. Exposed or buried, these blood-stained weapons still retain their sinister charge of *karma;* and this means that they cannot really turn into inanimate foundation-stones, but must be stirring—like the dragon's-tooth seeds that they are— to spring to the surface again in a fresh crop of slaying and dying gladiators.[95]

Several worship sites of Christians, Jews, Zoroastrians, and Hindus have been converted into mosques. The Al-Aqsa mosque in the Hague, the Netherlands, was formerly a synagogue until 1975. The great synagogue of Oran in Algeria has become a mosque. The Qutub Minar in Delhi India is built in AD 1198 on the ruins of the Lal Kot, the Red Citadel in the city of Dhillika, the capital of the Tomars and the Chauhans, the last Hindu rulers of Delhi. The complex initially housed 27 ancient Hindu and Jain temples, which were destroyed and their debris used to build the Qutub minar. The Iron Pillar in the courtyard bears an inscription in Sanskrit in Brahmi script of 4th century AD, according to which the pillar was set up as a Vishnudhvaja (Hindu god Vishnu) on the hill known as Vishnupada in memory of a mighty king named Chandra.[96] The Ajodhya temple in Allahabad, India is alleged to become the Babri Masjid, The Taj Mahal in India was also built on the ruins of the Tejo Mahalay, a Shiva Temple with its annexes, ruined defensive walls, hillocks, moats, cascades, fountains, majestic garden, hundreds of rooms arcaded verandahs, terraces, multi stored towers, secret sealed chambers, guest rooms, stables, the trident (Trishul) pinnacle on the dome and the sacred, esoteric Hindu letter "OM" carved on the exterior of the wall of the sanctum sanctorum now occupied by the cenotaphs. Today, there are two marble palaces in Agra, one is the Mausoleum of Idmat-ud-Daula, the father of Noorjahan and the other is Taj Mahal, and it is evident from the Munj Bateswar edict that, once upon a time, one of them was the temple of Lord Vishnu and the other was a temple of Lord Shiva. Experts believe that it is the temple of Lord Vishnu that has been made the mausoleum of Idmat-ud-Daula, and the temple of Lord Shiva has been converted into the mausoleum of the queen Arjumand Banu. (The Taj Mahal is called Bateswar and in 1900 A.D., General Alexander Cunningham, the then Director of the Archaeological Survey of India (ASI), conducted an excavation at Bateswar and discovered an edict, now known as the *Munj Bateswar Edict* and kept at the Lucknow Museum). The former St. Nicholas Cathedral in Cyprus is now the Lala Mustafa mosque, and the Armenian church of the 1000 BC is now the Umayyad mosque at Damascus, Syria, the largest, oldest, and holiest mosque in the world. Hagia Sophia in Constantinople, formerly an Eastern Orthodox patriarchal basilica, is now a mosque, as are the Pantheon in Rome and several churches in Spain.[97]

The Muslim world's decline in the Middle Ages resulted in a series of attacks against them by Mongols, Spanish Christians, Crusaders, and Zionists. Following the death of the Prophet Muhammad, the ills plaguing Islam included severe corruption, blatant distrust, deadly revenge, unrelenting tribal conflicts, and stagnation of ideas. The lack of freedom of thought, creativity, and self-determination, fiery mullah-fascism, discrimination against slaves and dhimmis, neglect of modern education, and the oppression of women, under brutal emperors such as Mogul Emperor Aurangzeb led down a dark path of decadence and decline. At the same time, there was tremendous scientific and technical advancement in Europe and colonial expansion by Western countries. The rapid rise of Western countries in science, technology, trade, industry, and military power eclipsed the glory of Islam. In their quest for territories, or to spread Islam by the sword, Muslim invaders had gained empires and colonies in Europe, Asia and Africa, from the eighth century until the dissolution of the Ottoman Empire (1600-1922). Arab invaders and conquerors had imposed the Islamic religion and culture upon their conquered subjects. These fanatical invaders often destroyed native cultures and civilizations or denied their subjects access to their indigenous culture, often taking the infidels to Arab lands as slaves. After the Muslim conquest of Persia and Syria in the seventh century, there were major cultural transformations in Syria and Iran. By contrast, British and French colonialists had never tried to change their colonies' language, culture, and religion. Today many Muslims aspire to return Islam to the past glory of the Ottoman Empire, when Islamic civilization was prevalent in Europe, or to reinstate the Mogul Empire in South and Central Asia, when Hindus and Buddhists were ruled by their Islamic conquerors. The decline and fall of these empires caused a great deal of resentment and anguish among the Muslims. During the decline of a civilization, loss of human life is coupled with the annihilation of cultural heritage. Islam has been marginalized and has lost its glamour due to the prevalence of secular, democratic governments and societies, Western influence, and the advent of Western colonization.[98]

For want of space, the decline of Islamic power will be outlined here in a few sentences. The earliest major attack on Islam was made by Mongols, who destroyed Baghdad in 1258. Egyptian armies were defeated by Napoleon at the Battle of the Pyramids in 1798. In 1924, the Turkish Caliphate was abolished. Islamic territories were further diminished by the European colonial powers that captured and controlled Muslim lands such as Morocco, Algeria, Egypt, Indonesia, and India. Stanley Wolpert comments that people who are descendents of the lost Asoka Empire, Roman Empire, or British Empire have not gone ravaging and pillaging to reclaim their lost glory.[99] British, French, and others have lost a lot of colonial territories, but they do not aspire to get back those territories. Barbaric tragedies have occurred due to the spread of Islam by sword.

In the words of two great historians David Frum and Richard Perle, militant Islam

> proposes to restore the vanished glory of a greater civilization through crimes that horrify the conscience of the world. It invokes the language of liberation—but it intends to fasten unthinking, unquestioning slavery on the minds of the people of one-fifth of the world. It claims the authority of God for its own cruelty and evil.[100]

History tells us that militant Islam is about action and not simply words: as President Dinesh D'Souza of the New York City College notes:

> Let us remember that before the rise of Islam, the region we call the Middle East was predominantly Christian. Inspired by Islam's call to jihad, Muhammad's armies conquered Jerusalem and the entire Middle East, then pushed south into Africa, East into Asia, and north into Europe.[101]

For most radical Islamists, there is a connection between the fall of Islam in the years after the golden age of the Ottoman Empire, and the fall of dignity of the jihadist. They justify mixing religion with politics, and feel sanctioned by their religion to pursue jihadist violence. Sharia is monolithic and unchangeable, and allows for no diversity. To the Islamist, secularism is considered perverted and corrupt, and democracy must be subordinated to Sharia. Even though Muslim countries, from Morocco to Indonesia, are culturally and ethnically diverse, these Muslims are not proud of their ethnicity. A Pakistani Muslim thinks he is more of an Arab than a man of the Indus Valley, his primal identity. To him the pre-Islamic period, including the primordial civilization of the Indus Valley, is only an object of disdain.

Unlike the followers of any other religion in the world, Muslims—in any region where there is a Muslim majority—are engaging in revolution to establish separate countries. These violent secessionist movements have unfolded in Xinjiang, China, in Narathiwat, Thailand, in Mindanao, the Philippines, in the Indian state of Jammu and Kashmir, and in Chechnya in Russia, among others. Muslim countries are either at war or engaged in hostile relations with every civilization that Islam abuts, from Nigeria to China. The 20 per cent or less of the population that was Muslim in British Colonial India asked for a separate country based on religion during the Indian independence movement. In many countries, Muslim minorities feel themselves to be beleaguered by the culture of the host country, and choose to confront the government. "Empathy among Muslims creates a big potential problem that does not exist with other immigrants."[102] This is often due to an obsession with the historical past of Islam, which is remembered as a golden age. They do not realize that Britain, France, Spain, Germany, Italy, and Russia have lost much of their former status, power, and hegemonies. By contrast, for the last one hundred years and with the help of the West, political Islam is in the ascendency.

The historic, political Islam existed in a wilderness of tyrannical grandeur, stolen treasures, and tortured civilizations. Yet in the Islamist's eyes, the Islamic world invented science, technology, art, architecture, medicine, agriculture, jurisprudence, and other advancements, and then the West inherited unfairly and deprived them of everything.

Underworld, Media, and the Internet

Many Islamic organizations own newspapers, magazines, television stations, and other media outlets in the Middle East and South Asia, which they use to promulgate and support their cause. These organizations patronize columnists to write articles about Islamic causes and their grievances, in the hopes of creating favorable public opinion. They also have affiliations with the world of crime through illegal gambling, drugs, money laundering, and the surreptitious investment of money in the movie industry. The films they sponsor on Islam and its mission, or about 'peaceful' Islamic terrorists, are popular in the Muslim world and serve as an advertisement for a terror-free-Islam. Lords of the underworld maintain several websites and host many Internet bloggers. They regularly publish hate literature, and warn of threats to Islam worldwide by cultural and political imperialism and exploitation. Some Muslim countries and organizations deny mass murder and genocide at the hands of Muslims. They also deny the Holocaust, during which six million Jews lost their lives, the genocide of 1.5 million Armenians in Turkey, and the existence of the mountains of infidel skulls in India, of those killed at the behest of Zahiruddin Muhammad Babur, the founder of the Mogul Empire. Babur recorded this event in *Baburnama,* his autobiography:

> With stones and matchlocks the Hindus all were reduced as low as the Elephanteers, the Ethiopian invaders of Mecca. Many mountains of bodies were created, and on every mountain running streams of blood.[103]

There are several Internet websites solely about jihad. One of these, *Minbar al-Tawhid wa'l-Jihad* (MTJ), is the website of Abu Muhammad al-Maqdisi, a prominent cleric and theorist of jihad living in Jordan. It includes the world's largest online library of jihadist literature. This website has served as a guide for some of the most brutal terrorists on earth. The Taliban, also maintains websites, making use of U.S. Web hosts such as The Texas Company, and another Web-hosting outfit called The Planet, which rented cyberspace to terrorists while having no clue about their Taliban connections. For more than a year, a militant group used the site to provide its users with their take on suicide bombings, rocket attacks, and raids against U.S. troops and their allies. This website, http://alemarah1.com, frequently claimed that the group's forces had killed coalition troops and even destroyed warplanes and tanks, all of which was utter misinformation. Another Taliban Website, http://Toorabora.com, continues to operate using the services of Free Web Town, a user-friendly template service run by Atlanta-based Tulix Systems. Tulix boasts over 1 million clients, while The Planet is the country's biggest supplier of Web-hosting services, with nearly 16 million accounts. The relatively cheap fees and high quality of U.S. servers seems to attract jihadists.[104] Professor Bernard Haykel of Princeton University has this to say about Maqdisi:

> Born in what is now the West Bank, Mr. Maqdisi spent time in Pakistan and Afghanistan in the 1980s, where his writings and speeches legitimizing violence influenced Osama Bin Laden and others. In the mid-1990s he

was sent to prison in Jordan and became the spiritual mentor of a fellow prisoner, Abu Musab al-Zarqawi, who later became notorious for decapitating hostages as the leader of Al Qaeda in Mesopotamia. For several decades, there has been a dynamic at work in the radical Sunni Islamist community where each new generation becomes less principled, less learned, more radical, and more violent than the one before it.[105]

The Internet has helped to connect desperate, frustrated radicals in the disparate underground radical Islamic movements of various nations, in a way that was unthinkable only three decades back.[106] *The New York Times* Columnist Thomas Friedman comments:

> The flattening of the world has also led to more urbanization and large scale immigration to the West of many of these young, unemployed, frustrated Arab-Muslim males, while simultaneously making it much easier for informal open-source networks of these young men to form, operate, and interconnect. This certainly has been a boon for underground extremist Muslim political groups. There has been a proliferation of these informal mutual supply chains throughout the Arab-Muslim world today—small networks of people who move money through hawalas (hand-to-hand financing networks), and who recruit through alternative education systems like the madrassas, and who communicate through the Internet and other tools of the global information revolution.[107]

A survey indicates that only 14 per cent of Americans had a positive opinion of Islam in 1993, and that this increased to 30 per cent after the 9/11 attack due to the fact that they had learned more about Islam from the media. This represents a victory for the terrorists, including AQ, which has been using multimedia propaganda through outlets such as al Jazeera satellite television to propagate its mission. AQ, Hamas, Hezbollah, the Popular Front for the Liberation of Palestine, HuM in Kashmir and others all have their own websites. The Internet provides instant communication for terrorists anywhere in the entire world, without very little censorship or approval. A terrorist can use cyberspace to foment violence, destruction, and death simultaneously to millions of people around the world, around the clock, with anonymity. The World Wide Web has given terrorists the unprecedented ability to extract information and disseminate it to millions of users (see Chapter 5). For example, a downloadable, thirteen-volume *Encyclopedia of Jihad* and a *Jihad Manual* are posted on the Internet. They have found a ready audience: It is estimated that more than 4000 websites are used by terrorists. Terrorist organizations can also raise funds via the Internet in various countries, and then send it to groups that train mujahedeen, in Afghanistan, Iraq, Chechnya, the Philippines, Bosnia, and Kashmir. For example, Lashkar-e-Taib (LeT), one of the largest and most active militant organizations based in Pakistan, relies on fundraising from the Pakistani diasporas and from Muslim countries to support and spread Islam by jihad. This group, which was founded by Hafiz Saeed, has links with Al Qaeda(AQ), Jaish-e-ohammad (JeM), Hizb-ul-Mujahidden (HuM), Indian Mujahidden (IM), and Student Islamic Movement of India (SIM). The LeT's goal is to restore Islam in South Asia by jihad.

Just three months after the September 11 attacks, militants from Lashkar-e-Taiba (L-e-T), meaning 'army of the pure,' and Jaish-e-Mohammed (J-e-M) bombed India's parliament building. L-e-T is the military wing of the well-funded Pakistani Islamist organization Markaz-ad-Dawa-wal-Irshad, which was founded in 1989 and recruited volunteers to fight alongside the Taliban. L-e-T and J-e-M, based in Pakistan, have connections to Al Qaeda. During the 1990s, it is reported (see Chapter 4) that LeT received instruction and funding from Pakistan's intelligence agency, Inter-Services Intelligence (ISI), in exchange for a pledge to target Hindus in Jammu and Kashmir and to train Muslim extremists on Indian soil. Pakistan's government has repeatedly denied allegations of supporting terrorism. Until it was banned in Pakistan in 2002, LeT claimed responsibility for numerous attacks, including an attack on the army barracks at Delhi's Red Fort in 2000, killing three people; a January 2001 attack on Srinagar airport that killed five Indians; and an attack in April 2002 against Indian border security forces that left at least four dead. But after being outlawed, it has not admitted to attacks. It denied responsibility for the November 2008 attack in Mumbai, the July 2006 attack on the Mumbai commuter rail, and the 2001 attack on the Indian parliament, despite the Indian government's allegations.[108] Frank Furedi comments:

> Videos celebrating the beheading of hostages and carefully orchestrated invasions of theaters and schools are designed to convey the message that "we will stop at nothing." While the Westerners love to live, terrorists love to die. By terrorists' attacks, the Westerners' risks are influenced by a one-dimensional concern with loss, whereas terrorists regard risk from the perspective of gain.[109]

Lack of Extradition Treaties

There is no universal extradition treaty among nations, only a few bilateral treaties. Transnational terrorists with material and military support from state or non-state actors commit terrorist acts in other countries, and then escape to their countries of origin. If they are accused of these terrorist acts, or if countries seek to try these terrorists, if denial does not work, the accusers are told that there is no extradition treaty between them. These perpetrators of bombings, killings, and arson often remain free to go about their business after committing atrocious acts of terrorism. Radicals of the Bombay underworld find safe havens across the borders of neighboring countries. Terrorists wanted in other countries are given welfare and citizenship in the United Kingdom and other countries, and are even allowed to form political organizations to raise funds that support terrorism. The United States does not have extradition treaties with many countries. But because of a bilateral extradition treaty with Pakistan, America in 1997 extradited Pakistani Mir Amal Kasi, who had been charged with the attack on the CIA headquarters in Langley, Virginia, in 1993. Unless the death penalty is abolished in the United States, the European Union nations and other nations of the world will not permit the extradition of alleged terrorists to America.

Injustice and Lack of Civil Liberties

There is no place in the world for unfairness, discrimination, or injustice based on religion, in terms of denying people jobs, education, career opportunities, political representation, and humane treatment in prison. Yet the inhuman and torturous treatment of prisoners held at Abu Ghraib, Iraq, and at the U.S. Naval Base at Guantanamo Bay, Cuba, has been confirmed. The treatment of these prisoners is outlined in a Congressional report: "U.S. military personnel subjecting Iraqi detainees to treatment that has been described as degrading, inhuman, and in some cases, tantamount to torture."[110] The abuse of Muslim prisoners has been reported worldwide through newspapers and television, causing serious resentment everywhere, and fomenting even more anger in Muslim countries. The Middle East-based television network, Al Jazeera, covered atrocities and injustices, including the story of the Guantanamo captives, some of whom repeatedly protested the abuse by U.S. military personnel.[111] The abuses by military prison guards at Abu Ghraib in Iraq were described by the New York Times reporter Kate Zernike, who reported that the following events had taken place: guards urinating and pouring phosphoric acid on detainees; sodomization; ropes being tied to the detainees' private parts and used to drag them across the floor.[112] Professor Alan Kruger has written:

> I argued that a lack of civil liberties seems to be a main cause of terrorism around the world. Support for civil liberty should be a part of the arsenal

in the war against terrorism, both at home and abroad. . . . However, just as we often say that correlation is not proof of causality, lack of correlation does necessarily imply lack of causality. This lack of correlation does, however, suggest to me that the burden of proof ought to shift to those who want to argue that low education, poverty, and other economic conditions are important causes of terrorism . . .

Zack Beuchamp argues:

These terrorists organizations are committed to a fundamentalist interpretation of Islam that preaches violence not primarily as a response to American foreign policy, but because it is at the core of their beliefs that the infidel must be subordinated to Islam.[113]

Former British Prime Minister Tony Blair made a similar point when he said: "The more people live under democracy, with human liberty intact, the less inclined they or their states will be to indulge terrorism or to engage in it."[114] In view of national security, the United States has taken three major measures that impact on civil liberties: The Patriot Act, racial profiling, and tourist and immigrant scrutiny.

The Patriot Act allows for: (a) Indefinite detention of non citizens, (b) Telephone and Internet monitoring, (c) Secret searches and seizures of documents and mail, (d) Authority to declare groups as terrorists, (e) Access to financial, medical, and educational records without court orders, (f) Phone wiretapping for domestic dissidents as well as following their political activities, and (g) Security agencies to have unlimited and unauthorized information sharing.[115]

The American Civil Liberties Union (ACLU) and others claim that the Act violates the First, Fourth, Sixth, Eighth, and Thirteenth Amendments of the Constitution. Using this Act, however, it was possible to dismantle terrorist cells in Buffalo, New York, Detroit, Michigan, Seattle, Washington, and Portland, Oregon. A total of about 225 suspected terrorists were arrested, with 132 convictions. Additionally, 90 per cent of Americans believes that there is no loss of civil liberty under this Act.

Racial profiling has no impact on terrorists except some inconvenience and humiliation. Terrorists can be male, female, or any age, race, or religion. They can be citizens, non-citizens, and speak any language. Terrorists can infiltrate local communities with money, or use other lucrative, seductive methods. A suicide bomber does not need robust health, strong features, fine clothes, or a Muslim name. There are plenty of extremist Muslim converts available to commit terrorist acts without being suspected.

Racial profiling has resulted in embarrassment, and in the searching of babies and innocent adults, such as Sikh gas-station owner Balbir Singh Sodhi and others. Additionally, racial profiling has caused severe resentment in minority communities—and it has not prevented terrorist acts. The latest terrorist attacks in the United States were conducted by U.S. citizens. These home-grown terrorists' intimate knowledge of Western cultures and languages, possession of Western passports and relative lack of overt ties to large terrorist organizations make their detection a difficult task. Their determination to strike in their own countries, combined with easy access to explosive substances and weapons, makes them an immediate threat to the security of Western and other countries.[116] Detaining a tourist or immigrant on the suspicion of terrorism is a precautionary and preventive measure that can only be justified when suspicions are substantiated by further information from an individual's past records. The expiration of visas is an immigration problem, not to be associated with possible future terrorism. In addition, all detainees should have access to legal services. The arbitrary detention of tourists who have visitor visas may reduce the number of terrorist who arrive in America as legitimate visitors, but not terrorists who sneak into the country. Furthermore, terrorists are usually careful not to get caught committing minor crimes. It is reported, however, that 84 detainees held at the Metropolitan Detention Center in New York were classified by the FBI as high-risk terrorists. Despite their frustration and anger toward the nation, Muslims are the largest group of tourists to visit America, and represent the largest group of foreign students studying in America.

When injustice is unbearable or when people feel repressed, harassed, or desperate, they resort to extreme violence like suicide bombing. Shibley Telhami writes:

> The true horror of suicide bombings is that they are immensely empowering to many people in the region who no longer believe that their governments can do anything to relieve their humiliation and improve their conditions. . . . Today many Israelis support the expulsion of Palestinians from their homes as a way of stopping the unbearable horror of suicide terror; and many Palestinians support terror as a way of ridding themselves of the unbearable pain of occupation.[117]

Terrorism used to be confined to the Israel-Palestine conflict, but it is now much more widespread. Injustices are no longer only confined to local conflicts.

The Afghanistan and Iraq Wars

The Afghanistan War started when Mullah Omar, the head of the Taliban government in Afghanistan, rejected President Bush's demands to hand over OBL after 9/11. The Iraq war was a result of concerns on the part of President Bush that Iraq had WMDs. The former was a war of necessity, the latter was a war of choice to overthrow Saddam Hussein (1937–2006). These two wars have spawned many Islamic jihadists who are eager to join their Muslim brothers and wage terror against the infidel armies.[118] The bombings in London and Madrid sent a clear a message to Britain and Spain about their joining in the Coalition Forces in the Middle East. During testimony before the Senate Foreign Relations Committee, Brookings Institute scholar Daniel Benjamin said that with

> the 2003 invasion of Iraq, we gave the radicals a shot in the arm, handing them a tableau that they could point to as confirmation of their argument. It is clear that Iraq was a major part of the motivation of the Madrid and London bombers as well as Mohammed Bouyeri, the murderer of Theo van Gogh. In countries such as Pakistan, it is also clear that anti-Americanism grounded in the invasion of Iraq is increasingly being used as a tool of mobilization for radicals. However benign our intentions were in going into Iraq to liberate the populace there of an evil dictatorship, in the context of the culture of grievance that exists in much of the Muslim world, the extremists have benefited from our missteps and their narrative has had a profound resonance.

A small number of jihadists (holy warriors) make a great difference and they are growing after the invasion.

> Against our most dangerous foe, our strategic position is weakening. Inspired by Usama bin Laden's boldness and outraged by America's recent actions, more Muslims are sympathizing with the radical Islamists and joining their movement. . . . In disparate places around the globe, from Indonesia to the Caucus and from Pakistan to Western Europe, the jihadist ideology has become the banner under which an array of grievances is being expressed, and often that expression is violent.[119]

The war on terror in Afghanistan has created a large number of Taliban extremists, and it has spread the Wahhabi version of Islam to Pakistan's Northwest Frontier Province. There have been several suicide bombings in both countries. It is reported:

President Barack Obama's new regional strategy puts Pakistan at its centre. Admiral Mike Mullen, the chairman of the Joint Chiefs of Staff, and Richard Holbrooke, the special envoy to the region, visited Pakistan this week. At a dinner for journalists the two men conceded that America was not winning in Afghanistan but seemed at odds over whether it was actually losing.[120]

The key to the debate over Afghanistan is the question of whether terrorists need a 'safe haven' the region, infested by Al Qaeda and the Taliban terrorists, from which they can launch attacks on America and the West. However, they can plan the bombing of America at an apartment in Germany as in the 9/11 attacks. Also, homegrown American terrorists don't need a safe haven. All they need is a place to buy a gun like the Muslim psychiatrist Nidal Hassan.[121]

The estimated size of the insurgency in Afghanistan as of 2010 is 30,000, while it was only 5,000 in 2005. The number of U.S. troops in Afghanistan has been increased from 18,000 in 2005 to 95,000 in 2010.[122] State Department spokesman PJ Crowley said the U.S. had a trillion dollar investment to protect in the country and wanted to honor the memory of the 4,415 U.S. troops who lost.[123] Former American Ambassador Peter Galbraith has mentioned Iraq war's unintended consequences (see Table 2.8).[124]

Table 2.8
Unintended Consequences

Intended	Unintended
1 Eliminate WMD	WMD with Iran and North Korea
2 Eliminate AQ terrorists	More terrorists worldwide
3 Undermine Iran	Iran back to Iraq after 4 centuries
4 For democracies in Iraq and the Middle East	More theocratic and despotic regimes
5 Intimidate and Isolate Syria	Threats to Israel increased
6 Enhance American power and prestige	All-time low and more anti-American

* Based on Peter Galbraith, 2008.

State-Sponsored Terrorism

State-sponsored terrorism is defined as suffering and destruction caused to innocent civilians by the state apparatus. Over a time span of more than three decades, Josef Stalin and his fellow Communists may have killed as many as 100 million Russians. The Nazis of Germany, led by Adolf Hitler, used state resources to kill Jews, Gypsies, and others between 1933 and 1945. More recently, Iranian students took fifty-three Americans hostage at the U.S. Embassy on November 4, 1979, holding them prisoner until January 20, 1981 and ushering in the Iranian Revolution. On December 21, 1988, two Libyan intelligence agents hijacked Pan Am Flight 103. The midair explosion over Lockerbie, Scotland, caused the deaths of 259 on the plane and 11 on the ground. On January 31, 2001, Ali Mohmed Al Megrahi, a Libyan agent, was convicted of this crime and sentenced to life imprisonment. He was released on August 20, 2009 by the Scottish Government, as he was suffering from terminal prostate cancer. Megrahi returned to Libya and received a hero's welcome, which insulted and shocked the world. British Prime Minister Gordon Brown said on August 22, 2009, that he was outraged and "repulsed" by the celebratory welcome given to the man convicted in the bombing of Pan Am Flight 103. The Abu Nidal Organization (ANO) has been sustained and supported by Syria, Libya, Iraq, and other Muslim nations. In Pakistan, nine university-style recruitment and training operations directly linked to Sipah-e-Sahaba Pakistan, JeM, HuM, and HuJ–Islami were operating out of Karachi. The U.S. State Department has listed several foreign organizations as terrorist organizations (Appendix 1), and has declared that Cuba, Iran, Libya, Sudan, Syria, and North Korea are home to state-sponsored terror.

State terrorism advances a political agenda, often surreptitiously through terrorist organizations. Professor Philip Bobbitt declares: "Terrorism is the use of violence in order to advance a political agenda by preventing persons from doing what they would otherwise lawfully do."[125] This definition enables us to differentiate between terrorists and freedom fighters. If a state harbors groups that meet Bobbitt's definition, it is a terrorist state. It has been alleged that Iran, Syria, Iraq, Saudi Arabia, and Pakistan, among others, provide financial support, military aid, and diplomatic services to several radical terrorist organizations. It is also reported that Iran has supported several Palestinian terrorist groups, such as the Islamic Jihad and Hezbollah in Lebanon, Hezbollah in Syria and Saudi Arabia, and the Taliban in Pakistan. Several militant groups, such as LeT, JeM, and Jamaat-al Dawa have settled in Pakistan to promote that nation's strategic depth in Afghanistan, India, and Central Asia, and to merge Kashmir with Pakistan. They are also linked to AQ. Saudi Arabia funds thousands of Wahhabi religious schools, or *madrassas,* and mosques around the world, particularly in poor countries where people cannot obtain basic necessities, education, and employment for themselves or their children. These constitute a part of state terrorism. In Pakistan, terrorist groups such as the Taliban, AQ, and LeT have established themselves as a state within a state. They have virtual free reign in the Federally Administered Tribal Areas (FATA), and a lesser but still substantial amount of leeway in the North West Frontier Province (NWFP), also known as Khyber Pakhtunkhwa (KP), and other provinces. That makes it all too easy for terrorists to launch attacks such as the ones that killed more than 170 people in Mumbai, and other attacks that killed NATO soldiers in Afghanistan. Government response in Pakistan to these attacks has been limited and ineffective. India, the United States, Afghanistan and other concerned nations have spent years begging Islamabad to crack down on terrorists. These pleas have been backed up by offers of aid, as well as threats if inaction continues. "Establish an international force to work with the Pakistanis to root out terrorist camps in Kashmir as well as in the tribal areas."[126] The graduates of these *madrassas* are vehemently opposed to non-Muslims and modern civilization, and are often recruited by terrorist organizations. The American historian Walter Laqueur states,

> The obvious tools of governments to engage in substitute terrorism are the use of Islamic groups, the link between Iran and the Lebanese Hezbollah has been the classic example. . . . Iran also kept contact with terror groups in Afghanistan before and after Taliban rule and it has undertaken efforts to destabilize the Jordanian government. The Iranian Revolutionary Guard Corps and Ministry of Intelligence and Security have been active in Syria, Lebanon, and Turkey and to a limited extent in Central Asia and Pakistan. It also reportedly made it possible for members of al Qa'ida to cross Iran on their way to the Caucasus after their defeat in Afghanistan. . . . Lastly, the radical terrorist Muslim groups do not hide or downplay the fact that they engage in violence but, on the contrary, intend to frighten and demoralize their enemies: Allah is with them and will protect them, their cause is invincible, and those opposing them are doomed and will be destroyed.[127]

In 2002, a right-wing party BJP in the State of Gujarat, India, was alleged to have been involved in the massacre of two thousand Muslims. It was said that this massacre was an aftereffect of several suicide attacks and passenger burnings in train, railway, and bus stations in Gujarat, Bombay, and other places, killing several hundred people. Muslims have accused India's right-wing parties of demolishing the sixteenth century Babri Mosque in ten hours in December 1992. While it is the moral and constitutional duty of every democratic government to defend minorities and their places of worship. India also did nothing to protect over one million Kashmir pundits who were either killed or thrown out of Jammu and Kashmir province by the Kashmiri Taliban in the process of ethnic cleansing during the 1990s.[128] By contrast, the entire world rallied against ethnic cleansing in Yugoslavia in the 1990s. America, with NATO forces, went to war twice to liberate Bosnia and Kosovo, and to free Muslims entrapped in these two countries. Ethnic cleansing of Jews in the Arab world has gone unnoticed; as the distinguished Professor Andre Aciman has said, President Obama has never acknowledged

> any of the other 800,000 or so Jews born in the Middle East who fled the Arab and Muslim world or who were summarily expelled for being Jewish in the 20th century. With all his references to the history of Islam and to its (questionable) "proud tradition of tolerance" of other faiths, Mr. Obama never said anything about those Jews whose ancestors had been living in Arab lands long before the advent of Islam but were its first victims once rampant nationalism swept over the Arab world.[129]

Several Western countries, including Russia and China, have conducted covert operations abroad through their intelligence agencies and provided financial assistance surreptitiously to militant groups. These groups have exploited religious, ethnic, and linguistic minorities to promote the strategic interests of these two countries. While Russia and China both have had problems with Islamic terrorists, in Chechnya and Xinjiang provinces, respectively, China deflects this menace by aligning with Muslim countries, particularly Pakistan.

Western countries and media downplay Chinese oppression of Muslims due to globalization and capital flow. Several think tanks and universities in the Western world are supported by grants from Saudi Arabia, Iran, and the Gulf countries, who offer exchange programs and participate in joint projects. Multitudes of Muslim scholars and statesmen act as advisors and consultants in interpreting the Islamic threat, and hundreds of Islamic centers and lobbying group exist in non-Muslim countries. Norman Podhoretz writes:

> [President] Bush declared we need to uproot and destroy the entire network of interconnected terrorist networks and cells that existed in as many as fifty or sixty countries. . . . The State Department itself had a list of seven state sponsors of terrorism (including all but two of which, Cuba and North Korea, were predominantly Muslim) and it regularly issued reports on terrorist's incidents throughout the world.[130]

Moral Decadence of the West

Muslim concerns about the moral decadence of the West is legitimate. The West is too obsessed with materialism and consumerism and there has been a blatant decline in sexual ethics. Additionally, faith in religion and attendance in church are decreasing yearly, while attendance in mosques is increasing. Western belief in the universality of Western culture may be seen as false, immoral, and dangerous. It is false because other civilizations have other ideals and norms; immoral because imperialism is the necessary, logical consequence of universalism; and dangerous because it could lead to a major intercivilizational war. To mitigate this decline, the United States should reaffirm its identity as a nation by repudiating multiculturalism at home, while adopting an Atlanticist policy of close cooperation with its European partners to protect and advance the interests and values of the unique civilization.[131]

The gap is widening between Muslim values and Western values. It is likely to lead to a clash of cultures and civilizations. Yet there is no conflict between spiritualism and materialism: Both can exist and thrive. Islam, by conversion, coercion, and reproduction, aggressively fills up the void of Western indifference to or perversion of their religion by adopting Sharia wherever they have a majority amidst non-Muslim populations. Muslims cannot live with non-Muslims, East or West, and have made it clear that the West cannot comprehend Islamic spirituality and religiosity as long as it is blinded by materialism. In the West, drug use, divorce rates, family violence, teenage pregnancy, single parents, same-sex marriage, homicides, immodest women's clothing, and obsessions with popular music and team sports franchises are on the rise. Islamists have highlighted this as proof of Western decadence. Imam Samudra of Jemmah Ismaiyyah (who was allegedly involved in the Bali bombing) was outraged by the "dirty adulterous behavior of the whites." With this in mind, it is ironic that in Las Vegas, also known as "Sin City," there is a large Muslim population and at least five mosques. Many Muslim terrorists, including the Mohammed Atta, Major Nidal Hassan, and others, are known to have visited strip clubs in Sarasota and in Daytona Beach, Florida, in Las Vegas, as well as in Canada and Italy. There are strip clubs in both Syria and Dubai which are often visited by Muslims.

Notes

1. Margulies, 2006, 66, Bukay, 2008, 27-36.

2. Wiktorowicz (Ed.), *Islamic Activism,* 2004, 25–26.

3. Sabrina Tavernise. "Pakistan Politics Take Nationalist, Anti-U.S." *New York Times,* November 19, 2009.

4. Chomsky, *9-11 (Nine-Eleven),* 79.

5. Dershowitz, 2002, 26.

6. Roberts, *1993,* 310, 304-309, 347-351.

7. Kepel, 2002, 17. Kepel. "Beyond terror and martyrdom." *The Economist,* Nov. 27, 2008.

8. Weaver, *Pakistan,* 3, 47.

9. "KLA (Kosovo Liberation Army) rebels train in terrorist camps." Jerry Seper, *The Washington Times,* May 4, 1999.

10. Podhoretz, 2008, 30–31.

11. Noam Chomsky. "What America has learnt/not learnt since 9/11." *The Age,* September 7, 2002, www.theage.com.au/articles/2002/09/06/1031115935 105.html.

12. Egendorf (Ed.), 2004, 68–69.

13. Wright, Lawrence, 2006, 106-107.

14. Allawi, 2009, 140.

15. Hiro, 2002, 375.

16. "Jihad? Abrogation in Islam." David Bukay. *Middle East Quarterly,* Fall 2007, 3–11; Rudolph Peters. *Jihad in Classical and Modern Islam.* Princeton, NJ, Markus Wiener, 1996, 1-8, 43–54, 108–12, 124, 132; Mustafa Akyol, Islam Without Extremes, New York: W.W.Norton & Company, 2011.

17. Frum and Perle, 2003, 187-188.

18. Hodson, *The Great Divide,* 1971, 470; Lars Blikenberg, *India and Pakistan, The History of Unsolved Conflict* (Odense: Odense University Press, 1997/ 1998) Vol. I, pp. 76, 78–82, 1997/1998. The Danish diplomat Lars Blinkenberg writes: "Almost all non-Pakistani writers have come to the conclusion that the accession is of J& K was legally complete."

19. Marguiles. 2006, 128.

20. Horowitz, 2004, 145.

21. Brendon, *Decline and Fall of the British Empire,* 405, 406; Hodson, *Great Divide,*1971, 321.

22. Luce, 2007, 224.

23. Brendon, 2009, 410, 420.

24. Muslim League. "Programme for the Day of Direct Action Day." *Star of India,* 13 August 1946.

25. Herman. *Gandhi and Churchill.* 2008, 554, 562, 567.

26. Mohanty. "Gandhi." *News India–Times,* February 7, 1997; Mohanty. "An Unprecedented Struggle to Achieve Liberty." *News India–Times,* August 15, 1997; Brendon. *Decline and Fall of the British Empire,* 405, 406.

27. Madhusree Mukherjee. *Churchill's Secret War*, New York, Basic Books, 2010, 258-259.

28. Hodson. *Great Divide*, 1971, 166.

29. Pape, 2005, 15.

30. Michael Mukasey. "Shahzad and the Pre-9/11 Paradigm in the 1990s." *Wall Street Journal,* May 12, 2010; Robert Wright. "The Making of a Terrorist." *New York Times*, May 11, 2010.

31. Naipaul, *Beyond Belief*, 1998, 251.

32. "Pakistan: A Wake-Up Call." 20 April, 2010 04:45:00 editor, Policy Research Group. *Strategic Insight*, http://policyresearchgroup.com/terror_updates/ pakistan_terror_updates/685.html

33. Barnett Rubin and Ahmed Rashid. "Pakistan, Afghanistan and the West." *Foreign Affairs,* November/ December 2008.

34. Chien Peng Chung. "China's War on Terror, September 11, and Uighur Separation." *Foreign Affairs*, September 11, 2002.

35. Julie Wilhelmsen. "Between a Rock and a Hard Place: The Islamisation of the Chechen Separatist Movement." Europe-Asia Studies, Vol. 57, No. 1, January 2005, 35–59, www.cfr.org/publication/9181

36. In *The Strangled Traveler: Colonial Imaginings and the Thugs of India* (2002), Martine van Woerkens suggests that evidence for the existence of a Thuggee *cult* in the nineteenth century was in part the product of "colonial imaginings"— British fear of the little-known interior of India and limited understanding of the religious and social practices of its inhabitants; *Juggernaut and the Black Hole of Calcutta*. Krishna Dutta, while reviewing the book *Thug: The true story of India's murderous cult,* by the British historian Dr. Mike Dash, in *The Independent*, argues:

"In recent years, the revisionist view that thuggee was a British invention, a means to tighten their hold in the country, has been given credence in India, France and the U.S., but this well-researched book objectively questions that assertion." Dash rejects skepticism about the existence of a secret network of groups with a *modus operandi* that was different from that of highwaymen.

Acting in the "Theatre of Anarchy": "The Anti-Thug Campaign" and Elaborations of Colonial Rule in Early-Nineteenth Century India, by Tom Lloyd (2006), "Parama Roy: Discovering India, Imagining Thuggee." In *Indian Traffic: Identities in Question in Colonial and Postcolonial India*. University of California Press, 1998.

37. Michael Crawford and Jami Miscik. "The Rise of Mezzanine Rulers." *Foreign Affairs*, November/December 2010.

38. Ajami. "Pakistan's Struggle for Modernity." *Wall Street Journal,* May 27, 2009.

39. Michael Mukasey. "Shahzad and the Pre-9/11 Paradigm in the 1990s." *Wall Street Journal,* May 12, 2010; Robert Wright. "The Making of a Terrorist," *New York Times*, May 11, 2010.

40. "Detention and Removal of Illegal Aliens." U.S. Department of Homeland Security, Washington, D.C., April 14, 2006 www.dhs.gov/xoig/assets/mgmtrpts/ OIG_06-33_Apr06.pdf.

41. Ajami. "Autocracy and the Decline of the Arabs." *Wall Street Journal,* Aug. 6, 2009.

42. "Arab Human Development Report 2009: Challenges to Human Security in the Arab Countries." United Nations Development Programme—Regional Bureau for Arab States, 11, United Nations Publications, 2 UN Plaza, DC2, Room 853, New York, NY, 10017, USA, by Helen Clark, Administrator, UNDP. (UNDP-RBAS) www.arab-hdr.org/contents/.aspx?rid=5.

43. "Madrassas and militancy." Dr Hasan-Askari Rizvi. *The Daily Times,* October 25, 2009; Llan Berman. "Pakistan's madrassas need reform: Road to moderation runs through its schools." *Washington Times,* August 20, 2010.

44. Ibrahim. *The Al Qaeda Reader,* 116-140; Sabrina Tavernise. "Hate Engulfs Christians in Pakistan." *New York Times,* August 2, 2009. This is related to the blasphemy laws of Pakistan.

45. Cole, 2009, 7.

46. Pape, 2005, 242.

47. J. Hector St. John de Crevecoeur. "Americans are the western pilgrims." *Letters from An American Farmer* (Letter III), 1782, http://xroads.virginia.edu/~HYPER/crev/home.html.

48. Paul Johnson. "Relentlessly and Thoroughly." *National Review,* October 15, 2001.

49. Schlesinger, 1991, 55.

50. Spain's migrants 'seek jobs not conquest' Leslie Crawford. "Madrid, September 8 2007." 03:00 | Last updated: September 8 2007 03:00, *Financial Times,* UK, June 30, 2011, http://www.ft.com/cms/s/0/9f4ea546-5da4-11dc-8d22-0000779fd2ac.html#axzz1QnDiYuSl.

51. Francis Fukuyama. "A Year of Living Dangerously." *Wall Street Journal,* November 2, 2005.

52. Phillips, 2006, 72.

53. Pamela K. Taylor. "On Faith." *Washington Post,* June 30, 2009.

54. "Sarkozy Says Burqas Are Unwelcome in France." Sausana Ferriera and David Gauthier-Villars, *Wall Street Journal,* June 22, 2009.

55. "Sarkozy Backs Drive to Eliminate the Burqa." Doreen Carvajal. *New York Times,* June 22, 2009.

56. "Muslim World: Majorities in Europe support 'burka ban'." Meris Lutz. *Los Angeles Times,* March 2, 2010.

57. Caldwell. *Reflections on the Revolution in Europe,* 2009, 349.

58. Steyn. *America Alone.* 2008, 83.

59. "Four bomb suspects 'had £500,000 in benefits'." Daniel McGrory and Sean O'Neill. *The Sunday Times,* August 6, 2005.

60. Caldwell. *Reflections on the Revolution in Europe,* 2009, 325.

61. Fallaci. *The Force of Reason.* 2006, 66.

62. "Rifqa Bary: A Florida Culture War Over Runaway Convert." *Time Magazine,* August 24, 2009, www.time.com/time/nation/article/0,8599,1918228,00.html.

63. "Madonna Booed In Bucharest For Defending Gypsies." Alina Wolff Murray; *The Huffington Post*, August 27, 2009, http://www.huffingtonpost.com/2009/08/27/madonna-booed-in-buchares_n_270176.html.

64. Bawer. *Surrender*. 2009, 21.

65. Naipaul. *Beyond Belief*. 1998, 141, 142.

66. Spencer. *Islam Unveiled*. 2002, 98, 157-258; Victor Sharpe. "Mosques of War." *American Thinker*, Sept. 1, 2010.

67. Lewis. *Islam and the West*. 1993, 186.

68. George J. Holyoake. *English Secularism*. Chicago, IL: The Open Court Publishing Company, 1986, 186.

69. Taylor. *Secular Age*. 2007, 560-679.

70. Sen. *The Argumentative Indian*. 2005, 16–19, 294–317.

71. Yusuf al-Qaradawi. "How the Imported Solutions Disastrously Affected Our Ummah." *The Lawful and Prohibited in Islam*. http://irn.no/old/halal/lawfull.PDF, 113-4.

72. Olivier Roy. *Secularism Confronts Islam*. New York, Columbia University Press. 2007, 10–91.

73. "Islam and Secularism." Sheikh Salman b. Fahd al-Oadah. *Islam Today*. Chapter 2, http://www.imanway.com/en/showthread.php?t=593&page=1.

74. Bernard Lewis. "License to Kill: Usama bin Ladin's Declaration of Jihad." *Foreign Affairs,* November/December 1998.

75. Bernard Lewis. "License to Kill: Usama bin Ladin's Declaration of Jihad." *Foreign Affairs,* November/December 1998.

76. Bernard Lewis. "License to Kill: Usama bin Ladin's Declaration of Jihad." *Foreign Affairs,* November/December 1998.

77. Stern. *Terror in the Name of God*. 2003, 283.

78. Pew Global Attitude Project. "World Publics Welcome Global Trade." released October 4, 2007.

79. Vidino. *Al Qaeda in Europe*. 89.

80. Bill Warner. "The Political Violence of the Bible and the Koran." *Political Islam* (Center for the Study of Political Islam), 10 September 2010, http://www.politicalislam.com/blog/the-political-violence-of-the-bible-and-the-koran/; John M. Broder. "For Muslim Who Says Violence Destroys Islam, Violent Threats." *New York Times*, March 11, 2006.

81. "The Lessons of Mumbai." Angel Rabasa, Robert D. Blackwill, Peter Chalk, Kim Cragin, C. Christine Fair, Brian A. Jackson, Brian Michael Jenkins, Seth G. Jones, Nathaniel Shestak, Ashley J. Tellis. Santa Monica, CA, Rand Corporation, 2009, http://www.rand.org/pubs/occasional_papers/OP249.html, 310; Nicole M. Warren. *Madrassa Education in Pakistan: Assisting the Taliban's Resurgence*. Salve Regina University, POL 372, Fall 2009, 23; Llan Berman. "Pakistan's madrassas need reform; Road to moderation runs through its schools." *Washington Times*, August 20, 2010.

82. "Human Development Challenges and Opportunities in Pakistan: Defying Income Inequality and Poverty." Ghazala Yasmeen and Razia Begum, University

of Peshawar; Bahaudin G. Mujtaba, Nova Southeastern University. *Journal of Business Studies Quarterly*, 2011, Vol. 2, No. 3, pp. 1-12.

83. Thomas Kean and Lee Hamilton. "Are We Safer Today?" *Washington Post*, Sept. 9, 2007.

84. Alberto Abadie. "Poverty, Political Freedom, and the Roots of Terrorism." Harvard University and NBER, October 2004, 9, 15, http://ksghome. harvard.edu/ ~ aabadie/povterr.pdf.

85. Gabriel. *They Must Be Stopped*. 2006, 202, 208-209.

86. Burleigh. *Sacred Causes*. 2007, 477, 479.

87. Eric Kaufmann. "Eurabia? The Foreign Policy Implications of West Europe's Religious Composition in 2025 and Beyond." paper prepared for the International Studies Association (ISA), Annual Conference, San Francisco, CA, March 25--29, 2008.

88. Durant, *Our Original Heritage*. 475.

89. Ruthven. *Islam in the World*. 278; Stern, Jessica (2000). "Pakistan's Jihad Culture." *Foreign Affairs,* Vol. 79, No. 6; Islamic Religious Schools, "Madrassas." Background by Christopher M. Blanchard, CRS Report for Congress, January 23, 2008. http://www.fas.org/sgp/crs/misc/RS21654.pdf.

90. Anatol Lieven. "Pakistan: A Hard Country." *Public Affairs*, New York, NY, 2011, 291.

91. William H. McNeill. "Decline of the West?" *The New York Review of Books*, Vol. 44, January 9, 1997; Huntington, *The Clash of Civilizations*, 1997, 209.

92. Bergen. *Holy War, Inc.*, 223.

93. Caldwell. *Reflections on the Revolution in Europe*. 116, 163, 173; German Survey: http://www.hudson-ny.org/1726/germans-sceptical-muslims-islam.

94. "On Bush's June 28th, 2005 Speech." Christine Smith. *The Ethical Spectacle*, August 2005, http://www.spectacle.org/0805/smith.html

95. Toynbee. *War and Civilization*. 157-158.

96. "World Heritage Monuments and Related Edifices in India." Ali Javid. *Tabassum Javeed*, July 1st 2008, New York, NY: Algora Publishing, 107.

97. Bostom (Ed.). *The Legacy of Jihad,* 2008, 354-368; Justin Marozzi Da Capo. *Tamerlane: Sword of Islam, Conqueror of the World*. New York NY: DaCapo Press/Perseus Publishing Group, 2006, 59.

98. Lewis. *Islam in History*. Chicago, Open Court, 2001, 103-114; Peter Mansfield. *A History of the Middle East*. Penguin Books, 2004, 252.

99. Wolpert. *A New History of India*. 61-66, 105-169.

100. Frum and Perle. *An End to Evil*. 276-277.

101. Dinesh D'Souza. "Liberal Myths about Radical Islam." *Town Hall Magazine,* March 26, 2007, http://townhall.com/columnists/DineshDSouza/2007/03/26/liberal_myths_about_radical_islam? = full.

102. Caldwell. *Reflections on the Revolution in Europe*. 326.

103. Mohanty. "Review of *The Baburnama: Memoirs of Babur, Prince and Emperor*." Washington, DC: Smithsonian Institution, 1998 (New York: Oxford University Press, 1996) in association with the Freer Gallery of Art and the Arthur

M. Sackler Gallery, Washington, DC: Smithsonian Institution, Translated by Wheeler M. Thackston, 386.

104. Joby Warrick and Candace Rondeaux. "Extremist Web Sites Are Using U.S. Hosts." *Washington Post,* April 9, 2009.

105. Robert F. Worth. "Credentials Challenged, Radical Quotes West Point." *New York Times,* April 29, 2009; "2003 Review of *The Prophet of Moderation: Tariq Ramadan's Quest to Reclaim Islam.*" Jonathan Laurence. *Foreign Affairs,* May/June 2007; John F. Cullinan. "Holy Challenge: A New Chapter in Christian-Muslim relations?" *National Review Online,* September 29, 2006.

106. "Botnets, Cybercrime, and Cyberterrorism: Vulnerabilities and Policy Issues for Congress." January 29, 2008, Clay Wilson, CRS Report for Congress, http://www.fas.org/sgp/crs/terror/RL32114.pdf; Andrew Parker. "Teachers' Muslim Dress Order." The Sun, October 31, 2007; "Jihad In Schools?" *Investor's Business Daily,* July 9, 2007; "Spread by the Sword? Is holy war against Christians and Jews—'infidels'—a perversion of Islam? Here's the evidence, from Islamic texts and history." Mark Hartwig. *By the Sword.* www.answering-islam.org/Terrorism/by_the_sword.html; Quintan Wiktorowicz, *Radical Islam Rising*, Lanham, MD: Rowman & Littlefield Publishers, Inc., 2005; James Taranto. "Islamic Supremacy." *Wall Street Journal*, January 16, 2009.

107. Friedman. *The World Is Flat*, 430.

108. "The Lessons of Mumbai." Angel Rabasa, Robert D. Blackwill, Peter Chalk, Kim Cragin, C. Christine Fair, Brian A. Jackson, Brian Michael Jenkins, Seth G. Jones, Nathaniel Shestak, Ashley J. Tellis. Santa Monica, CA, Rand Corporation, 2009, http://www.rand.org/pubs/occasional_papers/OP249.html, 308–310.

109. Furedi. *Invitation to Terror.* 128; James Taranto. "Islamic Supremacy." *Wall Street Journal,* January 16, 2009.

110. Jennifer K. Elsea. *U.S. Treatment of Prisoners in Iraq: Selected Legal Issues*. Washington, D.C.: Congressional Research Service, May 24, 2004, www.fas.org/irp/crs/RL32395.pdf.

111. Carol Rosenberg. "Fearful Guantánamo captive wants to stay behind." *Miami Herald*. July 7, 2009, http://www.miamiherald.com/news/breaking-news/story/1131597.html.

112. "Detainees Describe Abuses by Guard in Iraq Prison." Kate Zernike. *New York Times*, January 12, 2005.

113. Kruger, Alan. "Lack of Civil Liberties Causes Terrorism, Islamic Fundamentalism Causes Terrorism." in *Terrorism* by Mike Wilson, Farmington Hills, MI, Greenhaven Press, 2009, 140-149.

114. Daniel Benjamin and Steven Simon. "Terrorism Is a Serious Threat" in Wilson 2009, 22-30; Benjamin and Simon. *The Next Attack.* 2005, 4, 8, 14, 33.

115. The Patriot Act, H.R. 3162, 107th Congress, October 24, 2001, http://epic.org/privacy/terrorism/hr3162.html\.

116. Lorrenzo Vedino. "The Danger of Home-Grown Terrorism to Scandinavia." *Terrorism Monitor*, Vol. 4, issue 20, 19 October 2006; Ian Ayres. "The LAPD and Racial Profiling." *The Los Angeles Time,* October 23, 2008; "Peoples Against States:

Ethnopolitical Conflict and the Changing World." Ted Robert Gurr. *International Studies Quarterly,* Vol. 38, 1994, pp. 347–378.

117. Shibley Telhami. "Why Suicide Terrorism Takes Root." *New York Times,* April 14, 2002; David Bukay. "The Religious Foundations of Suicide Bombings, Islamist Ideology." *Middle East Quarterly,* Fall 2006, pp. 27-36.

118. Woodward. *Plan of Attack.* 5-8, 31, 37-38, 53; Woodward, *Bush at War.* 329-330, 335-336, 346-350.

119. "Terrorism is a Serious Threat." Daniel Benjamin and Steven Simon in *Terrorism* by Mike Wilson, Farmington Hills, MI, Greenhaven Press, 2009, 23.

120. "The slide downhill: In the world's most dangerous place." *The Economist,* April 11, 2009.

121. Lawrence Wright. "The Rebellion Within An Al Qaeda mastermind questions terrorism." *The New Yorker,* June 2, 2008; "How Terrorists Hijacked Islam." Jessica Stern. *USA Today,* October 1, 2001.

122. Michael O'Hanlon. "Staying Power." *Foreign Affairs,* September /October 2010.

123. "The last U.S. combat brigade in Iraq has left the country, seven years after the U.S.-led invasion." *BBC News, Middle East,* 19 August 2010. The BBC's Jane O'Brien in Washington says the brigade's departure is a significant step, http://www.bbc.co.uk/news/world-middle-east-11020270.

124. Galbraith. *Unintended Consequences.* 43-63.

125. Bobbitt. *Terror and Consent.* 530.

126. Max Boot. "Pirates, Terrorism and Failed States." *Wall Street Journal,* Dec. 9, 2008.

127. Laqueur. *No End to Terror.* 223-228.

128. *Ethnic Cleansing in Kashmir Valley.* K.N. Pandit. November 11, 2008, http://idp.world-citizenship.org/wp-archive/147; "White Paper on Kashmir." M. K. Teng and Gadoo, Joint Human Rights Committee for Minorities in Kashmir "Genocide of Hindus," January 20, 2011, www.kashmir-information.com/Whitepaper/ethnic.html.

129. Andre Aciman, The Exodus Obama Forgot to Mention, *New York Times,* June 8, 2009.

130. Podhoretz. *World War IV.* 52–53.

131. William H. McNeill. "Decline of the West?" *The New York Review of Books,* Vol. 44, January 9, 1997; Huntington. *The Clash of Civilizations.* 1997, 209.

Chapter 3

Radical Islam's Ideologies

> Religion is based primarily and mainly upon fear. It is partly the terror of
> the unknown and partly, as I have said, the wish to feel that you have a
> kind of elder brother who will stand by you in all your troubles and dis-
> putes. . . . A good world needs knowledge, kindliness, and courage; it
> does not need a regretful hankering after the past or a fettering of the free
> intelligence by the words uttered long ago by ignorant me.
>
> — Bertrand Russell

Religion has played a fundamental role in the development of our society
and its people. One of the major religions, Islam, with over one billion
followers, is a significant determinant of peace, prosperity, and globalization in our world civilizations. Yet the strand of Islam known as radical
Islam has been shaped and driven by succession conflicts and rivalries,
beginning with its inception in the seventh century. It has also been propounded by radical thinkers with a great deal of influence. Holy militants
want Islamic law, or Sharia, which regulates Muslim life, to be followed
worldwide. The law has been followed rigorously within the Wahhabi movement in various parts of the world, with funding from Saudi Arabia. In the
subcontinent, the Deobandi has been formed to propagate orthodox Islam.
The Caliphate movement, although abolished in Turkey by Kemal Ataturk,
is the focus of terrorists who are eager to restore it worldwide. AQ and its
leader OBL are determined to address Islamic injustices with terrorism and
suicide bombings. Meanwhile, on the African continent, the radical terrorist group al Shabaab is on the rise. Despite Islam's ethnic diversity and
sectarian conflicts, terrorists throughout the world are united in jihad.

A religion is a set of beliefs, principles, and codes, written or unwrit-
ten, that let a seeker gain enlightenment or follow a spiritual quest for divine

knowledge, love, truth, heavenly peace, and the realization of God. Morality, decency, and harmony among people are regulated through devotional and ritual practices, prayers, meditation and dedications. Ideally it is free and equally accessible to all people, regardless of color, race, age, gender, or location. It can be used to promote social solidarity, and it encourages the observance and celebration of ritualistic festivals. Some people are born into it, others join, and many do not have any religion at all. However, in all of these cases, religion should be a private matter. It is a tragedy that people kill each other in order to claim their own religion as the most authentic. Islamic civilization and culture have been governed and guided by two diametrically opposed categories of people—the intellectuals, known as *arbab al-aqlam* (bearers of pen) and martial people, *arbab al-suyuf* (bearers of swords).

The glamour, glitter, splendor, and acme of Islamic civilization were furnished by several Islamic scholars and philosophers, beginning with the Mutazilah in the eighth century. In recent times, the leading scholar of *arbab al-aqlam* (bearers of the Islamic pen) was Morocco-born Mohammed 'Abed al-Jabri (1936–2010). He is famous for his book *Contemporary Arab Discourse: A Critical and Analytical Study*, and his three-volume magnum opus, entitled *Naqd al-'aql al-'Arabi (Critique of Arab Reason)*. The epistemological system of demonstration based on inferential evidence al-Jabri saw as having its origins in Greek thought (especially the wisdom Aristotle), but he did not restrict it to those who had based their analysis on logic. His concept of demonstration is much wider, and encompasses the rationality of Ibn Rushd, the critical attitude of Ibn Hazm (994–1064, a Cordova-born philosopher), the historicism of Ibn Khaldun, and the fundamental theology of al-Shatibi. Al-Jabri's approach consists of the exploration of the conflict between modernity and tradition in the Muslim and Arab world. In his writings, Al-Jabri focused on the rationalism of the Avicenna (Abū Alī Sīnā; 980–1037), the Averroes, Ibn Rushd (1126–1198), and the Ibn Khaldoun (1332–1406). These scholars enriched the golden age of Islam.

The conquest of Persia, Egypt, Iraq, Syria, Spain, and India, among others, was furnished by *arbab al-suyuf*, by virtue of the sword. Islamic culture resonated from the river Amy Darya to the Nile, to the Tigris, and beyond. From the ninth to the thirteenth centuries, Islamic scholars contributed to the 400-year-long golden age of Islam through science, architecture, mathematics, astronomy, agriculture, navigation, art, literature, medicine, and the law, while the West was far behind. Islamic scholars were innovative and creative thinkers who accepted the knowledge and learning of all countries and cultures. Today, by contrast, radical Islam is driven solely by *arbab al-suyuf*, and the dominant desire to conquer the world by *jihad*. The

Islamists believe that jihad is the sacred duty of every Muslim believer, that Jews and Christians should be killed, and that this fight should continue until only the Muslim religion is left (Quran 8:30). The French writer and philosopher Voltaire spoke of wars of religion as having unleashed a type of barbarism that the Heruli, the Vandals, and the Huns never knew. Voltaire's critique of religion—along with other Enlightenment philosophies, from Bayle, Locke, and Hobbes through Hume, Diderot, Helvetius, d'Holbach, Lessing, and others—is not incidental to or detachable from the bulk of their thought. Ultimately, it was Kant who brought the campaign launched by the Enlightenment to a compromise conclusion. Among the prime beneficiaries of this transformation was the secular nation-state, which learned to derive its legitimacy from the people it governed rather than from God, and which assumed responsibilities for countless functions previously carried out by religious institutions: law, education, moral discipline and surveillance, social relief, record keeping, and others. The media of civil society—philosophy, literature, the arts, science, journalism, and popular culture—also gained at religion's expense, becoming prime venues in which ethical and aesthetic issues are seriously engaged and debated.[1]

As to the separation of church and state, which exists in tandem with the philosophical view of the development of secular state, the historian Mark Lilla commented:

> Those of us who have accepted the heritage of the Great Separation must do so soberly. . . . Our challenge is different. We have made a choice that is at once simpler and harder: We have chosen to limit our politics to protecting individuals from the worst harms they can inflict on one another, to securing fundamental liberties and providing for their basic welfare, while leaving their spiritual destinies in their own hands.[2]

Conversely, throughout the history of Islam and up until the present day, the state has been embedded in religion, while religion has been hijacked by radicals, fundamentalists, extremists, and iconoclasts in the name of Allah. God revealed the Quran to the Prophet Mohammed (570–632), the self-designated last of the prophets, who fought with his fellow Quraysh tribes. According to Islamic teaching, the Quran (also spelled *Qur'an* or *Koran*) came down to him as a series of revelations from Allah through the Archangel Gabriel. Mohammed gave his first public revelation in 613. His first wife was the rich widow Khadija, and his youngest wife was the virgin Aisha, daughter of the first caliph Abu Bakr. The Quran contains 114 chapters and 6346 verses. Though the Quran was revealed to Mohammed sequentially over some twenty years' time, it was not compiled in chronological order. It was finally compiled into book form under Caliph Uthman in 633–653. The *suras*, or chapters, were ordered from longest to shortest several years after the Prophet's death. As Muhammad could not write or read, the Quran was compiled by his followers. Any deviation from Islam or negative depiction of the Prophet Mohammed is considered blasphemous.

During the month of Ramadan in 624, Mohammed led a large Muslim contingent to intercept and seize caravans of wealth en route from Mecca to Syria and back. They were the property of Abu Sufyan (560–650), who was a leading man of the Quraysh (a dominant tribe of Mecca) and a virulent opponent of the Prophet. The ensuing conflict, which became known as the Battle of Badr, was a turning in the Prophet's life, since he almost died fighting the Quraysh army. Mohammed was knocked senseless, and word spread that he had been killed. In fact, he had only been stunned. Twenty-two Meccans and sixty-five Muslims had been killed, including Mohammed's uncle Hamzah, a renowned fighter. The Quraysh ran onto the battlefield and mutilated the corpses; one of them cut out Hamzah's liver and carried the gruesome trophy to Hind (Abu Sufyan's wife), who ate a morsel of it to avenge her brother, who had died by Hamzah's hand at Badr. She then cut off his nose, ears, and genitals, urging the other women to follow her example, and to the disgust of some of their Bedouin allies, they left the field sporting grisly bracelets, pendants, and collars. Before his army moved off, Abu Sufyan heard the disappointing news that Mohammed had not after all been among the causalities. The Prophet's involvement in war is as follows: Mohammed accepted booty and reassured the community; he divided the spoils equally, and began negotiations with the Quraysh for an exchange of prisoners.[3]

Enough has already been said about the religious motivation of the invaders, the power of the idea of martyrdom and paradise as incentives in battle. In one infamous episode, Muhammad cut the heads off hundreds of Jewish males of the Beni Quraiza tribe who did not side with him in battle, "then taken their wives and children hostsage, and spent that same night with the Jewish woman Safia, whose husband, father, and brother he had just killed." The prophet is quoted as saying (Albert L. Weeks),

> The sword is the key of heaven and hell; a drop of bloodshed in the cause
> of Allah, a night spent in arms, is of more avail than two months of fasting
> or prayer: whosoever falls in battle, his sins are forgiven, and at the day of
> judgment his limbs shall be supplied by the wings of angels and cherubim.

The Muslim Psychiatrist Sultan writes that anyone who openly rejected any one of these Islamic customs was considered an apostate and was punished by death. She has noted, "The great catastrophe came with the advent of Islam, which gave these customs divine sanctions and laid a sharp divisive sword between those who accepted them and those who did not."4

After the brutal victory at the battle of Badr (624), the Uhud battle (625) was a turning point of the Prophet's life, due to the miracle that had saved his life. There was no mercy for the Qurayzah tribe:

> all seven hundred men of the tribe should be executed, their wives and children sold into slavery, and their property divided among the Muslims. When he heard the verdict, [Mohammed] is reported to have cried, "You have judged according to the ruling of Allah above the seven skies." The next day, the sentence was carried out.5

In the battle of Uhud, in 625, Mecca won the battle against Medina Muslims; it was a big loss to the Prophet Mohammad, who believed that the defeat was due to the Muslims' interest only in the booty of war. Sunnis, the followers of Abu Bakr (the first Caliph), believe that Bakr was Mohammed's rightful successor. They constitute 85 per cent of all Muslims, while Arabs in 21 countries constitute 282 millions, 13.2 per cent of the Muslim population, in 2000. Shias believe that Mohammed divinely ordained his cousin and son-in-law Ali to be his successor. These followers of Ali constitute the remaining 15 per cent. Iran, Bahrain, and Iraq have a majority of Shias, while there are also large numbers of Shias in Pakistan, Yemen, Turkey, Afghanistan, and Iraq. Sunnis are a majority in South East Asia, China, India, Africa, and the rest of the Arab world. From the very beginning of Islam, Sunnis and Shias killed each other for hundreds of years. This conflict has resulted in the violent deaths of about a million people since 1990, as is characteristic of a chronic condition.6 In Pakistan alone, thousands have died in sectarian violence among the majority Sunni and minority Shi'ite sects over the past two decades. In the last week of August 2010, over ninety-eight Shias were killed in several suicide bombings. It may be recalled that the Prophet's family has stated with the Qurasysh tribe. It is fathered by Abd al-Uzzah, Abd Manaf, Abd ad-Dar, and Abd Qusayy. Abd Manaf's decedents were Abd al-Muttalib and Umayyah. Umaiyyads caliphs originated from Umayyah while Abbasid caliphs from al-Abbas and Prophet Muhammed from Abdallah. And descendents of Muhammad were Hasan, Husayn, and Shite Imamas were from Husayn. Abu Bakr, Umar, Uthman and Ali were four right-guided caliphs. The Shite–Sunni conflict is within the Prophet family, yet it has resulted thousand casualities in the last 1400 years of Islamic history.

Both Sharia (law) and Hadith (tradition) forgive corrupt rulers. On the other hand, non-Muslims "cannot be called human beings but are animals who roam the earth and engage in corruption" in the words of Ayatollah Ahmad Jannati.[7] Some translations of the Quran refer to "other villainy" on the part of non-Muslims (Quran 5:32), who "spread disorder" (Quran 5:33).[8] These verses are among those that have been misused by radical extremists.

The Quran divides people into Muslims, believers or *Dar al-Islam* (dwellers in the abode of peace) and *kafir*, infidels, or *Dar al-Harb* (denizens of the abode of war), as well as unbelievers, who include all non-Muslims. Non-Muslims living under Muslim sovereignty are called *Dhimmis,* and are treated as *Dar al-Harb.* Of the four rightly guided successors, Abu Bakr (ruled 632–634), Umar (634–644), Uthman (644–656), and Ali (656–661), only one of them, Abu Bakr, died in his bed. Three caliphs were assassinated, two of them by fellow Muslims. Ali, cousin and son-in-law of the Prophet and the fourth caliph, was the central figure in the contentious Shia/Sunni split that occurred in the decades immediately following the death of the Prophet in 632. Shias feel that Ali should have been the first caliph and that the caliphate should pass down only to direct descendants of Mohammed via Ali and Fatima. They often refer to themselves as *ahl al bayt* or "people of the house" [of the prophet]. Sunnis and Shias (Shiites) each believe that the other sect is heretic.[9] Table 3.1 compares Sunni and Shia (Shiite) Muslims.[10]

In 680, about fifty years after the death of Mohammed, his close male descendents were massacred at Karbala, Iraq. This began the Sunni-Shia split[11] (However, the Sunni do not accept the Shia interpretation of the hadith). The Ashura massacre at Karbala in 2004 and the destruction of the Askariya shrine in 2006 served to escalate this fourteen-hundred-year-old conflict.[12] For both sects, Mecca, Medina, and Jerusalem are holy cities, and they share major holidays: Eid al Adha and Eid al Fitr. For Shias, Najaf and Karbala are also holy cities, and they observe Ashura, mourning for the martyrdom of Husayn ibn Ali, the grandson of the Islamic Prophet Muhammad, which is related to the religion of Zoroastrianism (Roberts, 1993), and Ahura, which is distantly related to Hinduism. The powerful Barmakid family, which had advised the Caliphs since the days of al-'Abbas as viziers, gained greater powers under al-Mahdi's ruleAl-Mahdi continued to expand the Abbasid administration, creating new *diwans*, or departments, for the army, the chancery, and taxation. *Qadis* or judges were appointed, and laws against non-Arabs were dropped. The Barmakids, of Persian extraction, had originally been Buddhists, but shortly before the arrival of the Arabs, they converted to Zoroastrianism.[13] Harun al-Rashid, jealous of the enormous power the Barmakids had acquired, destroyed them overnight.

Table 3.1
Comparison of Sunni and Shia Sects

Areas	Sunnah	Shia/ Shi'ah/Shiite
Identity	Sunnis	Shiites/ Shi'i
Origin	632 CE-650CE	632-650 CE
Founder /Prophet	Muhammad	Muhammad

Successor	Abu Bakr
	 father of the
	   Prophet's wife
	 Aisha's husband
	 (elected by people
	   of Medina)
		Ali ibn Abi Talib
		 husband of the
		   Prophet's daughter
		 Fatima
		 (designated
		   by the Prophet)

Meaning	tradition	party
% of Muslims	85%	15%
Location	most countries	Iran, Iraq, Yemen
Subsects	all major schools	Ithna, Isma'iliah, Zaydah

Final Imam/
   Twelfth Imam
	Al Mahdi
	   will appear
		Al Mahdi is
		   already in earth as
		   hidden

He became the fifth caliph (763–809) and the most famous of the Abbasid dynasty.

Baghdad, the capital of Iraq, blossomed during al-Mahdi's reign. The city attracted immigrants from all of Arabia, and from Iraq, Syria, Persia, India, and Spain. Baghdad was home to Christians, Jews, Hindus, Zoroastrians, and Muslims. During this time, several generations of emigrants from Baghdad settled in India. For 1400 years, the swords of Islam ruled Persia, Babylonia, Mesopotamia, Armenia, Syria, Palestine, Egypt, Tunisia, Algeria, Morocco, Spain, Portugal, India and Central China—more territories than the Roman Empire. It is important to bear in mind that there are sharp differences among Arab Muslims, who represent 25 per cent of all Muslims, and non-Arab Muslims. Non-Arab Muslims include Persians and

Pakistanis, *Ahmadiyyas* (also known as *Ahmedis, Ahmadis,* and *Qadians*) and Sunnis. There are also differences among ethnic Muslims, Kurds, Turks, Punjabis, Bangladeshis, Sindhis, and Pashtuns. Forged from diverse ethnic groups, and linked together only by Islam, disparate nations including Pakistan, Afghanistan, Indonesia, and Bangladesh provided fertile soil for radical Islamism. In addition to the radical Islamists' unfair treatment of women, they treat Blacks,[14] sometimes known as *abeds* (slaves) as sub-human beings.

From the battle of Badr[15] onwards, jihad has been waged as a holy war against infidels (and Chapter 4). Holy warriors have ranged from sects Kharijites[16] (749–1258) to the Qarmatians (899–930, also known as the *Qarāmita*, a Shi'a Ismaili group centered in eastern Arabia (see Appendix 1) to the Assassins (1090–1275, also known as *Hasan Sabbah, Hashshashins,* or *Fadayeen*). Hanbalite scholar Ibn Taymiyah (1263–1328), the spiritual father of radical Islamists, Muhammad Wahhab (1703–1792), Hasan al-Banna (1906–1948), Sayyid Qutb (1906–1966), Abul Maududi (1903–1979) and others through Osama bin Laden (1957–2011) have also wielded the sword of Islam. The Islamic scholar Andrew Bostom has defined jihad as a devastating institution, not an individual striving. He has provided an historical account of *jihad* that discusses its brutality and the ruthlessness of the jihadists: The jihad first emerged out of the plundering raids of Arab nomads. They attacked merchant caravans and took their loot. Then they began to make raids into settled and civilized populations of the Byzantine (Greek-speaking Roman) Empires, and into the Sassanian and Sassanid-Persian Empires, not with the intention seizing these empires for themselves but merely to rob them. Not only the promise of paradise, but the desire for quick wealth also played a role in the war of jihad. Abu Sufyan, who opposed to and fought with the Prophet Muhammad, was converted to Islam.

The Abbas who was present with Muhammad told Abu Sufyan[17]: "Woe to you! Accept Islam and testify that Muhammad is the apostle of God before your neck is cut off by the sword". . . . Muhammad's practice and constant encouragement of bloodshed are unique in the history of religions. Murder, pillage, rape, and more murder are the Kuran and in the Traditions 'seem to have impressed his followers with a profound belief in the value of bloodshed as opening the gates of Paradise' and prompted countless Muslim governors, caliphs, viziers to refer Muhammad's example to justify their mass killings, looting, and destruction. . . . Starting in 712 the raiders, commanded by Muhammad Qasim, demolished temples, shattered sculptures, plundered places, killed vast number of men—it took them three days to slaughter the inhabitants of the port city of Debal—and carried off their wives and children to slavery. . . . Qasim obeyed (Iraq governor Hajjaj) and on his arrival at the town of Brahminabad, massacred between 6,000 and 16,000. . . . In the aftermath of the invasion (by Mahmud of Gazni), in the Ancient cities of Varanasi, Mathura, Ujjain, Maheswar, . . . Jwalamukhi, and Dwaraka, not one temple survived whole and intact. . . . The slaughter in Samantha, the site of a celebrated Hindu temple, where 50,000 Hindus were slain on Mahmud's orders, set the tone for centuries. . . . The Buddhist were the next to the subjected to mass slaughter in 1193, when Muhammad Khiliji also burned their famous library. . . . The Mogul emperor Akbar is remembered as tolerant and only major massacre was recorded during his long reign (1542-1605), when he ordered that about 30,000 captured Rajput Hindus be slain on February 24,1568, after the battle for Chitod. . . . Most westerners remember him (Shah Jahan) as the builder of Taj Mahal and do not know that he was cruel warmonger who initiated 48 military campaigns non-Muslims in less than 30 years. Taking his cue from his Ottoman co-religionists, on coming to the throne in 1628 he killed all his male relations except one who escaped to Persia. Shah Jahan had 5,000 concubines in his harem, but nevertheless indulged in incestuous sex with his daughters, Chamini and Jharana. During his reign, in Benares alone 76 Hindu temples were destroyed, Christian churches at Agra and Lahore was demolished. At the end of the three-month seize of Hugh, a Portuguese enclave near Calcutta, he had 10,000 inhabitants "blown up with the powder, drowned in water or burnt by fire." More than 4,000 were taken captive to Agra where they offered Islam or death. Most refused and were killed, except for the younger women who went to harems.

The massacres perpetuated my Muslims in India are unparallel in history, bigger in sheer numbers than the Holocaust, or massacre of the Armenians by Turks: more extensive even than the slaughter of the South America native populations by the invading Spanish and Portuguese.

Most Muslim historians of India have ignored the massacres and destruction of Hindu temples during the Muslim reign or invasion.

As Wolpert writes: "Mahmud (971–1030), the "sword of Islam," who led bloody raids into India from his Ghazni perch, waged jihad at least as much for plunder as for the promise of entry into paradise."[18]

The eminent author Deepak Chopra has recently written a novel entitled *Muhammad*, a supplement to Karen Armstrong's book covering the life of the Prophet.[19] As Chopra narrates, the founder of Islam did not see himself as another Jesus, the Son of God, or like Buddha, who achieved sublime, cosmic enlightenment. Chopra recounts that because of the bickering among the Prophet's wives, "God told the women around him to obey their husbands in all things." While this is now a major component of Sharia,[20] its modern relevance is questionable, as most men have a single wife and there is no need for the wife to obey her husband in all things. On the Islamic victory over territories from Spain to Persia, Chopra writes: "This vast expansion wasn't due to warfare, although the Muslims were fierce warriors." This contradicts the thinking of many scholars, although Chopra later concludes, "It took warfare to spread the new faith, but just over the horizon was a paradise in which one God welcomed all believers." This of course meant Muslims, not infidels. Chopra—a leading authority on spiritual matters—regrettably believes:

> The life dedicated by the Koran wasn't a prison deprived of free will—it was order in place of chaos. . . . Muhammad can be judged by the worst of his followers or the best. He can be blamed for planting the seeds of fanaticism and jihad, or praised for bringing the world of God to a wasteland. The message he brought wasn't pure, it never is.

Chopra has not done any service to the Muslim world by not providing an unbiased scientific study or by ignoring the threat of the resurgence of extremism. Instead, he is defensive of the seventh century's obscurantism and anachronistic legacy.[21] The fundamentalist interpretation of the Quran is not just impeding civilization's progress, but is inspiring radical groups who believe that every solution to the present distress in the Muslim world can be found in the Quran. The noted international affairs expert and liberal commentator William Pfaff writes:

> Because of Qur'anic teaching, Islam had difficulty in separating political from religious power or philosophy from the theology as Christians did very early in the history of church and state. This was vital to the West's eventual development of independent scientific and political thought. . . . Islamic political society today generally remains confined within a religious dogma that is considered immutable, as presented in the original Arabic text of the Qur'an, the canonical version of which was determined in the seventh century.[22]

Former U.S. Secretary of State Henry Kissinger has commented:

> Today it is radical Islam that threatens the already brittle state structure via a fundamentalist interpretation of the Koran as the basis of a universal political organization. Radical Islam rejects claims to national sovereignty based on secular state models, and its reach extends to wherever significant populations profess the Muslim faith.[23]

There are various schools of terrorism: abortion-related terrorism, state terrorism, religious terrorism, criminal terrorism, pathological terrorism, secular and political terrorism, Maoists terrorism, anti-capital and anti-globalization terrorism, and environmental terrorism. Naxalite Maoists in India have killed more people than Islamic terrorists and are now banned in India. Over 6500 people have died during this rebel group's decades-long fight for a Communist state in parts of India. Indian Prime Minister Manmohan Singh feels that these Maoists pose the most serious threat to national security in India.[24] While Maoist terror is a direct threat to Indian democracy, and has left several thousands dead, apologists like Arundhati Roy (author of *The God of Small Things*), compares their activities to the non-violent acts of Mahatma Gandhi. Roy foolhardly links the 2008 Bombay attacks with insurgents from Kashmir, and preposterously advocates annexing Kashmir to Pakistan. This would represent an abject surrender to Islamic terrorism.[25]

For Islamic revivalists, just as Muhammad challenged false gods and immoral ways, Islamism is seen as a path to justice and equality in opposition to Western corruption and worship of false gods. Radical Islamists believe that the solution to Western decadence is revitalizing Islam by reintroducing Sharia.[26] Orthodox Muslims believe that Sharia is divine law, whereas democracy is earthly law, created by man. But in light of the fact that, since its earliest history, Islam has espoused the cultivation of knowledge in all spheres, and from all places, it would appear that *jihad* (holy war) against Western values and culture is strangely unIslamic. There was a drive in early Islamic societies to amass knowledge, starting with that of other civilizations, including Byzantium, Rome, Greece, Egypt, India, China and the ancient Middle East. The theology and philosophy of Islam was strongly influenced by Neo-Platonism, and eventually by Aristotelian metaphysics. Once amassed, this knowledge in technology, science, philosophy, ethics, and other disciplines was critiqued and elaborated upon. Eventually new forms of knowledge were created, including social theory, whose advances were usually available only to small circles of elites. During the Golden age of Islam, scholars in centers of Islamic culture such as Baghdad and Cordoba nurtured Renaissance thinkers who worked simultaneously in the fields of medicine, science, philosophy, and theology. Islamic scientists developed the scientific experimental method, and while refining Indian mathematics and the Chinese material arts. They developed innovations in many of the sciences, including astronomy, medicine, and physics. This may be qualified as "waging good jihad."

As many would note, if America were to completely disengage itself from the Islamic world, and if Israel ceased to exist, conditions for the world's one billion Muslims would not improve, but would actually deteriorate. The purging of Western values and investment from Islamic countries does not fall under the heading of a good jihad. Saudi Arabian King Abdullah's audience with to Pope Benedict XVI at the Vatican on November 6, 2007 was meant to promote religious understanding, and to counter the Pope's characterization of Islam in terms of violent, intolerant, and virulently hateful Islamic *jihad*. The Pope was courteous and accommodating, but not in a denial mode. As John F. Cullinan, a former senior foreign-policy adviser to the U.S. Catholic bishops, explained: "Jihad—in the sense of armed conflict for religious reasons—remains a living element of Islamic thought and life."[27] Islam involves two sets of standards, one for Muslims and another for non-Muslims. Muslims can preach or build mosques anywhere, and can convert others to their religion. But there are no non-Muslim places of worship in Saudi Arabia and other Muslim countries; even carrying an idol or wearing a non-Islamic religious symbol is forbidden. While Muslims seek converts from other faiths, apostasy—the conversion of Muslims to other religions—is a crime punishable by death. The two most powerful Muslim nations in the world, Saudi Arabia and Iran, are ruled under a Sharia legal code that permits no dissent, allows no freedom of religion, and provides no equal rights for women for or non-Muslim minorities. It is, in the words of Lauren Langman and Douglas Morris, a cruel "system of religion-based behavioral control in which certain crimes are punishable by stoning, flogging, amputation, and beheading, punishments intended to inspire subjection and fear."[28] In Saudi Arabia, non-Muslim worshipers may be subject to arrest, imprisonment, lashing, deportation, and are sometimes tortured for drinking in public. Saudi Arabia forbids the construction of any non-Muslim missions or places of worship. Non-Muslims are also barred from entering holy cities, namely Medina and Mecca—the holiest cities in Islam from the days of the Prophet. In contrast, the largest mosque in Europe will be built with Saudi Arabian money in Rome, the bastion of Christianity. Many church leaders are demanding reciprocity in the form of permission to build churches and Christian schools in Muslim countries. According to the Freedom House's 2006 report, Saudi textbooks

> continue to promote an ideology of hatred that teaches bigotry and deplores tolerance. These texts continue to instruct students to hold a dualistic worldview in which there exist two incompatible realms—one consisting of true believers in Islam . . . and the other the unbelievers—realms that can never coexist in peace.[29]

(See also the Epilogue, on the proposed Islamic Center and Mosque at Ground Zero in Manhattan, where there are already approximately one hundred mosques.)

The Constitution of the Islamic Republic of Iran mandates that the official religion of Iran is Islam. Members of the Baha'i faith (see Appendix 4), Iran's largest non-Islamic religious minority, are cruelly persecuted, and hundreds of them have been executed since 1979. Other religious minorities live in a precarious state. Religious police continually crack down on displays of Western influence, such as movies, clothing styles, and music. Political dissidents, including students, professors, and journalists, are jailed under torturous conditions or are executed for such vaguely worded offenses as "insulting Islam" and "damaging the foundations of the Islamic Republic." There is persecution of Jews, Christians, Buddhists, and Hindus in Pakistan, Bangladesh, Malaysia, Nigeria, Sudan, Lebanon, Egypt, and Indonesia. Imams in most mosques preach hatred against unbelievers. They recite: "Allah has warned us in the Quran, do not befriend the *kuffar* [unbelievers], and do not align yourselves with the *kuffar*." Muslim countries living under Sharia believe that Islam should dominate the world. They believe that non-Muslims are innately inferior, and they preach a theology that rejects democracy and equality. Radical Islam has infiltrated Western educational systems and communities in the name of multiculturalism. Devout Muslims believe that Islam is the future, not only of the Middle East and South Asia, but also of Europe and the entire world. Not a few are prepared to sacrifice, suffer, and die to bring the world into submission to Allah, as their ancestors fourteen centuries ago sought to do. They dream of a resurrected caliphate and Islamic empire like the domain once ruled from Iberia to India, with converts all the way to the Philippines.

> Multiculturalism and antiracism were now the weapons with which minorities were equipped to beat the majority . . . And as multiculturalism thus unwittingly fomented Islamic radicalism in the sacred cause of "diversity," it simultaneously forbade criticism of Muslim practices such as forced marriages or polygamy, or the withdrawal of children from school to be sent for long periods to Pakistan . . . And so, as British identity was steadily eviscerated by multiculturalism, real human rights abuses on British shores were studiously ignored and its victims left abandoned in its name.[30]

Islamists also seek to rule *Maghreb,* "the place of sunset," a region encompassing Morocco, Algeria, Tunisia, Mauritania, Libya, and adjacent areas. All of these places have diverse ethnicities and cultures, and follow religions including Islam, Christianity, and Judaism. Maghreb combines the culture of Romans, French, Greeks, and Arabs with a population mix of Arabs and non-Arab Berbers. Historically, this region was moderate, tolerant, and secular. Yet two Moroccan terrorists, Zacarias Moussaoui in the United States and Mounir al-Mossadeg in Germany, participated in the 9/11 attacks. Radical terrorism is on the rise in these countries as seen in Algeria in 1995, in Tunisia in 2002 and in Morocco in 2003.

Political Islam was initiated in Egypt in the 1920s by the Muslim Brotherhood (MB) who declared at the time that "the Qur'an is our Constitution."[31] Later, Wahhabi's jihad was wedded to Reagan's anti-communism to produce a new form of political Islam. But in the democratic and secular West, religion is subordinate to the state, while in Islam, the state is a subordinate to religion. For this reason, even though the Taliban is not political, it is a form of political Islam in the sense that it is opposed to secularism, women's equality, and minority rights. Radical Islamists are opposed to secularism, modernism, democracy, women rights, and tolerance to other religions and cultures. They are even opposed to various Muslim sects as Shiites, Ahmediyyas, and Bahias, and Sufis. They want the whole world as the house of Islam (Dar al-Islam) or to be a part of the house of war (Dar al-Harb). However, these Islamists are obscuring and marginalizing the glorious achievements of Muslim Spain, among others, and the vast contributions of Islam from the antiquity to the modern worlds in sciences and philosophy by infusing with other civilizations and cultures, not by a denial of the modernism. Radical Islamists are a prisoner of the seventh century Islam.

The Founding Director of the Prince Alwaleed Bin Talal Center for Muslim-Christian Understanding in the Walsh School of Foreign Service at Georgetown University, Professor John L. Esposito has stated:

> In the 1990s political Islam, what some call 'Islamic fundamentalism,' remains a major presence in government and in oppositional politics from North Africa to Southeast Asia. Political Islam, in power and in politics, has raised many issues and questions and some possible answers.

- 'Is Islam antithetical to modernization?'—Yes
- 'Are Islam and democracy incompatible?'—Yes
- 'What are the implications of an Islamic government for pluralism, minority, and women's rights?'—Zero
- 'How representative are Islamists?'—Little
- 'Are there Islamic moderates?'—Very few
- 'Should the West fear a transnational Islamic threat or clash of civilizations?'—Yes

Political Islam is an intriguing concept with many scholars' many views: A person who espouses Islamic fundamentalist beliefs; A Muslim, particularly an orthodox Muslim; A person who specializes in Islamic studies; Motivated by Islamic beliefs, particularly in the political sphere (e.g., a supporter of the introduction of sharia law); Relating to Islam, particularly. It can be summarized as: Political Islam describes it as

a form of instrumentalization of Islam by individuals, groups and organizations that pursue political objectives: (a) Something unique in Islam that precludes separation between religion and state, and that religion dictates political action in Muslim countries, (b) It is a monolithic phenomenon, (c) Who are obsessed with implementing the sharia and enforcing God's sovereignty over everything (d) They will use non-violent and violent means, if necessary, to implement Sharia by democratic or theocratic means. Political Islam, a movement to gain political ascendency and intellectual revival in Islam, is in various shapes and sizes that jettison ethics and democracy and straddle in violence and radicalism with a sole political objective of establishing Sharia and irrdentism. Some apologists justify violence because in the hundred years back other religions have it against others. Some of them are Egypt's Syed Qutb's Muslim Brotherhood, Hamas, Hezbollah, Algeria's Islamic Salvation Front and Pakistan's Syed Maududi's Jamaat-e-Islami. Rejectionists maintain that Islam has its own forms of governance and that it is incompatible with democracy. This position is held by moderates and militant Muslims, from King Fahd to radical Islamists. Cognizant of a Western tendency to see Islam as a threat, many Muslim governments use the danger of Islamic radicalism as an excuse for their suppression of Islamic movements. Much as anti-Communism during the Cold War was a convenient excuse for authoritarian rule and the need for aid from Western powers, today some governments and experts charge that "there are no Islamic moderates."[32]

(See Chapter 2 for additional answers to these questions.) Radical Islamists do not hold significant voting power in Egypt or Pakistan, although the world's largest and oldest Islamist organization, Egypt's Muslim Brotherhood, and another large and prominent organization, Pakistan's religious party Jamaat-e-Islam, are strong in these countries. As discussed in Chapter 1, moderates in these countries are afraid of fundamentalists at home and abroad, and fear for their lives. Islamists stubbornly refuse to accept the Western hegemony and challenge not only the domestic status quo but the international status quo as well, keenly aware of Islamists the existential threat to their religion.[33] While Christians and Jews separated religion from politics several hundred years ago, most Muslim scholars justify interweaving the two.

During the regime of President Zia-ul Haq, Pakistan's civil and military establishments were radicalized to turn the country away from modernity and secularism, with the support of Islamic clerics. As Nobel Laureate Naipaul writes:

> Always in the background now were the fundamentalists who—fed by the ecstasy of the creation of Pakistan, and further fed by the partial Islamization of the laws—wanted to take the country back to the seventh century, to the time of the Prophet. There was as hazy a program for that as there had been for Pakistan itself: only some idea of regular prayers, of Quranic punishments, the cutting off of hands and feet, the veiling and effective imprisoning of women, giving men tomcatting rights over four women at a time, to use and discard at will.[34]

Al-wala' Wal-bara'

The doctrine of *al-wala' wal-bara'*[35] defines Islam and radical Islam on the basis of love for fellow Muslims and hatred for those in opposition to it. David Cook emphasizes the dysfunctional Muslim majority in the face of this doctrine:

> One cannot understand radical Islam, let alone globalist radical Islam, until one comprehends the importance of the doctrine known as *al-wala' wal-bara'* (loyalty or fealty and disloyalty or dissociation). Basically, this is a polarizing doctrine by which radicals—and this idea is emphasized almost exclusively by radicals, so virtually any book or pamphlet on the subject will be written by radicals—maintain their control over what constitute definitions of "Islam." Islam is defined according to this doctrine not only by its willingness to fight, but also by the polarities of love and hatred: love for anything or anybody defined as Islam or Muslim, and hatred for their opposites or opponents. The crucial fact is that Muslims in the vast majority, whatever they truly believe, are unwilling to dissociate themselves publicly from radical Islam. This passivity is the work of the doctrine of *al-wala' wal-bara'* ("love and hate for Allah's sake")."

From the seventh century onwards, *al-wala' wal-bara'* has been used to justify insane acts of savagery, including the murder of early caliphs and even of family members. Perpetrators of such religious violence, have included the Assassins, the Qaramatis, Ibn Taymiyah, Abd al-Wahhab, Mohammad Abduh, Hasan al-Banna, Ayatollah Khomeini, Abdus Salam Faraj, and Omar Abdel Rahman. As the journalist M. J. Akbar writes: "Jihad is the signature tune of Islamic history. . . . Radical movements in Islam turn to the past for inspiration, with faith as their sustenance."[36] In

March 632, the Prophet Mohammed stated: "I was ordered to fight all men until they say there is no God but Allah." On November 2001, OBL issued this statement: "I was ordered to fight the people until they say there is no God but Allah and Muhammad is God's Prophet." As to the doctrine of *al-wala' wal-bara'* in Islam. the theologian Ibn Taimiyya (1263-1328) has said,

> The declaration of faith, there is no god but Allah, requires you to love only for the sake of Allah, to hate only for the sake of Allah, to ally yourself only for the sake of Allah, to declare enmity only for the sake of Allah; it requires you to love what Allah loves and to hate what Allah hates.

One modern weapon of jihadists is using young children as suicide bombers. Suicide attacks were pioneered by the Assassins (1090–1275, also known as the Hashshashin, the Hashasi, the cult of Alamut, or the followers of the Shaikh al-Jabal). Taking their cue from these eleventh-century holy warriors, modern suicide bombers began to ply their lethal trade in Lebanon during the early 1980s. A decade later, in 1991, the Liberation Tigers of Tamil Eelam (LTTE) followed suit. The theory and practice of suicide bombing, as practiced during the Iran–Iraq war of a quarter-century ago, was established by a 13-year-old Iranian boy named Hossein Fahmideh: He strapped on explosives and blew himself up, along with an Iraqi tank. Some have argued that ending occupation in Iraq and other places is the key to solving the jihadist problem. But we should be disabused of the belief that withdrawal alone will appease the new martyrs. Instead, the countries affected by suicide attacks must step up the battle for the hearts and minds of alienated young Muslims.[37]

The fall of the Berlin Wall in 1989 marked not only the end of the Cold War, but the beginning of the spread of radical Islam in Europe and Asia. Many jihadists emerged, supported by Turkey, Iran, Pakistan, and Saudi Arabia, in order to expand the hegemonies of those nations. There is a myth that the two wars in Afghanistan and two wars in Iraq prompted OBL to instigate radical Islam. This is not true. Radical Islam planted its roots several centuries before, with widespread violence, death, and destruction in the Middle East. AQ and its ilk, even when diminished in strength, have the ability to stage terrorist attacks around the world, and have dominated large swaths of the Muslim world with radical Islam. Even before the United States invaded Iraq, polls in Muslim countries revealed support for OBL and for AQ's aims. If such thinking were to triumph in major Muslim countries beyond Iran—say, Pakistan, Egypt and Saudi Arabia—violent extremists would command vast mujahedeen with dreaded explosives.[38] As a historical note, the first victims of radical Islam on a national scale were Sassanid Persia and its religion of Zoroastrianism. In the years that followed, Arab armies invaded Syria, Iraq, and Jerusalem in 633, Egypt in 640, Khurasan in 655 and Kabul in 664. At the beginning of the eighth century, Arab armies crossed the Hindu Kush, in Afghanistan, to invade Sind in India. Prior to this the civilizations of Persia, Mesopotamia, and Egypt had experienced the early phases of radicalism. It is rare to find in Iran the early Persian heritage of the Sassanid period, but the early civilization of the Indus Valley, however neglected and in ruins, still exists in Mohenjo-Daro (named after the mound of the Hindu God Krishna, or Mohan), Chanhdaro, and Larkana in Sind, and in neighboring Punjab at Harappa and Taxila in Pakistan.[39] Pakistan is currently the worst victim of radical Islam. American current alliances with radical Muslim countries have been put in place as a strategy to defeat terrorism. Previously, in the 1980s, America's alliance with Pakistan and Saudi Arabia led to the defeat of the Soviet Union, and its occupation and Communist rule of Afghanistan. Just as everyone understood during World War II that defeating Germany justified the alliance with an equally evil regime in the Soviet Union, it should have been clear that America's alliance with Pakistan, a hotbed of Islamist radicalism, was necessary to the successful prosecution of the war against Islamofascism. The first description of the ruins of Harappa is found in the Narrative of Various Journeys in Balochistan, Afghanistan and Punjab of Charles Masson. It dates back to the period of 1826 to 1838. In 1857, the British engineers accidentally used bricks from the Harappa ruins for building the East Indian Railway line between Karachi and Lahore. In the year 1912, J. Fleet discovered Harappan seals. This incident led to an excavation campaign under Sir John Hubert Marshall in 1921–1922. The result of the excavation was discovery of Harappa by Sir John Marshall, Rai Bahadur Daya Ram Sahni and Madho Sarup Vats and Mohenjodaro by Rakhal Das Banerjee, E. J. H. MacKay, and Sir John Marshall.

An Islamic reform movement in Turkey led by Kemal Ataturk abolished the institution of the caliphate, an anachronistic holdover. In twentieth century Turkey, the caliphate remained as a ceremonial office, lacking significant power. In the Middle Ages, however, it had been the seat of the Ottoman Empire, and served as the center of the Arab Empire from the time of the Prophet. While Ataturk, the modernizer, swept away every mote and cobweb of the distant past in his own country, Egypt's Muslim Brotherhood and others wanted to bring back the tradition of the caliphate. The Muslim world's moral and martial decline was compounded by a series of attacks in the Middle Ages, from Mongols, Spanish Christians, Crusaders, and Zionists. Europe's scientific and technical achievement allowed it to snatch away Islam's glory, and to dominate the world. Europe inflicted its appalling social isolation on peoples and cultures in every corner of the globe.[40]

Suicide Bombing

Suicide bombing is a terrorist attack intended to kill others and inflict widespread damage, along with the death of the terrorist(s) carrying out the attack. It did not start with the Japanese kamikaze attacks in the World War II against U.S. warships in the Pacific, or in 1991, when a suspected Tamil Tiger of Sri Lanka assassinated former Indian Prime Minister Rajiv Gandhi. The Muslim Hashshashin (Assassins) of the late eleventh century perfected suicide attacks on their opponents, and were told by Persian Hassan-i Sabbah that after their death, they would enter Paradise. According to a report compiled by the Chicago Project on Suicide Terrorism, 224 out of 300 suicide terror attacks from 1980 to 2003 involved Islamist groups or took place in Muslim-majority lands.[41] Another tabulation found a massive increase in suicide bombings in the two years following Pape's study, and that the overwhelming majority of these bombers were motivated by the Islamist ideology of martyrdom. The world was shocked when, in October 1983, a Hezbollah operative drove his truck into the U.S. Marines' barracks in Beirut, killing 241 U.S. service members in an attack that remains the deadliest terrorist strike on Americans overseas. Since the fall of Saddam Hussein in 2003, an incredible 1121 Muslim suicide bombers have blown themselves up in Iraq, killing at least 14,132 men, women, and children and wounding a minimum of 16,612 people. The suicide attackers have arrived at the scene disguised as soldiers, police officers, tourists, worshippers, middle-aged housewives, and children's sweet-sellers. They have carried their bombs in rickshaws, vans, cars, fuel trucks, garbage trucks, or on flatbed trucks, donkeys, bicycles, motorcycles, carts, minibuses, date-vendors' vans, and lorries packed with chlorine.[42] On June 10, 2010, NATO and the Afghan government blamed a Taliban suicide bomber for the grisly scene at a wedding party in Kandahar province, where at least 40 people were killed by an intense explosion. Patrick Sookhdeo, Director of the Institute for the Study of Islam and Christianity, describes features of the suicide bombers last prayers as being

> Like the Western wedding video, that has some formulaic elements: the bomber will be sent at prayer; he will be dressed in white; there will be a message for his family; and then, once he has done his work, there will be the shots of brutal Israeli reprisals.[43]

The larger part of the training consists of pouring the venom of their hatred and rage onto the bomber's target. These trainings are rendered at the madrassas, so that their young students may learn how to participate in jihad and become martyrs who will die in the name of Islam. These students, who often come from poor families, are provided with food, shelter, and a free Islamic education. The system of madrassas has become a hatchery for tens of thousands of Islamic militants who have spread conflict around the world after their graduation. The distinguished political scientist Benjamin Barber describes Khuddamuddin, one such madrassas:

> Khuddamuddin is run by Mohammed Ajmal Qadri, leader of one of the three branches of the fundamentalist Jamiat Ulema Islam party, who told me that nearly 13,000 trained jihad fighters have passed through his school. At least 2,000 of them were in their way to India-held Kashmir (which is also claimed by Pakistan).[44]

Operation Iraqi Freedom and
Operation Enduring Freedom

Revenge is often more of a motivation for Islamic fighters than the lure of Paradise. American losses in Operation Iraqi Freedom (OIF) and Operation Enduring Freedom (OEF) in Afghanistan are listed in Table 3.2. Total deaths in the Iraq War are reported as being between 110,663 and 119,380. Of these, Iraqi civilian deaths number between 96,037 and 104,754, and Iraqi security forces' deaths total 9451.[45]

Table 3.2
Deaths and Wounded in OIF and OEF in 2001-2009

Causalities	OIF	OEF
Non-hostile deaths	836	220
Hostile Deaths	3,425	443
DOD civilian	11	1
Total Deaths	4,261	663
Wounded	31,131	2725

* Source: Department of Defense, www.defenselink.mil/news/casualty.pdf.
Biweekly updates of OIF and OEF can be found in Council of Foreign Relation, CFR Report RS21578, *Iraq: U.S. Casualties*, by Susan G. Chesser.
Note: Current as of March 20, 2009. United States Military Casualty Statistics: Operation Iraqi Freedom and Operation Enduring Freedom, Hannah Fischer, March 25, 2009.

So if religion is not the primary motive for suicide terrorism, what is? Robert Pape outlines three general trends:

1. Nearly all suicide attacks occur as part of organized campaigns.
2. Democratic states are uniquely vulnerable to suicide terrorism. The United States, France, India, Israel, Russia, Sri Lanka, and Turkey have been the targets of almost every suicide attack of the past two decades.
3. Suicide terrorist campaigns are directed toward a strategic objective. From Lebanon to Israel to Sri Lanka to Kashmir to Chechnya, the sponsors of every campaign have been terrorist groups trying to establish self-determination by compelling a democratic power to withdraw from the territories they claim. Since 2003, suicide attacks have been driven by radical Islam, in order to spread Islamic ideology by means of jihad. Radical Islamists are against political, educational, social, and economic freedom for women. They denounce secularism, democracy, pluralism, and the weakening of the mullahs' regimes. They wish to suppress freedom of expression and of religion, and hate the globalization of trade, finance, and services, as well as the intermingling of cultures and civilizations. Yet they also wish to possess modern armaments, including missiles and nuclear, biological, and chemical weapons. They crave the latest technology: satellite phones and cellular phones, SIM cards, VoIP capabilities, the Internet, digital television, GPS devices, small satellite dishes that receive worldwide TV and news, and all the amenities of modern living. Radical Islamists may be using ancient methods of assassination and suicidal attacks, but at the same time they are deploying modern weapons, and taking full advantage of the advances of new technology and globalization.

Radical Ideologues

Radical Islam is guided by the fear of *jahiliyya* (Godless), the ignorance and barbarism of pre-Islamic days. The Quran asks: "Is it a judgment of the time of [pagan] ignorance [*jahiliyya*] that they are seeking?" Who is better than Allah for judgment to a people who have certainty [in their belief] (5:50 and also 3:154, 33:33, 48:26) Many Muslim scholars have evoked *jahiliyya* in order to fight against it. They believe that it is the righteous duty of all Muslims to use extreme acts of terrorism against the *kuffar* (unbelievers), *takfiri* (those who are not fundamentalists), and *murtadd* (apostates), as in the days of *Salafi-jihad* following the period of the Prophet. There is a difference of perception regarding radical Islam. For the West, the nations of Iran and Syrian, as well as Hezbollah, Hamas, and Fatah are radical, but Saudi Arabia and Pakistan are not. For Russia, Chechnya is radical, and for China, so are the Uyghur Muslims of Xinjiang. In reality all of them are radicals who wish to spread Islam around the world by jihad.

On January 7, 2010, seven Coptic Christians were killed by radical Islamists in Egypt. In Malaysia on January 8. 2010, at least four Christian churches were burnt by radical Islamists and several Bibles seized by the government because Christians were translating God as "Allah." According to Professor John Esposito:

> Religious minorities in the Muslim world today, constitutionally entitled in many countries to equality of citizenship and religious freedom, increasingly fear the erosion of those rights—and with good reason. Interreligious and inter-communal tensions and conflicts have flared up not only in Egypt and Malaysia but also in Sudan, Nigeria, Turkey, Iran, Iraq, Afghanistan, Bangladesh, Indonesia and Pakistan. Conflicts have varied, from acts of discrimination, to forms of violence escalating to murder, and the destruction of villages, churches and mosques.[46]

Islamic theology contains some binary propositions: Was the Quran uncreated or created in time? Sects including the Ash'arites, traditionalists who practice a speculative form of Muslim theology founded by the religious scholar Abu al-Hasan al-Ash'ari (874–936), believed in absolute and total surrender to Allah without any questioning, because the Quran was coeval with Allah. Abu al-Hasan al-Ash'ari propagated the deterministic view that Allah created every moment in time and every particle of matter. He rejected that the Quran had been created other than by Allah, and this theology, which evolved between the ninth and twelfth centuries, is prevailing today. Another leader of this branch of theology was the Persian born al-Ghazali (1058–1111), one of the greatest Islamic jurists, theologians, and mystical thinkers and the author of brilliant classics on Islamic theology including *The Incoherence of the Philosophers*. His views on Islamic theology rejected the Islamic metaphysics influenced by Hellenistic philosophy, turning towards an Islamic philosophy based on cause and effect. His works delivered a deadly blow against Muslim Neo-Platonic philosophy, particularly against the work of the philosopher Ibn Sina (Avicenna).[47] Avicenna created an extensive corpus of works in which the translations of Graeco-Roman, Persian, and Indian texts were examined extensively. Those who

believed in the second proposition—that the Quran was created by men—
were influenced by Greek philosophers Aristotle, Plato, Socrates and others
during Islam's Byzantine and Sassanid periods. They were known as Ratio-
nalists, and were followed by the Mu'tazilites, including Muhammad Ibn
Rushd, who added their own rational views. The chief proponent of Rationalism, Ibn Rushd (known as Averroes in the West) was born in 1128 A.D.
in Cordova, Spain. He is regarded by many as the most important of the
Islamic philosophers,[48] and is known for his classic, *The Incoherence of the
Incoherence*.[49] A product of twelfth-century Islamic Spain, Ibn Rushd set
out to integrate Aristotelian philosophy with Islamic thought. For the justification of reason and *ijtihad*, or individual effort, the Mu'tazilites [The
Mu'tazilites also argued that the Qur'an was created and not eternal] cited
the Quran 2.164: "He revives the earth after its death, dispersing over it all
manner of beasts; in the disposal of the winds, and in the clouds that are
driven between earth and sky; surely in these there are signs for rational
men."

Rushd believed in integrating philosophy with the Islamic religion, but
his rational views did not last long. A Mu'tazilite master, Baghdad theologian Abd al-Jabbar, (935–1025) believed that God is not only power, but
He is reason, that God is removed from all that is morally wrong, and that
all His acts are morally good. On the other hand, the Persian Jamal al-Din
al-Afghani (1838–1897) claimed that there was conflict between faith and
reason in Islam. He is famous for the following statement: "I lived in the
West, I saw Islam, but I never saw any Muslims. I lived in the East, and I
saw the Muslims, but I never saw Islam." The Wahhabist Muhammad Rashid
Rida, a student of the Egyptian jurist Muhammad Abduh, founder of Islamic modernism, and of Jamal-al-Din Al-Afghani, was a radical Islamist.
Along with Abduh and Afghani, Rida blamed Muslim decline on the *Ulema*
(Muslim authorities), and was critical of the excesses of some Sufi sects.
Sunni Muslims are repugnant to Sufis because Sufi sect is considered as a
composite culture that emerged in the course of a thousand years of cohabi-
tation between Hinduism and Islam though there some Sunni Muslims who
are Sufis. On July 2, 2010, the Pakistani Taliban organized a double-suicide
bombing of the Data Darbar, the largest Sufi shrine in Lahore, Pakistan,
resulting in the deaths of 42 people. In May 2010, Peeru's Cafe in Lahore,
a cultural center with a troupe of Sufi musicians, was bombed. The tomb of
Haji Sahib of Turangzai, a Sufi, has been forcibly turned into a Taliban
headquarters. Two shrines near Peshawar, the mausoleum of Bahadar Baba
and the shrine of Abu Saeed Baba, have been destroyed by rocket fire. The
most devastating Taliban attack occurred in the spring of 2009 at the shrine

of the seventeenth-century poet/saint Rahman Baba, in northwest Pakistan, destroying the shrine.[50] The rejection of Sufism may have spelled the death of Islamic intellectualism. A Pakistani scholar, the late Fazlur Rahman, lamented: "A people that deprives itself of philosophy necessarily exposes itself to starvation in terms of fresh ideas—in fact, it commits intellectual suicide."[51] Modern Muslim intellectuals are responsible for the decline of Islamic excellence, partly because they have not pursued the rational views of Mohammed 'Abd al-Jabbar, Ibn Sina (Avicenna), al-Farabi, and Ibn Rushd, creators of the golden age of Islam. Tunisian-born Abdelwahab Meddeb, an outspoken critic of Islamic fundamentalism, is a staunch proponent of secularism and democracy, who would reconcile Islam with modernity. His erudite historical and cultural analyses of world events impacted by Islamic extremism have led to innumerable publications, including *The Malady of Islam*.[52] Professor Robert Reilly quotes Muslim thinker Meddeb:

> If Maududi reproached the West with the death of God, we can accuse him of having inaugurated the death of humanity . . . that the fulfillment of Qutb's vision of "liberation" would transform man into one of the living dead, on a scorched land.[53]

Radical Islam has a long, brutal history of holy war by violence, coercion, guerrilla warfare, and terrorism against unbelievers. This history begins with Abu-al-Faraj Ibn Al-Jawzi (508–597), an Islamic scholar whose family traces their lineage back to that of Abu Bakr, the first caliph. It continues with the Kharijites, an eighth-century Shia group who declared jihad against the unbelieving, apostate Muslims and carried out political assassinations to advance their cause. One of their victims was Caliph Ali, son-in-law of the Prophet Mohammed, in 661. An equally extreme sect that arose in the Middle East was the Qarmatians, a Shiite Ismailiyyah sect, known for their brutality. The Qarmatians flourished in Iraq, Yemen, and especially Bahrain during the ninth to eleventh centuries. They took their name from Hamdan Qarmat who led the sect in southern Iraq in the second half of the ninth century. They are most famed for their revolt against the Abbasid Caliphate, and particularly for their seizure of the Black Stone (in the center of the Grand Mosque) from Mecca and (the) desecration of the Well of Zamzam (near the Masjid al-Haram in Mecca, Saudi Arabia) with Muslim corpses during the hajj season of 930. The Assassins, who were sometimes known as the "new propaganda," are perhaps history's best-known holy terrorists. The term "assassin" originated with Shi'ite Muslims (Nizari Isma'ilis—also known as hashashins). They spread terror in the form of murder, including that of women and children. The first Assassins was al-

Hasan ibn-al-Sabaah, who died in 1124. He was probably a Persian from Tus, who claimed descent from the Himyarite kings of South Arabia. The Assassins murdered Muslim leaders from the eleventh through the thirteenth century, to cleanse Islam of corruption as well as to garner recognition for a new theological order. They considered killing to be a divine act, one that would guarantee entrance into heaven.

Ibn Taymiyah (1263–1328), a jurist of Egypt, was the spiritual source of jihad, serving as an insipiration to the Muslim Brotherhood of Egypt, and an inspiration for OBL. In the 1700s, radical Islam was espoused by Abd al-Wahhab of Saudi Arabia, who propagated jihadism based on the earliest Islamic principles and practices. The reward for holy warriors is a place in heaven, and beyond that, to be martyrs in the revival of Islamism worldwide. Radical Islamists believe that they are following the militant ideology of the Prophet Mohammed and successive Islamic leaders as to the use of jihad. Religious intellectuals have also espoused radical Islam. They have included Abd al-Wahhab (1703–1787) of Saudi Arabia, a founder of radical Islam, and Hasan al-Banna (1906–1949), who established the Muslim Brotherhood of Egypt in 1928. Al Banna defined Islam as ideology and faith, homeland and nationality, creed and state, spirit and action, book and sword. He, along with Ibn Taymiyah, had an impact on Qutb of Egypt, who is probably the most important Islamic scholar and radical thinker, and the author of *Social Justice in Islam, Islam: The Religion of the Future*, and *In the Shade of Qur'an Future*, among other books. Syed Maududi (also known as Abul Mawdudi [1903-1979]) of Pakistan was the founder of Jammat-e-Islam, and Muhammad al-Faraj (also known as Abd al-Salam Farag, 1952–1982) was a member of the Islamist jihad. In 1979 al Faraj, along with Karam Zuhdi, Ayman al-Zawahiri (AAZ), Abu Ayyub al-Misri (1968–2010), Abu Hamza al-Misri, and others, formed the Egyptian Islamic Jihad (EIJ) as a more radical offshoot of the Egyptian Jamaa Islamiya.

Maududi considered only non-Muslims to be *jahili*, ignorant or uncivilized and anti-Western. The Egyptian Qutb was more liberal and pro-reform, but stood against progressive, socialist secularist Gamal Abdel Nasser (1918–1970), president of Egypt. Qutb felt that Nasser's secularism was radical and distorted the message of Islam and the Prophet's life. He was sent to prison by Nasser for his membership in the MB. Qutb considered Nasser an apostate, and of course, Islam prescribes harsh and ruthless punishment to apostates. Nasser was also the most important leader in the Middle East and Muslim world. He defied British colonialism and brought about Arab pride with the nationalization of the Suez Canal. He successfully modernized Egypt's education systems, and improved its agricultural infrastructures. Qutb, at the age of sixty-one, was hanged in 1966 on the charges of conspiracy.

Maududi asserted that *jihad* is the central tenet of Islam. His students are Masood Azar, the founder of JeM (2000) and Hafiz Saeed, the founder of JuD (1985; also knwn as Markaz Daw'a wal Irshad; these are terrorist organizations in Pakistan (Appendix 1). Radical Islamists are urged to unite to fight against encroaching secularism and for their survival, even in the absence of threat. Maududi was overwhelmed by British colonial expansion and the spread of Western thoughts and values in the Indian Subcontinent. He was threatened by the rise of Indian nationalism and the loss of Muslim prominence. Maududi argued that Muslims must band together to fight this encroaching secularism, if they wanted their religion and culture to survive. He influenced Qutb to become a Muslim fundamentalist and to apply *jahiliyyah* (ignorance of monotheism) to contemporary Muslim society. Qutb was the pioneer of Islamic fundamentalism in the Sunni sect. He was distressed to see the torture and execution of Muslim Brotherhood members, and rejected Nasser's avowed determination to establish secularism in Egypt. He saw in this all the characteristics of *jahiliyyah,* which he defined as barbarism that was forever and for all time the enemy of faith, and which Muslims, following the example of the Prophet Muhammad, were bound to fight to the death. Qutb told Muslims to model themselves on Muhammad: to separate themselves from mainstream society (as Mohammed had made the *hijrah* from Mecca to Medina), and then engage in violent *jihad*.[54] Maududi's dream of an Islamic state of Pakistan was rejected, by Pakistan's national poet Muhammad Iqbal, who knew that such an occurrence would mean that Pakistan would lose its soul forever.

America's 9/11 Commission Report states that Tehran was in contact with AQ at various levels before the 2001 attacks. Tehran has admitted to the presence of AQ figures in Iran on a number of occasions, and has arranged for the repatriation of at least 13 Saudi members in the past five years. The OBL family tells us that at least one of Osama's sons, Sa'ad, has lived in Iran since 2002. Reports from Iran claim that scores of Taliban leaders and several AQ figures spend part of the year in a compound-style housing estate near the village of Dost Muhammad on the Iranian frontier with Afghanistan. One way to verify these claims is to allow the world media access to the area. But Tehran has declared large segments of eastern Iran a "no-go" area, even for its own state-owned media.

Any claim that AQ and the Khomeinists, not to mention other terrorist groups operating in the name of Islam, would not work together simply because they have theological differences is both naive and untenable. Qutb was famous for his book *Milestone*, which states that Salafism, based on the first three generations of Islam beginning in the seventh century with the Prophet Mohammed, and the two succeeding generations after them, the Tabi'al-Tabi'in, was a Sunni movement whose principle was derived from the Sunni *hadith* (tradition) attributed to Mohammed. Whereas Khomeinists are Shiites, they are considered to be heretics by Sunnis. These two groups have not buried the hatchets for centuries, except when they are killing *kuffir*.[55] Wahhabis, like the adherents of Salafism, wish to be true to the Prophet and are against any shrine or other form of idolatry.

Muhammad al-Faraj (1952–1982) inspired OBL and the Taliban leaders, following Wahhabi teaching, who destroyed two magnificent thousand-year-old mountain-high statues of Buddha at Bamyan in Afghanistan, a crossroads to many cultures and civilizations, in the pursuit of Islamist "perfection." He invented the sixth pillar of Islam—the jihad—and declared, in his 1980 pamphlet entitled *The Neglected Duty* that the idols of this world can only disappear through the power of the sword. *The Neglected Duty*, created by Anwar Sadat's assassins to explain and justify their use of violence, is perhaps the purest expression of this Islamist perspective on jihad. Faraj, executed along with the actual killers, argued that jihad as armed action is the cornerstone and heart of Islam, and that the neglect of jihad has caused the current depressed position of Islam in the world. Force must be used, he asserted, for it alone can destroy idols. Abraham and Mohammed both began their careers by smashing idols; the Islamists propose to follow their example. Muhammad al-Faraj characterized the rulers of the Muslim world as apostates, despite their profession of Islam and obedience to some of its laws, and advocates their execution. His pamphlet is explicitly messianic, asserting that Muslims must "exert every conceivable effort" to bring about the establishment of truly Islamic government, a restoration of the caliphate, and the expansion of *Dar al-Islam*. It states that their success is inevitable.[56]

The five pillars of Islam are as follows:

1. "There is no God but Allah and Mohammed is the messenger of God." (*la illaha il Allah-Muhammad rasul Allah*)—*Shahada*
2. Prayer five times a day at fixed times: dawn, noon, mid-afternoon, sunset, and night, facing towards the Kaaba in Mecca—*Salah*
3. Alms giving—*Zakat*
4. Fasting during the month of Ramadan (the ninth month of the Islamic calendar and the month the Quran was revealed to the Prophet Muhammad)—*Sawm*
5. Pilgrimage to Mecca, Saudi Arabia—*hajj*

Although Muslim scholars say that *jihad* means striving in the path of God, Faraj believes: "A glance at Muhammad's life and at the Qur'an establishes beyond doubt that striving is fighting, which means confrontation and bleeding."[57] This is significant because Faraj's influence is wide-reaching. David Rapport writes: "In the eyes of two of the most prominent scholars of Egyptian Islamism, Faraj is the most articulate spokesman of the gospel for the youth of the 1980s and may inaugurate a new era in Islamic thought."[58] Many believe that radical Islamists are actually preventing an Islamic revival. Nicholas Kristof writes:

> Muslim fundamentalists damage Islam far more than any number of Danish cartoonists ever could, for it's inevitably the extremists who capture the world's attention. If the Islamic world is going to enjoy a revival, if fundamentalists are to be tamed, if women are to be employed more productively, then moderate interpretations of the Quran will have to gain ascendancy.[59]

There has been some movement in reforming Islamic society in view of its harsh laws, gender inequality, and supremacy over the state. Scholar Ali Allawi notes: "It was difficult therefore to posit the reformation of Islam specifically in terms of reforming Sharia, if its provisions were no longer applicable outside the framework of family law or personal law."[60] Sharia was abandoned during the colonial and immediately post-colonial era. The conflict between Islam and democracy could not arise in the context of Muslim countries ruled by despotic regimes. The ideology of the terrorists was assessed alongside Islamic orthodoxy, to see if the two were intertwined. In Pakistan, the Taliban have taken away a part of a sovereign state, establishing a parallel judicial system that utilizes their version of Sharia. Their actions have been violent. On April 2009, Pakistan's daily newspaper, *The Dawn*, stated:

> The footage recently made public showing the flogging of a girl in Swat and the execution of a man and woman in their 40s reportedly in the Hangu district must have sickened anyone with respect for human rights and dignity. As such, these videos constitute a graphic reminder of the fact that behind the rhetoric of religion, the real face of the Taliban is one of unmixed brutality and murderousness.[61]

The turn to violence and terror by a small part of the Islamic movement, especially its signature mass murders of innocent civilians, is a decisive break with Islamic civilizational legacy.

Islam's detractors claim that there is a linear connection between the two best-known terrorist phenomena in Islamic history—the Kharijites and the medieval sect of Assassins—and the modern day jihadists. As for jihadists, they have relied on angry and disaffected individuals to forge violent and disciplined organizations, driven by a messianic ideology. AQ and other jihad organizations can be connected to the nihilist and terrorist movements of Tsarist Russia, or to the post-war groups that blurred the boundaries between national and social liberation struggle and terrorism in Indo-China, Sri Lanka, Palestine, Peru, Algeria, and South Africa. This recourse to terrorism in the name of a grand civilization confirms the disappearance of that civilization from the consciousness of the terrorists.[62]

The Kharijites, and after them, the Assassins, rebelled against unjust Muslim rulers known for killing targeted enemies, spawning other groups known for terrorism and violence. There are two major radical groups that can be found in most Muslim countries: the Muslim Brotherhood of Egypt and Jammat-e-Islami (JeI) of Pakistan. Egypt's MB, the world's oldest and largest Islamic political group, was founded by Hasan al-Banna in 1928 with a goal of establishing *Sunnah* (custom) and Sharia (law) throughout the world. Several Arab–Palestine groups, whose aim is to establish a Palestinian state or destroy Israel, are associated with al Banna. They include many organizations, as outlined in Appendix 1. Syed Abul Maududi, founder of the JeI, is famous for his writings on jihad in Islam; an excerpt follows: "The word 'Jihād' is commonly translated into English as 'the Holy War' and for a long while now the word has been interpreted so that it has become synonymous with a 'mania of religion.' The word 'Jihad' conjures up the vision of a marching band of religious fanatics with savage beards and fiery eyes brandishing drawn swords and attacking the infidels wherever they meet them and pressing them under the edge of the sword for the recital of *Kalima*. Islam wishes to press into service all forces which can bring about a revolution and a composite term for the use of all these forces is 'Jihad.' To change the outlook of the people and initiate a mental revolution among them through speech or writing is a form of 'Jihad.' To alter the old tyrannical social system and establish a new just order of life by the power of sword is also 'Jihad' and to expend goods and exert physically for this cause is 'Jihad' too."[63] Maududi was admired by Pakistani poet Muhammad Iqbal, and by Muhammad Ali Jauhar ("Muhammad Ali"), the famous leader of the Khilafat Movement. But he was fiercely opposed to the Muslim sect of Ahmadiyyas. He, along with Sayed Qutb, is considered a father of radical Islam He was mentor to Pakistani dictator General Zia-ul Haq, a devout Deobandi Muslim. General Haq hanged the former Pakistan Prime Minister Zulifikar Bhutto (1928–1979), father of former Prime Minister Benazir Bhutto

(1943–2007). Benazir was allegedly killed by Taliban terrorists. The deaths of the two Bhuttos had a major impact on Pakistani politics and militancy. Mr. Bhutto was patronizing radical mullahs, while Mrs. Bhutto was publicly against radicals. OBL's *jihad* goal to build AQ so that it might do battle with a Crusader–Zionist–Hindu conspiracy was provided in an audiotape aired by al Jazeera on April 23, 2006. For the first time, OBL spoke directly of India and the Kashmir dispute to support his claim that a Zionist-Hindu war was being waged against Muslims:

> A U.N. resolution passed more than half a century ago gave Muslim Kashmir the liberty of choosing independence from India. (President) George Bush, the leader of the Crusaders' campaign, announced a few days ago that he will order his converted agent (Gen. Pervez) Musharraf to shut down the Kashmir mujahedeen camps, thus affirming that it is a Zionist-Hindu war against Muslims.[64].

OBL is using Kashmir for his political and personal gain to please his Pakistani host. It is his AQ that is responsible for the current mayhem, turmoil, and upheaval in Kashmir. He went on to say:

> It is the duty for the Ummah with all its categories, men, women and youths, to give away themselves, their money, experiences and all types of material support, enough to establish jihad particularly in Iraq, Palestine, Afghanistan, Sudan, Kashmir, and Chechnya.[65]

The idea of a Crusader–Zionist–Hindu conspiracy has been thrown around for years in jihadist circles, with AAZ responsible for most of the anti-India and anti-Hindu statements. OBL's mention of India in his audio recording is intended to gear up existing militant outfits linked to the Kashmir dispute, including the Pakistani LeT and JeM, which have successfully staged attacks within Kashmir and in major Indian cities. Inspiration derived from OBL's message could drive these groups to heighten terrorist activity in Kashmir and other states of India.[66]

Several authors have dealt extensively with Islamist groups including Hamas, the PLO, Islamic Jihad, The Gamaa Islmiyya (GI), *Takfir wal Hijra*, Palestine MB, and radical Islamic movements in Algeria. All have a common objective of creating the pristine Islam of Mohammed by violent jihad.[67] The GI has caused several dozens of deaths in Egypt, where Christians are targeted and intellectuals killed, including Egypt's Nobel Prize winner Naguib Mahfuz and Columnist Farag Foda. Some people blame secularists Gamal Nasser (1918–1970), Anwar Sadat (1918–1981), and President Hosni Mubarak of Egypt for being at the root of this trouble.[68]

Jihad as carried out in South Asia by Ahmad Sirihindi (1564–1624), Shah Waliullah (1703–1762) and others is discussed in Chapter 4. Saudi Arabia has supported al-Banna, Qutb, Maududi, and other Egyptian dissidents all along, with funds and shelter. Radical Islam, from the days of the Kharijites of the eighth century right up to OBL of the twenty-first century, has treaded the path of violence and revenge, steadily and swiftly, to spread their version of Islam around the world. The leader of greatest consequence for our time, however, is OBL, who has changed our world radically since the 1990s with his quest for global jihad. Over 200,000 Muslim converts live in the West, most having been converted to Islam because their wives are Muslims (this is mandatory for marriage in Islam). Some 30,000–40,000 prisoners in American jails convert to Islam each year.[69] Some non-Muslims of the West joined radical Islamist networks in the 1990s in the aftermath of globalization. These cases are termed protest conversions[70] and they belong to the following four categories:

1. Politicized rebels who find a cause in radical Islam, and are fascinated its anti-system and anti-imperialist dimensions. These have included terrorists Christopher Caze and Lionel Dumont.
2. Religious nomads who are attracted to radical Islam after exploring other religions. These have included terrorists John Walker Lindh and David Hicks.
3. Former drug addicts and petty thieves hoping for a better life. Terrorists Jerome Courtailer and shoe bomber Richard Reid are examples.
4. Blacks, Latinos and persons of mixed race who feel that there is no racism in Islam, including terrorists Jose Padilla, John Bonte, and Jean-Marc Grandvisir.

Recently, several Muslim converts have targeted America and Germany. The suspect in the deadly shooting at a military recruiting center in Arkansas is the latest in a series of Muslim converts accused of planning or launching violent attacks in the United States, part of what security experts call an alarming domestic trend. The attack came less than two weeks after a foiled bomb plot on two synagogues in Riverdale, New York, allegedly led by four men who converted to Islam in prison or shortly after their incarceration. Abdulhakim Mujahid Muhammad, the 23-year-old accused of killing one U.S. soldier and injuring another in the attack in Little Rock, Arkansas, was born in Tennessee as Carlos Leon Bledsoe. He reportedly converted to Islam as a teenager, and court records show that he changed his name in March 2006.[71] White Muslim converts have brought the Islamic holy war

into the heart of Europe with a narrowly thwarted plot to blow up hundreds
of people in German airports, discotheques, and restaurants. Three men—
two Germans and a Turk who are believed to have received explosives
training at a terrorist camp in Pakistan—were arraigned by the German
federal prosecutor after a nine-month police operation.[72]

Sharia

All Muslim converts wish to live under Sharia. Sharia (also Shariah, al
Shariah) is the path to follow God's law, based on the *Quran* (to recite), the
Sunna (custom), and the *hadith* (tradition). Sharia was created by the Prophet
Mohammed, a religious, political, and military leader of Islam. Sharia deals
with every aspect of Muslim life, from family to finance to politics to social
issues covering civil, commercial, penal, and personal law, among others.
It is the legal framework of both public and private life (divorce, inheritance, childrearing, etc.), and is regulated by a legal system based on *fiqh*
(Islamic jurisprudence) as expressed in the Quran [verses 45:18, 42:13,
42:21, and 5:51]. According to Sharia, Muslim behavior is formulated on a
five-point scale: obligatory, meritorious, indifferent, reprehensible, and
forbidden. The major principles of Sharia are:

1. The Quran;
2. Sunnah (the way and manner of the Prophet);
3. Consensus (*ijma*) of Mohammed's consensus (*sahaba*);
4. Analogy (*quias*); and 5. Islamic jurists (*ulema*).

The treatises on Sharia normally contain a chapter on jihad, understood
in the military sense as regular warfare against infidels and apostates. The
first jihad was waged by the Prophet against the rulers of his birthplace and
ended with the conquest of Mecca in the month of Ramadan of the year of
the *Hijra*. In Sharia, the caliph is both Pope and Emperor, and there is no
separation of church and state. Sharia overrules democracy and political
parties. According to Sharia, a daughter inherits half as much as a son, and
the testimony of a female witness in court is worth only half that of a male
witness. In cases of murder, the compensation for a woman is less than that
given for a man. According to a 2007 poll conducted by the University of
Maryland, 66 per cent of Egyptians, 60 per cent of Pakistanis and 54 per
cent of Jordanians want Sharia. The Islamist political parties associated
with the Muslim Brotherhood in Egypt and elsewhere, and the Justice and
Development Party in Morocco, want to adopt Sharia if elected. In Iraq, for

example, the Constitution declares Sharia to be "the source of law," and it is up to the National Assembly to pass laws.

There are five major Sharia schools:

1. The *Hanbali* School, known for following the most orthodox form of Islam, is embraced in Saudi Arabia and by the Taliban in Afghanistan.
2. The *Hanafi* school, known for being the most liberal and the most focused on reason and analogy, is dominant among Sunnis in Central Asia, Egypt, Pakistan, India, China, Turkey, the Balkans, and the Caucasus.
3. The *Maliki* School is dominant in North Africa.
4. The *Shafi'i* School is dominant in Indonesia, Malaysia, Brunei Darussalam, and Yemen.
5. The *Ja'fari* school is most notably in Shia-dominant Iran.

These schools are molded by ethnic cultures and traditions, while retaining the principles of Sharia. All schools of Sunni Islam as well as mainstream Shi'ism consider idolatry (*shirk*), apostasy (*irtidad*), and hypocrisy (*nifiq, munafaqah,* or *riya'*) to be capital offenses.

There are three major crimes in Sharia: 1. *Hadd* (serious crimes); 2. *Tazir* (least serious crimes); and 3. *Quisas* (revenge crimes). Hadd crimes are: 1. Murder, 2. Apostasy, 3. Theft, 4. Adultery, 5. Defamation, 6. Robbery, and 7. Drinking alcohol. Punishments for *hadd* offenses may result in death, flogging, stoning, amputation, exile, or execution. Most Islamic fundamentalists reject secularism and democracy in favor of Sharia because of the Quran, which asserts (43:84): "Blessed be He who has sovereignty over the heavens and the earth and all that lies between them!" They see democratic and secular laws as being man-made, not God-made like Sharia.

Despite restrictions on women's behavior, the Muslim world has elected three women prime ministers, in Indonesia, Pakistan, and Bangladesh; however, these women were always subordinate to their armies, and were instated with the collaboration of religious extremists' organizations. Out of 192 worldwide governments, 121 countries have electoral democracies. In the 45 countries with significant Muslim populations, only 23 countries have democratically elected governments. In Afghanistan, Sharia has become state law. On August 14, 2009, ABC News reported that a controversial bill that Afghan President Hamid Karzai promised to review before implementing had quietly become law, allowing police to enforce language that stipulates a wife's sexual duties and restricts a woman's ability to leave her own home. Ultimately, the language in the law required Shiite women to give their husbands "their Sharia rights" when it comes to sex, a reference to Islamic law. It also allows women to leave their own homes "according to local customs." But human rights advocates say the new language is just legal cover for husbands to subjugate their wives. "It's symbolic with our society, which is a male dominated society—it somehow approaches a woman as a second class citizen and approaches a woman more as property than a human being," says Orzala Nemat of the Afghan Women's Network.[73]

Commenting on Sharia, Professor Hoffman notes,

> The language and terminology are, of course, reminiscent of the medieval Assassins' doctrine, invoking the paradise that awaits the holy war terrorists. This heaven is described today just it was 1400 years ago, as a place with 'rivers with milk and wine . . . lakes of honey and the services of seventy-two virgins,' where the martyr will see the face of Allah and later be joined by seventy chosen relatives. Indeed, the pleasures of alcohol—which all Muslims are forbidden in their lives on earth—and sex are permitted in this glorious afterlife, *where the commandants of the Shari'a (Islamic law) do not apply.*[74]

Bangladesh has rejected Sharia rule. Pamela Taylor of the *Washington Post* reported on July 11, 2010 that a Bangladeshi High Court had ruled that all judgments and punishments outside of the legal system, including those made by religious authorities, are illegal. The Court asserted that punishments such as caning, whipping, or stoning are in direct violation of the Bangladeshi Constitution, which states that no one shall be subject to cruel, inhuman, or degrading punishment. This was a direct blow against the religious authorities who issue *fatwa* (religious edicts) based upon their understanding of Sharia law.[75]

India, on the other hand, has accepted Sharia rule: Professor An-Na'im wondered why India has adopted Eurocentric conceptions of sovereignty, secularism, pluralism, and constitutionalism, instead of being neutral to all religions. While visiting India, he and met some fundamentalist scholars and historians who are in favor of Sharia of the Muslim period of India, and read their books. An-Na'im blamed British colonial rulers and Indologists William Jones and Max Mueller for portraying Muslims as outsiders. He noted the Morley–Minto reforms of 1909, which granted Muslims separate electorates. He made the strange comment that "the Hindu nationalists' organizations did not join with the struggle of the Congress." The entire Indian Congress was all Hindus, except for a very small number of Muslims, who included the noted scholar Maulana Azad. These "nationalist

Muslims" were waging a nonviolent struggle against British rulers, to win India's independence. That was the very reason the British colonial rulers gave Pakistan on a golden platter to the Muslim League leaders, who were hardly interested in India's independence movement. An-Na'im called Mahatma Gandhi and Jawaharlal Nehru "nationalist Hindus." "Nationalist Hindu" Gandhi vigorously campaigned with "nationalist Muslims" for the restoration of the caliphate. As An-Na'im writes, however: "In keeping with Nehru's legacy of viewing religion essentially as an obstacle to modernity, Indian intellectuals have tended to avoid engaging religion as *religion* in assessing its relationship to secularism." An-Na'im has noted that communal bias and riots in India have negated India's secularism, which is different from that of any other secular country, and for this he blamed the British. Despite secularism, Muslims in India are governed by Muslim Personal Law as it relates to marriage, inheritance, and owning property.[76] India is the only secular, democratic country in the world where the government-subsidized airfare in 2007 for the Hajj pilgrimage was $1323 million. As a gesture to minorities, India observes the Prophet's Birthday and Christmas as national holidays. India, from the beginnings of Muslim rule, has patronized sectarian education, offering support to the nation's more than twenty-three Muslim Universities and three traditional schools. These include Aligarh Muslim University, http://anjumaniislam.org/Jamia Millia Islamia, and two famous orthodox schools: Darul-uloom Nadwatul Ulama and Jamia Nizamia, both pioneers of *madrassa*. Most of them are totally funded by India, in spite of the fact that some faculty members of these elite schools support radicalism and jihad. Like the jihadi separatists, they believe that Kashmir, a Muslim majority area in J&K, should merge with Pakistan as per Sharia, which states that a Muslim area should not be joined to a non Muslim country—despite the fact that J&K has a Muslim Chief Minister and Muslim Provincial Assembly. These views are endorsed by some Muslim journalists, politicians, and Constitutional experts. Unfortunately, by law, India cannot close these institutions even when they are engaged in anti-India activities. Some of the graduates and faculties of these institutions went on to found the nation of Pakistan, and have rewritten Indian history so as to glorify Islamic savagery and the annihilation of Indus Valley civilization in the Muslim period. These historians have ignored the atrocities by the insolent, brazenly cruel Muslim rulers and disdainful invaders and their killing of thousands of local people. In the course of conquest, they demolished, desecrated, and pillaged thousands of temples and other institutions, burning manuscripts and idols, looting the treasury several times, and taking booty back to the invaders' own homelands. Jihad in India was carried out by barbaric killing, pillaging, and looting under the swords of Ghaznavi, Khiljis, Mamluks, Hammad, Ghori, Timur, Babur, Jahangir, Aurangzeb, and others, from the eleventh to the sixteenth centuries. The "destruction of temples during the early period of Muslim rule, which was justified in terms of *jihad* and motivated by the wealth of temples"[77] is outrageous, irrational, and provocative.

Aligarh Muslim University founder Syed Ahmad Khan (1817–1898) adopted the pro-British stance, and was ambivalent about the concept and the scope of citizenship of India. On the demolition of Babri Masjid in India, built in 1528, An-Na'im noted that 174,000 Hindus sacrificed their lives fighting against the Muslims when the temple was first demolished, and that 35,000 Hindus died in the 77 battles fought by Hindus to reclaim the temple.[78]

There have been more recent sources of friction between India's government and its Muslim constituency. In the case of Shah Bano, a divorced Muslim woman, the ultimate ruling by the Supreme Court of India was that she had the right to receive support from her ex-husband under Section 125 of the Indian Criminal Procedure Code, like any other Indian woman. The Supreme Court of India also invoked the need for a uniform civil code for national integration. The majority of Muslim organizations, including the All India Muslim Personal Law Board (AIMPLB), challenged this ruling as an attack on Islam. The AIMPLB also challenged the authority of non-Muslim judges of the Indian Supreme Court to interpret the Quran. Jawaharlal Nehru's grandson Rajiv Gandhi passed the Muslim Women Act of 1986, which deprived Muslim women benefits under the Criminal Procedure Code. Many Muslim intellectuals, including Muslim women, want a uniform civil code, and denounce the genocide, destruction, and vandalism of Hindu temples, manuscripts, and books carried out during Muslim rule in India. But a large number of Muslims are against a uniform civil code, insisting on Sharia for Muslims. Hindus believe in universality, equality, and respect for women, separation of religion from politics and state affairs, and strict adherence to nonviolence and tolerance. Islam, on the other hand, is a bellicose religion based on the Quran and Sunnah, and avows prejudice against "unbelievers" and women. As scholar Samuel Huntington has noted: "The Koran and other statements of Muslim beliefs contain few prohibitions on violence, and a concept of non violence is absent from Muslim doctrine and practice."[79] The author of the Constitution of India, B.R. Ambedkar (1891–1956), had this to say on the subject of Islam:

> As a consequence of the purda (veil) system, a segregation of the Muslim women is brought about. . . . Such seclusion cannot but have its deteriorating effects upon the physical constitution of Muslim women. . . . Purdah

deprives Muslim women of mental and moral nourishment . . . [they] become helpless, timid, and unfit for any fight in life.[80]

Muslim immigrants have brought Sharia to the United Kingdom. The UK *Guardian,* reported on January 13, 2010, that the ban on Islam4UK, an extremist group, announced that morning by the home secretary was "a victory for Islam and Muslims."[81] Islamists hung up a black banner proclaiming "Sharia for the UK" in a room at the back of the restaurant—for the benefit of the television cameras gathering for a press conference. Beside it they pasted neatly lettered posters saying "Islam will Dominate the World," "Democracy is Hypocrisy," and, as if to trump the slogans in Orwell's *1984,* "Freedom = Dictatorship." Britain's eminent writer Timothy Gordon Ash wrote that "an ineffective ban will be the worst of both worlds, and we know that the ban is likely to be ineffective, because Islam4UK itself emerged when two other offshoots of the original al-Muhajiroun organization were banned."[82] There are mixed opinions about the compatibility of Sharia with democracy. Democracy is not just about fair elections with participation from both genders, but it is also about protecting human rights for all people, (see Appendix A2), secular education, equal treatment of men and women, independence of judicial systems, and free press. In this context, whether Sharia contradicts democratic values or not, jihadists hate democracy because democracy respects others' views and equality.

Muslims believe that that Qur'anic verses from the Mecca period emphasize the freedom of faith and equal dignity of all human beings regardless of faith and gender, but that verses of the Medina period restrict the rights of women and non-Muslims. Discrimination against women and non-Muslims is intensified when legal scholars regard the verses from the Mecca period as being "abrogated and abolished" by those of later years from Medina.[83]

The Sudanese Muslim legal scholar Abdullahi Ahmed An-Na'im claims that "this process of abrogation" should be reversed to develop a modern version of Shariah that can guarantee the equal rights of women and non-Muslims.[84] Pakistan-born author Ziauddin Sardar writes:

The Shariah, Muslim intellectuals and thinkers in places like Indonesia, Morocco, and India are arguing, is not divine. It is socially constructed in history. . . . This argument is a seismic shift. Thus the future is not riddled with conflicts between Islam and the West, or traditionalism and secularism. On the contrary, the future will be shaped by mutual respect and collaboration. And it will be a multi-civilizational future where the two civilizations—and others, such as China and India—will nourish themselves from their distinct ways of being.[85]

Honor Killing

While precise statistics are scarce, the UN estimates that thousands of women are killed annually in the name of family honor. Honor killing is a penalty for marital infidelity, premarital sex, flirting, or even failing to serve a meal on time. All of these things can be perceived as impugning the family honor.[86] It is difficult to get precise numbers on the phenomenon of honor killing because the murders frequently go unreported, the perpetrators unpunished, and the concept of family honor justifies the act in the eyes of some societies. Other controversial practices that are woven into the Sharia debate include female genital mutilation, adolescent marriage, polygamy, and gender-based inheritance rules.[87]

While there are some challenges to the Islamic teachings that permit or sanction honor killings, the view of women as property with no rights of their own is deeply rooted in Islamic culture. Dr. Tahira Shahid Khan, a professor specializing in women's issues at the Aga Khan University in Pakistan, wrote, in *Chained to Custom:*

> Women are considered the property of the males in their family irrespective of their class, ethnic, or religious group. The owner of the property has the right to decide its fate. The concept of ownership has turned women into a commodity which can be exchanged, bought and sold.[88]

In Pakistan, however, there are other forms of Sharia, especially *riba*, and the *marufaat*, which do not punish people for not performing their *namaz* daily and not keeping beards, and other orthodox features.[89]

As the *Wall Street Journal* reported in an op-ed by Nidra Poller in on September 7, 2009:

> Five thousand honor killings testify to the danger Rifqa Bary faces. The 17-year-old (Rifqa Bary) had been practicing Christianity in secret for four years when she fled her home in central Ohio in July, fearing for her life after her parents discovered her defection. The Sri Lankan Bary family has been in the U.S. since 2000. Her story is related to "honor killing." The United Nations affiliate, Human Rights Watch, defines honor killing as, "Acts of violence, usually murder, committed by male family members against female family members, who are perceived to have brought dishonor upon the family." A woman can be targeted by (individuals within) her family for a variety of reasons, including: refusing to enter into an arranged marriage, being the victim of a sexual assault, seeking a divorce—even from an abusive husband—or (allegedly) committing adultery. The mere perception that a woman has behaved in a specific way to "dishonor" her family, is sufficient to trigger an attack.[90]

"[Mr.] Bary (Rifqa's father) is a middle-class jeweler with no documented history of abuse and no record of radical actions or beliefs," the Orlando Sentinel's Mike Thomas wrote in a piece alleging anti-Muslim bias in Miss Bary's case. Mr. Thomas seemed to see no reason why Mr. Bary would kill his daughter—after all, he said in court she would be free to worship as she chooses. Miss Bary affirmed in a sworn affidavit that her father said, "in a fit of anger that I had never seen before in my life . . . 'If you have this Jesus in your heart, you are dead to me! You are no longer my daughter . . . I will kill you!'"[91]

Five thousand victims of honor killings annually worldwide, according to a conservative U.N. estimate, bear witness against Mr. Thomas's placid supposition. Women in Muslim countries and immigrant communities everywhere fall prey to an elaborate legal code enforced by torture and murder that deprives them of their civil rights, their human rights, and their right to exist. Sharia-sanctioned death for apostasy was recently confirmed by Harvard chaplain Taha Abdul-Basser, who sparked controversy when a private e-mail discussing punishment for leaving Islam was made public. Mr. Abdul-Basser noted:

> There is great wisdom (*hikma*) associated with the established and preserved position (capital punishment) and so, even if it makes some uncomfortable in the face of the hegemonic modern human rights discourse, one should not dismiss it out of hand.[92]

European awareness of honor killings contrasts with the artificial ignorance surrounding Ms. Bary's case in the United States. Europeans cannot ignore the savage murders of "wayward" girls who want the freedoms of their adopted countries. Stories of runaways enticed to come home and let all be forgiven, only to be met by their executioners, abound on the continent. Banaz Mahmod, a 20-year-old Iraqi refugee in London, was murdered by her father and uncle in 2006 after police dismissed her requests for protection. In 2002, 17-year-old Sohane Benziane was burned alive in a Paris suburb by a fellow teenager. [Her crime: refusing to obey him.] In April 2002, a 20-year-old Turkish man was jailed for allegedly strangling, beating and ultimately killing his twin sister, Gulsum Semin, after learning of her abortion, Agence France-Presse reported.[93]

Dhimmis (Zimmis)

Dhimmi status was originally afforded to non-Muslims who had become People of the Book, *ahl-khitab* (i.e., Jews and Christians), and later to

Zoroastrians, Mandeans, Hindus, Sikhs, and Buddhists. This was initiated in 628 by the Prophet, after a long siege of Khaybar, the inhabitants surrendered under terms of a treaty known as the *dhimma*. According to this agreement, Mohammed allowed the Jews living there to continue to cultivate the land on the condition that they cede to him half of their produce, and to bear no arms, but he reserved the right to cancel the agreement and expel them whenever he desired. Sharia prescribes a discriminatory set of rules for non-Muslim *Dhimmis*, subjugated by *jihad*. The laws of Islam Governance by al Marwadi (d. 1058) calls it dhimmitude (the dhimmitude system is governed by Qur'an verse IX, 29) in which native infidels had to recognize Islamic ownership of their land, submit to Islamic law, and accept payment of the poll tax, *dhimma-jizya*, mentioned in the verse. *Dhimmis* had to maintain a low profile, had to have less valuable houses than Muslims, and could not ride camels and horses, only donkeys.[94] They also had to get down from their mount when they saw a Muslim, and were forbidden from walking on the good part of the road. Additionally, they had to wear special clothing to identify themselves as non-Muslims. They could not marry Muslims or convert them to their own faith. Muslim social history is fraught with random killing of dimmis when they overstepped their social limits.[95]

Wahhabi

Ultra-orthodox Sunni Islam is very similar to Salafism. The term *Ahl Hadith*, or *Ahl-I-Hadeeth*, is often used interchangeably with the Salafi *dawah*, and proponents prefer to call themselves "Salafis," although they are often called Wahhabis. It was founded in Saudi Arabia by Muhammad al-Wahhab (1703–1792). His influence and action were behind several Saudi battles and conquests, until the Saudis were checked by the Ottoman Empire. The Wahhabist-oriented Al-Saud dynasty conquered and unified the various provinces on the Arabian Peninsula, founding the modern day Kingdom of Saudi Arabia in 1932. Saudi Arabia has the largest deposit of oil and gas in the world (see Table 2.1). Enriched and enabled by huge price increases after the 1973 Arab–Israel war, Saudi Arabia has funded thousands of mosques and madrassas across the world. British historian Michael Burleigh wrote:

> The Saudis further institutionalized their political and financial reach through the Organization of the Islamic Conference (OIC) and the Islamic Development Bank, and by donating money to Western and Eastern universities to promote Islamic and Middle Eastern studies.[96]

Present-day followers of Wahhabism include OBL and Saudi Prince Nayef. Besides spreading in its birth place, Wahhabi influenced AQ, the MB of the 1940s and 1950s, al-Jihad, Gamaa Islamiya of the 1970s and 1980s, the National Salvation Front (FSN), JeI, and the Taliban. Wahabbis strictly observe the following:

1. Few Women's rights—women cannot drive a car, cannot go out alone, only with a male relative, and must cover the whole body with full veil, or *burqa.*
2. Dietary restrictions—no pork, no alcohol, no cigarettes, only *halal* meat and fish.
3. Modesty in women's clothing, wearing of the *burqa* and no display of jewelry.
4. Culture—no music, dancing, pictures or paintings, or long beards for men.
5. No worship of shrines, tombs, or graves.

Wahhabism has been completely funded by Saudi Arabia through its World Islam League since 1962, with the goal of promoting, propagating and preserving Wahhabi Islam. This is accomplished by building schools, mosques, libraries, educational institutions, Islamic centers, hospitals and charities around the world. Wahhabis are against Shiites and Sufis and have destroyed major Shi'a and Sufi shrines, tombstones, and cemeteries. They have also demolished Ottoman artwork with any human representation, along with architecture and its decoration, libraries, and even mosques in Kosovo and Bosnia, as well as Buddhist statues in Afghanistan. Wahhabis do not want to be associated with Kharijites, and reject Shi'ism as impure, illegitimate, and even apostate. Opponents claimed that Wahhabis, like the extreme Kharijites before them, divided the world into two spheres, the land of Islam (*dar al-Islam*), which was the exclusive realm of the Wahhabis, and the land of unbelief (*dar al kafir*), which was the domain of everyone else. This was carried out in order to declare jihad against all non-Wahhabis, who were categorized as unbelievers (*kafir*). The result was a portrayal of militant Wahhabism in conflict with Muslims, particularly Sufis and Sh'ias, and with non Muslims.[97] The AQ leader of Iraq, the late Abu Mussab al Zarqawi, a Sunni, wrote to fellow Sunni OBL in 2004: "The danger from Shi'a is greater than the Americans and the only solution is for us to strike the religious, military and other cadres among Shi'a with blow after blow until they bend to Sunnis."[98] It is reported that Abu Musab al Zarqawi, head of AQ in Iraq, wrote a letter to the AQ leadership in Afghanistan and Pakistan in January 2004 which stated that striking the Shiites in religious, political, and military terms would provoke them to show the Sunnis their rabies, as they bared the teeth and displayed the hidden rancor working within their breasts. The solution, he said, was for Sunnis to drag the Shi'as into battle, because that was the only way to prolong the fighting between Sunnis and the infidels.

Al Sahaaba Soldiers of Iraq claimed responsibility for an explosion in a Sh'ia temple in Saydia, on a busy commercial street. Afterwards they issued the following statement: "Thanks are unto Allah they were killed—those friendly with the Americans, the oppressors and the killers in Iraq."[99] Wahhabic extremism and terrorism were pursued rigidly and with messianic zeal by the Taliban, by OBL's AQ, and by Pakistan's Jamiyyat-I-Ulama-Islam, using funds from Saudi Arabia and military training provided by Pakistan Inter-Service Intelligence Agency, the ISI. Wahhabism has spread to Central Asia and Russia and has resulted in the suicide bombing of schools, hospitals, and marketplaces. It has also been used to topple many governments that are considered un-Islamic. While Islam prohibits fighting with and killing fellow Muslims, fighting with unbelievers is held to be a religious duty, even if they are Muslims. The armies of God have become agents of death and destruction for non-Muslim religious sites in Central Asia, and in Eastern Europe since the demise of the Soviet Union. Wahhabi-Taliban-AQ literalists have found a home in Pakistan and Afghanistan, and are exporting terrorism to the world in the name of God. Between 1995 and 2008, a total of 80,094 people have died in terrorists' attacks.

With the attacks in Bali, Indonesia was added to the list of countries that have fallen victim to major acts of terror. Abdur Wahid (1940–2009), a former President of Indonesia, expressed these concerns about the spread of Wahhabism:

> In recent decades, Wahhabi/Salafi ideology has made substantial inroads throughout the Muslim world. Islamic fundamentalism has become a well-financed, multifaceted global movement that operates like a juggernaut in much of the developing world, and even among immigrant Muslim communities in the West. To neutralize the virulent ideology that underlies fundamentalist terrorism and threatens the very foundations of modern civilization, we must identify its advocates, understand their goals and strategies, evaluate their strengths and weaknesses, and effectively counter their every move. The armed *ghazis* (Islamic warriors) raiding from New York to Jakarta, Istanbul, Baghdad, London and Madrid are only the tip of the iceberg, forerunners of a vast and growing population that shares their radical views and ultimate objectives.

According to Wahid, the formidable strengths of this worldwide fundamentalist movement include: immense funding from oil-rich Wahhabi sponsors; an appeal to Islamic identity; an ability to blend into the much larger traditionalist masses; networks of radical Islamic schools; a global network of fundamentalist imams, a strong organization established to translate, publish, and distribute Wahhabi/Salafi propaganda and disseminate its ideology throughout the world; and scholarships for study in Saudi Arabia, and worldwide Internet communication.[100]

Syed Qutb may be called the Islamic world's Solzhenitsyn, Sartre, or Havel, and he easily ranks with all of them in influence. He fused together the core elements of modern Islamism: the Kharijites' *takfir*, Ibn Taymiyah's *fatwa* and policy prescriptions, Rashid Rida's salafism, Maududi's concept of the contemporary *jahiliyya*, and Hasan al-Banna's political activism. Qutb asserted that human rule through man-made government is illegitimate, and that Muslims must answer to God, not democracy.[101] (Taymiyah did not accept Mongols as Muslims even after they were converted to Islam in 1295, because they were not observing Sharia literally.)

Deobandi

The Deobandi is a Sunni Islamic revivalist movement of radical Islamists that started in pre-independent India at Deoband, India, and has spread to other countries: Afghanistan, Pakistan, South Africa, and the United Kingdom. Deoband is a town one hundred miles north of Delhi, India, where a *madrassa* was established in 1867. The "Deobandi Tradition" itself is much older than the eponymous Dar-ul-Ulum madrassa at Deoband. In 1947, when Pakistan was created, there were 246 *madrassas* in India. This grew to 2861 in 1988, and today there are 28,982 *madrassas* with over 3 million students. Half of these *madrassas* belong to Deobandis. In Punjab alone, there are 2512 Deobandi *madrassas*. Over 15,000 people from Punjab, including 6,000 from *madrassas,* have died in fighting in Afghanistan and Kashmir.[102] The Deobandis believe that a Muslim's first loyalty is to his religion, and only secondarily to the country of which he is a citizen or a resident, that Muslims must regard only their Ummah as their community, and not their national frontiers; and that it is a Muslim's sacred duty is to go to any country in the world to wage jihad in order to protect the Muslims of that country. Deobandis follow the *fiqh* (observance of rituals and morals; law) of Iraq's Abu Hanifa (699–765), and the *aqidah* (creed) of Iran's Abu Mansur Maturidi (853–944). Deobandi has five main principles:

1. *Tawhid*: Abrahamic monotheism of God; no one shares his
   attributes.
2. *Sunna (the Quran and Hadith)*
3. Hubbus-Sahaba: Following the methodology of companions of
   Mohammed
4. *Taqlid wal-Ittiba*: Giving preference to the jurisprudence of
   one of the earliest jurists of Islam over that of later jurists
5. *Jihād fī Sabīlil-Lāh*: Doing jihad (striving for good, in the name
   of God)

In 1866, a group of Hanafi Islamic scholars (*Ulama*) led by Qasim
Nanotwi founded an Islamic seminary known as Darul Uloom Deoband.
While the scholars at Darul Uloom Deoband in India itself have been sup-
porters of a secular government in India, its branches in Pakistan have
supported militant Islamism. Deobandis control Muslim voters whose reli-
gion and *madrassa* are protected in secular India. According to The London
Times, about 600 of Britain's nearly 1400 mosques are run by Deobandi-
affiliated clerics, and 17 of the country's 26 Islamic seminaries follow
Deobandi teachings, producing about 80 per cent of all domestically trained
Muslim clerics.

The Taliban are said to follow the teachings of the Deoband School,
although some journalists, such as noted Pakoistani scholar Ahmed Rashid,
claim that they follow a simplistic version of the school's teachings. Some
Barelwi leaders have pronounced *takfir* on Deobandis for writings deemed
to be against the Quran and Hadith (*Sunna*). In May 2001, riots broke out in
Pakistan after the assassination of a leader of the Barelwi/Barelvi (see Appendix 4) movement by Sipah-e-Sahaba Pakistan, a Deoband-affiliated group.
Barelwi activists forcibly took control of several dozen Deobandi and Salafi
Mosques between 1992 and 2002, with methods that have often sparked
violence. A "cash-for-fatwa" scandal came to light following a sting operation, in which Pakistan's Star TV Channel showed clerics belonging to Darul
Uloom Deoband demanding and receiving cash for the issuance of fatwas.
The fatwa that was issued allegedly mandated that Muslims are not allowed
to use credit cards, double beds, or camera-equipped cell phones; that Muslims should not act in films, donate their organs, or teach their children
English; and that Muslim girls should not wear jeans.[103] Starting in 1979,
leading Deobandi madrassas in Pakistan welcomed Central Asian radicals,
who then received a free education and an allowance for living expenses. A
large contingent of Central Asian militants who arrived clandestinely, without passports or visas, were given scholarships.

There are more than 80,000 Deobandi madrassas, based on a 2008 estimate. Because of the Deobandis' close association with fundamentalist Islam, they vehemently oppose the Ahmadiyyas, a Muslim sect. Ahmadiyyas (also known as Qadians) were founded by Mirza Ahmed (1835–1908) of Qadin, India. Ahmadiyyas (who consider Mirza is the last prophet, not the Prophet Muhammad) have a large following, of approximately 200 hundred million, ranged throughout most countries of the world including the United States and the United Kingdom. On May 28, 2010, the Taliban carried out suicide attacks on Ahmadiyyas' two mosques in Lahore, Pakistan's cultural capital, which left more than 90 people dead. Pakistani radicals had, apparently, forgotten that Sir Zafarullah Khan (1893–1985), an Ahmadiyya and the first foreign minister of Pakistan, had drafted the Lahore Resolution, under the guidance of Viceroy Lord Linlithgow, which resulted in the creation of Pakistan. The Deobandi faction had been in the vanguard of the movement against the Ahmadiyya community (not accepting Prophet Muhammad as the last prophet), which General Zia ul Haq eventually declared non-Muslim in the 1970s in Pakistan. The Deobandis also orchestrated anti-Shia sectarian violence in the 1980s and 1990s. The Jamiat Ulema-e-Islam (JUI) is the largest Deobandi political outfit, which gave rise to terrorist organizations such as Lashkar-e-Taiba, LeT (also Jama'at-ud-Da'wah Pakistan (JuD) is a banned Islamic organisation that is considered by the United Nations to be an alias of the banned terrorist group Lashkar-e-Taiba), IM, SPS of Pakistan, and LeJ (see Appendix 1 and 5).

Not only have these organizations been active in Kashmir and other parts of the world but subsequently they also challenged the writ of the Pakistani state. In July 2007, Deobandi clerics' stiff armed resistance to the state agencies from Lal Masjid (Red Mosque), located in the very heart of Pakistani capital, Islamabad, demonstrates their potential to pose a challenge to the state.[104]

(Other forms of Deobandi Islamism, including Barelvi, Ahmadiyya, and Sufism, are discussed in Appendix 4.)

The principal reasons for the phenomenal growth of the *madaris* (plural of madrassas) in Pakistan (particularly the Deobandi sect) include the defeat of the Soviet Union by Taliban mujahidin; the Islamization of schools and public institutions from 1977–1988 under General Zia-ul Haq; the rise of radical Islam; free food and lodging for poor students funded by Saudi Arabia and other Gulf countries; and training the mujahedeen to serve as insurgents and in a guerrilla army. Madrassa students who went to the Afghanistan war, and to Kashmir in India during the Kargil war, are honored

as martyrs. The Deobandi–Taliban Islamic movement has spread to
Uzbekistan (IMU) and Tajikistan in Central Asia. Deobandi were associated with the Tablighi Jammat (TJ, Group for Preaching), established in
Mewat, India, in 1927. The TJ was designed as an apolitical, pietistic organization for proselytizing mission that sends missionaries across the globe
on with the objective of making converts to Islam. This group is planning to
build the largest mosque in Britain, which will house 70,000 people. Members of the Tablighi Jammat have included Jose Padilla, Richard Reid, John
Walker Lindh, and others charged with terrorism. The group is under investigation for terrorism in Britain, France, and the United States. One of
the major terrorist organizations that follow Deobandi is Sipah-e-Sahaba of
Pakistan (SeS Pakistan or SSP). It is a splinter group from the predominant
Deobandi political party in Pakistan, the JUI. Initially called Anjuman-e-
Sipah-e-Sahaba, it currently operates under the name Millat-e-Islamia Pakistan, but the latter name was banned in late 2003. SeS/SPS Pakistan, founded
in 1985 by Haq Nawaz Jhangvi, is a leading Sunni Deoband group in Pakistan. SSP wants to make Pakistan a Sunni state, under a narrow interpretation of Hanafi Islam that seeks to restore the caliphate. It is also adamantly
opposed to Pakistan's alliance with the United States of America. The United
States added Lashkar—Jhangvi (LeJ), a radical offshoot of SSP, to its list of
Foreign Terrorist Organizations in January 2003. The LeJ is reported to
have allied with the JeM and the HuM (Appendices 4 and 5) around 2002 to
form what appears to be an AQ-affiliated hit squad. Upon investigation, the
LeJ safe houses were found to hold chemical labs and toxic substances. This
led to speculation that the SSP and LeJ benefit from the support of other
Deobandi groups and wealthy patrons from Saudi Arabia and Pakistan.[105]
Deobandi *Ulema* have articulated jihad as a sacred right and obligation,
encouraging their followers to go to any country to wage jihad to protect the
Muslims of that country.[106] Deobandis advocate that no matter where they
live, their allegiance is to Islam, and preach *Qu'adt al Jihad* (global jihad)
for all Muslims everywhere. It is reported[107] that every militant organization that exists in Pakistan, including the JuD was Deobandi in orientation,
and that all terrorists in Pakistan are Deobandis.

The Khilafat Movement and the Moplah Rebellion

The Khilafat Movement (caliphate) and the Moplah (aka Mapilla) rebellion
have both played a major role in the worldwide Islamic movement. A major
goal of Islamists is to establish a worldwide caliphate by overthrowing 'infidel' governments. The Caliphate, a single Islamic state, was started in 632
in Medina (Yathrib), Saudi Arabia, after the death of Islam's founder

Mohammed. It expanded Islam's territories by conquest or treaty to encompass most of the Middle East, Central Asia, and North Africa. It ended when the Ottoman Turks began losing ground to the Christian West. The Khilafat movement seeks to retain or restore the Ottoman Caliphate (*khilafat-e-usmania*), and to prevent Muslim holy places from coming under the control of non-Muslims. It is essentially a radical Islamic movement on the order of the Deobandi, and follows Maududi's tenet of "Jihad in Islam." After World War I (1914–1918), the Ottoman Empire faced dismemberment. In the wake of the surrender of Turkey, Muslims heard a rumor that the British were bent on abolishing the caliphate. This motivated Muslims to campaign for the Khilafat movement, which urged the British to maintain the religious rights of the Turkish sultan as head of Sunni Islam. The Ali Brothers—Muhammad Ali Jouhar, cofounder of Jamia Islamia at Delhi, and Shaukat Ali—started the Khilafat movement (1919–1924) to restore the caliphate. Mahatma Gandhi linked the issue of *Swaraj* (self-rule) with the Khilafat, movement to associate Hindus with the movement to gain freedom for India from the British. Gandhi fused religion and politics in this movement to obtain Muslim allegiance in the freedom movement of India. But Gandhi's *Satyagraha*, the nonviolent resistance movement, was thwarted by the rise of the *hijrat*, or migration movement. Gandhi's movement was further damaged when some *ulema* announced that India was not *dar al-Islam*, the abode of Islam, but *dar ul Harb*, the abode of war, where it is permitted to wage jihad. This was a severe blow to Gandhi's concept of Hindu–Muslim unity, and ushered Pan-Islamism into India, under the leadership of Ismailia Aga Khan. Quitting Gandhi's Congress, the Ali Brothers joined the Muslim League with Mohammed Jinnah. In September 1921, both Ali brothers were arrested in connection with their role in the Khilafat movement, which delivered a severe blow to the Khilafat movement. Gandhi, who was using this movement to accelerate India's advance towards independence, withdrew his support from the Khilafat movement in the aftermath of the Chauri Chaura incident in February 1922, when policemen and British officers were killed by fanatics. In 1924, the Turks under Mustafa Kemal were consolidating their position in Turkey, and announced an end to the Khilafat. This was a major setback for Indian Khilafatists, who had been campaigning against the British to restore the caliphate in Turkey.

The failure of the Khilafat movement infuriated the Moplah Muslims of Malabar, India. The Moplah rebellion in 1921, a jihad against Hindus, was an offshoot of the Khilafat movement. Religious revivalism among the Muslim Moplahs, a Muslim community in the Malabar district of Kerala, India, led to a revolt against their landlord, the Hindu Nair Jenmi. As background, a large number of fanatic Muslims sailing from Arab countries had settled in

Moplah on the Malabar Coast in Kerala, India, during the eighth or ninth century, where they married Indian women. As reported by Annie Besant (1847–1933), a prominent Theosophist, women's rights activist, writer, and orator and supporter of both Irish and Indian self-rule, Moplah Muslims went on a rampage, raping, plundering, force-converting several thousand Hindus, and murdering several thousand others who would not renounce their faith. Approximately 100,000 people were driven from their homes with nothing but the clothes they had on, stripped of their homes and property. At the end of this campaign, there 2,339 Hindus were dead and 1652 wounded, while British casualties numbered 43 dead and 126 wounded.[108] In the aftermath of the revolt, Moplah's Mohamed Haji was declared the caliph of Malabar.

A Khilafat kingdom was proclaimed, and the flags of the Islamic caliphate were flown. This Khilafat movement proved to be an asset for Pakistan. It made clear to the Indian Muslims that they should trust neither the British nor the Hindus, but look to their own strengths for self-preservation. Mohammed Jinnah, the founder of Pakistan, was not in favor of the Khilafat movement. Later, Gandhi paid an appalling price for supporting the caliphate movement against the British, and for the Indian Congress's vote of neutrality in the Second World War (1939–1945). Jinnah took credit for not supporting the Khilafat movement against the British, and offered his full, unconditional support of the Muslim League towards the British war effort in the WW2. Repeated occupation of Muslim lands such as Chechnya, Kashmir, and Palestine, may be attributed to the absence of the "Khilafah systems."[109]

Al Qaeda and Osama bin Laden

Al Qaeda—the most dangerous and formidable terrorist group—was founded by Osama bin Laden (OBL) and his Palestinian mentor, Abdullah Azzam, on September 10, 1988 in Peshawar, Pakistan. AQ became famous after the formation of its global network, the World Islamic Front (WIF), in 1998. WIF brought the Egyptian Islamic Group (EIG) and Pakistani and Bangladeshi terrorists groups to the forefront of global jihad. In 1998 OBL, whose home country is, Saudi Arabia, brought together a Jihad Council with many prominent members: Ayman al-Zawahiri (AAZ), a wealthy Egyptian physician, and a student of Qutb; Abdullah Yusuf Azzam (1941–1989) of Jordan and Palestine, his former teacher, and the Godfather of militant global jihad; Syed al Sharif Fadl (also known as Dr. Fadl) a physician, of the Egyptian terrorist group Al Jihad; Abu Musab al-Suri from Syria; Sudanese Jamal al-Fadl; Abu Ayyub al-Masri (1968–2010), an Egyptian, Abu Musab al-Zarqawi

(1966–2006), a Jordanian; and the Egyptian Abu al-Yazid. AQ and its affiliate organizations are engaged in guerrilla warfare with Western forces in the Afghanistan and Iraq wars. They have also committed several terrorist attacks around the world, including 9/11 in America; the Bali bombing in Indonesia in October 2002; and the bombing of Superferry 14 in Manila, the Philippines, in February 2004, which killed 116 people. Although the WIF has been emboldened by its success in Afghanistan, it is keeping a low profile in various countries under the guidance of OBL.

Osama bin Laden (1957–2011) was born on March 10, 1957 in Saudi Arabia, and educated there as well. His mother is Syrian and his father is Yemeni. Prior to his life on the run as the world's most wanted criminal, he was a successful Saudi businessman. AQ was founded to topple pro-western governments in the Muslim world, to eliminate western influence and military bases in Gulf countries, to control oil and gas resources and operations in the Muslim world, and to serve as a base for jihadists training to fight in Afghanistan and beyond. AQ grew, assembling mujahedeen across the Muslim world, when America opposed the 1979 Soviet invasion of Afghanistan. OBL and Azzam recruited, trained, and financed thousands of foreign *mujahedeen,* or holy warriors, from more than fifty countries. Egyptian Abu al-Yazid served time in prison in the early 1980s with deputy leader AAZ for their role as conspirators in the 1981 assassination of Egyptian President Anwar Sadat. Abu Musab Suri has transformed AQ from a vulnerable cell into a decentralized movement, propagating international jihad through the Internet. The three Arab terrorists—the Saudis' OBL, the Egyptian AAZ, and the Syrian Al Suri—are the world's foremost modern international jihadists. Dean Schabner and Karen Travers of ABC News reported on May 1, 2011 that

> Osama bin Laden, hunted as the mastermind behind the worst terrorist attack on U.S. soil, has been killed, President Obama announced tonight. The president called the killing of bin Laden the "most significant achievement to date" in the effort to defeat al Qaeda. "Justice has been done," Obama said. Bin Laden was located at a compound in Abbottabad, Pakistan, which was monitored and when the time was determined to be right, the president said, he authorized a "targeted operation." "A small team of Americans carried out the operation," Obama said. "After a firefight, they killed Osama bin Laden and took custody of his body." He was replaced by Ayman al-Zawahri, Al Qaeda's second-in-command.

Egypt's president, Anwar Sadat (1918–1981) was assassinated by jihadists because he signed a peace treaty with Israel. Ironically, he had released these jihadists from prison to propagate radical Islam, while placing the names of Egyptian Christians onto a list of suspected anarchists. Sadat even legalized the Muslim Brotherhood, allowing it to publish and organize once again, and encouraged the formation of so-called Islamic Groups at universities. Sadat did this to offset the power of the Leftists on campus, a relic of the days of Socialist Abdel Nasser. But Egypt's two terrorist groups, the MB and the WIF, wished to subvert the Egyptian government. Linked with al-Qaeda is the Gama'at al-Islamiyya (or Jamaat al-Islamiyya, also known as the Islamic Group, GI/IG) a radical organization founded in 1973 that seeks to install an Islamic regime in Egypt. One of its spiritual leaders, Omar Rahman, was convicted and jailed in the United States as the perpetrator of the 1993 World Trade Center attacks. It is a radical offshoot of the much older and more grassroots-oriented MB. Its strength is unknown, but there are probably several thousand hardcore members and another several thousand sympathizers. One of its members is AAZ, the deputy of OBL, collaborated with the Egyptian Islamic Jihad in the assassination of Egyptian President Anwar Sadat in 1981, and were suspected in an unsuccessful assassination attempt against President Hosni Mubarak of Egypt in Addis Ababa, Ethiopia, in 1995. In September 1997, this group killed nine German tourists and their driver near the Egyptian Museum, and in November of that year, they killed fifty-eight foreign tourists and four Egyptians in a shooting spree at the Luxor Resort. They work in tandem with Al-Jihad, which started in 1970s and has branches in Yemen, Afghanistan, Pakistan, and Lebanon, merging with AQ in 2001. It has conducted attacks against several high-ranking Egyptian officials through the use of car bombs and means of assassination.[110]

Let us recall this passage from the 9/11 Commission Report:

> Usama bin Laden and other Islamist terrorist leaders draw on a long tradition of extreme intolerance within one stream of Islam (a minority tradition), from at least Ibn Taimiyyah, through the founders of Wahhabis, through the Muslim Brotherhood, to Qutb. That stream is motivated by religion and does not distinguish politics from religion, thus distorting both. It is not a position with which Americans can bargain or negotiate. With it there is no common ground—not even respect for life—on which to begin a dialogue. It can only be destroyed or utterly isolated.[111]

The AQ Manual prescribes eight principal reasons to join the *jihad*:

1. Identity as a Muslim
2. Commitment to the need to increase numbers of Muslim fighters
3. Fear of hellfire (an afterlife reserved for unjust and unrighteous persons)

4. Fulfilling the duty of jihad and responding to the call of Allah
5. Obeying Allah, his Messenger, those charged with authority, and their pious predecessors
6. Establishing a base for Islam
7. Protecting those Muslims who are oppressed in the land
8. Seeking martyrdom

OBL returned to Afghanistan in 1996 where he had left behind a vast organization, yet he was distrustful of Afghanis. Since the year 2000, AQ is alleged to have been associated with the following attacks:

1. The February 2006 attacks on the Abqaiq petroleum processing facility, the largest such facility in the world, in Saudi Arabia
2. The July 2005 bombings of the London public transportation system
3. The March 2004 bomb attacks on Madrid commuter trains, which killed nearly 200 people and left more than 1,800 injured
4. The May 2003 car bomb attacks on three residential compounds in Riyadh, Saudi Arabia
5. The November 2002 car bomb attack, and a failed attempt to shoot down an Israeli jetliner with shoulder-fired missiles, both in Mombasa, Kenya
6. The October 2002 attack on a French tanker off the coast of Yemen
7. Several spring 2002 bombings in Pakistan
8. The April 2002 explosion of a fuel tanker outside a synagogue in Tunisia
9. The September 11, 2001, hijacking attacks on four U.S. airplanes. Two of these crashed into the World Trade Center; and a third aircraft crashed into the Pentagon, and fourth crashed into a field in Pennsylvania
10. The October 2000 bombing of the *U.S.S. Cole*
11. AQ is also suspected of carrying out the December 2007 bomb and suicide attacks in Algiers, or of directing sympathetic groups to do so.

There also have been hundreds of arrests of terrorists linked to AQ in Germany, Belgium, Spain, France, England, Turkey, Malaysia, Indonesia, and the Philippines. AQ is associated with the following terrorist groups: Egyptian Islamic Jihad, The Libyan Islamic Fighting Group, Islamic Army of Aden (Yemen), *Jama'at al-Tawhid wal Jihad* (Iraq), LeT, JeM , IMU, AIQM, Salafist Group (see appendices 1 and 5) for Call and Combat, Armed Islamic Group, GSPC, ASG (Malaysia, the Philippines), Jemaah Islamiya (Southeast Asia), and the KLA.

OBL chose to go Sudan when he was persuaded or forced to leave Saudi Arabia. There he met National Islam Front (NIF) leader Hasan al-Turabi, a firebrand preacher of violent hatred of the *kafir*. Together, using OBL's money, they started an international network of radical Islam that brought together fellow Arab jihadists of the Afghanistan war. Both OBL and al-Turabi built a huge number of companies, industries, investment firms, weapons factories, and chemical plants in Sudan. Their intent was to make money that would be used to overthrow both moderate and oppressive rulers, and to establish a pure caliphate.

In Sudan, OBL was exposed to factors including (1) rampant anarchism and corruption, (2) anti-colonialist struggle by African nations, particularly in Ghana, (3) racial prejudice and discrimination, (4) violent separatist movements in Europe and Asia, (5) left-wing radicalism in Egypt, Algeria, and Somalia, which is considered un-Islamic, (6) Palestinian *intifada*, or uprisings, and (7) religious terrorism in Uganda, Somalia, Sudan, and Ethiopia (see Figure 3.2). Even while doing business in Sudan, where he became resentful of the corruption, ineptitude, and inefficiency he found there, OBL remained a clean-living man with a very austere life. He had several radical lieutenants, including Mohammed Khalifa, Ramzi Yousef, and Khalid Muhammad, who were sent to the Philippines, Chechnya, and elsewhere with money and arms. The tone of OBL's movement was austere, simple, and stark, and they never organized, observed, or celebrated any social event. OBL's associates were equally committed to an ascetic life.

OBL's strategy for AQ was to take advantage of a situation in which a Christian government was attacking a weaker Muslim country. This allowed the terrorist group to rally jihadists from many countries to come to the aid of their religious brethren. If this strategy succeeded, the Muslim region would become a radical Islamic state, a part of the eventual network of Islamic states that would make up the great new caliphate, or Muslim empire. OBL was motivated by the Egyptian Islamists al Banna and Qutb, radical groups, Gamma Islamiyya, *Takfir wal Hijra,* Islamic Jihad, Sheik Ibn Taymiyah, and Maududi. According to Sheik Ibn Taymiyah, it is legitimate in Islam for a Muslim to adapt to a non-Muslim ethos including dress, food, drinks, gambling, and any other things *haram* in Islam, for the beneficial goal of pursuing Islam. OBL also found inspiration in Faraj's book *The Neglected Duty*.[112] After his return to Afghanistan in 1996, OBL established cave-based military operations, guiding the jihad networks through the Internet, and avoiding and evading all attempts by NATO forces in Afghanistan and covert operations to catch or kill him. OBL is still at large, and poses a great threat to the world. His goals remain the same, as does his basic strategy. He seeks to "provoke and bait" (as he puts it) the United States into "bleeding wars" throughout the Islamic world; he wants to bankrupt America much as he helped bankrupt, as he claims, the Soviet Union in Afghanistan in the 1980s. The demoralized "far enemy" would then go home, allowing AQ to focus on destroying its "near enemies," Israel and the "corrupt" regimes of Egypt, Jordan, Pakistan, and Saudi Arabia. The U.S. occupation of Iraq helped move his plan along, and OBL has worked diligently to turn it into a trap for Washington. OBL's views on uniting Muslims around the world are powerful. He feels that that true believers originate from many different places and regions, representing a wide spectrum of the unity of Islam, which recognizes neither race nor color and pays no heed to borders and walls.[113] It is likely that OBL has settled in FATA/KP (Federally Administratered Tribal Agency/Khyber Pakhtunkhwa, formerly North West Frontier Provonce, NWFP), Pakistan. From there he has been able to collaborate with the Taliban on making bombs.[114] Ahmed Rashid comments:

> It was from there the bomb plots in London, Madrid, Bali, Islamabad and later Germany and Denmark were plotted. With the help of AQ and Pakistani extremists, the Taliban have also set up a lethal cottage industry along the Afghanistan-Pakistan border—the manufacture of improvised explosive devices (IED). OBL believes that the infidel must be subordinated to Islam and enmity and hate shall forever reign between us (Muslims and Infidels).[115]

Osama Bin Laden hates secularism so much that he hates PLO leader Yasser Arafat despite his fight against Israel. OBL has sacrificed millions of dollars of his wealth to propagate radical Islam. He has slept on floors, most days eating raisins and chickpeas and only drinking water. He is shy, speaks very softly, and keeps a low profile. He reads a great deal, and even reads the Quran while pointing his gun on the battlefield. With the Quran in one hand, and an AK-47 in the other, he inspires other terrorists, most of whom follow his AK-47 culture. The Journalist Lawrence Wright comments:

> The fierce idealists who did respond to Azzam's message viewed Afghanistan as the beginning of Islam's return to international domination, which would see not only the liberation of the Afghans but also eventual recapture of all territory, from Spain to China, that had been under enlightened Muslim domination while Europe was mired in the Middle Ages. The

restoration of the former empire was only the first step, however. The next stage was final war against unbelievers, culminating in the Day of Judgment.[116]

Throughout history, and throughout the world, invaders, kings, Sultans, military commanders, and Imams, have like OBL, selectively used Islam in the name of God. Both mainstream and extremist movements, including "holy warriors" like OBL, have selectively used the pattern of *hijra* and jihad for their own purposes. OBL was a celebrity in the Afghanistan war with the Soviets (1978–1989), having created a formidable mujahedeen army. Even President Ronald Reagan called the Afghan mujahedeen "freedom fighters."[117] OBL was happy when America, in Operation Desert Storm (August 1990–February 1991), liberated Kuwait from the secularist Saddam Hussein's invasion. America indirectly supported OBL by furnishing arms to the KLA to liberate Bosnia. Although by joining hands with the KLA, the United States had become partners of a sort with OBL, in 1998 the U.S. State Department listed the KLA as an international terrorist organization that supported itself with drug profits and through loans from OBL.

Iran benefited when America, in Operation Iraqi Freedom (2003–present), invaded Iraq to overthrow Saddam Hussein: As an unintended consequence of the Iraq war, Shiites took power in Iraq. Professor Barnett Rubin and the Pakistani journalist Ahmed Rashid write,

> And some Iranians speculate that in preparation for the coming of the Mahdi [i.e., the guided one; Muslims believe the Mahdi is coming to stay on earth and will rid the world of error, injustice and tyranny], God has blinded the Great Satan to its interests so that it would eliminate both of Iran's Sunni-ruled regional rivals, Afghanistan and Iraq, thus unwittingly paving the way for the long-awaited Shiite restoration.[118]

Radical Islam's rejection of modernity and its adherence to the tribalism of the seventh century cannot take Islam back to its golden age of empire.

Instead, Muslims were falling behind, not only because they did not espouse modernity, but because they actively rejected all but the dark shadows of modernity—the totalitarian ideologies that sprung up as the corruption of modernity: Bolshevism, fascism, and Nazism. Modern jihad is the modern form of Mahdism. It is Islamic in its cultural idiom, form, and content. There is no firewall between Mahdism and mainstream Islam, since it is all "in the Book" in the Quran, in the *hadith* literature, in the *fiqh*, and in the jurisprudence derived from both.[119] As Sunni Muslims, both OBL and his Sunni host, Taliban leader Mohammad Omar Abdullah, went into hiding without surrendering in the American war on Afghanistan (2001–

present). OBL masterminded the 9/11 attacks in America from his secret caves, protected by the former state military and intelligence personnel of the neighboring country of Pakistan. The counter-insurgency expert David Kilcullen has called AQ *takfiri* (unbeliever, apostate) terrorists who are *Salafists* (the first three generations of Islam) and are considered impure by their fellow Muslims.[120] Unlike other insurgents who operate locally, AQ seeks to take the entire world for its territory, and the political order it seeks to overthrow is that of the entire Muslim world. It also seeks to control the relationship between the world's Muslim population (the *ummah*) and the rest of world society. And *takfiri* terrorists use physical operations (bombings, insurgent activity, and beheadings) to support an integrated armed propaganda campaign.

OBL's attacks in Spain, Indonesia, India, Jordan, Nigeria, Algeria, Egypt, Russia, Turkey, France, Italy, Kenya, Somalia, Morocco and Britain represent a global jihad by militants. He vindicated the clash of civilizations with the attack on 9/11. He views the Israel–Palestine conflict and India–Pakistan conflict as civilization-wide wars, in which he is fighting against the War on Terror. The distinguished legal scholar Phillip Bobbitt writes:

> The preemption of terrorism, the preclusion of humanitarian crises brought by genocide or ethnic cleansing and natural catastrophe, the prevention of the proliferation of weapons of mass destruction for compellance, all require this (we achieve a greater facility in dealing with possible futures). But the greatest of these trials of imagination will be Wars against Terror themselves.[121]

OBL is the most articulate leader of the Muslim world, championing all Islamists. His effectiveness is based on many factors, which include: the use of *jihad* to pursue violent radicalism; his vocal opposition to the presence of American troops in the Persian Gulf War (1990–1991) to protect holy sites in Saudi Arabia; his admiration for the success of the Palestinian intifada that openly challenges Israel; his hatred for America's support of repressive regimes in the Middle East; his belief that there is an existential threat to Islam; his anger about American support for the seizure of Jerusalem; Israel "the statelet" of the Jews; his resentment of American involvement in the Iran–Iraq war (1980–1988), his vehement opposition to the American war in Afghanistan (October 2001–present) and the Iraq war (March 2003–present); his willingness to attack American interests to spread global jihad; and his role in the defeat and demise of the Soviet Union (1979–1988). Like OBL, the wider Muslim population voices deep and widespread discontent with their rulers and their Western patrons, yet they need American support to throw them out. For example, Egypt, Saudi Arabia, and Jordan have pro-Western governments while Iran and Syria have anti-Western governments. "This leads to a paradox—namely, that countries with pro-Western regimes usually have anti-Western populations, whereas the populations of countries with anti-Western regimes tend to look to the West for liberation."[122]

Since OBL and his deputy AAZ went underground, several AQ commanders have surfaced, including Abu Hafa al Masri, Khalid Sheikh Mohammed (KSM), Abu Faraj al Libi, Hamza Rabia, and Abdur Rahman al Muhajir—but there is no strong cross-fertilization with war veterans of Iraq and Afghanistan. It is likely, however, that some war veterans from Iraq and Pakistan may infiltrate Afghanistan, Kashmir, and Chechnya. The violence in Iraq and Afghanistan is not diminishing, and AQ objectives and goals are on the march, not on the run.[123]

Where recruitment is concerned, not only does OBL have a messianic character, but he has been established as a Saladin by his effort to defeat the Soviet Union and wound America. His terrorists group AQ and its affiliates have utilized mosques, madrassas, prisons, and restive Muslim regions, as well as social, political, cultural, and religious groups, for the recruitment of suicide bombers. Two Western mosques, the Finsbury Park Mosque in London and the al-Farouq Mosque in Brooklyn, have preached jihad. It is an Islamic duty to think as a unitary community of the faithful, a part of *ummah*, despite differences in race, ethnicity, and nationality. This religion dictates almost every aspect of life in the Muslim world, and has become one of the biggest factors that drives an individual towards terrorism. By way of blackmail, its leaders allege that if mosques are not built in Western countries, non-Muslim troops, embassies, and citizens will be under attacked in the Muslim world. The world is waiting to see whether there will be a mosque at Ground Zero in New York City, a Babri *masjid* in Ayodhya, India, or higher minarets on the mosques in Europe.

It was Khalid Sheikh Mohammed (KSM), however, masterminded the 9/11 attacks. He was inspired by the Ayatollah Khomeini's overthrow of Reza Pahlavi of Iran, the Soviet Union's withdrawal from Afghanistan, his unpleasant college years in America, and his working relationship with the MB. He single-handedly raised funds, recruited mujahedeen pilots, and organized the operations and funds with the consent of OBL. KSM was also involved in several terrorist acts in Asia. The noted reporter Terry McDermott writes: "We tend to think of jihad and Islamism and associate it with Afghanistan. It's really a Pakistan based movement."[124] Daniel Byman, Professor at Georgetown University, concurs: "The focus is on Afghanistan, but all things that make this movement hum are in Pakistan."[125] Sheikh Mohammed thrived in the chaos of Pakistan, and that chaos still exists. The melding of the various jihadi groups with Al Qaeda and the Taliban has resulted in a chaotic mess. For example, one of the premier field commanders for Al Qaeda in Pakistan is Ilyas Kashmiri. In Kashmir, he was sponsored by the Pakistani government; now he is fighting it. In some sense, most of the terrorists who have attacked the West in the name of Islam are sparks thrown off by the fires in Pakistan. Byman and others believe that this has implications that have not been given due consideration in the current Afghan war.[126] Douglas Murray, director of the London-based Centre for Social Cohesion, writes:

> Two British citizens are among those reportedly killed in the Pakistan drone strikes, along with several German nationals. Lashkar-e-Taiba certainly has links to the United Kingdom, the Western center of jihad. A comprehensive report published in July by the Centre for Social Cohesion, "Islamist Terrorism: the British Connections," revealed that 5 per cent of the Islamists convicted of terrorism-related offenses in Britain over the past 10 years have links to the group. Shehzad Tanweer, one of the suicide bombers who attacked the London transport system in July 2005, was associated with Lashkar-e-Taiba. So were British-born Omar Sheikh, convicted in a Pakistani court for his role in the killing *Wall Street Journal* reporter Daniel Pearl, and Rashid Rauf, the suspected ringleader of the 2006 trans-Atlantic airline plot (himself reportedly killed in a missile strike in Pakistan two years ago). A further five men with links to Lashkar-e-Taiba have been convicted of terrorism-related crimes in the U.K. They include Dhiren Barot, the head of a U.K.-based terror cell that planned a series of attacks against major targets including financial buildings, and Omar Khyam, convicted in 2007 for heading a cell that aimed to use fertilizer bombs to attack targets including a shopping center in Kent and a nightclub in London.[127]

It has been announced that Khalid Sheikh Mohammed and others will be tried in a civilian court in New York, rather than by military commission. The national security expert Marc Thiessen writes:

> When KSM was first captured in March 2003, he refused to answer questions, informing his captors: "I will tell everything when I get to New York and see my lawyer." Now he is getting that trip to New York he requested, courtesy of Eric Holder and Barack Obama. The civilian trial will be an intelligence bonanza for al Qaeda, as KSM and his lawyers use discovery rules, and compel testimony from government officials, that will force the revelation of national defense secrets to the enemy."[128]

The eminent author Dinesh D'Souza writes,

> Obama has been careful to define Al Qaeda operatives not as terrorists or enemy combatants, as President Bush did, but rather as common criminals. . . . What Obama has never explained, however, is why the rights of the U.S. Constitution extend to people who are not U.S. citizens.[129]

The trials will be at the expense of American taxpayers, and will give jihadis the same protections as U.S. citizens.

Within a hundred days of September 11, 2001, the U.S. Army had wiped the Taliban regime from the face of the earth. OBL was on the run, his secret cells dismantled or disbanded. Today, OBL remains the most wanted militant Islamist, and as NATO Secretary General Willy Claes has declared, Islamic militancy has emerged as the single gravest threat to the NATO alliance and to Western security since the end of the Cold War. He also stated in February 1995 that the scale of the danger was greater, for militant Islam encompassed elements of terrorism, religious fanaticism, and the exploitation of social and economic injustice.[130] OBL has been reassuring his followers in AQ and the Muslim world that guerilla warfare defeated the United States in Vietnam and the Soviet Union in Afghanistan, and his own violent jihad has forced the United States to withdraw its troops from Lebanon and Somalia. He also claims that these tactics may be credited with the liberation of Bosnia. OBL predicts that due to his violent jihad, consisting of guerilla and urban warfare, the United States will be forced to withdraw from Iraq and Afghanistan. His movement has produced more than 70,000 militants, from 1979 to 2003.[131] A congressional investigation into the Sept. 11 attacks has concluded that between 70,000 and 120,000 terrorists were trained by AQ in the "skills and arts of terrorism."[132] They have been dispatched to more than 60 countries to establish OBL's version of jihadist Islam. OBL has in his possession a billion dollars to support various separatist and radical organizations that are bent on overthrowing un-Islamic regimes, and propagates his message through his website, alneda.com. He also has the support of many Islamic countries. Professor Robin Wright has vividly described the pre- and post-9/11 terrorists activities in and outside America. Here she explains the distinction between Muslim militancy and Islamist activism.

> One is malignant and the other can be benign—potentially even positive. As Islamic sentiment grows, policy makers in the West face two stark alternatives: One is to use this important juncture—when interest in both democracy and Islam is expanding—to press Muslim dominated countries on political pluralism, to encourage action that will include rather than

exclude troubled populations, and then to accept the results of free and fair elections even if Islamist parties gain significant votes.[133]

A *Washington Times* report on September 11, 2009, stated:

Lt. Gen. Ronald Burgess, director of the Defense Intelligence Agency, called the U.S. record against AQ "mixed." While AQ leaders OBL and AAZ remain at large, the organization has been forced to "perpetually rebuild," he said. Still, AQ remains a "determined adversary" and has had success in recruiting Americans to fight with it, he said. He noted incidents of Somali-Americans going to fight alongside extremists in Somalia and said "others travel to Pakistan and Afghanistan" to battle U.S. and allied troops. Both Gen. Burgess and Leon Panetta, director of the CIA, said AQ's popularity may be waning among Muslim populations. "AQ's own vicious ideology, founded on the murder of innocent people, has proven to be a major weakness,' Mr. Panetta told the agency's work force on the eve of Sept. 11 commemorations. "But we cannot wait for popular disgust to isolate and overcome the extremists. We and our allies must continue to press the offensive, eroding their ability to plot and kill." Former CIA Director Michael Hayden pointed to recent successes in targeting AQ's [UT] leadership. He said there have been a "dozen or so AQ leaders who have died since last July [2008]" and that this "has been the most compressed or rapid-fire loss of leadership that al Qaeda has had to adapt to, and I think it has had a dramatic impact on them. . . . You can replace one person at a time; when you have a series of folks who have been dying, it is harder," he told *WT*. Among those killed in the past 14 months are Khalid Habib, a veteran combat leader and operations chief; Rashid Rauf, considered the mastermind of a 2006 plot to bring down trans-Atlantic jets; Abu Khabab al-Masri, an expert on explosives and chemical and biological weapons; and Baitullah Mehsud, leader of the Pakistani Taliban affiliated with AQ.[134]

OBL has remained a determined, deadly adversary for the last eight years, and he and his AQ members are still active and in unknown areas. With his help, the Taliban are fighting vigorously in Afghanistan and in Pakistan from their hideout sanctuaries. The governments of Afghanistan and Pakistan are negotiating with the Taliban for a truce and for possible power-sharing. AQ's doctrine for insurgency is rendered by 'Abd Al-'Al-Muqrin's: A *Practical Course for Guerrilla War*. Al-Muqrin calls all unconventional wars guerrilla wars, and has borrowed guerrilla warfare tactics from Karl von Clausewitz, Mao Tse-tung, Chie Guevara, Ho Chi Minh, and Sun Tzu. His book covers in detail basic preconditions for successful guerrilla war, force structure, covert operations, the dead drop, assassinations, hostage taking, planning, and operational techniques within cities.

The essence of his doctrine is illustrated by the following statement:

> Yet, one passage above all reveals the depth of hatred and the unappeasable
> global ambition of al-Qa'ida: We must target and kill Jews and Christians.
> To anyone who is an enemy of God and His Prophet (this includes Kafir,
> infidel, *takfir*, apostates, and Shiites) we say, "We have come to slaughter
> you." In today's circumstances, borders must not separate us nor geogra-
> phy keep us apart, so that every Muslim country is our country and their
> lands are our lands. We must turn the idolaters' countries into a living hell
> just as they have done to the Muslim countries. . . . All the active cells in
> every corner of the world must pay no attention to geography borders that
> enemies have drawn. Instead, these cells must make every effort to trans-
> form the infidel countries into battlefronts and to force the infidel and
> collaborationists countries to deal with that. Just as Muslim countries have
> been turned into test labs for their weapons and inventions, so also their
> countries must be turned into hell and destruction. The sons of the Islamic
> Ummah (Community) are capable of doing that (God willing).[135]

The research fellow Norman Cigar denotes:

> Al-Muqrin's doctrine presents a complex challenge that is more than just
> in the terrorist—or even the military realm, due to his parallel emphasis on
> politics, economics, and religion. To be effective in the long term, the
> responses must be as complex as the challenge, with the military compo-
> nent playing a supporting role, providing a shield of time and security for
> the sword of socioeconomic, political, and ideological response to occur
> and win the war.[136]

While simultaneously engaging the West with jihad warfare in the enemy
land, information warfare including cyber-terrorism, and with the economic
warfare of hitting strategic and commercial assets, AQ terrorists often recruit disgruntled youths and Muslim converts from non-Muslim countries,
as well as citizens from lawless regions. They are then trained to commit
suicide or bomb attacks in distant places, which have included India, the
United States, London, Madrid, Yemen, Germany, the Netherlands, Algeria, and Somalia. As the Georgetown University Professor Bruce Hoffman
writes:

> A survey of terrorist incidents in the past seven months alone underscores
> the diversity of the threats arrayed against us and the variety of tactics Al
> Qaeda is using. These incidents involved such hard-core operatives as
> (Humam) Balawi, the double agent who played American and Jordanian
> intelligence to kill more CIA agents than anyone else has in more than a
> quarter-century. And sleeper agents such as David Headley, the U.S. citi-

zen whose reconnaissance efforts for Lashkar-i-Taiba, a longtime Al Qaeda ally, were pivotal to the November 2008 suicide assault in Mumbai. And motivated recruits such as Abdulmutallab, the alleged Northwest Airlines bomber, and Najibullah Zazi, the Afghan-born U.S. resident arrested in New York last September and charged with plotting a "Mumbai on the Hudson" suicide terrorist operation. And "lone wolves" such as Maj. Nidal Hassan, accused of killing 13 people at Fort Hood in November, and Abdulhakim Muhammad, a convert to Islam who, after returning from Yemen last June, killed one soldier and wounded another outside an Army recruiting center in Little Rock.[137]

Force, sword, belligerence, and violence are essential for Islam to succeed and survive. The Al Qaeda training manual spells this out for the world to see:

> The confrontation that we are calling for with the apostate regimes does not know Socratic debates, . . . Platonic ideals, . . . or Aristotelian diplomacy. But it knows the dialogue of bullets, the ideals of assassination, bombing, and destruction, and the diplomacy of the cannon and machinegun. Islamic governments have never and will never be established through peaceful solutions and cooperative councils. They are established as they [always] have been by pen and gun by word and bullet by tongue and teeth.[138]

Numerous books have been written on how to defeat AQ, the source of modern violent jihad. Pakistan has been a training site, headquarters, and safe haven to AQ and the Taliban terrorists and their leaders OBL and Mullah Omar. The former presidential advisor, Bruce Riedel writes that "the hardest part of trying to defeat al Qaeda lies in meeting the challenges in Pakistan."[139] OBL has significant support in his home country of Saudi Arabia, whose wishes include the creation of a Palestinian state; and in Pakistan, which wants Kashmir annexed. It has been suggested that peaceful resolution of the Palestinian and Kashmir issues will weaken OBL's effort and popularity, resulting in a loss of the two supporter states Saudi Arabia and Pakistan. The governments of these two allies of the United States will not provide any support to OBL. The United States has been providing huge economic and military aid to Afghanistan and Pakistan for the last decade, in the hunt for OBL and Mullah Omar. But as of 2010, this multibillion-dollar aid has not earned any love for America; it has only served to strengthen the terrorist's networks for destabilizing these regions and others. Besides, OBL's interest is in restoring a worldwide caliphate, and Saudi Arabia and Pakistan have orthodox religious organizations that embrace OBL's radical Islam. The *New York Times* reported on July 14,

2010 that from their base in the frontier area near the border of Pakistan and Afghanistan, the networks of Sirajuddin Haqqani, aligned with AQ, the Taliban, and the ISI, are suspected of running much of the insurgency around Kabul and other areas in Afghanistan, carrying out car bombings and kidnappings, including spectacular attacks on American military installations.[140] Mullah Omar's trusted colleague Abdul Zaeef, Afghan ambassador to Pakistan before the U.S. invasion of Afghanistan and a spokesman for the Taliban, writes of Taliban's link with Pakistan:

> Pakistan, which plays a key role in Asia, is so famous for treachery that it is said they can get milk from a bull. They have two tongues in one mouth, and two faces on one head so they can speak everybody's language; they use everybody, deceive everybody. They deceive the Arabs under the guise of Islamic nuclear power, they milk America and Europe in the alliance against terrorism, and they have been deceiving Pakistani and other Muslims around the world in the name of the Kashmiri jihad. . . . He (Mullah Omar) has not only gathered remnants of the former Taliban under his leadership but he has also recruited new members from the madrassas in Pakistan.[141]

The Taliban

The Taliban, a Sunni Islamist Group, came to power in Afghanistan in 1994 under the patronage of Pakistan, and was recognized by Saudi Arabia and the United Arab Emirates. They followed Qutb's ideology of *jihad*, with a vision of establishing fundamentalist Islam and immediately putting Sharia into effect throughout the whole country. They sheltered OBL and his AQ organization during their rule in Afghanistan from 1994 to 2001. During their rule, women were barred from schools and jobs, and were forced to wear *burqa* in public. All forms of entertainment, cinema, dancing, music stores, kite flying, and even clapping during sports events were banned, and men were required to grow long beards. The exhibit of drawings, paintings, photographs, pictures, posters, and dolls were forbidden. They were against any idols, tombs, or sculptures and ordered in 2001 the demolition of two 1500-year-old Buddha statues carved into cliff-sides at Bamiyan, one 125 feet tall and the other 174 feet tall. The Taliban are against music and dancing because they feel it creates a strain in the Muslims' mind and hampers the study of Islam. The Islamic punishment of stoning, amputation for small crimes, and mutilation were reinforced. Women were even beaten in public for not covering their toes (see Figure 3.1).

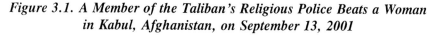

Figure 3.1. A Member of the Taliban's Religious Police Beats a Woman in Kabul, Afghanistan, on September 13, 2001

RAWA (Revolutionary Association of the Women of Afghanistan) insists that suicide among women rose significantly under the Taliban as a result of depression induced by cabin fever. They cite not only being kept within four walls but also the various assaults on women's honor and feelings of helplessness as driving this phenomenon which often took the form of self-immolation.[142]

Prior to 1994, the various governments in Afghanistan were inept, corrupt, and bankrupt, and were dominated by brutal, incessant fighting among mujahedeen warlords. The Taliban consisted of mujahedeen from many Muslim countries, Europe, and China. Some of them were indoctrinated in Pakistan's madrassas. The Taliban's extremely strict and "anti-modern" ideology has been described as an innovative form of Sharia combining Pashtun tribal codes, the Pashtunwali, with Deobandi, Jamaat ul-Islami (JUI) Wahhabism, and AQ ideologies. The Taliban government, which consists almost exclusively of Pashtuns (also known as Pathans), was initially greeted with enthusiasm and relief in Afghanistan. Like the Wahhabi and Deobandis, the Taliban do not consider Shias to be Muslims, declaring the Hazara ethnic Shia group, which comprises 10 per cent of Afghanistan's population, non-Muslims. The Taliban are also against another Muslim sect, Sufis (see Appendix 4).

The Taliban leader Mohammad Omar Abdullah refused to hand over OBL when America demanded this after the 9/11 attacks. The Afghan government fell after the American invasion. When the Taliban were defeated in the war, Mullah Muhammad Omar and OBL allegedly escaped to Pakistan along with many Taliban soldiers. Pashtuns are a majority in Afghanistan, and there is a significant Pashtun population in adjacent Pakistan, in the Khyber Paktunkhwa (KP) province. Pashtuns cross the boundary from both sides of Pakistan and Afghanistan for trade, socialization, and business. Once ensconced in Pakistan, the Taliban formed terrorist camps along the border and sent insurgents to Afghanistan to destabilize the country. With the alleged help of the Inter-Services Intelligence Directorate (ISI), the Taliban conduct guerrilla warfare operations based in the mountainous and largely lawless tribal area along the Pakistan–Afghanistan border.[143] The Taliban leaders, including Mullah Muhammad Omar, are directing the movement and military campaign from Quetta, Pakistan.

With the Pakistan military, and its intelligence service (ISI) publically offering to help initiate and broker talks with the Taliban, this could be the first opportunity for a breakthrough in ending the Afghan war. At this writing, negotiations and reconciliation efforts by Afghanistan President Hamid Karzai and others are in progress, with Taliban leaders including former Afghanistan ruler Mullah Omar, Jalalladin Haqqani, Mullah Nazir, and Gulbuddin Hekmatyar of Hizb-e-Islami. In an effort to help the United States end the war, Karzai convened a *loya jirga,* a mass meeting of Pashtun and other leaders, in June 2010. But this has not much impact on the peace process. The Pakistani Taliban is dominated by three powerful commanders—Baitullah Mehsud, Hafiz Gul Bahadur and Maulavi Nazir—who are based in North and South Waziristan, the hub of insurgent activity in Pakistan's tribal border regions. These three have often clashed among themselves. In late April 2010 the Taliban's advance into the Swat Valley appeared to spread to the adjacent district of Buner. The apparent takeover of the district on April 22, 2010, left the Taliban just 70 miles from Islamabad, the capital of Pakistan, and raised new international alarms about the ability of the Pakistani government to defend itself.[144]

In a peace agreement with the Pakistan government, the Taliban are occupying Swat in Pakistan's KP and have imposed Sharia on the whole area. The Taliban in Pakistan may be able to possess nuclear weapons after they control other areas of Pakistan, possibly causing the disintegration of Pakistan as well as Afghanistan. The Taliban can then spread to Central Asia. Their possession of nuclear weapons is the gravest danger our world faces. There are 4.5 million Tajiks in Afghanistan, and more than two hundred thousand Tajiks living in Xinjiang, the restive Muslim province of

China. Tajiks, who are almost exclusively Pashtun, are against the Taliban. Their leader, Ahmad Shah Masood, was assassinated on September 9, 2001 by two terrorists posing as journalists, just prior to 9/11. His assassination turned the tide in favor of the Taliban, who then had no opposition.

The Uighurs in Xinjiang have been waging war by jihad against Beijing to effect their separatist demands since the 1980s. Hundreds of Uighurs studied in Pakistan madrassas and honed their skills in Afghanistan, first with the Hizb-i-Islami Party and later with the Taliban. Maintaining their base of operations with the Taliban over the past few years, the IMU (Islamic Movement of Uzbekistan) has become one of the region's biggest threats. IMU aims to topple the regime of neighboring Uzbekistan's President Islam Karimov, as part of a jihad that will reach Central Asia. Central Asia, comprising the republic of Kazakhstan, Kyrgyzstan, Tajikistan, Turkmenistan, and Uzbekistan, is the new battleground for radical Islamists (see Chapter 4).[145] After their occupation of the large areas of KP, the Taliban demanded that minority Sikhs in the Swat Valley pay a non-Muslim tax, or *jizya,* under Sharia law for Dhimmis. Although they paid this jizya to the Taliban, the militants want more money and have auctioned the Sikh's property. Yet some commentators believe that the Taliban's goal is localized, with the aim of establishing a greater Afghanistan. The Taliban, who (as mentioned previously) are mostly Pashtuns from the mountainous borderlands of Pakistan and Afghanistan, have fought to keep out Punjabi plainsmen. Pashtuns from the KP are seeking an independent Pashtunistan that would include 41 million people who live in large areas of Pakistan and Afghanistan.[146] Like AQ, the Taliban have been supportive of terrorists' activities outside Pakistan and Afghanistan. All jihadi groups, whether AQ or other terrorist organizations, such as Algeria's Armed Islamic Group or Kashmir's Harakal ul-Mujahideen, cannot operate on their own, and are provided with training facilities by the Taliban. They have terrorized people, making them afraid to speak publicly. The Taliban has beaten and beheaded teachers, school children, doctors, and nurses, and have blown up schools.[147] They have been militarized by the Pakistani Army since the term of General Zia-ul Haq (1924–1988) in the 1980s. Haq was instrumental in developing Pakistan's nuclear capability, with the aid of Dr. Abdul Khan. Haq received generous aid from the Regan Administration, which, upon entering office, set about restoring Pakistani trust in the reliability of the American commitment to Pakistan's independence and territorial integrity. The Administration arduously negotiated a six-year, 3.2-billion-dollar aid package evenly divided between economic and military assistance. The Administration avoided the Symington Amendment by supporting legislation exempting Pakistan from the amendment for the duration of the aid package. The United

States agreed to sell them 40 F-16 fighter bombers to replace the increasingly obsolescent warplanes of the Pakistani Air Force. In addition, U.S. military assistance was designed to fulfill two objectives: to give Pakistan the military capability to repel limited cross-border threats posed by Soviet-backed Afghan forces, and to dissuade Moscow from thinking it could coerce or subvert Pakistan with impunity.[148]

The *New York Times* reporter Dexter Filkins notes that the Taliban machinery would have collapsed long ago without Pakistani advisors and money. "There has been a palpable change in the public perception of the Taliban," says Rifaat Hussain at Qaid-i-Azam University in Islamabad. "When the savagery of their rule was exposed, people began to think, 'This is not the kind of Islam that we want in Pakistan.'" At the same time, Hussain said, the military has navigated its own shift. Previously, the Taliban were seen as "Pakistan's second line of defense against India. Now they're being seen as a very serious threat."[149]

"These people were certified as God's holy warriors by the White House itself. Now they've been transformed into the world's darkest villains. That's complicated," notes Ayaz Amir, a Member of Parliament and a newspaper columnist and army veteran. "But the opinion that Pakistan has no choice other than to fight these people is becoming stronger."[150]

The Taliban, after escaping to Pakistan from Afghanistan, have established Sharia rule in certain areas, including Swat, Waziristan, FATA, and the KP in Pakistan. They have entered into a peace accord with Pakistan, on the condition that they will not interfere with the Pakistani administration. But they have tried to trespass into Burner, which is close to the Pakistan capital Islamabad. In this they were aided and guided by the Taliban leader Baitullah Meshud. Pakistan continues to fight against an existential threat from the Pakistani Taliban and the Afghanistan Taliban at home and abroad.

The Taliban was initially a mixture of mujahideen who fought against the Soviet invasion of the 1980s, and a group of Pashtun tribesmen who spent time in Pakistani religious schools, or *madrassas*, and received assistance from Pakistan's Inter-Services Intelligence agency (ISI). The group's leaders practiced Wahhabism, an orthodox form of Sunni Islam similar to that practiced in Saudi Arabia. With the help of government defections, the Taliban emerged as a force in Afghan politics in 1994 in the midst of a civil war between forces in northern and southern Afghanistan. They gained an initial territorial foothold in the southern city of Kandahar, and over the next two years expanded their influence through a mixture of force, negotiation, and payoffs. In 1996, the Taliban captured Kabul, the Afghan capital, and took control of the national government.[151] The militants (Taliban) are said to be backed up by the jihad organizations, especially the Jaish-e-Mohammad (JeM) and Hizb-ul-Mujahidden (HuM). JeM has been involved in several assassination attempts on top Pakistani officials, including former President Pervez Musharraf. The Taliban members were also responsible for the kidnapping and murder of *Wall Street Journal* reporter Daniel Pearl, and are said to have carried out the attack on the Indian parliament. HuM is the JeM's parent organization and one of the largest militant groups in the world.[152] The Pakistani supported Taliban are linked with the SSP and the LeJ, which are fomenting unrest with respect to Pakistan's sectarian conflicts.

The Taliban receive huge sums of money from the narcotics trade, opium taxes, charities, and other resources outside Afghanistan, despite the U.S. Treasury department's restrictions on channeling funds to terrorists. On October 19, 2009, The *New York Times* reported that terrorists' proceeds from the illicit drug trade alone range from $70 million to $400 million per year worldwide.[153] The Pakistan-based Lashkar-e-Taiba (see Chapter 4) is allied with AQ. It has become a global terrorist organization whose intent is to install a worldwide caliphate and recover past Muslim territories. Along with AQ and the Taliban, LeT is involved in insurgency in Afghanistan. Decision makers within the Pakistani security establishment have not yet internalized the fact that American concerns about LeT date back to the 1990s, and, particularly after the events in Bombay, have increased because of the growing conviction—with much supporting evidence from the U.S. intelligence community—that LeT's activities in Afghanistan, South Asia (outside of India), the Middle East, China, Europe, and North America, make it a direct threat to the United States. AQ in the Arab Peninsula (AQAP), headquartered in Yemen, has become a potential threat to America in the aftermath of 9/11, due to a change in AQ's strategy towards decentralization and the recruitment of new mujahidin in Arab peninsula. One of its top leaders, the Saudi-born American Adnan el-Shukrijumah, has—at age 35—taken over a position once held by 9/11 mastermind Khalid Sheikh Mohammed. A Yemen-American cleric named Anwar al-Aulaqi is another top leader of the AQAP. AQAP has shared its chemical bomb-making technology with al-Shabaab.

And for all her pretensions to Western liberalism, Benazir Bhutto, who followed her father's footsteps to become Prime Minister, was midwife to the Taliban in Afghanistan and stoked jihadist terror in Kashmir—all part of her geopolitical maneuvering against India.[154]

Al-Shabaab

Al-Shabaab, (also known as al-Sahab or al-Shabab, "the Youths") affiliated with AQ since 2007, is a group of Somali Islamists based in Somalia. It has AQ members from Pakistan, Afghanistan, and Sudan, while its top commander, Omar Hammami, is an Islamic convert from Alabama and an American citizen. On February 29, 2008, Secretary of State Condoleezza Rice designated al-Shabaab as a Foreign Terrorist Organization. The consequences of this designation include a prohibition against the provision of material support or resources to al-Shabaab, and blocking of all property and interests in property of the organization that are in the United States. Members of Al Shabaab are prohibited from visiting the United States. These designations play a critical role in fight against terrorism and are an effective means of curtailing support for terrorist activities and pressuring groups to renounce terrorism. Many of Al-Shabaab's senior leaders are believed to have trained and fought with al-Qaida in Afghanistan. Al-Shabaab has used intimidation and violence to undermine the Somali government and has threatened activists who are working to bring about peace through political dialogue and reconciliation.[155] In December of 2008, The *Economist* reported on the rise of the Shabaab:

> Several thousand have signed up in the past year. They attend large training camps in southern Somalia to join the Shabaab, the armed wing of the former Islamic Courts Union where one of the instructors is said to be a white American mujahedeen. They are expected to disavow music, videos, cigarettes and qat, the leaf Somali men chew most afternoons to get mildly high. Thus resolved, they wrap their faces in scarves and seek to fight the infidel. In return, they get $100 a month, are fed, and can expect medical treatment and payments if they are wounded, as well as burial costs and cash for their families if they are killed. Al Shabaab now controls much of south Somalia and chunks of Mogadishu. It took Kismayo a few months ago. The port of Marka, which takes in food aid, fell more recently. Many fighters are loosely grouped around two older jihadist commanders with strongholds near Kenya's border, Mukhtar Robow and Hassan Turki. Mr. Robow celebrated the recent festival of Eid al-Adha by hosting prayers in Mogadishu's cattle market. How sweet it would be at Eid, he told the gathering, if instead of slaughtering an animal in praise of Allah, they would slaughter an Ethiopian. On a visit to Marka he was only slightly less belligerent. He urged reconciliation—except with enemies of Islam. There are many of those, it seems. Hundreds of Somali aid workers, human-rights campaigners and journalists have been killed or exiled. Foreigners have been shot and kidnapped, in two cases just across Somalia's border, in Kenya and Ethiopia [see Figure 3.2]. Where it cannot exert

control, the Shabaab excuses banditry. Borrowing tactics from Afghanistan's
Taliban, it spreads chaos to build a new order.[156]

It controls much of southern Somalia, excluding the capital, Mogadishu. It
is responsible for the insurgency against Somalia's transitional government
and its Ethiopian supporters since 2006. Estimates of Shabaab's size vary,
but analysts generally agree that the group contains ten thousand fighters
and armed men, many of whom are from the Hawiye clan. Experts say the
number of rank-and-file members is less important than the number of
hardcore ideological believers, which could range between three hundred
and eight hundred individuals. Foreign fighters have traveled to Somalia to
fight with Shabaab, as have Somalis from the United Kingdom and the
United States. The FBI says as many as two-dozen Somalis have disappeared from Minneapolis in the past two years. The FBI director Robert S.
Mueller III says one of these individuals was a suicide bomber in an October 2008 attack in Somalia.[157] When it began its insurgency in late 2006, it
used classic guerrilla tactics—suicide bombings, shootings, and targeted
assassinations—to oppose the Somali government and what it perceives as
its allies, from aid groups to the Ethiopian military to African Union peacekeepers. Much of the violence was concentrated in Mogadishu; battles between the Ethiopian military and Shabaab in August 2007 caused roughly
400,000 people to flee the city. The strongest tie between Shabaab and AQ
seems to be ideological. In September 2008, a senior Shabaab leader released a video in which he pledged allegiance to OBL and called for Muslim
youth to come to Somalia. In February 2009, AAZ, AQ's second-in-com-
mand, released a video that began by praising Shabaab's seizure of the
Somali town of Baidoa. The group will "engage in Jihad against the Ameri-
can-made government in the same way they engaged in Jihad against the
Ethiopians and the warlords before them," Zawahiri said.[158] Looking ahead,
there are several measures that will indicate Shabaab's level of strength and
internal coherence: first, whether the group is able to extend its territorial
control to Mogadishu; second, whether Somalia's business community decides to support the group; third, whether the Somali Diaspora continues to
fund Shabaab through the *hawala* money transfer system. (It is not clear
how much money Shabaab currently receives from the diaspora or other
sources.)

Africa recorded 6,177 casualties from 296 acts of terrorism between
1990 and 2002, positioning the continent to rank second in the world, after
Asia, for having the most casualties during that period. Ten countries in
Africa have been subjected to three categories of terrorists' threat: high
(Somalia, Sudan, Algeria, Kenya, and Uganda), intermediate (Nigeria, Ethio-

pia, South Africa), and low (Ghana and Senegal). It is reported that AQ has moved to Somalia and Yemen, leaving Pakistan after being driven from the Swat Valley. The conflict between Muslims in the north and Christians in the south in Sudan (the largest country in Africa) has created more than 3 million refugees in Darfur. In the west of Sudan, Chad is facing an influx of fundamentalists, and in the East of Sudan, Christians of Ethiopia are worried about terrorists inspired by al Shabaab—the most violent terrorists in Africa (see Figure 3.2). Sierra Leone, in the west, with a 60-per cent Muslim population, has been harboring Islamic terrorists for many years. It is famous for its diamond industry—the cause of its decade-long civil war. The United Nations Mission in Sierra Leone (UNAMSIL) released a report stating that in the months prior to 9/11, AQ and the Revolutionary United Front (RUF) of Sierra Leone had purchased massive amounts of weapons by trading native diamonds. The religious genocide in Africa is the worst in recent history. Attacks by the Somalia-based al-Ittihad al-Islami (AIAI) were directed against civilian targets in Ethiopia in the 1990s. The Sudan-based Eritrean Islamic Jihad (EIJ) has conducted attacks inside Eritrea that have killed several civilians and military personnel. The third category of terrorist threats comes from groups including indigenous organizations such as the Lord's Resistance Army (LRA) and Allied Democratic Front (ADF) in Uganda, and the militant wing of the Ogadeni National Liberation Front (ONLF) and Oromo Liberation Front (OLF) in Ethiopia. Both have committed terrorist attacks inside these countries (see Figure 2.3). The LRA has operated out of southern Sudan and the ADF out of the eastern Congo, while the OLF has had, at various times, state support from Somalia, Eritrea, and Sudan.[159] Two Somali Islamic fundamentalist organizations—al-Ittihad and al-Islah—have ties to Wahhabism and receive funding from Saudi Arabia and the Gulf States. The more dangerous of the two is al-Ittihad, which has been on the U.S. terror list since 2001. East Africa, Kenya, Tanzania, Uganda, Somalia, Djibouti, Ethiopia, Eritrea, and Sudan are engulfed in Islamic fundamentalism and terrorism in sub-Saharan Africa. Terrorists killed sixteen people in 1980 at an Israeli-owned hotel in Nairobi. AQ sponsored attacks destroyed the U.S. embassies in Tanzania and Kenya in 1998, they bombed an Israeli-owned hotel north of Mombasa, Kenya in 2002. Sudan has a history of attacks including Black September's 1973 assassination of the American ambassador and deputy chief of mission in Khartoum. Sudan has supported international terrorist organizations; OBL and his deputy al-Zawahari lived in Sudan from 1991 to 1996. All of these countries are either predominantly Muslim or have important Muslim minorities. Sudan, Somalia—including self-declared independent Somaliland—and Djibouti are predominantly Muslim. Ethiopia and Eritrea are about fifty per cent Muslim. Kenya, Uganda, and Tanzania have significant Muslim minorities, while Tanzania's islands of Zanzibar and Pemba are overwhelmingly Muslim. Muslim Sufi sects, who tend to resist the philosophy of Islamic fundamentalism, are strong throughout the region.

These local terrorists accommodate the plans of international terrorists who operate in the area, and are relatively well financed by Saudi Arabia and some Gulf States. The *Washington Post* reports that Al Shabaab, one of the archetypal twenty-first century terrorist groups, claimed responsibility for the coordinated bombings of July 11, 2010, that killed more than 76 people in Kampala, Uganda, as crowds were watching the final match of the World Cup.[160] Al Shabaab's leader, Fazul Abdullah Mohammed, a native of the Comoros Island, was one of the architects of the 1998 bomb attacks on the U.S. embassies in Kenya and Tanzania. He has recruited hundreds of militants to join his organization, including veterans of Iraq and Afghanistan and at least 20 U.S. citizens. His campaign, aligned with al Qaeda, poses a serious risk to the stability of Uganda, Kenya and Ethiopia (see Figure 3.2), all of which have tried to prevent an al-Shabaab takeover in Somalia. Al Shabaab has many sympathizers in America and beyond. Mohammed Mahmood Alessa and Carlos Omar Almonte, two New Jersey Muslim men, were arrested on June 2010, at John F. Kennedy airport in New York, shortly before boarding an Egypt-bound flight. They were allegedly en route to Somalia, possibly to join Al Shabaab.

For over a decade, the United States has considered the Horn of Africa—Kenya, Ethiopia, Djibouti, Somalia, Eritrea, and Sudan—to be a major source of terrorism. Following the 9-11 attacks against the United States, the Horn has come under increased scrutiny as a strategic focal point in the war against terrorism. Here are the situations with respect to each country:

Kenya: In May 2003, the government admitted that a key member of the AQ terror network was plotting an attack on western targets.

Ethiopia: Muslims have not been receptive to Islamic fundamentalism, and they lack centralized power. They tend to identify first with their ethnic kin. Muslims and Christians are geographically intermixed throughout most of the country. Islam in Ethiopia has been benign during the past century.

Djibouti: Its terrorists derive from its transit capabilities rather than its potential as a base for international terrorist organizations. Events since 1999, however, may have increased Djibouti's attractiveness to international terrorists.

Radicalism in Islam

*Figure 3.2. Africa. North of Somalia are Djibouti and Eritrea,
Adjacent to the Red Sea. Ethiopia Lies Between Two
Restive Countries, Somalia and Sudan*

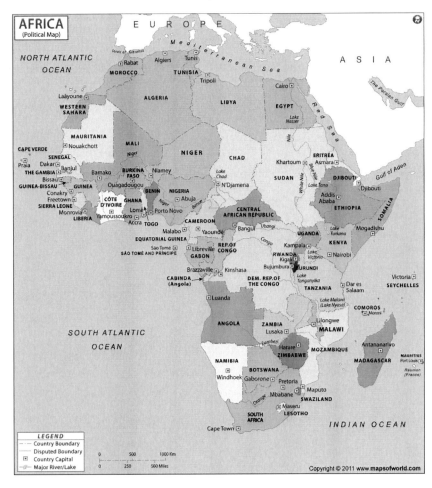

* Courtesy of Kartik Suri.

Somalia: It has played a role in Islamist terrorism, albeit a special-ized one. It has served primarily as a short-term transit point for movement of men and materiel through the porous and cor-rupt border between Somalia into Kenya. Somalia Muslims believe that the Sufi version of Islam, which stresses tolerance, mysticism, and a personal relationship with God, is more con-gruent with their traditions than the Wahhabi Islam espoused by the Shabaab, which calls for strict separation of the sexes and harsh punishments like amputations and stoning.

Eritrea: Its "coalition of the willing" threatens to widen the gap between moderate and radical Eritrean Muslims due to the regime's use of the "war against terrorism" to eliminate all dissent.

Sudan: It is attempting to move in a new direction through serious peace negotiations with the Sudan People's Liberation Army (SPLA) and improved relations with the United States.[161]

Al Qaeda in the Islamic Maghreb

AQ in the Islamic Maghreb (AQIM), based in Algeria, is a violent Sunni terrorist group in Algeria (see Figure 3.2) that has replaced the militant Salafist Group for Call and Combat (GSPC). The GSPC, formed in 1998, is an outgrowth of the extremely violent Groupe Islamique Armée (GIA). All these groups are responsible for killing thousands of civilians. They are spread throughout Algeria, Mali, Mauritania, Niger, Chad, Senegal, Nige-ria, and Somalia. (The Maghreb Union in 1989 was established to promote cooperation and economic integration among Morocco, Algeria, Tunisia, Libya and Mauritania). In the Islamic insurgency following the cancellation of the Algerian 2002 parliamentary election results, there were 200,000 deaths. This insurrection had its beginnings when Algeria's military regime canceled the second round of parliamentary elections in 1992, when it seemed that the Islamic Salvation Front, a coalition of Islamist militants and moder-ates, might win and take power. A government amnesty program and a persistent counter-terrorism campaign by the Algerian Army significantly decreased the number of local terrorists, which at its highest point in the 1990s was estimated to be as high as 28,000. According to the U.S. State Department, the AQIM's membership is now only in the hundreds. Origi-nally, its aims included the overthrow of Algeria's secular military govern-ment and the establishment of an Islamic caliphate: a theocracy based on Islamic law that for twelve centuries spanned the Muslim world. Counter-terrorism experts, however, say that the group's folding into the global AQ structure may indicate a shift to take up the banner of global jihad and collude on future attacks in North Africa, Western Europe, and Iraq. With only a few hundred insurgents, the AQIM maintains control over a vast tract of land that stretches from just north of Timbuktu (Mali), 370 miles (600km) north to Taoudenni near the Mauritanian and Algerian borders. Fuelled by ransoms and income from drug trafficking, it carries out attacks against tourists, police, and other government authorities in Niger, Mauritania, and Algeria, with the ultimate aim of establishing the western end of a future Islamic caliphate that would stretch across North Africa and the Middle East. There is also evidence of contacts between the AQIM and the Shabaab terrorists, creating "an arc of fire" across North Africa.

The LeT group trained many foreigners in their camps in Pakistani-occupied Kashmir, including citizens from France, the United States, and Britain in order to send them back to conduct missions in their home countries. All of these men were directly supported by active members of the Pakistani military and intelligence forces, who provided them with arms, ammunition, and training In order to reinforce his operational capability during the Iraqi insurgency against the United States, the late Abu Musab al-Zarqawi, who headed AQ in Iraq, reached out to high-ranking members of the Algerian group GSPC (Fighting and Preaching Salafist Group). After Zarqawi's death in 2006, the leadership of GSPC swore formal allegiance to AQ, meeting with high-ranking AQ members (who probably included AAZ) in the tribal zones of Pakistan, and changing its name to "AQ in the Maghreb Lands" (AQIM). The aim of AQIM is to destabilize the Maghreb, mainly Algeria, and extend its activities into the Sahara using Mali—a very weak country—to set up a stronghold in Mauritania. It is now recruiting members in Senegal and has established operational connections with cells in Niger, some of which are suspected of links with radical Islamists in Nigeria. This is a visible sign of the increasing role of Africa as a breeding ground for terrorism.[162]

Slavery

Slavery, which makes one individual the property of another, is the ultimate denial of human freedom and dignity. From the days of the Islamic conquests, Muslims forced their culture and heritage onto occupied lands, eradicating all remnants of local customs and civilizations. Arab conquerors took *kuffar* (non-Muslims, or infidels) as slaves to keep and to sell. Slavery was practiced in the days of the Prophet Mohammed, with slaves auctioned in bazaars and Muslim markets. Slaves have been used as domestic help, sex workers, concubines, and warriors. Islamic slavery is based on the Trilogy of the Quran, the *Sira* (which tells of Mohammed's life) and *Hadith* (tradition; see, e.g., Quran 2.178, 4:92, 5:89, 12:29, 12:30, 16:71, 16.75; 30.28). The Islamic scholar Ibn Taymiyya comments: "Slavery is justified because of the war itself; however, it is not permissible to enslave a free Muslim. It is lawful to kill the infidel or to enslave him, and it also makes it lawful to take his offspring into captivity."[163] The history of slavery goes back to the inception of Islam. Ronald Segal writes:

> The harem of Abdal Rahman III (912–961) in Cordoba contained over 6000 concubines! And the one in the Fatimid Palace in Cairo had twice as many. The Caliph in Baghdad at the beginning of the 10th Century had 7000 black eunuchs and 4000 white eunuchs in his palace.[164]

Mohammad disliked the black race immensely and referred to them as "raisin heads" several times in the *Hadith* (which contains sayings and actions of the Prophet or his approval of something said or done in his presence). Throughout the *Hadith* blacks are also referred to as *abeds*, which means "black" in Arabic, and is also synonymous with the words "slave" or "filth." In fact, Arab Muslims have enslaved blacks for 1400 years, and the black slave trade is still thriving in the Sudan and Mauritania. In examining the relationship between blacks and Islam, readers will be surprised to find that throughout history, Islam has placed blacks on the same level as barn animals. Moreover, the barn is where most enslaved blacks are relegated after they are kidnapped and forced to convert to Islam or die. It is reported that in Islam, several millions of slaves in 1400 years of Islam, with a multimillion of Africans.[165] The slave trade was associated with Muslim imperialism, supremacism, and a culture that seeks to subjugate non-Muslims, or convert them to Islam by force. This is slightly different from white supremacy, in that there is no such thing as a racial conversion—but the analogy is close enough to be useful. Sadly, that supremacy is inherent in Islam, inasmuch as it claims to be the one true religion and seeks converts. Islamic supremacy and slavery have been intermingled through the ages, and in the eyes of many Muslims, they are thought to be part of the lost glory of Islamic civilization. OBL and others are using jihad to try and restore this antedated worldview, in which Islam remains a prisoner of its historic memory. The Prophet himself possessed at least fifty-nine slaves at one stage or other, besides thirty-eight servants both male and female.[166] As Bostom relates, slavery, tribute, and booty became the main props of the new Arab aristocracy. The slavery in Islam is interwoven with the laws of marriage, sale, and inheritance, and its abolition would strike at the very foundation of the code of Mohammedism. According to Will Durant:

> In the year 997 a Turkish chieftain by the name Mahmud became sultan of the little state of Ghazni, in eastern Afghanistan. Pretending a holy zeal for destroying Hindu idolatry, he swept across the frontier with a force inspired by a pious inspiration for booty. He met the unprepared Hindus at Bhimnagar, slaughtered them, pillaged their cities, destroyed their temples and carried away the accumulated treasures of centuries. . . Sometimes he spared the population of the ravaged cities, and took them home to be sold as slaves.[167]

Rejecting slavery and suppression, the Vikings of Scandinavia and other invaders of the Roman empires adopted native cultures and eventually blended in with those they had conquered. But the Arab invaders converted conquered lands to Islam and then imposed Islamic culture and language on other far more civilized cultures. This was accomplished by force in Persia, Syria, South Asia, and South East Asia. Christian missionaries, on the other hand, have failed to gain any significant foothold in Muslim countries by either persuasion or economic benefits, after centuries of attempting to do so.

Jihad, Hanbalists, and Reformists

Beginning in the eighth century, Persian Emperors and Central Asian Kings came to the Indian Subcontinent to plunder, smashing countless Hindu idols and looting India's cities of as many of their jewels, women, and rare animal species as they could carry back. The first to arrive was Mohammed Bin Qasim of Iran (695–715) who invaded Sindh (Pakistan). In 997, the Afghanistani Mahmud of Ghazni razed ten thousand temples including those at Thanesar, Mathura, and Somanath. He took their fabled wealth of gold and jewels to Ghazni to convert it into one of the world's greatest Islamic centers, after having killed more than fifty thousand Hindus. In 1738, Nadir Shah of Iran sacked Delhi, slaughtering an estimated thirty thousand people, and looting a billion rupees worth of gold and jewels—including the fabulous Peacock Throne, which he took back to Iran with him.[168] But injustices to Hindus have remained unnoticed and unaccounted for, largely because they have been non-violent and disinclined to seek revenge. The foundation of Indian civilization and culture was not immoral, brutal, and godless acts of occupation, plundering, forced conversion, and murder, but a divine spirituality. Nobel Laureate V.S. Naipaul writes of Arab imperialism:

> The Arab faith, the Arab language, Arab names, and the fez: twelve hundred years after the conquest of Sindh (Pakistan), this affirmation of separateness, of imperial and racial and religious authority: there probably has

been no imperialism like that of Islam and the Arabs. The Gauls, after five hundred years of Roman rule, could recover their old gods and reverences; those beliefs hadn't died; they lay just below the Roman surface. But Islam seeks as an article of faith to erase the past; the believers in the end honor Arabia alone; they have nothing to return to.[169]

The Sepoy mutiny in the nineteenth century was a jihad against British. In 1803, Shah Abd al Aziz Dihlawi proclaimed India as a *Dar al Harb*, house of war. Wahhabist Syed Ahmad wrote that "jihad was a means by which Muslims could regain their supremacy in India," on the pretext of expelling the British. He continues: "The Muslims were fighting for a renewal of Muslim domination, not for freedom for all Indians." Thus, their fight in 1857–1858 was clearly conceived as a jihad. Syed Ahmad's goal was to renew the Muslims' domination of the Hindus.

For this reason he was killed by the Sikhs in 1831. Nonetheless, Indian Muslim writings—from this period until the present day are dominated by apologists concerning the role of jihad, the Muslim relationship toward the Hindus.[170]

From the ninth to the twelfth centuries, Islam in all Muslim regions (with the exception of Cairo and Baghdad) underwent a cultural and a territorial crisis under the influence of Ash'arite and Imam al-Ghazali. Yet it found a safe, nonbelligerent territory in India, with its tolerant and mystical people. The seven hundred years of Muslim ruler in India is a history of coercion, abduction, forced conversion, and the destruction and desecration of thousands of temples and educational places. It is also a history of terrible brutality, looting, subjugation, barbarism, and rampant immorality, marking one of the grimmest periods in Indian and world history. Unlike in Iran, Iraq, Syria, Egypt, Turkey, and some parts of Northern Africa, Central Asia, and Europe, Islam could not vanquish Hinduism. Yet it did tarnish India's Hindu culture, including its cuisine, art, music, architecture, and literature, depleting the country's wealth and plunging it to poverty and misery. More recently, however, Indian Muslims have remarkably enriched music, films, the software industries, science, painting, and the freedom movement.

Worldwide Islamization and terror had a new beginning in 1938, with the discovery oil in Saudi Arabia, and the subsequent rise of fundamentalist schools in Asia and Africa. People from Asian and African Muslim countries adopted Arabic culture, because they and their children wanted to be Saudi. When they migrated to the West, as mentioned in Chapter 2, they carried the baggage of Arabic culture and customs to their adopted countries. With the establishment of radical mosques and anti-Western values in these countries, they became the breeding ground for terror whose object is to install Sharia throughout the world.

The Muslim intellectual Sir Ahmed Khan (who was opposed to India's independence) warned that if people do not shun blind adherence, if they do not seek that Light which can be found in the Quran and the indisputable *Hadith*, and do not adjust religion and the science of today, Islam will become extinct in India.[171] Traditional Islam, formulated by Persian al-Afghani, his student Egyptian Muhammad Abduh, and his student the Tripoli-born Rashid Rida, was reinforced by the radical views of Persian Ibn Hanbal (founder of Hanbal *fiqh*), the Iranian bornal-Ghazali, and the Muslim theologian Ibn Tayymiyya. With this theological support, radical Islam grew under the twentieth century revolutionaries like al Banna, Qutb, Maududi, and OBL and his associates. These revolutionaries were guided by Abdallah Ibn al-Mubarak (736–797), Muhammad Ibn Isma'il al-Bukhari (810–870), and Muhammad Jarir al-Tabari (838–923). Al-Bhukari, born in Bukhara in Central Asia, is the leading author on radical Islam. *Sahih Al-Bukhari* his book on *Hadith*, is acknowledged as being comparable in importance to the Quran.

United in Hatred

Muslims regularly kill each other in Pakistan, Lebanon, Turkey, and Iraq. Hamas and Fatah are fighting to take control of Gaza. Kurds have lost more people in Turkey than Palestinians in Israel. King Hussein bombed Palestinians in Jordan. Iran and Iraq have fought huge wars with millions of casualties. Hafez al-Assad leveled several PLO refugee camps and the Muslim Brotherhood terrorist training sites. Saddam Hussein used poison gas in Yemen and Iraq. Despite their centuries-old religious and sectarian differences, as well as ethnic national and territorial conflicts, Sunni and Shiite extremists are united in their hatred of the infidels and in their desire to establish Sharia around the world. It is naïve and dangerous to ignore the following collaborations:[172]

1. Iran provides help to Afghan Sunnis and to the Algerian FIS.
2. Islamic Parliament Speaker Ayatollah Mehdi Karrubi, a Shiite mullah, supporting Sunnis OBL, AAZ, Turabi, and the Algerian Abdallah Jaballah.
3. The operation carried out by the Hezbollah in Hejaz, an Iranian-financed outfit, with the help of the Sunni militant group "Sword of the Peninsula."

4. Sunni groups linked to AQ killed 17 U.S. servicemen in a suicide attack on the USS Cole off the coast of Yemen, with help of Teheran.

5. In Central Asia's Tajikistan and Uzbekistan, Tehran has for years supported two Sunni movements, the Rastakhiz Islami (Islamic Awakening) and Hizb Tahrir Islami (Islamic Liberation Party).

6. In Azerbaijan, Iran supports the Sunni Taleshi, an-anti American group opposed to the Azeri Shiite, a pro American party.

Terrorism in Other Religions

Religion should be a non-violent, spiritual process that rejects violence in any form, even as a means to get closer to God. But violence and religion have merged to become the new mantra for terrorism. "What is striking about religious terrorism," writes the UC Santa Barbara Professor Mark Juergensmeyer,

> is that it is almost exclusively symbolic, and performed in remarkably dramatic ways. Moreover, these disturbing displays of violence have been accompanied by strong claims of moral justification and an enduring absolutism, characterized by the intensity of the religious activists' commitment and the trans-historical scope of their goals.[173]

Further, the historian John Dower of MIT believes that the religion does still matter and the religion has impacted the World wars, in particular to the World War II.[174] Terrorism has no place in religion, as it is contrary to the concepts of love, tolerance, forgiveness, kindness, and compassion. It may be said that terrorism has no religion. However, Juegensmeyer observes that: "This is one of history's ironies, that although religion has been used to justify violence, violence can also empower religion."[175] Some of this religious violence has been glorified as "cosmic war" that will imitate victories in the religious wars of the past; for example, the battle of Badr.

Terrorism is not just the work of Muslim fanatics. A Hindu fanatic, Nathuram Godse, gunned down Mahatma Gandhi during a prayer meeting; a Tamil Hindu girl carried out the suicide bombing of India's prime minister Rajiv Gandhi; Yigal Amir of Israel assassinated prime minister Yitzhak Rabin; Lord Mountbatten (the last Viceroy of India) was killed by an Irish Republican Army (IRA) terrorist; and Timothy McVeigh, a Christian, bombed the Alfred Murrah building in Oklahoma City, killing 168 people. McVeigh was indoctrinated by Christian Patriots and other right-wing extremist and White supremacist groups, and by reading the book *The Turner Diaries*, written by their leader William Pierce. The book serves as a Bible to many White Supremacist groups.[176] There is the notorious Ku Klux Klan, a radical Christian supremacy group, which has burned black churches and schools, and has been involved in the murders of civil rights leaders. Religious violence occurs in all five major religions, Buddhism, Christianity, Hinduism, Judaism, and Islam. In the name of religion, terrorism has been prevalent for centuries.

Buddhism

The noble truths of Buddhism—the fourth largest religion after Christianity, Islam, and Hinduism—are as follows: mental suffering arises from attachment to desires; suffering ceases when attachment to desire ceases; and freedom from suffering is possible by practicing the Eightfold Path. Buddhism is based on freedom from cravings, desire, and anger, and on universal peace and harmony, known as *Nirvana*. A religion with one billion followers in China, Japan, South East Asia, and India, it was founded by Gautama Siddhartha (563–483 B.C.). The edict not to kill or inflict pain on others is integral to Buddhist thought. Periodically, however, Buddhist monks have encouraged or initiated violence. The primary examples in the twentieth and twenty-first centuries have taken place in Sri Lanka, where Sinhala Buddhist groups have committed and encouraged violence against local Christians and Tamils. The leader of Aum Shinrikyo, a Japanese cult, committed a lethal sarin gas attack in the Tokyo subway on March 20, 1995. He used misguided interpretations of Buddhist and Hindu beliefs to justify killing 12 people and injuring 5000. Aum Shinrikyo was founded by Shoko Ashara. In the spring of 1985, as he claimed, while meditating on the beach, he was visited by the Hindu God Shiva, who appointed him God of Light with responsibility for building an ideal society. Buddhism remains more tolerant than the other great religions and ideologies—which is no small matter at a moment in history when the world seems threatened once more by fundamentalism.[177]

Christianity

Christianity has been described as a synthesis of Jewish metaphysics and Greek ideas of political freedom. Christianity has around 2.2 billion adherents, making it the largest religion in the world. It is a monotheistic, Abrahamic religion like Islam and Judaism. During the Reformation, the Catholic Popes tortured and killed millions of Protestants. In the sixteenth century, ten thousand to possibly one hundred thousand Calvinist Protestants were killed by Catholic mobs. The Christian Crusades (1071–1291) inspired the most bloodthirsty cruelty and the greediest vandalism of medieval times, in which millions of non-Christians were killed. Christian armies and missionaries, even devout Christians, as ordered by their ecclesiastical leaders, have pillaged, plundered, and committed both forced conversion and mass murder. These heinous acts have been carried out in Rwanda, Tahiti, Hawaii, and other places in the Pacific, the Caribbean, North America, Mexico, the Philippines, India, Burma, and China.[178] The Army of God (AOG) (1982–present; United States; Christian radicals), an underground extremist anti-abortion group, is responsible for abortion clinic bombings and attacks on doctors who perform abortions. For more than a generation, the Ugandan military has been fighting a brutal Christian terrorist organization—the Lord's Resistance Army (L.R.A.)—which originally wanted to overthrow the Ugandan government but now slaughters and maims people in the name of fighting for the Ten Commandments.[179] Christian terrorist groups, in India, most notably the National Liberation Front of Tripura (NLFT) and the National Democratic Front of Bodoland, are responsible for thousands of deaths and the destruction of Buddhist shrines in North East India: at Assam, Nagaland, Manipur, Tripura, Meghalaya, Mizoram and Arunachal Pradesh, Sikkim, and the Darjeeling district of West Bengal. Their objective is to create a separate Christian country. These terrorist groups are funded by Christian charities from America, Australia, and New Zealand. There has been a significant increase in Christian conversion by violence and threats in the North East of India by several Christian missionaries (see Table 3.3).

Table 3.3
The Percentage of Christians in North East India

State	1901	1951	1991
Arunachal Pradesh	NA *	NA *	10.29
Assam	0.4	2.00	3.32
Manipur	0.016	11.84	34.12
Meghalaya	6.16	24.66	64.58
Mizoram	0.05	NA	85.73
Nagaland	0.59	46.05	87.47
Tripura	0.08	0.82	1.69

* Not available: 051 in 1961
* Source: Christian Conversions and Terrorism in North-East India (3-29)

Many violent White Supremacist groups have been formed under the auspices of race and religion. These include: the American Nazi Party, Aryan Nations (AN), Aryan Youth Movement, Church of the Creator (COC), Ku Klux Klan (KKK), National Democratic Front, National Socialist White Peoples' Party, National Socialist White Workers' Party, Skinheads, The Holy Order or the Order (Bruders Scheweigen), The New Order, The Silent Brotherhood, United White Peoples' Party, White Aryan Resistance, and White Revolution. The KKK, founded in 1866, is probably the largest of these, with more than 150 chapters, and 6000 members. They are against Jews, Africans, Asians, Hispanics and other people of color. At least one Democratic Senator, the late Robert Byrd of West Virginia, was at one time a member of the KKK, but later regretted it. Byrd said: "I know now I was wrong. Intolerance had no place in America. I apologized a thousand times . . . and I don't mind apologizing over and over again. I can't erase what happened."[180]

Hinduism (aka *Santana Dharma*)

Hinduism was founded between 5500 and 2600 B.C., or possibly even earlier. Today it has more than one billion adherents. Unlike Judaism and Christianity, Hinduism does not accept religious converts. The belief is that you cannot be Hindu unless you have both a Hindu father and a Hindu mother. Hinduism does not possess an empire other than its cultural heritage in South East Asia. Its philosophy was best described by Radhakrisnan.[181] There is no terrorism or organized violence within Hinduism, as this religion is kept completely separate from state governments and politics. Some authors mistakenly label the Thugs as an early terrorist group in Hinduism. Thugs were not even a cult, just robbers who attacked and executed travelers or caravan merchants. They were outcasts, living in jungles and remote places, and not part of any one cult. While they did kill as *bhog*, an offering, to Kali, the goddess of destruction and death, to earn her blessings to go heaven, true followers of Kali are not Thugs. British historian Dr. Mike Dash estimated that the Thugs killed 50,000 persons in total, based on his assumption that they were around 150 years before their eradication in the 1830s. (See Mike Dash, *Thug: the true story of India's murderous cult*, Granta Books, London, 2005). Thugs came from all backgrounds and castes: they were Muslims, Hindus, Sikhs, Brahmins, and untouchables, warriors and farmers, as desperate a bunch as one could hope to gather.[182]

In 1984, Hindu fanatics killed Sikhs in the aftermath of their assassination of Indian Prime Minister Indira Gandhi (1917–1984). Gandhi had tried to crush the secessionist movement of Sikh militants led by Jarnail Singh

Bindranwale, and in June 1984, she ordered an assault upon the holiest Sikh shrine in Amritsar, the Golden Temple. This "Operation Bluestar" was intended to flush out the militants holed up inside the temple. The operation caused the death of Bindranwale and damaged of the Golden Temple. On October 31, 1984, Mrs. Gandhi was assassinated at her residence by two of her own Sikh bodyguards. The 1984 anti-Sikh riots were triggered by this event. Over the next four days, as many as 3100 Sikhs were killed in retaliatory attacks in Delhi and other places. It is alleged that three Hindu fundamentalist groups, the Rashtriya Swayamsevak Sangh (RSS), Vishwa Hindu Parishad (VHP), and the Bajrang Dal, were involved in the 1999 killing of an Australian priest, Graham Staines, and his two sons for his role in converting local tribes to Christianity in Orissa, India. A noted French journalist, Francis Gautier of *Le Figaro*, refutes the murder of Staines on religious grounds. He writes, "if ever there was persecution, it was of the Hindus at the hands of Christians."[183] He gave, as an example, the burning of churches in Andhra Pradesh on June 8, 2000, which was attributed to the RSS. Later it was proved that this was actually the handiwork of Indian Muslims, at the behest of the Pakistani Inter Services Intelligence Agency, to foment hatred between Christians and Hindus. Gautier charges Christian missionaries with not realizing that they have been honored guests in India for two thousand years, and that they are betraying those that gave them peace and freedom. He notes, "Hinduism, the religion of tolerance, the coming spirituality of this millennium, has survived the unspeakable barbarism of wave after wave of Muslim invasions, the insidious onslaught of Western colonialism."[184]

On December 23, 2007, Swami Laksmanananda Saraswati, a Hindu monk aged 82, was coming home at night to his hut at Khandamal, Orissa, in India. A bus carrying Sugriba Singh, a Christian BJD Member of Parliament (affiliated with the BJP) obstructed the road. As reported, the Swami was attacked and was mortally injured. This murder caused a riot among Hindu and Christian tribes in the tribal lands of Khandamal, resulting in three deaths (one Christian and two Hindus) and the burning of churches and Hindu places of worship. It was alleged that Maoists had fomented the riot. In 1992, Hindu radicals demolished a mosque, and in 2002, they killed several thousand Muslims in Gujarat, India. Terrorists from Pakistan shouted to the victims in The Taj hotel that the Mumbai attacks on November 2008 were a revenge of Muslims for these acts by Hindus.

Another major act of desecration was the destruction of the Babri Masjid, an ancient mosque close to the city of Ayodhya in the Indian state of Uttar Pradesh. The location of the building was traditionally believed by Hindus to be the birthplace of Lord Ram (Ram *Janmabhoomi*). According to some sources, in 1528 a Hindu temple had been destroyed by Emperor Babur to build the mosque. The issue of the mosque had already been raised by Hindu militants in 1949-1950, but mobilization against it was stopped by the determination of the Government, led by Jawaharlal Nehru. The problem was brought up again in the 1980s, when the Indian political landscape had deeply changed, in neglect of Nehru's strict secularism. Nehru, along with his father Motilal, had authored the *Nehru Report* of 1928, emphasizing the secularism in the Indian Constitution: "There shall be no state religion; men and women shall have equal rights as citizens."[185] As Samuel Huntington writes: "Only in Hindu civilization were religion and politics also so distinctly separated In Islam, God is Caesar; in China and Japan, Caesar is God, in Ortodoxy, Godis Caesar's junior partner."[186] Jinnah rejected the 1928 report, but his August 11, 1947 report to the Pakistan Constituent Assembly was similar. In fact, the religious nationalist movement had grown dramatically, mainly due to the efforts made by the RSS—the main nationalist organization in India, with more than one million members—and its affiliated groups, collectively known as Sangh Parivar. The BJP leader, Prime Minister Atal Vajpayee, characterized the December 1992 destruction of the Babri mosque, by a Hindu fundamentalist group, as a "blunder of Himalayan proportions." This had been the oldest Muslim shrine in India, built in honor of the Mogul Emperor Babur in 1527. In the ensuing riots that took place in many major Indian cities, more than 3000 people were killed. The demolition of the Babri Masjid was barbaric and sacrilegious. On several occasions, Vajpayee made it clear that discrimination on the basis of religion "is not our way in India, not in our blood or in our soil."[187]

India's Shiv Sena (the Army of Shiv, referring to the Emperor Shivaji) was founded in 1966 as a far-right political party with a parochial objective. Although the party's primary base is still in Maharashtra, India, it has tried to expand with the objective of securing a pan-Indian base, in support of a broader Hindu nationalist agenda. To this end, it has aligned itself with the BJP. The Sena started placing more weight on the Hindutva ideology in the 1970s, as did RSS. The Sena's founder, Bal Thackeray, is known to have made xenophobic remarks against Muslims and neighboring Pakistan.

Judaism

This ancient Abrahamic religion has some beliefs in common with Christianity and Islam. It has over fifteen million adherents around the world, comprising a very powerful community. Jews believe that African Americans and other inhabitants of North and South America are the twelve lost tribes of Israel. They have been persecuted by Christians and Muslims in several countries, particularly by the Nazis. To avoid this persecution, they have migrated to many other countries, even to India several thousand years back. Judaism was one of the first foreign religions to arrive in India in recorded history, and they have never been discriminated against in India. Most of them live in Manipur, Calcutta, and Mizoram; one fourth of India's Jews live in the city of Mumbai.

Historically, as far back as AD 66–73, the Jewish sect known as the Zealots were engaged in public assassinations of Roman officials and their Jewish collaborators. One former prime minister of Israel was alleged to have been involved in terrorism: Menachim Begin, who was associated with a terrorist group called Irgun that took part in terrorist acts in the 1940s. This included the attack on the King David Hotel in Jerusalem, which killed 91 people. Nevertheless, Begin received the Nobel Peace Prize in 1978. Yitzhak Shamir was associated with the Stern Gang, a terrorist group that was responsible for a string of political assassinations. Ariel Sharon was indirectly responsible for the Sabra–Shatila massacre in which over 1000 people (mostly Palestinians) were murdered. The Zionist movement began in the 1880s, in the hopes that the Jewish nation might return to the land of Israel. Jewish people were suffering from discrimination and persecution in Europe and elsewhere, and many of them emigrated from Europe to Israel. Their principal leader was Theodore Herzl. On November 29, 1948 the State of Israel was established, and in February 1949, David Ben-Gurion became its first prime minister. The land was divided into two states, Palestine and Israel. This Arabian–Palestinian–Israeli land, particularly the city of Jerusalem, is a sacred place for three monotheistic religions, Islam, Judaism, and Christianity. Terrorist groups have formed to pursue a Jewish state with political sovereignty in Israel. Some Jewish terrorists groups are listed below:

Hashomer: Zionist organization founded in April 1907. The purpose of the Hashomer was to provide guard services for Jewish settlements. It was headed by a committee of three: Israel Shochat, Israel Giladi, and Mendel Portugali. They adopted local dress, and many of the customs of the Bedouins, Druze, and Circassians. It ceased to operate after the founding of the Haganah in 1920.

Irgun: A militant Zionist group that operated in Palestine between 1931 and 1948. The Irgun was the armed expression of the ideology of Revisionist Zionism, which was founded by Ze'ev Jabotinsky. He expressed this ideology as "every Jew had the right to enter Palestine."[188] Some infamous attacks by Irgun were the bombing of the King David Hotel in Jerusalem on July 22, 1946, and the Deir Yassin massacre (perpetrated together with the Stern Gang) on April 9, 1948.

Stern Gang: A Zionist extremist organization in Palestine, founded in 1940 by Avraham Stern (1907–1942). Fanatically anti-British, the gang repeatedly attacked British personnel in Palestine and even invited aid from the Axis powers. The British police retaliated by killing Stern in his apartment in February 1942.

Lehi: An armed, underground Zionist faction (established in 1940) in Palestine that had as its goal the eviction of the British authorities from Palestine, to allow unrestricted immigration of Jews and the formation of a Jewish state. The name of the group became "Lehi" only after the death of its founder, Avraham Stern.

Kach: This Jewish extremist group was founded by Israeli–American rabbi Meir Kahane, who sought to restore a Biblical, "ethnically pure" Israel. After Kahane was assassinated in the United States, his son, Binyamin Kahane, formed Kahane Chai, or "Kahane Lives." Both groups were involved in several terrorist acts.

Religion and Politics

Is there a solution to defeating religious violence? A negotiated settlement by an international body? On November 13, 2008, a high-level meeting of the UN General Assembly decried the use of religion to justify the killing of innocent people, and demanded that terrorist acts of intolerance, discrimination, and harassment among those of different faiths and cultures be stopped. The idea that God's sovereignty over the universe makes Islam's Sharia laws "ethically superior to those of other civilizations" is an ignorant and illiterate view of other religions, to say the least. To claim that "Islamic teachings are more humane than the Sermon on the Mount and the message of (Gandhi, 1983)" (non-violence) is partisan, thoughtless, and untenable. A society becomes cruel and brutal only when it is devoid of compassion, love, and equanimity. The murder of the Arya Samaj leader, Swami Shraddhananda, by a Muslim in December 1926 caused deep Hindu rage. Professor Ayesha Jalal writes:

> Some Hindus baldly asserted that there could be no peace on earth unless the Quran was banned. Such erroneous and ill-founded charges, Maududi complained, led even Gandhi to say that Islam was born in an atmosphere

of violence where the sword was paramount and that it was still in too
much evidence among Indian Muslims[189]

(Gandhi later issued a retraction). In the wake of the 9/11 attacks and the
London bombing, the whole world is gravitating to have the Quran banned;
even many prominent Muslims and a silent majority Muslim women and
girls have echoed the feelings of Hindus.

The Muslim world, in turn, was misled by Maududi. Pakistani scholar
Fazlur Rahman was critical of Maududi's Jamaat-e-Islami (JI), terming it
"not merely inadequate, but positively harmful" in Islamic education. He
also wrote that Maududi was "by no means an accurate or a profound scholar"
and "blatantly he contradicted himself from time to time on such basic issues as economic policy or political theory. . . . Maududi displays nowhere
the larger and more profound vision of Islam's role in the world."[190] The
BBC News reported on July 16, 2010, that the Bangladeshi government had
ordered mosques and libraries across the country to remove all books written by the late Maududi, who had encouraged "militancy and terrorism."[191]
The Bangladeshi government has ordered nearly 24,000 libraries attached
to mosques to remove his books immediately. Maududi's JI (founded in
Lahore, Pakistan on August 26, 1941) had terrorist links with the Hizbul
Mujahideen (HuM). A 1993 U.S. Congressional Report stated that Hizbul
Mujahideen has been supported by and is closely affiliated with Jamaat-i-
Islami, "from which they receive funding, weapons and training assistance
beyond the ISI's contribution."[192] The All-Parties Hurriyat Conference
(APHC)'s former chairman Syed Ali Shah Geelani, who also headed the
political wing of the Jamaat-e-Islami and was a follower of Maududi, became active in the secessionist movement in Jammu and Kashmir. In the
summer of 2008, matters came to a head after the J&K state government
granted temporary land-use rights for facilitating the annual pilgrimage to
the Amarnath shrine in south Kashmir. Geelani claimed this was a conspiracy to settle Hindus in the region: the authorities were working "on an
agenda of changing the demography of the State." "I caution my nation,"
he warned, "that if we don't wake up in time, India and its stooges will
succeed and we will be displaced."[193] Jammu and Kashmir Chief Minister
Omar Abdullah's key lieutenant, Devinder Rana, offered Geelani the right
to lead the protests in return for calling off rioters who had paralyzed
Kashmir's civic life that summer. "In essence, the deal involved ceding
control of urban Kashmir to the Islamist movement—in return for peace."[194]

Homegrown Terrorists

According to F.B.I. Director Robert Mueller:

> Groups affiliated with al Qaeda are now actively targeting the United States
> and looking to use Americans or Westerners who are able to remain unde-
> tected by heightened security measures—as seen with the attempted airline
> bombing on Christmas Day 2009 and the failed car bombing in New York's
> Times Square in May. In addition, it appears domestic radicalization and
> homegrown extremism is becoming more pronounced, based on the num-
> ber of disruptions and incidents.

The terrorists include: a. Domestic Terror: Jose Padilla, Detroit Sleeper
Cell. Six days after September 11, 2001, Nidal Hasan, Lackawanna Six.
Nearly a year after September 11, Fort Dix Plot, The Portland Seven, and
Mohamed Osman Mohamud, b. Terror Abroad: Anwar al-Awlaki, John
Walker Lindh, David Headley. Pakistan Five, Somalia Plot, and Shirwa
Ahmed.[195] There has been an emergence of many homegrown, radicalized
expatriates, and even third-generation immigrants or visiting students in-
volved in attacks in Britain, America, Denmark, Sweden, Spain, France,
Norway, Italy, Canada, and Australia. Countries including Britain and
America provide support to these expatriates by providing asylum or by
patronizing their extremist mosques and organizations, thus supporting the
efforts of separatist movements such as those in Kashmir and Xinjiang. As
the journalist Marc Sageman notes:

> The concept of home grown indicates that the members of these Muslim
> Diaspora groups in the West were born and radicalized in the host coun-
> try. In the second wave, host Western governments did not appreciate that
> these groups radicalized locally because their ideology was foreign, im-
> ported from the Middle East. It was assumed that the second generation of
> Muslim immigrants would not pose problems to their host countries, but
> would direct their ire against the Middle East (Egypt, Jordan, Yemen, and
> Algeria), Europe (Bosnia), Central Asia (Chechnya), or South Asia (Kash-
> mir).[196]

These home-grown terrorists have been brainwashed by radical mosques,
Internet propaganda, multiculturalism, segregated living, separatist organizations, and relentless radical visitors who beg their support for the separatists' movement, or to establish theocratic governments in their lands. An
active plot to wage Mumbai-style shooting sprees in Europe has been seeded
in Pakistan's tribal areas. Europeans worry about citizens who have traveled to Pakistan to train at militant camps. It was reported in the *Washington*

Post of September 30, 2010 that the head of Germany's Federal Office of Criminal Investigation, as quoted in a recent interview with the Berlin newspaper *Der Tagesspiegel*, said that there was evidence that at least 70 Islamic radicals from Germany had undergone paramilitary training in Pakistan, and that 40 are thought to have gone on to fight coalition forces in Afghanistan.[197] Despite the two wars in Afghanistan and Iraq, American drone strikes of possible terrorist sanctuaries in Pakistan's tribal areas, and the choking off of terrorists' international funding, AQ continues to be a great threat. By 2007, if not before, it was clear that AQ had enjoyed a resurgence in Pakistan's tribal belt, and that it remained committed to conducting attacks on a global scale, not just in Afghanistan and Pakistan. In 2007, officials drew worldwide attention when they broke up an AQ cell in Denmark and an Islamic Jihad cell in Germany. In 2008, police and intelligence forces uncovered several terrorist plots in Europe (including Spain and France) linked to militants in Pakistan's tribal areas. Jihadists taking part in each of these operations received training and other assistance in Pakistan. British authorities initially believed that the July 2005 terrorist attacks in London were purely the work of home grown Muslim terrorists. But subsequent evidence compiled by British intelligence agencies indicated that key participants, including Mohammed Sidique Khan and Shahzad Tanweer, visited Pakistani terrorists' camps where they were trained by AQ operatives between November 2004 and September 2005. In September 2005, Ayman al-Zawahiri said that AQ had been "honored to launch" the London attacks. Several authors[198] have documented AQ activities: "In the Wills of the hero brothers, the knights of monotheism," al-Zawahiri remarked, "may God have mercy on London attackers, make paradise their final abode and accept their good deeds."[199] The jihadist-salafist AQ network imagined them to be the spark that would ignite the volatile frustration of the disenchanted ones in the Muslim world and stoke a firestorm. They believed that once the great American Satan was defeated, a sweeping tide of jihad could overtake the modern world.

The Terrorist's Mind

Terrorism is a psychological weapon that is used to instill the fear of death and destruction, at a relatively low dollar cost. This low-intensity, asymmetric warfare is designed to inflict the maximum amount of damage and panic on the largest number of people. It can be accomplished with bullets, bombs or by a keyboard via the Internet. Terrorists are in general violent people, aggressive, action oriented, and stimulus hungry, with narcissistic mental disorders. They are eager to destroy their enemies, and are easily moved by propaganda supplied by terrorists' networks. They believe in the *Umma*, the worldwide community of Muslims: "I am a Muslim; Muslims are oppressed in a faraway land, so I am oppressed. And one Muslim to another is like a single body. If one part is in pain, the other part will also feel it."[200] It has been observed that some of the terrorists are not successful in their personal, educational, and professional lives and they have bleak futures. They are in the 18–22-year-old age group, and many come from crowded refugee camps with high unemployment rates. The mullahs indoctrinate these youths to commit aggression by subjecting them to emotional stress, and enticing them a place in Paradise, as a *saheed* (martyr) after their deaths. Mullahs exploit the suffering of youth in the camps and cloud their minds with deep prejudice against non-Muslims, whom they say are threatening the existence of their race. Terrorists beg to be suicide bombers so as to become a *saheed*. They believe that passage to heaven is their reward. Many come from broken families and have felt abandoned by their parents. According to noted psychologist Jerrold Post:

> The combination of personal feelings of inadequacy with the reliance on the psychological mechanisms of externalization and splitting leads them to find especially attractive a group of like-minded individuals whose credo is, "It's not us—it's them; they are the cause of our problems."[201]

Some terrorists just love flying first class, and being visible in TV footage. They feel that violence brings them success, and they enjoy having their families supported generously by terrorist groups or State-sponsored organizations. Some terrorists are attracted by power, privilege, prestige, and wealth, others by revenge, hatred, revulsion, and an eagerness for political change. Some psychologists believe that terrorists are psychopaths, due to the terrorists' violent nature, hatred of others, and willingness to participate in indiscriminate killings. As psychologist Walter Reich wrote in *Understanding Terrorist Behavior,* "Anarchist with millenarian visions, anticolonialists with broad but realizable goals, and groups that simply want to call attention to particular situations they find offensive, all use terror."[202] Terrorists are motivated by radically alienated, frustrated, bitter individuals, and support aggrieved communities and extremist ideologies. In exchange for committing acts of terrorism, they are promised a safe shelter in a neighboring country, besides a place in heaven. They feel that their death at the hands of the law would be condemned by human rights agencies, and would provoke denunciations and retaliation, besides having a receptive audience of billions of people. They are aware that there is no global consensus on combating terrorism, because there is divergence in strategic and economic interests. Many wish to become terrorist celebrities.

FBI agent Art Cummings, who has interrogated young jihad prisoners, finds these terrorists to be determined and dedicated. He concluded that coercive and degrading techniques would not change terrorists' mindsets, though most terrorists look at their future and are susceptible to creature comforts as well. The New York Times' best selling author, Ronald Kessler puts it this way,

> You are going to somehow coerce a young jihadist who has just traveled a thousand miles through desert and unfamiliar territory to go put his ass on the line to die in really austere, dirty, nasty, rocky conditions, wholly untrained. And you think you're going to somehow make this guy uncomfortable? You found this guy in a cave and drinking only water. And what are you doing to this guy that will compel him to do anything except hate you more.[203]

As noted earlier, the terrorists are not depressed, severely disturbed, or crazed fanatics. Jerrold Post has observed: "It is not individual psychopathology, but group, organizational, and social psychology, with particular emphasis on "collective identity," that provides the most powerful lens through which to understand terrorist psychology and behavior.[204] For Muslim groups, especially nationalist–separatist terrorist groups, this collective identity is established extremely early, so that from childhood on, "hatred is bred in the bone," probably in madrassas and mosques. It has been found that very young boys and girls become suicide bombers even without knowing what Islam is.

Radicalization and Deradicalization

Radicalization is a process of indoctrination to violent jihad. Deradicalization, a reverse process of radicalization, is a non-violent component of counter-terrorism. Radicalization is a psychological war against unbiased and emotional minds, transforming a passive mind into militancy, as with adopting the extreme political and religious ideologies of jihad, to become *fidayeen,* suicide bombers. The main reason for radicalization is the group dynamics of the radical madrassas and mosques, in which terrorists learn about real or perceived injustices, and are trained in preparation for future actions, including state repression. Sometimes terrorists are promised jobs and challenging assignments. Radicalization permeates them through friends, schools, and environments, as happened to a young Nigerian man, Umar Farouk

Abdulmutallab. On December 25, 2009, Abdulmutallab allegedly tried to set off an explosive device on Northwest Airlines Flight 253 between Amsterdam and Detroit. Radicalization is occurring far away from Muslim lands, at prestigious institutions from British universities to American college campuses elsewhere. For example, Abdulmutallab was the past president of the Islamic society of the College of Engineering in London. In fact, the past three presidents of the Islamic Society have been affiliated with terrorism. Some of these Islamic societies have connections with Hizb ut-Tahrir, which has been banned by several governments. It is reported that Muslim countries in the Middle East have donated $400 million or more to British universities, while disregarding the ostentatious refusal by British academics to acknowledge that they have Islamist extremists among their students. An Islamist underworld exists within these universities, in Muslim prayer rooms and Islamic societies, all of which are passively tolerated by their administrations and faculty.[205] According to the *Wall Street Journal* of January 9, 2010,

> The list of Muslim students from the U.K. who had become active in Islamist terrorism is substantial and growing. . . . A poll (YouGov) showed that one in three Muslim students believed that killing in the name of their religion could be justified. That figure almost doubled to 60 per cent among respondents who were active members of their universities' ISOCs (British university Islamic Society). Other results included the discovery that 40 per cent of Muslim students polled supported the introduction of sharia law into British law, and that 58 per cent of students active in their ISOC supported the idea of the introduction of a worldwide Caliphate.[206]

The radicalization of prison inmates through conversion to Islam is on the rise. They are told that child molestation and rape are not considered crimes in Islam, and that Islamists are fighting to abolish injustice in society. Several imams and as well as prison chaplains have been involved in the conversion of the inmates. On May 23, 2009, the *New York Post* reported:

> Amid all the shocking details in the disrupted plot to bomb Bronx synagogues and fire missiles at American military aircraft, one component of the case should come as no surprise—three of the alleged culprits converted to radical Islam in prison. Radical Islamists have targeted prison populations for recruitment for years. That's where Jose Padilla, suspected of plotting to detonate a dirty bomb and convicted of conspiracy to murder people overseas and of providing material support to terrorists, converted and was radicalized. That's where a California man, Kevin James, created his own cell, called the Jam'iyyat Ul-Islam Is-Saheeh (JIS), and recruited

other inmates to plot attacks against military and Jewish targets in and around Los Angeles. In New York, the man who was the head Muslim chaplain for state prisons considered the 9/11 hijackers to be martyrs. Warith Deen Umar spent 20 years working with New York prisons, overseeing the hiring of Muslim chaplains and leading prayer services.[207]

Radicalization of prison inmates with state funding is regrettable, and needs to be reviewed by Counter-Terrorism organizations. The *New York Times* reporter Sarah Kershaw writes that "researchers often differ over the path to radicalization. Some boil it down to religion, others to politics and power, others to an array of psychological and social influences."[208] Programs for deradicalization, sometimes called disengagement, dialogue, or rehabilitation, are available to counter the radicalization process. De-radicalization is a process of working to combat extremism in groups or individuals that have already committed violence. Yet it implies a cognitive shift. There are three aspects to these deradicalization programs:

Behavioral—requires the abandonment of violence (disengagement)
Ideological—de-legitimizes the use of violence
Organizational—focuses on structural changes within an organization's leadership

The United Nations refers to these tactics as counter-terrorism. Their own programs include: the Counter-Terrorism Implementation Task Force (CTITF); the "1267 Committee" of the Security Council; the UN Educational, Social and Cultural Organization (UNESCO); the UN Office on Drugs and Crime (UNODC); and the Counter-Terrorism Executive Directorate (CTED). The UN's four key action areas are: addressing conditions conducive to terrorism; preventing and combating terrorism; building and developing state capacity to counter terrorism, and developing the UN's role in this regard; and ensuring respect for human rights in counter-terrorism activities. In the aftermath of a series of deadly terrorist attacks in 2003, the Saudi Arabian government created a counter-terrorism strategy focused on rehabilitating extremists and preventing their violent ideology from spreading. Roughly 1400 out of 3000 individuals have completed the program, and only 45 have been re-arrested. The Saudi program uses the three main tools, "force, money, and ideology." This program of prevention, rehabilitation, and aftercare ("PRAT") targets detainees who have been identified as supporting terrorism—a multi-pronged approach to dealing with "deviant groups." The primary approach of the government has been to work with doctors, psychologists, and clerics on eroding support for extremist ideologies. Famously, a fatwa issued during Ramadan 2007 called for high-profile ideologues to recant their positions. The deradicalization programs in Saudi Arabia and Europe attempt to rectify terrorism as a psychological matter. They include psychological counseling, vocational training, art therapy, sports, and religious reeducation. The Saudi government also runs a terrorism prevention program that monitors religious leaders, schoolteachers, and websites. In summary, the process includes the abandonment and delegitimization of violence, and structural changes within an organization's leaderships, along with material, economical, educational, and psychological rehabilitation. Disengagement is a behavioral change, breaking off participation in terrorism, whereas deradicalization is seen as a cognitive change in belief or ideology. Most important, it is necessary to establish an amnesty program that transforms terrorists into dignified citizens.

Several studies have shown that the process by which disaffected people are radicalized into homegrown terrorists takes place in four steps:

1. Pre-radicalization (via mosques, schools, the workplace, prison, friends and socialization, radical Imams, other radical groups, and outside financial support, and the lure of instant notoriety, impressing and attracting sexual partners, and the promise of marriage)
2. Identification and Belonging (exploring and adopting the ideological tenets, perceived injustice and humiliation, obsession of the loss of past glory, Sharia as the cure for Muslims' problems, intolerance, vengeance, victimization, and hatred)
3. Indoctrination (irrational beliefs and commitment to ideas such as the illegitimacy of civil government, corrupt democratic process, selective passages from the Quran, martyrdom)
4. Action (Muslims are under siege and it is a holy duty to engage in violent jihad)

Deradicalization[209] is a vital component of the counter-terrorism (see Chapter 6). Without it, the terrorist's mind will mutate from holy virtues to unholy vagaries.

Notes

1. Lincoln. *Holy Terrors Talking about Religion after September 11*, 2003, 57–58.

2. Mark Lilla. *The Stillborn God.* New York, NY, Random House, 2008, 308-309.

3. Armstrong. *Muhammad.* 2006, 119, 132.

4. Albert L. Weeks. *The Choice of War: The Iraq War and the Just War Tradition.* Santa Barbara, CA: ABC-CLIO, 2009, 34; Wafa Sultan. *A God Who Hates.* New York, St. Martin's Press, 2009, 45, 208.

5. Armstrong. *Muhammad.* 2006, 162.

6. *Shia versus Sunni, the World's Longest Running Feud,* Nazeer Ahmed, 2009, http://www.irfi.org/articles/articles_551_600/shia_versus_sunni.htm; "History of a conflict." Rachel Aspden, Published 12 February 2007, *New Statesman,* http://www.newstatesman.com/politics/2007/02/sunni-shia-iran-iraq-lebanon; Kung, Hans. *Islam,* 2007, 195.

7. Adnkronos International, *Regime Change in Iran,* November 28, 2005, http://regimechangeiniran.com/index.xml.

8. Dawood. *The Quran,* 1990, 83.

9. Armstrong, *Muhammad,* 119, 132, 150.

10. The Origins of the Shia-Sunni Split, by Mike Shuster, February 12, 2007, http://www.npr.org/templates/story/story.php?storyId=7332087.

11. "Behind the Sunni-Shi'ite Divide," Bobby Ghosh, *Time Magazine,* February 12, 2007, http://www.time.com/time/magazine/article/0, 9171, 1592849, 00.html.

12. Hazleton. *After the Prophet.* 2009, 10, 62-64, 108, 194, 209.

13. Frederik Coene. *The Caucasus: An Introduction.* Oxford, UK, Routledge, 2009, 77-78.

14. Bostom, *Legacy of Jihad.* 65, 365, 479, 523.

15. Armstrong, *Muhammad.* 2006, 119, 132.

16. Ruthven, *Islam in the World.* 1984, 96, 129, 146.

17. Serge Trifkovic. *The Sword of the Prophet.* Boston, MA, Regina Orthodox Press, 2002, 48, 51, 109-113; Warraq. 2003, 349.

18. Wolpert, *A New History of India,* 2004, 107.

19. Armstrong, *Muhammad,* 2006, 21-165.

20. Ruthven, *Islam in the World,* 1984, 24, 30, 99, 131, 141-180.

21. Chopra, *Muhammed,* 2010, 261-267.

22. Pfaff, *The Irony of Manifest Destiny,* 2010, 651–652.

23. Kissinger, "The Debate We need to Have." *New York Times,* April 7, 2008.

24. Maoist Insurgency:India's War Within, by Devyani Srivastava, la renaissance de l'Inde, 2009, 77-86, http://www.societe-de-strategie.asso.fr/pdf/agir43txt8.pdf; Terror Groups in India by Carine Zissis, November 27, 2008, CFR Backgrounder, http://www.cfr.org/india/terror-groups-india/p12773.

25. Arundhati Roy, *The God of Small Things,* New York, N.Y. HarperCollin Publishers/ India Ink, New Delhi, India, 1997, 215.

26. Fareed Zakaria, "Learning to Live with Radical Islam." *Newsweek,* February 28, 2009; Daniel Markey, *Securing Pakistan's Tribal Belt,* Council on Foreign Relations Press, July/August 2008 http://www.cfr.org/pakistan/securing-pakistans-tribal-belt/p16763; Jalal, Transcript before the United States Commission on Inter-

national Religious Freedom, March 17, 2009; U.S. Muslim Engagement Project, *A New Direction for U.S. Relations with the Muslim World*, Report of the Leadership Group on U.S. Muslim Engagement, September 2008, http://www.sfcg.org/programmes/us/pdf/Changing%20Course.pdf, compiled by Madeline Albright and others and Klein, *Surrendering to Islam,* FrontPageMagazine.com | Wednesday, November 14, 2007, http://archive.frontpagemag.com/readArticle.aspx? ARTID=28875.

27. *Holy Challenge: A New Chapter in Christian–Muslim Relations*, by John F.Cullinan, National Review Online, September 29, 2006.http://www.nationalreview.com/articles/218859/holy-challenge/john-f-cullinan.

28. Laurent Langman and Douglas Morris, "Islamic Terrorism: From Retrenchment to Ressentiment and Beyond." in Harvey Kushner (Ed.), *Essential Readings in Political Terrorism* (New York: Gordian Knot Press, 2002).

29. Freedom House, Annual Report, 2006. Peter Ackerman, *Chairman,* Freedom House, 1301 Connecticut Ave. N.W. Fl. 6, Washington, DC 20036 *http://www.freedomhouse.org/uploads/special_report/49.pdf.*

30. Buchanan, *Day of Reckoning*, 143-149; Phillips, *Londonistan, 60, 69*; *Schlesinger,* 1991, 55, 58, 67, 70, 71-79.

31. *Allah is our goal; the Messenger is our model; the Quran is our constitution; jihad is our means; and martyrdom in the way of Allah is our aspiration.* September 18, 2007, http://rightvoices.com/2007/09/18/%E2%80%9Callah-is-our-goal-the-messenger-is-our-model-the-quran-is-our-constitution-jihad-is-our-means-and-martyrdom-in-the-way-of-allah-is-our-aspiration%E2%80%9D/; John Esposito, *Political Islam*, Boulder, Colorado, Lynne Riener Publishers, 1997, 218, 241.

32. John Esposito, "Claiming the Center: Political Islam in Transition." *Harvard International Review, Political Islam in Transition*; May 6, 2006 HIR Issue: http://www.unaoc.org/repository/Esposito_Political_Islam.pdf; https://www.csidonline.org/9th_annual_conf/Mohammed_Ayoob_CSID_paper.pdf

33. Mohammed Ayoob, "Political Islam: Image and Reality." *World Policy Journal,* Vol. XXI, No. 3, 2004.

34. Naipaul, 1998, 251.

35. Douglas Streusand, "What Does Jihad Mean?" *Middle East Quarterly*, September 1997. Bernard Lewis, *The Political Language of Islam*, 72. David Cook, *Understanding Jihad*, Berkeley, CA, University of California Press, 2005, 141, 165-166.

36. al-Ghazali, *The Book of the Decisive Treatise*, translated by Charles Butterworth, (Provo, UT: Brigham Young University Press, 2001); al-Ghazali, *The Incoherence of the Philosophers*, translated by Michael Marmura (Provo, UT: Brigham Young University Press, 1997). Raymond Ibrahim, *Qaeda Reader*, 116, 137.

37. "Suicide bombers go global." by Assaf Moghadam November 21, 2005; *New York Times*, November 21, 2005.

38. Joshua Muravchik, "For Radical Islam, the End begins." *Washington Post,* June 27, 2009; David M. Haugen, Susan Musser, and Kacy Lovelace (Eds.), *Islam*, 63-74, 158-165; John Esposito, *The Unholy War*, 5-9, 15, 18, 29-35; Chaliand and

Blin (Eds.), *The History of Terror, 221-398*; Norman Podhoretz, *World War IV,* 188; Paul Berman, *Terror and Liberalism*, 74-75.

39. Jonathan Mark Kenoyer, *Ancient Civilization of the Indus Valley*, New York: Oxford University Press, 2005, 62-64, 139, 161.

40. Joshua Muravchik, "For Radical Islam, the End begins." *Washington Post,* June 27, 2009.

41. Pape, *Dying to Win*, 27-126.

42. Andrew Hansen and Lauren Vriens, *Al-Qaeda in the Islamic Maghreb (AQIM)*, Council on Foreign Relations, July 21, 2009 www.cfr.org/publication/ 12717/.

43. Lauri Freedman, *A Choice of Enemies*, 2008, 109-192.

44. *Pakistan's Jihad's Factories*, by Ben Barber, (Islamic Terrorism in India) http://islamicterrorism.wordpress.com/2009/02/20/.

45. Robert Fisk, "The Cult of the Suicide Bomber." *The Independent,* March 14, 2008; Dan Eggen and Scott Wilson, "Suicide Bombs, Potent Tools of Terrorists Deadly Attacks, Have Been Increasing and Spreading Since Sept. 11, 2001." *Washington Post*, July 17, 2005.

46. John Esposito, "On Faith." *Washington Post*, January 11, 2010.

47. al-Ghazali, *The Book of the Decisive Treatise*, translated by Charles Butterworth, (Provo, UT: Brigham Young University Press, 2001); al-Ghazali, *The Incoherence of the Philosophers*, translated by Michael Marmura (Provo, UT: Brigham Young University Press, 1997). Raymond Ibrahim, *Qaeda Reader, 116, 137*; Praveen Swami, The Autumn of Kashmir's Islamist Patriarch, *The Hindu*, August 20, 2010. Nabil Nofal, Al Ghazali, *Prospects: the quarterly review of comparative education* (Paris, UNESCO: International Bureau of Education), vol. XXIII, no. 3/4, 1993,. 519-542 www.ibe.unesco.org/publications/ThinkersPdf/ghazalie.pdf; Hans Kung, *Islam*, 195, 547-576.

48. Maulana Maududi, "Jihad in Islam," *Islamist Watch*, www.islamistwatch. org/texts/maududi/maududi.html.

49. Ibn Rushd, *The Incoherence of the Incoherence*, translated by Simon Van Den Bergh London: E.J. W. Gibb Memorial Series, 2008.

50. "The Muslims in the Middle." by William Dalrymple, *The New York Times*: August 16, 2010.

51. Fazlur Rahman, *Islam and Modernity*, 157–158. Fazlur Rahman, *Revival and Reform in Islam*. Fazlur Rahman, *Islam*, 217.

52. Abdelwahab Meddeb, *The Malady of Islam* New York: Basic Books, 2003, 54.

53. Reilly, *The Closing of the Muslim Mind*, 2010, 200.

54. Armstrong, *Islam*, 281-285, 293; *Muhammad*, 79, 119, 143-144.Bostom, 2008, 165-174.

55. "The Sunni-Shiite Terror Network." by Amir Taheri, *The Wall Street Journal*, March 29, 2008.

56. Raymond Ibrahim, *The Al Qaeda Reader*, 105, 117-118, Malise Ruthven, *A Fury for God*, London, UK, Granta Books, 2002, 185, 278., Gilles Kepel, *Jihad,* Cambridge, MA, HUP, 2002, 86-87, 221, 282.

57. Douglas Streusand, "The Neglected Duty." *The Middle East Quarterly,* September 1997.

58. Anthropoetics 8, no. 1 (Spring / Summer 2002) *The Four Waves of Rebel Terror and September 11* David C. Rapoport. http://www.anthropoetics.ucla.edu/ap0801/terror.htm.

59. Nicholas Kristof, "Islam, Virgins and Grapes." *New York Times*, April 22, 2009.

60. Allawi, *The Crisis of Islamic Civilization*, 97, 113, 114, 253-254.

61. "What the Taliban ideology means." Editorial, *The Dawn*, April 19, 2009.

62. Allawi, *The Crisis of Islamic Civilization*, 253-254.

63. Abul Maududi, *Jihad in Islam*, www.muhammadanism.org/Terrorism/jihad_in_islam/jihad_in_islam.pdf.

64. "The Kashmir Connection: A Puzzle." by Tim Weiner, *New York Times*, Dec. 7, 2008.

65. *Bin Laden Targets India, International Terroism Monitor: Paper No.47*, by B.Raman, April 25, 2006, http://www.southasiaanalysis.org/%5Cpapers18%5Cpaper1776.html.

66. *Stratford Global Intelligence*, April 26, 2006 www.stratfor.com/india_bin_ladens_call_kashmirs_militants.

67. Lee Harris 2007, 228. Ruthven, *Islam in the World*, 196-197; Bawer, *Surrender, 44, 175, 186, 255.*

68. Joshua Muravchik, For Radical Islam, the End begins, *Washington Post,* June 27, 2009; John Esposito, *The Unholy War*, 21-32; Chaliand and Blin (Eds.), *The History of Terror, 200, 225, 286-291;* Norman Podhoretz, *World War IV*, 188; Paul Berman, *Terror and Liberalism*, 74-75.

69. Burleigh, *Blood and Rage*, 346-352.

70. Olivier Roy, *Globalized Islam*. New York, N.Y. Columbia University Press, 2006, 317; Jeffrey Cozzens, "The Culture of Global Jihad: Character, Future Challenges, and Recommendation," *The International Center for the Study of Radicalization and Political Violence*, October 2008 www.icsr.info/publications/papers/1238519802ICSRJeffCozzensReport.pdf; *Jihad Networks in Pakistan and Their Influence in Europe*, July 2008 Evan F. Kohlmann Presentation before the III International Course on "Jihad Terrorism: Contingency Plans and Response" organized by Pablo Olavide University and the Granada University; July 10, 2008; www.nefafoundation.org/miscellaneous/FeaturedDocs/nefapakcamps0708.pdf.

71. "Little Rock Shooting Suspect Joins Growing List of Muslim Converts Accused of Targeting U.S." by Joseph Abrams, Fox News, June 2, 2009.

72. "Muslim converts target Germany." by Roger Boyes, *Times*, London, September 6, 2007.

73. "Afghanistan President Hamid Karzai Passes Controversial Law Limiting Women's Rights." by Jim Sciutto, Bruno Roeber, and Nick Schifrin, Kabul, *ABC News*, August 14, 2009, Chalind and Blin, 2007, 55.

74. Hoffman, *Inside Terrorism,* 161.

75. Pamela Taylor, "A Modern Muslim." *Washington Post*, July 11, 2010.

76. An-Na'im, 2008, 132-133, 146, 148, 155-157, 163, 169, 171; Delong-Bas, 2004, 93-123.

77. Durant, *Our Oriental Heritage,* 1935, 459, 460.

78. An-Na'im, 2008, 163.

79. Huntington, *The Clash of Civilization.* New York, Touchstone Books, 1997, 263.

80. *Thoughts On Pakistan,* by Dr Ambedkar, by Sanjeev Nayyar, March 2003 [esamskriti@suryaconsulting.net] http://www.esamskriti.com/essay-chapters/Thoughts-on-Pakistan-by-Dr-Ambedkar-11.aspx; Pakistan or The Partition of India, by B.R. Ambedkar, Part IV. http://www.ambedkar.org/pakistan/40E1.Pakistan%20or%20the%20Partition%20of%20India%20PART%20IV.htm; Dr. *Babasaheb Ambedkar and Women's Question,* compiled and edited by Lalitha Dhara, http://www.ambedkarcollege.org/forms/Ambedkar_Book_women.pdf.

81. "Media-savvy designer Islamists must not distract us from the real danger, From Denmark to Detroit the threat of violence is ever present." Timothy Garton Ash, *Guardian,* January 13, 2010.

82. *Developments in Radicalisation and Political Violence,* Editor Prof. Harvey Rubin, University of Pennsylvania, Dr. John Bew, ICSR, King's College London, January 2, 2010., Al Muhajiroun andIslam4UK; May 2010 http://icsr.info/publications/papers/1276697989CatherineZaraRaymondICSRPaper.pdf.

83. *The Abrogator and Abrogated Qur'anic Verses,* http://www.answering-islam.org/BehindVeil/btv10.html, David Bukay, "Peace or Jihad, Abrogation in Islam." *Middle East Quarterly* Fall 2007, 3-11; Kung, *Islam:* 2007, 573-574.

84. Delong-Bas, *Wahhabi Islam,* 243-244; Ruthven, *A Fury for God 160;* Ruthven, *Islam in the World,* 160, 197, 207-212 Esposito, *Political Islam.* 1997, 98, 100-103.

85. Ziauddin Sardar, The struggle for Islam's soul, *The New Statesman,* 18 July 2005; 2007, 105, 110.

86. Hillary Mayell, *Thousands of Women killed For Family Honor,* National Geographic News, February 12, 2002.

87. Dennis J. Wiechman, Jerry D. Kendall, and Mohammad K. Azarian, "Islamic Law: Myths and Realities," CJ International, V 12, N 3, May-June 1996.

88. Tahira Shahid Khan, *Chained to Custom* "The Review", 4-10 March 1999, 9; http://www.universitydissertations.com/dissertations/Religion/Honour-killings.php.

89. *Pakistan: Honour Killings of Girls and Women* (Amnesty International, 1999) www.amnesty.org/en/library/asset/ASA33/018/1999/en/9fe83c27-e0f1-11dd-be39-2d4003be4450/asa330181999en.PDF. A. C. Niemeijer, *The Khilafat Movement in India, 1919–1929* (Netherlands: N.V. De Nederlandsche Boek-en Steendrukkerij V/H. Yossef Bodansky (2007), 362.

90. Nidra Poller, Sharia-Sanctioned Death vs. Western Toleration, *Wall Street Journal,* September 7, of 2009; Susie Steiner, *Sharia Law,* Guardian.co.uk, 20 August 2002.

91. Mike Thomas, *Orlando Sentinel,* Sunday, August 23, 2009, Mike Thomas, Orlando Sentinel Advocates for Honor Killing: "the rule of law will send Rifqa

back to Ohio," http://atlasshrugs2000.typepad.com/atlas_shrugs/2009/08/mike-thomas-orlando-sentinels-advocates-for-honor-killing-the-rule-of-law-will-send-rifqa-back-to-oh.html.

92. The Muslim Chaplain of Harvard University advocates the killing of ex-Muslims. Taha Abdul-Basser: Wa-iyyakum. http://www.skepticfriends.org/forum/topic.asp?TOPIC_ID=11420.

93. Nidra Poller on Rifqa Bary in the Wall Street Journal: Sharia-Sanctioned Death Vs. Western Toleration, September 07, 2009, http://atlasshrugs2000.typepad.com/atlas_shrugs/2009/09/nidra-poller-on-rifqa-bary-in-the-wall-street-journal-.html.

94. Lewis, *Islam and the West*, 173.

95. Bostom (Ed.), *The Legacy of Jihad, 199* Delong-Bas, *Wahhabi Islam*, Bat Ye'or, *Juifs et Chrétiens sous l'islam, les dhimmis face au défi intégriste* (Paris: Berg International, 1994). This theme is developed in Bat Ye'or, *Jihad and Dhimmitude. Where Civilizations Collide* (Cranbury, NJ: Farleigh Dickinson University Press /Associated University Press, 2002).

96. Burleigh, *Blood and Rage*, 349.

97. Delong-Bas, *Wahhabi Islam*, 243-244; Filkins, *The Forever War,* 41, 274, 276.

98. Text from Abu Mus'ab al-Zarqawi Letter (a letter that shows the path to victory and defeat in Iraq) globalsecurity.org; Zarqawi Posted on Thursday, February 23, 2006 5:09:29 PM by jmc1969 Filkins, 2008, 269, http://www.freerepublic.com/focus/news/1584456/posts.

99. Delong-Bas, 2004, 243-244.

100. A. Wahid, "Right Islam vs. Wrong Islam: Muslims and non-Muslims must unite to defeat the Wahhabi ideology." *Wall Street Journal,* December 30, 2005.

101. Benjamin and Simon, *The Age of Sacred Terror*, 62.

102. Ali K. Chishti, "Punjab: the New FATA." *The Daily Times*, June 7, 2010.

103. *Deobandi Islam: The Religion of the Taliban, 2001, The Deobandi Debate Terrorist Tactics in Afghanistan and Pakistan*, by Tayyab Ali Shah: Terrorism Monitor Volume: 8 Issue: 21, May 28, 2010, www.globalsecurity.org/military/library/report/2001/Deobandi_Islam.pdf.

104. Tahir Kamran, *Evolution and Impact of Deobandi Islam in the Punjab* (Lahore: G.C. University, 2008) www.gcu.edu.pk/FullTextJour/Hist/V3N205/P28-50.PDF.

105. "The Jihadi Terrain in Pakistan: An Introduction to the Sunni Jihadi Groups in Kashmir." by Nicholas Howenstein, *Journal of International. . .* "India in 2008," *Asian Survey*, January/February 2009, Gilles Kepel, *Jihad:* 2002, 100-104. Peter Bergen and Swati Pandey, "The Madrassa Scapegoat." *Washington Quarterly* 29, no. 2 (Spring 2006): 117-125; Alexander Evans, "Understanding Madrasahs." *Foreign Affairs* 85, no. 1 (January-February 2006); *Studies in Conflict & Terrorism,* 27:489–504, 2004; "Militant Recruitment in Pakistan: Implications for Al Qaeda and Other Organizations." C. Christine Fair, U.S. Institute of Peace.

106. Haqanni, *Pakistan*, 4-50.

107. Yasser Latif Hamdani, "Extremists' War on People's Islam." *Daily Times* (Lahore, Pakistan), July 5, 2010.

108. Malabar Rebellion, ttp://www.enotes.com/topic/Malabar_Rebellion, "The Mappilla Rebellion, 1921: Peasant Revolt in Malabar." Robert L. Hardgrave, *Modern Asian Studies*, Vol. 11, No. 1 (1977), Cambridge University Press, 58.

109. *Pakistan: Honour Killings of Girls and Women* (Amnesty International, 1999) www.amnesty.org/en/library/asset/ASA33/018/1999/en/9fe83c27-e0f1-11dd-be39-2d4003be4450/asa330181999en.PDF. A. C. Niemeijer, *The Khilafat Movement in India, 1919–1929* (Netherlands: N. V. De Nederlandsche Boek-en Steendrukkerij V/H. H. L. Smits's Gravenhage, 1972), Yossef Bodansky (2007). 362.

110. Holly Fletcher, "Jamaat al-Islamiyya." *Foreign Affairs*, May 30, 2008. Audrey Kurth Cronin, Huda Aden, Adam Frost, and Benjamin Jones, "CRS Report for Congress: Foreign Terrorist Organizations," (Washington, DC: Library of Congress Congressional Research Service, February 6, 2004) www.fas.org/irp/crs/RL32223.pdf.

111. Nine/eleven Commission report, final report of the National Commission, 362.

112. Douglas Streusand, "The Neglected Duty." *The Middle East Quarterly,* Sept. 1997.

113. Steve Coll. 2008, 103–123. Esposito, *The Unholy War.* 21, 23, 25, 29.

114. Riedel, "AQ Strikes Back." *Foreign Affairs,* May/June 2007.

115. Rashid, *Descent into Chaos*, 265, 361.

116. Wright, *The Looming Tower*, 109.

117. *Freedom Ride, what is ur opinion of the quote 'one mans freedom fighter is another mans terrorist'?* Posted on December 15th, 2009 by admin.http://www.svitakfreedomride.com/freedom-quote/what-is-ur-opinion-of-the-quote-one-mans-freedom-fighter-is-another-mans-terrorist.

118. Barnett Rubin and Ahmed Rashid, "Pakistan, Afghanistan and the West." *Foreign Affairs,* November/ December 2008.

119. Murawiec, *The Mind of Jihad*, 2008, 324–325.

120. Kilcullen, *The Accidental Guerrilla,* 35, 83, 87, 224, 230-231.

121. Bobbitt, *Terror and Consent*, 545.

122. Bernard Lewis, "The Arab World in the Twenty-first Century." *Foreign Affairs,* March/April 2009.

123. Christopher Blanchard, *Congressional Research Service Report RL 32759, AQ: Statements and Evolving Ideology* (Washington, DC: Library of Congress Congressional Research Service, June 20, 2005).

124. Terry McDermott, "The Mastermind." *The New Yorker*, September 13, 2010.

125. *New Yorker Magazine*, Sept. 13, 2010. "The Mastermind, Khalid Sheikh Mohammed and the making of 9/11." by Terry Mcdermott, http://tmcdermott.com/911stories.aspx.

126. Marta Sparago, *Terrorist Recruitment: The Crucial Case of Al Qaeda's Global Jihad Terror Network* (New York, NY: New York University Center for

Global Affairs, Spring 2007) www.scps.nyu.edu/export/sites/scps/pdf/global-affairs/
marta-sparago.pdf; John Farmer, Jr., How to Spot a Terrorist, *New York Times*,
September 27, 2010.

127. Douglas Murray, "Preventing the Next Mumbai." *Wall Street Journal,* Oct.
5, 2010.

128. Thiessen, *Courting Disaster,* 476-483.

129. D'Souza, *The Root of Obama's Rage,* 195; Charles Krauthammer, "Obama
Hovers From on High." *Washington Post,* June 12, 2009.

130. William Drozdiak, "NATO Turns Attention to Islamic Extremists." *International Herald Tribune,* 9 February, 1995.

131. "Al Qaeda Trained at Least 70, 000 in Terrorist Camps, Senator Says."
Los Angeles Times, July 14, 2003.

132. "Senator Bob Graham Remarks to the Council on Foreign Relations." Moderator: Gerald Seib, Washington Bureau chief, *The Wall Street Journal,* Speaker:
Bob Graham, Member, U.S. Senate (D-Fla.) March 26, 2004, Council on Foreign
Relations. A congressional investigation into the Sept. 11 attacks has concluded
that between 70, 000 and 120, 000 terrorists were trained by al-Qaida and some are
still in the United States, Sen. Bob Graham, D—Fla., said Sunday. http://
www.democraticunderground.com/discuss/duboard.php?az = view_all&address
= 102x12027.

133. Wright, *Sacred Rage*, 54-56, 162, 163, 243-269 Wright, *Dreams and Shadows*, 37, 269.

134. "Al Qaeda 'determined' foe despite losses." by Eli Lake *Washington Times,*
Sep. 11, 2009.

135. *'Abd Al-'Al-Muqrin, A Practical Course for Guerrilla War.* by Norman
Cigar, Dulles, Virginia, Potomac Books, Inc. 2008 Julian Lewis MP, London,
August 2008 http://www.potomacbooksinc.com/resrcs/frontm/1597972533_
foreword.pdf.

136. Cigar (Tr.), *Al Qaeda's Doctrine for Insurgency*, xi, 55.

137. Bruce Hoffman: "Al-Qaeda Has A New Strategy. Obama Needs One, Too."
The Washington Post, Jan. 10, 2010.

138. *The Al Qaeda Manual, The al Qaeda manual presented here was made
available by the FBI which distributed the manual on their website: www.fbi.gov*
Presentation IntroductionFirst Lesson—General Introduction, Second Lesson—Necessary Qualifications And Characteristics For The Organization's Member, Third
Lesson—Counterfeit Currency And Forged Documents, Fourth Lesson—Organization Military Bases "Apartments Places"—Hiding, Fifth Lesson—Means Of Communication And Transportation, Sixth Lesson—Training, Seventh Lesson—Weapons: Measures Related To Buying And Transporting Them, Eight Lesson—Member
Safety, Ninth Lesson—Security Plan, Eleventh Lesson—Espionage (1) Information-Gathering Using Open Methods, Twelfth Lesson—Espionage (2) Information-Gathering Using Covert Methods Eighteen Lesson—Prisons And Detention Centers, http://www.disastercenter.com/terror/index.htm; www.au.af.mil/au/awc/
awcgate/terrorism/alqaida_manual/manualpart1_1.pdf.

139. Riedel, *The Search for Al Qaeda, 2008, 152.*

140. "U.S. May Label Pakistan Militants as Terrorists." by Mark Landler and T. Shanker *New York Times*, July 14, 2010.

141. Zaeef, *My Life with the Taliban,* 235, 240; David Hunt, *On the Hunt*, New York, Crown Forum, 2007, 19; "'Taqiyya': How Islamic Extremists Deceive The West." by Dr. Andrew Campbell, *National Observer*, Winter 2005, 12-21, http://www.vananne.com/serpentdove/taqiyya%20how%20islamic%20extremists%20deceive%20the%20west.pdf.

142. Juan Cole, *Engaging Muslim World*, 2009, 147; Madeline Albright and others and Klein, *Surrendering to Islam,* FrontPageMagazine.com, Wednesday, November 14, 2007.

143. Bob Woodward, *Obama's Wars*, 2010, 203-286, 355, 356.

144. "Taliban Seize Vital Pakistan Area Closer to the Capital." by Jane Perlez April 22, 2009 *New York Times*, April 30, 2009, (http://www.nytimes.com/2009/04/23/world/asia/23buner.html?_r=1&hp).

145. Rashid, *Jihad*, 141-142.

146. "Shafqat Ali, Taliban Tax Forces Sikh Exodus." *The Asian Age,* May 1, 2009; Selig Harrison, "Pakistan's Ethnic Fault Line." *Washington Post,* May 11, 2009 David Hunt, 2007, *On The Hunt*, New York, N.Y.Crown Forum/Random House, 5, 12-13, 19, 23, 24, 36, Peter Bergen, *Holy War*, 24-40, 83-86.

147. Shafqat Ali, "Taliban Tax Forces Sikh Exodus." *The Asian Age,* May 1, 2009; Selig Harrison, "Pakistan's Ethnic Fault Line." *Washington Post,* May 11, 2009 Peter Bergen, *Holy War Inc,* New York, N.Y. Simon and Schuster, 2001, 125, 221-235, 247.

148. James A. Phillips, *Backgrounder #232: The U.S. and Pakistan at the Crossroads* (Washington, D.C.: The Heritage Foundation, 1982).

149. Dexter Filkins, *The Forever War*, 40, 48-61, 269-271; "Pakistanis Confront Bonds of Faith, Country in Battle With Taliban." Griff Witte, *Washington Post*, Friday, June 12, 2009.

150. Griff Witte, "Pakistanis Confronts Bonds of Faith, Country in Battle with Taliban." *Washington Post,* June 12, 2009.

151. Greg Bruno and Eben Kaplan, *Backgrounder: The Taliban in Afghanistan* (Council on Foreign Relation, August 3, 2009) http://www.cfr.org/publication/10551/taliban_in_afghanistan.html.

152. Foreign Terrorist Organizations, February 6, 2004, Audrey Kurth Cronin; Foreign Affairs, Defense, and Trade Division, CRS Report for Congress, 111 pages. http://www.fas.org/irp/crs/RL32223.pdf.

153. "Many Sources Feed Taliban's War Chest." by Eric Schmitt, *New York Times,* Oct. 18, 2009.

154. McCarthy, *The Grand Jihad: How Islam and the Left Sabotage America,* New York, N.Y. Encounter Books, 2010, 168.

155. "On the Rise of the Shabaab." *The Economist*, December 18, 2008; Stephanie Hanson, *Backgrounder: Al-Shabaab*, Council on Foreign Relations, February 27, 2009.

156. *The menace of Al-Shabaab: A rising threat for Kenya and for Africa,* Annette Theron, July 1, 2011, http://www.consultancyafrica.com/index.php?option=com_

content&view=article&id=787:the-menace-of-al-shabaab-a-rising-threat-for-kenya-and-for-africa-&catid=60:conflict-terrorism-discussion-papers&Itemid=265.

157. "Militants Drew Recruit in U.S., F.B.I. Says." by David Johnson, *New York Times*, Feb.23, 2009.

158. *Terrorism Havens*, by Julie Cohn; http://www.cfr.org/somalia/terrorism-havens-somalia/p9366; *Bin Laden urges jihad against new Somali government*, June 2010, http://www.cfr.org/somalia/terrorism-havens-somalia/p9366, *The Terror Journal*, March 20, 2009. "A Journal on errorism and Genocide." *Opinion*, http://theterrorjournal.wordpress.com/2009/03/20/680.

159. David Shinn, "Al Shabaab's Foreign Threat to Somalia." *The Journal of Conflict Studies,* Fall 2003.

160. "Shabaab suicide bomber kills Somali interior minister." by Bill Roggio, *The Longwar Journal*, June 10, 2011, http://www.longwarjournal.org/archives/2011/06/shabaab_suicide_bomb_1.php#ixzz1RL7WuZ8v.

161. *Special Report 113: Terrorism in the Horn of Africa* (U.S. Institute of Peace, January 2004) 16 pages. http://www.usip.org/files/resources/sr113.pdf Gettleman, Jeffrey. "For Somalia, Chaos Breeds Religious War, " *New York Times*. May 23, 2009, http://www.nytimes.com/2009/05/24/world/africa/24somalia.html; Andrew Natsios, "Beyond Darfur, Sudan's Slide Toward Civil War." *Foreign Affairs,* May/ June 2008.

162. Jean-Louis Bruguiere, "The Holes in America's Anti-Terror Fence." *International Herald Tribune,* January 12, 2010; David H. Gray and Erik Stockham, "Al-Qaeda in the Islamic Maghreb: The Evolution from Algerian Islamism to Transnational Terror." *African Journal of Political Science and International Relations*, Vol. 2(4), December 2008, pp. 91-97; Julian Borger, "AQIM: Jihadists with a Global Name." *The Guardian,* June 3, 2009; Yaroslavl Trofimov, "Islamic Rebels Gain Strength in the Sahara." *Wall Street Journal,* August 15, 2009.

163. Kung, *Islam*, Oxford, U.K. Oneworld, 2007, 392, 547-549, 600-601.

164. Segal, *Islam's Black Slaves,* 39, 204.

165. Gabriel, *They Must Be Stopped*, 84; Peter Hammond, *Slavery, Terrorism & Islam: The Historical Roots and Contemporary Threat,* Fourth Edition, Longwood, Florida, Xulon Press, 2010.

166. Bostom (Ed.), *The Legacy of Jihad*, 531–532.

167. Durant, *Our Oriental Heritage*, 460.

168. Wolpert, *A New History of India*, 174.

169. Naipaul, *Beyond Belief*, 251, 331.

170. Cook, *Understanding Jihad*, 79–81.

171. Graham, George Farquhar Irving. *The Life and Work of Sir Syed Ahmed Khan*. Karachi: Oxford University Press, 1974., Troll, Christian W. *Sayyid Ahmad Khan: A Reinterpretation of Muslim Theology*. New Delhi: Vikas Publishing House, 1978.

172. Taheri, "The Sunni–Shiite Network." *Wall Street Journal,* March 29, 2008.

173. Juergensmeyer, *Terror in the Mind of God*, 217.

174. John Dower, *Embracing Defeat*, New York, N.Y. W.W. Norton & Company, 1999, 26, 61, 307-308.

175. Juergensmeyer, *Terror in the Mind of God*, 242.

176. For more on American Christian White Supremacists, see Hoffman, *Inside Terrorism*, 101–118.

177. Daniel Bell, "Revolutionary Terrorism: Three Justifications." *An International Review of Culture & Society*, Issue No. 9, Spring 2002 http://iranscope. ghandchi.com/Anthology/Bell-Terrorism.htm.

178. Christopher Tyerman, *God's War: A New History of the Crusades*, (Cambridge, MA: Belknap Press /Harvard University Press, 2006); and Nikolas Jaspert, *The Crusades*, (Florence, KY: Routledge, Taylor and Francis, Inc, 2006); www.burningcross.net/crusades/christian-missionary-atrocities.html.

179. Ivan Eland, *Battling Christian Terrorists*, (Center on Peace and Liberty: February 14, 2009), www.antiwar.com/eland/?articlei d = 14244.

180. "Sen. Robert Byrd, One-Time KKK Member, Backs Barack Obama, May 19, 2008." Don Frederick, *The Los Angeles Times*.

181. Radhakrishnan, *The Principal Upanishads*, New Delhi, India, HarperCollins, 1995, 131-147, Nirad C. Chaudhri, *Hinduism,* New Delhi, India, B.L. Publications, 1979, 125-129, Sri Aurobindo, *The Life Divine*, New York, N.Y. The Greystone Press, 1949, 58-68, 292-330.

182. Kevin Rushby, *Children of Kali; Through India in Search of Bandits, the Thug Cult, and the British Raj*, (New York, NY: Walker and Company, 2002), page 145.

183. Dudley, *India and Pakistan*, 76.

184. *Rewriting Indian History: Complete Book*, by Francois Gautier, Revised Edition for Bahri & Sons: 2002, http://francoisgautier1.blogspot.com/2008/04/re-writing-indian-history-complete-book.html.

185. "Toward Fifty Years of Constitunalism And Fundamental Rights In India: Looking Back To See Ahead (1950-2000)." Vijayshri Sripti, *American University International Law Review*, 414, http://www.auilr.org/pdf/14/14-2-2.pdf.

186. Samuel Huntington, 1997, 70.

187. Luca Ozzano, "Religious Terrorist Groups and Political Power: An Ambiguous Relationship" Torino: University of Torino, 2007, http://turin.sgir.eu/uploads/Ozzano-paper_sgir_to_2007_def.pdfhttp://archive.sgir.eu/uploads/Ozzano-paper_sgir_to_2007_def.pdf; Almond, Appleby, and Sivan, *Strong Religion*, 2003, 139–140.

188. *Zionist political violence*, http://zionist-political-violence.co.tv/; *Jabotinsky. . . The Man and the Vision*, William Mehlman, Jerusalem, January 2010 http://www.afsi.org/pamphlets/JabotinskyPamphlet20100714.pdf.

189. Jalal, *Partisans of Allah*, 243.

190. Rahman, *Islam and Modernity,* 116.

191. "Bangladesh bans books written by radical Islamic author." by Anbarasan Ethirajan, Dhaka *BBC News,* July 16, 2010.

192. *The New Islamist International, Task Force On Terrorism & Unconventional Warfare*, House Republican Research Committee (Chairman: Bill McCollum, Florida), February 1, 1993, (1993 Congressional Reports, Intelligence and Security.http://www.fas.org/irp/congress/1993_rpt/house_repub_report.html; Ter-

rorism in South Asia, August 9, 2004, K. Alan Kronstadt, and Bruce Vaughn, http://fpc.state.gov/documents/organization/35167.pdf.

193. "Kashmir's rising tide of hate." by Praveen Swami, *Peace Kashmir, A journey through Spriritual and Secular Ethos of Jammu and Kashmir*, http://www.peacekashmir.org/columnist/Kashmirs%20rising%20tide%20of%20hate.htm.

194. "The autumn of Kashmir's Islamist patriarch?" Praveen Swami, *The Hindu*, August 19, 2010.

195. Robert S. Mueller, Statement Before the Senate Committee on Homeland Security and Governmental Affair, September 22, 2010. http://www2.fbi.gov/congress/congress10/mueller092210.htm; *Threat of Homegrown Islamist Terrorism*, by Toni Johnson, December 10, 2010; http://www.cfr.org/terrorism/threat-homegrown-islamist-terrorism/p11509.

196. Sageman, *Leaderless Jihad*, 134.

197. "New focus on Europeans who have traveled to Pakistan to train at militant camps." by Peter Finn and Greg Miller, *Washington Post,* September 30, 2010.

198. Jones, 2009, 281; Kessler, Ronald, *The Terrorists Watch*, 2003, 375–376; Pipes, *Militant Islam Reaches America*, 245; Bruce Riedel, *The Search for Al Qaeda*, Wasington, D.C., Brookings Institution Press, 2008, 32.

199. Report of the Official Account of the Bombings in London on 7th July 2005, May 11, 2006, http://www.official-documents.gov.uk/document/hc0506/hc10/1087/1087.pdf.

200. "Should American Muslims Work Through The American Political Process To Try To Change American Foreign Policy Towards The Muslim World?" 26 Jan, 2011 *Debates About Foreign Policy*, Muslims for a Safe America, http://muslimsforasafeamerica.org/?p=514.

201. Reich, *Origins of Terror*, 31.

202. Reich, *Origins of Terror*, 261-281.

203. Kessler, *The Terrorist Watch*, 95.

204. Post, *The Mind of Terrorists, 8*; Sarah Kershaw, The Terrorist Mind: An Update, *New York Times,* January 9, 2010.

205. Burleigh, *Blood and Rage*, 487–494.

206. "British Radicalization Studies: The U.K.'s universities offer the most conducive environment an Islamic extremist could inhabit outside Waziristan." by Douglas Murray, *Wall Street Journal,* January 9, 2010.

207. "Radicals in Our Prisons: How to Stop The Muslim Extremists Recruiting Inmates to Terrorism." by Steve Emerson, *New York Post*, May 23, 2010.

208. Sarah Kershaw, "The Terrorist Mind: What moves people to kill themselves and innocent bystanders?" *New York Times*, January 9, 2010.

209. Robert Litwak, "Walking Away: Disengagement and De-Radicalization from Terrorism." *International Security Studies,* November 13, 2009; Omar Ashour, "Perspective on Terrorism, De-Radicalization of Jihad? The Impact of Egyptian Islamist Revisionists on AQ." *Journal of the Terrorism Research Initiative,* Vol. II. Issue 5, 2008–2009.

Chapter 4

Islamic Radicalization in Asia, Europe, and Africa

> Give up the old ways—
> Passion, enmity, folly.
> Know the truth and find peace.
> Share the way.
>
> —*Dhammapada*
> —*The Sayings of the Buddha*

Freed from the shackles of colonialism and Communism in the twentieth century, violent Islamic extremists and victorious mujahedeen from the Afghan wars of 1979–1989, emerged in the fertile, restive soil of Asia and Africa. Money, along with mosques based on Wahhabism, poured into Asia to fill the void of one hundred years of atheism, autocratic rulers, religious oppression, and segregation of religion and state politics. Afghanistan in Central Asia, Pakistan in South Asia, and the Philippines in South East Asia became the breeding ground for terrorists. Terrorism emanated into Uzbekistan, Tajikistan, and Turkmenistan in Central Asia, to Bangladesh and India in South Asia, and to Thailand, Indonesia, and Malaysia in Southeast Asia. This chapter discusses the radicalization of Islam in these regions where poverty, unemployment, and illiteracy are feeding the roots of terrorism. It includes sections on radicalization, and on deradicalization as a non-violent component of counter-terrorism, as well as a discussion of the resurgence of radical Islam in Africa and in Europe. However, the South Asian terrorists are the most brutal, savage, fanatic, perverted, and worse than the worst criminals.

The culture of brutal violence and Islamic radicalism, as discussed in previous chapters, has existed in Asia since the days of the Kharijites, after the demise of the prophet. It extended from the time of Taqi ad-Din Ahmad ibn Taymiyyah in the thirteenth century, to the eighteenth century of Muhammad Wahhab, the nineteenth century of Al Afghani and Muhammad Abduh, the twentieth century of Hassan Banna, Qutb, Maududi, Ali Shariati, and the Ayatollah Khomeini, into our own twenty-first century. Asia has seen the emergence of powerful fundamentalists, including, Azzam, Sheikh Omar Abdel Rahman, AAZ, al-Maqdisi, OBL, Abu Musab al Suri, Khalid Sheikh Mohammed (KSM), Encep Nurjaman, alias Riduan Isamuddin, alias Hambali, from Indonesia, and the late Juma Namangani. Among them, Maqdisi is considered to be the most influential jihadi intellectual. Most of these radical fundamentalists are veterans of either the Afghan or Bosnian war. In Asia, the jihadi movement—unlike the French Revolution of 1789, the Bolshevik movement of 1917, or Mao Tse Tung's Cultural Revolution of 1950—is intellectually bankrupt, culturally obscurantist, socially violent, perverse and introverted, and politically irredentist. The jihadists have adopted irrational choices, such as slitting throats and suicide bombing. They are engaged in a global jihadi movement to establish the caliphate worldwide, utilizing radical Islamic theology and extremely barbaric methods. This cult of insurrection is perfunctory, illegitimate, and anti-human. Jihad is not included in the five pillars of the Islamic religion, though some interpret that the first pillar Tawhid (oneness of God) implies that holy war should be waged against infidels. It is a human tragedy and a travesty of this interpretation that two giant Buddha statues in Afghanistan were destroyed, along with thousands of cultural artifacts in other parts of Asia. One of the jihadists, Abu Zarqawi, has commented:

> Shi'ism is an imminent plague and a real challenge. Shi'ism is a religion that has nothing to do with Islam more than Christians and Jews under the name of the People of the Book. . . . It is a proven idolatry: worship of the tombs (of their Imams) and the rite of walking around them.[1]

However, a visit to the Kaaba in Mecca or to the tomb of Prophet Muhammad at Medina, both in Saudi Arabia, is not considered idolatry.

For most jihadis and Islamic scholars, other religions and Gods are nothing, but the first part of Tawhid—"there is no God but Allah"—is an idolatry. Some of the Islamist terrorists and their fiery imams do not know very much about Islam. For them, jihad is an honorable way to achieve martyrdom and get 72 Houris. Some of them complained at a rehabilitation center in Saudi Arabia that they had been sexually abused by their imams and in training schools. The global jihad's cultural mission includes: 1. creating a "parity of suffering" with Islam's enemies; 2. defending Islam wherever one resides; 3. understanding martyrdom as both an operational, communal, and personal boon; 4. internalizing one's obligation to physical jihad to the degree that one supports it logistically or through direct action; 5. believing that the jihadi movement is the apocalyptic "saved sect" (*al-ta'ifa al-mansoura*) whose constant fighting will usher in the end of time; 6. promoting the notion of "brotherhood" to establish clear identity boundaries between both nominal Muslims (who fail in their obligation to support the *mujahedeen*, or whose actions or statements are believed to take them outside of Islam) and *kefir* (unbelievers); and 7. believing that God's sovereignty has a direct impact on the success or failure of jihadi operations, and that he intervenes miraculously on behalf of the *mujahedeen* when they display the requisite levels of belief (*iman*).[2]

Asian jihadists want to establish Islamic culture, civilization, and Sharia from Spain to Southeast Asia by killing people, destroying their property, and pursuing secessionist movements in restive provinces. The jihadists appear may take the form of liquid bombers, shoe bombers, or underwear bombers. There were also fertilizer bombers affiliated with the UK-based Al Muhajiroun, led by Omar Bakri of Saudi Arabia heritage, and Anjem Choudary of Pakistani heritage. The group became notorious for its conference, called "The Magnificent 19," which praised the September 11, 2001 attacks on America. "Democracy is dying, communism is dead, Islam is the only way for revival" is a slogan used by the Al-Muhajiroun. These jihadist use children of seven or eight years old as suicide bombers, with bombs strapped to their bodies for remote detonation. Some parents let their children be used in this manner so they can attain martyrdom. They have been blessed by many famous ulemas (Islamic scholars), muftis (Islamic legal experts), and imams (prayer leaders): Egyptian cleric Sheikh Yusuf al-Qaradawi; Sunni Iraqi cleric Sheikh Ahmad Al-Qubeisi; the Imam of the Grand Mosque in Mecca, Abd Al-Rahman Al-Sudayyis; the former President of Al-Azhar University, Ahmad 'Omar Hashem; and Sheikh Ibrahim Mudeiris, a cleric of Gaza, have all urged on suicide operations by Muslims, as has Yemen-based preacher Anwar al-Awlaki, an extremist cleric with links to AQ and Abu Hamza of Britain. It is reported that 7 per cent of the 1.3 billion, 90 million, Muslims support jihadism.[3]

Whether in the West or East, global jihadism has benefited from globalization, radical preachers with abundant monetary resources, nostalgia, disenchantment, and new generations of frustrated, segregated Muslims. This has helped the jihadists to remake Muslim identity. They remind them of the glory and glamour of the sword of Islam, and focus on how the submissiveness of Muslim governments to America and the presence of American forces in the Muslim holy land have caused humiliation and loss of dignity in the Muslim world. Muslims are terribly upset with the loss of the Ottoman Empire in World War I and the abolition of the caliphate in Turkey by Kemal Ataturk in 1924. This was exacerbated by the Arab–Israeli war of 1948–1949, the 1956 Suez war, the 1967 Arab–Israeli war, and the 1973 Arab–Israeli war. With the mujahedeen's victory in Afghanistan against the Soviet army, Islamic radicals, with their tremendous power of destruction, flocked to Asia to spread global jihad. As a result, martyrdom has gained a great deal of currency and honor in the region. According to the Paris based Professor Farhad Khosrokhavar remarked:

> As a global movement, Jihadism in the Muslim world has its credentials in the history of Islam within a subculture of violence. The crisis of the Muslim world has increased its attraction vis-à-vis many new generations that have been educated and therefore are able to read the Quran and inherited texts directly themselves without the moderating influence of the traditional ulama.[4]

Several Muslim cultural and public relations organizations in America and other regions are imparting and interpreting Islam for the benefit of a new generation of Muslims.

Muslims in East Asia do not feel victimized or threatened by Western civilization, culture, and secularism. Despite a few brutal, bigoted emperors and savage, plundering invaders, Asia remained peaceful. Neighboring countries with diverse cultures, religions, and ethnicities lived in harmony for a thousand years. There was no transnational aggression or territorial expansion. The coexistence of pluralism, "unto you your religion and unto me my religion" (Quran 109:6), changed with the advent of colonialism, Communism, Wahhabism, and radical Islam. Based on obscurantist and violent versions of the religion, some rulers destroyed idols, burned places of worship, or built their own temples over them. They also enforced conversion, practiced the abuse and rape of women, imposed strict seclusion upon them, and stoned people in public executions. The containment of Communism by Islamic fundamentalism, in their struggle against the Soviet Union in the 1980s, has yielded an unintended rise of global jihad. Even Muslim women who have been treated as second-class citizens, deprived of equality and freedom, are wearing the *burqa* in public places to show their Muslim identity, and wish to return to *purdah* (seclusion). Since 9/11, terrorist attacks and casualties have increased by 45 per cent, and 11,800 people have died in the last eight years,[5] with the majority of casualties in

Asia. While Hezbollah of Lebanon, Hamas of Palestine, and the Mahdi Army of Iraq are responsible for the terrorist related deaths in the Middle East, the Taliban (essentially Ghilzai Pashtuns), IMU, JI, AQ, and ASG are deeply involved in the terrorist acts in Asia. The assassination of Benazir Bhutto in 2008 marked the apex of terrorism in the region. There were also several attempts to assassinate Pakistan's former president Pervez Musharraf. The Taliban, a Wahhabi Islamic political movement, has killed hundreds of people in Pakistan—in Karachi, Islamabad, Lahore, Peshawar, Muzaffarabad and other locations—with roadside bombs, suicide bombs, and rocket attacks. A Hong-Kong based research organization, International Risk, has observed that these are dangerous times for Pakistan and the potential descent into anarchy is one of the biggest sources of geo-strategic concern for the international community, particularly because of Pakistan's possession of nuclear weapons. Conflicts between Muslims and non-Muslims and the subsequent terrorist attacks are on the rise in Asia, with Afghanistan and Pakistan emerging as the epicenter for the training of terrorists. The Uighur terrorists are killing Hans in Xinjiang, China, while the Taliban terrorists are killing Hindus in Jammu & Kashmir in India, while Jemaah Islamiah (JI) are killing Christians and Buddhists in Southeast Asia.

As per the *CIA Handbook,*[6] in 2009 the world population was 6,780,584,602, with 1,634,948,648 Muslims, or 24.11 per cent of the world population. In Asia, Muslims constitute 30 per cent of the population. Indonesia has the largest Muslim population, with 206,873,780, and Pakistan, the next highest, at 170,955,661. Asia has been a safe haven for terrorists, looters, and assassins from the very inception of Islam. With the collapse of the Soviet Union in 1991, several Muslim states emerged. The overwhelming majority of Muslims were Sunni, except for the Shiite Azerbaijanis. The Central Asian republics with large numbers of Muslims (see Figures 2.4 and 2.5) are Azerbaijan, Kazakhstan, Kirghizia, Tajikistan, Turkmenistan, and Uzbekistan (six out of fifteen republics). There are significant numbers of Muslims in Central Russia's Bashkiria and Tatarstan, and in Chechnya, Dagestan, and Transcaucasia. Muslims made up 15 per cent of the population in the former Soviet Union; the regions where they lived became volatile with the rise of fundamentalist Islam. Currently, the world is focused on Afghanistan and Pakistan, where the Taliban and AQ have found sanctuaries and may destabilize Asia. Selig Harrison writes: "Unless the (Barack) Obama administration can get Pakistan's army to stop supporting the Taliban with weapons and logistic support, the insurgency will continue."

Pakistan, with 10.45 per cent of the world's Muslim population, is an important country for the West because of its possession of nuclear weapons. Additionally, the defeat of the Soviet Union in Afghanistan in 1989 by the Pakistan sponsored Taliban gave credence, visibility, and prominence to Pakistani military schools, *madrassas,* and training camps. Terrorists around the world who are part of the Muslim diaspora came to Pakistan for an education in jihad operations, courtesy of Pakistan's military intelligence agency, the ISI, and terrorist training camps. The insurgency in South Asia and Central Asia is due to terrorists based in Pakistan, along with Saudi-supported Wahhabi mosques and *madrassas* (see more on funding and the ISI).[7]

Prior to the Muslim invasion, Asia was a non-Muslim continent. The Arab invasion of Iran began in 640, with the abolition of the Zoroastrian religion in Iran. It was followed by the invasion of Afghanistan in 642, and the eventual banishing of Buddhism from Afghanistan. Khyber Pass (also known as the Hindu Kush) in Afghanistan served as an entry point for remorseless Muslim invaders to South Asia, while some Iranian invaders crossed to Sindh, India, just after the Arab conquest of Iran. But Sindhi, the language of Sindh, is now 70 per cent Sanskrit, even after centuries of Islamic heritage. Through the Hindu Kush came Genghis Khan, Timur, Babur and others. They carried out massacres of non-Muslims and coercive religious conversions on a massive scale in tolerant, peaceful, hospitable India. After the partition of India in 1947, many of their radical Muslim descendents—fraught with Deobandi hatred of Hindus—remained in pluralistic, secular India to propagate Salafi-Wahhabism in India. The radical religious and educational institutions that nurtured separatists and religious bigotry, promoted orthodox Islam, undermined Indian civilization and culture, and stoked communal disaccord are still thriving in India, which remains weak and restive in many respects. Three famous Indian-born Pakistanis, the former President Zia-ul Haq, the former President Pervez Musharraf, and the nuclear scientist Abdul Khan, nuclear scientist, have made Pakistan strong against India.

Central Asia

During the last thousand years, the countries of Central Asia have undergone metamorphosis, transmutation, and cataclysm, from the Arab Caliphate (875–999) to the Bolshevik Revolution (1917), to Islamic extremist convulsion (1990s). With the collapse of the Soviet Union, mosques and *madrassas* proliferated, and preachers from the Middle East arrived to spread the word of political and radical Islam.[8] While Serb militiamen fought their Croat and Bosnian neighbors, insurgencies emerged in Afghanistan, Chechnya, and in Uzbekistan with the rise of Juma Hojiev Namangiani (1969–2001), the leader of the Islamic Movement of Uzbekistan, IMU, a terrorist organization whose political vision was greatly influenced by Wahhabism. Namangiani's final aim, like that of OBL, was to re-establish the storied Islamic caliphate in the newly formed Central Asian republics of Uzbekistan, Tajikistan, and Kyrgyzsta see Figures 2.4 and 2.5). Islamism provided a forum for rejecting Western culture and hegemony. The IMU, based in the Ferghana valley, clandestinely operates in the region that encompasses southeast Uzbekistan, southwest Kyrgyzstan, and northern Tajikistan. Their intent is to foment radical Islam, in order to topple pro-Western or pro-Russian governments. This mission was also supported by Hizb ut Tahir al-Islami (The Party of Islamic Liberation, HTI/HT) and the Islamic Revival Party of Tajikistan (IRPT). The IRPT was officially formed on December 4, 1991, with the following objectives: (a) spiritual revival of all citizens of Tajikistan, (b) political and legal rights with a view to realizing Islamic norms, (c) expansion of Islam in all its manifestations, (d) Muslim participation and representation in all spheres of the republic of Tajikistan, (e) safeguarding the unity and fraternity of relations among the people of Tajikistan, and (f) ensuring the political, economic, and cultural independence of Tajikistan. The HTI/HT has organizations in 40 countries, and hopes to establish Islamic states and unite them under a single caliphate. As part of their efforts to overthrow democracy and establish a worldwide Islamic theocracy, HTI/HT has distributed leaflets to young Muslims inciting them to resist the occupation of Islamic lands, according to a TV documentary by a former group member. One leaflet read: "Your forefathers destroyed the first crusader campaigns. Should you not proceed like them and destroy the new crusaders? Let the armies move to help the Muslims in Iraq, for they seek your help." Another leaflet, handed out in August of 2009, pours scorn on the UN and tells followers to embark on a Jihad (holy war).[9]

Saudi-funded Wahhabi mosques in Asia have been at the center of recruiting suicide bombers, as well as fundraising and the training, arming and nurturing of terrorists. They put out messages such as: "You have atomic bombs, we have suicide bombers," and "You have watches and we have no time." It was reported that the mosque networks have funded French-born Zacarias Moussaoui, and others and have provided them with false passports and ID cards. Sheikh Omar Bakri–Mohammad, the founder of al-Muhajiroun, an Islamic group based in London, claimed that mosques and university campuses in the United Kingdom recruit a yearly average of 18,000 British-born Muslims to fight abroad with Islamist armed groups. Mohammad Ibrahim Azhar is another British-based Islamist. He served time in an Indian prison between 1994 and 1999, and was released as part of deal to free hostages in the Indian Airline plane hijacking. Azhar had also set up

Harakat ul-Ansar (also known as Harakatul-Mujahedin or Jaish-e-Mohammad), in Pakistan, Chechnya, Somalia, and Central Asia. He is the brother of Masood Azhar, founder of the JeM, one of the leading Islamist Kashmiri armed groups. Azhar traveled at least once to Birmingham, well-known as a hotbed of Islamism in the United Kingdom, to recruit jihadists to fight against India. Riduan Ismuddin, the leader of the Indonesian JI, has been proselytizing Wahhabism for a decade to achieve a unified Islamic state encompassing Indonesia, the Philippines, Malaysia, and Singapore, to be ruled as a single caliphate governed by Sharia.

AQ jihadists, Taliban jihadists and other global jihadists are modern Kharijites, heterodox Muslims bent on carrying out their obscurantist, reductionist, and anachronistic views of Islam through violence. They are more interested in orthodoxy than economic deprivation, and favor the removal of *jahiliyya* above the removal of illiteracy, *Sharia* above national sovereignty, *da'wa* above tolerance, imposing the *burqa* above freedom and equality for women, and monotheism above pluralism and polytheism. Famed American author Mark Twain had this to say about religion and polytheism:

> Man is a religious animal. He is the only animal that has the True Religion—several of them. He is the only animal that loves his neighbor as himself and cuts his throat if his theology isn't straight. He has made a graveyard of the globe in trying his honest best to smooth his brother's path to happiness and heaven. . . . The higher animals have no religion. India has two million gods, and worships them all. In religion all other countries are paupers; India is the only millionaire.

According to the John Hopkins University Professor Mary Habeck (2006), based on their definition of *tawhid,* the extremists argue that democracy, liberalism, human rights, personal freedom, international law, and international institutions are illegal, illegitimate, and sinful.

In Afghanistan, the Taliban became a major power with the support of majority Pashtuns who used AQ as their global base. From Afghanistan AQ leader OBL launched an appeal to the Muslim world: "The people of Islam (have) suffered from aggression, iniquity and injustice imposed on them by the Zionist Crusaders' alliance and their collaborators," he wrote in 1996. To justify his call to arms he reminded his followers of the slaughter of Muslims across the world. "Their blood was spilled in Palestine and Iraq as well as Lebanon, Tajikistan, Burma, Kashmir, the Philippines, Somalia, Entrea, Chechnya, Bosnia-Herzegovina and Indonesia."[10] As mentioned earlier, Pakistan's Inter Service Intelligence Agency (ISI), with the help of the CIA, recruited Muslim youth to fight the holy war against the Soviets. The best selling of author of *Terror Incorporated and Insurgent*, Loretta Napoleoni[11] claims that after the anti-Soviet war, the ISI continued to export Islamist warriors from Pakistan to Central Asia and the Caucasus.

> A stream of covert operations was launched in Central Asia . . . (where) the ISI played a pivotal role in supporting Islamist armed insurgencies. OBL's International Islamic Front, formed in 1998, became an umbrella organization for various militant activities coordinated by Pakistan's LeT, an organization whose purpose, according to Mariam Abou Zahab and Olivier Roy, was to Islamize Kashmir and India, then embark on global conquest with the goal of restoring the caliphate. . . . If anyone in a prominent military position exemplifies Pakistan's official tolerance, if not support, of militant Islamism it is Lieutenant General Hamid Gul, former head of the ISI, whose involvement with various Islamist causes has gone unchallenged over many years. . . . Between 1988 and 2001 Gul was OBL's principal Pakistani advisor.[12]

BBC South Asia News reported on that Pakistani military intelligence not only funds and trains Taliban fighters in Afghanistan but is officially represented on the movement's leadership council, giving it significant influence over operations. This information was contained in a report published by the London School of Economics, a leading British institution, on June 13, 2010. The report strongly suggested that support for the Taliban was the "official policy" of ISI. Another report, written by Harvard University academic Matt Waldman, said that support for the Taliban, far from being carried out by rogue spies, is "official ISI policy." Based on extensive interviews, he reports that Pakistan appears to be playing a double game of astonishing magnitude. The Taliban insurgence in Afghanistan has caused the deaths of over 1,000 American and 700 other foreign military personnel; thousands of Afghan soldiers, police, officials and civilians; and an unknown number of Afghan, Pakistani, and other foreign insurgents, costing America more than $400 billion. The Taliban get more than $4000 for killing each enemy soldier, and they are paid by America through ISI.[13] A report appearing in *The Sunday Times* of London agreed with this view, while noting that such support was "officially sanctioned at the highest levels of Pakistan's government." Most of the Taliban are from Punjab, which is home to SSP at Jhang, JeM, based in Bahawalpur (where it has a huge seminary) and LeT at Muridke, near Lahore. Punjab has had these extremist bases since the late 1980s, when Punjabi veterans of the anti-Soviet Afghan Jihad *returned* home, and the ISI decided to use them against India.

In addition, the Afghan Jihad (1979–1989), in conjunction with regional terrorists' organizations, was involved in terrorist attacks in the Philippines, Myanmar (Burma), Bosnia, Indonesia, Kosovo, Chechnya, Algeria, Egypt, Jordan, and Yemen.

The religion is on rise worldwide with the resurgence of Islamic fundamentalism abetted by modern communications, sophisticated technology, nano-oriented weaponry and explosives, computer and satellite networks, text messaging, face book, twitters, research in motion (RIM) boundaryless Internet, undetectable cybercafé, Google, handheld computer and phones, Blackberries with encryption capabilities, GPS Navigation systems, and globalization.

> Islam is experiencing a genuine revival, one that extends beyond the more extreme Islamic fundamentalist movements. More Muslim women are wearing the veil; more Muslim men are growing beards, more Muslims are attending mosques more often. According to the Gallup Center for Muslim Studies, Islam is thriving with 86 per cent of Turks, 90 per cent of Indonesians, and 98 per cent of Egyptians surveyed reporting that religion plays an important part in their lives. Muslims are also an important force in Russia, making up between 12 and 15 per cent of the population. Russia has more Muslim inhabitants than any other country in Europe. Battles with Muslims in the North Caucus—Chechnya, Dagestan, and Ingushetia—have left Moscow viewing Islam as a source of extremism, separation, and secession.[14]

Northwestern China is home to more than 20 million Muslims and is now facing unrest and upheaval in Xinjiang province. The problems faced by Central Asian countries were documented by the 180th United States Congress, 1st session, on October 29, 2003:

> Economic collapse, isolation from global markets, high birthrates and high unemployment, the absence of social safety nets, inadequate education and increasing illiteracy, heroin trafficking and intravenous drug use, public health crises, the erosion of traditional social institutions, and the infiltration of radical ideologies, challenge each of the states to a greater or lesser degree. Broader regional development issues like water resource management, energy development, and trade can also not be tackled without the concerted effort of all states.

These circumstances have contributed to the rise of radical Islam in Thailand, the Philippines, Malaysia, and Indonesia. The unrest was also vitalized by veterans from the Afghanistan war with the Soviets, and by students and scholars returning from *madrassas* and universities in Pakistan, Afghanistan, Egypt, and Yemen. Besides the link to OBL's AQ, there was an historical link between Central Asia (and Yemenis in Southeast Asia). In the last ten years, the number of *madrassas* and mosques in these countries, as funded by the Gulf nations, has increased tenfold. The problems of unrest, insurgency, external religious funding, drug trafficking, and the impact of AQ and other terrorist organizations, have created turmoil and mayhem in Afghanistan, Uzbekistan, Tajikistan, South Asia and South East Asia, and Africa's underdeveloped and restive regions (see more on funding, the ISI).[15]

Afghanistan

Afghanistan, known as the graveyard of empires, is a multi-ethnic country with a majority of Pashtuns, who comprise 42 per cent of the population. For centuries it encompassed the trade route from the West to the East, which was also known as the Silk Road. Afghanistan has been a battlefield for many empires, including those of Britain, the Soviet Union, and America, because of its strategic location in relation to the Middle East, Iran, and Central Asia. It is fiercely independent. *Afghanistan,* a variation of the Sanskrit word *Upaganasthan,* means "land of the allied tribes." Alexander's march to Afghanistan through the Hindu Kush was followed by Islamic conquest in 652 A.D., but mountain tribes that were a conglomerate of Hindus, Buddhists, and Zoroastrians resisted the Muslim invaders. Afghanistan was a Hindu kingdom until the eleventh century A.D. Zoroastrianism might have originated in Afghanistan circa 1800 to 800 B.C., as Zoroaster lived and died in Balkh, Afghanistan. The last province that was converted to Islam, by Abdul Raman Khan in the nineteenth century, was "Kufirstan," the land of unbelievers, also called Nuristan. People in Kufirstan still retain their culture, even after hundreds of years of forced conversion and killing. They are known for dancing, feasting, and singing in which both sexes freely participate. Zahir ud-din Muhammad Jalal ud-din Babur (1483–1531), founder of the Mogul Empire, was from Central Asia, most likely a native of Afghanistan's Ferghana Valley. In its capital of Kabul, Babur's tomb lies in the beautiful Babur Garden. His autography, the *Baburnama* (Chapter 2) is the first true autobiography in Islamic literature. Ahmad Shah Durrani founded the modern state of Afghanistan in 1747, and although it remains a hybrid of several civilizations, it is now a Muslim country, of which 87 per cent are Sunnis and 10 per cent Shiites. There are five major ethnic groups, Pashtuns (Sunnis), with a population of 42 per cent per CIA estimates in 2006, Tajiks (Shias) 27 per cent, Hazaras (Shias), 9 per cent, and Uzbeks

(Sunnis), 9 per cent. There are also significant numbers of Pashtuns in KP and Baluchistan in Pakistan. Afghanistan has served as a buffer state between the British Empire in India and the Soviet Union. The British made several unsuccessful attempts at conquest and control of Afghanistan starting in the nineteenth century, to counter the Russian presence and its territorial expansion towards the Indian Ocean. In 1893 the *Durand Line Treaty*, named after Mortimer Durand, the foreign secretary of British Colonial India from 1884 to 1894, effected the demarcation of the border between Afghanistan and Pakistan. It was signed by Durand and Amir Abdur Rahman Khan (1840–1901), Emir of Afghanistan from 1880 to 1901. Afghanistan has never accepted the 1600-mile-long Durand Line, and was the only country that objected to Pakistan's entry into the United Nations, mainly because the Durand line separated Afghanistan's ethnic Pashtuns from those of Pakistan.

The tumultuous history of Afghanistan entered a new era on December 24, 1979, when the Soviet Union sent its troops into Afghanistan to support the Communist oriented regimes of Noor Mohammad Taraki and others. Over the next decade, the Taliban and AQ mujahedeen from several countries, supported and trained by the ISI and the CIA, fought and eventually defeated the Soviet Union Army. On February 15, 1989, the last of the Russian Army, under the command of Soviet General Boris Gromov, left Afghanistan. The Taliban, headed by Mullah Omar, took over Afghanistan, and enforced the radical version of Sharia at the behest of AQ leader OBL. They turned soccer stadiums into killing fields, resumed the stoning of women for adultery and the closure of girl's schools, and also banned women's employment. Mullah Omar destroyed anything he considered to be an idol, including the famous mammoth Buddha statues at Bamyan. He was also against kite flying, and images of people displayed in shops, hotels, or taxis, as these were all forms of idolatry; women's liberation, education, and employment; and music, among other things (for a list of sixteen prohibited items,[16] He was anti-Shiite and anti-Sufi, and had sent the Taliban to Nimroz, so that they might kill all the males and marry all the females in order to put an end to unbelievers. During his reign, as reported by Lutz Rzehak, the local library with more than fifteen thousand books, was burned down. Some eight thousand Turkic Uzbeks are said to have been killed in Mazar-e-Sharif in 1998 alone, when the Taliban reconquered it. Within three months, the Taliban closed sixty-three schools affecting 103,000 girls.

The Taliban and others believe that those in the West criticize women in Islam based on their hatred of Islam. Yet by any standards, the Taliban's cruelty to women and girls is barbaric, inhuman, and an outrageous abuse of religion. Two Afghani women, Latifa and Zoya, have documented this treatment in their autobiographical accounts; it has also been documented by the RAWA (Revolutionary Association of the Women of Afghanistan). Juan Cole (2009) provides a vivid description of women's condition in *The Taliban, Women and the Hegelian Private Sphere*.[17] At certain times during the month of Ramadan, women are not even allowed on the streets. Girls have been forbidden from going to school as the Taliban view schools as the gateway to Hell for them, and the first step on the road to prostitution. Women are not allowed to laugh or even speak loudly, because this might sexually excite men. They cannot wear high heels, makeup, or nail polish. Women who failed to respect such edicts can be beaten, whipped, or stoned to death. For the Taliban, if a woman was sick, it was better for her to die than to be treated by a man. If she refused to let a male doctor touch her, she could be certain of going to Heaven. RAWA has found that suicide among women rose significantly under the Taliban as a result of depression induced by cabin fever. Physicians for Human Rights (PHR) reports that 81 per cent of women participants in a study reported a decline in their mental condition while living under Taliban rule. A large number of respondents (42 per cent) met the diagnostic criteria for post-traumatic stress disorder (PTSD), based on the *Diagnostic and Statistical Manual of Mental Disorders*, and major depression (97 per cent). (The overall literacy rate is thought to be around 20% among Afghan males and less than 5% among females; Around 50% of students and 60% of teachers at Kabul University were women before the Taliban seized control; Up to 40% of Afghanistan's doctors were women before the Taliban took over in 1996, source: The Revolutionary Association of the Women of Afghanistan and The Feminist Majority Foundation). They also demonstrated significant symptoms of anxiety (86 per cent). Twenty-one per cent of the participants indicated that they had suicidal thoughts "extremely often" or "quite often." It is clear from the PHR's forty interviews with Afghan women that the general climate of cruelty, abuse, and tyranny that characterizes Taliban rule has had a profound effect on women's mental health. Zoya, an Afghani woman who shared her life story in a written account, had many disturbing stories to tell. One describes a mother who was rushed to the hospital by her daughter when she was having a severe asthma attack. While there, her condition worsened because of her burqa, which she removed to fight for her breath in the ward. A talib (member of the Taliban) burst into the ward to give the mother forty lashes for removing her burqa while her daughter watched, helpless to intervene. The nurses did nothing to stop the beating.[18]

Muslims fully integrate Islam into their lives, including their style of dress, as urged by Islamic extremists. This is known as Islamic Integrism. As a result, orthodox Muslims are easily recognized, and may become objects of fear: On October 18, 2010, the African-American veteran journalist Juan Williams made these comments about Muslims on the "O'Reilly Factor" (Fox News): "But when I get on a plane, I got to tell you, if I see people who are in Muslim garb and I think, you know, they're identifying themselves first and foremost as Muslims, I get worried. I get nervous." Two days later, as a result of these comments, he lost his job at National Public Radio (NPR).

When Mullah Omar refused to hand over OBL after the 9/11 attacks, America invaded Afghanistan. Despite terrorist activities there, the Taliban scarcely challenged Nuristan's autonomy, and eventually in Afghanistan's political struggle, Nuristan became the base of Gulbuddin Hekmatyr, LeT, and possibly AQ. With remarkable speed, between October 7 and November 12, 2001, America triumphed and drove out the Taliban government. The defeated Taliban and AQ escaped from their stronghold on Tora Bora Mountain into Pakistan. With the significant withdrawal of American forces in 2003, however, the Taliban and AQ became leaders of worldwide terrorism and several attacks followed. These included the March 2004 bombings in Spain, the July 2005 bombing in the London suburbs, the plot unearthed in the summer of 2006 to use explosives to blow up transatlantic flights to America, and a 2007 plot master-minded by the Islamic Jihadi Union cell in Germany, led by Fritz Gelowicz, to inflict terror in Europe.

Rand Corporation security analyst and political scientist Seth Jones[19] writes:

> In 2008, police and intelligence forces uncovered several terrorist plots in Europe (including in Spain and France) linked to militants in Pakistan's rural areas. People taking part in each case of these operations received training and other assistance in Pakistan.

What had started out as a U.S.-led war in Afghanistan had developed into a region-wide insurgency. In nuclear-armed Pakistan, militant groups were destabilizing the KP, the FATA, Baluchistan Province, and urban areas. The U.S. Ambassador to Pakistan, Anne Patterson, circulated a memo in early 2008 warning that "militant extremists in Pakistan have sharply increased attacks, both in tribal areas along the Pak-Afghan border and into settled areas." These attacks were undermining regional stability and effective prosecution of the war on terror by Coalition Forces in Afghanistan, and the Pakistan military was hindered by significant capability gaps and fears of civilian casualties, which could undercut already weak public support for offensive operations.

U.S. financial resources that could have been devoted to Afghanistan were going to Iraq, squandering a momentous opportunity. In addition, insurgents were also able to gain significant assistance from the international jihad network and neighboring states, such as Pakistan and Iran. In one of his final reports before leaving Afghanistan in 2008 as the European Union's special representative, Francesc Vendrell reflected on his decade of experience in Afghanistan:

> . . . [W]e blinded ourselves to growing evidence that Pakistan, contrary to assurances, was condoning the presence of, and probably providing assistance to, the Taliban, with its old policy of supporting extreme Islamist groups as the best means of installing a pliable government in Kabul.[20]

Ironically, Pakistan was not immune to the spreading militancy: The Taliban monsters have turned against Pakistan itself. It is alleged that the ISI is supported by rogue elements of the Pakistan Army. However, America cannot attack terrorist sanctuaries in Pakistan, even while aiding the Pakistan Army. It is sad and highly dangerous to support the ISI. As Ambassador Patterson says: "You cannot tolerate vipers in your bosom without getting bitten."[21]

An NBC report of from Kabul, Afghanistan reported that the 91,000 documents published by WikiLeaks appear to show, among other things, that agents for Pakistan's ISI have been working in close collaboration with the Taliban for years.

> President Hamid Karzai was furious to observe in his news conference on July 29, 2010, why his allies (America and NATO) were not doing more to shut down insurgent havens in other countries (Pakistan). "The international community is here to fight terrorism, but there is danger elsewhere and they are not acting," he said. "The war against terrorism is not in the villages or houses of Afghanistan . . . but in the sanctuaries, sources of funding and training and they lie outside Afghanistan."[22]

Between July and October, 2009, the Taliban attacked the Pakistani Army's national headquarters at Rawalpindi, killing a dozen and taking hostages. They also blew up the Indian mission in Kabul, conducted separate attacks on an Italian Army patrol and NATO forces in Kabul. They also attacked a U.S. military base in Kamdesh, causing heavy casualties, and bombed the World Food Program office of the United Nations in the capital, killing five people. After Taliban leader Baitullah Mehsud was killed in a U.S. predator drone attack, new leader Hakimullah Mehsud attacked vigorously in Waziristan, Lahore, and Rawalpindi. On October 15, 2009, the Taliban attacked three law enforcement agencies in Lahore, Pakistan, killing more than 30 police and military officials. They have also been active in the state of Punjab, where they have killed hundreds of soldiers and civilians, burned hundreds of NATO fuel supply trucks and several fleets of Humvees, and captured fifty containers of military supplies. On October 16, 2009, in an attempt to free arrested militants, Taliban terrorists conducted a suicide bombing at a police station in Peshawar, KP, killing about a dozen people. The BBC News (South Asia) reported on October 16, 2009, that in the months of September and October 2009, there were 160 deaths due to terrorist attacks in Pakistan.

At least nine Taliban suicide attacks hit Pakistan's security forces that October. These included a devastating and embarrassing siege at the army's General Headquarters (GHQ) in Rawalpindi, which claimed twenty-two lives, and three attacks on a single day in Lahore. Over 150 people were killed and several hundred injured. As of October 2009, there were 8,375 fatalities from terrorist violence, up from 189 in 2003. In the past six years, 22,110 were killed in Pakistan.[23]

U.S. aid has only consolidated and modernized the Pakistan army, without being used to rid the country of terrorists. Pakistani journalist Rashid states:

> Between 1954 and 2002, the United States provided a total of $12.6 billion in economic and military aid to Pakistan, of which $9.19 billion was given during twenty-four years of military rule, while only $3.4 billion was provided to civilian governments over a nineteen-year period. Between 2001 and 2007, the United States gave more than $10.0 billion to the Musharraf regime. Yet what has been the gross profit of this aid?[24]

Today, seven years after 9/11, Mullah Omar and the original Afghan Taliban Shura still live in Baluchistan province (Pakistan). The powerful Western world is terrorizing Muslims. They are now regrouping, rearming, and resurging. William Dalrymple writes:

> The Taliban have reorganized, advanced out of their borderland safe havens, and are now massing at the gates of Kabul, threatening to surround and throttle the capital, much as the U.S.-backed Mujahedeen once did to the Soviet-installed regime in the late eighties. Like the rerun of an old

movie, all journeys out of the Afghan capital are once again confined to tanks, armored cars, and helicopters. Members of the Taliban already control over 70 per cent of the country, up from just over 50 per cent in November 2007, where they collect taxes, enforce Sharia law, and dispense their usual rough justice; but they do succeed. . . . The army's senior military brass were convinced until recently that they could control the militants whom they had fostered. In a taped conversation between then-General Pervez Musharraf and Muhammad Aziz Khan, his chief of general staff, which India released in 1999, Aziz said that the army had the jihadist by their *"tooti"* (their privates). Yet while some in the ISI may still believe that they can use jihadists for their own ends, the Islamists have increasingly followed their own agendas, sending suicide bombers to attack not just members of Pakistan's religious minorities and political leaders, but even the ISI headquarters at Camp Hamza itself, in apparent revenge for the army's declared support for America's war on terror and attacks made by the Pakistani military on Taliban strongholds in FATA.[25]

It is reported that the ISI was giving refuge to the entire Taliban leadership after it fled from Afghanistan after the October attacks by America. The Taliban leader Mullah Omar was kept in an ISI safe house in the town of Quetta, Pakistan. Both Gulbuddin Hikmetyar and Jalaluddin Haqqani were given sanctuary by the ISI in Pakistan. Terrorist groups LeT, JeM, Tehrek-e-Taliban (TeT), LeJ and SSP have been patronized by Pakistan. Professor C. Christine Fair[26] describes how Pakistan has waged a partial war against the terrorists.

Pakistan is now paying the heavy price for its earlier attempts to use terrorist groups as strategic tools. Pakistan's efforts to fight the bad terrorists while protecting the good militants cannot be sustained. The latest string of attacks and bombings shows the high cost the policy is inflicting on Pakistan itself.

Fair continues:

For some six decades, the country has benefited from FATA being a "black hole" from which it could launch operations into Afghanistan and train militants operating in Afghanistan, Kashmir, . . . and the rest engage in a modicum of political liberalization apart from permitting adult franchise in 1996.

She reports that Pakistan provided extensive military, financial, and political support to the Taliban during Prime Minister Benazir Bhutto's second term of office (1993–1996). General Nasrullah Babar, Bhutto's Minister of the Interior, shaped Pakistan's clandestine activities in Afghanistan during her father's tenure (Zulfiqar Ali Bhutto served as president from 1971 to 1973, and as prime minister from 1973 to 1977). Pakistan's pro-Taliban policy continued during Nawaz Sharif's second term as prime minister (1997–1999). Pakistan has also supported the so-called Kashmir jihad, which has enabled numerous militants, many if not most of whom are not Kashmiri, to operate in Indian-administered Kashmir and other places in India.

In order to curb Islamic militancy, America and the international community have been aiding Pakistan for years.

> All told, since 2001, the United States has spent about $12 billion to help Pakistan. Yet last month, Secretary of State Hillary Clinton declared Pakistan a "mortal threat" to international security. Faced with a Taliban offensive and the threat of Pakistan's nuclear arsenal falling into jihadists' hands, the United States is proposing to spend an additional $1.5 billion each year until 2013 on civilian aid programs and to increase funding for Pakistan's security forces. Last month in Tokyo, international donors pledged $4 billion to help Pakistan.[27]

But American deployment and aid in Afghanistan is significantly low compared to troop levels in other places: Under the umbrella of air power supplied by bases in surrounding countries and the Indian Ocean, the Pentagon deployed more than 20,000 troops to this country of some 31 million in 2007. By 2009, NATO and U.S. forces in Pakistan had grown to some 40,000 troops. In Iraq, which has some 26 million inhabitants, American troop levels in Iraq reached a maximum of roughly 160,000 in the summer of 2007. Peacekeeping operations in Somalia, Haiti, Kosovo, Bosnia, Northern Ireland, Iraq and elsewhere all had higher ratios of peacekeepers per inhabitants. In comparative terms, for every 1,000 Afghans, there was less than 1 American or coalition solider (0.5) to provide security in 2002 (versus 23.7 per 1,000 in Kosovo in 1999, 6.1 per 1,000 in Iraq in 2003, and 3.5 per 1,000 in Haiti in 1994). Even before American attention shifted to Iraq in the winter and spring of 2002–2003, per capita aid levels—$57 per Afghan—remained well below those of other war-torn environments, such as East Timor ($233), Kosovo ($526), or Bosnia ($679).[28]

Dr. Richard Haass, President of the Council of Foreign Relations wrote:

> The one issue that should be at the core of the United States' Afghan strategy is Pakistan. It is there, not Afghanistan, where the United States has vital national interests. These stem from Pakistan's dozens of nuclear weapons, the presence on its soil of the world's most dangerous terrorists, and the potential for a clash with India that could escalate to a nuclear

confrontation. The United States is doing a great deal in Afghanistan—and is considering doing more—because it sees the effort as essential to protecting Pakistan. But this logic is somewhat bizarre. Certainly, allowing the Taliban and AQ to reestablish a sanctuary in Afghanistan would make it harder to defeat them in Pakistan. But the Taliban and AQ already have a sanctuary in Pakistan itself. It is the government of Pakistan that is tolerating the very groups that the United States is fighting in Afghanistan in the name of Pakistan's stability.[29]

Former Secretary of State Henry Kissinger observes:

The special aspect of Afghanistan is that it has powerful neighbors or near neighbors—Pakistan, India, China, Russia, and Iran. Each is threatened in one way or another and, in many respects, more than we are by the emergence of a base for international terrorism: Pakistan by AQ; India by general jihadist and specific terror groups; China by fundamentalist Shiite jihadists in Xinjiang; Russia by unrest in the Muslim south; even Iran by the fundamentalist Sunni Taliban. Each has substantial capacities for defending its interests. Each has chosen, so far, to stand more or less aloof.[30]

Afghanistan's neighbors have other interests in that nation's material and strategic assets. Afghanistan has vast deposits of copper, iron, gold, uranium, and precious gems. A Chinese company is engaged in exploring and processing its minerals, and so China is very much interested in the stability of Afghanistan. China has constructed port facilities at Gwadar in Baluchistan, a deep-sea, warm-water port at the apex of the Arabian Sea and at the entrance of the Persian Gulf. This port lies about 286 miles west of Karachi, Pakistan, and approximately 46 miles east of Pakistan's border with Iran. It can serve as a naval base, and has been operational since 2008. China is now a player in the great game of rivalry for strategic gains in the Middle East, Central Asia, and South Asia, and for access to the Indian Ocean.

The National Correspondent for the Atlantic Monthly, Robert Kaplan comments:

China will find a way to benefit no matter what the United States does in Afghanistan. But it probably benefits more if we stay and add troops to the fight. The same goes for Russia. Because of continuing unrest in the Islamic southern tier of the former Soviet Union, Moscow has an interest in America stabilizing Afghanistan (though it would take a certain psychological pleasure from a humiliating American withdrawal). In nuts-and-bolts terms, if we stay in Afghanistan and eventually succeed, other countries will benefit more than we will. China, India and Russia are all Asian

powers, geographically proximate to Afghanistan and better able, therefore, to garner practical advantages from any stability our armed forces
would make possible.[31]

The Washington Post columnist Jim Hoagland cautions that the

Obama administration must not slip back into letting Pakistan present itself as an aggrieved party whose delicate national sensibilities are unjustly
offended by suggestions that its army and intelligence services might be
ripping off U.S. aid ($7.5 billion for 5 years) and covertly encouraging
terrorism. Pakistan's spread of nuclear technology to Iran and North Korea and continued its support for the Taliban and AQ networks are for its
own perverted reasons of national security—not out of hurt pride.[32]

In the present American deliberations on Afghanistan, it seems that global
security and human rights in Afghanistan are secondary to annoying Pakistan. Afghani women are concerned about the possibility of America pulling out from Afghanistan or the goal of the 2001 war of necessity seeming
inconsequential in 2009, as demonstrated by giving in to the Taliban. An
Afghani woman graduate student in the UK is worried:

At this time of violence and anxiety, it is important for the international
community and the United States to reaffirm their commitment to Afghanistan rather than questioning whether it is worth defending an entire
people against those who would install another brutally repressive regime
under which women cannot be educated or seek to improve their lot, where
"justice" is meted out in mass public executions, where repression is the
rule—and where new terrorist plots will inevitably be hatched to attack the
United States and its allies.[33]

The security analyst Ashley Tellis notes that the U.S. has missed a
momentous opportunity to stymie terrorist incursions, insurgency, and infiltration into Afghanistan and to help Pakistan rid itself of its long addiction
to terrorism, by not pressing Pakistan to relinquish all of its terrorist clients
once and for all during the present crisis, as Washington previously compelled Islamabad to forsake the Taliban on September 13, 2001.[34] Pakistan
is known to have been instrumental in seizing several AQ terrorists, including Abu Zubaidyah, Ramzi Bin al Shibh, Khalid Sheikh Mohammed, and
Abu-Faraj-al-Libi. As strategic specialist Professor Sumit Ganguly reiterates:

Pakistan's geo-strategic utility to the United States came to the fore a third
time after September 11. Once again, a squalid dictator, Gen. Pervez
Musharraf, became the instrument for the prosecution of Washington's

goals. Though Musharraf had little use for AQ, his willingness to help topple the Taliban regime in Afghanistan was limited at best.[35]

Afghanistan has had a series of deadly tragedies since 1929. The NPR reporter Gregory Feifer quotes an Afghan Radio Kabul correspondent:

Habibulah was hanged in 1929. His successor Nadir Khan was shot, his successor Zahir Shah fled, Daoud was killed, Taraki suffocated, Amin murdered, and Najibullah hanged; even Massoud was blown up. Deaths of heads of state in other countries are followed by periods of mourning and visits by heads of state abroad. That never happens in Afghanistan. . . . Never mind the failure of Brezhnev's great gamble, and the billions of Soviet rubles and American dollars poured into Afghanistan in the 1980s helped create a ruin of humanity and a homeland for today's worldwide fundamentalist terrorist network.[36]

What has helped terrorists and the Taliban are Afghanistan's formidable terrain, hostile climate for foreigners, and fierce tribal groups who are determined to live by their traditions, and are prepared to fight to uphold them, using the huge amount of armaments abandoned by the retreating Soviet army. Terrorists depend on active sanctuaries in neighboring countries including Pakistan, where they are given arms, money, and supplies. Until these sanctuaries of terrorists are completely destroyed, their infrastructures in neighboring countries are diffused, dismantled and demolished, their narcotic income and other illegitimate income are stopped, and borders are safeguarded from insurgents, Afghanistan will remain a killing field for terrorists.

The security situation in Afghanistan has not improved during the last decade. Roadside bombings soared by 94 per cent in the first four months of this year compared with the same period in 2009. In addition to roadside bombings, the report says suicide attacks occur at the rate of about three per week, half of them in the ethnic Pashtun areas of the south. Assassinations of Afghan officials also rose by 45 per cent in the first four months of the year compared with the same time in 2009. With the announcement of Obama's decision to withdraw American forces in July 2011, there was a surge of activity by the Taliban, AQ, Pakistan and others to install the old Taliban regime in Afghanistan. The parties and individuals involved are located in Pakistan's North Waziristan and Kandahar, and areas in Afghanistan. They include Mohammad Omar of the Taliban, and an allied group headed by Gulbuddin Hekmatyar, as well as Sirajuddin Haqqani and his father Jalaluddin Haqqani, a legendary Afghan mujahidin leader. After the elder Haqqani passed the reins to Sirajuddin in recent years, the organization has swelled in lethality and in size, to as many as 10,000 fighters.[37] Pakistan and Afghanistan are negotiating with the Taliban leaders to bring peace to the region. American aid to Pakistan and Afghanistan has not contained terrorism as the surge of terrorists and their grievances do not arise from poverty or deprivation. The announcement of the withdrawal of American forces from Afghanistan next year has also caused concern in Afghanistan, Pakistan, India, Central Asia and the Middle East. Former Secretary of State Henry Kissinger observes:

> "All of them, from a strategic perspective, are more threatened than is the United States by an Afghanistan hospitable to terrorism. China in Sinkiang, Russia in its southern regions, India with respect to its Muslim minority of 160 million, Pakistan as to its political structure, and the smaller states in the region would face a major threat from an Afghanistan encouraging, or even tolerating, centers of terrorism." On the other hand, *Newsweek* reports that Hafiz Muhammad Saeed, one of LeT's founders and its top spiritual leader, has repeatedly proclaimed that the Western world "is terrorizing Muslims,"

he says.

> We are being invaded, humiliated, manipulated and looted. We must fight against the evil trio, the United States, Israel and India. Suicide missions are in accordance with Islam. In fact, suicide attack is the best form of *jihad*.

And John R. Bolton, former U.S. ambassador to the United Nations, suggests American forces must stay in Afghanistan to defeat the Taliban and AQ terrorists and to ensure that nuclear arsenals are not taken over by terrorists.[38]

Uzbekistan

After the Iranian Revolution in 1979, the Muslim nation of Uzbekistan became an important state. Not only is it the most populous nation in Central Asia, it is also the cultural, historical, and political hub of the that region, and has the strongest economy. Three of its biggest cities are Tashkent, the capital; Samarkand, the second largest city, with the beautiful Bibi-Khanym mosque, and Bukhara. Bukhara is located on the Silk Road and has served as a region wide center of trade, scholarship, culture, and religion for several centuries. Bukhara is a republic with one legislative body; its president as the head of state and prime minister as head of the government. Genghis Khan received the territory as his inheritance in the 13th century.

The Mongols ruled over a number of Turkic tribes, with intermarriage with the Mongols to form the Uzbeks and other Turkic peoples of Central Asia. In the early 16th century a federation of Mongol-Uzbeks invaded and occupied settled regions, including an area called Transoxania that would become the permanent Uzbek homeland. By the early 19th century the region was dominated by the khanates of Khiva, Bukhara, and Kokand, all of which eventually succumbed to Russian domination. The Uzbek S.S.R. was created in 1924. In June 1990 Uzbekistan became the first Central Asian republic to declare sovereignty, with full independence from the Soviet Union in 1991.

Most of the governments in Central Asia, including this one, are weak, repressive, and abusers of human rights. In addition to these repressive measures, after the collapse of the Soviet Union, the deterioration of economic conditions, the abolition of the welfare system, and high unemployment rates led Uzbekistan to become a hotbed of radicals in Central Asia. It is a doubly landlocked country in Central Asia—bordering Kazakhstan to the west and to the north, Kyrgyzstan and Tajikistan to the east, and Afghanistan and Turkmenistan to the south. Uzbekistan and its capital Tashkent were at the crossroads of many invasions and cultures including Arabs, Persians, Ottoman Turks, and Mongols. The most ferocious terrorist organization in the region is the Islamic Movement of Uzbekistan (IMU). Its goal is to establish an Islamic state in Uzbekistan, remove Uzbekistan's President Islam Karimov, and establishing a caliphate throughout Central Asia.

Samarkand-born engineer Karimov, an Uzbek politician who has been the first President of Uzbekistan since 1990, is a secular leader, married to a Russian botanist. After the September 11, 2001 attacks, Uzbekistan became a strategic ally for the United States because of a mutual opposition to the Taliban. The IMU is based in the Ferghana Valley, which is famous for its cotton and other textiles, and borders Tajikistan and Kyrgyzstan. The IMU is associated with AQ, Hizb ut-Tahrir, the Salafi movement, and Tabligi Jamaat of Pakistan. The U.S. State Department has declared it a terrorist organization. IMU started in 1998 as an activist spinoff, known as Adolat (or Justice), of the Uzbekistan branch of the Islamic Renaissance Party (IRP). The IRP participated in politics but was not fully committed to turning the nation into an Islamic state. The triggering incident was the seizure of the Communist Party offices in the eastern city of Namangan, after the mayor refused to give a group of unemployed young Muslims land to build a mosque. Their leaders were Tohir Yuldeshev, a veteran of the Afghan War, and Jumaboi Khojaev Namangani, a former Uzbek Soviet paratrooper. Both were killed during or after the American invasion of Afghanistan in 2001.

After 9/11, thousands of Uzbek militants escaped into Waziristan, Pakistan. The IMU is alleged to have been responsible for several terrorist attacks and hostage-takings; these included the 2006 armed attack in a detention center in Kyrgyzstan that killed the Center's Chief; a 2005 bombing in Dushanbe, Tajikistan, killing one; a 2004 suicide attack on U.S. and Israel embassies in Tashkent; a 2003 bombing of a currency market, killing one; a 2002 bombing of a market in Bishkek, Kyrgyzstan, killing 6; a 2000 hostage-taking of 4 U.S. mountain climbers; and a 1999 car bombing and hostage-taking of 4 Japanese citizens. The IMU has fought for the Taliban against the Coalition Forces in Afghanistan, and for the Taliban in the Swat Valley in Pakistan against Pakistan's Army. It collaborates with another terrorist movement, Hizb-ut-Tehrir (HT/HuT), which was founded in Jordan and is now based in London. HT has 10,000 members in Central Asia, most of who are from Uzbekistan. Like the IMU, the HT is an Islamic movement focused on establishing Sharia in Central Asia and beyond. The IMU is also collaborating with the Islamic Movement of Turkestan (IMT) and with Muslim Uyghur to create an autonomous Xinjiang province in China.

The Islamic Jihad Union (IJU), with breakaway members from the IMU, was among the groups that claimed responsibility for attacks in Tashkent and Bukhara in late March and early April 2004 that left 47 people dead. The IJU resurfaced in 2007 when German police arrested three men with alleged ties to the organization for plotting domestic terrorist attacks against the U.S. military base at Ramstein and the U.S. and Uzbek Consulates. German police arrested three more suspected IJU members in September 2008. German and Uzbek authorities have been in frequent contact since the first arrests, indicating that German officials see a link that goes back to Uzbekistan. In the case of the May 2005 violence in Andijan, the Uzbek government blamed supporters of Akramiya (a splinter group of Hizb-ut-Tehrir based on the teachings of Akram Yuldashev). The group allegedly entered Uzbekistan from Kyrgyzstan, ambushed a police station, and attacked a prison before briefly taking over administrative buildings in Andijan, killing hundreds. The Uzbek government claimed that the IMU and the Hizb ut-Tahrir organized the 2005 protests and unarmed uprising in Andijan (the birthplace of the Mogul emperor Babur. These rebels were aided by Afghanistan, Pakistan, Kyrgyzstan, and Kazakhstan with the objective of toppling Karimov's government. Twenty-three businessmen connected to the terrorist organization Akramiya were arrested and were kept in jail pending a hearing. On May 11, 2005, nearly 4000 demonstrators assembled to hear the verdict, but the judge deferred the hearing. On May 12, the jail was raided and several guards were killed. The terrorists released the businessmen and eight other inmates from the jail. They also seized the building and demanded the resignation of President Karimov.[39] The Andijan massacre occurred when Uzbek troops fired into a crowd of protesters killing more than 1000 people: a disastrous and brutal killing, under the cover of counterinsurgency. Human rights organizations condemned the massacre, which was also denounced by the governments of the United States and several European nations, while Russia and China supported the action by the Uzbek government. In the aftermath of these events, Uzbek President Karimov ordered the closing of the American air base in Karshi-Khanabad. Vitaly Naumkin, a Russian scholar on Central Asia, has commented that an essential aspect of the rise of militant Islam in the region was its relationship with organized crime, because income from drug trafficking, hostage taking, and looting helps fund extremist groups.

> Extremism in turn creates conditions in which criminal groups can flourish because it destabilizes society and exerts pressure on governments. Local traditional networks—regional groups, extended families, clans, and so on—are exploited by both secular authorities in the government and radical Islamists, both of whom compete to dominate these networks.[40]

Tajikistan

Tajikistan became independent in 1991 following the breakup of the Soviet Union. Today it has one of the lowest per capita GDPs among the 15 former Soviet republics. It borders Afghanistan in the south, Uzbekistan in the west, Kyrgyzstan in the north, China in the east, and also lies adjacent to Pakistan-controlled Kashmir. Tajikistan is largely a nation of Muslim Sunnis. Its capital is Dushanbe. The population of 7.5 million is 79.9 per cent Tajiks, who speak Tajiki, 15.3 per cent Uzbek, who speak Turkic, 1.1 per cent Russians, and 3.7 per cent others minorities including Arabs and Iranians. Tajikistan has been invaded since the eighth century by Arabs, Persians, and Mongols. During the years 1860 to 1900, Tajikistan was divided, with the north coming under Tsarist Russian rule while the south was annexed by the Emirate of Bukhara. Tajiks have emphasized their historical pre-Islamic roots with the beliefs of Zoroaster, and the government named its online news agency Avesta in 2004. Written in the ancient Persian language of Pahlavi, the Avesta is the scripture of Zoroastrianism, which flourished in the region then populated by the Aryan tribes. These Aryan tribes fanned out from Sogdiana and Tukhara to Europe and the Indian subcontinent.

> In an anti-Islamic campaign, modeled along Karimov's in Uzbekistan, [President Rahmanov's] government banned head scarves in schools, im-

posed official examinations on clerics, and closed hundreds of unauthorized mosques. Within two summer months of 2007, the authorities in
Dushanbe—its population being nearly 600,000—shut 300 mosques, leaving only 57 intact. The closed places of worship were transformed into
beauty salons, public baths, community centers, or police stations. This
was a repeat of the pattern set in Soviet times.[40]

There have been several terrorist attacks in Tajikistan. Dushanbe blames
much of the increased violence on a resurgence of activity by the IMU.
Three men arrested at a checkpoint in eastern Tajikistan on July 22, 2005,
as reported by the police, were IMU members who were carrying firearms,
grenades, communications equipment, and homemade bombs. Another alleged IMU operative was arrested in Khujand in connection with the murder
of two police officers on August 4, 2005. Two IMU militants were reportedly shot by security forces in separate incidents on August 9, 2005. Forty-
six members of the Tablighi Jamaat, a Pakistani-based Islamic revival group,
were arrested in the Khatlon region, near Pakistan, on July 16, 2005. The
Tablighi Jamaat was banned in March 2006 due to the belief that the movement aims to subvert constitutional order in Tajikistan and establish an Islamic caliphate. Tajikistan also is home to an unknown number of Hizb-ut-
Tahrir members, primarily in the northern part of the country, as well as
other Islamist groups including AQ. Because of its proximity to Pakistan,
terrorists from Afghanistan find sanctuaries in Tajikistan. In January 2007 a
Tajik court found Makhmudzhon Shokirov, a member of Hizb ut-Tahrir[41]
(HuT), guilty of "publicly calling for violent change of the constitutional
order in Tajikistan" and "inciting ethnic, racial, and religious enmity."
Tajikistan is embroiled in ethnic rivalries between North and South, religious tension among Sunnis and Shias, and cultural conflict among Tajiks
and Iranians and with neighbors. Meanwhile, political Islam receives foreign funding through the Islamic Party of Tajikistan's Renaissance (IPRT),
Islamic Jihad Union (IJU), and the HuT in Central Asia—funding that is
used to arm and train radical Islamists. Dormant religious and political organizations in Central Asia have made a chaotic dive into turmoil and instability, replacing atheist, secular Soviets with fanatic firebrand radicals. From
2005 onward, an average of one bomb per month explodes in Dushanbe,
terrorizing the people there. The government of Tajikistan blamed Islamist
militants, some with ties to Afghanistan and Pakistan, for an assault on a
military convoy in Tajikistan that killed at least 23 soldiers in September
2010.[42]

In Central Asia, the East Turkestan Islamic Movement (ETIM), designated a terrorist organization by the United States, is linked to AQ and the

Turkestan Islamic Party (TIP). The ETIM has been stoking Islamic separatism and violence in Xinjiang, China, and other places for decades. It is alleged that the IMU changed its name to the TIP in 2001, expanding its goal to the creation of an Islamic state in all of Central Asia. Islamist terrorists, including AQ and the International Islamic Brigade (IIB), have been involved in suicide bombing in Chechnya and Dagestan. The TIP is involved in deadly attacks in several Chinese cities, including deadly bus explosions in Shanghai and Kunming.[43]

Between 2000 and 2005, more than 800 people were killed in 25 different suicide attacks carried out by over 100 terrorists in Chechnya. During the years 1994 to 1996, this conflict was primarily been depicted as a struggle for independence from Russia. Yet its second stage, from 1999 to 2009, has revealed trends of Islamic extremism within the Chechnya campaign.

Jalāl ad-Din Muhammad Rum, also known as Rumi (1207–1273), was born in Tajikistan and lived in Central Anatolia. He proclaimed that "all religions were one, all manifestations of the same divine reality," According to Talat Halman, the leading Turkish Rumi scholar:

> Rumi's brand of Sufism represents the free spirit of Islam . . . the liberal spirit that I think needs to be recognised at a time when Islam has come to be considered almost synonymous with terrorism. The Sufi spirit softens the message of the Qur'an by emphasizing the sense of love, and the passionate relationship between the believer and the beloved, God of course being the ultimate beloved. So in the eyes of Rumi and the Sufis, God becomes not the angry god of punishment, nor the god of revenge, but the god of love. Rumi advocated an individual and interior spirituality, and it is the love, rather than the fear, of God that lies at the heart of his message. He attempts to merge the spirit of the human with the ideal of a god of love, whom Rumi locates within the human heart. Rumi's first biographer, Aflaki, tells of a man who came to Rumi asking how he could reach the other world, as only there would he be at peace. "What do you know about where He is?" asked Rumi. "Everything in this or that world is within you." One way Rumi did, however, most certainly diverge from some of the more austere ulema of his time was in that he believed passionately in the use of music, poetry and dancing as a path for reaching God, as a way of, as he put it, opening the gates of paradise. For Rumi, music helped devotees to focus their whole being on the divine, and to do this so intensely that the soul was both destroyed and resurrected.[44]

Rumi's poems were close in spirit to the Indian sect of Vaishnavists' *Bhakti (devotion)* movement, who propagated devotion to God through music, dance, and spiritual love. (Many of the ancient Indian kings, beginning with

Chandragupta II (Vikramaditya), were known as Parama Bhagavatas, or Bhagavata Vaishnava).

> Every prophet, every saint has his path
> But as they return to God, all are one.

> Love's folk live beyond religious borders
> The community and creed of lovers: God.[45]

Rumi's creed was followed in some parts of Northern India, including Jammu & Kashmir. He influenced South Asian poets including Sir Mohammad Iqbal, Thir ul-Qadri, and Kazi Nazrul Islam, and the Persian liberal reformist Abdolkarim Soroush. He was a great Sufi poet who propounded Sufism or Islamic mysticism, the most accessible, tolerant and pluralistic incarnation of Islam, and a uniquely valuable bridge between east and west at this moment of crisis, finds itself suppressed by the Islamic world's two most pro-western governments: fundamentalist Saudi Arabia and secular Turkey. In some Islamic countries Rumi's music, dance and accompanying instruments are banned.

South Asia

With the independence of India, territorial disputes and resource sharing among the decolonized states of India, Bangladesh, and Pakistan gave rise to militancy and animosity. There were several wars between India and Pakistan, while Pakistan and Afghanistan could not accept the Durand Line demarcated by the British. Then came the Soviet invasion of Afghanistan, and later, the American intervention. From 1979 to 2009, there was an emergence of several terrorist organizations in the region, creating the global jihadi movement.

Terrorism in South Asia and beyond continues unabated even after the American strikes in October 2001 and the continuing war in Afghanistan. Terrorists have found safe havens on the borders of Pakistan and Afghanistan and use these bases to launch jihadi attacks around the globe. Pakistan denies their presence on its soil and insists that it does not help terrorists. Frustrated British Prime Minister Gordon Brown left unstated what has been a common assumption among Western governments dealing with Pakistan on the issue of Islamic extremism: that powerful elements of the government in Islamabad, including its military intelligence agency, ISI, have been following a two-track policy, accepting billions of dollars in Western aid on the pledge of fighting the Taliban and AQ while covertly assisting them, or at least avoiding a confrontation with them.[46]

More than half of the world's Muslims live in South Asia and South East Asia. The influx of terrorists during the Afghanistan war in 1979–1989, aided by the use of Middle Eastern funds to build Wahhabi mosques and schools, has generated communal hatred and Islamic extremism. Many former Afghanistan war veterans have gone to fight with the Americans and Allied forces in Afghanistan and Iraq. In spite of the fact that these wars are waged to combat terrorism, Muslim extremists believe they are actually a war against Islam, and that the 9/11 attacks in America were fabricated.

Syed Maududi, founder of Jamaat-e-Islami (Islamic Party), was the foremost proponent of modern jihad in South Asia. Maududi, along with Qutb, is considered one of the founding fathers of the global Islamic revivalist movements. Yet Maududi has been more strongly influenced by Stalin or Mussolini than by the Qur'an and Hadith and the example of seventh-century Medina. The majority of Muslims regard his views as being born of ignorance and a hatred of Islam. Maududi was not a nationalist and scholar like Maulana Abul Kalam Azad (1888–1958), or a poet and philosopher like Muhammad Iqbal (1877–1938), or a supporter of colonialism like Syed Ahmad Khan (1817–1898),

> who had himself protected the British during the uprising, devoted himself in the decades following to fostering intellectual and political reconciliation between the Muslim service elite and the colonial power. Within two decades, Muslim elites had, in fact, come to be seen, like the princes, as a pillar of loyalty, a role not uncommon for "minorities" in authoritarian settings.[47]

Maududi was not a separatist and Muslim nationalist like Jinnah, who established the first Islamic state in Pakistan in 1947. After the partition of India in 1947, Maududi migrated to Pakistan and was involved in much political activity. He was imprisoned there for his views, and his extremism caused the persecution of Ahmadiyyas in Pakistan, along with the passage of highly problematic "blasphemy" and "Hudood" laws. Maududi was influenced by jihadi preachers Ahmed Sirhandi (1564-1624) and Shah Waliullah Dehlvi (1703–1762), in addition to Ibn Taymiyya (1263-1328). Waliullah, a Muslim of Arab origins who lived in colonial India, urged Muslim rulers to enact a jihad against the enemies of Islam, hoping to restore the Ulama's former power and influence and to unify all Indian Muslims against non believers. He was a bigoted, insecure and paranoid intellectual who urged that the universal domination of Islam was not possible without jihad. He pioneered jihad in South Asia, and was against Turks, Shias, and Hanafi's liberal laws, besides being virulently anti-Hindu. However, a few Pakistani Muslim scholars believed he was the greatest Islamic scholar of his time and that he would restore the integrity of Islam, by rejecting Emperor Akbar and his grandson Dara Shikoh's' vision of assimilating Sufism with Hindu mysticism.

Dara Shikoh, murdered by his brother Aurangzeb in August 30, 1659, is famous for his work, *Mujma-ul-Bahrain*, "The Mingling of the Two Seas." He was involved in the mystical and universal confluence between Sufism and Vedantic philosophy. Being a liberal scholar, he understood the need for the harmonious coexistence of heterodox traditions of the Indian Subcontinent.[48] Maududi, a virulent critic of the West, died in America. But Maududi's jihadi legacy was pervasive in Pakistan. The Pakistani born Muslim scholar Aesha Jalal expounds upon this legacy:

> Parents, who are encouraged to send their sons to battle Hindu infidels, celebrate news of their death by distributing sweets and offering prayers of thanksgiving to Allah. Jihad has done a roaring business in Pakistan because it appeals to the imagination of people whose prospectus are severely limited.

Religion can make some people mentally blind, destroys their analytical minds, scientific reasoning and rationality, debunks their humanity and scholarship, and incarcerates them in the most anachronistic obscurantism. Many radicals live in America and enjoy privileges, freedom, and equality, yet denounce secularity, and are against Muslim women not wearing burqa in America. South Asia's Islamist political movements trace their inspiration back to Ahmed Sirhandi's challenge in the sixteenth century to the ecumenism of Mughal (Mogul) Emperor Akbar. Despite Emperor Akbar's tolerant views of Hinduism, Encyclopadia Britannica mentions that he "ordered the massacre of about 30,000 captured Rajput Hindus on February 24, 1568 AD, after the battle for Chittod, a number confirmed by Emperor Akbar's court historian Abul Fazl."

In the nineteenth century, the first jihadi group emerged in India and operated in the country's northwest frontier, which included parts of present-day Pakistan and Afghanistan. This puritanical militant movement fought the region's Sikh rulers. The movement's founder, Syed Ahmed of Bareili, organized cells throughout India to supply the frontier movement with men and money to kill infidels. Calling themselves "mujahidin," the movement's followers interpreted the Islamic concept of jihad in its literal sense of holy war. Sirhandi wrote that cow-sacrifice in India is the noblest of Islamic practices. The kefirs may probably agree to pay jiziya but they shall never concede to cow-sacrifice.

Animesh Roul (NBR Analysis) highlights five features of the terrorist landscape in South Asia. First, the region has the highest concentration of Islamist jihadist groups in the world; second, many groups operate across national borders; third, India has the greatest number of jihadi groups; fourth, some of the groups have achieved an impressive degree of cross-national coordination; and fifth, several of the most violent and well-coordinated groups have ties with international jihadi organizations based in Pakistan, Afghanistan, and Uzbekistan. Roul concludes that in Pakistan and Bangladesh the Muslim leadership's tolerance of extremist interpretations of Islam has contributed to the rise of Islamist radicalism. In India, Roul observes, the major contributor to Islamist radicalism has been the upsurge in anti-Muslim violence, particularly since the destruction of the Babri Mosque in 1992. Roul adds:

> In Bangladesh, government crackdowns pushed the extremist forces into hiding initially, although now they are regrouping and recruiting cadres in rural pockets. Both Pakistan and Bangladesh are serving as major hubs for ideological and material support to the South Asian radical Islamic networks. In India, homegrown jihadists are emerging, while radical elements are attempting to exploit the alienation of India's Muslim youths. With these three South Asian countries increasingly under the militant Islamic grip, the Sunni-majority Maldives could become the next safe haven for radical elements. This region has the highest concentration of Islamic *jihadist* groups in the world: a rough estimate is that nearly one hundred Islamic extremist groups and jihadi organizations with cross-border linkages are operating with impunity throughout South Asia. India tops the list with more than 50 active or dormant terrorist *tanzeems* (organizations). Several anti-India and anti-Hindu Islamic groups fighting in Kashmir are based in Pakistan or Bangladesh.

Bangladesh

In 1947, Sonar Bangla (see 1913 Nobel laureate Rabindranath Tagore's famous poem, "Golden Bengal") was divided, with East Bengal becoming East Pakistan. In 1971, East Pakistan became Bangladesh. Bangladesh's national poet Kazi Nazrul Islam (1899–1976), known for composing 4000 songs and authoring many works including *The Rebel, The Song of Destruction, The Comet,* and *Decomposition of a Political Prisoner*, assailed fanaticism in religion, denouncing it as evil and inherently impious. In 1920, Islam expressed his secularism in an editorial in *Yuga Bani,*

Come brother Hindu! Come Musalman (Muslims)! Come Buddhist! Come Christian! Let us transcend all barriers, let us forsake forever all small-ness, all lies, all selfishness and let us call brothers as brothers. We shall quarrel no more.

Sheikh Mujibur Rahman (1920–1975), head of the Awami League, won a majority in Parliament in the 1970 elections in Pakistan but was denied the seat of Prime Minister. Following agitation and revolt, President Yahya Khan arrested him in the early hours of March 26, 1971, and launched Operation Searchlight, a sustained military assault on East Pakistan. Esti-mates of those massacred throughout the war number up to 3 million. With more than one million East Pakistani refugees streaming into West Bengal, India intervened and Pakistan was defeated on December 16, 1971. India then declared a unilateral ceasefire. According to the historian Richard Sisson and Leo Rose.[49] Generals Niazi and Farman Ali immediately prepared plans for surrender; their intention was signaled to the Government of India through the U.S. diplomatic service. The terms of the surrender were initiated by General Manekshaw, presented to General Niazi by General Jacob on De-cember 16, and signed by Generals Niazi and Aurora at the Ramna Race Course, the scene of Sheikh Mujibur Rahman's most significant political moments. Ironically, it was here too that General Niazi, Commander of the forces of Muslim Pakistan, surrendered his arms to three generals of "Hindu" India—one a Parsi, another a Sikh, and the third a Jew.

On his return from the Pakistani prison, Mujibur Rahman became Bangladesh's first Prime Minister. He, an avowed secular socialist, was assassinated in a military coup on August 15, 1975. There were several political assassinations, and much turmoil and unrest under military and presidential rule. From a liberal, secular, socialist, democratic Bangla, the country is on its way to becoming Islamic Bangla. Bangladesh is a Muslim country of 163 million, with 83 per cent Muslim, 16 per cent Hindu, and 1 per cent other. It is one of the poorest countries in the world, with a per capita GDP of $520 according to a 2008 estimate. This poverty and political instability have laid the ground for terrorism. Several terrorist organiza-tions have cropped up, all with the intent of transforming secular Bangladesh into Islamic Bangladesh, to be governed by Sharia. One terrorist organiza-tion forced the feminist writer, Taslima Nasreen (also spelled Nasrin), to leave the country due to her views on the Quran.

When elections were finally held in late December 2008, Sheikh Hasina Wajed, daughter of Mujibur Rahman, was reappointed prime minister. Eight grenades, 28 firearms, large amounts of ammunition, and 30 motorbikes have been seized from potential terrorists in a nationwide crackdown since

Prime Minister Sheikh Hasina's government took power in January 2009. "We have detained 15 hardcore Islamists and about 3,000 suspected militants in the past two days," a senior police officer said. The most prominent terrorist organizations in Bangladesh are: Jama'at ul-Mujahedeen Bangladesh (JuMB), Allahr Dal, Harkat-ul Jihad al Islami (HuJI), and Hizb-ut Tawhid (HuT). There is also a new jihadi outfit, Islam-o-Muslim (IoM), in addition to the LeT and the transnational criminal network of Dawood Ibrahim, the underworld gang leader from Bombay. These organizations have been involved in terrorist attacks in several places including Varanasi, New Delhi, Ajodhya, and Mumbai, India. The HuJI Bangladesh (HuJI-B) has been added to the U.S. U.K. and UN lists of terrorist organizations. HuJI-B was behind the 2004 grenade attacks on British High Commissioner Anwar Choudhury. The HuMB on August 17, 2005, coordinated 459 synchronized bomb explosions in Bangladesh, killing two people and injuring hundreds. They also assassinated two judges, on November 14, 2005.

The JuMB has more than five thousand cadres, including female militants. Many of these cadres have crossed the border into India and have links with two Indian terrorist groups, Muslim United Liberation Tigers of Assam (MULTA) and the United Liberation Front of Assam (ULFA). It is believed that 1000 Bangladeshi mujahidins came back to Bangladesh after the war in Afghanistan in the 1990s, and an Afghanistan war veteran has served as the chief of HuJI-B. The HuJI-B has taken much of its training and arms supply from Muzaffarabad in Pakistan Occupied Kashmir (PoK) as part of its partnership with Harakat-ul-Jihad-i-Islami Pakistan (HuJI-P), and from the LeT and the JeM. On returning to Bangladesh, some of these Afghan veterans formed terrorist organizations in conjunction with Jagrata Muslim Janata Bangladesh (JMJB), which is headed by Siddiqul Islam and Bangla Bhai. In 2004, after seizing power from the authorities, Bangla Bhai imposed Sharia in certain section of Rajshahi, Bangladesh. The MULTA, affiliated with Jamaat-e-Islami (JI) of Pakistan, has been collaborating with other terrorist organizations such as the ULFA and the Students Islamic Movement of India (SIMI), which are both allies of OBL's International Islamic Front (IIF). Hizb ut-Tahrir was banned by the government of Bangladesh on October 22, 2009 for "anti-state, anti-government, anti-people and anti-democratic" activities in the country. None of the Bangladeshi terrorists are illiterate or poor. Table 4.1 provides statistics on terrorist attacks in Bangladesh from 1999 to 2005.

It is believed that much of the funding that allows these groups to operate comes from the Middle East, from organizations such as the now-officially defunct Al-Haramain Islamic Foundation. But financial contributions also come from individuals (Arabs, expatriate Bangladeshis, and others),

Table 4.1
Terrorist Attacks in Bangladesh (Jugantara, August 2005)

1999	18
2000	Not Available
2001	25
2002	21
2004	42
2005 May	48

and the Islamic Bank of Bangladesh has been accused of handling these transactions.[50]

South Asian analyst Selig Harrison observes:

> While the United States dithers, a growing Islamic fundamentalist movement linked to Al Qaeda and Pakistani intelligence agencies is steadily converting the strategically located nation of Bangladesh into a new regional hub for terrorist operations that reach into India and Southeast Asia. . . . For Pakistan's intelligence agencies, especially Inter-Services Intelligence (ISI), the legacy of the independence war has been a built-in network of agents within the Jamaat and its affiliates who can be utilized to harass India along its 2,500-mile border with Bangladesh. In addition to supporting tribal separatist groups in northeast India, the ISI uses Bangladesh as a base for helping Islamic extremists inside India. After the July 11 train bombings in Bombay, a top Indian police official, K.P. Raghuvanshi, said that his key suspects "have connections with groups in Nepal and Bangladesh, which are directly or indirectly connected to Pakistan."[51]

Links to India and Pakistan: In the last two decades, due to the fall of secular, democratic governments and instability in Bangladesh, its territory has been used as a sanctuary for various militant groups operating in India's northeastern states. Groups such as the HuJI, the LeT, the JeM, and the HuM are still focusing on India, while receiving support from the ISI and its Bangladeshi counterpart, the Director General Field Intelligence (DGFI), who have formed a deadly alliance against India. Terrorist leaders such as Masood Azhar (JeM), Hafiz Saeed (LeT), and Syed Salauddin (HuM) have sponsored many terrorist acts in India while dominating the radical Islamic landscape for more than a decade. The HuM has strong links with the Students' Islamic Movement of India (SIMI) and the Tabligh-i-Jamaat (TJ), and is largely supported by Pakistan's ISI and JI. Unlike the HuM, the JeM has perpetrated major attacks on Indian establishments within the very short span of its existence. Having direct affiliations with AQ and Taliban militants, the JeM became the first terrorist group to adopt suicide terror tactics when it targeted the J&K State Legislative Assembly and Indian parliament in 2001. The LeT's military wing, Jamaat-ud-Dawa, has a pan-Islamic Wahhabi ideology. The LeT masterminded the 2006 Mumbai train blasts and 2005 Delhi market blasts with HuJI's support.

The Asia analyst Bruce Vaughan reports:

> HuJI is thought to remain active in the area south from Chittagong and the border with Burma. A report sourced to a former senior Indian intelligence official alleges that HuJI is training Burmese Muslim Rohingyas, as well as small groups from Thailand, Cambodia, Indonesia, and Brunei. . . . AQ had reportedly recruited Rohingyas from refugee camps in southeastern Bangladesh to fight in Afghanistan, Kashmir, and Chechnya. Bangladesh has been ruled by the military for approximately 15 of the past 35 years. Ganguly asserts that the military's desire for legitimacy led them to "wrap themselves in the mantle of Islam" and this created new political space for Islamists in Bangladesh. As a result, "they not only altered the terms of political discourse in Bangladesh but also helped fashion a new political culture that could accommodate a shift toward a more pristine, austere, and parochial vision of Islam."[52]

India

The strategic location of India, including Kashmir, was one of the main reasons the British Empire sought to occupy the country. Its advantages include wide access to the Indian Ocean, to Afghanistan and Iran through the Khyber Pass, and to China along the Himalayas. Colonial occupation of India made it possible for the British to keep the Soviets away from the great game:

> The material self-interest was economic and strategic. India was a captive market, for long prevented by a system of counterveiling excise duties from protecting its cotton-manufacturing industry from the products of Lancashire.[53]

The British first encountered strong resistance from Marathas and Sikhs. In June 1818, Maratha power was finally crushed. Baji Rao, the Maratha ruler, was pensioned off and shipped north of Bithur, to a castle on the outskirts of Kanpur (Cawnpore), which would later become the center of the 1857 'mutiny.'[54] The Sikh hegemony of the Punjab was finally overthrown not by Muslims but by the British in the 1940s, and it was in the services of the new rulers of India that the Sikhs last warred against the

Muslims, at the siege of Delhi in 1857–1858.[55] The rebellion against British rule started in 1857 with the Sepoy Mutiny, when a large number of Hindus revolted under the leadership of kings, queens, and common men, including Rajput Lady Laksmibai of Jhansi, Tartia (Tantiya) Topee, Nana Sahib, U. Kiang Nongbah, Rao Tularam, and Mangal Pandey; Muslim Sepoy Shaikh Patu helped arrest Pandey. The British colonialists were looking for partners to pursue their strategic objective before leaving India. The nationalist sentiments of the Indian National Congress (INC) were strongly against Colonial rule, and wanted full independence. India's independence movement started in 1885 with the formation of the INC, while the All India Muslim League (AIML), founded in 1906, sought a Muslim nation-state. The Colonialists thwarted the independence movement, proposing a two-nation theory that the INC would reject. Imperial rule was disastrous under this horrible theory, which partitioned on the basis of religion. Things became violent in 1857 when rumors spread that rifles were greased with beef and pork fat. The terrorist attacks in India originated from the partition of India based on religious and communal identities. The British could put down the non-violent movement of Mahatma Gandhi's INC, but were cowed by the violence of Direct Action Day, espoused by the AIML. The Indian rebellion, led by Hindus against the British occupation of India, was unacceptable to the British Raj. The British used Muslim elites including Sir Syed Khan (1817–1878; he founded Aligarh Muslim University in 1875 to provide Islamic-based education to Muslims), Allama Iqbal (1877–1938), M.A. Jinnah (1876–1948), and Liaquat Ali Khan (1896–1951) to secure their support, in order to impede the independence movement by the INC, which was dominated by a majority of Hindus. Even education in India was communalized and segregated by the British rulers, with the establishment of Banaras Hindu University in 1916, in addition to the AMU in 1875. It was said that the infusion of separatist politics for Muslims had been "preventing the growth of a national spirit and national parties characterized by social or economic beliefs rather than religion."[56]

The history of South Asia from 1857 to 1947 was marked by a violent struggle between the INC's Indian nationalism and the AIML's Muslim separatism. The British struggled too, trying to keep the Empire by any means, and rewarded the AIML for its pro-British policy. This brought India not simply partition into two dominions, but also the division of Punjab and Bengal, with Hindus and Muslims almost equally represented in each province. Muslim-dominated districts of Punjab and Bengal joined Pakistan, while the Hindu-dominated sections joined India, even though the populations were intertwined. However, Baluchistan and the KP, being Muslim majority provinces, were forced to join Pakistan against their wishes.

The Cabinet Mission, appointed by the British Empire to transfer power, never cared about their democratic rights, or their cultural and ethnic differences.

Communal Reservation: Reservations based on Islam were the beginning of the divide-and-rule policy of the British Raj. The British exhorted the Muslim elites to shun the Indian National Congress. They encouraged and favored the Muslim community, encouraging them to equals with the Hindu majority, despite their very small numbers (about 20 per cent of the population). A number of seats on local government boards, based on religion, not on population, were assigned by the Rippon Reform of 1882–1883, the Morley Minto reforms of 1909, and the Montague–Chelmsford Reform of 1919.

The Act of 1909 stipulated, as demanded by the Muslim leadership:

- that Indian Muslims be allotted reserved seats in the Municipal and District Boards, in the Provincial Councils and in the Imperial Legislature;
- that the number of reserved seats be in excess of their relative population (less than 25 per cent of the Indian population); and,
- that only Muslims should vote for candidates for the Muslim seats ('separate electorates').

These concessions were a constant source of strife from 1909 to 1947. British statesmen generally considered reserved seats as regrettable in that they encouraged communal extremism, as Muslim candidates did not have to appeal for Hindu votes and vice versa. As more power was shifted from the British to Indian politicians, in 1919, 1935, and thereafter, Muslims were ever more determined to hold on to, and if possible expand, reserved seats and the power associated with them.[57]

The separate electorate for Muslims damaged the concept of Indian nationalism. The Muslim communitarians, based on Islam, were pitted against Indian nationalists. The establishment of the AIML in 1906 consolidated communal separatism further and deeper.

The Fourteen Points of Jinnah, proposed by M.A. Jinnah in March 1929 at the AIML meeting, was based on religious reservations, in contrast to Nehru's secular report on the constitution. Jinnah never went to prison, like Mahatma Gandhi or Pundit Nehru. Viceroys made Jinnah the sole spokesman of the AIML, even though he did not have the majority support of the party like any other chief minister of Punjab, Sindh, or Bengal. He was also designated the spokesman for the Muslims of India. In a blatantly undemocratic act, Viceroy Wavell remarked that unless Congress accepted the Muslim League as the sole representative of all Muslims of India, there could be no agreement. This happened when the Congress had won eight out of eleven States.

Communal Politics: In 1920, Indian National Congress leader Mohandas Gandhi and the Khilafat leaders, Mohammad Ali and his brother Shaukat Ali and others, promised to work and fight together for the causes of Khilafat—a nationwide campaign of peaceful mass civil disobedience to restore the caliphate, based on the seventh century Islamic concept of Sharia rule. It is strange that Gandhi, an ardent secularist, supported the religious-based Khilafat movement. The British were against the Khilafat movement as was M.A. Jinnah (who was well aware of British interests), although a vast number of Muslims in India supported it. With the victory of Mustafa Kemal, Turkey became a secular republic, and the Kilafat movement was buried. The AIML's support of World War II: The INC and the AIML were divided over World War II, as Lord Linlithgow declared that India would join the Allies with an Indian army of more than 200,000. As a vehement protest to Lord Linlithgow's action, the entire Congress leadership resigned from the local government councils. Soon after the outbreak of war in 1939, the eight Congress ministries in the provinces and the pro-Congress North-West Frontier Provinces ministry resigned. The AIML, led by M.A. Jinnah, stepped into the vacuum, forming ministries in Assam and Sind, which had INC-led coalition ministries, and in the KP, where the pro-INC ministry of Dr Khan Saheb was in power. The British were pleased with Jinnah's decision.

The Pakistan Resolution (Lahore Resolution): On March 12, 1940, Viceroy Lord Linlithgow wrote to the Secretary of State for India:

> Upon my instruction Zafarullah (Khan) wrote a memorandum on the subject, *Two Dominion States*. I have already sent it to your attention. I have also asked him for further clarification, which, he says, is forthcoming. He is anxious, however, that no one should find out that he has prepared this plan. He has, however, given me the right to do with it what I like, including sending a copy to you. Copies have been passed on to Jinnah, and, I think, to Sir Akbar Hydari (of Punjab). While he, Zafarullah, cannot admit its authorship, his document has been prepared for adoption by the Muslim League with a view to giving it the fullest publicity. The Viceroy explains this further. Since Zafarullah was a Qadiani he had to be cautious. The Muslims would become irritated if they found that this scheme was prepared by a Qadiani.[58]

The Cabinet Mission and Direct Action Day: The Cabinet Mission for the Partition of India was formed on February 19, 1946, with Lord Patrick-

Lawrence (Secretary of State for India), Sir Stafford Cripps, and Mr. A.V. Alexander. On the March 13, Prime Minister Attlee declared: "It was for India to decide what form of Government should replace the existing regime, though he (Attlee) hoped that she would elect to remain within the British Commonwealth." Mr. Attlee added:

> We are mindful of the rights of minorities, and the minorities should be able to live free from fear. On the other hand, we cannot allow a minority to place their veto on the advance of the majority. Sir Stafford found it impossible to pin him (Jinnah, the leader of the minorities' party, AIML) down to anything beyond vague phrases. The Muslim leader's technique of getting the other man to make an offer so that he (Jinnah) could turn it down and ask for more was difficult to counter, except for ignoring it, and that was dangerous in the existing crisis. . . . At the same time the Congress would never agree to the partition of India.[59]

The meeting at Simla produced no agreements between the INC and the AIML. The Indian National Congress was also opposed to parity between groups in the executive or legislature, and held that it was not open to suggestions for the division of India. The three-tier structure was a recipe for a deadlock in the parliament because of the veto power of each party. The Cabinet Mission left India on the of June 29, 1946, after securing the following agreement on May 16, 1946, agreed to by both the INC and the AIML: if there is to be internal peace in India it must be secured by measures that will assure Muslims control in all matters vital to their culture, religion, and economic and other interests. But it rejected the AIML's demand for a Pakistan consisting of all six provinces, since substantial portions of those provinces contained non-Muslim minorities.[60] The three-tier constitutional structure of the Cabinet Mission consisted of a top level which would be a Union of India embracing British India as well as the Indian States, but dealing only with foreign affairs, defense, and communications, with equal numbers of majority and minority members for parity. The second one was comprised of "groups" to be formed by Provinces, to deal with certain common subjects. The third one was to consist of Provinces and States in which all residuary powers would be vested. At a press conference on July 10, 1946, Pundit Nehru said:

> Moreover, the scope of the Center would have to include (as the corollary of foreign affairs, defense and communications) defense industries, foreign trade, currency and credit, adequate taxing power. The Mission's proviso about power arrangements for minorities was a domestic Indian problem. We accept no outsider's interference with it, certainly not the British Government's.

Asked at the press conference whether he meant that the Cabinet Mission's plan could be modified, Nehru replied that the Congress regarded itself as free to change or modify the plan in the Constitutional assembly as it thought best. Nehru's undiplomatic blunt remarks were not against decentralization, but were against religious groupings as a dysfunctional construct. "Concerning the central powers of the union executive, Nehru argued that it would require 'some over-all power to intervene in grave crisis breakdowns and that such central power 'inevitably grows.'"

The Cabinet Mission had no objections to Nehru's press conference. The AIML passed a resolution in Bombay on the July 27 rejecting the Cabinet Mission, and revoking the agreement of May 16, 1946. That was the death sentence for the Cabinet Mission's plan.[61] What follows is the sequence of events that led to a jihadi agenda in the wake of the Partition of India: The Cabinet Mission rejected the demand for Pakistan because such a state would still have considerable non-Muslim minorities living in it. On June 16, 1946 the Cabinet Mission made a proposal for forming an interim government. But it observed that major difficulties existed between the INC and the AIML, and therefore they were unable to agree on the formation of an interim government, as M.A. Jinnah demanded a 50–50 Muslim representation, whereas the Muslim population at that time was less than twenty-two per cent of the total population of India. On August 15, 1946, the Muslim League withdrew its support for the Cabinet Mission Plan and fixed the date for direct action as August 16. M.J. Akbar, Editor of the Asian Age, wrote:

> The demand for Pakistan was accompanied by the rhetoric of a simulated jihad. A jihad is valid if Muslims are denied the right to practice their faith, or against the invasion of a Muslim's homeland. And so Muslims were warned that in post-British India mosques would be destroyed and the call to prayer forbidden and they must resort to violence if necessary to protect their separateness. A typical pamphlet, circulated after the Muslim League announced a "Direct Action Day" on 16 August 1946, said, "The Bombay resolution of the All-India Muslim League has been broadcast. The call to revolt comes to us from a nation of heroes. . . . The day for an open fight which is the greatest desire of the Muslim nation has arrived. Come, those who want to rise to heaven. Come, those who are simple, wanting in peace of mind and who are in distress. Those who are thieves, goondas (thugs), those without the strength of character and those who do not say their prayers—all come. The shining gates of Heaven have been opened for you. Let us enter in thousands. Let us all cry out victory to Pakistan." The themes are immediately recognizable, with Heaven, as usual, playing a prominent part.[62]

The Mayor of Calcutta (the present Kolkata), Mohammed Usman, gave a call for waging jihad against Hindus through another inflammatory leaflet titled, "Munajat for Jihad." It reminded the Muslims of the Battle of Badr in which "kafirs" were annihilated by a small army of soldiers of Islam.

On the Direct Action Day in Calcutta city, within 72 hours over 5000 were murdered and over 20,000 were injured and a hundred thousand residents were left homeless. It plunged Calcutta to an orgy of communal violence, terror, and slaughter that spread from Calcutta to Dhaka, from Bihar to Bombay, and from Ahmedabad to Lahore.[63]

> One *"jehad"* was recorded in Iskander Mirza's book. Mirza had no hesitation about mounting an attack on India using the tribals of Waziristan, Tirah and Momand. These British minions had in their employ Pirs and Faqirs who could be used to create unrest among the tribals. . . . Jinnah explained that if Pakistan cannot be won by negotiations he would achieve it by combat. Mirza [at the time, the Joint Secretary, Ministry of Defense, later President of Pakistan] wrote that Jinnah wanted him to resign from service, go into the tribal territory and start a *Jehad*.[64]

The root of the terrorist attacks is Kashmir: Pakistan considers Kashmir disputed territory, and has gone to war with India several times over it, including in 1947, 1965, 1971, and 1999. The most dreaded terrorist organization involved in this struggle is the LeT. The number of deaths due to the terrorist attacks in India over this conflict is the highest in the world, barring Iraq. The U.S. Congress Researcher Alan Konostadt states: The U.S. State Department's Country Reports on Terrorism 2007 identified "India as being 'among the world's most terror afflicted countries and counted more than 2,300 Indian deaths due to terrorism in 2007 alone. This number is set to be equaled or exceeded in 2008.'" In the aftermath of the terrorist attacks in Mumbai, India on November 26, 2008 in which more than 170 people were killed by 10 gunmen, came another terrorist incident. It involved terrorists who sailed from Karachi, Pakistan, to the shore of Bombay by hijacking a fishing trawler on the high seas. Upon reaching India's territorial waters, the terrorists transferred their operation to inflatable speedboats, which landed at two different locations near the Port of Bombay. The Carnegie Endowment scholar Ashley Tellis commented on this incident in *Yale Global* (December 2008):

> "Lashkar-e-Taiba (LeT)'s objectives from the beginning have had less to do with Kashmir and more to do with India and beyond. To begin with, India's achievement in becoming a peaceful, prosperous, multi-ethnic and secular democracy remains an affront to the Laskar-e-Taiba's vision of a

universal caliphate begotten through tabligh, or preaching, and jihad. Further, India's collaboration with the United States and the West in general against terrorism has marked it as a part of what the Lashkar-e-Taiba calls the detestable 'American-Zionist-Hindu' axis that must be confronted by force. Finally, New Delhi's emergence as a rising global power represents an impediment to the LeT's objective of, in the words of its leader, Hafiz Saeed, recovering 'lost Muslim lands' that once spanned much of Asia and Europe. Given this ideology, the LeT's attack is an attempt to cripple India's economic growth, destroy national confidence in its political system, its open society, and to provoke destabilizing communal rivalries, all while sending a message that India will remain an adversary because its successes make it a hindrance to the LeT's larger cause. In this context, the struggle over Kashmir is merely instrumental. To quote Saeed, Kashmir is merely a 'gateway to capture India' en route to the LeT's other targets. Outside of Al Qaeda, the Lashkar-e-Taiba today represents the most important South Asian terrorist group of 'global reach.' With recruitment, fundraising and operations extending to Afghanistan, Iraq, Central Asia, Europe, Africa and Australia, the LeT has rapidly become a formidable threat. . . . Saeed has unequivocally declared that the Lashkar intends to 'plant the flag of Islam in Washington, Tel Aviv and New Delhi.' However absurd it might sound, his words could launch thousands of zealots to commit horrible crimes worldwide."[65]

The *Washington Post* reported:

"Groups active in Kashmir and listed by the State Department as terrorist organizations include Laskar-e-Taiba, Hizb-ul-Muhammaed, and Jaish-e-Muhammad. The group suspected of playing the central role in terrorist attacks on Indian soil since 9/11 is Laskar-e-eTaiba, or 'Army of the Pure.' The LeT is the armed wing of a Pakistani-based group of Markaz-ud Dawawal-Irshad, known for preaching Salafi views of Islam. During the 1990s, the group received instruction and funding from the ISI, in exchange for a pledge to target Hindus in Jammu and Kashmir and to train Muslim extremists on Indian soil. After 9/11, when the United States named LeT a terrorist group and Islamabad banned it, the group went underground, splintered and began using different names, and stopped claiming responsibility for attacks. However, the Lashkar-e-Taiba is suspected of involvement in the December 2001 attack of New Delhi's Parliament, the 2006 Mumbai train bombings, and the February 2007 blast of a train running between India and Pakistan. A little known group called Lashkar-e-Qahar, was associated with the LeT and orchestrated the Mumbai bombings. New Delhi has also accused the Student Islamic Movement of India (SIMI) of having connections with the LeT and the Mumbai blasts, as well as terrorist attacks in August 2003."[66]

It is reported in *Los Angeles Times*:

"U.S. officials often tout U.S.-Pakistani intelligence cooperation. The CIA payments are a hidden stream in a much broader financial flow; the U.S. has given Pakistan more than $15 billion over the last eight years in military and civilian aid. . . . The ISI is a highly compartmentalized intelligence service, with divisions that sometimes seem at odds with one another. Units that work closely with the CIA are walled off from a highly secretive branch that has directed insurgencies in Afghanistan and Kashmir.[67]

Designated as a Foreign Terrorist Organization (FTO) under U.S. law in late 2001, the LeT is based in Muzaffarabad, Pakistani Kashmir, and Muridke, Lahore, Pakistan. Jamaat-ud-Dawa (JuD) is alleged to be the new name of the LeT, which is now disguised as a charity organization. The JuD operates 2500 offices and 11 religious seminaries in Pakistan. Ambassador Husain Haqqani, Pakistan's current Ambassador to the United States, has commented upon Pakistan's "state sponsorship of jihad against India" and described the LeT as "backed by Saudi money and protected by Pakistani intelligence services." In a 2005 book[68] on the relationship between Pakistani Islamists and the Pakistani military, this diplomat wrote of how, earlier in the decade, the ISI provided significant "severance pay" to jihad leaders in return for their promise to "remain dormant for an unspecified duration." Among the alleged recipients of this ISI largesse were the LeT's Saeed, and Masood Azhar, chief of the Pakistan-based, FTO-designated Jaish-e-Mohammed (JeM). In addition, there are two major terrorist groups: Jaish-e-Mohammad (JeM) and Hizb-ul-Mujahiddeen (HuM). The JeM, founded by Masood Azhar, is closely connected with the Binori Seminary, the largest Deobandi *madrassa* in Pakistan. Azhar was released on December 31, 1999, from an Indian prison in a hostage swap. The HuM is numerically the largest terrorist group in Jammu and Kashmir (J&K), India, accounting for up to 60 per cent of the total terrorist cadres in the State. The HuM, founded in 1989 as the militant wing of the *Jamaat-e-Islami* (JI), is headed by Syed Salahuddin, who is located in Islamabad, Pakistan. All three of these organizations have links with AQ and are allegedly funded and trained by the ISI. Over the years, Pakistan's Deobandis have insisted that Muslims must recognize only the religious frontiers of their *Ummah* and not the national frontiers. In recent years, Deobandi *Ulema* have articulated jihad as a sacred right and obligation, encouraging their followers to go to any country to wage jihad, in order to protect the Muslims of that country. Deobandis advocate that no matter where they live, their allegiance is to Islam, and not to their adopted country. Deobandis preach Qu'adt al Jihad (global jihad) for all Muslims everywhere. In addition to the Deobandis, two more terrorist organizations have emerged in India: Indian Mujahedeen (IM) and Deccan Mujahidin (DM). Both of them are associated with the LeT.

Of all the terrorist groups the ISI has sponsored over the years, LeT has been especially favored because its dominant Punjabi composition matches the primary ethnicity of the Pakistani Army and the ISI. Additionally, its puritanical Salafism (also called *Ahl al-Hadith*) undergirded its willingness to engage in risky military operations throughout India. The state of J&K in India has been the cause of several wars between India and Pakistan. The historical background of the state is outlined briefly: The Princely State of Jammu and Kashmir came into existence after the First Anglo-Sikh War of 1845, when Gulab Singh, a Sikh who had fought on the British side in the First Anglo-Sikh War, bought what is now the Kashmir Valley for 7.5 million Indian rupees. His son, Ranbir Singh, expanded the territory to include most of modern-day J&K. The state was ruled autonomously until the province came under British rule following the Indian Rebellion of 1857. It remained a princely state within British Colonial India. Kashmir has its own language, the Indo-European tongue Kashmiri, and a unique culture known as *Kashmiriyat,* a blend of Sufism and Hinduism. Kashmire has three regions. There is the Kashmir Valley, which has a Muslim majority; Jammu, with a majority of Hindus; and Ladakh, with a majority of Buddhists. There were never any communal riots in J&K, even during the creation of Pakistan. After the Indian Partition on August 15, 1947, the princely states of India (which included J&K) were given the option of joining either India or Pakistan. The prevailing belief in Pakistan was that Kashmir, with its large Muslim population, rightfully belonged to Pakistan. But the government in Islamabad, recognizing the popularity of Sheikh Abdullah of the National Conference, grew suspicious of the Sheikh's close ties to Jawaharlal Nehru of India. As a result, Pakistan sent troops to the Poonch district, which was largely sympathetic to Pakistan and the Muslim league, to incite a revolt against the state. Pakistani troops nearly reached Srinagar, the largest city in the Vale, forcing Hari Singh, the ruler of J&K, to flee to Jammu. On October 27, 1947, along with the British Viceroy of India, Lord Mountbatten, Hari Singh signed the Instrument of Accession Act of 1947, conceding his territory to India.

Kashmir-Kashmiriyat: Due to the huge influx of insurgence and terrorists across the border, since 1979, the Kashmiriyat culture has eroded significantly, and even the language Kashmiri has almost been forgotten.

In ancient Kashmir, Shaivism and Buddhism flourished in complete harmony with each other and when Islam arrived here in the 14th century AD, it did not meet with any resistance as the people of this land had learned over centuries to assimilate what is good in other religions. The interface of different religions gave birth to a new society whose defining identity was tolerance, amity and unconditional surrender to knowledge and wisdom. This unique identity is also known as Kashmiriyat and stands for the sublime and higher values of humanity. Laleshwari and Sheikh Nooruddin Noorani are the embodiments of this identity. While the former, a Hindu mystic, was Lal Ded for her Muslim fellow citizens, the latter, a great Muslim saint, was revered by Hindus as Nund Rishi.[69]

The Indian portion of J&K is in the foothills of the Himalayas, north of India, and has an area of 222,236 square kilometers. The Valley is an area of 4,320 sq.km in Kashmir, which has an area of 78,900 sq.km. The veteran journalist B.G. Verghese[70] has briefly narrated the history of Jammu and Kashmir:

> Kashmir, as much as Jammu, has been part of India's political and cultural domain and spiritual consciousness for some 3000 or more years going back to Mahabharata legend. The Ganpatyar and Khir Bhavani Temples in the Valley, the Shankracharya shrine dominating Srinagar and the giant Buddha statutes in Gilgit speak of this connection. The Emperor Asoka brought Buddhism to Kashmir in the 3rd century B.C. and it was here that Kanishka held the Third Buddhist Council. Lalitaditya's reign (697-738 A.D.) marked the golden age.

A forced mass conversion took place when Buddhists and Saivites were given a choice to either surrender to Islam, or surrender to the sword of Islam. The Kashmir Valley, once a place of pristine, idyllic, and placid beauty, with a unique culture, became one of the most dangerous places in the world—a nuclear flashpoint, due to its location between India and Kashmir.

> The direct involvement of the Pakistan army in Kashmir [during the uprising and insurgence at the behest of radical Islam], not previously confirmed, represented for the UNCIP [UN Commission on India and Pakistan] a material change in the situation. The Kashmir dispute was now understood to be a fully fledged international political conflict, a more serious and potentially much more dangerous affair.[71]

Even former President Pervez Musharraf of Pakistan implied that "if India insists on launching all-out war to attack Pakistan's support for Kashmiri militants, Pakistan is prepared to go nuclear," Musharraf did not impose any restrictions on Fazl-ur-Rahman Khalil, the head of the Harakat-ul-Mujahideen, and Qari Saifullah Akhtar, the head of the Harakat-ul-Jihad Islami, in order to maintain his link with the insurgents for strategic purposes. The distinguished scholar Mohammed Ayoob has noted that the American illusion about a negotiated settlement feeds the Pakistani delusion that it will be able to change the territorial status quo in Kashmir by manufacturing a crisis that threatens to escalate into nuclear confrontation.[72] The Kashmiriyat culture is fast diminishing, with the establishment of ninety-four Ahl-I-Hadeeth mosques in Srinagar in 2004 alone. During the jihadist insurrection from 1979 to 2009, with infiltration of insurgents from Pakistan, over 50,000 people have lost their lives. The main causes of this insurgency include:

1. The British colonial strategy to keep their strategic and commercial interests in the Subcontinent (1946–1948);

2. Prime Minister Nehru of India's anti-imperial policy (1947–1964), non-alignment policy, socialistic government (considered anti-Western), and Mahatma Gandhi's peasant movement, as seen in the light of Cold War rivalries;

3. The rise of Jihadist terrorists in Pakistan and Afghanistan, with the support of Saudi Arabia and America, and the collapse of the Soviet Union (1979–1990);

4. China's aggressive policy towards India, and its collaboration with Pakistan after the 1962 border war with India (1962–2009), in which Pakistan gave China 4853 square miles of a part of J& K that was occupied by Pakistan. This was done to obtain Chinese favor and collaboration. The Chinese now occupy 20 per cent of J&K, Pakistan 35 per cent, and India 45 per cent. Pakistan also occupied in 1947 four small semi-independent kingdoms, Baltistan, Skardu, Gilgit, and Hunza, where very few Muslims used to live through 1947. These areas constitute a part of Pakistan known as The Northern Area Province. Only 6 million Muslims live in Kashmir, but more than 160 million Muslims live elsewhere in India, as many as there are Muslims in Pakistan. In 1947, Ladakh was 10 per cent Muslim; in 2001, it was 46.5 per cent Muslim. In 1947, Jammu was 20 per cent Muslim; in 2001, it was 34 per cent Muslim. Indira Gandhi's (1917–1984) insecure and weak gov-

ernance, under the faulty Simla Accord with Pakistani Prime Minister Z.A. Bhutto, did not accept the Line of Control (LoC) as the boundary between India and Pakistan. Gandhi's overarching zeal to extend the Congress government throughout India, particularly in Punjab and J&K, along with her criticism of Nixon and Kissinger's Vietnam policy, tilted Nixon's policy in favor of Pakistan. As reported in the *Glasgow Herald:*

> The Nixon administration cut off economic aid to India and the president himself decided to "tilt" towards Pakistan, supporting it in the UN in 1971, and pressuring the Soviets to discourage India with hints that a U.S.-USSR detente would be damaged if Moscow did not comply. Nixon eventually ordered the U.S. carrier Enterprise into the Bay of Bengal in the 1971 India-Pakistan war and instructed Kissinger to try to persuade China to offer military support to Pakistan.[73]

5. The resurgence of the Taliban and AQ to spread jihad in J&K and beyond. Pakistan has not accepted the accession of J&K with India. In that context, the entire state of J&K as of 1947 belongs to the family of the late Maharaja Hari Singh. Currently it should belong to Dr. Karan Singh, son of Maharaja Hari Singh, as per international law or the Instrument of Accession Act. Pakistan has violated the 1948 UN Security Council Resolution on Kashmir, and other resolutions, by (a) not withdrawing its forces from the occupied J&K territory, Azad Kashmir; (b) building its military bases in the Azad Kashmir, and controlling both civilian and military establishments; (c) absorbing the Northern Area Province into its territory (in 1947, there were almost no Muslims in NAP, and in 2001, there were no non-Muslims); (d) transferring 20 per cent of J&K territory to China; (e) not allowing free elections in Azad Kashmir, just as in the KP, which was forcibly annexed to Pakistan in 1947; (f) sending a large number of armed Pakistani insurgents over the border since 1979, to destabilize and occupy J&K, and pretending the insurgents are freedom fighters or indigenous separatists; (g) allowing people from Punjab and other provinces, and retired military personnel and others, to settle in Azad Kashmir so as to change its demography; (h) having militants carry out ethnic cleansing through killing Hindus or forcing them to leave Kashmir; and (j) in 1998, General Pervez Musharraf's launching of the Kargil attack in J&K by Pakistan's armed forces, in total violation of the UN Security Council Resolution of August 1948.[74]

As footnotes to the causes of insurgency: In 1999, former President Bill Clinton asked Pakistan to withdraw its forces unconditionally from Kargil. The UN Security Council Resolution provides J&K with only two options: to join Pakistan or join India. Most of the western media favors self-determination for J&K, which is not an option; they ignore the fact that only 45 per cent of J&K is in India, while 55 per cent is occupied by Pakistan and China. There have been several elections in India's J&K including a very free and fair election in 2008. It is now ruled by a National Conference headed by Sheikh Abdullah's grandson, Omar Abdullah.[75]

In the Indian Parliament on August 25, 2010, former chief minister Farooq Abdullah, who heads the state's ruling National Conference party,[76] made the following statement: "Today, I am surprised that nobody has talked about Kashmir under Pakistan occupation which they call Azad Kashmir, nobody talked about Northern Areas of Gilgit Baltistan and Skardu, nobody talked about the territory Pakistan gave away to China, Those in Kashmir demanding "azadi" (independence) have not realized the consequences of such a demand. Kashmir too faces a threat from Taliban elements and a situation similar to Afghanistan and Pakistan will arise in the state too. Most Kashmiris[77] want to find a solution to the problems within India. We want to find a solution to the problem within India and not in Pakistan, China or in America." Robert Bradnock, an Associate Fellow at the Chatham House think-tank in London, conducted a survey in Indian- and Pakistani-administered Kashmir, dated May 26, 2010. It revealed that 44 per cent of respondents in Pakistani-administered Kashmir and 43 per cent in the Indian state of Jammu and Kashmir desire independence. These similar figures conceal wide regional disparities. But in the four districts of the predominantly Hindu Jammu part of Indian-administered Kashmir, there was virtually no support for independence. Only 27 per cent of all Kashmiris are in favor of the LOC (Line of Control) in its present form, while 22 per cent are in favor of it in Pakistani-administered Kashmir, and 29 per cent in the Indian state of J&K. In light of this, it is not surprising that in Poonch and Rajouri, two key border districts in the Indian state of J&K, more than 90 per cent are in favour of keeping the LOC.[78]

Jammu and Kashmir (J&K), one of the 562 princely states in British India, became an official territory of India after Governor General Lord Mountbatten and Maharaja Hari Singh (the Maharaja of J&K) signed the Instrument of Accession on October 27, 1947. Each princely state was given the option of joining either Pakistan or India.[79] According to historian H.V. Hodson:

Lord Mountbatten's part in this debate can be recorded in his own words to H.M. King: It was unquestionable that, if Srinagar was to be saved from pillage by the invading tribesman, and if the couple of British residents in Kashmir were not to be massacred, Indian forces would have to do the job. . . . The accession would fully regularise the position and reduce the risk of armed clash with Pakistan forces to a minimum. "I shall relate a little further on," he continued, "how lucky it was that this accession was accepted."[80]

This account is sustained by American scholars Sumit Ganguly and Devin Hagerty.[81]

In October, some 2,000 to 3,000 armed raiders, mainly Pathans from Pakistan's Northwest Province, crossed the border between West Pakistan and Kashmir [J&K], rallying behind the rebels. The Pakistan government provided material support to the Poonch rebels and their Pathan allies, who together made fast progress toward the state capital of Srinagar. With his domain on the verge of collapse, Hari Singh signed Kashmir's accession to India on October 26, 1947. The next day, the Indian government began airlifting troops and supplies to Srinagar. In the ensuing fighting, the Indian army drove the insurgents out of the capital.

The AIML was adamant that their choice of the ruler must be accepted as final. The rulers of Baluchistan and Bahawalpur wanted their states to become part of India, but India declined in view of their geographical distance and demographic composition. They were forced militarily to join Pakistan in April 1948, against their wishes as expressed in the Baluch legislature in January 1948. The fate of the KP was similar: They wanted to be independent, but were forced to join Pakistan. As the Muslim administrator of India, Wajahat Habibullah reflected: "As I have sought to show throughout this book, the dignity of a people smarting from what they have seen as humiliation after accession to India in 1947 lies at the heart of any sustainable resolution."[82] Unlike Baluchistan, Bhalawapur, and the KP with respect to Pakistan, J&K was not forced to join India. Instead, they were given more federal aid than any other states in India, and were assured of their demography because Indians were denied the right to migrate to there. Since 1947, India has strictly observed Article 370 of the J& K constitution, which states that no Indian can buy land in J&K. In 1946, M.A. Jinnah asked Sheikh Abdullah to annex J&K with Pakistan, and Sheikh Abdullah declined. Prime Minster Z.A. Bhutto and others were not in favor of independence for J&K.

J&K's ruler, Maharaja Hari Singh, urged the accession of his state with India, to repel Pakistani aggression led by Major General Akbar Khan of the Pakistani Army. The accession was endorsed by the largest Muslim party, the National Conference, and its leader Sheikh Abdullah of J&K. This state is now ruled by the democratically elected Muslim National Conference Party. The elections were free and fair, with a heavy turnout. The election, however, has been boycotted by jihadists. In addition, millions of Indian Muslims chose to stay in India, negating the two-nation theory. The separatists, who only follow orders from Islamabad, use bullets and violent strikes, not the ballot box, to try and establish self government in J&K. Some people, who believe in Muslim exclusiveness while advocating the Pakistani position towards J&K, cannot accept that the Muslim dominated Valley, with its approximately 5.4 million Muslims, can be a part of India—even though over 150 million Muslims live elsewhere in the country. Some people still quote misinformed Josef Korbel's outdated, inconsequential book, *Danger in Kashmir*,[83] despite the Simla Agreement of 1972 and the annulment of the UNO resolution by the former UN Security Council General Secretary Kofi Annan. During the 1947–1948 India–Pakistan war, there was no uprising by the people of J&K in support of Pakistan. Again, when Pakistan launched Operation Gibraltar in 1965, there was not a single person in J&K that supported the invasion. Yet some remain blind to the fact that the people of Baluchistan, Bhalawpur, and KP did not suffer humiliation or loss of dignity as a result. Instead, the dignity of J&K is threatened by the invasion of Pakistan-sponsored terrorists and by hundreds of radical mosques, armament warehouses, and a command center, which are engaged in ethnic cleaning and have been destroying the culture and heritage of Kashmir since 1947. India insists that the security forces of India have been in J&K to check terrorism, the infiltration of Pakistani insurgents, mass murder, rape, and killing. India reiterates that any demilitarization will put the state into calamity and greater chaos. In fact, peace and prosperity will come to the region only when Pakistan cleans up all terrorist schools and camps.

Tribesmen from Pakistani-controlled areas, with the active support of the Pakistani army, invaded J&K in 1947. Maharaja Hari Singh asked for military help from India, which was airlifted to Srinagar, the capital of Kashmir, under the direction of Governor General Lord Mountbatten. The state of J&K legally joined the Indian Union on October 26, 1947. At that point it seemed imminent that India and Pakistan would go to full-scale war for Kashmir. H.V. Hudson, Constitutional Advisor to Lord Mountbatten (1941–1942), has described what happened next: "At the advice of Mountbatten, when first I suggested bringing U.N.O to this dispute, India approached the UNO under article 35 of the Charter."[84] The Maharaja Hari Singh's reluctance to assent to J&K's joining India was his fear of Nehru's socialism and Mahatma Gandhi's peasant movement, which had also turned away many Muslim landowners and wealthy people. At the behest of Lord Mountbatten, Indian Prime Minister Nehru requested on January 1, 1948 that the UN Security Council put an end to Pakistani aggression in J&K, an act of aggression against India. If Pakistan did not do so, he stated, the Government of India might be compelled, in self-defense, to enter Pakistan territory, in order to take military action against Pakistani invaders. He considered the matter one of extreme urgency, and called for immediate action by the Security Council. As Hudson continues:

> The Indian Government, however, was grievously disappointed by the reception of its appeal to the Security Council, which it had naively hoped would at once take India's part, without reserve, as the victim of aggression. . . . Pundit Nehru was shocked to find that power politics and not ethics were ruling the UNO. He considered that the United States did not intend to deal with the issue on its merits but merely help Pakistan against India. He said that he thought that Mr. Noel Baker (the Secretary of State for Commonwealth Relations and the leader of the United Kingdom Delegation) had been nearly as hostile to India as was American Senator Warren Austin, except he had been more polite and had wrapped his phrases in more careful language.

In the U.N.C.I.P. Resolution of August 13, 1948, S/1100, the UN asked Pakistan to remove its troops, after which India was also to withdraw the bulk of its forces. Once this happened, a "free and fair" plebiscite was to be held, to allow the Kashmiri people to decide their future. India, having taken the issue to the UN, was confident of winning a plebiscite, since the most influential Kashmiri popular leader, Sheikh Abdullah, was firmly on its side. An emergency government was formed on October 30, 1948 with Sheikh Abdullah as the Prime Minister. Pakistan ignored the UN mandate and continued fighting, holding on to the portion of Kashmir under its control. On January 1, 1949, a ceasefire was agreed upon, with 45 per cent of the territory to remain under Indian control and the remainder with Pakistan. The ceasefire was intended to be temporary, but the Line of Control remains the de facto border between the two countries to this day.[85] This is the most significant UN Resolution on Kashmir passed by the UN on the state of Jammu & Kashmir. It clearly stated that Pakistan was to vacate its troops from the whole of the state. It also mentions, albeit indirectly, that Pakistan had consistently lied on the question of whether or not its troops were involved in the fighting in Jammu & Kashmir. Once the then-Pakistani

Prime Minister conceded that Pakistani troops were indeed involved, the UN had no option but to ask for their withdrawal. That the withdrawal never took place is another story. Pakistan in 1963 ceded over 2000 square miles of Pakistani-occupied Jammu and Kashmir (PoK) to China. There was no protest from J&K's leaders, including its separatist leaders.

Nehru made no secret of his disappointment over what he considered was an "equivocal attitude" of the United States and the United Kingdom towards the situation in Kashmir. And when in 1954, Pakistan joined Western Treaty Alliances and obtained American military aid, Nehru responded by declaring that: "The military pacts had destroyed the roots and foundations of the plebiscite proposal in Kashmir." He also demanded withdrawal of 18 American military observers, as "they could no longer be treated as neutrals in the dispute." Nehru declared in August 1963:

> Our record is one of honesty and integrity, which does not warrant admonitions. So far as Kashmir is concerned, I would not give an inch. I would hold my ground even if Kashmir, India, and the whole world go to pieces. . . . There is no question of considering any proposal for internationalisation or division of the Valley or joint control of Kashmir and the like.

Sheikh Mohammed Abdullah (1905–1982), the leader of the National Conference, Kashmir's largest political party, and one of the most important political figures in the modern history of Jammu and Kashmir, ruled J&K as its Prime Minister from 1948 to 1953, and as Chief Minister from 1975 to 1982. His son, Dr. Farook Abdullah, was the Chief Minister of J&K from 1982 to 1984 and from 1986 to 2002, while his grandson Omar Abdullah, a former Foreign Minister of Government in India, has been Chief Minister since January 2009. Omar became Chief Minister by virtue of ballots in a fair and free election in 2008, defying the separatist call for a boycott of the elections, as had happened before. After the 2008 elections in Jammu and Kashmir, when more than 62 per cent of the people voted as compared to around 43 per cent in 2002, many argued that this historic referendum was the last nail in the coffin of separatist parties and "azaadi" (freedom) sentiments in the Valley.[86] Three per cent of Indian Muslims live in the Kashmir Valley, a majority area of Muslims in India. Their teenagers, throwing stones and attacking police stations for the glamour of martyrdom, supported by the invisible hands of separatists with external funds, are testing the limits of Indian secularity and seeking international media coverage. They probably do not know that their forefathers were non-Muslims. Pakistan-born novelist Tariq Ali, an atheist and a secularist, believes in the power of violence in Islam. He censures the Abdullah dynasty of Kashmir because for three generations, they have supported secular India, not Islamic Pakistan. In the *London Review of Books* (July 22, 2010), he declared:

> Now a new generation of Kashmiri youth is on the march. They fight, like the young Palestinians, with stones. Many have lost their fear of death and will not surrender. Ignored by politicians at home, abandoned by Pakistan, they are developing the independence of spirit that comes with isolation and it will not easily be quelled.

Lal Krishna Advani, leader of the Bharatiya Janata Party (BJP), believes the government of India is pandering to terrorists by letting the separatists sheltering behind the stone pelting teenagers, under the guidance of the hidden hands of Pakistani insurgents. On September 7, 2010, he told the Indian Prime Minister

> that the Centre should take no steps which would embolden the azadi-seeking separatists and weaken the government. New Delhi has never shown weakness in the last 63 years. It would be akin to rewarding the separatists.

The Muslim author and administrator Wajahat Habibullah[87] is of the opinion that India's argument (in the UNO) would have been more convincing had it asserted that its case was based on the public will. He wrote:

> And indeed, Sheikh Abdullah spoke for Kashmir at the United Nations in February 1948, stridently declaring, "we shall prefer death rather than join Pakistan. We shall have nothing to do with such a country. Whether Kashmir has lawfully acceded to India—complaints on that score have been brought before the Security Council on behalf of Pakistan—is not the point at issue. If that were the point at issue then we should discuss that subject. We should prove before the Security Council that Kashmir and the people of Kashmir have lawfully and constitutionally acceded to the Dominion of India, and Pakistan has no right to question that accession." (Excerpts of the speech by Sheikh Mohammed Abdullah, UN Security Council Meeting No. 241, held on February 5, 1948)

Sheikh Abdullah's son, former Chief Minister Farook Abdullah, said on June 14, 2010, that Kashmir was an integral part of India. National Conference leader and Union Minister Farooq added that J&K was the crown of India and would remain so. Farooq recounted a visit to Pakistan in 1974:

> The entire bureaucracy of Pakistan and Bhutto's secretary himself told me that a final solution has been arrived at; there can be nothing more. What

we (the Pakistanis) have got (in Kashmir) we are keeping, what they have got they are keeping and that is how it is.

Raja Muzaffar Ali, who accompanied Abdullah on that visit, agreed with him. The timing of the UNO resolution in 1948 was very much in Pakistan's favor. When Pakistani forces were retreating, India's were advancing. Indians accepted the UNO resolution on December 31, 1948, under the British influence.[88] Lord Mountbatten's appointment as Chairman of the Cabinet's Defense Committee, by virtue of being Governor General of India,

> rendered a great service to Britain—and, incidentally, to Pakistan—by restraining India's military initiatives on more than one critical occasion. He made sure that India did not extend operations up to the Pakistan border in the Poonch and Mirpur districts, going to the extent of sabotaging his government's plans for creating a *cordon sanitaire* along the border by aerial action. He foiled his government instructions for preparing contingency plans for a counter-strike across the Pakistani border, while prevailing upon Nehru to take the Kashmir issue to the UN. Contrary to popular belief, he achieved his ends mainly by exercising his official powers, not by influencing Nehru's thinking behind the scenes. . . . British political and strategic interests dictated a tilt in favor of Pakistan. The Foreign Office feared that antagonizing Pakistan might "align the whole of Islam against us," jeopardizing British interests in the Middle East. . . . Under British inspiration, the Security Council next turned its attention to the question of a ceasefire linked to an arrangement with plebiscite, brushing aside the question of Pakistan's involvement in the invasion.

In addition to Mountbatten's effort to get the UNO involved, he and his staff Field Marshal Claude Auchinleck, the Commander-in-Chief of the Indian Army, prevented Nehru from approving General K.S. Thymayya, commander of the 19th Infantry Division in J&K, to drive the raiders and the Pakistan Army out of the Kashmir Valley. General Thmayya succeeded in driving them beyond Uri, and ordered Stuart Light Tanks of the 7th Light Cavalry to the dizzy heights of the Zoji La Pass, to drive out the entrenched raiders and Pakistan Army regulars. But Nehru denied his pleas for three more months to drive the raiders back to Muzzarfarbad. Since that time, J&K has become the epicenter of jihadists in South Asia. Mountbatten always insisted that any political, security, and administrative decisions by Prime Minister Nehru and Home Minister Vallabhbhai Patel (1875–1950) be approved by the defense committee headed by him and his defense staff, if they were even remotely connected to Pakistan.[89] As reported in its issue of October 4, 2009, Pakistani President Zardari told the *Wall Street Journal* that India and Pakistan should open trade as the first step toward broader economic cooperation. India has "never been a threat to Pakistan," he said, and the Muslim insurgents fighting Indian rule in Kashmir are "terrorists."

The demography of Jammu and Kashmir (Figures 2.2 and 2.3) is outlined in Table 4.2. (India's population as of July 2009 is estimated to be 1,166,079, 217, including about 150 million Muslims, or 13.4 per cent of the total.)

Table 4.2
Demography of Jammu and Kashmir in India

Division	Population	% Muslim	% Hindu	% Sikh	% Buddhist/ Other
Kashmir (53.9%)	5,476,970	97.16%	1.84%	0.88%	0.11%
Jammu (43.7%)	4,430,191	30.69%	65.23%	3.57%	0.51%
Ladakh (2.3%)	236,539	47.40% Shia	6.22%	–	45.87%
Jammu & Kashmir	10,143,700	66.97%	29.63%	2.03%	1.36%

* Statistics calculated from the 2001 Census India District Profiles.
* An estimated 50-100,000 Kashmiri Muslims and 150-300,000 Kashmiri Pundits have been internally displaced due to militancy.

Unlike any other state in India, J&K has its own constitution. In addition, article 370 of the Indian Constitution provided, on November 17, 1952, special status to the state of J&K, "which will have autonomy in all matters except defense, communications, and foreign affairs." Indian citizens cannot buy property in J&K even after marrying one of its citizens. There have been several wars between India and Pakistan, with the possibility of a nuclear exchange, regarding the merger that Pakistan refused to accept. The 1972 Simla Agreement[90] between the two nations led to the establishment of the Line of Control (LOC) between Pakistan's J&K (known as Azad Jammu and Kashmir, AJK or Pakistan-occupied Kashmir —PoK) and India's J&K (IJK). The 2009 population of J&K is as follows: in Jammu, 4 million with 30 per cent Muslims, in Kashmir, 5 million with 95 per cent Muslims, and in Ladakh, 0.25 million with 46 per cent Shia Muslims. The Hindu population, particularly Kashmir Brahmins and Pundits in the Kashmir Valley, was 14 per cent in 1940 and 0.01 per cent in 2006. On minorities in India-held J&K, Sumantra Bose writes:

For example, it is possible that non-Muslim minorities—Hindus, Sikhs, and Buddhists—who total about 35 per cent of IJK's population, adhere nearly unanimously to an Indian national identity and wish to live under Indian sovereignty, a preference overriding the social diversity and lower order of political conflicts within these groups. The entire Hindu and Sikh populations of Muslim majority districts like Muzaffarabad, Bagh, Rawalakot (Western Poonch), Kotli, Mirpur, and Bhimbar were killed or expelled.[91]

Great powers also play a role in the Kashmir dispute. Partition was the direct result of British decisions, and the British government bears some responsibility for the outcome. Pakistan became a Cold War ally of the United States, and was the recipient of considerable U.S. military assistance and training. After a decade-long rift, Pakistan again became a valued ally in the 1980s, during the brutal Soviet occupation of Afghanistan. Most recently, the United States and Pakistan agreed to cooperate in the war on terrorism."[92] The rivalry between India and Pakistan for the possession of J&K, based on its strategic value, goes back many years. As a historical note, Pravin Swami[93] writes:

> Long before anyone had ever conceived of the modern states of India and Pakistan, Jammu and Kashmir (J&K) had become a key piece in the infinitely complex covert battle waged by imperial Great Britain and Russia for control of Asia: a contestation immortalized by Rudyard Kipling as the Great Game.

Following British diplomat Noel Baker's input to the UNO, the U.S. foreign policy in South Asia became involved in the Kashmir dispute because of its strategic interests. It also indirectly fomented terrorism and violence in the region while combating Communism from 1947 to 1979. Along with Afghan, Pakistani and other foreign mujahedeen, and with the help of former Pakistan President Zia-ul Haq, America indirectly waged war with the Soviet Union from 1979 to 1990. Haq radicalized Pakistan's army, educational institutes, and other civil and religious organizations including the Islamic proselytizing organization Tabligh-i-Jamaat. All the while, he was given a free hand in developing Pakistan's nuclear weapon, and in supporting radical religious parties. America aided Pakistan, militarily and economically, because of Pakistan's membership with SEATO and CENTO, while opposing India's non-alignment policy under Pundit Nehru. With the fall of the Communist empire and the rise of Muslim fundamentalists, including OBL and his group AQ, the Taliban, and other jihadists, America followed an anti-terrorist policy to wage war against the Taliban and AQ.

After the 9/11 attacks, America turned again to Pakistan, led by former Pakistan President Musharraf, to fight with the Taliban and AQ. "I hereby designate the Islamic Republic of Pakistan as a major non-NATO ally of the United States for the purposes of the Arms Export Control Act," as President George W. Bush's statement said. The BBC's Rob Watson in Washington commented:

> Pakistan's new status means that it is now eligible for a series of benefits in the areas of foreign aid and defense co-operation, including priority delivery of defense items. During the stint of Musharraf, terrorist organizations flourished and jihadists found safe haven in Pakistan. Musharraf arrested the leaders of some terrorist organizations and later released them. These organizations appeared under different names. He considered this necessary for his survival and also for strategic assets against Afghanistan, Afghanistan Taliban, and India. He protected them in Baluchistan, Pakistan and other places while modernizing his army with U.S. aid which was given to contain terrorists. His strategies have created more terrorism and more infiltration of terrorists operating in the region.

According to the *Wall Street Journal* of December 24, 2009:

> If Pakistan truly has given up on its old double game of claiming backing America while allowing a Taliban sanctuary within its borders, now would be a good time to show it's serious. If not, the U.S. has leverage with Islamabad through foreign aid, as well as various military options. U.S. drone strikes can be expanded, including for the first time to Baluchistan, and Special Forces might be deployed across the porous border.[94]

In the aftermath of the Pakistani army assaults in Waziristan and Swat in late 2009, followed by several Taliban suicide attacks that caused more than three hundred deaths, as well as additional terrorist attacks in Afghanistan, Taliban specialist and Pakistan's well known journalist Ahmed Rashid echoed the Pakistan army's position that terrorism can only be contained if: (a) India surrenders J&K to Pakistan, (b) America gives unconditional massive aid to Pakistan for development, and (c) Afghanistan accepts the Durand Line, the line of demarcation of the border between Afghanistan and Pakistan. This flawed, absurd logic is based on manufacturing crises in order to be rewarded for terrorism. Terrorists are responsible for attacks on the Pakistan Army headquarters, Lal Masjid (The Red Mosque), universities and schools, the Meena market, security offices, and the UNO offices, and for killing Shiites in their Ashura processions and elsewhere. Pakistan has supported these terrorists for their strategic advantage against Afghanistan and India. Hundreds of Shiite Muslims, considered apostates by Sunni

Muslims, are attacked and killed in Karachi, Muzaffarabad, and other places during the Muharram celebration in honor of Imam Hussein, the grandson of the Prophet Mohammed. It is alleged that Pakistan has been exporting terrorists or has been involved in terrorist attacks all over the world, including those in London, Madrid, and Bali, among other places. This death and devastation is not related to the liberation movement in J&K, or to American and Afghan interference in Pakistan. America and others simply want to wipe out AQ and other terrorists who are sheltered in the Pakistan–Afghanistan border areas, Kandahar and Quetta. The AIQM and al Shabaab are spreading terrorism and radical Islam to Yemen, Nigeria, Niger, Mali, Mauritania, and other countries in West Africa (see Figure 3.2). They are murdering and kidnapping diplomats and teachers in Mali, Niger, and Mauritania. Recently, the attempted downing of Northwest Airlines Flight 253 from Amsterdam to Detroit is a chilling reminder that there are people out there who want to kill us. The latest failed martyr claiming ties to AQ is a Nigerian. And if the details that have emerged so far prove correct, that's further evidence that the enemy the United States faces is not confined to or by a national border.[95] Terrorists and Jihadists in J&K: Several jihadi organizations with links to the ISI, and its political organization, Jamat-i-Islami (JI) have attempted to wage violent insurgency and jihad in J&K. To this end, they have tried to disguise themselves as indigenous, homegrown freedom fighters. The journalist Jamal Afridi[96] provides an overview of the major terrorist organizations in the region: 1. Harakat ul-Mujahideen (HuM) was established in the mid-1980s. Based first in Pakistan and then in Afghanistan, it has several hundred armed supporters in Pakistan and Kashmir. The group is responsible for the December 1999 hijacking of an Indian airliner, and numerous attacks on Indian troops and civilians in Kashmir. 2. Jaish-e-Mohammed (JeM) was founded in 2000 by Masood Azhar, a Pakistani cleric. The group seeks to incorporate Kashmir into the state of Pakistan and has openly declared war on the United States. JeM has carried out attacks on Indian targets, the Pakistani government, and various sectarian minority groups within Pakistan. Acts of terrorism attributed to the group include the 2001 attack on the Indian Parliament and a series of assaults in 2002 on Christian sites in Pakistan. 3. Hizb-ul-Mujahideen (Hizbul Mujahideen, "party of holy warriors," founded by Ahsan Dar), headquartered in Muzaffarabad, Pakistan-occupied Kashmir, is a group of Pakistani-sponsored Kashmiri militants. They have been designated a terrorist group by India and the United States. Hizb-ul-Mujahideen is now headed by Sayeed Salahudeen (Syed Mohammed Yusuf Shah). Its members are affiliated with al-Fatah, another terrorist organization from the 1970s. They are also connected to the "Master Cell," which is linked to the Pakistan ISI. They became known as ruthless and barbaric after they killed 36 innocent Sikh villagers and hundreds of Hindu peasants who were out working in the fields. 4. United Jihad Council (UJC), also known as the Muttahida Jihad Council (MJC). It was formed in 1994, as an amalgamation of several armed resistance organizations, to coordinate efforts of Hizb ul-Mujaheden and other terrorist organizations to infiltrate and terrorize J&K. The UJC distributes resources including arms, ammunition, propaganda materials, and communications equipment. It has fifteen organizations including Hizb-ul-Mujahideen, Harakat-ul-Ansar, Hizb-ul-Mujahideen, Jamiat-ul-Mujahideen, Al-Jihad, Al-Barq, Al-Badr, Ikhwan-ul-Mussalmin, Tehrik-ul-Mujahideen, Lashkar-e-Toiba, Harkat-ul-Mujahideen, Al-Badr, and Tehrik-i-Jihad. Many of these organizations are banned by the United States and the United Nations.

Forty-five years ago, Fazal-ul-Haq Qureshi helped lay the foundations of the jihadist movement in Jammu and Kashmir. Released from jail in 1992, Qureshi helped found the All Parties Hurriyat Conference (APHC), which started out as a 23-party alliance of secessionist groups. By 1999, though, it was clear to him—and other doves in the APHC, like Abdul Gani Lone—that the armed struggle had outlived its utility. In 2000, he played a key role in brokering a unilateral ceasefire by the Hizb ul-Mujahideen and the initiation of talks between Dar and representatives of the Government of India. Pakistan, however, soon withdrew support from the ceasefire, fearing India would cut a deal with the Hizb ul-Mujahideen. The key APHC leaders had met with Ashan Dar, and agreed to endorse the ceasefire—but later refused to do so being fearful of reprisals from anti-ceasefire jihadists. Fifteen days after it went into force, Hizb ul-Mujahideen chief Mohammad Yusuf Shah withdrew the ceasefire. . . . In the years that followed, Qureshi watched as his allies in the peace effort were murdered one by one. Abdul Lone was shot dead in 2002, by a LeT hit-squad. His son, Sajjad Lone contested in the 2008 election defying the call of boycott by the All Parties Hurriyat Conference (APHC), but he lost the election. Ashan Dar was killed by Hizb ul-Mujahideen hardliners the following year; his wife is now confined to a wheelchair, as a consequence of a terrorist attack which left her crippled.[97]

5. Lashkar-e-Taiba (LeT, also spelled Lashkar-e-Tayyaba, Lashkar-e-Tayyiba, or Lashkar-e-Toiba) was formed as the military wing of the well-funded Pakistani Islamist organization Markaz-ad-Dawa-wal-Irshad. LeT, the most dreaded terrorist organization worldwide, is one of the largest and most active Islamist militant organizations in South Asia. Hafiz Muhammad Saeed founded LeT in 1989. It is affiliated with Jama'at-ud-Da'wah (JuD), which Hafiz had previously Lahore, Pakistan, in 1985. The JuD occupies more than 190 acres of land at Murdike, near Lahore, Pakistan, as a center

for preaching and training, yet it claims to be an Islamic charity and educational organization. Both the LeT and the JuD have been declared terrorist
organizations by the UNO. LeT is one of the largest and most proficient of
the Kashmir-based terrorist groups, and has claimed responsibility for a
number of high-profile attacks on Indian targets in Jammu and Kashmir, as
well as within India. Over the last several years, the group has split into two
factions, al-Mansurin and al-Nasirin. There is wide speculation that LeT
was responsible for the July 11, 2006 series of bombings on Mumbai's
commuter railroad, though a spokesman for the group denied any involvement. "Very few things," said United States counter-terrorism official David
Benjamin in a recent speech, "worry me as much as the strength and ambition of the Lashkar-e-Taiba." The arrest of Pakistani-American jihadist David
Headley, alleged to have carried out the reconnaissance that enabled a 10-
man assault team to kill more than 160 people in Mumbai in November of
2008, could prove a significant step forward in delivering justice to the
victims of the horrific attack. But the arrest has also underlined the reach of
LeT's transnational networks, which give South Asia's most dangerous
jihadist group global lethality. British-born Dhiren Bharot, held in 2005 for
attempted bombings in the U.S., had trained with t LeT and fought with it in
Jammu and Kashmir. French national Willie Brigitte, held for planning
terrorist attacks in Australia, was another product of LeT's transnational
operations. Lebanese national Assem Hammoud, held in April 2006 for
planning to target Port Authority Trans-Hudson commuter trains running
between New Jersey and New York, was preparing to travel to Pakistan to
acquire the expertise he needed to do so. And five Washington, D.C. men
were picked up in Sargodha, Punjab, where they had traveled to acquire
military training.[98]

> The Mumbai massacre ranks as one of history's grisliest acts of retail
> terrorism. In the fall of 2008, a dozen young Muslim men armed with AK-
> 47 assault rifles, grenades, and plastic explosives stormed a train station,
> the Taj Mahal Palace hotel, a Jewish center in Mumbai, India, and slaugh-
> tered in cold blood about 160 people, including six Americans. They singled
> out Western tourists and Jews for attack. The barbaric terrorists sexually
> humiliated some of the hotel guests by first forcing them to strip, then
> shooting them. Police found the blood-drenched bodies of a rabbi and his
> wife completely nude, their genitals mutilated. The jihad-crazed troglo-
> dytes, who were ordered to kill until the last breath in the name of Islam,
> carried out their killing spree after training in neighboring Pakistan. Over
> five months they practiced their assault at a camp run by terrorist group
> LeT, an AQ subcontractor.[99]

Some Pakistani journalists blamed the massacre on India, for its not having solved the Kashmir dispute to the satisfaction of Pakistan.

Other terrorists and jihadists groups in J&K include the J&K Liberation Front (JKLF, founded by Amanullah Khan and Maqbool Bhat, in Birmingham, U.K.), Hizb-ul-Mujahidin, Al Jihad, Tehrek-e-Taliban (TeT), Lashkar-e-Jhangvi (LeJ), and Sipha-e-Sahaba Pakistan (SSP). Most of these terrorist organizations and the Taliban and AQ leadership are ensconced in Quetta, Baluchistan, where they are allegedly protected by the Pakistani ISI. Most of these terrorist organizations are on the U.S. terror list. One of the important members of JI was Syed Ali Gilani, who was willing to publicly support armed jihad. He is an influential member of the All Parties Hurriyat Conference (APHC), an alliance of twenty-six separatist organizations in J&K including Jamaat-i-Islami (JI) and JKLF. Maulana Maududi, the late violent Pakistani radical, preached that Islam will destroy the West. "The objective of Islamic jihad is to put an end to the dominance of the un-Islamic systems of government and replace them with Islamic rule," wrote Maududi, founder of Pakistani religious party Jamaat e-Islami.

Until 1980, there was little friction in J&K. This changed dramatically with the influx of JI terrorists from Pakistan during with the war in Afghanistan, between 1979 and 1989. The JI was responsible for destroying 800 villages, desecrating temples, and smashing idols. There were a series of political murders of Hindu personalities in 1988–1989. Pakistani journalist Arif Jamal writes:

> In many cases, killers left the JKLF tags on the bodies, claiming responsibility of the organization. The Allah Tigers, which took direct orders from Syed Ali Shah Geelani, carried out most of these murders in the name of the JKLF. Following the foundation of the HM, hundreds of Hindus were killed, many brutally. For example, a twenty-year-old girl, Girija kumara Tiku, was cut into two halves by a mechanical saw after she was kidnapped and gang raped by the jihadists. As a part of ethnic cleansing, jihadists had destroyed ninety-seven temples between 1990 and 1997 and forced the Hindu population of the entire Valley of Kashmir to leave. During 2001 to 2008, 16,047 people were killed by terrorist attacks in J&K. Unfortunately the massacres and the destruction did not receive much attention, not even from human rights groups. President Musharraf proposed a few out of the box solutions for the settlement of the Kashmir dispute on a bilateral basis with India, declaring that Pakistan is not demanding a plebiscite as part of the solution. However, during his tenure, there are more jihadi groups than ever. Jihadists were banned and arrested, but released later. He needed their support to remain in the power.[100]

Jamal also points out:

> The ISI-backed jihadi groups and Jamat-i-Islami had also become involved
> in militant operations outside Kashmir, alarming American official's ac-
> tions. In addition to Afghanistan, the ISI backed Jamat-i-Islamia of Paki-
> stan had become involved in military actions in several Central Asian
> states during the early 1990s. Uzbekistan and Tajikistan accused the
> Islamabad government of doing nothing to stop what they called Pakistani
> interference. The gunfights between security forces and Islamist militants
> last week, the first clashes with Islamists in Kyrgyzstan for three years, on
> June 10, 2010, had caused over 2000 deaths and a million Uzbek homeless
> and refugees. It is reported Islamists are trained in Pakistan. "The leader
> of the destroyed terrorist group (was) Khasan Suleimanov, born in 1977 in
> Osh, Kyrgyzstan, trained at the international terrorist centers in Pakistan.
> The (Kyrgyzstan State National Security) Committee said both Suleimanov's
> group and five militants killed days before in the nearby town of Jalalabad
> likely had links to the Islamic Movement of Uzbekistan (IMU), The ISI
> was also supporting the Chinese Muslim separatists in the Xinjiang Prov-
> ince, and jihadi groups in Central Asia."[101]

Pakistan considers the APHC to be a voice of the Kashmiri people, although
the APHC never contested any election in J&K. The APHC is not recognized by the Hindu-dominated Jammu or the Buddhist-dominated Ladakh
people. The APHC members are provided with security protection costing
millions of dollars. It is not known who has the maximum support of the
citizens of J&K—the APHC, Sheikh Abdullah's National Conference (ANC),
the Indian National Congress (INC) headed by Ghulam Nabi Azad, or the
People's Democratic Party (PDP) headed by Mufti Mohammed Sayeed,
former Home Minister of India. In the 2008 state election in J&K, which
had a massive turnout, despite boycott calls and threats by the separatists,
the National Conference won the maximum number of 28 seats. This was
compared to the PDP with 21 seats, and the INC with 17 seats. J&K has a
democratically elected government headed by Omar Abdullah of the National Conference, a pro-India party. (Only one AHPC member contested
the election, but failed to get elected.)

In order to capture J&K, President Pervez Musharraf conducted the
Kargil war with India in 1999, when he was Chief of the Pakistani Army
under Prime Minister Nawaz Sharif. But Sharif had to withdraw the Pakistani Army after a humiliating defeat, as President Clinton demanded a
unilateral and unconditional withdrawal.

> Pakistan could stoke the flames of violence without getting burned, be-
> cause its now-demonstrated nuclear posture would deter New Delhi from

responding robustly or escalating the fighting, while at the same time causing severe anxiety in an international community already fearful of Kashmir's potential to be a "nuclear flashpoint."[102]

Musharraf also tried to sabotage the peace talks between Prime Minister Sharif and Prime Minister Vajpayee in Lahore. India's Prime Minister Atal Vajpayee invited President Pervez Musharraf, the architect of the Kargil war against India, to Agra to settle the J&K dispute, but there was no resulting agreement. Musharraf initiated a back-channel process to re-draw the border with India during the last phase of his stint as President. "I have made it clear to President Musharraf that any redrawing of the international border is not acceptable to us. Any proposal which smacks of further division is not going to be acceptable to us," Prime Minister Manmohan Singh told a crowded press conference in Srinagar, the capital of Kashmir, on November 17, 2004. Prime Minister Yousuf Raza Gilani of Pakistan said that Musharraf's proposal was "half baked." Prime Minister Gilani reassured the people of Kashmir that Pakistan would not abandon them and that there was no change in Pakistan's Kashmir policy. "We will not sit idle till the resolution of the Kashmir issue according to wishes of the people of Kashmir and the implementation of the United Nations resolutions," he assured the separatist leadership of Kashmir.[103] On the other hand, President Asif Zardari has created several peace incentives: He has declared that jihadis are not "freedom fighters" and that Pakistan would agree to a "no first use" policy with India for its nuclear weapons. The Kashmir issue, he said, should be put on the backburner, since India was not the real enemy. "He was blamed directly for the put-down of the Army in the Kerry-Lugar legislation, its incorporation of Indian concerns about the Lashkar-e-Toiba and Jaish-e-Mohammed."[104] The India–Pakistan peace talks have been stalled since the jihadist attacks in Mumbai, India, in 2008. Jihadi attacks continue. Secularists and human rights groups are quiet and blind when minorities in J&K are harassed, humiliated, denied rights, and brutally killed, or when Hindu women are raped, as the separatists pursue their agenda of secession from India, supported by Pakistan since 1947.

A veteran ambassador and scholar, Howard Schaffer, has some thoughts on the Kashmir issue, concerning the main lines of an eventual settlement:

> [T]he Line of Control as an international boundary, greater autonomy for both sides, free movement of people and goods and all Kashmir institutions, which will also have to include a considerable degree of demilitarization on both sides of Kashmir."[105]

Many in the ISI are deeply sympathetic to LeT's vision of recovering "lost Muslim lands" in Asia and Europe and resurrecting a universal Islamic Caliphate through the instrument of jihad. Active LeT operations in Pakistan's northwestern border areas involve close collaboration with Al Qaeda, the Afghan Taliban, the Haqqani network, and Jamiat al-Dawa al-Quran wal-Sunna. Such a strategy is designed to make Islamabad the kingmaker in determining Kabul's future. This too promises to become one more in the long line of cruel illusions that has gripped Pakistan since its founding.

Pakistan

The declassified documents of correspondence between Viceroys of India, Secretaries of State for India, and others have revealed conspiracy, injustice, and even calls for jihad and fanning of the communal hatred in the partition of India, to support the case for a separate state in Jammu and Kashmir.[106] Yet many questions remain to be answered, many intrigues to be unfolded. Pakistan was created by British colonialists on the premise that Muslims of India constituted a separate nation state, as proposed by the AIML in March 1940 at Lahore. But the INC, a secular, progressive party, represented all of India, Hindus, Muslims, Sikhs, Parsees, Buddhists, and Christians, and sought independence for India from Great Britain. Yet landlords and landowners viewed the INC as a peasant movement meant to abolish the feudal systems and privileges of kings and maharajas. Neither the AIML or any other Muslim party ever claimed to represent all Muslims from 1857 to 1940.

> The very party claiming to represent all Indian Muslims had staked an apparently separatist demand for independent Muslim states. There was no reference at all in the resolution to a center, weak or strong, Muslim or Indian. Moreover, there was no mention of either partition or Pakistan. The nub of the League's resolution was that all future constitutional arrangements be considered 'de novo' since Indian Muslims were a 'nation' and not a minority, as had been presumed in the past. H.V. Hudson, the British reforms commissioner, discovered in 1941 that every Muslim Leaguer . . . interpreted Pakistan as consistent with confederation of India for common purposes like defense, provided the Hindu and Muslim element therein stood on equal terms.[107]

The equal-terms concept emanated from the two-nation theory. Gandhi claimed, however, that the two-nation theory "was not true." The vast majorities of Muslims in India are converts to Islam or are descendents of converts. "They did not become a separate nation as soon as they became converts," argued the Mahatma. His argument was strongest when he focused upon Bengali Muslims, whose language, dress, appearance, food, and social life made them virtually indistinguishable from Bengali Hindus.[108] Since India was a pluralistic, diverse, multiethnic, multireligious, multilingual, multicultural state, and had been sustained as such for thousands of years, many felt that there was no need for a separate state-nation for Indian Muslims. As celebrated Muslim poet Sir Allama Muhammad Iqbal wrote:

> Religion does not teach mutual discord
> Strung on a single strand we are one we are Indians.

Even Syed Ahmed Khan as well as Allama Iqbal did not consider Hindus and Muslims as two nations. Khan's speeches are categorically against the two-nation theory. For instance, in his speech at Gurdaspur in January 1884, he said, "We [i.e., Hindus and Mohammadans] should try to become one heart and soul and act in union. In old historical books and traditions you will have read and heard, and see even now, that all the people inhabiting one country are designated by the term one nation. Remember that the words Hindu and Mohammadan are meant for religious distinction; otherwise, all who reside in this country in this particular respect belong to the same nation." In another speech delivered at Lahore in 1884, Khan explicated the two-nation theory in detail, "These are the different grounds upon which I call both these races which inhabit India by one word, i.e. Hindu, meaning that they are inhabitants of Hindustan," he said.

Khan went to the extent of calling all Indians Hindus, and gave a clear verdict that in this respect, whoever inhabited Hindustan should be called Hindu irrespective of his faith or creed. This was precisely the approach of Iqbal. He said, "We are all Indians, we are all Hindus and our homeland is Hindustan." He found an Islamic justification for this reasoning that states that religion does not teach hatred. It is axiomatic that the tenets of religion are immutable. Muslims believe that after the Prophet no one has any authority to make the slightest change in the basic tenets of Islam. The question, therefore, arises: How can religious tenets vary with changing political ideology? Even Sir Mohammad Iqbal, like Sir Syed Ahmed Khan, had gone to the extent of saying in one of his Persian verses:

> Plant Islam and Hindu holy flowers in one pot, make it right,
> Have no opinion, if thou see only black or white.

This verse illustrates the underlying unity and brotherhood between Hindus and Muslims. The poet suggests that the beads of the *tasbih* (to count the repetitions of prayers) of a Muslim should be threaded by the sacred thread of the Hindus. He goes on to say that, if you make a distinction between the two, if unity appears to be a duality to you due to your defective eyesight, alas, you have become blind.[109] On August 11, 1947, three days before the creation of Pakistan, Jinnah rejected the two-nation theory in a speech before the Constituent Assembly of Pakistan.

> You are free; you are free to go to your temples, you are free to go to your mosques or to any other place of worship in this State of Pakistan. You may belong to any religion or caste or creed that has nothing to do with the business of the State. We are starting with the fundamental principle that we are all citizens and equal citizens of one State. Now I think we should keep that in front of us as our ideal and you will find that in the course of time Hindus would cease to be Hindus and Muslims would cease to be Muslims, not in the religious sense, because that is the personal faith of each individual, but in the political sense as citizens of the State.[110]

Muslims are religiously different from Hindus, as are Sikhs, Jains, and Parsees (one of the earliest minorities in India, who escaped there from Iran fleeing persecution). Yet culturally, socially, historically, and ancestrally, Muslims have been the same as other Indians for thousands of years. They have had no single identity or single language. There was no politico-cultural-linguistic-historical entity construct. The adopted official language in Pakistan is Urdu, which is the same as Hindustani spoken by other non Muslim Indians. Even Muslims of India are heterogeneous; there are Shias, Sunnis, Sufis, and Ahmadiyyas. All ethnic groups, including Sindhis, Baluchis, Punjabis, and Pashtuns in Pakistan, have diverse identities. In 1971, Bengalis were separated into a new country, Bangladesh, the birthplace of the AIML. By every measure, Pakistan is a failed nation–state. If the British had not defeated the Marathas and Sikhs early in the nineteenth century, and had not given special privileges to Muslims in education and employment, they would have been marginalized. Out of a total of 600 princely Indian states, only 10 were Muslim. One-third of Indian Muslims remained in India after the partition, so that India has almost the same number of Muslims as Pakistan. Even after sixty years of existence, there has been a significant existential threat to Pakistan as a nation–state. In the opinion of the The Brookings Institution scholar Stephen Cohen, "The larger issue facing Pakistan is not total state failure or collapse, but an exploration of the kind of nation-state that Pakistan will become."[111] Could the Muslims of India qualify for a nation-state? This has always been a debatable point. It is inconceivable and incomprehensible that secular, democratic Britain, a pioneer in jurisprudence, could award a separate country to Muslims in British India. Jinnah (also known as Quaid-i-Azam), a Shia, became the sole spokesman of the Sunni-dominated AIML, thanks to Viceroys Lord Linlithgow and Archibald Wavell of India, and Sir George Cunningham. The AIML, founded in Dhaka (now Bangladesh) in 1906, was opposed to the August 1942 Quit India movement, which was launched by the INC at the behest of Mahatma Gandhi. Jinnah was able to found Pakistan with East Bengal, West Punjab, Sindh, and the KP in August 1947, thanks to his unconditional and energetic support of World War II. But in four provinces- —Punjab, Sindh, the KP, and Baluchistan—the AIML was not in the majority, failing to win the last election prior to the partition. It was neither a referendum for the partition, nor recognition of Jinnah's leadership of Muslims. Jinnah married a Parsee woman, his personal doctor was a non-Muslim (Hindu, as was his home steward), and his only child married a Christian man. He drank whisky, ate pork, and did not regularly attend Friday prayers. Due to all this, some people considered him secular. Notwithstanding, he insisted that the constitution of Pakistan would be made on the basis of Sharia. But the intent of establishing Sharia is not secularism. Jinnah's views were extremely communal—he was against the Muslim coalition government of the Unionist Ministry in Punjab, and alliances between Muslim and non-Muslim parties in Bengal, two provinces where Muslims were barely a majority. Punjab's Chief Minister was Sikandar Hayat Khan of the secular Unionist Party, Sindh's Chief Minister was Allah Baksh Somuru of the secular Nationalist Party, and Badshah Khan's Khudai Khidmatgars Party dominated KP, the largest Muslim province. Badshah Khan and his Khudai Khidmatgars party were strongly against partition and were also opposed to the AIML. In the 1937 elections called by the British, the AIML could not get a majority in any of the eleven provinces of India. In the 1946 elections, the AIML again failed to form governments in any of the eight major provinces. The Indian National Congress formed the governments each time, even in Muslim-majority provinces. In every election, the AIML could not get any seats in Sindh or in the KP, and only one seat in Punjab. Despite the poor performance of the AIML, the imperial British dictatorially declared that Jinnah was to be recognized as the sole spokesman of Indian Muslims. Jinnah, a Muslim educated in British law schools, refused to shake hands with the his fellow Muslim, INC leader Maulana Azad, because as a Muslim Azad should not have served in the INC (which had several Muslim presidents and chief ministers). While deliberating on the Cabinet Mission, Jinnah insisted the communal groupings in each state be based on religion, and the communal parity at the Center. But Mahatma Gandhi and Nehru of the Congress Party objected to such communal groupings, whether they were in the State or the Center. For this reason, Pakistani historians' asser-

tion that it was Congress that insisted on partition and Jinnah who was
against it is questionable. The Awami National Party leader Wali Khan
(1899–2002) of Pakistan's KP, who read the declassified documents prior
to writing his book, *Facts are Facts* writes:

> It was an absurd situation. The British had accepted the principles of par-
> tition, but the Congress (INC) was violently opposed. And how could the
> Congress be overlooked? It was the Congress' efforts which had shown up
> all the way, Congress movement, Congress protest, Congress sacrifice,
> Congress imprisonment, Congress abdication. The Congress did all the
> work and the Muslim League got all the plaudits! The Muslim League
> remained a party minus a movement, minus sacrifices, minus seats in the
> Elected Assemblies and minus any political power. Blinded by their self-
> interest, the British lost all sense of principle or fair play. Despite the fact
> that the Muslim League was a political non-entity, the British regarded it
> the sole representative of all Muslims.

Communal bloodshed and mass migration—the worst in the history of
the nation—was a result of the AIML's decision for partition based on the
two-nation theory, particularly on its call for Direct Action Day. NWFP/KP
leader Khan Abdul Ghaffar Khan, a Pashtun, variously known as Badshah
Khan and Bacha Khan, has also been called "the frontier Gandhi." He founded
the Khudai Khidmatgars, which was banned by Pakistan after the partition.
Wali Khan describes the partition of India and the role of Ghaffar Khan,
who was vehemently against the two-nation theory and the partition. These
rebelling Pashtuns wanted to be a separate nation as the Bengalis in East
Pakistan were. Baluchistan, at 48 per cent of the area of Pakistan, was
forced to join Pakistan as a Muslim majority province, despite its wishes to
become a separate state. The rebelling Baluchis formed a separatist organization, the Baluchistan Liberation Army (BLA). Jinnah was fuming when
Maharajah Hari Singh of J&K—a Muslim majority province—signed the
Instrument of Accession to join India instead of Pakistan. He could not
accept the fact that Sheikh Abdullah, as the sole leader of J&K, did not want
to join Pakistan. In addition to Kashmir terrorists, there are Baluchi terrorists, Pashtun (Pakhtoon) terrorists, and Sindh terrorists in Pakistan.[112]
(Sindhis have been complaining since 1947 about the central interference
and domination as well as the inflow of muhajirs and refugees who migrated
from India after the partition. A separatist group, the Sindhu Desh movement, probably became dormant under the Sindhi's Asif Ali Zardari as
president of Pakistan).
    Many charitable Pakistani historians, laden with a deep hatred and abomi-
nable prejudice of India, and blinded by historical misjudgment, have com-

pared Jinnah with Saladin, a Kurdish Sunni Muslim, who regained Palestine from the Crusaders. Unlike Saladin, Jinnah was not fighting back; he simply sold Pakistan to Imperialists in exchange for being crowned sole spokesman. The Viceroy assured his superiors that Jinnah was one-hundred-percent a British stooge! The interesting conundrum is that if Jinnah lacked power and organization, how could he be considered the custodian of Muslim rights?[113]

Selig S. Harrison, director of the Asia Center for International Policy in Washington, wrote of Pakistan's separatist movements in the issue of *La Monde*:

> Only 2,260 Baluch fled their villages to escape bombing and strafing by the U.S.-supplied F-16 fighter jets and Cobra helicopter gunships of the Pakistan air force, but as casualty figures mount, it will be harder to ignore the human costs of the Baluch independence struggle and its political repercussions in other restive minority regions of multi-ethnic Pakistan. Already, in neighboring Sindh, separatists who share Baluch opposition to the Punjabi-dominated military regime of General Pervez Musharraf are reviving their long-simmering movement for a sovereign Sindhi state, or a Sindhi-Baluch federation, that would stretch along the Arabian Sea from Iran in the west to the Indian border. Many Sindhi leaders openly express their hope that instability in Pakistan will tempt India to help them, militarily and economically, to secede from Pakistan as Bangladesh did with Indian help in 1971. Some 6 million Baluch were forcibly incorporated into Pakistan when it was created in 1947. This is the fourth insurgency they have fought to protest against economic and political discrimination.[114]

There is now a new generation of terrorists in Pakistan, and terrorist attacks increased significantly in 2009. According to the South Asia Terrorism Portal (SATP), a terrorism database, 2155 civilians were killed in terrorist violence in 2008 and nearly 1800 in the first ten months of 2009, as compared to around 1600 civilian deaths from 2003 to 2006. In his January 2008 testimony before a U.S. House Foreign Affairs Subcommittee, security and strategic affairs analyst Ashley J. Tellis, a senior associate at the Carnegie Endowment for International Peace, outlined five categories of terrorists:

1. Sectarian: Groups such as the Sunni SSP and the Shia Tehrik-e-Jafria, which are engaged in violence within Pakistan;
2. Anti-Indian: Terrorist groups that operate with the alleged support of the Pakistani military and the LeT, the JeM, and the HuM;

3. Afghan Taliban: The original Taliban movement and especially its Kandahari leadership, centered around Mullah Mohammad Omar, believed to now be living in Quetta (with links to veteran Afghan warlords Jalaluddin Haqqani and Gulbuddin Hekmatyar);
4. AQ and its affiliates: The organization led by OBL and other non-South Asian terrorists believed to be ensconced in the FATA (Rohan Gunaratna of the International Centre for Political Violence and Terrorism Research in Singapore says other foreign militant groups such as the IMU, Islamic Jihad group, the Libyan Islamic Fighters Group, and the Eastern Turkistan Islamic Movement are also located in FATA);
5. The Pakistani Taliban: Groups consisting of extremist outfits in the FATA, led by individuals such as Hakimullah Mehsud, of the Mehsud tribe in South Waziristan, Faqir Muhammad of Bajaur, and Qazi Fazlullah of the Tehrik-e-Nafaz-e-Shariat-e-Mohammadi (TNSM).[115]

Other groups include Tehreek-e-Taliban Pakistan (TTP), which has been blamed for the assassination of former Pakistan prime minister Benazir Bhutto; and LeJ, an anti-Shia, Sunni-Wahhabi group that wants a Taliban-style Islamic state. It was reportedly behind the abduction and murder of *Wall Street Journal* reporter Daniel Pearl, the killing of twelve French nationals in a bomb attack in Karachi, and the attack on the U.S. Consulate, Karachi, in 2002. This group works with JeM and HuJI.

Terrorizing civilians and issuing a warning to the security establishment have been part of the terrorists' new agenda. For example, on March 3, 2009, terrorists attacked a Sri Lankan team that was visiting Pakistan to play with the Pakistani Cricket team. *BBC News* reported that the gunmen attacked a bus carrying the Sri Lankan cricket team on its way to play in the Pakistani city of Lahore. At least six policemen escorting the team bus were killed, along with a driver, while seven cricketers and an assistant coach were injured. Pakistani officials said that about 12 gunmen were involved, and that grenades and rocket launchers have been recovered. Annual fatalities due to terrorist attacks in Pakistan are given in Table 4.3.

Terrorist attacks in Pakistan significantly increased despite a general decline in such violence and its casualties worldwide, according to U.S. Government figures. In 2009 alone, 3317 people were killed in Pakistan due to terrorist attacks and sectarian conflict.[116] Meanwhile, the death toll from worldwide terrorism fell from 22,508 to 15,765 in 2007, and the number of attacks dropped from 14,506 to 11,770, according to data compiled

Table 4.3
Annual Fatalities in Terrorist Violence in Pakistan, 2003–2008

Year	Civilians	SF Personnel	Terrorists	Total
2003	140	24	25	189
2004	435	184	244	863
2005	430	81	137	648
2006	608	325	538	1471
2007	1523	597	1479	3599
2008	2155	654	3906	6715
Total	5291	1865	6329	13485

* Source: Institute for Conflict Management (SATP), SF—security force (www.satp.org/
satporgtp/countries/pakistan/index.htm)

by the U.S. intelligence community and released in a U.S. State Department report.[117] It was reported in the American media that from January 1, 2010 to July 9, 2010, there were over 514 deaths and over 877 wounded by suicide attacks in Pakistan; most of the victims were Shias and Ahmadiyyas. As reported by the Washington-based Pew Research Center: 9 per cent of Pakistanis gave Al Qaeda a favorable rating in 2009, which rose to 18 per cent in 2010, a gain of 9 per cent. The Taliban had a 10-per cent favorable rating in 2009, which rose to 15 per cent in 2010, a gain of 5 per cent. Meanwhile, Pakistan gave LeT a 25-per cent favorable rating in 2010. In terms of threats to their country, 53 per cent of Pakistanis named India 53, while only 23 per cent of respondents named the Taliban 23, and 3 per cent cited Al Qaeda.[118] Clearly, India is seen as the greatest enemy in Pakistan. Pakistan's military dimension and other topics are discussed elsewhere.[119] Today, LeT's close ties with AQ in Pakistan, its support for the Afghan Taliban's military operations (despite the ideological divide between the Deobandi and the *Ahl-e-Hadith* interpretations of Islam), and its close collaboration with Jamiat al-Dawa in operations directed at American troops in Afghanistan's Korengal Valley, are only the latest in a long string of hostile activities affecting U.S. citizens, soldiers, and interests. The concerted focus on India since 1996—one that still continues—is largely due to the interests of America's strategic interest in Pakistan. Since the mid-1990s, the ISI favored LeT as its preferred instrument for war against India: the group's dominant Punjabi composition, which matched the ethnicity of most of the Pakistani Army and the ISI, its willingness to engage in risky military operations throughout India, its demonstrated savagery in encounters with the Indian military, its readiness to inflict high and indiscriminate levels of violence on its targets, and above all, its absolute loyalty to its state sponsors, made it favored above among other state-supported groups, such as JeM, HuM, HuJI, and even the dominantly Kashmiri HM.[120] Particular attention will be given as to how these groups receive funding and support from each other through state sponsors such as Pakistan's Inter-Services Intelligence (ISI) agency and non-state sponsors such as al-Qaida and Wahhabi idealists in Saudi Arabia, as well as arms supplies from Iran and potentially China.First, the local *madrassas* have provided Mehsud with funding for his insurgency.*Madrassas* receive funding from prominent Muslims in Saudi Arabia and the Gulf states, which is then often funneled through the madrassa system into the hands of the TTP. Second, the TTP is indirectly funded fromwealthy benefactors who share a common ideology of shar'ia law and subscribe to the Wahhabi sect of Islam. This radical view of Islam originated in Saudi Arabia and has spread throughout Pakistan in response to the continued presence of U.S. forces in the region. Finally, The TTP participates in opium smuggling and heroin production in South Waziristan.Funding from this smuggling accounts for the vast majority of TTP.[121]

U.S.–Pakistan Relations: To address Pakistani security anxieties, the Obama administration has taken several little-noticed steps. One is to implicitly accept Pakistan's status as nuclear-armed state, and thereby counter conspiracy theories that the United States is secretly plotting to seize Pakistani nukes. The administration has repeated Obama's assurance of last June 2009 that "we have no intention of sending U.S. troops into Pakistan." The Pakistanis are concerned of late that the United States may negotiate a peace deal with the Afghan Taliban that cuts them out as an intermediary. "In reconciliation talks, Pakistan must have a seat at the table," insists one Pakistani government.[122] While America has alleged that the ISI is helping the Taliban, it is well-known that the ISI rarely allows civilian governments to devise an independent Afghan or India policy. Despite Obama's assurance, Pakistan has remained a problem state. The Pew Research Center's survey of 22 countries was basically conducted to judge Obama's popularity, or lack of it, among the participating countries. Only eight per cent of Pakistanis approve of the U.S. president's foreign policy, in sharp contrast to India, where 73 per cent approve of it. Although no fewer than 69 per cent in Pakistan worry that extremists could take control of the country, support for suicide bombings has gone up slightly in the past year. Pakistan is ranked tenth among the ten states that top the 2010 Failed State Index, as designated by the America's *Foreign Policy* magazine. The Freedom House survey for 2009 places Pakistan in the company of Iraq, Afghanistan, Somalia, and Yemen where, "violent Islamic extremism" continues to plague the countries' internal affairs.

Several radical or jihadists organizations in Pakistan have been state sponsored. It is amusing to observe that several Pakistani dictators and others, who seized democratic governments and promoted radicals, have been patronized by American presidents:

> Ayub Khan (1958–1969)—John F. Kennedy—Pakistan was allowed
>   to join SEATO and CENTO
> Yahya Khan (1969–1973)—Richard M. Nixon—initiating America–
>   China dialogue
> Zia-ul Haq (1977–1988)—Ronald Reagan—supporting mujahedeen
>   in 1979–1989
> Pervez Musharraf (1999–2008)—George W. Bush—sheltering the
>   Taliban and AQ

India–Pakistan: The jihadists gloated over their international fame and acceptance of their jihadist ideology among fellow Islamists with the victory against the Shah Reza Pahlavi of Iran, the defeat of the Soviet Union in Afghanistan, the withdrawal of American forces from Somalia, Hezbollah's accomplishments against Israel in Lebanon, the West Bank, and Gaza, and India's yielding to holy warriors in J&K. Beijing has used its prerogative as a permanent member of the Security Council to prevent international condemnation of Pakistani support for terrorist incursions across the Line of Control in Kashmir, a *de jure* part of India. There is strong collaboration in weapons program development between China and Pakistan. In 1990, thousands of Hindus were killed by terrorists in Kashmir, constituting a huge genocide and ethnic cleansing, and the perpetrators were not held accountable. Hindus who fled the massacre are living as refugees in Delhi and elsewhere in India. The separatist party APHC is demanding autonomy, annexing with Pakistan, or independence, merely to establish Sharia which would destroying the *Kashmiriyat* culture as well as the accord of 1952 between Sheikh Abdullah and Pundit Nehru.[123]

Our politicians, who salivate for Muslim votes and are willing to go to any extent to appease "minority sentiments"—including approving the absurd inclusion of Muslims in the list of BPL (below the poverty line) beneficiaries of the Indian state's munificence in keeping with the Prime Minister's "Muslims first" policy—would rather pretend this particular event never happened. Our judiciary, which endlessly agonizes over terrorists and their molls being killed in Gujarat, has not thought it fit to set up a Special

Investigation Team to identify the guilty men of 1990 and bring them to justice. It would seem Hindu pride is responsible; Hindu dignity and Hindu lives are irrelevant in this wondrous land of ours.

These murders are being supported by neighboring state networks that hold religion above human lives and dignity. They have not been subjected to international criminal justice or to UNO sanctions.

The threat has taken a syndicated shape with more terrorist attacks in Afghanistan and Pakistan. Robert Gates, who was involved in coordinating American military aid to Pakistan in the 1980s as the Number Two CIA official under President Reagan, remarked during a visit to Pakistan: AQ, the Taliban in Afghanistan, Tariki Taliban in Pakistan, the LeT, the Haqqani network—this is a syndicate of terrorists that work together. And when one succeeds they all benefit, and they share ideas, they share planning. They don't operationally coordinate their activities, as best I can tell. But they are in very close contact. They take inspiration from one another; they take ideas from one another. Religious prosecution continues in 2010 with a trial in Iran for blasphemy. The Baha'i community of 300,000 or more is facing arrest, vandalism, dismissal from jobs, denial of education, and other forms of religious bigotry inflicted by the Shiites, who consider Baha'ism an intolerable blasphemy for its belief in a nineteenth-century prophet, as the Prophet Muhammad is held to be the last prophet in Islam.

In this conflict, savagery, violence, and terror have wielded power and gained territory, while tolerance and nonviolence have been subdued, humiliated, and disgraced by the most brutal warfare in human history. The sword is more powerful than prayer with folded hands. The political terrorism of Stalin, Lenin or Mao is also brutal and gross. The brutal repression and killing of civilians by despotic rulers, leftists, and military dictators using army or guerrilla forces in Asia (massacres in Cambodia, the Suharto regime in Indonesia, the Pakistani Army's massacre in Bangladesh), Africa (the Algerian Army, Charles Taylor in Liberia, and others), and Latin America (The Revolutionary Forces of Columbia, the National Liberation Army, the Shining Path in Peru), under the guise of combating terrorism, are no less barbaric and colossal. The insane acts of Islamic savagery go back to the seventh century, with the murder of early caliphs, even family members, and has been prolonged through the Assassins, the Qaramatis, Ibn Taymiyyah, Abd al-Wahhab, Mohammad Abduh, Hassan al-Banna, Ayatollah Khomeini, Abdus Salam Faraj, Omar Abdel Rahman,[124] and others, to inculcate *al-wala' wal-bara'* (love and hate for Allah's sake). The journalist M.J. Akbar writes:

Jihad is the signature tune of Islamic history. Radical movements in Islam turn to the past for inspiration, with faith as their sustenance. The nineteenth century was one during which Indian Muslims declared more than one jihad against the British, who were forced into a serious enquiry into the nature of the Muslim mind and asked if rebellion was compulsory in Islam. A division in the mind became, through the agitational politics of an extremely determined leader, Mohammad Ali Jinnah, a division of the land.[125]

The *Book of Jihad* states: "Know that Paradise is under the shade of swords." Yet as the former diplomat Narendra Sarila asserts:

Many of the roots of Islamic terrorism sweeping the world today lie buried in the partition of India. Once the British realized that the Indian nationalities who would rule India after its independence would deny them military cooperation under a British Commonwealth defense umbrella, they settled for those willing to do so by using religion for the purpose. Their problem could be solved if Mohammad Ali Jinnah, the leader of the Muslim League Party, would agree in his plan to detach the northwest of India, abutting Iran, Afghanistan and Sinkiang and establish a separate state there—Pakistan. The proposition was a realizable one as a working relationship had been established between the British authorities and Jinnah during the Second World War and he was willing to cooperate with the British on defense matters if Pakistan was created. Jinnah "represents a minority and a minority that can only hold its own with our assistance." Jinnah said disdainfully: "We eat cow, the Hindus worship it." The warriors (Archibald) Wavell and (Winston) Churchill could agree on this much: the malevolence of Gandhi, whose half-naked frame, hair splitting arguments, and refusal to put up his fists encapsulated all that was repugnant to them about Hindus. (Leopold) Amery wrote in his diary that Wavell was refusing to see that his insistence on consensus before freedom means Pakistan and break up of India.[126]

India's Viceroy Lord Linlithgow made Jinnah the sole spokesman for Muslims in India, shepherding all the Muslims into the Muslim League fold to oppose the "Hindu Congress," and thus burying the tenets of secularism, democracy, and free and fair elections. Jinnah's Muslim League, however, could not get one fourth of the seats reserved for Muslims in the 1937 election. Furthermore, with 95 per cent Muslims, the League lost to Gandhi's Congress Party. Jinnah walked out of the AIML meeting when it supported the Khilafat movement, as it is unconstitutional for the AIML to go against the government's foreign policy. He then resigned in protest. Even the Jamaat-e-Islami founder, Indian-born Sunni Muslim, Syed Abul Maududi, went against the Shia Muslim Jinnah—a non practicing Muslim—as he believed that he was unfit to lead the Muslims of India. The Shia Political Conference also did not support Jinnah. It is ironic that Shia Muslim M.A. Jinnah and Ahmadiyya Zafrulla Khan—pioneers of Pakistan—are declared un-Islamic in Sunni dominated Pakistan.

The radicalism is largely fomented by madrassas and radical mosques. As a former intelligence official recently noted on Fox News,

> When you finish an education in a madrassa, you are good for one of two things: You can be a mullah, or you can be a jihadist. Madrassas drew added attention when it became known that several Taliban leaders and Al Qaeda members had developed radical political views at madrassas in Pakistan, some of which allegedly were built and partially financed by donors in the Persian Gulf states. These revelations have led to accusations that madrassas promote Islamic extremism and militancy, and are a recruiting ground for terrorism.[127]

It is widely acknowledged that the Saudi government, as well as wealthy Saudi individuals, have supported the spread of the Wahhabist ideas in several Muslim countries and in the United States and Europe. Some have argued that this proselytizing has promoted terrorism and has spawned Islamic militancy throughout the world. Saudi funding of mosques, *madrassas*, and charities, some of which have been linked to terrorist groups such as Al Qaeda, has raised concern that Wahhabi Islam has been used by militants who tailor this ideology to suit their political goals and who rely on Saudi donations to support their aspirations.

After a lull, several militant outfits have now again raised their heads and increased their activities in and around Muzaffarabad, the capital of Pakistan-occupied Kashmir (PoK), to wage 'jihad' against India, BBC Urdu Service has reported. A 25-year-old engineering student from Lahore, fresh from a training stint in one of the camps told BBC from POK that a large number of youths from Pakistani universities and abroad are undergoing training in PoK under supervision of a militant group to wage jihad against India.

Southeast Asia

Southeast Asian countries, unlike South Asia and the Middle East, were secular, tolerant and peaceful in the presence of significant Muslim populations. The region has 13 countries and 9 territories, and a total population of 581 million. Only three countries—Brunei, Indonesia, and Malaysia—are Muslim majority countries, with populations that are 67 per cent, 86 per cent, and 60 per cent Muslim, respectively. Indonesia is the largest country in the region, with 230 million people. About 250 million Muslims live in Malaysia, Indonesia, the Philippines, Thailand, and Singapore, making up almost one fourth of the Muslims in the world. After the defeat of the Soviet Union in 1989 and the emergence of the victorious AQ and the Taliban, the rebellion and unrest of Muslim separatists began. Muslims came in large numbers to Pakistan and Afghanistan to be trained as mujahedeen, and from there they would carry jihad to SE Asia. After the 2001 invasion of Afghanistan by American-led Coalition forces, AQ terrorists found safe havens in South Asia and Southeast Asia. Mujahedeen who had fought against Soviet troops in the 1980s returned to their respective countries to continue jihad, for the establishment of Sharia and regional AQ branches. Radicals now seek to establish an Islamic state encompassing Indonesia, Malaysia, Singapore, Southern Thailand, and the Southern Philippines, with strict Sharia law replacing current secular legislation systems. One thousand Southeast Asian Muslims were trained and fought in Afghanistan; these veterans now want to Talibanize Southeast Asia. The most famous of these Afghan war veterans are: Riduan Isamuddin Hambali, the leader of the Indonesian terrorist organization Jemaah Islamiyah (JI; Abu Bakar Bashir is their spiritual leader and founder); Abdurajak Janjalani (founder of Abu Sayyaf Group, ASG, in the early 1990s); Jafar Umar Thalib (founder of Laskar Jihad, or LJ, in 2000); and Nik Abdul Aziz Nik Mat (a Malaysian politician who is also an Islamic ulama).

Other recent factors have contributed to the rise of terrorism in the region. They include (1) lack of security, plus corruption; (2) a resurgence of tourism in the face of problematic visa standards (some countries do not have visa requirements and there are no boundary controls, no computerized data on visitors, and there is forgery in passports and other documents); and (3) under-regulated Islamic banks in Malaysia, Indonesia, and Thailand, which has enabled money laundering, drug trafficking, and people smuggling. Southeast Asia terrorist specialist Zachary Abuza[128] writes:

> In the Middle East, these informal banking systems (the unregulated systems) are known as the hawala, or trust systems in which no money is wired, no names or accounts of senders or receivers are used, and no records are kept. With a commission of only 1 to 2 per cent, compared to average fees up to 15 per cent, they are the transfer systems of choice. In Pakistan, for example, of the $6 billion in foreign exchange that is remitted to the country annually, only $1.2 billion arrives through the banking system. This type of money exchanging is common throughout South Asia. . . . Over $6 billion is remitted annually to the Philippines, mainly through the *hawala* systems, which has considerable financial exchanges due to the 1.4 million guest workers in the Middle East alone.

Additional factors stoking to the rise of terror in Southeast Asia include: (4) This region is now the world's largest manufacturing center for electronic and computer hardware and software productions. AQ terrorists took advantage of this modern technology development in communication and computer systems, to give their networks more efficient and wider area accessibility. (5) There is an abundant supply of arms and ammunitions for purchase by terrorists; and (6) tax money from zakat-Muslim donations of 2.5 per cent were diverted to terrorist organizations.

After the end of the Afghanistan war in 1989, as AQ members and war veterans returned to their respective countries, AQ began to establish regional branches in Southeast Asia, where Arab migrants from Yemen and Sudan have settled for decades and where a majority of Muslims live. AQ's Manila cell, which was founded in the early 1990s by a brother-in-law of OBL, was particularly active in the early-to-mid-1990s. In the late 1990s, the locus of AQ's Southeast Asia activity appeared to have moved to Malaysia, Singapore, and—most recently—Indonesia. In 1999 and 2000, Kuala Lumpur and Bangkok were the sites for important strategy meetings among some of the September 11 plotters. AQ's leadership also has taken advantage of Southeast Asia's generally loose financial controls, to use various countries in the region as places to raise, transmit, and launder the network's funds. By 2002, roughly one-fifth of AQ's organizational strength was centered in Southeast Asia. AQ Southeast Asian operatives helped create what may be Southeast Asia's first indigenous regional terrorist network, JI, which has plotted attacks against Western targets. Additionally, AQ's local cells worked to cooperate with indigenous radical Islamic groups by providing them with money and training. Until it was broken up in the mid-1990s, AQ's Manila cell provided extensive financial assistance to Moro militants such as the ASG and the Moro Islamic Liberation Front (MILF).[129]

The Southeast Asian countries formed the Association of Southeast Asian countries Nationals (ASEAN) in August of 1967, with members including Indonesia, Malaysia, the Philippines, Singapore, Thailand, Brunei, Burma (Myanmar), Cambodia, Laos, and Vietnam. Its object was to promote economic development, peace, security, culture, trade, and other regional issues. The 7th Summit of ASEAN leaders in Brunei Darussalam in November 2001 adopted the 2001 ASEAN Declaration on Joint Action to Counter Terrorism. The specific measures that ASEAN member-nations are implementing based on the Declaration include:

1. Reviewing and strengthening national mechanisms to combat terrorism.

2. Early signing/ratification of or accession to all relevant anti-terrorist conventions including the International Convention for the Suppression of the Financing of Terrorism.

3. Deepening cooperation among ASEAN's front-line law enforcement agencies in combating terrorism and sharing "best practices."

4. Studying relevant international conventions on terrorism with the view to integrating them with ASEAN mechanisms on combating international terrorism.

5. Enhancing information/intelligence exchange to facilitate the flow of information, in particular, on terrorists and terrorist organizations, their movement and funding, and any other information needed to protect lives, property, and the security of all modes of travel.

6. Strengthening existing cooperation and coordination between the ASEAN Ministerial Meeting on Transnational Crime (AMMTC) and other relevant ASEAN bodies in countering, preventing and suppressing all forms of terrorist acts. Particular attention would be paid to finding ways to combat terrorist organizations, support infrastructure and funding and bringing the perpetrators to justice.

7. Developing regional capacity building programs to enhance existing capabilities of ASEAN member countries to investigate, detect, monitor and report on terrorist acts.

8. Discussing and exploring practical ideas and initiatives to increase ASEAN's role in and involvement with the international community to make the fight against terrorism a truly regional and global endeavor.

9. Strengthening cooperation at the bilateral, regional and international levels in combating terrorism in a comprehensive manner and affirm that at the international level the United Nations should play a major role in this regard.[130]

The specific measures outlined in the Declaration have been incorporated in the terrorism component of the Work Programme to Implement the ASEAN Plan of Action to Combat Transnational Crime, adopted in May 2002. Yet there are mutual suspicions among the states—Singapore against Malaysia and Indonesia, Thailand against Myanmar (Burma) and Indochina, Indonesia against Malaysia, and the Philippines against Malaysia regarding Malaysia's support of the Philippine terrorist groups Moro National Liberation Front and Moro Liberation Front (MNLF and MILF). All these factors have impeded a multilateral terrorist campaign. There is no multilateral extradition treaty, as only the terrorized states of the Philippines, Thailand, and Indonesia perceive jihadists as threats. In these countries, security, police, and intelligence are scattered in various ministries, with no collaboration or sharing of information. Bureaucrats heading these ministries are often corrupt and inefficient and are engaged in rivalry for state funds. For example, in Indonesia there is immense rivalry among BIN (the State Intelligence Agency), the National Police, and even the Ministry of Justice. There are many in the BIN who support Islamists in Indonesia. Counterterrorism using security forces sometimes leads to violations of human rights and dignity, and suppression of minorities' grievances of torture and long detentions. American economic assistance and subsidized trade are supposed to uproot poverty, illiteracy, and inequality to contain the spread of radicalism. It should be repeated here, however, that poverty does not always correlate with terrorism. Saudi Arabia, one of the richest countries in the world, supports and propagates radical Islam and terrorist organizations, whereas Mauritania, one of the poorest countries, is not affected by terrorism. Many well-known terrorists come from rich, respected families, have received higher education, and have had good employment opportunities. Instead, terrorism is more typically born from issues of Islamic identity, dignity, and socio-political injustice. The destruction of the caliphate some 80 years ago, the inception of European colonialism in Muslim and Arab land, and Western endorsement of the creation of a Jewish state in Palestine seem to better explain political Islam's grudge against the West than simplistic socioeconomic argument.[131]

The Philippines

The Philippines is a country of 92 million, of whom 90 per cent are Christian and 5 per cent Muslim. For decades, the southern Philippines have been a breeding ground for terrorist activity. It is estimated that 120,000 people have been killed since the insurgency in the 1970s and the property damage is estimated at more than $3 billion. The Philippines is home to a number of militant groups, including the ASG, the Communist Party of the Philippines/New People's Army, JI, the Alex Boncayao Brigade, the Pentagon Gang, the MNLF, and the MILF. These organizations are associated with AQ. The 2008 U.S. State Department estimates the ASG to consist of between two hundred and five hundred members. The terrorist attacks and number of deaths since 1999 are provided below.

In 1999, 105 bombing and grenade-throwing incidents claimed 59 lives and injured 525 people across the Philippine archipelago. In 2000, 268 terrorism-related incidents resulted in 142 dead and 989 wounded. The most telling of these was the December 30, 2000, Rizal Day bombing of Metro Manila's Light Rail Transit system and several buses, where twenty-two people were killed and more than a hundred injured. In the six-month period from October 2002 to March 2003, twenty-five bombing incidents were reported, beginning with the October 2 bombing in Malagutay, Zamboanga that killed three soldiers, including one American. The greatest damage, in terms of human lives and public confidence in government, was caused by a bomb that exploded at the waiting shed in front of the arrival area of the Davao City International Airport on March 4, 2003. Twenty-three people were killed and 162 were injured in that blast. On April 2, another bomb exploded at the passenger terminal of Davao City's Sasa Wharf, killing sixteen people and injuring fifty-seven others. This was followed a few hours later by grenade explosions at three different mosques in the city, which injured at least fourteen Muslim scholars. In 2004, a ferry bombing at sea resulted in 111 deaths; in 2006, eight people died in bombings in central Mindanao. In 2007, the Moro Islamic Liberation Front killed fourteen members of the Philippine Marines, beheading eleven of them, on the Philippine island–province of Basilan. In 2009, a Christian church was bombed, resulting in six deaths. The Philippine government has taken significant steps to combat terrorism, but terrorists continue to use the country as a base to organize, raise funds, train, and operate.[132]

Thailand

Over the past four years, an Islamic insurgency in Thailand's southern, predominantly Muslim provinces has claimed nearly three thousand lives. The Malay–Muslim provinces of Yala, Narathiwat, and Pattani in southern Thailand are fighting for a separate state, to be placed under Sharia law. In 2005, these provinces had a population of 1.8 million, with 79 per cent Muslim, while the population of Thailand is 62 million, with 94.6 per cent Buddhists, 4.6 per cent Muslims, 0.7 per cent Christian, 0.1 per cent Hindu, and 0.1 per cent other (including Judaism).[133]

The principal groups at the forefront of this unrest are:

1. Barisan Revolusi Nasional-Coordinate (BRN-C). Possibly the largest and best organized of the separatist groups, the BRN-C is the only active faction of an organization founded in the early 1960s to fight for an independent, religious state. The group recruits members from Islamic schools.

2. Pattani United Liberation Organization (PULO), part of a second wave of more secular separatist groups, established in 1968. A splinter called New PULO split from the group in 1995, but the two factions allied again two years later. Most of its leaders are based abroad.

3. Bersatu, an umbrella organization of various southern terrorist groups, founded in 1989. The coalition counts PULO and BRN-C among its members. This merger may have resulted from their weakening during the 1980s.

4. Gerakan Mujahedeen Islam Pattani (GMIP), established in part by Afghan veterans in 1995 to support a separate Islamic state. GMIP likely has connections to a Malaysian counterpart called Kumpulan Mujahedeen Malay.

It is alleged that foreign mercenaries and foreign funding support the secessionist movement, possibly from the Philippines, Malaysia, Indonesia, and AQ. The insurgents want to be part of the Muslim Malay majority in Malaysia rather than remaining in Thailand. Malaysia denies the existence of any support to the insurgents or any training camps in Malaysia. The insurgency-ridden provinces are some of the poorest provinces in Thailand. To boost economic development in the area, the government included them in the Indonesia-Malaysia-Thailand Growth Triangle, started a special economic development zone with tax incentives for those willing to invest in the area, and is working bilaterally with Malaysia to develop the border region. The level of unrest has increased steadily since 2001: 6 attacks in 2001, 75 incidents in 2002, 119 in 2003, and 7,743 incidents were recorded in southern Thailand from January 2004 to the end of August 2007, leaving 2,566 dead (an average of 58 per month or roughly two a day) and a further 4,187 wounded. Estimates of the number of people actively engaged in violent attacks vary greatly, from 5,000 to 6,000 to as many as 20,000 to 30,000.

Several Western and regional commentators have expressed concern that the altered and more acute nature of post-2004 unrest in the Malay-Muslim provinces is indicative of a growing penetration involving radicals with links to the Indonesia-based Jemaah Islamia (JI, appendices 1, 4) and, through this movement, to the broader global jihadist network. In particular, a fear remains that a process of fanatical Arabization, similar to that which has occurred in the outlying areas of the Philippine archipelago, may now be taking place in Thailand's deep south, possibly heralding the emergence of a new tactical center for anti-Western attacks in Southeast Asia. Compounding these fears are reports that money from Saudi Arabia, the United Arab Emirates, and Pakistan is increasingly being channeled to fund the construction of local Muslim boarding schools, private colleges, and mosques dedicated to the articulation of hard line Wahhabist and Salafist teachings. General Sondhi Boonyaratkalin, a Muslim, who orchestrated the military takeover of Thailand and who was instrumental in appointing new members of an interim administration, immediately signaled that he was ready to negotiate with rebels in the south. His designated prime minister, Surayud Chulanont, issued a public apology for past hard-line government policies and, in November 2006, specifically affirmed that Islamic law should be given a bigger role in the south and explicitly recognized the need for a long-term strategy that combines three main strands: (1) reconciliation, (2) security (promoting hard and soft approaches), and (3) dialogue.[134]

The general who led the September coup, Sondhi Boonyarataglin, said he was ready to talk to representatives of the insurgents. But the immediate response from the insurgents was far from conciliatory. The day after Surayud issued his apology, forty-six violent incidents were recorded, compared with a daily average of nine the previous month, according to the International Crisis Group, a Brussels-based organization that has been monitoring the situation in southern Thailand.[135] In 2009, Amnesty International reported:

> The current violence has led to at least 3,500 deaths so far; with the number of total deaths increasing each year through at least 2007. In March 2008 government statistics showed that 66 per cent of those killed in the south since 2004 were civilians. Just over half of those killed were Muslims. Anti-government forces have been particularly brutal. Since 2005 the insurgents have engaged in bombings of civilian areas, beheadings, and drive-by shootings of both Buddhist and Muslim security forces and civilians, including local officials seen as cooperating with the government. The insurgents have targeted state schools and teachers, and tried to frighten Buddhist residents away from the area.[136]

Indonesia

In the sixteenth century, the waning power of the Javanese Hindu–Buddhist Majapahit kingdom saw the advent of Islam, which brought violence to Indonesia's islands. Many Javanese people fled to Bali, where over 2.5 million refugees kept Hinduism alive. There were tensions between orthodox Muslims and more syncretistic, locally based religions, tensions that were still visible in the early 1990s. This tension was expressed in a contrast between *santri* and *abangan*, an indigenous blend of native and Hindu-

Buddhist beliefs with Islamic practices that are sometimes called Javanism or *kebatinan*. Indonesia still remains the most tolerant, pluralistic Muslim country. It has been a moderate, progressive secular country for decades, particularly under President Sukarno's reign (1950–1965) and President Suharto's regime (1967–1998). Indonesia has preserved the largest Islamic mosque, Istiqlal; the giant Hindu temple complex, Prambanan; and the largest Buddhist monument, Borobudur. In the 1980s, the governments of Indonesia and Malaysia sent 80,000 and 15,000 pilgrims to the *hajj* at state expense. In spite of this tradition of religious pluralism and tolerance, the Islamic movement *Darul Islam* (Islamic state), which aims for the establishment of an Islamic nation of Indonesia, was founded in 1942 by a group of Muslim militias, and coordinated by a charismatic radical Muslim politician, Kartosuwiryo. There has been a proliferation of paramilitary wings associated with Islamist extremists; for example, Lashkar Prembela Islam (LPI), Lashkar Jihad (LJ), founded by Ja'far Umar Thalib, Lashkar Mujahedeen Indonesia (LMI), and Jamaah Islamiyah (JI). Umar Thalib raised a 4000-man army to wage sectarian violence against Christians in the Malkus in May 2000, resulting in thousands of deaths.[137] In the last decade, poverty, unemployment, and underdevelopment have made the country into a fertile ground for terrorists, Islamic extremists, and mercenaries who say secularism has failed and the answer lies in adopting Sharia. Islamic fundamentalists are enraged in the wars in Iraq, Afghanistan, and the proxy war in Palestine. The poor, the uneducated, and the young are devoured by the extremists, and lured by Islamic subsidies poured in by the rich Gulf countries. There were 421 terrorist attacks in Indonesia between 1970 and 2007. The vast majority (92 per cent) of the terrorist activity in Indonesia has happened since 1994. From 1995 to 2007, there has been an average of thirty events per year, although the frequency of attacks has been declining since 2000. For those incidents in Indonesia where the perpetrator is known, the most active has been Free Aceh Movement (FAM, which was responsible for 113 terrorist attacks in Indonesia. GAM was most active in 2001, taking responsibility for 58 incidents that killed 65 people in that year alone, while Jemaah Islamiya (JI) was responsible for 11 attacks that killed more than 273 people.[138]

Sidney Jones, an expert on Southeast Asian terrorism, comments on terrorist bombings:

> Southeast Asia's most notorious jihadist organization, the Indonesia-based JI, is largely dormant but far from dead. Its leadership is not interested in Western targets, but its members still constitute a potentially important recruitment pool for other terrorist groups. Noordin Top, the Malaysian

national who heads the splinter group of JI is reportedly responsible for major anti-Western bombings in 2003, 2004, and 2005, remains at large in Indonesia. His capacity to mount another attack appears low, but his capacity for recruitment should not be discounted. It is worth noting that two of his key aides were released from prison in 2007. Most other known Indonesian jihadist groups appear to be more interested in stirring up communal tensions than in attacking the United States and its allies; "Christianization" is seen as the bigger threat.[139]

On September 18, 2009, Indonesia's chief police official, General Bambang Hendarso Danuri, confirmed that officers had killed Noordin Mohammed Top, the most wanted terrorist in Indonesia, and perhaps in South-East Asia.

Southeast Asian Muslims are more tolerant, culturally, socially, and politically, than other Muslims in the world and are proud of their heritage. Separatists in Thailand and the Philippines will probably settle for more autonomy and religious space rather than becoming separate states, provided there is no external influx of AQ and the Taliban-type terrorists into the region, and radicalization supported by foreign money. The South East Asian expert Joseph Liow writes:

> There are legitimate concerns that heightened religiosity—if not managed and channeled properly—could threaten the social and cultural pluralism that defines much of Southeast Asia. . . . Yet despite the diverse nature and expression of political Islam in Southeast Asia, it should also be clear that, whatever the national and local context, Islam is gaining strength politically and will likely remain a major point of reference for Muslims in the region seeking to locate their place in a rapidly globalizing world.[140]

ACEH Terrorists: The Free Aceh Movement (Indonesian: *Gerakan Aceh Merdeka* or simply GAM), a separatist group seeking independence for the Aceh region of Sumatra from Indonesia, was founded by a former Darul Islam foreign minister, Hasan di Tiro in December 1976. They fought against Indonesian government forces from 1976 to 2005, at a cost of over 15,000 lives. There have been alleged reports of stoning following the adoption of Sharia law. Now the question that confronts Indonesian President Susilo Bambang Yudhoyono is whether Aceh, which adopted Sharia in 2001 as part of efforts to broker a peace agreement, will remain a part of Indonesia. The alternative is for Indonesia to become, in effect, an extension of Aceh.[141]

> The trends aren't encouraging. Despite its reputation as one of the world's most inclusive Muslim-majority democracies, Sharia-inspired laws have been multiplying across the country in recent years with Saudi sponsored

madrassas (*pesantren*). These laws do things like restrict women from leaving the house at night or mandate that Muslims seeking marriage be able to read the Quran in Arabic. They can be unilaterally imposed by local politicians even if they don't enjoy widespread popular support.[142]

Terrorists may take over Indonesia if they spread Sharia from Aceh province, resulting in more bloodshed in secular Indonesia and engulfing all of the nations in Southeast Asia. These edicts would appear to violate Indonesia's secular constitution, which guarantees "all persons the right to worship according to their own religion or belief."

Jama'ah Ansharut Tauhid (JAT): This is another jihadi movement in Indonesia, founded in 2008 and led by Indonesia's best-known radical cleric, 72-year-old Abu Bakar Ba'asyir. Ba'asyir is alleged to have been involved in the 2002 Bali bombing that killed 202 people. JET preaches jihad against Islam's enemies, and has extended its membership to Jema'ah Islamiyah (JI). Ba'asyir has turned JAT into a nationwide structure within two years of its founding. On May 6, 2010, Indonesian police raided its Jakarta headquarters and charged three officials with raising funds for a militant training camp. They claim that democracy is antithetical to Islam, that only an Islamic state can uphold the faith, and that Islamic law must be the source of all justice.[143] A secular, democratic country with the world's largest population of Muslims, Indonesia faced terrorism in the form of 500 violent attacks between 1970 and 2010. Given the similar violence in its two sister democracies, India and Israel, it is clear that democracy is not a remedial answer to radical Islam. Yet despite poverty and a weak central government, Indonesia is not a fertile ground for radical Islamists, as a 2009 survey indicates that only 27 per cent of the people there want Sharia.

Radicalization in Africa

The radicalization of Islam in Africa has been dealt with by Angel Rabasa.[144] The growth of radical Islam in East Africa in recent decades has manifested itself in the spread of *Salafi* and Wahhabi ideologies, which has put pressure on traditional tribal cultures and Sufi practices. The emergence of extremist and terrorist groups is also impacted by African diasporas, and by money from the Gulf countries. Both of these things have been facilitated by weak governance and collapsed states, alternative power centers, prevalence of the informal economy, porous borders, widespread access to illegal weapons, proximity to the Arabian Peninsula, and operational access to attack venues. Civil and communal wars are pervasive and brutal throughout the entire region. Thousands have been killed or made homeless in the violence. It is reported that Djibouti, Egypt, Eritrea, Iran, Libya, the Lebanese terrorist group Hezbollah, Saudi Arabia, and Syria had provided arms, train-ing, and logistical support to the ICU (Islamic Courts Union), while Ethio-pia, Uganda, and Yemen have provided military assistance to the Transnational Federal Government (TFG). As reported by UPI on March 10, 2010, the takeover of Somalia's al-Shabaab Islamists by AQ veteran Fazul Abdullah Mohammed,[145] alleged mastermind of the 1988 U.S. em-bassy bombings in East Africa, could rally the divided jihadists as they brace for a U.S.-backed government offensive. According to counter-ter-rorism operatives in Kenya, Somalia's northern neighbor that sides with the beleaguered TFG in Mogadishu, officials believe Fazul took command of the jihadist forces following the assassination of Saleh Ali Saleh Nabhan by U.S. Navy SEALs on Sept. 14, 2009.

Fazul was born in the Comoros Islands in the Indian Ocean off the coast of Mozambique, in 1972. He was trained as a computer expert and speaks five languages, including English, French and Arabic. While pursuing Is-lamic studies in Pakistan in 1991, he was recruited by AQ and was sent to Somalia to help train Islamist militiamen, and has been closely linked to them ever since. Fazul took over leadership of AQ's East Africa cell fol-lowing the embassy bombings there, and was heavily involved in the Afri-can "blood diamonds" trade to fund AQ. The rapid and recent rise of AQ in Yemen—which spawned the Christmas Day airliner attack by 23-year-old Umar Farouk Abdulmutallab of Nigeria—is seen by U.S. officials as evi-dence that North African militants could just as quickly take on a broader jihadist mission and become a serious threat to the U.S. and European al-lies. The Mali-based militants have yet to show that they are capable of launching such foreign attacks, but are widening their involvement in kid-napping and the narcotics trade, reaping profits that could be used to expand terror operations. The world's "ungoverned spaces," which include Yemen, Somalia, and the Sahel (the Sahel covers parts of the countries of Senegal, Mauritania, Mali, Burkina Faso, Niger, Nigeria, Chad, Sudan, Somalia, Ethiopia, and Eritrea), are ideal for radicalization and have been a "breed-ing ground" for AQ.[146] As *Newsweek* reported in on November 20, 2009: "Still, American policymakers see the violence in the Sahel as proof that AQ in the Maghreb is threatening to transform the region into a hotbed of radical Islam, undermining the stability of local governments and threaten-ing Western interests. Gen. James Jones, President Obama's national-secu-rity adviser, has argued that the Pan-Sahel region 'provides opportunities to Islamic extremists, smugglers, and other insurgent groups.'"

The fact that AQIM and al Shabaab are fighting for control of Somalia, along with Nigeria's homegrown sects, illustrates the fact that radical Islam is taking hold in sub-Saharan Africa, albeit in many varied forms. One of these sects is Boko Haram, a Taliban-inspired militant Islamic group whose name means "Western education is a sin," and which seeks to unite Muslims under a Caliphate. In July 2009, Boko Haram carried out simultaneous attacks in four northern Nigerian states. Since 2008, the north and east of Mali, near the Algerian border, have served as a refuge for armed Islamists who have kidnapped westerners. Six Europeans abducted in Mauritania since November 2009 are thought to be held there. In January 2010, Al Shabaab militants tried to kill Danish cartoonist Kurt Westergaard at his home in Aarhus, Denmark, and on February 15, 2010, they attempted to assassinate Somalia's state minister for defense, Yusuf Mohamed Siyad.

Terrorism in Europe and Crossroads of Culture

The main objective of terrorists is to recover Muslim lands that they occupied during the Abbasid Empire (750–1258), Ottoman Empire (1299–1923), and Moghal Empire (1527–1857), and that they later lost to the British in India, the French in North Africa, and the Russians in Central Asia, among others. They lament the loss of the golden ages of Islam, the Islamic renaissance—the period from the eighth century to thirteenth century, when Islamic civilization, culture, and science reached their acme, in contrast to the dark ages of Europe. At the beginning of the eighth century, the Arabs brought one of history's greatest revolutions in power, religion, culture, and wealth to Dark Ages Europe.[147] But there are certain lingering myths. During the Muslim occupation, the contributions to science, theology, architecture, jurisprudence, astronomy, and medicine were originated by non-Muslims and non-Arabs from France, Italy, Spain, Austria, and other places in Europe and India. Muslim countries had inherited civilizations and scientific discoveries from other cultures, including the Babylonian, Byzantine, Sassanian, Persian, Hindu, Chinese, Mesopotamian, Greek, Roman, and other Empires. The noted scholar Peter Watson writes:

> In the late eighth century, an Indian merchant brought to Baghdad two seminal mathematical works. One was the Brahmasphuta Siddhanta (origin of the universe), known to Arabs as the Sindhind, the work of the great seventh-century Indian mathematician Brahmagupta (598–668). This contained early ideas about al-jabr, to give algebra its Arabic name. It was this work that Muhammad ibn-Musa al-Khwarizmi in the ninth century was to expand on so successfully. Khwarizmi became known as "the father of algebra" and gave his name to algorithms. . . . (The decimal system (numerals) was discovered in India in the eighth century, along with the solution of quadratic equation, cosmology, and astronomy.) In addition to Khwarizmi, this group included Ibn Turk, al-Karkhi, al-Biruni, al-

Haytham (called Alhazen in the West), Nasir Eddin and Omar Khayyam (he of "Rubaiyat" fame). . . . Finally, Aristotle. As a pagan, he posed a problem for Muslims—as he did for Christians a couple of centuries later. Nevertheless, the power of his ideas triumphed, and a whole slew of Arab "falasafahs" were influenced by Aristotle—al-Ghazali, Ibn Sina (Avicenna) and Ibn Khaldun among them. In addition, al-Farabi glossed Plato, al-Rhazi (Rhazes) built on Galen and Hippocrates, and Ibn Qurrah added to Euclid and Archimedes. Other luminaries of that period are Ibn Rushd (1126–1198), Abu al-Razi (865–925), and Yaqub al-Kindi (801–873). Ibn Rushd's *The Distinguished Jurist's Primer* is still today used in Islam.

Many of the scholars who translated the manuscripts of the Greeks, Indians and Chinese, and who flocked to Baghdad in the golden age, were Christians, Jews and pagans. Although the West as we know it did not exist in the ninth and tenth centuries, one could say that the Arab world was, for a time, part of the intellectual circle that would become the West. Many of the Greek classics reached Europe via Muslim Toledo, in Spain, where they were translated from Arabic into Latin. According to the Muslim scholar Kamran Mirza:

> Besides, all the ancient luminaries like Plato, Aristotle, Socrates, Buddha, Confucius, Euclid, Epicurus, Democritus, Lucretius and Aristarchus et al. were born long before Prophet Muhammad and his Islam but they all had direct and profound influence in laying the foundation of today's world of science, education, politics, human rights and justice.[148]

In the words of the Ahmediyya Nobel prize winner Dr. Abdus Salam (1926–1996), science is universal:

> There is only one universal Science; its problems and modalities are international and there is no such thing as Islamic Science just as there is no Hindu Science, nor Jewish Science, no Confucian Science, nor Christian science.[149]

The Western Terrorist Groups

Terrorism finds support among the liberal, secular democratic governments in Europe and America, where politicians are eager to protect their minority constituencies while balancing security concerns and civil liberties. Terrorist cells are operating in Belgium, France, Germany, Italy, the Netherlands, Spain, Sweden, and the United Kingdom. Terrorist groups in Europe and America include the Red Army Faction, Revolutionary Cells, Red Brigades, and others.

The Red Army Faction (RAF), founded in 1970, was organized by Andreas Baader and Ulrike Meinhof. It was the most violent and anti-imperialist "urban guerrilla" group to engage in armed resistance, and was held responsible for thirty-four deaths in Germany. Although it was more well-known, the RAF conducted fewer attacks than the Revolutionary Cells (RZ), which was responsible for 296 bomb, arson, and other attacks between 1973 and 1995. The Red Brigades, formed in 1970, was a Marxist-Leninist left wing terrorist group active in Italy in the 1970s and early 1980s. Known as "Brigate Rosse" in Italian, which was sometimes shortened to BR, their main aim was to force Italy to leave the NATO alliance. BR's boldest move took place in 1978 when BR groups headed by Mario Moretti kidnapped the former Christian Democrat Prime Minister Aldo Moro, killing five men of his entourage and murdering him 54 days later. During their long history of political and at times somewhat random violence, they carried out approximately 14,000 violent acts.

Euro-terrorist groups also include Action Directe in France, Fraktion Roter Armee in Germany, the Basque movement in Spain, the Corsican movement in France, Sin Fein in Northern Ireland, and environmental terrorists. In addition, there has been a resurgence of Islamic terrorism, particularly since 1979. Most of the Muslim population in Europe are immigrants from the former European colonies, lost to Islam in the aftermath of the Muslim golden age. These immigrants are usually poor, uneducated, unemployed, and remain segregated. While most first-generation immigrants had loyalties to their former homeland, some second and third-generation immigrants are loyal neither to their ancestral countries nor to their adopted countries. They are susceptible to Islamic radicalization, although their counterparts in America are affluent and have mostly integrated with the mainstream. A 2009 Gallup report found that 70 per cent of American Muslims have a job, compared with 64 per cent of the U.S. population as a whole. Muslim men have one of the highest employment rates of any religious group; Muslim women are as likely as Catholic women to say that they work. After Jews, Muslims are the most educated religious community in the United States. Muslim women (unlike their Jewish counterparts) are as likely as their male counterparts to have a college degree or higher; 40 per cent of women have a college degree as compared to 29 per cent of Americans overall. Yet there are some homegrown terrorists in America. Nidal Malik Hassan, a U.S. Army major serving as a psychiatrist, was charged with thirteen counts of premeditated murder and thirty-two counts of attempted murder on November 5, 2009. Colleen LaRose posted messages online under the name Jihad Jane, expressing her desire to participate in jihad, or holy war. Arrested in October 2009, Ms. LaRose had exchanged emails over the course of 15 months to recruit fighters for "violent jihad" (*BBC News*). The recent arrest in Pakistan of five young men from Northern Virginia who were suspected of terrorist activities precipitated new, dire warnings. In addition to the Northern Virginia case, four previous arrests in 2009 are noteworthy: Najibullah Zazi, the Denver airport shuttle driver charged with testing explosives for an attack; Bryant N. Vinas, a Hispanic-American convert to Islam, who pleaded guilty to receiving training from AQ in Pakistan; David C. Headley, a suspect in the November 2008 terrorist attacks in Mumbai; and the Minnesota American Somali youths accused of joining an Islamist insurgency in Somalia.[150] In Europe, the Muslim population has increased in recent decades, in some countries by up to 15 per cent. Their citizenship allows them to travel visa-free to any country in Europe, and they are also free to visit America under the visa-waiver program. There are also a significant number of converts. The 2004 murder of Dutch filmmaker Theo Van Gogh,[151] the Madrid train bombings the same year, and the following year's attacks on London's transportation systems demonstrated that European citizens and residents are capable of conducting horrendous acts against their adopted countries. On September 4, 2007, the German security services arrested three men for plotting car-bomb attacks in Germany, targeting the U.S. military base at Ramstein and pubs and nightclubs frequented by Americans. Two of the three were German-born converts to Islam. This plot was not the first involving German converts. In 1997, Israeli security services detained Steven Smyrek at Ben Gurion International Airport as he tried to enter Israel to survey possible Hezbollah terror targets. Christian Ganczarski, a Polish immigrant of German descent who had converted to Islam in 1986, played a major role as the intermediary between AQ's leadership and the suicide bomber who carried out the 2002 bombing of a Tunisian synagogue in Djerba, which killed twenty-one people. In 2006, the German police arrested Sonja B., a 40-year-old German convert who sought to travel to Iraq with her 1-year-old son and to carry out a suicide attack. Richard Reid, a British convert to Islam, attempted to blow up an airliner with explosives hidden in his shoes and boarded a flight to the United States under the visa waiver program. Some converts emphatically champion Islam as the best alternative to post-industrial Western society. Such is the rationale for Murad Wilfried Hofmann, a former German diplomat who converted to Islam in 1980 and has since acted as an intellectual leader for German converts. Ayyub Axel Köhler, the current chairman of the Zentralrat der Muslime in Deutschland, who converted to Islam in 1963, has remarked that Islam is a way of life and thus offers its adherents the chance to avoid the alienation of life in Western societies.[152]

Terrorist laws, including immigration asylum and counter-terrorism laws, vary with different countries. The French-Algerian journalist Mohammed Sifaoui commented that

> "the most sought-after terrorists in the world have found shelter in the UK . . . [t]hey propagate their ideology there [and] . . . Islamists considered the UK as a secondary base for their actions." The French have mockingly labeled the United Kingdom's capital city "Londonistan" and "*l'antechambre de l'Afghanistan.*"[153]

Belgium has become a support center for terrorists in Europe, offering a safe haven, false documents, and financing, including money for the alleged terrorists who were linked to a bombing that killed 190 in Madrid last year. Dutch researchers investigated the stories of 242 people who, between 2001 and 2006, were organized in 28 networks, planned 31 attacks and, in some cases, executed or allegedly executed these attacks. The list includes some little-known plots, such as the attempt to attack the Spanish Supreme Court in 2004, as well as prominent terrorist attacks, the murder of Dutch filmmaker Theo van Gogh in 2004 and the 2005 London bus and subway bombings. Great Britain and the Netherlands have proven to be at the greatest risk during the period studied, with twelve of the networks operating in Great Britain, seven in the Netherlands, four in France, and three each in Spain and Belgium. A total of 29 nationalities are represented, but there are clear clusters. The fifty-five Algerians in the study make up almost one-fourth of the entire sample. The second largest group consisted of twenty-four attackers of Pakistani ethnic origin whose attacks were planned primarily for Great Britain. The authors of the study believe that they have confirmed that "homegrown terrorism" is the new megatrend among Europe's jihadists, who include many converts. The balance of bridging and bonding has been successful for immigrant communities and their offspring in Britain, where Indians from Uganda expelled by Idi Amin in the 1970s have become remarkably successful in today's United Kingdom. In Germany, a conference was held in on to explore how to reach out to secular Muslims who want to climb the economic ladder and who identify themselves primarily as musicians, doctors, teachers, engineers or students. European countries are expelling radical Islamic clerics who praise acts of terrorism, in hopes of stemming the tide of extremism among impressionable Muslim youth. The expelled, unwelcome, or soon-to-be expelled imams include the following individuals. Raed Hlayhel, who was very active for some time in stirring up hatred against Denmark in the Arab world. Britain has banned controversial Indian Islamic preacher Zakir Naik from entering the country, citing his "unacceptable behaviour." Naik had declared that Muslims should beware of people saying OBL was right or wrong, adding: "If you ask my view, if given the truth, if he is fighting the enemies of Islam, I am for him. If he is terrorizing the terrorists, if he is terrorizing America the terrorist, the biggest terrorist, every Muslim should be a terrorist." Deported to Egypt by the French authorities was radical imam Ali Ibrahim Al-Sudani, who for months had been inciting followers in Paris-area mosques to rise up against the West. Suhayb Salam, an Islamic teacher from Tilburg, the Netherlands, taught his students to hate all infidels. Bouriqi Bouchta, the self-proclaimed imam of the northern city of Turin, Italy, was taken by police and put on a flight back to his home country of Morocco.[154]

Radicalization occurs due to the alleged anti-Muslim policies of the European government, as reported earlier. Perceptions regarding European foreign policy towards the Muslim world, which are ridden with double standards, are equally to blame. This situation is untenable. Since the inception of Pakistan, America has had a strong pro-Pakistan policy that translates into billions of dollars of economic and military aid, but Pakistanis and the Pakistani diasporas hate America more than their enemy India. (In Pakistan, 64 per cent of the public regards the United States as an enemy, while only 9 per cent describe it as a partner, according to a 2009 PEW Survey.) A Turk in Amsterdam is more worried about Muslim problems in Chechnya than ill-treatment of the Kurdish people in Turkey. A Bangladeshi Muslim in Britain is upset about Palestine rather than the ill-treatment of Shias in Pakistan. These Muslims should realize that they are better off living in Europe than in their country of origin. They never analyze why some Muslim countries are far behind Israel, which Muslim terrorists want to annihilate. For example: Egypt got independence in 1922 and Israel in 1948. Egypt's GDP PPP (Gross Domestic Product purchasing power parity) per capita was $4,200 in 2006 while that of Israel was $26,800, compared to Britain's $31,800, Saudi Arabia's $13,600 (founded in 1932), and Pakistan's $2,410 (created in 1947).

Britain's jihadists far outnumber those in all other European countries combined. The Dutch security service has identified several hundred jihadis, Spain around 300 radicals, and, Britain more than 4,000 active terrorists. Hizb-ut-Tahrir, a virulently anti-Semitic group wishing to pursue jihad and install Islamic regimes by coup d'état, is said to have 10,000 members in Britain. Germany's Party of Liberation has 300 members and Denmark's has fewer than 200. In most European countries, Muslim immigrants receive public assistance including unemployment insurance, health care and housing subsidies, subsidies for a wide range of religious and social organizations, reserved jobs, bilingual education, and sometimes free legal aid services. The failure of these policies has caused the West to review its liberal policies along with its multiculturalism and tolerance. The United States' offer of visa waivers to European citizens enables jihadists to travel to America and launch terrorism that is planned from the European countries. Global jihadist terrorism is dealt with from different perspectives in America and in Europe. The key difference between them is that while the former is fighting outside America, Europeans are fighting an enemy "in their midst in the shape of North African, Bangladeshi, and Pakistani second- or third-generation citizens, as well as those to whom they have sometimes been foolish enough to grant asylum."[155]

Afghanistan and Kashmir, two dangerous areas in Asia, are being attacked by the insurgent terrorists to seize these areas to their control. In Afghanistan, the Haqqani network is Al-Qaeda's dangerous patron. The Haqqani network, along with the Taliban militant organizations in Pakistan and Afghanistan, is fighting U.S. troops in eastern Afghanistan. With the drawdown of the U.S. forces in 2014, the Haqqani and the Taliban militants may grip Pakistan, Afghanistan and beyond to impose Sharia, as in 1990s. They are formidable obstacles to the success of the U.S. strategy in the region.[156] Kashmir, claimed by Pakistan and India, has been in the turmoil since 1947 when India was divided. The mujahedeen forces, supported by Pakistan, have been fighting proxy war with Indian forces since 1990s. The Kashmiri diasporas and Islamists in the U.S. and Britain render diplomatic and monetary support to influence the legislative branches in each country and are urging international organizations to have plebiscite in Kashmir, a region of Muslim majority area in Indian state of Jammu and Kashmir. It is alleged that Pakistan's powerful spy agency, ISI, has spent $4 million over two decades in a covert attempt to tilt American policy against India's control of much of Kashmir—including funneling campaign donations to members of U.S. Congress and presidential candidates. The Federal Bureau of Investigation (FBI) made the allegations with the indictment of two United States citizens on charges that they failed to register with the Justice Department as agents of Pakistan, as required by law. One of them is Zaheer Ahmad, who is now in Pakistan, but the other, Syed Ghulam Nabi Fai, the director of the Kashmiri American Council, lives in Virginia and was arrested on July 19, 2011.[157]

Muslims believe that when one Muslim is subject to an injustice anywhere anytime , then the whole community, ummah, is subject to that injustice, but when a few jihadists are creating the violence and bloodshed, ummah does not take responsibility for those few radical Islamists. Even an editorial cartoon in a Danish newspaper has the potential to cause violent protests in many Muslim countries and in Muslim neighborhoods. However, Peter Gottaschalk and Gabriel Greenberg observe:

> Any depiction of him (the Prophet Muhammad) as a militant not only denigrates this beloved figure but also stains the character of Islam and, by default, impugns their own dignity, already sensitive to Western disparagements and suspicions during centuries of European imperial domination followed by today's American hegemony.[158]

Notes

1. Khorsrhavar, 2009, 38, "Killing in the Name of Islam," *Middle East Policy Journal*, Vol. X. # 2; Summer 2003, www.mepc.org/journal_vol10/wiktorowicz kaltner.pdf

2. Jeffrey B. Cozzens. *The Culture of Global Jihad: Character, Future Challenges and Recommendations*, www.icsr.info/publications/papers/1238519802ICSR JeffCozzensReport.pdf (October 2008)

3. "Pakistan & Afghanistan: Domestic Pressures and Regional Threats: India-Pakistan Rivalry in Afghanistan." by Nicholas Howenstein, Sumit Ganguly, *Journal of International Affairs*, Vol. 63, No. 1, Fall/Winter 2009 Page 127-140, Kux, Dennis 2000, 53.

4. Khorshavan, 2009, 295.

5. Berman, 2009, 3, http://mitpress.mit.edu/books/chapters/0262026406chap1. pdf.

6. Muslim Population, CIA Handbook: www.factbook.net/muslim_pop.php; Harrison, Selig. *Pakistan Aids the Taliban in The Taliban* By Noah Berlatsky, Farmington, MI, Greenhaven Press, 2011, 126; Smith, Greg. "The Tangled Web of Taliban and Associated Movements." *Journal of Strategic Security*, 31-38, 2009.

7. "On the trail of Pakistani terror group's elusive mastermind behind the Mumbai siege." By Sebastian Rotella, ProPublica, *Washington Post*, November 14, 15, 2010; "Pakistan bombshell: Candid narratives explode myths about our purported ally." by Arnaud de Borchgrave, *Washington Times*, November 16, 2010; "Pakistan's madrassas need reform: Road to moderation runs through its schools." by Ilan Berman, *Washington Times*, August 20, 2010.

8. Hero 2009, 125-310, Naumkin, 2005, 49-87, Tamerlane: Sword of Islam, Conqueror of the World, by Justin Marozzi, www.missionislam.com/knowledge/ alwalawalbara.htm, http://en.wikipedia.org/wiki/Jihad

9. Islamists 'urge young Muslims to use violence,' Tom Harper, 30 Sep 2007, *Telegraph*, UK, www.telegraph.co.uk/news/uknews/1564616/Islamists-urge-young-Muslims-to-use-violence.html

10. *Man Is A Religious Animal. He Is The Only Religious Animal,* http://www.anvari.org/fortune/Miscellaneous_Collections/168544_man-is-a-religious-

animal-he-is-the-only-religious-animal.html; *Observations & Views:* Some Famous Quotations About India, http://www.jainstudy.org/JSC7.07O%26VA.

11. Syed Mansoob Murshed and Sara Pavan, *Identity and Islamic Radicalization in Western Europe*, Microcon Research Working Paper 16, August 2009.www. microconflict.eu/publications/RWP16_MM_SP.pdf

12. Crews and Tarzi, 2008, 224-225.

13. C. Christine Fair, 2009, "A Better Bargain for Aid to Pakistan." *Washington Post*, May 30; Moqtedar Khan. "Obama's Afghan Predicament?" *The Daily Times*, October 15, 2009. Ahmed Rashid, BBC News—South Asia, October 16, 2009. Shuja Nawaz, "The Battle for Pakistan." *Wall Street Journal*, October 20, 2009. William Dalrymple, Pakistan in Peril, *The New York Review of Books,* February 12, 2009. Napoleoni, *Modern Jihad.* 2003, 83, 87–88, 97, 132; "Islamists urge young Muslims to use violence." Tom Harper, 30 Sep 2007, *Telegraph*, UK, www.telegraph.co.uk/news/uknews/1564616/Islamists-urge-young-Muslims-to-use-violence.html; Ashley J. Tellis, Pakistan's Record on Terrorism: Conflicted Goals, Compromised Performance, *The Washington Quarterly*, Spring 2008, www.twq. com/08spring/docs/08spring_tellis.pdf; Matt Waldman, The Sun in the Sky: The Relationship between Pakistani ISI and Afghanistan Insurgents, Discussion Paper 18, *London School of Economics*, June 2010, www.crisisstates.com/download/dp/DP%2018.pdf; Rita Cristofari, Latifa, Visage Vole: Avoir vingt ans a Kabul, Anne Carriere, Paris, 2001, by the PHR (Physicians for Human Rights, 1999 Report: The Taliban War on Women—A Health and Human Rights Crisis in Afghanistan, www.phrusa.org/research/health_effects/exec.html.

14. "A Globalized God." by Scott Thomas, *Foreign Affairs*, Nov/Dec 2010; Just Like Us! Really? Gallup says only 7 per cent of the world's Muslims are political radicals. Yet 36 per cent think the 9/11 attacks were in some way justified; May 12, 2008, Vol. 13, No. 33, by Robert Satloff.

15. "Islamic Religious Schools, Madrassas: Background." Christopher M. Blanchard, *Foreign Affairs*; "Saudi Arabia, Wahhabism and the Spread of Sunni Theofascism." Ambassador Curtin Winsor, Jr., Vol.2, #1, June/July 2007, *Middle East Monitor*; "Wahhabism: State-Sponsored Extremism Worldwide." Testimony by Alex Alexiev, Senior Fellow, Center for Security Policy, U.S. Senate Subcommittee on Terrorism, Technology and Homeland Security, June 26, 2003; "Pakistan's ISI problem." Opinion, *The Boston Globe*, February 11, 2009.

16. Juan Cole, 2009, 135-136.

17. Robert Crews and Amin Tarzi, 2008 118-155, Rita Cristofari, *Latifa, Visage Vole: Avoir vingt ans a Kabul,* Anne Carriere, Paris, 2001, by the PHR (Physicians for Human Rights, 1999 Report: The Taliban War on Women—A Health and Human Rights Crisis in Afghanistan, www.phrusa.org/research/health_effects/exec.html.

18. Robert Crews and Amin Tarzi, 2008, 149.

19. Jones 2009, 281.

20. Jones, 2009, 281, 308,316,

21. Patterson says Quetta Shura high on U.S. list, by, Dawn, September 30, 2009; http://archives.dawn.com/archives/100135.

22. Pakistan civilian-military ties hit new low, BBC News, October 16, 2009. *BBC News*, South Asia, July 29, 2010.

23. Shuja Nawaz, The Battle for Pakistan, *Wall Street Journal*, Opinion, October 20, 2009. Rashid, 2008, 400-404.

24. (Former President Pervez Musharraf says the U.S. military aid given to Pakistan during his tenure was used to strengthen defenses against India, BBC News, September 14, 2009).

25. William Dalrymple, Pakistan in Peril, *The New York Review of Books*, February 12, 2009.

26. "Pakistan's Partial War on Terror, The deadly results of cooperation with terrorists." C. Christine Fair, *Wall Street Journal*, October 13, 2009.

27. C. Christine Fair, "A Better Bargain for Aid to Pakistan." *Washington Post*, May 30, 2009.

28. Robert Crews and Amin Tarzi, 2008, 325.

29. Richard Haass, "In the Afghan War, Aim for the Middle." *Washington Post,* October 11, 2009.

30. "Deployments and Diplomacy: More troops is a start. But to win in Afghanistan, we'll need help from its powerful neighbors." Henry A. Kissinger, *Newsweek*, Oct 12, 2009.

31. Robert Kaplan, "Beijing's Afghan Gamble." *New York Times*, October 7, 2009.

32. Jim Hoagland, "Obama's Afghan Squeeze." *Washington Post,* October 18, 2009.

33. Wazhma Frogh, "Risking a Rights Disaster." *Washington Post,* October 18, 2009.

34. Ashley J. Tellis. "Pakistan's Record on Terrorism: Conflicted Goals, Compromised Performance." *The Washington Quarterly*, Spring 2008, www.twq.com/08spring/docs/08spring_tellis.pdf

35. Ganguly. "Breaking America's Silence on Pakistan, Hillary Clinton's truth-telling is necessary and overdue." *Wall Street Journal,* November 3, 2009; Ganguly. "Pakistan's Fickle Ally Washington Must Stick by Islamabad." *Newsweek,* October 9, 2009.

36. Gregory Feifer. *The Great Gamble: The Soviet War in Afghanistan.* New York, N.Y., Harper Collins, 2009, 290.

37. Karin Brulliard and Karen DeYoung. AP, Pakistan. "Afghanistan begins talks about dealing with insurgents." *Washington Post,* June 19, 2010.

38. John R. Bolton. "We must crush the Taliban and Al Qaeda in a 'long war' in Afghanistan." *Los Angeles Times,* July 1, 2010; Najam Sethi. "The Road to Kabul Runs Through Islamabad." *Wall Street Journal,* June 30, 2010; Henry A. Kissinger. "America needs an Afghan strategy, not an alibi." *Washington Post,* June 24, 2010; Chinmaya R. Gharekhan. "The winners and losers of the Afghan war." *The Hindu,* June 25, 2010; Mohammad Shehzad. "Suicide bombing is the best form of jihad." *The Friday Times,* April 11–17, 2003, URL: www.thefridaytimes.com/.

39. Dilip Hero, 2009, 188.

40. "Militant Islam in Central Asia: The Case of the Islamic Movement of Uzbekistan." *Vitaly V. Naumkin Spring 2003,* Berkeley Program in Soviet and Post-Soviet Studies.

41. Hero, 2009, 356.

42. "Tajikistan Says Militants Were Behind Attack on Troops." M. Schwirtz, *New York Times*, September 20, 2010.

43. Holly Fletcher, Jayshree Bajoria. "The East Turkestan Islamic Movement (ETIM)." *Council on Foreign Affairs.* July 31, 2008.

44. William Dalrymple. "What goes 'round." *Guardian.* November 5, 2005.

45. William Dalrymple. "The Muslims in The Middle." *New York Times,* August 17, 2010.

46. John Burns. "Britain Presses Pakistan and Afghanistan on Militants." *New York Times*, November 30, 2009.

47. Barbara Metcalf. "A Historical Overview of Islam in South Asia." http:// press.princeton.edu/Chapters/i9061.pdf; Madhusree, Mukherjee. *Churchill's Secret War.* New York, Basic Books, 2010.

48. Mir Mohammad Ali. "Dara Shioh Still Prosecuted." *Daily Times,* August 1, 2010; Robert Wright. "The Making of a Terrorist." *New York Times*, May 11, 2010; Ishtiaq Ahmed. "The Cabinet Mission Plan." *The Daily Times*, August 10, 2010; M.B. Mukasey. "Shahzad and the Pre-9/11 Paradigm in the 1990s." *Wall Street Journal,* May 12, Halima Bashir, 2008, 2-30; Current Trends in Islamist Ideology, Edited by Hillel Fradkin, Husain Haqqani, and Eric Brown, Center on Islam, Democracy, and The Future of the Muslim World, The Hudson Institute, Washington, D.C. (2005), Vols.1 and 2, www.hudson.org/files/publications/ Current_Trends_in_Islamic_Ideology_vol_1.pdf (and _v2); Jalal 2008, 287; Haqqani, 2002, 2005; NBR analysis: volume 19, number 4, August 2008; Aspects of Islamism in South and Southeast Asia. Introduction: Islamism and U.S. Policy in South and Southeast Asia, Robert W. Hefner; South Asia: Hotbed of Islamic Terrorism, Animesh Roul; The Fluid Terrain of Islamism in Southeast Asia, Joseph Chinyong Liow; The National Bureau of Asian Research, faxnbr@nbr.org e-mailwww.nbr.org.

49. Sisson and Rose, 1990, 234.

50. Ron Clark. *The Blind Spot of Counter-Terrorism: Bangladesh,* www.bipss. org.bd/Terrorismpercent20inpercent20Bangladeshpercent20-percent20Ryan percent20Clarke.pdf

51. Selig Harrison. "A New Hub for Terrorism? In Bangladesh, an Islamic Movement With AQ Ties Is on the Rise." *Washington Post,* August 2, 2006.

52. Bruce Vaughan. "Islamist Extremism in Bangladesh." CRS Report for Congress, http://hrcbmdfw.org/blogs/bangladesh/archive/2008/03/23/818.aspx; *Bangladesh: Background and U.S. Relations,* August 2, 2007, www.fas.org/sgp/ crs/row/RL33646.pdf; Ganguly. "Pakistan's Fickle Ally Washington Must Stick by Islamabad." *Newsweek,* October 9, 2009.

53. Hudson, 1971, 3.

54. H.V. Hudson, 1971, 18.

55. Wolpert, 237-238.

56. H.V. Hudson, 1971, 137.

57. http://en.wikipedia.org/wiki/Government_of_India_Act_1909.

58. Wali Khan. *Facts are Facts, The Untold Story of India's Partition, 2nd Edition,* 2004, www.awaminationalparty.org/books/factsarefacts.pdf

59. Hudson, 1971, 135-136; Ganguly. "Breaking America's Silence on Pakistan: Hillary Clinton's truth-telling is necessary and overdue." *Wall Street Journal,* November 3, 2009.

60. Stanley Wolpert, 2004, 343-348.

61. Hudson, 1971, 163-164.

62. M.J. Akbar. "The Home of Jihad." *The Asian Age*, August 4, 2005.

63. Wolpert. 2004, 346.

64. Wali Khan. "Facts are Facts, 2004." www.awaminationalparty.org/books/factsarefacts.pdf

65. Ashley Tellis. "Terrorists Attacking Mumbai Have Global Agenda: Pakistan's Lashkar-e-Taiba, not as well known as Al Qaeda threatens India, the West and even Pakistan." *Yale Global,* 8 December 2008.

66. "Terror Groups in India." Carin Zissis. *Washington Post*, December 1, 2008.

67. "CIA Pays for Support in Pakistan." Greg Miller. *Los Angeles Times.* November 15, 2009.

68. Husain Haqqani. "The Ideologies of South Asian Jihadi Groups." *Current Trends in Islamist Ideology*, April 2005; Husain Haqqani. *Pakistan: Between Mosque and Military.* Washington: Carnegie Endowment for International Peace, 2005, 306.

69. Madanjeet Singh in Kashmiriyat. The Pluralist Sufi-Bhakti-Rishi Culture, Madanjeet Singh/SAF/UNESCO 2009.

70. Verghese, 2007, 8.

71. Ganguly. "Breaking America's Silence on Pakistan: Hillary Clinton's truth-telling is necessary and overdue." *Wall Street Journal,* November 3, 2009; Ganguly. "Pakistan's Fickle Ally Washington Must Stick by Islamabad." *Newsweek,* October 9, 2009.

72. Mohammed Ayoob. "South Asia's Dangers and U.S. Policy." *Orbis*, Vol. 45, No.1, Winter 2001, 123-134.

73. "A brief history of the Kashmir conflict." *Daily Telegraph* (UK), September 24, 2001.

74. "Kashmir: India and Pakistan's bitter dispute." M. Basu. CNN, September 29, 2010, http://articles.cnn.com/2010-09-25/world/india.kashmir.explainer_1_pakistani-backed-forces-kashmir-conflict-india-and-pakistan?_s=PM:WORLD.

75. Sarkar, Jadunath. *How the Muslims forcibly converted the Hindus of India, Pakistan and Bangladesh to Islam.* K. S. Lal: *Growth of Muslim Population in Medieval India*, 1973, Tamerlane: Sword of Islam, Conqueror of the World. by Justin Marozzi (www.missionislam.com/knowledge/alwalawalbara.htm, http://en.wikipedia.org/wiki/Jihad,)

76. Jagmohan. "A Bone-Deep Issue." *The Asian Age,* March 3, 2010. (www.missionislam.com/knowledge/alwalawalbara.htm, http://en.wikipedia.org/wiki/Jihad,)

77. Lars Blikenberg. *India and Pakistan, The History of Unsolved Conflict.* Odense University Press, Odense, Denmark, Vol. I, 76, pp. 78–82; Justin Marozzi, Tamerlane: Sword of Islam, Conqueror of the World, www.missionislam.com/knowledge/alwalawalbara.htm, http://en.wikipedia.org/wiki/Jihad.

78. "Pakistan Has Mistreated the Kashmir People." *The Statesman*, July 3, 2002; Dudley, 2003, 88-96.

79. Ganguly. 2001, 150–151.

80. Hudson, 1971, 453.

81. Ganguly and Hagerty, 2006, 91-92.

82. Wajahat Habibullah, 2008, 98.

83. *Danger in Kashmir.* Princeton University Press, Princeton, New Jersey, 1954.

84. Hudson, 1971, 466, 469–470.

85. "Pakistan Has Mistreated the Kashmir People." *The Statesman.* July 3, 2002; Dudley 2003, 88-96.

86. "Kashmir insurgency, 20 years after." Happymon, Jacob. *The Hindu.* December 25, 2009.

87. Habibullah 2008, 20.

88. *Jihad in Kashmir.* Girdhari Lal Jalali Vakil Publications, New Delhi, 2010. http://ikashmir.net/gljalali/docs/Jihad%20in%20Kashmir%20-%20Girdhari%20Lal%20Jalali.pdf

89. Hudson, 1971, 466, 469–470.

90. Text of Simla Agreement Between India and Pakistan. http://india97780.yuku.com/topic/897/Text-Of-Simla-Agreement-Between-India-and-Pakistan

91. Sumantra Bose, 2003, 11, 40.

92. Timothy Hoyt, *American Military Strategy in the 21st Century*, Cambridge, U.K. Polity Press, 2011, 123–124.

93. Swami, 2007, 9.

94. "Obama, Pakistan and Mullah Omar, Why Islamabad resists going after the Quetta shura." Opinion, *Wall Street Journal*, December 24, 2009.

95. Abdulhakim Muhammad, Arkansas Army Center Shooting Suspect, Claims Al Qaeda Ties, Andrew Demillo, *Huntington Post*, January 22, 2010

96. "Kashmir Militant Extremists." Jamal Afridi. Council on Foreign Relations, *Backgrounder,* July 9, 2009.

97. "Patriarch of Jammu & Kashmir jihad turned peacemaker." Praveen Swami. *The Hindu,* December 5, 2009; "Pakistan Has Mistreated the Kashmir People." *The Statesman.* July 3, 2002.

98. "Lashkar-e-Taiba's Long Arm." *The Hindu.* Editorial, December 12, 2009.

99. Gaubatz and Sperry, 2009, 27, 77.

100. "Pakistan's Islamists take center-stage." Arif Jamal, March 11, 2011, *Foreign Policy*, March 11, 2011, Jamal, 2009, 173.

101. Arif Jamal, 2009, 243-244.

102. Ganguly and Hagerty, 2006, 4-41.

103. *The News*, September 20, 2009.

104. Jim Hoagland. "Obama's Afghan Squeeze." *Washington Post*, October 18, 2009; Nirupama Subramanian. "The hazards of being Zardari." *The Hindu*. November 12, 2009.

105. "The Limits of Influence: America's Role in Kashmir." July 25, 2009; http://brookingspress.typepad.com/bipblog/2009/06/schaffer-kashmir.html

106. Wali Khan. *Facts are Facts, The Untold Story of India's Partition, 2nd Edition,* 2004, www.awaminationalparty.org/books/factsarefacts.pdf.

107. Bose and Jalal, 2004, 144-145.

108. Wolpert, 2004, 333.

109. Wali Khan. *Facts are Facts, The Untold Story of India's Partition,* 2nd Edition. 2004. 126,www.awaminationalparty.org/books/factsarefacts.pdf

110. Wali Khan. *Facts are Facts, The Untold Story of India's Partition,* 2nd Edition. 2004. 174, 175, 185. www.awaminationalparty.org/books/factsarefacts.pdf; *Dawn,* Independence Day Supplement, August 14, 1947.

111. Cohen, Stephen. "The Nation and the State of Pakistan." *The Washington Quarterly* 25:3, pp. 109-122, 2002.

112. Mustafa Malik. "Pakistan: Can U.S. Policy Save the Day." *Middle East Policy Journal,* Vol. XVI, #2, 2009.

113. Wali Khan. *Facts are Facts, The Untold Story of India's Partition,* 2nd Edition, 2004, 67, www.awaminationalparty.org/books/factsarefacts.pdf

114. Selig Harrison. "Pakistan's Baluch insurgency." *Le Monde Diplomatique.* October, 2006, http://mondediplo.com/2006/10/05baluchistan; "Pakistan's Ethnic Fault Line." *Washington Post,* May 11, 2009.

115. "Pakistan's New Generation of Terrorists." *Jayshree Bajoria,* October 26, 2009, www.cfr.org/publication/15422/; CTC Sentinel: Defining the Punjabi Taliban Network: Hassan Abbas. April 2009, www.cfr.org/publication/20409/ctc_sentinel. html; CTC Sentinel: AQ's Pakistan Strategy, Don Rassler; June 2009, www.cfr.org/ publication/20498/ctc_sentinel.html.

116. *Pakistan's Security Reports,* June 2011, PAK Institute for Peace Studies, http://san-pips.com/index.php?action=reports&id=psr_1

117. Reuters, April 30, 2009.

118. Public Opinion in Pakistan: Concern About Extremist Threat Slips, America's Image Remains Poor, July 29, 2010 and see previous years as well.

119. David Ignatius. "To Pakistan, almost with love." *Washington Post,* March 4, 2010; Arif Nizami, The Way the World Sees Us, *The News,* Pakistan, June 26, 2010, www.thenews.com.pk/editorial_detail.asp?id=247198' Imtiaz Gul, Challenges in Afghanistan, *The Dawn,* 06 Mar, 2010, Imtiaz Gul, 2010, 183, Ayesha Siddiqa, *Military Inc—Inside Pakistan's Military Economy,* Pluto Press, London, 2007.Daniel Markey, Terrorism and Indo-Pakistani Escalation, Memo # 6. January 2010, Council of Foreign Affairs. Seth G. Jones, C. Christine Fair, *Counterinsurgency in Pakistan,* Rand Report, Rand Corporation, Santa Monica 2010015059, June 20, 2010, RAND URL: www.rand.org,Riaz Hassan, What

Motivates the Suicide Bombers? Study of a comprehensive database gives a surprising answer, *Yale Global,* 3 September, 2009.

120. Ashley Tellis, Congressional Testimony, March 11, 2010; "Pakistan and the Afghanistan End Game—Part II: Pakistan sees no reason to stop supporting terrorists." Ashley J. Tellis, *Yale Global,* 15 March 2010; Bad Company, Testimony by Ashley J. Tellis, United States House of Representatives Committee on Foreign Affairs, Subcommittee on the Middle East and South Asia, March 11, 2010; "The Tangled Web of Taliban and Associated Movements." Greg Smith. *Journal of Strategic Security*, 31-38, 2009.

121. "Pakistan's madrassas need reform, Road to moderation runs through its schools." Ilan Berman. *Washington Times*, August 20, 2010.

122. Bruce Riedel and Pavneet Singh. "U.S.-China Relations: Seeking Strategic Convergence in Pakistan, Foreign Policy, China, Pakistan, Relations." The Brookings Institution, Foreign Policy Paper #18, January 24, 2010.

123. "Strategic Asia and the War on Terrorism." William P. Pope, Principal Deputy Coordinator for Counterterrorism, Luncheon Keynote Address at the Carnegie Endowment for International Peace, National Bureau of Asian Research, Washington, D.C. September 22, 2004, http://merln.ndu.edu/archivepdf/terrorism/state/37410.pdf

124. Jessica Stern. "5 myths about who becomes a terrorist." *Washington Post*, January 10, 2010; Robin Wright. "Islam and Liberal Democracy: Two Visions of Reformation." *Journal of Democracy* 7.2 (1996) pp. 64–75.

125. "Global Jihad and its Implications for the Hindu Identity of India." Ram Kumar Ohri. http://hindurenaissance.com/index.php/yugabda-5107/2007100125/articles/islam/global-jihad-and-its-implications-for-the-hindu-identity-of-india/menu-id-34.html, "In Defense of Jihad." *The Hindu.* July 7, 2002. "'Abdullah ibn Abi Awfa wrote to us that the Messenger of Allah, may Allah bless him and grant him peace, had said, 'Know that the Garden is under the shadow of the swords.'" Sahih al Bukhari's *Book of Jihad,* http://noorulislam.wordpress.com/jihaad/sahih-al-bukharipercentE2percent80percent99s-book-of-jihad/; David M. Haugen, S. Musser, and K. Lovelace (Eds.) (2009); Omar Abdel Rahman, Egyptian scholar on jihad: "If God . . . says, 'Do Jihad,' it means do jihad with the word, with the cannon, with the grenades, and with missiles. This is jihad," Andrew McCarthy, 2008, 71.

126. Sarila, 2005, 11, 26, 77, 299, 354–355; Madhusree Mukherjee. *Churchill's Secret War.* New York, Basic Books, 2010, 131-132, 244, 245, 250, 251.

127. "Saudi Arabia, Wahhabism and the Spread of Sunni Theofascism." Ambassador Curtin Winsor, Jr., Vol. 2, #1, June/July 2007, *Middle East Monitor*; Kanchan Gupta, To forget would be to forgive, *Sunday Pioneer*, January 24, 2010.

128. Zachary Abuza, 2003, p. 21.

129. "Terrorism in Southeast Asia, The Rise of Islamist Militancy in Southeast Asia." Bruce Vaughn, Coordinator, Emma Chanlett-Avery, Mark E. Manyin, and Larry A. Niksch, CRS Report to Congress, September 11, 2007, http://fas.org/sgp/crs/terror/RL34194.pdf; Sidney Jones in *The Annals of the American Academy of Political and Social Science* 25 June 2008, www.crisisgroup.org/home/

index.cfm?id=5519; Christopher S. Bond and Lewis M. Simons. "The Forgotten Front." *Foreign Affairs*, November/December 2009.

130. Abuza, 2003, 5-37.

131. "Islam and Terrorism: Lebanese Muslim Views on September 11." S. Haddad and H. Khashan, *Journal of Conflict Resolution*, 2002, 46: pp. 81-828.

132. Terrorism and Counterterrorism in Asia: The Philippine Perspective, November 19-21, 2003, www.pctc.gov.ph/updates/tandctia.htm; "Terrorism Havens: Philippines." Preeti Bhattacharji, June 1, 2009, Council on Foreign Relations, *Backgrounder*, www.cfr.org/publication/9365/; Abu Sayyaf Group, May 27, 2009, www.cfr.org/publication/9235/abu_sayyaf_group_philippines_islamist_separatists. htm Background on Terrorism and Public Opinion in Indonesia, by START—Study of Terrorism and Response to Terrorism, Homeland Security Center at University of Maryland, July 17, 2009; www.start.umd.edu/start/media/Background_on_Terrorism_Public_Opinion_Indonesia.pdf; *NBR analysis*: volume 19, number 4, August 2008; *Aspects of Islamism in South and Southeast Asia.* "Introduction: Islamism and U.S. Policy in South and Southeast Asia," Robert W. Hefner; "South Asia: Hotbed of Islamic Terrorism," Animesh Roul; "The Fluid Terrain of Islamism in Southeast Asia," Joseph Chinyong Liow, (The National Bureau of Asian Research (NBR), www.nbr.org).

133. "The Muslim Insurgency in Southern Thailand." Jayshree Bajoria, Carin Zissis, Council on Foreign Relations, September 10, 2008, http://www.cfr.org/thailand/muslim-insurgency-southern-thailand/p12531

134. "The Malay-Muslim Insurgency in Southern Thailand Understanding the Conflict's Evolving Dynamic." Peter Chalk, Rand Report, 2008; "In Thailand, a New Model for Militants?" John M. Glionna, October 01, 2006, *LAT*; http://articles.latimes.com/2006/oct/01/world/fg-thaiterror1; "The Amnesty International, Thailand: Torture in Southern Counterinsurgency." www.amnesty.org/en/library/asset/ASA39/001/2009/en/45c1226f-dcd6-11dd-bacc-b7af5299964b/asa3900 12009eng.pdf; "After the bombings, Jul 23rd 2009, Bangkok." *The Economist.*

135. Thomas Fuller, Southern Thai towns increasingly rely on militia, *New York Times,* March 18, 2007; "Aceh passes adultery stoning law." BBC News, September 14, 2009. http://news.bbc.co.uk/2/hi/8254631.stm; "Free Aceh movement in Indonesia." May 13, 2002. www.cdi.org/terrorism/aceh.cfm; "In Nangro Aceh Darussalam, Indonesia." http://units.sla.org/division/dmah/tsunami_3.pdf.

136. "Will Aceh Dominate Indonesia? A province's embrace of stricter Shariah law is part of a worrying trend." Opinion, *Wall Street Journal,* November 2, 2009.

137. "Radical Islam in Indonesia: the case of Ja'far Umar Thalib and the Lashkar Jihad." Saiful Umam, *Exploration in Southeast Asian Studies,* Vol. 6, No 1, Spring 2006; www.hawaii.edu/cseas/pubs/explore/Umam2006.pdf

138. "Background on Terrorism and Public Opinion in Indonesia, by START—Study of Terrorism and Response to Terrorism." Homeland Security Center at University of Maryland, July 17, 2009.

139. "Briefing for the New President: The Terrorist Threat in Indonesia and Southeast Asia." Sidney Jones. *The Annals of the American Academy of Political and Social Science,* 25 June 2008, www.crisisgroup.org/home/index.cfm?id=5519.

140. *NBR analysis*: volume 19, number 4, August 2008; "Aspects of Islamism in South and Southeast Asia. Introduction: Islamism and U.S. Policy in South and Southeast Asia." Robert W. Hefner; "South Asia: Hotbed of Islamic Terrorism." Animesh Roul; "The Fluid Terrain of Islamism in Southeast Asia." Joseph Chinyong Liow. The National Bureau of Asian Research, faxnbr@nbr.org e-mailwww.nbr.org.

141. Free Aceh movement in Indonesia, May 13, 2002www.cdi.org/terrorism/aceh.cfm; In Nangro Aceh Darussalam, Indonesia, http://units.sla.org/division/dmah/tsunami_3.pdf; "Will Aceh Dominate Indonesia? A province's embrace of stricter Shariah law is part of a worrying trend." Opinion, *Wall Street Journal,* November 2, 2009.

142. *The Wall Street Journal,* November 2, 2009.

143. Radical Islam in Indonesia: the case of Ja'far Umar Thalib and the Lashkar Jihad, Saiful; Umam, *Exploration in Southeast Asian Studies,* Vol. 6, No 1, Spring 2006, www.hawaii.edu/cseas/pubs/explore/Umam2006.pdf; International Crisis Group, Asia Briefing #, 107, Jakarta/Brussels, 6 July 2010; www.crisisgroup.org/en/regions/asia/south-east-asia/indonesia/B107-indonesia-the-dark-side-of-jamaah-ansharut-tauhid-jat.aspxIslam, http://countrystudies.us/indonesia/37.htm

144. Angel M. Rabasa et al. *The Muslim world after 9/11.* Rand Corporation, Santa Monica, California, 2004; "Gallup says only 7 per cent of the world's Muslims are political radicals. Yet 36 per cent think the 9/11 attacks were in some way justified." May 2, 2008, Vol. 13, No. 33. Robert Satlofff, *The Weekly Standard*; John L. Esposito, founding director of Georgetown University's Prince Alwaleed bin Talal Center for Muslim-Christian Understanding. The authors define Muslim radicals as those who say the 9/11 attack was "completely justified," which was seven per cent of the sample; "Support for Terror Wanes Among Muslim Publics, Islamic Extremism: Common Concern for Muslim and Western Publics." http://pewglobal.org/2005/07/14/islamic-extremism-common-concern-for-muslim-and-western-publics/; "Muslim Networks and Movements in Western Europe." September 16, 2010; http://pewresearch.org/pubs/1731/muslim-networks-movements-western-europe

145. "Al Qaeda names Fazul Mohammed East African commander." BILL ROGGIO. November 11, 2009, *The Longwar Journal*, http://www.longwarjournal.org/archives/2009/11/al_qaeda_names_fazul.php

146. Jeffrey B. Cozzens. "The Culture of Global Jihad: Character, Future Challenges and Recommendations." October 2008, www.icsr.info/publications/papers/1238519802ICSRJeffCozzensReport.pdf

147. John R. Bolton. "We must crush the Taliban and Al Qaeda in a 'long war' in Afghanistan." *Los Angeles Times,* July 1, 2010; Najam Sethi. "The Road to Kabul Runs Through Islamabad." *Wall Street Journal*, June 30, 2010; Henry A. Kissinger. "America needs an Afghan strategy, not an alibi." June 24, 2010, *Washington Post*; Chinmaya R. Gharekhan. "The winners and losers of the Afghan war." *The Hindu,* June 25, 2010; *Newsweek*, February 26, 2010; December 29, 2008 http://sharonchadha.blogspot.com/2008_12_01_archive.html; Mohammad Shehzad. "Suicide bombing is the best form of jihad." *The Friday Times,* April 11–17, 2003,

www.thefridaytimes.com/; Steve Coll. "Between India and Pakistan, A changing role for the U.S." *Washington Post,* May 26, 2002.

148. Syed Kamran Mirza. 07 Nov, 2007, watch.org/SyedKamranMirza/Nostalgia-of-Islamic-Gold; "Crossroads of Culture." Peter Watson. *New York Times,* April 21, 2003.

149. *History of Science and Religion.* Syed Kamran Mirza. Syed_mirza @hotmail.com, http://www.islam-watch.org/SyedKamranMirza/history_of_ science_and_religion.htm

150. John Esposito. "Is America Facing a European-Like Domestic Terrorist Threat?" *The Huffington Post,* April 18, 2010; Milena Uhlmann. "European Converts to Terrorism." *Middle East Quarterly,* Summer 2008, pp. 31–37; Syed Mansoob Murshed and Sara Pavan. "Identity and Islamic Radicalization in Western Europe." MICROCON Research Working Paper 16, August 2009; "On the trail of Pakistani terror group's elusive mastermind behind the Mumbai siege." Sebastian Rotella. ProPublica, *Washington Post,* November 14, 15, 2010; "Pakistan bombshell: Candid narratives explode myths about our purported ally." Arnaud de Borchgrave. *Washington Times,* November 16, 2010; "Militant Islamist Terrorism in Europe." W. Jason Fisher. *Washington University Global Studies Law Review,* Vol. 6: 2007; Yassin Mushabash. *Terrorism in Europe: OBL's Eurofighters,* www.spiegel.de/ international/world/0,1518,476680,00.html; Robert S. Leiken. "The Menace in Europe's Midst." *Current History,* April 2009.www.microconflict.eu/publications/ RWP16_MM_SP.pdf

151. Theodore Dalrymple. "Why Theo Van Gogh Was Murdered, The filmmaker focused on the shameful abuse of Muslim women by Muslim men in Europe." 15 November 2004, *City Journal,* http://www.city-journal.org/html/ eon_11_15_04td.html; "A Framework for Understanding Radical Islam's Challenge to European Governments." Jonathan Paris. *The Hudson Institute, Transatlantic Issue* No. 15, May 7, 2007. www.hudson.org/files/publications/ TransatlanticInstituteMay7_2007.pdf

152. Milena Uhlmann. "European Converts to Terrorism." *Middle East Quarterly,* Summer 2008, pp. 31–37.

153. "Militant Islamist Terrorism in Europe." W. Jason Fisher. *Washington University Global Studies Law Review,* Vol. 6: 2007.

154. Yassin Mushabash. "Terrorism in Europe: OBL's Eurofighters Militant Islamist Terrorism in Europe." W. Jason Fisher, *Washington University Global Studies Law Review,* Vol. 6: 2007, www.spiegel.de/international/world/0,1518,4766 80,00.html

155. Michael Burleigh, 2009, 499.

156. "The Haqqani network: Al-Qaeda's dangerous patron." Jason Ukman. *Washington Post,* July 18, 2011.

157. "Pakistan's Military Plotted to Tilt U.S. Policy, F.B.I. Says." Charlie Savage and Eric Schmitt. *New York Times,* July 19, 2011; "Patriarch of Jammu & Kashmir jihad turned peacemaker." Praveen Swami. *The Hindu,* December 5, 2009; Dudley 2003, 88-96, Sarila 2006, 396-414, Weaver, 2002, 249-275, Hudson, 1971, 441, 517.

158. Peter Gottaschalk and Gabriel Greenberg, *Islamophobia,* Lanham, MD: Rowman & Littlefield Publishers, 2008, 146; Walid Phares, *The Confrontation*, New York: Palgrave Macmillan, 2008; Hillel Frisch and Efrain Inbar(ED) *Radical Islam and International Security*, New York: Routledge, 2008.

Chapter 5

Weapons of Mass Destruction, Technology, and Cyberterrorism

> I am Time, the mighty cause of world Destruction,
> Here come forth to annihilate the worlds.
> Even without any action of thine, all these warriors
> Who are arrayed in the opposing ranks, shall cease to exist
> —*The Bhagavat Gita, XI, 32*

Weapons of mass destruction, and unconventional weapons—namely biological, chemical, and nuclear weapons systems—pose the gravest threat to mankind. The possibility of terrorists using these weapons to carry out a global nuclear jihad cannot be ignored, especially with the disclosure of relationships between Pakistani nuclear experts and OBL. The secrecy surrounding nuclear weapons, the secret trade in nuclear weapons, and the proliferation of nuclear weapons is "the number one threat to the world at this moment in time." Technological developments in the areas of communications, networks, and weapons systems are aiding terrorists' capabilities. Additionally, the threat to information infrastructures by cyberterrorism has the potential to cause severe and significant damage to our daily lives and our national and global infrastructures.

Weapons of mass destruction (WMD) usually refer to nuclear, biological, and chemical weapons. But massive destruction can take place even without the use of these weapons, and cause thousands of deaths and devastation of infrastructure. These atrocities can be caused by suicide bombings in crowded cities. As just one example, there was the failed attempt of a "Muslim soldier," in May of 2010, who packed an SUV with explosives meant to kill thousands of people in New York City. Some U.S. agencies refer to these unconventional weapons as nuclear, biological, and chemical (NBC) weapons. Traditionally, bombs, grenades, rockets and IEDs have been used to terrorize and kill people, along with kidnapping, hijacking, and hostage taking, and are considered to be conventional terrorist weapons. On September 11, 2001, hijacked planes were used to destroy the World Trade Center, killing more than three thousand people. No NBC weapons were involved, even though airplanes were an unconventional weapon for terrorists.

Since the end of the Cold War in 1991, materials and technologies related to weapons of mass destruction (WMDs)—nuclear, radiological, biological, and chemical weapons—have become increasingly available in the former Soviet Union, to rogue states and terrorist groups. Terrorists' interest in chemical and biological weapons is not surprising, given the relative ease with which some of these weapons can be produced and detonated to inflict large numbers of casualties, without being detected. The United States has long recognized the dangers inherent in the spread of NBC weapons and missiles, and has focused on the potential acquisition of such weapons by terrorist organizations such as AQ and the Taliban, and by criminal organizations, alone or via middlemen. In April of 2004, the UN Security Council adopted a unanimous Resolution (1540), continuing an effort that began with Resolution 1373 in 2001. The 2004 resolution was designed to prevent individuals and organizations from acquiring and spreading WMDs as well as their means of delivery. In particular, it removed the possibility of safe havens for terrorists seeking to acquire WMDs, and covered all three kinds of WMDs as well as their means of delivery and related material. It put in place prohibitions and controls, under domestic law, of a wider range of activities, and set up a single committee to monitor all three types of these weapons, which had previously been regulated separately.[1]

Nuclear and Radiation Terrorism

The test of nuclear weapons the size of 20 Ktn (20, 000 tons) of TNT in the desert at Alamogordo, New Mexico, on July 16, 1945 (the Trinity Test) released dust and debris from the ground into a giant mushroom cloud that was horrifying in its magnitude and its capacity to annihilate instantly. The brightness of the nuclear debris prompted the nuclear physicist Robert Oppenheimer to recite:

If there should be in the sky
A thousand suns risen all at once,
Such splendid would be
Of the splendor of that Great Being
—*The Bhagavat Gita, XI 12*

A nuclear detonation (which may be an airburst, surface burst, or high-altitude burst) creates a severe environment including the blast, thermal pulse, neutrons, X- and Gamma-rays, radiation, electromagnetic pulse (EMP), and ionization of the upper atmosphere. Depending upon the environment in which the nuclear device is detonated, blast effects are manifested as ground shock, water shock, "blueout," cratering, and large amounts of dust and radioactive fallout. The energy of a nuclear explosion is transferred to the surrounding medium in three distinct forms: blast, thermal radiation, and nuclear radiation. Because of the tremendous amounts of energy liberated per unit mass in a nuclear detonation, temperatures of several tens of millions of degrees centigrade develop in the immediate area of the detonation. In an atmospheric detonation, this electromagnetic radiation, consisting chiefly of soft X-rays, is absorbed within a few meters of the point of detonation by the surrounding atmosphere, heating it to extremely high temperatures and forming a brilliantly hot sphere of air and gaseous weapon residues—the so-called fireball. Immediately upon formation, the fireball begins to grow rapidly, and rises like a hot air balloon. Within a millisecond after detonation, the diameter of the fireball grows from a 1-megaton (1000, 000T) airburst into a 150-megaton airburst. This increases to a maximum of 2200 megatons within 10 seconds, at which time the fireball is also rising at the rate of 100 meters per second. The initial rapid expansion of the fireball severely compresses the surrounding atmosphere, producing a powerful blast wave. As it expands toward its maximum diameter, the fireball cools, and after about a minute its temperature has decreased to such an extent that it no longer emits significant amounts of thermal radiation. The combination of the upward movement and the cooling of the fireball give rise to the formation of the characteristic mushroom-shaped cloud.[2]

Nuclear scintillation effects on electromagnetic signal propagation affect Command, Control, Communications, Computers, and Intelligence, Information, Surveillance and Reconnaissance (C4I2SR), via high-altitude detonation that could interrupt satellite-to-satellite communications, satellite-to-aircraft links, or satellite-to-ground links (since most satellites are not protected from nuclear scintillation), and also disabling the Global Positioning System (GPS), yielding erroneous data and messages. All communication links will be damaged by a high altitude nuclear explosion.[3]

On August 6, 1945, an atomic bomb (A-Bomb; given the nickname "Little Boy"), the first Uranium-based detonation, was detonated at Hiroshima, Japan. It exploded with a destructive power equivalent to between 13 and 18 kilotons (13, 000–18, 000 tons) of TNT and killed approximately 140, 000 people. On August 9, 1945, over Nagasaki, Japan, another bomb ("Fat Man") was detonated at an altitude of about 1800 feet (550 m). The bomb had the same yield as about 21 kilotons of TNT, or 8.78×1013 joules = 88 TJ (terajoules). An estimated 39, 000 people were killed outright; a further 25, 000 were injured. Thousands more died later from related blast and burn injuries, and hundreds more from radiation illnesses following exposure to the bomb's initial radiation. On March 1, 1954, one Hydrogen bomb (H-bomb) of 15 megatons (15, 000, 000 tons), or 750 times the size of Little Boy, was tested. This bomb could devastate three or four hundred square miles, generating lethal quantities of radioactive fallout. Realizing the gravity of mutual nuclear annihilation, the United States and the Soviet Union entered into a doctrine of "Mutually Assured Destruction" (MAD) of no first strike, providing a mutual deterrence. America was not and is not expecting a nuclear attack from China or the Soviet Union, but it cannot be sure that it is safe from a terrorist nuclear weapon strike on its own soil or that of its allied nations.

In Russia and other places, there are stockpiles of weapons-grade enriched uranium and plutonium that can be used to make bombs of 1 ktn (1000 tons) or larger, which can fit into a briefcase or pickup truck. Despite their small size, such bombs could cause great damage, having a blast radius of 1600 feet. For example, a ten-kiloton nuclear device could kill one million people if detonated in New York City. Terrorists could also make a nuclear explosive by obtaining reactor-grade plutonium from MOX, a mixture of plutonium oxide and uranium oxide. Additionally, nuclear terrorism can be carried out by sabotaging nuclear power plants and storage facilities, transporting nuclear bombs, stealing or purchasing enriched uranium and plutonium, and using the help of unauthorized personnel to assemble nuclear material into a bomb, which would then be detonated in a public place. These activities can be conducted by privately funded groups, or state-sponsored agencies.

The International Atomic Energy Agency (IAEA), based in Vienna, Austria, is concerned with the regulation and monitoring of nuclear technology, the safety and security of radioactive material, and safeguarding against any misuse. The IAEA can be authorized by the UNO resolutions to prevent nuclear terrorism. On October 28, 2008, Dr. Mohamed El Baradei, Director General of the International Atomic Energy Agency (IAEA), stood at the rostrum of the United Nations General Assembly and warned the world about nuclear terror:

> The possibility of terrorists obtaining nuclear or other radioactive material remains a grave threat. The number of incidents reported to the Agency involving the theft or loss of nuclear or radioactive material is disturbingly high. Equally troubling is the fact that much of this material is not subsequently recovered. Sometimes material is found which had not been reported missing. We live in a time of increasing nuclear peril. Terrorist organizations are intent on acquiring nuclear weapons or the material, technology, and expertise needed to build them. Trafficking in nuclear technology is a serious, persistent, and multidimensional problem.[4]

Radiation Terrorism

A piece of highly radioactive material stolen from a nuclear reactor site can be hidden in the trunk of a car and left in a public place, such as a water reservoir (to contaminate water resources), or near a school (to terrorize and injure the public). The sabotaging of a nuclear power plant would cause widespread panic. Industrial sites and hospitals are other sources of radioactive materials. The first radiation terrorism, using a device that consisted of dynamite and cesium-137, occurred in 1995 in Chechnya, Russia at the hands of Muslim terrorists. A discarded radiation therapy machine containing cesium-137 was found in Goifinia, Brazil, by a scavenger looking for scrap metal, and caused twenty-four cases of radiation burns and four deaths. There may be I-cubed attacks (for ingestion, inhalation, and immersion) by radiation terrorists. The analysts' favored isotope for a radiological terrorist attack is cesium-137, which emits very energetic gamma radiation capable of traveling many yards in the air or penetrating lead shielding. Even its non-radioactive form is highly poisonous. I-cubed attacks are enabled by the easy availability of comparatively large alpha-emitting sources (sources 10 per cent of the size of a lethal dose can be bought with a specific license). Cesium-137 is normally supplied for use in cancer therapy machines, hospital blood sterilizers, and elsewhere in industry as a water-soluble powder—the most dangerous possible form.[5]

Nuclear Weapons Proliferation

AQ terrorist Abu Zubaydah told U.S. investigators that AQ had the ability to make dirty bombs with the above types of radiation devices. In the 1990s, AQ tried to purchase enriched uranium from South Africa and Germany. After the 9/11 attacks on the United States, OBL contacted Pakistan's top nuclear scientists, Sultan Bashiruddin Mahmood and Abdul Majeed in Kabul, to develop nuclear weapon capability for AQ. It is still mysterious.

The international community has attempted to stop nuclear proliferation to non-nuclear countries with the Nuclear Proliferation Treaty (NPT). This agreement was authorized in 1968, to stop the transfer of unauthorized weapons-grade enriched uranium and plutonium to rogue states, and to prevent terrorist organizations from acquiring it. AQ and the Taliban terrorists are alleged to have camps in Pakistan whose purpose is to store nuclear materials and create the technology to build dirty bombs. Several authors including Ophir Falk and Henry Morgenstern have discussed the perils of dirty bombs. Dirty bombs[6] known also as radiation dispersal devices (RDD) are weapons that use conventional explosives to disperse radioactive materials, augmenting the injury and property damage caused by the radioactive explosion. However, this type of device lacks the complex nuclear-fission chain reaction that makes a nuclear bomb a weapon of dangerous and devastating proportions with the capability of mass destruction instantly. Radiological weapons are dynamite, packaged with radioactive material that scatters when the bomb is detonated. Some terrorists groups are alleged to have links with the Inter Services Intelligence Directorate (ISID) of the Pakistan Army. Graham Allison writes:

> In the summer of 2002, an American spy satellite detected a Pakistani C-130 cargo plane loading missile parts near Pyongyang, the capital of North Korea. Intelligence analysts recognized immediately what was happening: Pakistan was trading nuclear centrifuge technology for North Korean ballistic missile parts in order to enhance its nuclear deterrent against its archrival India. . . . Its (Pakistan's) clandestine networks for procuring and selling nuclear technology span the globe from China, North Korea, Malaysia, and Myanmar, to the Netherlands and Germany, and on to Iran, Iraq, Saudi Arabia, and the United Arab Emirates. A recently declassified State Department memo confirms that Pakistan may have originally acquired the technology for "fissile material production and possibly also nuclear device design" from China and North Korea. Following a pattern of reciprocal back-scratching that characterizes much of its nuclear proliferation activities, Pakistan offered China improved centrifuge designs years later that A.Q. Khan had stolen from the Dutch centrifuge plant where he worked during the 1970s.[7]

> Estimates of the size of Pakistan's arsenal by outside experts range from 60 to 100, with more being produced each year. Pakistan can deliver its weapons by both intermediate range missiles and jet aircraft, including its F16s. The bombs and the delivery systems are dispersed around a country twice the size of California, often buried deep underground.[8]

It is reported that Dr. A.Q. Khan, father of Pakistan's nuclear bomb, is involved in nuclear proliferation with many countries. One of Khan's associates is Sultan Bashiruddin Mahmood, the founder of Umma Tamer-e-Nau (UTN), a Pakistani nongovernmental organization (NGO) to establish social welfare projects in Afghanistan. He is also author of the book *Doomsday and Life After Death: the Ultimate Failure of the Universe as Seen by the Holy Quran*. Other Pakistani scientists, including C. Abdul Majeed, have had contact with the Taliban and AQ and have met with OBL in Afghanistan.

According to former CIA Director George Tenet:

> However, the information suggested that UTN had another purpose: they hoped to lend their expertise and access to the scientific establishment in order to build chemical, biological, and nuclear programs for al-Qa'ida. (NGO can be a convenient vehicle for providing cover for terrorist organizations, as they have legitimate reasons to traffic in expertise, material, and money) . . . The book's basic message—from the leader of a group that had offered WMD capabilities to al-Qa'ida—was that the world would end one day soon in the fire of nuclear holocaust that would usher in judgment day and thus fulfill the prophecies of the Quran.[9]

Tenet then flew to Islamabad for an emergency meeting with Pakistan's President Musharraf, and the scientists, including Dr. Mahmood, were placed under house arrest. The nuclear proliferation experts David Armstrong and Joseph Trento offer the following commentary:

> While U.S. concern about the incident was clearly warranted, the reaction is notable for the contrast to Washington's approach to dealing with the Khan network. U.S. policy makers chose not to confront Musharraf about Khan's nuclear trade with Libya, Iran, and North Korea, ostensibly for fear of exposing the joint CIA-MI6 operation that had penetrated Khan's network. . . . Whatever operations the CIA mounted in hopes of stalling the nuclear programs of A.Q. Khan's customers, the fact remains that that the United States allowed dangerous weapons technology and know-how to spread unnecessarily for decades.[10]

President George Bush remarked:

> Over time, it became clear that (Pervez) Musharraf either would not or could not fulfill all his promises. Part of the problem was Pakistan's obsession with India. In almost every conversation we had, Musharraf accused India of wrong-doing. . . . Some in the Pakistani intelligence service, the ISI, retained close ties to Taliban officials.[11]

President Ronald Reagan turned a blind eye to Pakistan's nuclear program in the 1980s because he needed General Zia and the ISI to fight the Soviets in Afghanistan.[12] It is also reported that it was National Security Advisor Zbigniew Brzezinski who urged President Carter (1977–1981) to close his eyes to Pakistan's nuclear weapon programs, in order to secure Islamabad's help in backing anti-Soviet Muslim insurgents—mujahedeen, the Taliban, and AQ—in Afghanistan. Successive presidents followed this policy, even after the extinction of the Soviet Union. The development of an Islamic bomb in Pakistan was started in 1974 with funds that may have come from Saudi Arabia, Libya, and other Muslim nations.

The late Zulfikar Ali Bhutto, who was then Pakistan's Prime Minister, warned that "we will eat leaves and grass, even go hungry" to build the country's own nuclear weapon. In July 2009, "There's a Hindu bomb, a Jewish bomb and a Christian bomb," Bhutto once wrote. "There must be an Islamic bomb."[13] His daughter,

> then-Prime Minister Benazir Bhutto herself acceded to AQ Khan's request to travel to North Korea in December 1995. There she took delivery of a bagful of computer disks and other materials containing the blueprints for the advanced ballistic missiles Pakistan needed for its nuclear weapons delivery system.[14]

No one can be sure if American economic aid and military aircraft sales to Pakistan from 1974 to present have been funneled to the program as "there's not a lot of transparency." However, OBL and his followers are determined to acquire the WMD—the Islamic bomb—as their holy duty to destroy the Western world. American officials continue to be concerned about the existential threat posed by nuclear weapons in a destabilized Pakistan. General David H. Petraeus, Commander, U.S. Central Command, testified on March 31, 2009, that "Pakistani state failure would provide transnational terrorist groups and other extremist organizations an opportunity to acquire nuclear weapons and a safe haven from which to plan and launch attacks."[15]

The nuclear proliferation by A.Q. Khan is a major concern for the international community.

> The Pakistani metallurgist deserved to be imprisoned for life. But he caught a scandalous break. As the father of Pakistan's nuclear weapons program, he is a national hero. And despite the tearful, televised confession in which Mr. Khan insisted that he alone was guilty, it is widely believed that Pakistan's powerful military, including Gen. Pervez Musharraf, who was then president and is a former army chief of staff, was complicit in this exceedingly vile trade.[16]

It was President George W. Bush (2001–2009) who closed his eyes to Khan's nuclear proliferation activities, in order to secure Pakistan's help in backing the War on Terror. Brzezinski's visionary inaugural of the world's worst nightmare has led to nuclear jihad and nuclear proliferation.

Professor Walter Laqueur, Chairman of the International Research Council at the Center for Strategic and International Studies, has written:

> In Pakistan, quasi-religious shrines have been erected to honor the Islamic bomb in major cities, and there is little doubt that if terrorist groups of this kind would gain possession of such weapons, they would not hesitate to use them even if the consequences would be suicidal. For here again a jihadist's belief could offer comfort, for everyone will die, the soul of the true believer will be saved or because they are invulnerable by the grace of God: "A thousand shall fall at thy side, and ten thousand at thy right hand, but it shall not come nigh thee." Or as Muhammad Atta (coordinator of the 9/11 terrorist attacks) advised his comrades: 'God is with the believers and the angels are guarding his steps.[17]

The nuclear weapons experts believe:

> Today, we face one tyrant (bin Laden) with a handful of nuclear weapons, another enthralled by first-use fantasies, and a terrorist with an effective propaganda machine—dangerous, vexing, but not the end of the world, not the end of the nation, not the end of a single city.[18]

"Pakistan was awash with extremists"[19]:

> Taliban, neo-Talibs, AQ, Sunni irregulars, and a hodgepodge of non-aligned, live-to-fight muscle-mullahs who would pack their bags and a Quran to take off at a moment's notice for a battle in the name of Islam anywhere in the world. What most alarmed the masters of "old think" in the West was the prospect of these hordes (acting on Abu Musab al Suri's plan that involved jihadist obtaining WMDs, gaining access to Pakistan's nuclear complex, whether through the instability of the weapons program, the dissatisfaction of its scientists, or through the political intent of an impoverished and unprincipled government in Islamabad which understood the value in hard cash of KRL (Khan Research Laboratories). So with the White House and 10 Downing Street unable to countenance an alternative, Musharraf's Pakistan remains an epicenter of terror, a disingenuous regime with its hands on the nuclear tiller.[20]

> The nuclear proliferations occurred when clandestinely North Korea swapped missiles with Pakistan, and China provided Pakistan warhead blueprints in exchange for centrifuge technology. Iran and North Korea

owe much of their current capabilities to the Khan enterprise. Libya was offered and it accepted, a complete nuclear weapons program, using entirely external materials and know-how. . . . It appears that nuclear weapons states will in fact hand over their dearest national treasures to persons who will convey them to a non-state entity, the Khan network itself. If the state was unwitting, the matter is even more damning. . . . Ultimately, the A.Q. Khan story is about the difficulty of curtailing the exchange of knowledge. Khan acquired his skills, and precious centrifuge technology, as the employee of a Dutch engineering firm. Is it so unlikely that there is a similar young man or woman today, working for Pfizer or GlaxoSmithKline or another international pharmaceutical company, who will one day use the knowledge acquired there to create biological weapons? And for what reason must it be that, were this capability to be sold, the only willing buyers would be states?[21]

It was reported that Pakistan's highest authority was aware of the clandestine operation of the Khan network.

Khan said Gen. Pervez Musharraf, the chief of the army staff from 1998 to 2007 and president from 2001 to 2008, and "his right-hand man"—including Kidwai "knew everything and were controlling incoming and outgoing consignments." Kidwai heads the group that controls Pakistan's arsenal, estimated by some U.S. government analysts at more than 100 weapons.[22]

In a speech at the West Point military academy in New York on December 1, 2009, President Obama said:

The stakes are even higher within a nuclear-armed Pakistan, because we know that AQ and other extremists seek nuclear weapons, and we have every reason to believe that they would use them.[23]

Former President Musharraf felt that nuclear jihad can be waged, when necessary, as a first strike. He boasted that Pakistan's command and control structure, the National Command Authority, was better than India's. "The fear of Pakistan's resort to a possible nuclear threat was paramount in the minds of Indian decision makers, thereby inhibiting a resort to all out war."[24] But the instability and insurrection of jihadist elements in Pakistan have caused a great deal of international concern. General David H. Petraeus, Commander of the U.S. Central Command, testified on March 31, 2009, that "Pakistani state failure would provide transnational terrorist groups and other extremist organizations an opportunity to acquire nuclear weapons and a safe haven from which to plan and launch attacks."[25]

The Harvard Professor Graham Allison (2010) warns:

> If Pakistan were to lose control of even one nuclear weapon that was ulti-
> mately used by terrorists, that would change the world. . . . The Commis-
> sion, of which I am a member (Commission on the Prevention of Mass
> Destruction Proliferation and Terrorism), issued its report to Congress
> and the new administration in December 2008. It included two provoca-
> tive judgments: first, that if the world continued on its current trajectory,
> the odds of a successful nuclear or biological terrorist attack somewhere in
> the world in the next five tears were greater than ever, and second, were
> one to map terrorism and weapons of mass destruction today, all roads
> would intersect in Pakistan.[26]

Nuclear weapons development in South Asia, based on deterrence capability, has major political implications for nuclear weapon developments
in Korea and Iran.

> Unlike Pakistan, North Korea does not harbor revisionist ambitions; it
> primarily seeks to ensure regime survival. . . . And while the Pakistanis
> can look to the United States to help extricate them from crises with India
> and to advance their interest with New Delhi, North Korea possesses no
> such external ally. Thus the North Koreans are far less likely than the
> Pakistanis to use their nuclear capability as a means of challenging the
> territorial status quo. . . . Unlike North Korea, Iran does not yet possess a
> nuclear weapons capacity. . . . If Iran does acquire a nuclear weapons
> capacity, how is it likely to behave? Many analysts and policy makers
> believe that, as a "rogue" state, a nuclear Iran will almost certainly adopt
> destabilizing and dangerous policies.[27]

But the overwhelming, swift nuclear retaliation by the Unites States is a
major deterrence to a possible Iranian nuclear weapons attack. If these weapons are obtained by extremists and Islamist terrorists in Palestine, Iraq, and
Lebanon, by renegade Iranian Revolutionary Guards Corps (IRGC) or rogue
dissidents, as in Pakistan, the United States will hold Iran as responsible
and would inflict nuclear devastation. The possession of a nuclear arsenal
by Iran, apart from the prestige, will not help Iran to settle the Israel-Palestine crisis, just as it didn't settle the India and Pakistan crisis over the territory of J&K, the North Korea-South Korea conflict, or the China-Taiwan
issue. In the case of the South Asia crisis, both India and Pakistan can
deploy nuclear arsenals unlike other involved asymmetrical states. The symmetry of the possession by India and Pakistan is precarious and perilous in
the unsettled, restive region and beyond, with possible clandestine collaboration of other regional powers, Iran and China.

While the characterization of South Asia as the most 'dangerous place in the world' is exaggerated, India-Pakistani relations do rank with Israel-Palestine affairs, China-Taiwan issues, and the North Korea-South Korea conflict as global problems of first order significance. . . . In addition, nuclear weapons loom larger in the Indo-Pakistani conflict than they do in West Asia, the Taiwan strait, or the Korean peninsula.[28]

In 1998, India and Pakistan tested their nuclear bombs despite internal pressures. This brings the number of nuclear powers to eight: the United States, the United Kingdom, France, Russia, China, India, Pakistan, and Israel. According to The nuclear proliferation specialist George Perkovich:

India is well positioned to assume a major place in the twenty-first century. This will be a world in which economic capacity is the determining source of power and the real value of nuclear weapons continues to decline. The October 2008 agreement facilitating nuclear cooperation between America and India is a watershed in U.S-India strategic relations.[29]

The presence of nuclear weapons in Pakistan and the withdrawal of NATO forces from Afghanistan are related and are causing concern worldwide. British historian and author Timothy Gordon Ash, urged that

. . . if for the next decade, with a residual security presence, Afghanistan must not become a safe haven and breeding ground for terrorists, that will be the avoidance of complete failure. It is in Britain's vital interest to ensure that Pakistan does not become a failed state with, in the worst case, its nuclear weapons falling into the hands of terrorists.[30]

Bioterrorism

A bioterrorism attack is the deliberate release of viruses, bacteria, or other germs (known as agents) that are used to cause illness or death in people, animals, or plants. Biological agents can be spread through air, water, or food. Terrorists may use biological agents because they can be extremely difficult to detect and do not cause illness for several hours to several days. Some bioterrorism agents, like the smallpox virus, can be spread from person to person and some, like anthrax, cannot.[31]

The definition of bioterrorism is generalized as:

Bioterrorism is the intentional use of any microorganism, virus, infectious substance, or biological product that may be engineered as a result of biotechnology, or any naturally occurring or bioengineered component of any such microorganism, virus, infectious substance, or biologic product, to cause death, disease, or other biological malfunction in a human, an animal, a plant, or another living organism in order to influence the conduct of government or to intimidate or coerce a civilian population.[32]

There are three categories of biological agents (see Table 5.1):

Table 5.1
Categories of Biological Agents

Category	Biological Agent	Profile/Risks
A	Anthrax, ^ Smallpox, ^^ Plague, Botulism*	high mortality, 90% for anthrax, 30% for Smallpox
B	Q fever, **	Rician toxin, low mortality
C	Yellow fever /TB	Potential to morbidity and mortality

*   Can cause paralysis (paralytic illness),
** Most acute cases of Q fever begin with sudden high fevers, with cough, nausea, severe headache, abdominal and chest pain.
^   not contagious
^^ contagious

When people are exposed to a pathogen such as anthrax or smallpox, they may not know that they are infected as they may not be sick immediately. The release of biological weapons remains undetected as germs are not visible to the naked eye and take time to cause death or symptoms. However, they can cause infections to large numbers of people. Anthrax, a biological agent, can be found in nature in domesticated animals or manufactured in laboratories. The symptoms (warning signs) of anthrax are different depending on the type of the disease:

1. Cutaneous: The first symptom is a small sore that develops into a blister. The blister then develops into a skin ulcer with a black area in the center. The sore, blister, and ulcer do not hurt.
2. Gastrointestinal: The first symptoms are nausea, loss of appetite, bloody diarrhea, and fever, followed by bad stomach pain.

3. Inhalation: The first symptoms are cold or flu-like symptoms that can include a sore throat, mild fever, and muscle aches. Later symptoms include cough, chest discomfort,
4. Shortness of breath, tiredness, and muscle aches. (Caution: Do not assume that just because a person has cold or flu symptoms, they have inhalation anthrax.)[33]

Antibiotics are used to treat all three types of anthrax. During World War II, the Imperial Japanese Army used biological agents like cholera, anthrax, plague and others to kill thousands of Chinese and Japanese soldiers. In 1970, Hamilton Smith and Daniel Nathans invented recombinant DNA (Deoxyribonucleic Acid) by cutting and pasting genes from one organ into another. They were awarded the Nobel Prize in medicine for this in 1978. RDNA has been used in mass quantities of human insulin for diabetics and is useful in cancer treatment. The Soviet Union has used RDNA to generate biological warfare that can cause several diseases, such as plague and deadly viruses. It is now thought that terrorists can use RDNA technology to enact biological terrorism.[34]

In September and October 2001, several cases of anthrax broke out in the United States, while people were still in panic mode from the 9/11 terrorist attacks. Letters laced with infectious anthrax powder combined with chemical additives were delivered to news media offices and the U.S Congress. The letters killed five people and sickened twenty-two others. The perpetrators have never been identified. In 2001, the invading U.S. forces destroyed anthrax laboratories in Kandahar, Afghanistan. In January 2003, traces of the toxin ricin were found in the apartment of people linked to AQ in London. The police also found recipes and ingredients for toxins including ricin, cyanide, and botulinum, as well as a bomb design, at the apartment. Later that month, Spanish police arrested 16 North Africans in connection with this incident. There is no international treaty to ban biological weapons, like the 1968 nuclear proliferation treaty, nor is there a treaty for the banning of chemical weapons. Because of the thousands of commercial jets that cross the world each day to every continent, infected people traveling by air to various regions can unknowingly contaminate other people. All nations should be concerned with bioterrorism, and there is a need for international collaboration to combat it. Because of the time lag between the moment of a terrorist attack with biological agents and the duration of time before the onset of the disease, the detection of the attack and attackers remain a technical and law enforcement dilemma. There is also ambiguity as to the provenance of the disease, since it can be either natural or induced and injected by terrorists.

Chemical Terrorism

Chemical warfare has been used in several wars because it is cheap to produce, easy to carry, and effective to kill and to incapacitate the enemy. The effects of chemical warfare are torturous and horrible. During the First and Second World Wars, it was used by Germany and France in the form of toxic gas. In the 1980s, one of these chemical agents, mustard gas, was used in the Iran–Iraq war (1983–1988) to kill several hundred thousand people. Phosgene and mustard bombs killed at least 1400 people during the Yemeni civil war (1963–1967) in Egypt. Massive chemical weapon assaults were seen during the Iran–Iraq War and in the Iraqi suppression of its Kurdish minority (1987–1988). On March 17, 1988, Iraq attacked the Kurdish village of Halabja with suspected nerve agents, killing hundreds of civilian refugees. The U.S. waged chemical warfare in Southeast Asia (1961–1972), when riot control agents (similar to tear gas) and chemical defoliants and herbicides (Agent Orange) were used extensively. In Bhopal, India in 1984, a disgruntled pesticide plant employee is believed to have caused the release of 40 metric tons of methyl isocyonate into the atmosphere, killing more than 2, 000 and injuring 100, 000, of whom an estimated 50, 000 suffered permanent disabilities. As mentioned in Chapter 3, a Japanese terrorist group called Aum Shinrikyo released sarin gas, a chemical agent, the Tokyo subway system in 1995, killing 12 and injuring 5, 000. In 1999, a Muslim separatist group in Chechnya, Russia used the chemical agent chlorine gas in battle against Russian forces. In 2007, AQ terrorists used chlorine gas in Iraq, injuring 400 people.

Major chemical agents are categorized according to their effects:

1. Nerve—Tabun, Sarin, Cyclosarin (damages the nervous system)
2. Blister—Sulfur mustard, Nitrogen mustard (burns eyes, skin, and tissues)
3. Choking—Phosgene, Chlorine, Chloropicrin (restricts respiratory systems)
4. Blood—Cyanide (blocks the blood circulation and flow)

Because the delivery of chemical agents by individuals or groups is difficult, it requires state sponsorship. In all cases there is a close connection between international terrorism and the illegal movement of potentially deadly materials. Individual member states must enact nationwide precautions to eliminate this danger through the Chemical Weapons Convention (CWC), an international control agreement designed to contain the threat of chemical terrorism. In January 1993, 143 countries including the United

States and Russia signed the CWC. Implementation of the CWC is based on a regime of declaration and verification for the chemical industry, through declaration and verification by on-site inspections; and for chemical weapons. Along with the CWC, an Organization for the Prohibition of Chemical Weapons (OPCW) has been established to oversee the implementation of the CWC at the international level, particularly through verification measures. The OPCW consists of three main organs: the Conference of the State Parties, an Executive Council, and a Technical secretariat that provides support to the CWC, verifies the declarations sent to it by member states, and carries out the inspections specified in the Convention.[35] Despite these precautions, *Jane International Review* has reported that Syria is rebuilding its chemical weapons capability.[36]

The severity of chemical, biological, and nuclear weapons is outlined in a chart by security analyst Anthony Cordesman (Table 5.2). It is noted that nuclear weapons of 1, 000, 000 tons can damage any big city like New York, Los Angeles, and Washington D.C. for several months. For a 1 MT (10, 000, 000 ton) explosion, lethal ellipses will reach 40–80 miles against unsheltered populations after 18 hours. Areas of extreme lethality (3000 radius) can easily reach over 20 miles. The comparative effects of WMD are provided by Anthony Cordesman, Arleigh A. Burke Chair in Strategy, Center for Strategic and International Studies.[37]

The comparative effects of biological, chemical, and nuclear weapons delivered against a typical urban target using missile warheads are outlined in Table 5.2. This assumes one Scud-sized warhead with a maximum payload of 1, 000 kilograms, and assumes that the biological agent would not make maximum use of this payload capability because this method is inefficient.

Dual-use materials and equipment can be used to produce WMDs. There are almost no regulations to monitor or control dual use technology. The threat from terrorists acquiring and using this technology is greater than that of a nuclear strike against the U.S. The theft of these nuclear and fissile materials, including dual use materials, during transport for maintenance, refurbishment, storage or construction of an improvised nuclear device (IND) by terrorists remains a menace. State sponsors of terrorism and non-state facilitators could provide the technology to terrorists. If terrorists acquire WMDs, they can use blackmail to obtain their demands, wielding the power of a nuclear state without ever having to launch a missile. Small-scale chemical- and biological-related weapons materials and instructions, or the intent to use them, have been uncovered, including Midhat al-Mursi's weapons plans, found in AQ camps in Afghanistan before 9/11, Abu Musab al Zarqawi network's plot to use ricin and cyanide in multiple attacks in Europe in

Table 5.2
WMD Damages

Types	Area Covered (sq. km.)	Death (assuming 3,000–10,000 people/sq.km.)
Chemical: 300 kilograms of Sarin nerve gas with a density of 70 milligrams per cubic meter	0.22	60–200
Biological: 30 kilograms ofAnthrax spores with a density of 0.1 milligram per cubic meter	10	30,000–100,000
Nuclear: One 12.5 kiloton nuclear device achieving 5 pounds per cubic inch of over-pressure	7.8	23,000–80,000
One 1 megaton hydrogen bomb	190	570,000–1,900,000

* Source: Adapted by the Anthony H. Cordesman from Office of Technology Assessment, Proliferation of Weapons Mass Destruction: Assessing the Risks, US Congress OTA-ISC-559, Washington, August, 1993, pp. 53-54.

2002–2003, and a Bahraini terrorist's attempts to use a crude cyanide gas device in an attack on the New York City subway in 2002.[38]

The security strategist John Measheimer argues:

> Because nuclear weapons are horribly destructive, no national leader would ever use them, even in self defense. Thus, nuclear weapons do not dampen security competition in any significant way, and the balance of conventional military power still matters greatly.[39]

Technology and Terrorism

Digital technology in communications, including computer networks, wireless cell phones and computers, and the Internet, have revolutionized information technology.[40] In addition, the digitized messages and images use data compression and decompression, encryption and decryption, to protect message bandwidth, reliability, and authenticity. Fiber optic and satellite channels provide huge bandwidth (frequency space) simultaneously to multiple users without interference or noise corruption. All analog messages and imagery are converted into digital signals of 0s and 1s (binary digits, or bits), for use in message security and bandwidth preservation. These 0s and 1s are transmitted via digital modulations, changing phase frequency, or amplitude of a sinusoidal signal, using radio-frequency (rf) carriers that perform source and channel coding, compression, and encryption, then multiplexed and modulated to distant receivers through microwave channels, optics channels, and satellites. Once received, their information is demodulated, demultiplexed, decoded, decompressed, and decrypted in the reverse order and converted back to an analog signal of the sounds and imagery. The digital communications systems are shown in Figure 5.1.

Fiber optics communications use pulse coded modulation and demodulations. With very wide bandwidth (broadband), the speed of the transmission is multiple gigabits (1, 000, 000, 000 bits) per second, reducing transmission time compared to the use of a telephone line. The main advantages of digital communications are that digits are regenerated easily in the presence of noise using the coding for correction of errors, and that the receiver is simple to implement. The digitized voice signal has a rate of 64K bps (64, 000 bits per seconds). The data are fragmented into data packets with header bits and trailer bits. The number of bits in a packet is fixed or variable. In computer networks, packets travel via store-and-forward packet-switching methods to avoid congestion. The Internet uses packet switching. In packet switching networks (PSN), routing directs packet forwarding according to header bits, which means the transit of logically addressed packets from their source users toward their ultimate destination users through several intermediate nodes: hardware devices called routers, bridges, gateways, firewalls, or switches. Routing involves two basic activities: determination of optimal routing paths with the least delay, and the transport of data packets through an internet. Path determination, on the other hand, requires adaptive algorithms based on traffic intensity and priority. One protocol that addresses the task of path determination is the Border Gateway Protocol (BGP). The BGP performs inter-domain and intra-domain routing in Transmission-Control Protocol/Internet Protocol (TCP/IP) networks. BGP is an exterior gateway protocol (EGP), which means that it performs routing between multiple autonomous systems or domains, and exchanges routing and reachability information with other BGP systems. The PSN is the core in digital communications systems for data and voice communications.

Figure 5.1. Digital Communications Systems, Showing the Flow of Data When Someone Uses a Telephone or a Laptop Computer to Contact Another Telephone or Laptop User in Another Location

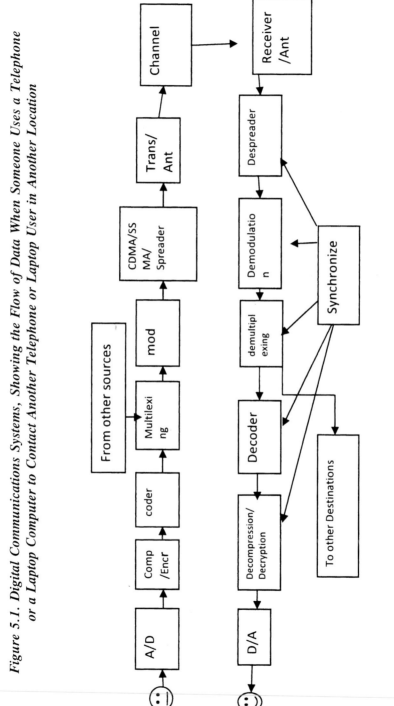

There are several kinds of communication networks: Ethernet Networks, Local Area Networks (LANs), Fiber Distributed Data Interface Networks (FDDI), and Wide Area Networks (WANs). Asynchronous transfer mode (ATM) networks operate using both LAN and WAN networks. The speed of an ATM network is 10G bps (10, 000, 000, 000 bits per seconds) while an Ethernet is 10M bps (1, 000, 000 bps). The old AT&T T-1 pared cable carrier had 24 voice circuits, while fiber network has 4032 voice circuits. These digits are used in compression, encryption, coding for self-error correction, and for mixing various data streams. The fiber optic network is robust against noise and interference. The speed, packet switching, compression and decompression, and encryption and decryption have enabled the Internet to provide various services, including electronic mail (e-mail), world wide websites (www), video on demand, on-line shopping, and teleconferencing that combines voice and video signals among multiple participants. Voice is transmitted on the Internet using Internet protocol (IP)—the method or protocol, a set of rules to access each others' computers, by which data is sent from one computer to another. This is known as VoIP. VoIP can connect personal computer to personal computer, personal computer to telephone, and telephone to telephone. VoIP involves sending voice information in discrete packets using packet switching and statistical multiplexing, instead of the traditional circuit-committed protocols of the public switched telephone network (PSTN).

All the message signals, as in cell phones, are transmitted using code division multiple access (CDMA) systems, which are also known as spread spectrum multiple access (SSMA) systems. They provide anti-jamming capability, which consists of rejecting unwanted signals and noise, and sharing the channel among a large number of users. Small ground-based antenna dishes can receive satellite signals.[41] BlackBerry[TM] is a modern wireless, handheld device, also known as a smart phone. It provides e-mail, telephoning, text messaging, internet faxing, web browsing, and other wireless information services via a multi-touch interface. The device gives:

1. The ability to listen to music, with no need for mp3 or mp4 players. It supports a multimedia environment that combines text, graphics, audio, and video, and allows users to download films, songs, books, posters, etc.
2. A built in GPS receiver for navigation and position location. GPS is carried out via twenty-four or more geosynchronous, stationary, earth orbiting satellites that cover most parts of the world except the polar region. This system provides an accu-

rate position location within 50 feet or less, year-round and around the clock, anyplace in the world.

3. Access to on-line books
4. Access to radio and TV news
5. Detailed information about locales around the globe. This makes BlackBerry a handy tool for terrorists to carry around with them.

The Internet is a global system of interconnected computer and communications networks that are linked via modems and telephone or cable lines. It uses the transmission control protocol/Internet Protocol (TCP/IP) to serve billions of users worldwide, and provides a convenient sanctuary for terrorists. Terrorist may use laptops, video cams, and DVDs to share information, whether they are holed up in secret hideouts or in sitting in neighborhood Internet cafés. The Internet lets them stay connected to the outside world from disparate places via multiple and simultaneous connectivity, while remaining concealed and anonymous. The Internet has become a great weapon to use in damaging communal harmony and peace, and to propagate messages and brainwash young minds to become jihadists. Muslims around the world can use the Internet to demonstrate their allegiance to Islam, or to their country of origin. Through the Internet, terrorists send instructions on how to make bombs, fire rocket-propelled grenades, destroy bridges, raid houses, or use SA-7 surface-to-air missiles to blow up planes and cars, a building or a plant where toxins are kept. It also provides instructions for hostage taking, posts military training manuals and target information, offers computer-based courses on kidnapping and assassinations, and conducts recruitment of *jihadists*. A fifteen-page Arabic language document, "Biological Weapon," was sent from Abu Musab Suri's website. Computer-savvy terrorists, operate more than 5000 websites and maintain a variety of e-mail accounts. They can access the Internet to receive information, faxes, and data from worldwide networks, and to transmit their hateful messages instantly to other websites and terrorist camps. In this way, they can incite terror through violence, propagating radical ideologies of jihad and instructing attacks on terror targets. They possess satellite phones and GPS receivers and are capable of breaching the radio frequencies of the enemy. Terrorists use mobile phones for surveillance and operational missions. They make use of tweeters (text-based posts of up to 140 characters;[42] and Facebook accounts for social networking. In Mumbai, India, attackers affiliated with LeT navigated their November 2008 terror spree using GPS-guided boats, Blackberrys[TM], and Google Earth imagery. In addition to communications and navigational technology, the terrorists use weapons technology including dirty bombs, transportation technology, war-games methodologies, and weapons available only on the black market. They engage in electronic fund transfers, exploit globalization of scientific knowledge and technologies, and invest in the narcotics trade. Terrorists often carry AK 47s, use IEDs, grenades, and missiles, and plot the use of WMDs, of which nuclear weapons are the most deadly and devastating. Terrorists use the Internet to coordinate travel on high-speed trains, private cars and buses, commercial jets, or ships, often while carrying weapons.

The noted social scientist Frank Furedi writes:

> A mood of suspicion and apprehension towards science and technology is constantly conveyed through popular culture, and particularly through the environment movement. Pessimism about the accomplishment of modernity and science has a direct bearing on how the threat of terrorism is perceived. Many believe that the destructive power of technology intensifies the threat of terrorism.[43]

Surveillance, Biometrics, and Information Technology

Surveillance with smart devices including radar, infrared, and electro-optical sensors, is required to check the inflow of illegal drugs, explosives, contraband, WMDs, and other undesirable products across borders via ground, air, or water. A cutting-edge technology, Fast Pulsed Neutron Analysis, is used to scan objects.

> It uses a pulsed beam scanned on vehicular traffic to examine cargo. The pulsed neutrons (n) interact with the elements of scanned objects, creating distinctive gamma rays that correspond to particular chemical elements.[44]

Explosives, narcotics, and other contraband materials contain various chemical elements such as hydrogen, carbon, nitrogen, oxygen, and chlorine, in quantities and ratios that differentiate them from each other and from other innocuous substances. Neutrons and ã-rays (gamma rays) have the ability to penetrate through various materials to large depths. In this way, security personnel may investigate, in a non-intrusive manner, volumes ranging from that of suitcases to Sea-Land containers. Pulsed Fast/Thermal Neutron Analysis (PFTNA) is a neutron-based technique that utilizes the (n, n?ã), (n, pã), and (n, ã) reactions to identify and quantify a large number of elements. The elements emit characteristic ã rays that are the "fingerprints" of each isotope. This technique is being employed in a variety of applications: bulk coal analysis, contraband detection, and detection of explosives.[45]

In 2007, the Swedish defense research agency (FOI) developed a fast neutron analysis (FNA) to detect biological, chemical, radiological, and nuclear agents and their combinations. A nuclear magnetic resonance (NMR) method is also used to scan baggage. The San Diego-based company Quantum Magnetics has developed magnetic resonance imaging (MRI) to detect explosives. This method uses an apparatus to screen individuals specifically for paramagnetic or ferromagnetic objects they may be carrying or wearing, before they enter the high-field region of an MRI suite. The device comprises either a screening portal or a compact, hand-held magnetic gradiometer and its electronics. It places all of the sensor arrays in close proximity to all parts of a subject's body, for screening purposes. (US7315166—Magnetic resonance imaging screening method and apparatus—01/01/2008)

Biometrics (Measures of Life)

This type of analysis is designed to recognize and interpret personal data based on certain physical or behavioral characteristics. The assessed features can be physical (facial geometry, palm-vein pattern, fingerprints, iris or retina pattern), or behavioral (keystroke, voice, or speech prints, and handwriting). These features are compared with corresponding information stored in a database to identify individuals. The interrelationships between these biometric structures is shown in Figure 5.2.

Figure 5.2. Biometric Structures

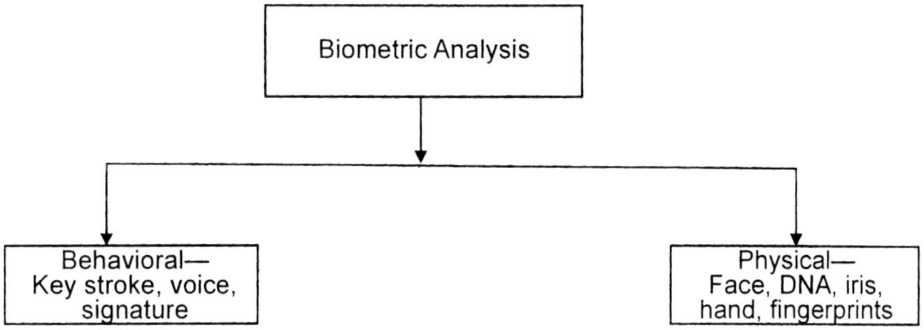

Among the various biometric personal identification systems, DNA provides the most reliable identification method. This is because the information is digital, and the means of recording it are stationary.

DNA differs from standard biometrics in several ways: DNA requires a tangible physical sample as opposed to an impression, image, or recording. DNA matching is not done in real-time, and currently not all stages of comparison are automated. DNA matching does not employ templates or feature extraction, but rather represents the comparison of actual samples.[46]

Another popular method is gait recognition. This technique looks to identify someone by the way that he or she walks (their gait). Unlike most other biometric technologies, gait recognition is based on dynamic movement. In other words, the subject needs to be in motion. Several variables affect gait recognition technologies, including:

1. the subject's clothing;
2. the surface on which the subject walks;
3. fatigue or injury, causing the subject to walk different;
4. the type of shoes the subject is wearing;
5. the presence of items such as handbags, briefcases, umbrellas and the like;
6. background or extraneous noise, including lighting and changes in the external environment.[47]

There are many commercially available software programs for DNA analysis. These include software developed by a Virginia-based company, Future Technologies Inc (FTI).

All communications data has to be secured, reliable, robust, and unalterable. The scheme is presented in Figure 5.3.

Certain elements of society use IT for political, financial, or sabotage purposes. These unauthorized or undesired users include hackers. A hacker is "a person who enjoys exploring the details of programmable systems and how to stretch their capabilities" and who is capable of "creatively overcoming or circumventing limitations." Activism is defined as "a policy of taking direct and militant action to achieve a political or social goal." A combination of the two has been dubbed *Hacktivism*—a policy of hacking, "phreaking," or creating technology to achieve a political or social goal.

Cyberterrorism

Terrorism that disrupts computer-communications networks, infiltrates and destroys information infrastructures, or propagates violence through coercive access of the network for political and religious gain or criminal purposes, to the cause deaths of innocent people and the destruction of property, is known as cyberterrorism. It may involve the loss of data integrity,

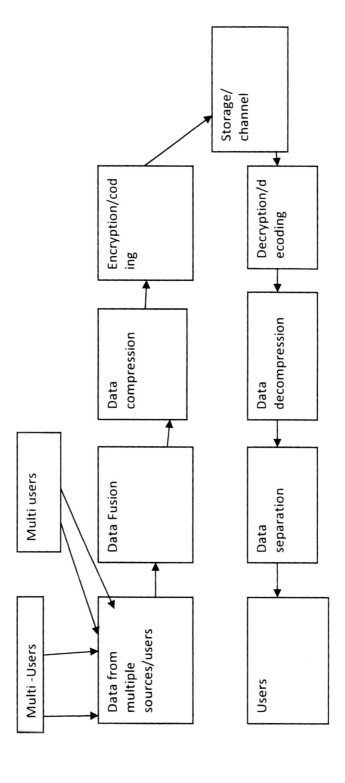

Figure 5.3. Secured Information Technology

of confidentiality, of availability, and physical destruction as well. Using cyberterrorism, terrorists have the advantages of anonymity, simultaneous diverse targets, a low risk of detection and personal injury, and minimal investment of finances. They may operate from nearly any location, using only a computer and some commercially available software. The terrorists' typical tools include backdoor, e-mail, and IP spoofing, logic bombs, sniffers, Trojan horses, viruses, worms, and Zombies.[48] The computer-communications network, with thousands of nodes and links, is accessed by millions of authorized users at every moment of every day, across the globe. Failure of, or damage to, any node or link within the networks is considered a "denial of service," which denies computer resources to intended users. A basic cyber war technique, Distributed Denial of Service (DDOS), is often used by criminals or terrorists. In a DDOS, in which an Internet site or router is flooded with more data than the maximum capacity of the network can respond to or to process. As a result, legitimate users cannot access the site, which then becomes dysfunctional. Botnets may be used for such attacks. The Border Gateway Protocol (BGP), an interautonomous system routing protocol of one network system (e.g., AT&T), is designed to be compatible with another network (e.g., the Juniper network. A network may be vulnerable to cyberwarriors located at any nodes of that network.

Information generated by computers is transmitted through communications links, telephones, cables, fiber optics, undersea cables, microwave links, and satellites to other computers and to several users at once. Multiple computers are used for large-scale computing in mapping, image processing, synthetic-aperture radar or data storage, nuclear detonation modeling, weather and navigation systems, hospital records and patient-care systems, economic modeling, finance, banking, crime detection, and many other types of systems. Such information is sensitive, private, proprietary, and designed for immediate use. Computers are used to control traffic, power generation, and distribution, water management, launching of space vehicles, missiles, and weapon systems, modeling and simulation, and many more applications. The application of information and communication theory and control systems as related to parts of the human body, including the nervous system, is known as cybernetics. Norbert Wiener, in his classic paper of 1948, coined this word and founded the modern information theory and systems.[49]

Cyberspace refers to thousands of computer-communications networks aided with servers, switches, routers, software engineering, computer hardware, sensors, signals, connections, processors, and controllers. Cyberspace provides users with instant accessibility regardless of their geographic location, via microwave, satellite, or fiber optic channels. It allows for the interdependent networks of information technology infrastructures and telecommunications networks—such as the Internet, computer systems, integrated sensors, system control networks, and embedded processors and controllers common to control and communications systems. The authenticity, confidentiality, and reliability of data are secured in a variety of ways, within both software and hardware. Any unlawful use or alteration of this data for economic gain is a computer crime. In the realm of terrorism, this can result in unimaginable and terrible consequences. While cybercrime is defined as crime in cyberspace, cyberterrorism is defined as terrorism in cyberspace. Cyberterrorism is a far bigger threat than cybercrime in terms of damage and violence in the name of religious and political gain. Cybersecurity is concerned with protecting systems against both cybercrime and cyberterrorism, which may take the form of exploiting system vulnerability, and sending unauthenticated messages.

> Cybersecurity is the prevention of damage to, the protection of, and the restoration of computers, electronic communications systems, electronic communication services, wire communication, and electronic communication, including information contained therein, to ensure its availability, integrity, authentication, and non-repudiation.[50]

The secured cyber-architecture must deny any unauthorized access to computers and communications systems, and must prevent espionage, interception, sabotage, fraud and false alarms, trespassing, and unauthorized disclosures. It must provide and preserve the integrity of data in real time everywhere around the clock. The United States and others are totally dependent on cyberspace, and any infraction of the cyberspace infrastructure will be disastrous to all sectors, including utilities, banking, emergency, homeland security, air traffic control, defense, manufacturing, electronic computing, and broadcasting networks. The U.S. government defines critical areas as banking and finance, insurance, chemicals, oil and gas, electric utilities, law enforcement, higher education, transportation, information technology and telecommunications, and water. Lead agencies of the information infrastructure include: the Department of Homeland Security (DHS), Department of the Treasury, Department of Defense (DOD), Department of Health and Human Services, Department of Energy, Department of Agriculture, the Environmental Protection Agency, Department of Justice, Department of Transportation, , Federal Bureau of Investigation (FBI), and the Federal Aviation Administration (FAA). It is vital to provide availability, integrity, and privacy to LL these systems.

Computer and Network Security

Electronic Communication: The U.S. Federal Code defines "electronic communication" as any transfer of signs, signals, writing, images, sounds, data, or intelligence of any nature transmitted in whole or in part by a wire, radio, electromagnetic, photo-electronic or photo-optical system that affects interstate or foreign commerce, but does not include:

1. Any wire or oral communication;
2. Any communication made through a tone-only paging device;
3. Any communication from a tracking device (as defined in section 3117 of this title); or
4. Electronic funds transfer information stored by a financial institution in a communications system used for the electronic storage and transfer of funds.[51]

According to U.S. Code Title 10, Subtitle A, Chapter 112, § 2200e: (1) The term "information assurance" includes the following:

1. Computer security
2. Network security
3. Any other information technology that the Secretary of Defense considers related to information assurance.

The National Security Agency (NSA) defines information assurance as measures that protect and defend information and information systems by ensuring their availability, integrity, authentication, confidentiality, and nonrepudiation. These measures include providing for restoration of information systems by incorporating protection, detection, and reaction capabilities.[52]

Authentication: Security measure designed to establish the validity of a transmission, message, or originator, or a means of verifying an individual's authorization to receive specific categories of information.

Availability: Timely, reliable access to data and information services for authorized users.

Confidentiality: Assurance that information is not disclosed to unauthorized individuals, processes, or devices.

Integrity: Quality of an IS [information system] reflecting the logical correctness and reliability of the operating system; the logical completeness of the hardware and software implementing the protection mechanisms; and the consistency of the data structures and occurrence of the stored data.

Nonrepudiation: Assurance the sender of data is provided with proof of delivery and the recipient is provided with proof of the sender's identity, so neither can later deny having processed the data.

Prevention[53]:

1. Reduce opportunities to criminals to develop elaborate system designs so that hacker does not hack the computer.

2. Use Authentication Technology—Use password bio-metric devices, fingerprint or voice recognition technology and retinal imaging, to greatly increase the difficulty of obtaining unauthorized access to information systems. Attention to be paid to bio-metric technology as this recognizes the particular user's authentication for using the particular computer.

3. Lay a trap—Bait a trap to catch the attacker in our computer.

4. Develop technology of encryption and anonymity, and also for protecting infrastructure, as hackers or cyberterrorists can attack over any nation's infrastructure, resulting in massive losses.

5. Understand cybercrime—For volume, impact and legal challenges, understand the benefit of proper equipment training and tools to control cybercrime.

6. Think about Nature of Crime—Computer crime is diverse. Consider what cybercrime can take place in one's particular organization, so that different types of monitoring/security systems can be designed and proper documentation can be written for security systems.

7. Adopt Computer Security—Avail yourself of new sophisticated products and advice for computer crime prevention, which are available free or paid in the market.

8. Use Blocking and Filtering Programs—For detecting viruses, since viruses can identify and block malicious computer codes. Anti Spyware software helps stop criminals from taking hold of one's PC and helps to clean up the PC if it has been hit.

9. Monitoring Controls—Separate monitoring to be done for (a) monetary files (b) business information.

10. Design Different Tools—For different needs rather than using one particular tool.

11. Data Recovery—Develop tools for data recovery and analysis.

12. Reporting—Always report the crime to cyberfraud complaint center in one's country as they maintain large amounts of data and have better tools for controlling cybercrime.

13. Educate Children.

14. Design Alert Systems—Design an alert system to sound when there is actual intrusion.

15. Install Firewalls—(a) as they block particular network traffic according to security policy. (b) Patches are generally installed automatically and automatically fix the software security flaws.

16. Install Original Software—As they contain many security measures. Pirated software does not contain many security abilities which exist in original software.

17. Online Assistance—Develop regular online assistance to employees. Learn Internet to one's advantage only and understand all tips to stay safe on line.

18. Avoid infection rather than cleaning afterwards. Keep browser up to date for security measures.

19. Avoid Bogus Security Products—As many anti-spyware activists run a website that lists bogus security products. Read the license agreement before installing any program.

20. Attachments—Avoid opening attachments or e-mails that you were not expecting and have come from unknown sources or persons.

21. Cross check regularly the statements of financial accounts and Internet banking.

22. Lack of Funds (whereas lawbreakers have enough funds for best hardware and software) National Repository to be established for investigation into cybercrime. More funds for training computer forensic personnel. Sufficient funds to be kept aside every year for upgrading security system in future.

23. Lack of Latest Technology and Good Equipment—Investigators to be provided with latest equipment. Easy access to technology required, to conduct computer investigation. Use of specialized software and training.

24. Lack of Training—Investigators to be continuously trained for (a) proficiency in investigating cybercrimes, (b) projecting the future complexes of cybercrimes, (c) locating computer based evidence, (d) understanding cybercrime legal challenges.

25. Documentation and Procedures Are Not Adequately Defined—Describe advance search and seizure procedure in documentation to handle high volume crimes. Since cybercrimes are diverse in nature different kinds of documentations are required for security systems. Reporting standards to be developed for investigating the crime.

26. Lacking Forensic Support—Computerized forensic support required for making strong forensic imaging and verification in order to follow "footprints" both on the computer and on the Internet. Creating forensic software and using high storage hard drives and good equipment to maintain high standards for recovery and preservation of evidence.

27. No Specialized Unit—Create cybercrime unit in the country. Create emergency cyber response team.

28. No Defined Jurisdiction—The victim and criminals may be in two different places, and may be overseas, hence adequate jurisdiction to be defined.

29. Accountability—Fixing responsibility on the investigator who investigates the cybercrime.

30. Lack of Manpower—Proper training in investigating complex cybercrimes.

31. Lack of Centralized Information and Sharing/Coordination—Sophisticated crime to be centralized in order to conduct forensic computer investigation and access to a computer lab environment. Law enforcement agencies should share information in the state and country so as to reach the key point as early as possible.

32. Lacking Storage Data Facilities—Law enforcement agencies to store past and present data for predicting future attacks. Large devices are required to store data.

There are several organizations that deal with standardization, interoperability, and cyber security—the protection required to ensure confidentiality, routing, integrity, and availability of the information communication network. These are:

1. The American National Standards Institute (ANSI)
2. The International Standardization Organization (ISO)
3. The Joint Technical Committee on Information Technology (JTCI)
4. The Internet Engineering Task Force (ITEF)
5. The International Electrotechnical Commission (IEC)
6. The National Institute of Standard and Technology (NIST)

ISO and the IEC have formed joint technical committees in an effort to combat cybercrime. These include ISO/IEC 13335-1:2004, ISO/IEC 27001:2005, and ISO 17799.[54] NIST has established a Smart Grid Cyber Security Coordination Task Group (CSCTG).

Cyber security is being addressed in a complementary and integral process that will result in a comprehensive set of cyber security requirements. Cyber security must address not only deliberate attacks, such as from disgruntled employees, industrial espionage, and terrorists, but inadvertent compromises of the information infrastructure due to user errors, equipment failures, and natural disasters. Vulnerabilities might allow an attacker to penetrate a network, gain access to control software, and alter load conditions to destabilize the grid in unpredictable ways.[55]

Cyberterrorists who are politically motivated can inject systems with cyberweapons including: malicious software (malware), viruses, Trojan horses (which facilitate unauthorized access to the user's computer system), worms, self-replicating computer program logic bombs, and sophisticated computer codes, to corrupt, erase, or change data. Terrorists indulge in these acts to advance political, religious or ideological causes by violence. Cyberterrorists (cyber attackers) are capable of breaking into firewalls and crypto software, and can alter or erase the control parameters in SCADA (Supervisory Control and Data Acquisition) Systems. Although such an attack is difficult to carry out, it may cause terrible damage in the chemical and energy industries, shutting down power grids. These acts can result in deaths in hospitals or in transportation systems and can damage infrastructures. Tough nuclear weapons and other sensitive sites are not connected physically to the Internet, but battlefield command, communications, control, and Intelligence (C 3 I) systems are linked to the Internet and are therefore subject to cyberterrorism.

It is being reported that hackers breached the Pentagon's biggest weapons program, the $300 billion Joint Strike Fighter, and stole data.[56] There have been cyber attacks in the past including one in Estonia on April 27, 2007, which wiped out several websites including that of its Parliament, several banks, ministries, newspapers, and broadcast stations. In 2008, Georgian and Azerbaijani sites were attacked. Recently,

> in the United States, the (cyber) attacks primarily targeted Internet sites operated by major government agencies, including the departments of Homeland Security and Defense, the Federal Aviation Administration and the Federal Trade Commission, according to several computer security researchers.[57]

There is a difference between cybercrime and cyberterrorism; one is done for monetary gain, usually by targeting financial services, the other for political gain, targeting government organizations and information infrastructures towards realizing violent objectives. Both of these disruptions are referred to as cyberattacks, and both cause loss of data integrity, denial of services, unauthorized disclosures, and damage to infrastructures, all of which can have devastating results. Cybercrime also includes credit card theft and identity theft, two crimes that are committed by terrorists, as reported by the DHS. At least two views exist for defining the term "cyberterrorism." Effects-based: Cyberterrorism exists when computer attacks result in effects that are disruptive enough to generate fear comparable to a traditional act of terrorism, even if done by criminals. Intent-based: Cyberterrorism exists when unlawful or politically motivated computer attacks are done to intimidate or coerce a government or people to further political objectives. The main targets of government agencies in the United State are the DHS, FBI, CIA, NSA, DOD, and FAA.

As reported by cyber security experts Jon Rollins and Clay Wilson:

> A 2004 survey by an internet security company, covering 450 networks in 35 countries, found that hacking (breaking into computers through knowledge of administrative controls to modify settings) had become a profitable criminal pursuit. Hackers sell unknown computer vulnerabilities (commonly called "zero-day exploits") on the black market to criminals who use them for fraud. Hackers with networks of compromised computers (also known as "bot nets") rent them to other criminals who use them to launch coordinated attacks against targeted individuals or businesses, including banks or other institutions that manage financial information. In autumn 2004, organized cybercriminals appear to have infiltrated the computer systems of the London offices of Sumitomo, the Japanese bank, in an attempt to steal £220 million. The cybercriminals reportedly planned to transfer the money to other bank accounts around the world. Officials at the London police fraud squad reportedly stated that Sumitomo is the only incident so far in which an attack by external cybercriminals has nearly succeeded against a major bank.[58]

A report by the DHS predicts that other possible sponsors of terrorist attacks against the United States may include groups such as Jamaat ul-Fuqura, a Pakistani-based organization allegedly linked to Muslims of America; Jamaat al Tabligh, an Islamic missionary organization; and the American *Dar al-Islam* Movement. The new IPV6, a secure communications protocol, may protect the Internet from hackers and cyber terrorists. The DHS has the following to be concerned with:

> Islamic terrorist groups such as Al Qaeda, Hamas, and Hezbollah incorporate information technology to support their operations and use it for communications, fundraising, propaganda, recruitment, target reconnaissance, and training. A statement posted on the website azzam.com used by Al Qaeda-related jihadists urged Muslim Internet professionals to disseminate information through e-mail, online discussion groups, and websites. The statement claimed, "The more websites, the better for us. We must make the Internet our tool." Islamic extremist groups use websites to provide information on their activities, organization, plans, and political, re-

ligious, and social objectives. Groups such as Hamas and Hezbollah, Islamic Jihad, and insurgents in Iraq use websites to glorify their violent actions by posting videos and pictures of executions and bombings, and statistical updates of daily attacks against the enemy. Many sites publish online exhortations by religious figures encouraging readers to undertake jihad, speeches and declarations of their leaders, and statements and claims of responsibility for attacks. Hamas and Hezbollah are especially technologically savvy with a strong Internet presence and have an interest in collecting information on the U.S. infrastructure weaknesses. They routinely use computerized e-mail, encryption to support their operations, and files. They facilitate fundraising and money laundering online by credit card fraud and the establishment of fronts such as charities and technology companies.[59]

Tech-savvy terrorists can use the Internet to sabotage the information, transport, power, and security infrastructures.[60] The former U.S. Army General Wesley Clark and specialist Peter Levin (2009) have reported:

> In 2007, there were almost 44, 000 reported incidents of malicious cyber activity—one third more than the previous year and more than ten times as many as in 2001 . . . (The) chip-level attacks are so attractive to adversaries, so difficult to detect, and so dangerous to the nation.[61]

Several terrorist groups have attempted to possess WMDs including AQ and its associates Islamic Jihad, Jemaah Islamiya, and LeT. To avoid detection of nuclear missiles by surveillance satellites, WMDs are kept in mobile delivery systems—yet those can be stolen or hijacked by terrorists. The threat of terrorists acquiring a nuclear weapon (or the material to make one) is terrible and plausible. The International Weapons of Mass Destruction Commission believes that this threat requires a tightening of controls over nuclear and other sensitive material, equipment, and technology. OBL was reported to have developed anthrax for use in a mass casualty attack in the United States, in addition to acquiring nuclear weapons. For global jihad, the development of tactical chemical, biological, and radiological weapons can be decentralized and pursued by terrorists in prime locations. Material and manpower are available around the world, and OBL has reiterated his 2006 statement that AQ will return to the United States.[62] The former defense officials and consultants Richard Clarke and Robert Knake[63] have evaluated the strength of cyber war capabilities in three categories, offense, defense, and dependence—in other words, the extent to which a nation is wired and reliant upon networks and system that could be vulnerable in the event of cyber attacks (see Table 5.3).

Table 5.3
Cyber War Strength

Country	Offense	Defense	Dependence	Total
U.S.	8	1	2	11
Russia	7	4	5	16
China	5	6	4	15
Iran	4	3	5	12
North Korea	2	7	9	18

Cyberterrorism or cyberwar is a new silent and powerful weapon for holy warriors. It lets them remain hidden, in unknown locations, as they attempt to gain unauthorized access to information infrastructures. It is difficult to identify the source of a cyber attack, and for this reason there are no effective ways to deter further damage, either by retaliating or taking preventive measures. There is also some ambiguity involved, because computer games by eccentric scientists as well as model building by computer entrepreneurs may be mistaken for malicious attacks. In cyberattacks, damage can range from an individual computer malfunctioning, to distorting an entire country's cell phone networks, jamming espionage, communications, and navigational satellites, or crashing its electrical grid or air traffic control systems. In terms of human and property loss, it can be no less damaging than the detonation of a WMD.[64] Dennis Blair, Director of National Intelligence, [65] has announced the formation of the Comprehensive National Cybersecurity Initiative (CNCI), which was designed to mitigate vulnerabilities being exploited by America's cyber adversaries, and to provide long-term strategic operational and analytic capabilities to U.S. Government organizations. By enabling the development of these new technologies and strategies, as a core component of a broad strategic approach to strengthening cybersecurity for the nation, the CNCI will give the United States additional tools to respond to the constantly changing cyber environment.

Notes

1. Nuclear, Biological, and Chemical Weapons Policy Team Report to the Commission, December 4, 2000, www.ussc.gov/NBCreport/NBCfinalreport.pdf. Nuclear, Biological, and Chemical Weapons and Missiles: Status and Trends, Updated February 20, 2008, CRS Report for Congress, www.fas.org/sgp/crs/nuke/

RL30699.pdf. Terrorism and Weapons of Mass Destruction: United Nations Security Council Resolution 1540, Gabriel H. Oosthuizen and Elizabeth Wilmshurst, International Law Program BP 04/01, www.chathamhouse.org.uk/files/ 9266_bp0904unsc1540.pdf. Resolution 1540 (2004) Adopted by the Security Council at its 4956th meeting, 28 April 2004, www.securitycouncilreport.org/atf/cf/ %7B65BFCF9B-6D27-4E9C-8CD3-CF6E4FF96FF9%7D/1540%20SPV%204 956.pdf.

    2. Federation of American Scientists, www.fas.org/nuke/intro/nuke/ effects.htm.

    3. Mohanty, 1991, 517–543.

    4. Commission on the Prevention of Weapons of Mass Destruction Proliferation and Terrorism, www.preventwmd.gov/world_at_risk_nuclear_proliferation_ and_terrorism/.

    5. How to stop radiation terrorism, Peter D. Zimmerman, James M. Acton and M. Brooke Rogers, New York Times, August 1, 2007.

    6. Radiological Attack: Dirty Bombs and Other Devices, A fact sheet from the National Academies and the U.S. Department of Homeland Security, http:// www.nae.edu/File.aspx?id=11317.a.

    7. Allison, 2004, 74–75.

    8. *Deception: Pakistan, the United States, and the Secret Trade in Nuclear Weapons*, Adrian Levy and Catherine Scott-Clark, New York, N.Y. Walker Books, 2007.

    9. Tenet, 2007, 262.

    10. Armstrong and Trento, 2007, 202, 229.

    11. George Bush, *Decision Points*, New York, N.Y. Random House, 2010, 213-214.

    12. Bruce Riedel, Pakistan and the Bomb, *Wall Street Journal*, May 30, 2009.

    13. Pakistan: Islamic Bomb, Time Magazine, July 9, 1979, http://www.time. com/time/magazine/article/0, 9171, 920461-1, 00.html. Nuclear Anxiety: The Know-How; U.S. and China Helped Pakistan Build Its Bomb, by Tim Weiner, June 01, 1998, *New York Times*, http://www.nytimes.com/1998/06/01/world/nuclear-anxiety-the-know-how-us-and-china-helped-pakistan-build-its-bomb.html?src=pm.

    14. A. Q. Khan and onward proliferation from Pakistan, Chapter three, A.Q.; Khan and Onward Proliferation from Pakistan, The International Institute of Strategic Studies.

    15. Pakistan's Nuclear Weapons: Proliferation and Security Issues, Paul K. Kerr and Mary Beth Nikitin, June 12, 2009, Congressional Research Service 7-5700, www.crs.gov, RL34248, http://assets.opencrs.com/rpts/RL34248_2009 0612.pdf. Nuclear Theft, http://america-hijacked.com/2009/08/13/pakistan-nuclear-thefts-foiled/. The Security of Nuclear Weapons in Pakistan, Shaun Gregory, 18th November 2007, http://spaces.brad.ac.uk:8080/download/attachments/748/ Brief_22finalised.pdf. China and Nuclear Proliferation: Rethinking the Link, Henry Stokowski, The Nonproliferation Policy Education Center, Washington, D.C., www.npec-web.org, Testimony before the U.S.–China Economic and Security Review Commission, "China's Proliferation Practices, and the Development of its

Cyber and Space Warfare Capabilities," May 20, 2008, Dirksen Senate Office Building Washington D.C. www.npec-web.org/Testimonies/20080520-Sokolski-USCC-PreparedTestimony.pdf. Pakistan as a Nuclear Power, Oliver Thranert and Christian Wagner, June 2009, www.swp-berlin.org/common/get_document.php? asset_id=6081. Pakistan–U.S. Relations, K. Alan Kronstadt, February 6, 2009, www.law.umaryland.edu/marshall/crsreports/crsdocuments/RL33498_03272008.pdf. Pakistan–U.S. Relations, Alan Kronstadt, July 1, 2009, http://fpc.state.gov/documents/organization/127297.pdf. Also: CRS Report for Congress, Prepared for Members and Committees of Congress, and Pakistan's Capital Crisis: Implications for U.S. Policy, Michael F. Martin and Alan Kronstadt, March 6, 2009, www.fas.org/sgp/crs/row/RS22983.pdf. Why Has the United States Not Been Attacked Again? Dallas Boyd, Lewis Dunn, and James Scouras, *The Washington Quarterly,* July 2009, www.twq.com/09july/docs/09jul_BoyddDunnScouras.pdf. Born to Jihad, Clare M. Lopez 05/12/2009, *Human Events,* www.human events.com/article.php?id=31820. Pakistan: The Islamic Bomb, Monday, Jul. 09, 1979Time/CNN, www.time.com/time/magazine/article/0, 9171, 920461, 00.html.

16. No Freedom for Mr. Khan, The New York Times, Editorial, September 6, 2009, Pakistan as a Nuclear Power, Oliver Thranert and Christian Wagner, June 2009, www.swp-berlin.org/common/get_document.php?asset_id=6081, Pakistan–U.S. Relations, K. Alan Kronstadt, February 6, 2009, www.law.umaryland.edu/marshall/crsreports/crsdocuments/RL33498_03272008.pdf. Pakistan–U.S. Relations, Alan Kronstadt, July 1, 2009, http://fpc.state.gov/documents/organization/127297.pdf. Also: CRS Report for Congress, Prepared for Members and Committees of Congress, and Pakistan's Capital Crisis: Implications for U.S. Policy, Michael F. Martin and Alan Kronstadt, March 6, 2009, www.fas.org/sgp/crs/row/RS22983.pdf. Why Has the United States Not Been Attacked Again? Dallas Boyd, Lewis Dunn, and James Scouras, *The Washington Quarterly,* July 2009, www.twq.com/09july/docs/09jul_BoyddDunnScouras.pdf. Born to Jihad, Clare M. Lopez 05/12/2009, *Human Events,* www.humanevents.com/article.php?id=31820. Pakistan: The Islamic Bomb, Monday, Jul. 09, 1979Time/CNN, www.time.com/time/magazine/article/0, 9171, 920461, 00.html.

17. God is with the believers and the angels are guarding his steps; Laqueur, 2003, 227; Marvin Perry and Howard Negrin, (Ed.), *Theory and Practice of Islamic Terrorism,* New York: Palgrave Macmillan, 2008, 21.

18. Jenkins, 2008, 377.

19. Armstrong and Trento, *America and The Islamic Bomb,* 2007, 21, 27, 30, 32.

20. *Deception: Pakistan, the United States, and the Secret Trade in Nuclear Weapons,* Adrian Levy and Catherine Scott-Clark, Walker Books, N.Y. 2007, 418–421, 439, 449.

21. Bobbitt, 2008, 117, 121.

22. Pakistan's nuclear arsenal is estimated at more than 100: WP, The Nation, July 17, 2011, http://www.nation.com.pk/pakistan-news-newspaper-daily-english-online/Politics/31-Jan-2011/Pakistans-nuclear-arsenal-tops-100-WP.

23. Al-Qaida wants Pakistan's nuclear weapons: Obama, Press Trust of India, Dec 2, 2009, 10.41am IST, The Times of India, http://articles.timesofindia.india times.com/2009-12-02/us/28077739_1_qaida-al-qaida-loose-nuclear-materials.

24. Pakistan's Nuclear Weapons: Proliferation and Security Issues, Paul K. Kerr and Mary Beth Nikitin, October 15, 2009, Congressional Research Service, 7-5700, www.crs.gov, RL34248, Ganguly (2006), Ganguly and Paul Kapur (2009).

25. Secure Cyberspace, National Academy of Engineering, 2008, www. engineeringchallenges.org/cms/8996/9042.aspx.

26. Graham Allison, Nuclear Disorder, *Foreign Affairs,* January/February, pp. 74–85, 2010.

27. Rogue States and Proliferation: *How Serious is the Threat?* Institute For National Strategic Studies, Strategic Assessment, 1999, 219-227.

28. Sumit Ganguly and Devin Hagerty, 2006, 10.

29. Perkovich, 2001, 462.

30. Obama has charted an Afghan course. Britain must lead the way on Pakistan, Timothy Gordon Ash, *Guardian*, December 2, 2009.

31. Center for Disease Control (CDC) and Prevention, www.bt.cdc.gov/ bioterrorism/overview.asp.

32. The Model State Emergency Health Powers Act—Draft As of 23 October 2001, Washington, D.C.: Center for Law and the Public's Health at Georgetown and Johns Hopkins Universities.

33. Centers for Disease Control, Anthrax: What you need to know, www.bt.cdc. gov/agent/anthrax/needtoknow.asp.

34. Langwith, 2008.

35. The risk of chemical and biological terrorism: discussing chemical disarmament in relation with the risk, Armand Lattes, www.sfc.fr/Articles/ChemicalBiol Terrorism.pdf. Organization For The Prohibition Of Chemical Weapons (OPCW) Inventory of International Nonproliferation Organizations and Regimes© Center for Nonproliferation Studies Last Update: 5/11/2011, http://www.nti.org/e_research/ official_docs/inventory/pdfs/opcw.pdf.

36. Syria developing chemical weapons site: Jane's (AFP)—Feb 18, 2009. Rolf Mowatt-Larssen, Al Qaeda Weapons of Mass Destruction Threat: Hype or Reality? A Timeline of Terrorists' Efforts to Acquire WMD, Belfer Center for Science and International Affairs, January 2010, http://belfercenter.ksg.harvard.edu/publication/ 19852/al_qaeda_weapons_of_mass_destruction_threat.html. Statement of Rolf Mowatt-Larssen, April 2, 2008, www.congressional.energy.gov/documents/ April_2_-_Homeland_Sec-Larssen(1).pdf.

37. Adapted by the Anthony H. Cordesman, Office of Technology Assessment, Proliferation of Weapons Mass Destruction: Assessing the Risks, U.S. Congress OTA-ISC-559, Washington, August, 1993, 53-54. Revised: November 19, 2007; http://csis.org/files/media/csis/pubs/071119_iran.is&nuclearwar.pdf.

38. The International Weapons of Mass Destruction Commission met in Washington on 30 April 2009 under the chairmanship of Dr. Hans Blix to refocus attention on the comprehensive; Rolf Mowatt-Larssen, Al Qaeda Weapons of Mass Destruction Threat: Hype or Reality? A Timeline of Terrorists' Efforts to Acquire

WMD, Belfer Center for Science and International Affairs, January 2010, http://belfercenter.ksg.harvard.edu/publication/19852/al_qaeda_weapons_of_mass_destruction_threat.html. Statement of Rolf Mowatt-Larssen, April 2, 2008, www.congressional.energy.gov/documents/April_2_-_Homeland_Sec-Larssen (1).pdf.

39. John Measheimer, 2001 *The Tragedy of Power Politics*, New York, N.Y. W.W. Norton & Company, 2001, 128.

40. Mohanty, 1991, 1-210; 2006 Report, *Weapons of Terror: Freeing the World of Nuclear, Biological and Chemical Arms, 231 pages.* http://www.blixassociates. com/wp-content/uploads/2011/02/Weapons_of_Terror.pdf).

41. Mohanty, 1986, 1989, and 1990., Warland and Varaiya, 2000 Technology and Terrorism, www.tbmm.gov.tr/ul_kom/natopa/raporlar/bilimpercent 20vepercent20teknoloji/AUpercent20121percent20STCpercent20Terrorism.htm. Digital Technology, http://books.google.com/books?id=My7Zr0aP2L8C&pg= PA5&lpg=PA1&ie=ISO-8859-1&output=html.

42. U.S. Army warns of twittering terrorists, http://news.cnet.com/8301-1009_3-10075487-83.html, Twitter 'could be used by terrorists', claims U.S. army, www.telegraph.co.uk/technology/3358932/Twitter-could-be-used-by-terrorists-claims-US-army.html. Network Technologies for Networked Terrorists Assessing the Value of Information and Communication Technologies to Modern Terrorist Organizations, www.rand.org/pubs/technical_reports/2007/RAND_TR454.sum.pdf.

43. Furedi, 2007, 82.

44. Clarke, 2004, 65.

45. Vourpoulos and Womble, 2001, 459–468., G. Vourpoulos and P.C. Womble, *Pulsed Fast/Thermal Neutron Analysis: A Technique for Explosives Detection,* TALANTA, 54 (2001) 459-468, G. Eiceman, Editor, Elsevier Publisher, New York, 2001.

46. Sandra Maestre, Sean Nichols, ISM 4320-001, DNA Biometric, http://danishbiometrics.files.wordpress.com/2009/08/nst.pdf.

47. Ravi Das, Biometric technologies of the future, www.biometricnews.net/articles/Biometrics_Article_Biometrics_Of_The_Future.pdf.

48. DCSINT Handbook No. 102, Cyberoperation and Cyberterrorism, August 15, 2005, http://stinet.dtic.mil/cgi-bin/GetTRDoc?AD=ADA439217&Location= U2&doc=GetTRDoc.pdf.

49. Nobert Wiener, 1961., Mathematics of Terrorism, http://globalguerrillas. typepad.com/globalguerrillas/2009/04/journal-power-laws-and-terrorism.html.

50. CRS Report for Congress, Creating a National Framework for Cybersecurity: An Analysis of Issues and Options, Eric A. Fischer, Senior Specialist in Science and Technology, Resources, Science, and Industry Division, February 22, 2005, www.dtic.mil/cgi-bin/GetTRDoc?AD=ADA463076&Location=U2&doc= GetTRDoc.pdf; and The White House, *National Strategy to Secure Cyberspace,* February 2003, www.whitehouse.gov/pcipb/cyberspace_strategy.pdf. Also see, for example, F. William Connor and others, *Information Security Governance: A Call to Action,* Report of the Corporate Governance Task Force, April 2004,

www.cyberpartnership.org/init-governance.html, www.cs.georgetown. edu ~ den ning, www.nautilus.org/info-policy/workshop/papers/ ~ denning.html.

51. § 2510.Tittle 18, www.law.cornell.edu/uscode/18/2510.htm.

52. Cyber terrorism, J.J. Prichard and L. MacDonald, *Journal of Information Technology Education,* Vol. 3, 2004, http://jite.org/documents/Vol3/v3p279-289-150.pdf.

53. Govil 2007, Ramifications of Cyber Crime and Suggestive Preventive Measures, *IEEE, 43*(4), 610–615:

54. Cybercrime, http://electronics.ihs.com/news/iso-cyber-crime.htm, http://17799.denialinfo.com/Chapter6.htm.

55. Gary Ackerman and Jeremy Tamsett (Eds.), *Jihadists and Weapons of Mass Destruction,* CRC Press, Boca Raton, Florida, 2009, www.wordtrade.com/society/politics/counterterrorismR.htm, www.wordtrade.com/society/politics/counterterrorismR.htm. David Sanger, Obama Meets With a Parade of Leaders *New York Times*, April 11, 2010. Steven C. Welsh, Nuclear Terrorism Convention: International Convention for the Suppression of Acts of Nuclear Terrorism, May 17, 2005, www.un.int/usa/a-59-766.pdf. www.cdi.org/news/law/ntc.cfm. Annabelle Lee, Tanya Brewer (Ed.), Smart Grid Cyber Security Strategy and Requirements Advanced Security Acceleration Project—Smart Grid September 2009, NISTIR 7628 Smart Grid Cyber Security Strategy and Requirements —http://csrc.nist.gov/publications/drafts/nistir-7628/draft-nistir-7628.pdf.

56. Computer Spies Breach Fighter-Jet Project, By Siobhan Gorman, August Cole and Yochi Dreazen, *Wall Street Journal*, April 21, 2009.

57. U.S., South Korea Targeted in Swarm of Internet Attacks by *Ellen Nakashima, Brian Krebs and Blaine Harden,* July 9, 2009 *Washington Post,* July 9, 2009.

58. Terrorist Capability for Cyber Attack: Overview and Policy Issues, Jon Rollins and Clay Wilson, January 22, 2007, CRS Report, www.dtic.mil/cgi-bin/GetTRDoc?AD = ADA463774&Location = U2&doc = GetTRDoc.

59. Potential Terrorist Threat to the U.S. Information Infrastructure, 5 June 2007, http://nefafoundation.org/miscellaneous/FeaturedDocs/JHSA_Info Infrastructure.pdf.

60. CRS Report, Botnets, Cybercrime, and Cyberterrorism, Clay Wilson, January 29, 2008, http://fas.org/sgp/crs/terror/RL32114.pdf. Terrorist Capability for Cyber Attack: Overview and Policy Issues, Jon Rollins and Clay Wilson, January 22, 2007, CRS Report, www.dtic.mil/cgi-bin/GetTRDoc?AD = ADA463774& Location = U2&doc = GetTRDoc.pdf. Cyber Terrorism and Information Security, Brett Pladna, 2007, www.infosecwriters.com/text_resources/pdf/BPladna_Cyber_ Terrorism.pdf. *Trends in Terrorism*, July 21, 2006, Raphael Perl, CRS Report for Congress. http://fpc.state.gov/documents/organization/69479.pdf.

61. Clark and Levin, Securing the Information Highway, *Foreign Affairs*, November/December 2009.

62. The International Weapons of Mass Destruction Commission met in Washington on 30 April 2009 under the chairmanship of Dr. Hans Blix to refocus attention on the comprehensive recommendations of its 2006 Report, *Weapons of Ter-*

ror: Freeing the World of Nuclear, Biological and Chemical Arms, and in particular on those relating to nuclear non-proliferation and disarmament to redouble their efforts at the present hopeful and crucial time. (www.wmdcommission.org/) Rolf Mowatt-Larssen, Al Qaeda Weapons of Mass Destruction Threat: Hype or Reality? A Timeline of Terrorists' Efforts to Acquire WMD, Belfer Center for Science and International Affairs, January 2010, http://belfercenter.ksg.harvard.edu/publication/ 19852/al_qaeda_weapons_of_mass_destruction_threat.html.

63. Clarke and Knake, 2010, 11, 287; Reconsidering State Military Strategy for Strategic Cyberwarfare by Clement Guitton, Geneva School of Diplomacy and International Relations University Institute, 2010/2011. http://clement-guitton.eu/ data/GSD/Reconsidering%20state%20military%20strategy%20for%20strategic%20 cyberwarfare.pdf.

64. Gary Ackerman and Jeremy Tamsett (Eds.), *Jihadists and Weapons of Mass Destruction,* CRC Press, Boca Raton, Florida, 2009, www.wordtrade.com/society/politics/counterterrorismR.htm, www.wordtrade.com/society/politics/counter terrorismR.htm. Steven C. Welsh, Nuclear Terrorism Convention: International Convention for the Suppression of Acts of Nuclear Terrorism, May 17, 2005, www.un.int/usa/a-59-766.pdf. www.cdi.org/news/law/ntc.cfm. Annabelle Lee, Tanya Brewer (Ed.), Smart Grid Cyber Security Strategy and Requirements Advanced Security Acceleration Project—Smart Grid September 2009, NISTIR 7628 Smart Grid Cyber Security Strategy and Requirements–http://csrc.nist.gov/publications/drafts/nistir-7628/draft-nistir-7628.pdf. Franklin D. Kramer, Stuart H. Starr, and Larry Wentz (Eds.), 2009.

65. Dennis C. Blair, Director of National Intelligence, February 2, 2010, Annual report, Annual Threat Assessment of the U.S. Intelligence Community for the Senate Select Committee on Intelligence, www.dni.gov/testimonies/20100202_ testimony.pdf.

Chapter 6

Mitigation Strategies and Structures

> The Moving Finger writes; and, having writ,
> Moves on: nor all your Piety nor Wit
> Shall lure it back to cancel half a Line,
> Nor all your Tears wash out a Word of it.
> —*Ruba'iyat of Omar Khayyam (1048–1131)*

Preventive measures have been taken in various countries, in the aftermath of the 9/11 attacks. There are several counterinsurgency methodologies that can be used to combat terrorism, and they are currently being used in Afghanistan and Iraq. Psychological mitigation strategies can also prove effective.

To prevent terrorist attacks and threats, to take steps to foil holy militants' cultural war and global jihad, and to address their grievances, mitigation schemes have been developed and implemented in several countries. Mitigation strategies include a multitude of technical, economic, psychological, legal, diplomatic, and operational techniques. There are preemptive deterrence based on the nature of terrorist threats, dynamics, environments, and intelligence inputs. Military and non-military deterrence includes blocking economic aid, blocking ports, denying access to infrastructures, trade and other sanctions, declaring sponsoring states as terrorists and severing diplomatic ties, bombing terrorists' strongholds, and commando actions.

Counter-Terrorism in America, Asia, and Europe

Counter-terrorism provides offensive and defensive strategies intended to prevent belligerent acts, monitor and track terrorists, detect WMDs, stop terrorists by destroying their infrastructures, freeze their financial support, take multilateral actions to curb terrorist activities, and to implement both non-military and military responses. Terrorists work with local dissidents or religious groups before attacking targets in foreign countries or in their own country. They usually make contact with community cultural centers, clubs, and work places, and attend religious schools. These places usually have contacts with foreign embassies. Surveillance and monitoring of foreign visitors and others are carried out by many organizations, including the FBI and DHS in the United States, FSB/FSO in Russia, JIC/MI5 in the United Kingdom, BFV/LFV in Germany, IB/CBI in India, DGSE/DCRI in France, and MSS/PAP in China. They also keep track of information on terrorist activities. The classical approach is to detect and disrupt, prevent, protect, and prepare for response to terrorism. Figure 6.1 narrates the various structures and functionalities of the mitigation approaches.

According to the legal and counterterrorism expert, Professor Richard Posner:

> Some effort at attaching geographic and time coordinates to potential attacks may be feasible. Al Qaeda is likely to continue to focus on symbolic targets. Home grown Muslim terrorists are likely to operate in areas of substantial Muslim population, where they would not stand out from their surroundings.[1]

Symbolic targets have included the World Trade Center in New York City, the Pentagon and the White House in Washington, D.C., India's Parliament House, Taj Mahal Hotel, and the Gateway of India, and tourist resorts in Bali.

South Asia

As a geographic location, South Asia is a prime site for the serious observation and study of terrorism. A report from the Center on Global Counterterrorism Cooperation states:

> There was also discussion about the state of counterterrorism-related legislation across South Asia. It was noted that India, for example, has passed comprehensive anti-money-laundering and counter-terrorist financing legislation and set up a financial intelligence unit, while other States in the region are not as far along. Measures such as these, it was pointed out, were mandated by the UN Security Council in the aftermath of 9/11. The CTED (the UN Security Council's Counter-Terrorism Committee's Executive Directorate) and the United Nations Office on Drugs and Crime's Terrorism Prevention Branch, it was stressed, have been working with

Analytical Approaches

(i) Intelligence gathering: It is required in detecting and preventing terrorist attacks. The RAND Corporation has developed a seven step algorithm to analyze the intelligence input.

> The tool envisaged within the ASAP (Atypical Signal Analysis and Processing) concept is a computer network that would use a wide variety of "agents"—software applications that perform a specific function on data they receive as inputs—to collect, link, and analyze "dots" of intelligence information. These agents would move data through a series of steps. 1. The network would gather information from a set of external databases, 2. The network would store this data within a structured information pool, 3. *Detection agents* would find the "dots" in this pool, 4. *Relationship agents* would search for other information related to the "dots," 5. *Hypothesis agents* would create possible interpretations of what the linked dots mean (presence or absence), 6. *Testing agents* would run tests to determine whether these hypotheses are correct. If a hypothesis that indicates certain linked data are threatening proved to be accurate, the data would warrant significant concern, and 7. The network would prioritize the results of the tests, forwarding high-priority outcomes to human analysts.[4]

(ii) Data Mining (extraction and classification): Mining of financial, travel, and other data regarding personal actions and circumstances other than mere association with questionable individuals and groups is one such technique. The potential for such data mining goes well beyond current usage. Yet, data mining for counter-terrorism purposes will always require a major investment in obtaining and manipulating the data in return for only a modest narrowing of the search for terrorists. Numerous practical difficulties in gaining access to personal information, significant privacy issues, and the lack of a reliable algorithm for processing the data all inhibit the effectiveness of this technique.[5]

(iii) Counter-Terrorism Rules and Handbook:[6] This Handbook describes in plain language the most critical counter-terrorism measures in effect as of March 15, 2004 of relevance to U.S. nonprofits and grant makers: (a) Executive Order 13224, (b) The Patriot Act and Related Laws, (c) Embargoes and Trade Sanctions, (d) IRS Rules, (e) Treasury Guidelines—"Voluntary Best Practices," and (f) Additional Requirements for Organizations Funded by USAID.

The detailed prosecution is discussed in the Department of Justice, Counterterrorism White Paper, June 22, 2006, using the Patriot Act, financial monitoring, immigration fraud and surveillance.[7]

The DHS provides the following counter-terrorism measures,[8] besides border security and measures related to immigration: protecting, analyzing and sharing information, protecting infrastructure, protecting against fraud and counterfeiting, aviation security, cyber security, chemical security, law enforcement, and secure identification. The DHS is concerned with cyber-infrastructures, which include information and communications systems and services and the information contained in these systems and services. Information and communications systems and services are composed of all hardware and software that process, store, and communicate information, or any combination of all of these elements. Processing includes the creation, access, modification, and destruction of information storage, routing, and distribution of computer systems. For example: computer systems; control systems (e.g., SCADA); networks, such as the Internet; and cyber services (e.g., managed security services) are part of the cyber infrastructure. (See Chapter 5)

The DHS provides the following guidelines: "The Seven Signs of Terrorism:

1. Surveillance: Someone recording or monitoring activities. This may include the use of cameras (either still or video), note taking, drawing diagrams, annotating on maps, or using binoculars or other vision-enhancing devices.
2. Elicitation: People or organizations attempting to gain information about military operations, capabilities, or people. Elicitation attempts may be made by mail, fax, telephone, or in person.
3. Tests of security: Any attempts to measure reaction times to security breaches or to penetrate physical security barriers or procedures in order to assess strengths and weaknesses.
4. Acquiring supplies: Purchasing or stealing explosives, weapons, ammunition, etc. Also includes acquiring military uniforms, decals, flight manuals, passes or badges (or the equipment to manufacture such items) or any other controlled items.
5. Suspicious persons out of place: People who don't seem to belong in the workplace, neighborhood, business establishment, or anywhere else. Includes suspicious border crossings and stowaways aboard ship or people jumping ship in port.
6. Dry Run/Trial Run: Putting people into position and moving them around according to their plan without actually committing the terrorist act. This is especially true when planning a kidnapping, but it can also pertain to bombings. An element of

this activity could also include mapping out routes and determining the timing of traffic lights and flow.

7. Deploying assets: People and supplies getting into position to commit the act. This is a person's last chance to alert authorities before the terrorist act occurs."[9]

European Approaches

Several European countries, including Belgium, France, Germany, Italy, Spain, and the United Kingdom, are working with the United Sates in the aftermath of the terrorist attacks in the United States, the U.K., and Spain, but none has a separate homeland security organization. In each of these countries, security and counterterrorism efforts are scattered throughout various ministries.

> Different countries maintain different priorities in spending for homeland security, but most have devoted increased funds over the last several years to intelligence and law enforcement efforts against terrorism. Funding for measures to strengthen transport security, improve emergency preparedness and response, counter chem-bio incidents, and protect critical national infrastructure are more difficult to determine and compare among the countries, given that responsibility for these various issues is often spread among the budgets of different government ministries.

The approaches of many European countries to protecting their publics and infrastructure have grown out of decades of experience in dealing with domestic terrorist groups. Even after the terrorist attacks of the last few years, European countries have continued to view combating terrorism primarily as a task for law enforcement and intelligence authorities. The United Kingdom has a cross-departmental strategy of prevent, pursue, protect, and prepare in the context of counterterrorism. Germany, the home of three 9/11 attackers, revoked the immunity of religious groups and charities from investigation or surveillance by authorities, as well as their special privileges under right of assembly, allowing the government greater freedom to act against extremist groups. It is now possible to prosecute terrorists in Germany, even if they belong to foreign terrorist organizations, curtail the ability of extremists to enter and reside in Germany, and strengthen border and aviation security. However, the European Union wants to address the rise of young Euro-Islamist immigrants who live in Europe, who are well educated and ostensibly integrated, shut off from Western values, but nevertheless thriving in the heart of Europe, and interested in pursuing global jihad.[10]

The Organization for Security and Cooperation in Europe (OSCE) is a European organization whose focus is combating terrorism. It recognizes that the United Nations plays the leading role in counter-terrorism matters from a global perspective. The OSCE is a regional arrangement under Chapter VIII of the UN Charter. It is actually the largest regional organization of its kind, with fifty-six participating states, spanning North America to Central Asia. It also has eleven partner countries in North Africa, the Middle East, and Asia. Moreover, the OSCE has a comprehensive security mandate, as opposed to the specialized mandates of some other organizations. The position of the OSCE vis-a-vis terrorism was highlighted in a decision adopted unanimously in the aftermath of the 9/11 attacks against the United States. Terrorist acts, in all aspects, committed no matter when, where or by whom, are a threat to international and regional peace, security and stability. Those terrorists who are perpetrating, financing, harboring or otherwise supporting those responsible for such criminal acts, should be denied any safe heaven and shelter. Terrorism, whatever its motivation or origin, has no justification to commit suicide attacks and bombing civilian targets.

Overall, OSCE is an important counter-terrorism organization that has five main objectives:

1. Building political support;
2. Enhancing the capacity of states to counter terrorism;
3. Identifying cutting edge threats and options for response;
4. Fostering international co-operation on counter-terrorism issues, and
5. Promoting security within the framework of human rights.

"Countering terrorism requires minimizing the recruitment of new members by terrorist groups. Thus, countering radicalization and violent extremism that lead to terrorism is a strategic area of importance." (Countering Terrorism: the OSCE as a Regional Model, Raphael F. Perl, testimony before the U.S. Congress.

Like AQ, the GIA (Armed Islamist Group) of Algeria wanted to spread global jihad. They considered France to be the center of the anti-Islamic movement in the 1990s. French authorities found connections between the GIA, Algerian terrorist Ahmed Ressam, who came from Canada with a trunk full of explosives to attack the Los Angeles International Airport on December 14, 1999, and AQ terrorists.

The French government eventually concentrated its efforts at home and created a system for monitoring, preventing, protecting against and pursuing terrorists that far outstrips, in terms of its invasiveness and effectiveness, anything the U.S. has been willing to do even after 11 September.[11]

Modeling and Simulation[12]

A simulation of terrorist threats can be performed utilizing game theory. Game theory, a branch of mathematics, has been applied to modeling the strategic situation in terrorism, both at the micro level and the macro level, and in counter terrorism. Hijacking and hostage taking are micro-level infractions, while a country's response, like a war on terror, is a macro-level response to a large-scale terrorist event like the 9/11 attack. Terrorists want to pursue their demands and counter terrorists want to deny them. Much decision-making is necessary on both sides. A payoff matrix can be generated by each player, the terrorist and counter terrorist. Consider an example in which terrorists want to bomb an oil site and the counter terrorist is a guard (ready or not ready) to prevent it. The possible outcomes are as follows (a). Terrorists drive through checkpoint unnoticed; (b). Terrorist drives through the checkpoint and shoots the guard, killing him; (c). Terrorist drives through the checkpoint, shoots the guard, misses, and gets killed; (d). Terrorist gets caught by the guard. In each outcome a payoff matrix can be constructed. One is that getting caught is the only situation that provides the terrorist with deep embarrassment. Planting the bomb and escaping as well as shooting the guard and escaping provides the greatest level of utility (slightly less so if they are noticed by an unready guard). This is because both of those situations allow the terrorist to complete the objective and return home and continue helping out the group. The next level down is shooting the guard and dying.

Although seemingly nonsensical, it is preferable for the terrorist to die in a shoot-out with guards rather than be caught and imprisoned. The utility values are determined based on cardinality that implies that the individual numbers don't matter, but rather the relations of each number to other numbers does matter. It would be possible for those protecting against terrorist attacks to conduct data-mining and come up with actual utility values. This data would be invaluable to people on the ground because it would enable them to make the most intelligent strategic interactions in their particular situation. Knowing how much more the terrorist prefers dying than being caught is important in coming up with strategic plans to fight terrorists in this situation and similar situations. Nash equilibrium (named after John Nash, a concept of game theory where the optimal outcome of a game is one where no player has an incentive to deviate from his or her chosen strategy after considering an opponent's choice, other player), basically speaking, is an equilibrium wherein all sub-matrices are optimally selected. Game theory is used to an allocation of resources between defense and preemption in the counter-terrorism world. Assume that America and Canada, two partners in the war against terrorists, are equally targeted by the same terrorist group. The United States can preempt terrorists, or they can defend against them, or do nothing (inaction). Canada has the same options. Preemption: Assume that it costs 8 points to preempt, and the return on that expenditure is 6 points. The U.S. preempts and gets a -2 (6 – 8 = -2), and Canada does nothing and gets a 6 (6+0), i.e., the outcome for USA and Canada is (-2, 6). If each country does nothing, it leads to a zero-zero, (0.0) outcome for both countries, which is a Nash Equilibrium because neither country has incentive to preempt, regardless of what the other country does. But this is vulnerable to terrorism. Defending: defending costs 6 points and returns 8 points to the defending country alone. But, the defenders' efforts make the other country more vulnerable and cost them 6 points. If they both defend, they each spend 6, get 8 back, but are cost another 6 by the other country's defense (8 – 6 – 6 = -4).This gives (-4, -4). If USA preempts and Canada defends, the outcome is (-8, 8) or America defends and Canada preempts, the outcome is (8, -8). The Nash Equilibrium is mutual defense, because the other two options have one country losing 8.[13]

Counterinsurgency (COIN)

An insurgency is a rebellion within a country with extraterritorial affiliations, often paid for by other countries, or by an invading army that works with dissident groups, against a legitimate, ruling regime through subversion, mobilizing dissident civilians, and sporadic armed conflict. The insurgency's objective is to overthrow the government or seize the country by force. Insurgents are also called militants, extremists, terrorists, radicals, jihadists, holy warriors, or freedom fighters. An insurgency is being operated by the Taliban in Afghanistan, Iranian supported sectarian groups in Iraq, Palestinian groups in Israel, and separatists in Chechnya in Russia, Xinjiang in China, and Kashmir in India, among other places. In Palestine, the insurgency is called the Intifada, "the uprising." There are political, religious, separatist, and ideological radicals, and sectarian insurgents. They are often supported by outside powers for strategic, territorial gain, trade, or for oil exploration. They find safe havens in neighboring countries. Like terrorists, insurgents are an invisible, proxy army. Counterinsurgency is meant to dispel the rebellion by comprehensive military, paramilitary, political, economic, psychological, diplomatic, and civic actions at all levels and to address the roots of insurgency.[14] Insurgency is an offensive approach involving all elements of national and international power; it can take place across the range of operations and spectrum of conflict. Religious insurgents are against secularism, democracy, pluralism, gender equality, education and employment for women, and modernism. The main goal of the Islamic radical insurgency is to establish a worldwide caliphate on the rubble of Western democracy and non-Muslim civilizations. That resolve can be defeated by a joint effort by all civilized countries that are, or can be, subject to such terrorism. Some measures on counterinsurgencies have been proposed by the counterterrorism and military experts Daniel Marston and Carter Malkasian. They have noted the fundamental issues of complexities of counterinsurgency strategies of General Sir Frank Kitson: The first thing must be apparent when contemplating the sort of action which a government facing insurgency should take, is that there can be no such thing as a purely military solution because insurgency is not primarily a military activity. At the same time, there is no such thing as a wholly political solution either, short of surrender, because the very fact that a state of insurgency exists implies that violence is involved which will have to be countered to some extent at least by the use of force. The counterinsurgency, COIN, mainly includes political processes, economic development, educational and employment inducements to youth, social reform, security measures and surveillance, border controls, the checking of insurgent funds, contacts, and movements, media persuasions, demographic transfers, and strong administrative, law enforcement, and judicial organizations. Some time, known as nation building, cannot be successfully implemented by a regular army. It may require to divide them, bribe them, and to offer amnesty indirectly, but not yielding to their illegitimate demands. Jihadists want to establish Sharia. When the Taliban came to power in Afghanistan, they adopted Sharia, adopting very orthodox systems, and regressive ideologies of the seventh century. African countries like Sudan, Somalia, Nigeria and others are fighting with terrorists over their version of Sharia. Terrorists want the worldwide Islam through jihad. Any counterinsurgency must deal with the insurgents who are an army of martyrs. It is naïve to suggest that the withdrawal of troops from Afghanistan and Iraq and a reasonable settlement of the Palestine problem will end terrorism and insurgency. The 9/11 attacks were planned much before these wars, even while America initiated several peace accords between Israel and Arab countries. Military actions are not always the correct answer to insurgency. There are two classic counterinsurgency models devised by Gallieni in French Indochina and Sir Robert Thompson in British-run Malaya.

America has been providing aid to Muslim countries and others for counterinsurgency measures. The top 16 recipients of U.S. foreign aid in

2005 (in billions) are: 1. Israel 2.58, 2. Egypt 1.84, 3. Afghanistan 0.98, 4. Pakistan 0.70, 5. Colombia 0.57, 6. Sudan 0.50, 7. Jordan 0.48, 8. Uganda 0.25, 9. Kenya 0.24, 10. Ethiopia 0.19, 11. South Africa 0.19, 12. Peru 0.19, 13. Indonesia 0.18, 14. Bolivia 0.18, 15. Nigeria 0.18, and 16. Zambia 0.18.[15] It is alleged that most of the aid has been channeled to terrorists and insurgents by the recipient countries. The priority must be to completely dry up the resources of the insurgents, and their supporters and sympathizers, who may be disguised as human rights organizations, charity organizations, or nongovernmental organizations. It must be recognized that these insurgents are often trained in other countries, such as Afghanistan and Pakistan. The outside training posts are to be taken out militarily, diplomatically, or by economic sanctions. America has lately been successful in targeting insurgents' safe havens in the Pakistan-Afghanistan badlands with aerial drone attacks. Insurgents use human rights organizations to protest when civilians, particularly women and children, are killed. The counterterrorism specialist Daniel Benjamin[16] has warned:

> Terrorism is going to be a fact of life for the foreseeable future. In the case of jihadist terror, the ideology is durable and has, for some Muslims, a compelling authenticity because of its appropriation of canonic Muslim texts. To a significant extent, the ideology cannot be disproven, though repeated setbacks may convince followers that it is a dead end.

Insurgents and terrorists know no Eastern or Western sensibilities, compassion, kindness, or mercy. They will shoot people who feed them or help them when they are traveling toward their targets. They believe that their lives will only improve after physical death. Sebestyen Gorka[17] has conducted a survey of the trends in counterinsurgency, which have also been studied extensively by David Ucko,[18] Ganesh Sitaraman,[19] David Kilcullen,[20] Army,[21] K.I. Sepp,[22] Cohen,[23] and N.A. Foster.[24] Although counterinsurgency is largely a military matter, it also encompasses constitutional concerns for domestic and international purposes.[25] Counterinsurgency is temporary, transitional, and tactical, designed to ensure stability, allowing the constitutional systems come later. It can be made permanent, constant, and normal. But the conflicts in Iraq and Afghanistan demonstrate the fallacy of these perceptions. Counterinsurgency and constitutional design took place simultaneously that required high-level political agreement, ground realities, accommodating politics, law, and security. Iraq and Afghanistan demonstrate that these two enterprises are not different and disconnected, but rather intricately interconnected and desirably useful. Graeme Steven and Rohan Gunaratna write:

In combating terrorism, the criminal justice model (CJM) prioritizes the preservation of democratic principles as being fundamental in the fight against terror, even at the expense of reduced effectiveness of counter-terrorism measures. The war model (WM) places a stronger emphasis on restraining or countering terrorism rather than upholding liberal democratic rights. . . There are three stages in building a COIN system. First, it must proceed in *phases* over a prolonged time to observe the system. 2. It must adapt to the conditions, culture, and characteristics of the place and 3. It must interact with local, provincial, national, and global administration. The main purposes of the counterinsurgencies are: 1. Democratization—a very fair, transparent election that includes the participation of people, particularly minorities. (For example, representation of Hazras and Tajiks, and others in Afghanistan and Sunni, Turks, and Christian minorities in Iraq), 2. Development of local and national police, and army and civilian governments to provide clean and fair administrations, and to create an irregular army, that never yields to communal or sectarian threats, 3. External support, military and economic, of insurgency must be eliminated, 4. Preserve local culture, tradition, language, and sensibilities, 5. Secular education and freedom to worship, 6. Economic development, creating employment opportunities, and 7. Reservation and representation of women in all areas.[26]

A counterinsurgency model has been constructed in Figure 6.2, similar to the work of counterterror expert David Kilcullen.

Insurgents take advantage of the sympathy and support of the religious community, as they are fighting, and dying for the cause of their religion and their culture. They use and exploit the community mosques as their command and control centers to hide their weapons, knowing that the counterinsurgency forces will not desecrate the sacred spaces. Insurgents and terrorists avoid visibility in their dress, appearance, luxuries, and other categories. They mingle with their community and stay in secure places that are not visited by police and military personnel. There they meet with community leaders, recruit possible jihadists, and collect information. In Iraq, insurgents live in urban areas and take refuge in sacred places so that American forces will not attack those places. In Afghanistan, insurgents move to rural places where they find support and shelter with a few security forces. In Najaf, Iraq, the U.S. military avoided direct attack against the Imam Ali shrine, the most sacred place for Shiite Muslims. The most sacred Muslim places prohibit the entrance of non-Muslims, and the Grand Mosque at Mecca does not allow non-Muslims within a 20-mile radius of the mosque.

What follows is a discussion of counterinsurgency measures in Afghanistan, Iraq, and India.

***Figure 6.2. Counterinsurgency Model Showing
Interconnections and Functional Interface***

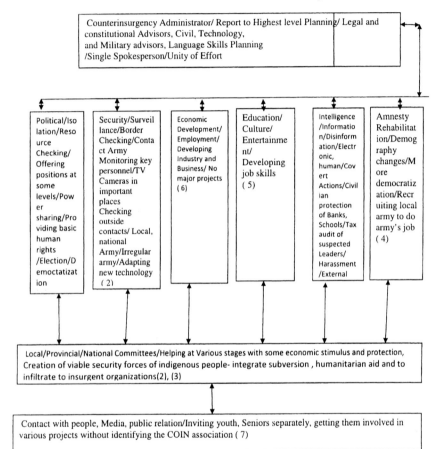

Afghanistan

Afghanistan served as a buffer country between British India and the former
Soviet Union. Its populace is largely Pashtun (also known as Pakhtuns or
Pathans), comprising 42 per cent of the population, but it has a significant
number of other minorities including Tajiks, Uzbek, and Hazras. Most of
them are Muslims (80 per cent Sunnis and 20 per cent Shiites, or Hazras).
When India attained independence in 1947, Afghanistan was demarcated
with the Durand Line, which divided the Pashtuns between Pakistan and

Afghanistan. The Durand Line was deliberately set where it would bring chaos among the Pashtuns in the Khyber Pakhtunkhwa (KP. aka North West Frontier Province, NWFP) in Pakistan, and in the Pashtun provinces of Farah and Ghazni in Afghanistan. The area was part of the famous Silk Road, the first international highway. (Besides silk, paper, spices and other goods, the Silk Road carried religion, the arts, literature, and painting, which was equally significant to world history. The spread of Buddhism was launched from northwestern India to modern Pakistan, Afghanistan, Central Asia, Xinjiang, China, Korea, and Japan.) Afghanistan was the only country that opposed Pakistan's entry into the UNO, because of the disputed boundary. The Afghanistan insurgency has been and continues to be a conflation of poor governance, ethnic conflict, difficult economic conditions, and the dominance of warlords. Part of the problem was Pakistan's strategic use of the Pakistani Taliban against the Tajik forces led by Burhauddin Rabbani and against the Uzbek forces led by General Rashid Dostum. Sunnis and Shiites killed each other in ethnic conflict with deaths numbering 8,000. In 1996, OBL came to Afghanistan as a refugee and supported the Taliban with his money and his AQ organization. Afghanistan's minority communities formed the Northern Alliance to fight against Pashtun-dominated Taliban rule. Two days before 9/11, two AQ members, posing as journalists, killed the Northern Alliance's Tajik Commander General Massoud. With the American invasion after 9/11, alienated, disgruntled Pashtuns became insurgents.

The counterinsurgency began with the coalition forces fighting against the Taliban insurgents and other factions, which had been led by Haqqani Networks and Hizb-e-Islami's Gulabuddin since 2001. All these groups used Pakistan's FATA as their sanctuaries. The counterinsurgency campaign under Lt. General David Barno conducted an operation based on the theories of Robert Thompson (Malaysia), David Galula (French Indochina), and Frank Kitson (Northern Ireland). By 2007, the United States had more than 22,000 personnel working in counterterrorism and counter insurgency along with the British-led Provincial Reconstruction Team (PRT), U.S.-led Operation Enduring Freedom (OED), NATO-led International Security Assistance Force (ISAF), and indigenous local forces including the Afghanistan National Police (ANP) and the Afghanistan National Army (ANA). The insurgents have access to the Afghani narcotics trade that accounts for 50 per cent of Afghanistan's GDP. As the insurgency requires both political and military solutions, the counterinsurgency theorists are against a total military solution. The abolition of the opium trade (which accounts for 90 per cent of the world's opium production) will foment more insurgency. Insurgency in Afghanistan is not like in Vietnam, Malaysia, or Northern Ireland. The enemy is spread everywhere and can use a variety of effective tools. Plus, Afghanistan is strategically important to Pakistan, Iran, India, China, America, and Russia, and has the ingredient of global jihad due to the support of countries like Iran, Egypt, Syria, and Libya, all of which are behind the resurgence of radical Islam (see Chapter 2).

One of the most important ways of curbing the insurgency is to eliminate external support. Rand security specialist Seth G. Jones writes that

> Another U.S. intelligence assessment unambiguously concluded: Al-Qa'eda has been able to retain a safehaven in Pakistan's Federally Administered Tribal Areas (FATA) that provides the organization many of advantages it once derived from its base across the border in Afghanistan, albeit on a smaller and less secure scale. The FATA serves as a staging area for al-Qa'eda attacks In support of the Taliban in Afghanistan as well as a location for training new terrorists operatives, for attacks in Pakistan, the Middle East, Africa, Europe and the United States. . . . In addition, insurgents were also able to gain significant assistance from the international jihadi network and neighboring states, such as Pakistan and Iran.[27]

The insurgency in Afghanistan has sponsors and financial backers outside Afghanistan. Many experts, including the counter insurgency expert David Kilcullen, have reported that members of Pakistan's armed services, civil armed forces, and other government agencies have directly and indirectly supported the insurgency. Whether the insurgency inside Afghanistan is now self sustaining or would wither without its active sanctuary on the Pakistani side of the Durand Line is something of an open question. In his views, since there is very little practical prospect of the active sanctuary diminishing anytime soon. It is likely to continue with the outside support. (Afghanistan has never accepted the Durand Line that favors Pakistan.)

According to the journalist Cathy Gannon (2005),

> The endorsement by Pakistan of Afghanistan insurgency goes back to 1979. For jihad in Afghanistan, against the Soviets, the CIA and the ISI were two strands of one thread. The relationship between jihad and the Pakistan military is as old as the Pakistan army. Jihad has been the motivating concept for the USA troops since day one. The United States also pumped out inspirational literature of its own for the Afghan refugee camps, where U.S.-printed school books taught the alphabet by using such examples as J is for Jihad, and K for Kalashnikov, and I for infidel.[28]

The counterinsurgency in Afghanistan is being foiled by another Afghan warlord, Siraj Haqqani, who is sheltered in Pakistan with the help of the Pakistani Army. Pakistan supports Mr. Haqqani and his control of large areas of Afghan territory as it is vital to Pakistan in the jostling for influence that will pit Pakistan, India, Russia, China and Iran against one another in the post-American Afghan arena. Siraj Haqqani has around 12,000 Taliban under his command. He is technically a member of the Afghan Taliban leadership based in Quetta, the capital of Pakistan's Baluchistan Province. That leadership is headed by Mullah Omar, the former leader of the Taliban regime. But Mr. Haqqani operates fairly independently of them inside Afghanistan. He funds his operations in part through kidnappings and other illicit activities. The Haqqani network held David Rohde, a correspondent for *New York Times*, for seven months.

Afghanistan's national security advisor, former foreign minister, Rangin Spanta has reportedly said that dismantling the terrorist infrastructure is a central component of Afghanistan's anti-terror strategy, and this requires confronting the state that still sees terrorism as a strategic asset and foreign policy tool. But global efforts to counter terrorism will not succeed until and unless there is clarity on who are Afghanistan's friends and foes. While Afghanistan is losing dozens of men and women to terrorist attacks every day, the terrorists' main mentor (Pakistan) continues to receive billions of dollars in aid and assistance.

Sajid Mir (of LeT, a retired major of Pakistan army) had spent two years using a Pakistani-American operative named David Coleman Headley to conduct meticulous reconnaissance on Mumbai, according to investigators and court documents. "Lashkar is not just a tool of the ISI, but an ally of al-Qaeda that participates in its global jihad," said Jean-Louis Bruguiere, a French judge who investigated Mir. "Today Pakistan is the heart of the terrorist threat. And it may be too late to do anything about it."[29]

Pakistani strategists built Lashkar into a proxy army against India in the disputed territory of Kashmir. Mir went into Lashkar's international operations wing, which embraced global jihad in the 1990s. Lashkar militants joined wars in Afghanistan, Bosnia and Chechnya and built global recruitment and financing networks. Lashkar trained tens of thousands of holy warriors. After the Sept. 11 attacks, Mir began grooming foreign volunteers who had come to Pakistan to wage war on the West.

Mir's recruits included four militants from the Virginia suburbs. They were part of a multiethnic crew of college graduates, U.S. Army veterans and gun enthusiasts whose spiritual leader was Ali Al-Timimi, an Iraqi-American imam based in Falls Church. The Pakistani army supplied crates of weapons with filed-off serial numbers. The mountains (in Pakistan) teemed with more than 3,000 trainees. Although Pakistanis dominated the ranks, there were Americans, Arabs, Australians, Azeris, Britons, Chechens, Filipinos, Kurds, Singaporeans, Turks and Uzbeks. In summer 2007, Bruguiere met at the White House with a top security adviser to President George W. Bush. The French judge shared his fears about Lashkar and his suspicion that Pakistani President Pervez Musharraf was playing a double game (see Epilogue).

Iraq

It was a grave mistake on the part of the U.S. to jump into a unilateral war in Iraq just after the Taliban and AQ retreated to the Tora Bora Mountains in Afghanistan near the legendary Khyber Pass. This action alienated Muslims, and ignored the worldwide public opinion, which was negative in light of the fact that there were no insurgents, no AQ, and no WMD in Iraq. It was a blunder strategically, politically, and militarily. Whether Saddam Hussein was a brutal or benign dictator, he was not a threat to America or Israel because he was against radical Islam, AQ, and its sponsors, Saudi Arabia and Iran. Iraq's arch enemy, Shiite Iran, was delighted with President George W. Bush's decision to invade Sunni Iraq. America's invasion of Iraq was meant to oust secularist Saddam Hussein, a former ally of America, and to destroy all its WMDs. Saddam Hussein fled into hiding and later died at the hands of Iraq's Shia dominated judicial system, which vehemently loathed him. The majority Shias were against America's occupation, but were not able to wrest power from the Sunnis, who were in control during Saddam Hussein's reign. On the advice of a few Pentagon consultants and flawed intelligence, America believed that Iraqis would welcome them and that they would be able to establish democracy. AQ's Abu Musab al-Zarqawi, founder of al-Tawhid wal-Jihad, the AQ of Iraq (AQI), was killed on June 7, 2006 by a U.S. aerial bombing, and Shiite religious leader Ayatollah Ali Sistani has become a powerful force. Iraq's population consists of Shias (65 per cent), Sunnis (32 per cent, Arabs are 10% of the Muslim world), and Christians (3 per cent, down from 7 per cent 50 years ago). Sunnis and Shiites had always fought, killing untold hundreds[30] and destroying each other's mosques and shrines, including the famous and fabulous Askriya Mosque in Samarra on February 22, 2006. On the toppling of Saddam Hussein, the Shia expert Professor Vali Nasr[31] writes:

> By toppling Saddam Hussein, the Bush administration has liberated and empowered Iraq's Shiite majority and has helped launch a broad Shiite revival that will upset the sectarian balance in Iraq and the Middle East for years to come. This development is rattling some Sunni Arab governments, but for Washington, it could be a chance to build bridges with the region's Shiites, especially in Iran.

It is indeed complex because of the powerful Ba'athists party.

> Shi'a leaders, including Prime Minister Nuri al Maliki's new government, considered militias merely a form of protection against the real threat to Iraq—the Ba'athists (Saddam Hussein's party) and AQI. The growth of the Iraqi Army (as well as the Badr Corps and Jayash al Mahdi) and majority control over the new democratic government gave Shi'a leaders little reason to compromise. Consequently, they rejected serious attempts at political reconciliation or restraining attacks upon the Sunnis.

Fallujah city leaders, a stronghold of Sunnis, were of the opinion that "Baghdad is in chaos. Iran hands are everywhere."

As of June 10, 2009, deaths from invasion and occupation reached more than 92,489, a number compiled by an independent UK/U.S. group, the Iraq Body Count project (IBC). With the removal of Saddam Hussein, there was severe turmoil amounting to near anarchy, with the emergence of several militia groups supported by AQ. As of August 30, 2009, according to a CNN count, there had been 4,657 coalition troop deaths—4,340 Americans, 2 Australians, 1 Azerbaijani, 179 Britons, 13 Bulgarians, 1 Czech, 7 Danes, 2 Dutch, 2 Estonians, 1 Fijian, 5 Georgians, 1 Hungarian, 33 Italians, 1 Kazakh, 1 South Korean, 3 Latvians, 22 Poles, 3 Romanians, 5 Salvadorans, four Slovaks, 11 Spaniards, 2 Thai and 18 Ukrainians. America's Abrams tanks and Bradley fighting vehicles were idling in the urban areas of Iraq while insurgents and Ba'athist forces (Saddam Hussein's party) were taking shelter inside urban neighborhoods, conducting roadside and suicide bombings, and mortar shelling. The army was also targeting high-value terrorists hideouts with all its battalions, brigades, and divisions, causing a great deal of collateral damage and further alienating the population. With the arrival of General David Petraeus, the counterinsurgency took a different path, securing populations' participation, particularly that of the Sunnis. The main two objectives of the counterinsurgencies—democratization and the formation of a national Iraq Army—have been unsuccessful mainly because the Sunnis think that the Maliki government, which is based on Iraq's having a Shia majority, is not the answer to Iraq's prosperity and peace. It also denies them safety, security, power, and their religious grandeur. In addition to several thousand deaths and cultural devastation, the cost of the failed war in Iraq from 2001 to 2010 is $1.1 trillion. The U.S. troop level in Iraq was 130,000 in November 2009 and may be reduced to 100,000 in 2010. (Lives Lost in Iraq: at least 186,924, March 20, 2003 to Sept 17, 2009, U.S. & Coalition casualties in Iraq are 4,662.)

In spite of both counterinsurgency operations, in Afghanistan and Iraq, insurgents' access to neighboring countries for arms, training, personnel, and supplies have continued unabated. The noted author Michael Scheuer writes,

> In Afghanistan, Washington refused to close the border with Pakistan, and as we are seeing today, the Taliban and AQ escaped to regroup, rearm, train, and fight another day. In Iraq, the president did not order the U.S. military to close the borders, and so the country's Islamist insurgents, Sunni and Shia, have had a constant and religious flow of fighters, ordinance, and funding, provided by the private and public sectors of neighboring countries, with which to kill U.S. service personnel.[32]

In Iraq, the insurgents are two mutually opposing armies of Sunnis and Shiites fighting on behalf of Iran and Saudi Arabia, while America's counterinsurgency is caught between them in a religious war going back to the inception of Islam. The noted NBC jouralist Richard Engel notes:

> Sunni purists like Wahabis and Salafists claim Shiites are not true monotheists because of their reverence of Ali and Hussein as saints. They call them refuters because they do not accept the Sunnah, or the teachings and traditions of the Prophet Mohammed as described by his disciples.[33]

The refuters are considered worse than infidels and more dangerous because they corrupt Islam from within. The most holy places of Wahhabis and Salafis are in Saudi Arabia, while the most holy places of Shiites are in Najfa—the tomb of Ali Ibn Abi Talib, the founder of Shiite Islam, and Karbala—the tomb of Ali's martyred son Hussein, both in Iraq. Iran's involvement in Iraq, in whatever extent or manner, or the Shiite victory in elections is not acceptable to Sunnis. In the second week of December 2009, five explosions were set off by Sunni suicide bombers targeting ministries, a university, and the Institute of Fine Arts, killing more than 127 in Bagdad.

COIN in India

The number, nature, and diversity of India's counterinsurgencies were born out of the partition of India in 1947, an event that was finalized hastily with strategic interest as the top criteria. COIN in India was not planned and manned properly, and has been particularly unsuccessful in Jammu and Kashmir, as Pakistan has foiled the strategy with the influx of trained mujahedeen veterans of the Afghan. Some of the deradicalization methods include economic support to individuals and their families, employment to individuals, secular modern education in *madrassas,* isolation from radical mosques and the attendant socialization processes, educational and cultural exchanges, constructing civil facilities such as hospitals, roads, and amusement parks following the Saudi method (see Chapter 4), and respecting the Kashmiriyat—the ethnonational and social consciousness and cultural values of the Kashmiri people (see Chapter 4). Radicalization with indoctrination to jihad is provided by a centralized network and by distributive networks through mosques, *madrassas,* training centers, Internet, CDs and DVDs, and personal communications. Deradicalization involves the dismantling and destroying of these networks, and the COIN does not have that capability.

Besides sending Afghanistan war–mujahedeen veterans to the Kashmir Valley since 1990s, funded and operated by its ISI, to foment unrest and destabilization of Jammu and Kashmir, Pakistan started its nuclear weapons arsenal as a deterrence against India. Pakistan, however, has denied of possession of any nuclear arsenals. By the end of May 2001, the world's two new nuclear powers were almost engaging in a nuclear war. A senior State Department official said:

> When she (Benazir Bhutto) stood on the floor of the United States Congress (June 1989), promising, to thunderous applause, that Pakistan neither possessed nor intended to assemble a nuclear bomb—the very day after she had received a detailed briefing on the weapons program from the director of the CIA—her worth was diminished in the eyes of the United States.

General Musharraf was using the Islamist's fervor for the battle of Kashmir.

> For bin Laden—along with many Pakistani Islamists—there were three signposts along the road: the jihad, which politicized him; the Persian Gulf War, which radicalized him; the Palestine intifada—combined with his sharp criticism of the repressive policies of Arab regimes—which gave him a cause that resonated on Arab streets. For Pakistanis, there was also the battle of Kashmir.[34]

The COIN in India is complicated by the possession of nuclear weapons by India and Pakistan. The threat of nuclear weapons use by the South Asian states is dissimilar to nuclear weapons possession by the West and the Soviet Union (which are separated by a large distance), because of the lack of spatial and temporal distance in a the launching, as well as the lack of monitoring. Detonation would cause instant catastrophic consequences to both sides. It has not, however, prevented the Kargil war misadventure by Pakistan in Kashmir in 1999, despite the 1998 Indo-Pakistan nuclear tests. This could have escalated into a nuclear war, which was prevented by President Clinton's demand that the Pakistan Army immediately and unconditionally withdraw from Kargil. Justine Hardy notes:

> There was the nuclear issue, and the threat in Pakistan of the fundamentalists' getting too close to the center of power for India's comfort. And there was the Indian Army line of how they felt encroached on by the heavy American presence in the region, on one side nearby in Iraq, and with NATO in Afghanistan on the other, and of how this created a sense of strategic encirclement.[35]

The Obama's AF-Pak policy is linked to the India's counter-terrorism policy.

> The success of the COIN in India depends on Obama's AF-Pak policy. If the COIN fails in Afghanistan, it will be disastrous for the entire region and for the world. The nuclear weapons in Pakistan have acquired a new dimension in Pakistan's strategy. The advent of nuclear weapons in the Pakistani arsenal only reinforced Islamabad's commitment to pursuing the bold and provocative national strategy centered on aiding insurgencies abroad. Unable to secure its political objectives through conventional war against its stronger neighbor, the Pakistani military began to exploit its evolving strategic capabilities as cover to support various insurgencies within India as a means of either realizing its territorial claims or merely wearing India down. Both these actions operated on the premise that New Delhi would be unable to retaliate conventionally against Islamabad's subconventional offensive for fear of provoking a major war that could end up in a nuclear holocaust.[36]

COIN measures of flushing out insurgents from urban areas or sacred places are challenging in view of collateral damage and profound religious sensitivity. Insurgents take cover in urban areas, and conduct their operations and hide their weapons in shrines and mosques, as these places are immune to search. In J&K, insurgents, both Pakistani and home grown, take shelter in urban areas like Srinagar, the capital, find sanctuary in several historic shrines. Any assault on these places tends to breed more insurgents and communal riots. In cases of sacred spaces, the terrain, surrounding, weather, and the type of terrorists are to be considered when planning COIN. To internationalize the demand for secession or independence of J&K, local insurgents seized the famous sacred Hazratbal Mosque in 1993, where a precious relic—the sacred hair (*Moi-e-Muqaddas*) of the Prophet Mohammed was preserved. In Srinagar, in 1995, mercenaries seized Charar-e-Sharief, the most sacred fifteenth-century shrine of Sheikh Nooruddin Noorani, located 30km southwest of the capital. The culprits at the Hazratbal

Mosque surrendered and a cache of weaponry was found on the premises of the mosque. But terrorists at Charar-e-Sharief relinquished the shrine in the dark of night after setting fire to it. India's counterterrorism effort to dispel the terrorists in both cases was partly successful. The seizure of the two sacred places by the militants was supported by Muslims of J&K and some top officials, who were not outraged by the militants' act of sacrilege. In both cases, the terrorists were not crushed by the fear of international condemnations, or Muslim backlash. However, the Hazratbal crisis was resolved peacefully, and the Charar-e-Sharief episode had caused the destruction of the shrine in the gun battle.

Analytic Measures and Social Science

Terrorism is deeply ensconced in political violence and social instability. For terrorists who are radical Islamic separatists, public support in Muslim countries is very important. The counterinsurgency experts Paul Davis and Kim Cragins[37] have written on the importance of public support to terrorist organizations. They have identified several structural dependencies of root causes of terrorism associated with low and incompetent, repressive, greedy governments, globalization with technological changes, urbanization, lack of education, lack of economic prosperity, unemployment, poverty, lack of health care, crime feasted environment, foreign occupation, inference in social and religious laws, lack of social and family values, loss of identity, cultural imperialism, segregated and alienated neighborhood.

Apart from public support, the success of terrorists and terrorist organizations relies on resources, including money, materials, technology, and sponsoring states who provide training, shelter, manpower and diplomatic support. There has been a resurgence, regrouping and rearming of terrorists in Afghanistan, Iraq, Pakistan, Sudan, Yemen, and elsewhere, and no real decline anywhere. The analytical model of Benjamin Bahney[38] can be represented by a control theory model, as seen in Figure 6.3.

The objective is to reduce the radicalization, damage and death. Some output parameters are unobservable or random processes. The parameters can be estimated from several measurements.

The number of terrorist attacks is a random event and number of deaths is also a random event, N (â), â a random parameter. They are governed by discrete distributions. When random events vary with time, t, they are called random process, N (â, t). In addition, when they vary with space, (x, y, z), they are called a random field that is donated by N (â, t, x, y, z), where â could be random parameters. The traffic intensity or number of people arriving at a bank counter is given by Poisson distribution, and an amount of

Figure 6.3. Modeling Terrorism

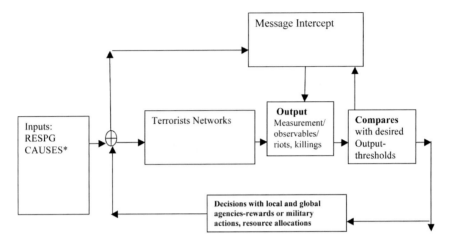

wealth in any country is given by Pareto distribution. The prediction of earthquakes including Tsunamis, a random field, still lacks accuracy, despite thousands of sensor networks around the globe. Likewise, there are not enough observation posts and surveillance systems to predict terrorist attacks. Without sufficient study, the distribution of terrorist's attacks cannot be concluded as either Poisson or Pareto. The study of random variables, random process, estimation, and prediction is dealt with[39] in Mohanty, among others.

The output of terrorist networks can be riots, hijackings, kidnappings, deaths, suicide bombings, and damage to infrastructures and to military installations. Terrorists also change the strategy of organizational structures and modus operandi. The lower number of terrorist attacks in 2003 did not constitute the demise of terrorism, as there was quiet for a while after the 9/11 attacks. This was because the terrorist organizations are decentralized, without being diminished in strength and capability. Terrorism picked up again in 2005 with several attacks in Europe and several terrorist attempts in America between 2006 and 2009.

The need for an alliance structure to counter terrorism is different from the anti-Communist alliance in the Cold War. Although Britain, France, and Israel remain the core alliance members (along with Saudi Arabia, Egypt, and Turkey, as important Muslim countries), there is a need for restructuring to include other countries that have a large number of Muslims and are devastated by terrorism. In view of the AQ presence in several countries of Asia and Africa, it would be prudent to include Afghanistan, India, Indonesia, Iraq, Pakistan, Kenya, Jordan, Mali, Nigeria, Pakistan, Somalia, Sudan, and Yemen. Some of the countries feel that their enemy is not terrorists but the neighboring country, and this may conflict with the broader counterterrorism goals of America. There are conflicting counterterrorism objectives between India and Pakistan, Pakistan and Afghanistan, and among both Sudan and Somalia and their respective neighbors, among others. Professor Daniel Byman[40] has noted that

> Defeating the jihadists menace is vital for America's security and if anything, more important for the rest of the world. Jihadist operatives seek to kill thousands of Americans at home and abroad and foment deadly insurgencies around the world.

With the help of the Taliban, Pakistan wants to establish a pro-Pakistani government in Kabul and wants to wrest Kashmir from India, but it is against the U.S. aim of eliminating the remnants of the Taliban and disrupting Al Qaeda's recruitment and logistics network. As al-Qaeda networks are interwoven with those of Kashmir jihadist, Kashmiri militants have recently been found fighting American forces in Iraq. Further, Director of National Intelligence Dennis Blair (see Chapter 5) recounts that Pakistan has not consistently pursued militant actors focused on Afghanistan, although Pakistani operations against TTP (Tehrik-i-Taliban of Pakistan) and similar groups have sometimes temporarily disrupted al-Qaeda. While Islamabad has maintained relationships with other Taliban-associated groups that support and conduct operations against U.S. and ISAF forces in Afghanistan. Pakistan has been providing support to its militant proxies, such as Haqqani Taliban, Gul Bahadur group, and Commander Nazir group.

Psychological Mitigation and Deterrence

Five major elements of a psychological program designed to counter terrorism are:

1. Inhibiting potential terrorists from joining terrorist groups
2. Producing dissension within groups
3. Facilitating exit from groups
4. Reducing support for groups and their leaders
5. Insulating the target audience, the public, from the intended goals of the jihadists, which is to terrorize people.

What can be done to open pathways for ambitious young people within their society? Support for programs that encourage economic development and opening of societies, be it Pakistan, the West Bank, or Gaza, can shrink the reservoir of dispirited youngsters. Both measures—educational support and economic programs—require funding by government agencies or nongovernmental organizations, but the investment would go a long way toward reducing the population that sees no path other than terrorism. Rehabilitation of the defected terrorists will help them to obtain jobs and other amenities. Public diplomacy and multimedia campaigns, including peace verses from the Quran, can be conducted via the Internet and satellite channels to educate unemployed youth. Governments can also offer assistance for education and employment, and aid to their parents.

Paris based Muslim scholar Farhad Khosrokhavar writes,

> In many respects, Jihadism is a regressive, repressive, and dangerous trend within the Muslim world. Its enemies are not only Western societies but also Muslims themselves, beside a tiny minority of Islamic radicals. Jihadism is also overwhelmingly a modernization vis-a-vis traditional Islam, but a perverse one. The jihad Akbar, greater jihad, based on spirituality, submission and sacrifice is holy and its descent to *jihad asqar,* lesser jihad, is unholy.[41]

Jihadism has been sponsored by state strategic agencies and has been used as a strategic asset for a territorial gain and hegemony. For example, Pakistan's ISI has been funding the Kashmiri Councils in Washington, London and Brussels to influence respective governments to urge India to hold plebiscite in Jammu and Kashmir.[42]

There is a common approach in the sharing of information and resources among terrorists and criminal gangs, in the context of organized crime and global terror, a part study of investigative psychology. The United Nations Office on Drugs and Crimes (UNODC) monitors transnational drug trafficking and other criminal activities. The UN Security Council resolutions have, over the years, imposed sanctions—such as the freezing of assets, travel ban and arms embargo, on members of the Taliban, Al-Qaida and their associates. According to the UNODC's World Drug Report 2007, the total potential value of Afghanistan's 2006 opium harvest is about $3.1 billion. Besides, being sponsored by some oil rich countries and weak states, terrorism is also financed by several criminal organizations, involved in human smuggling, money laundering, drug trafficking, kidnapping, counterfeiting money and bank robbery.

There exists a symbiotic relationship between organized crime and terrorist organizations. While organized crime's goal is clearly economic profit, terrorism is seeking territorial gain. Outfits such as Hamas, Hezbollah, al-Qaeda, and the Taliban are reportedly linked to tobacco and cigarette smuggling. The Iran-backed Lebanese group is involved in narcotics and human trafficking. Hezbollah smuggles weapons, document traffickers, narcotics, and alien and human contraband along routes used by drug cartels—enlisting Shiite expatriates to negotiate contracts with Mexican crime syndicates. Each year over 700,000 women disappear from Russia, China, Burma and other countries.

Though the Bombay attacks were conducted by terrorists, the funding was apparently provided by Dawood Ibrahim. Ibrahim's D-Company is the largest organized crime industry in South Asia, South East Asia, South Africa, and United Arab Emirates. In addition to narcotics, money laundering and contract killing, the infamous D-Company is allegedly working jointly with LeT. According to Ryan Clarke:

> In early 1990s, (Pakistan's) ISI formed a partnership with D-Company and jointly planned and executed the 1993 Mumbai blasts. Following these attacks, ISI facilitated the development of ties between LeT and D-Company, thus forming a trilateral nexus that often functions independently of the political system and greatly complicates diplomacy between New Delhi and Islamabad on a wide range of issues.[43]

The transnational organized crime—terror nexus would pose some of the gravest challenges to the world order in the foreseeable future.

Notes

1. Posner 2007, 215.

2. Center on Global Counterterrorism Cooperation: Countering Terrorism in *South Asia: Building Capacities and Strengthening Multilateral Engagement,* 20 May 2009.

3. Daniel Benjamin, *Strategic Counterterrorism*, Foreign Policy paper 7, Brookings Institution, Washington, D.C. October 2008; Counter terrorism.www. wordtrade.com/society/politics/counterterrorismR.htm; David G. Gompert, The Cognitive side of Counterinsurgency, www.rand.org/pubs/occasional_papers/2007/RAND_OP168.pdf.

4. *Connecting the Dots in Intelligence,* Research Brief, Rand Corporation, 2005, www.rand.org/pubs/research_briefs/RB9079/RAND_RB9079.pdf.

5. Paul Pillar, Counterterrorism after AQ, *The Washington Quarterly,* Summer 2004.

6. Handbook on Counterterrorism Measures, www.independentsector.org/PDFs/counterterrorism.pdf.

7. Counterterrorism White Paper, June 22, 2006, http://trac.syr.edu/tracreports/terrorism/169/include/terrorism.whitepaper.pdf.

8. Homeland Security–Counter terrorism, www.dhs.gov/files/counter terrorism.shtm; www.homelandsecurity.ms.gov/docs/msaic_seven_signs_terrorism.pdf.

9. Kristin Archick, Coordinator, European Approaches to Homeland Security and Counterterrorism, CRS Report RL 33573, July 24, 2006, http://italy.usembassy.gov/pdf/other/RL33573.pdf; French Approach, J. Shapiro and B. Suzan, *Survival,* Vol. 45. No1, Spring 2003, pp. 67–98. The International Institute for Strategic Studies; www.brookings.edu/views/articles/fellows/shapiro20030301. pdf; Countering Terrorism: the OSCE as a Regional Model, Remarks by Raphael F. Perl, Head of the OSCE Action against Terrorism Unit (ATU) International Terrorism Conference, Royal United Services Institute for Defence and Security Studies, London, 2 October 2008, www.osce.org/documents/atu/2008/10/33845_ en.pdf; Global Security, Testimony of Raphael F. Perl, Specialist in International Affairs, Foreign Affairs, Defense, and Trade Division, Congressional Research Service, www.globalsecurity.org/security/library/congress/2005_h/050512-perl.pdf; International Terrorism: Threat, Policy, and Response, Updated January 3, 2007, Raphael F. Perl, www.fas.org/sgp/crs/terror/RL33600.pdf.

10. Shapiro and Suzan, 2003, 6–18; Kristin Archick, Coordinator, European Approaches to Homeland Security and Counterterrorism, CRS Report RL 33573, July 24, 2006, http://italy.usembassy.gov/pdf/other/RL33573.pdf; French Approach, J. Shapiro and B. Suzan, Survival, Vol. 45. No1, Spring 2003, pp. 67–98.

11. Joel Watson, *Strategy: an introduction to game theory,* W.W. Norton, New York, 2002; Modeling Terrorism: A Game Theoretical Approach, Adam Samson, www.adamsamson.com/writing/asamson-terrorism-game-theory.pdf.

12. Sandler & Enders, "Applying Analytical Methods to Study Terrorism," *International Studies Perspectives,*2007, 8,287-302, (http://russwbeck.wordpress.com/2009/01/24/sra211review2/).

13. USA Counterinsurgency Guide, January 13, 2009; www.state.gov/documents/organization/119629.pdf; Luttwak, Edward, Dead End: Counterinsurgency Warfare as Military Malpractice, *Harper's Magazine,* February 2007, www.harpers.org/archive/2007/02/0081384, Counterinsurgency Operations, 2006, www.fas.org/irp/doddir/army/fmi3-07-22.pdf.

14. Vali Nasr, When the Shittes Rise, *Foreign Affairs*, July/August 2006, www.foreignaffairs.com/articles/61733/vali-nasr/when-the-shiites-rise; Daniel Marston and Carter Malikasian (Eds.), 2008, 238.

15. CRS Report for Congress: Foreign Aid: An Introductory Overview of U.S. Programs and Policy, Updated January 19, 2005, http://shelby.senate.gov/legislation/ForeignAid.pdf.

16. Daniel Benjamin, Strategic Counterterrorism, Policy Paper #7, October 2008, Foreign Policy at Brookings, www.brookings.edu/ ~ /media/Files/rc/papers/2008/10_terrorism_benjamin/10_terrorism_benjamin.pdf.

17. Will America's New Counterinsurgency Doctrine Defeat AQ? Sebestyen L.V. Gorka, 10/01/2008, www.itdis.org/Portals/11/Gorka_Counterinsurgency_AQSpain.pdf.

18. Innovation or Inertia, The U.S. Military and the Learning of Counterinsurgency, David Ucko, Foreign Policy Research Institute, Spring 2008.

19. Counterinsurgency, the War on Terror, and the Laws of War, Ganesh Sitaraman, Harvard Law School, http://papers.ssrn.com/sol3/papers.cfm?abstract_id=1354677.

20. Three Pillars of Counterinsurgency, Dr. David J. Kilcullen, Remarks delivered at the U.S. Government Counterinsurgency Conference, Washington D.C., 28 September 2006, www.au.af.mil/au/awc/awcgate/uscoin/3pillars_of_counterinsurgency.pdf; David Kilcullen, Counterinsurgency Redux, http://smallwarsjournal.com/documents/kilcullen1.pdf.

21. Counter insurgency-Army, www.fas.org/irp/doddir/army/fm3-24fd.pdf; New Counterinsurgency Manual, www.military.com/features/0,15240,1208 10,00.html.

22. K.I. Sepp, Best Practices in Counterinsurgency, *Military Review,* May–June 2005, www.au.af.mil/au/awc/awcgate/milreview/sepp.pdf.

23. Principles of Counterinsurgency, Eliot Cohen, *Military Review,* March–April 2006, www.smallwars.quantico.usmc.mil/search/articles/Cohen2.pdf.

24. Brigadier-General N.A. Foster, Changing the Army for Counterinsurgency, http://usacac.army.mil/CAC/milreview/download/English/NovDec05/aylwin.pdf.

25. The article refers to Afghanistan and to Iraq where the United States is an occupying force. Notes, Counterinsurgency and Constitutional Design, Harvard Law Review, April 2008, Vol.121, #6, www.harvardlawreview.org/issues/121/april08/notes/counterinsurgency_and_constitutional_design.pdf.

26. Steven and Gunaratna 2004, 100–101.

27. Jones, 2009,280, 316, Counterinsurgency in Afghanistan, Seth Jones, Rand Report, 2008 www.rand.org/pubs/monographs/2008/RAND_MG595.pdf.

28. Gannon, 2005, 141.

29. Getting Away with Muslims Mass Murdering in Mumbai? "It's a balancing act" Sunday, November 14, 2010, Pamela Geller, Atlas Shrugs, http://atlas shrugs2000.typepad.com/atlas_shrugs/2010/11/getting-away-with-muslims-mass-murdering-in-mumbai-its-a-balancing-act-.html.

30. Iraq's Sectarian and Ethnic Violence and Its Evolving Insurgency Developments through Spring 2007, Anthony H. Cordesman, Arleigh A. Burke Chair in Strategy, with the Assistance of Emma Davies, Updated: April 2, 2007, http://csis.org/files/media/csis/pubs/070402_iraq_spring.pdf; Iraq: Trends in Violence and Civilian Casualties: 2005-2009, Anthony H. Cordesman, Arleigh A. Burke Chair in Strategy, May 5, 2009, http://reliefweb.int/rw/RWFiles2009.nsf/FilesByRW DocUnidFilename/ASHU-7RR48S-full_report.pdf/$File/full_report.pdf; Testimony to the Senate Foreign Relations Committee, January 10, 2007, Yahia Khairi Said, Revenue Watch Institute, London School of Economics, http://foreign.senate.gov/testimony/2007/SaidTestimony070110.pdf; Annual Threat Assessment, Statement before the Committee on Armed Services, United States Senate, 10 March 2009,

Lieutenant General Michael D. Maples, U.S. Army Director, Defense Intelligence Agency, http://armed-services.senate.gov/statemnt/2009/March/Maplespercent2003-10-09.pdf.

31. Vali Nasr, When the Shittes Rise, *Foreign Affairs*, July/August 2006, www.foreignaffairs.com/articles/61733/vali-nasr/when-the-shiites-rise.

32. Scheuer, 2008, 256.

33. Engel, 2008, 102.

34. Weaver, 2002, 207, 271.

35. Hardy, 2009, 203.

36. Ashley J. Tellis, Pakistan sees no reason to stop supporting terrorists, *Yale Global*, 15 March 2010.www.carnegieendowment.org/experts/index.cfm?fa=expert_view&expert_id=198&more=1,http://www.dni.gov/testimonies/20100 202_testimony.pdfwww.meforum.org/1927/european-converts-to-terrorism.

37. Davis and Cragins, 2009, 46.

38. Davis and Cragins, 2009, 459–483; David Tucker, Terrorism, Networks, and Strategy: Why the Conventional Wisdom is Wrong. *The Journal of the Naval Postgraduate School Center for Homeland Defense and Security,* Vol.IV, no.2, June 2008.

39. Mohanty, 1986, 212, 412.

40. Byman, 2008, 5.

41. Khosrokhavar, 2009, 297; Jerrold Post, *Psychological Operation and Counterterrorism,* Joint Force Quarterly, April 2005, Issue 37.

42. Pakistan's Military Plotted to Tilt U.S. Policy, F.B.I. Says, By Charlie Savage and Eric Schmitt, New York Times, July 19, 2011, Pak took Fai route to discredit UK MP, Dipankar De Sarkar, Hindustan Times, London, July 22, 2011.

43. Ryan Clarke, Crime-Terror Nexus in South Asia, New York, Routledge, 2011, 177; *Evil Twins: The Crime Terror Nexus* by Frank S. Perri, Terrance G.Lichtenwald, and Paula M. MacKenzie, The Forensic Examiner,® *Winter 2009,* www.acfei.com.

Epilogue

Unto Allah belong the East and the West,
and whithersoever ye turn,
there is Allah's countenance.
Lo! Allah is All Embracing, All-Knowing.
—*The Quran: 2-115*

The hydra of unholy jihad is alive. The threats of jihadi terrorism and radicalization have been decentralized with no abatement of vigor, from Somalia and Yemen to Swat Valley, Pakistan, to Southern Afghanistan, to Fort Hood, Texas. The relentless Taliban are coming back in Afghanistan with the old gospel of global unholy jihad, *qital,* battle and aggression. Holy warriors have yielded to unholy warriors of *al-musallah,* armed jihad, aided by radical fundamentalists, and alienated diaspora youth. They tread on a path from holy jihad to unholy jihad—from the light of spirituality to the darkness of death and destruction—for the reward of passage to the "garden of paradise" as a *shaheed,* to achieve the highest level of *Shahada,* martyrdom.

The smoke from the rubble of the Twin Towers, destroyed in the 9/11 attacks, has been extinguished, the Pentagon building has been repaired, and a Flight 93 National Memorial has been erected, but jihadi terror waves in the Atlantic have remained turbulent. The destruction of the Twin Towers, the center of American pride and fortune, has brought joy in the streets of the Muslim world. The historian John Dower of MIT believes: "Religion does still matter. Great struggles over conflicting ideals do remain integral to some if not all wars: World War II remains the proof positive of this." Further, "in the eyes of Islamic fundamentalists and many of their fellow travelers, the flaming towers in Manhattan," writes Professor Dower, "were as awesome and beautiful as the billowing, multicolored pillars of nuclear smoke and fire that carried American observers of the earliest nuclear explosion to a transport of near rapture."[1]

A monument to the terrorism is proposed to be erected at Ground Zero, two blocks away from the 9/11 attacks site, to express freedom of religion, pluralism, and diversity. Any monument there

> belongs to those who suffered and died there . . . such ownership obliges us, the living, to preserve the dignity and memory of the place, never allowing it to be forgotten, trivialized or misappropriated.[2]

Partly because there are already more than 100 mosques in New York City and seven Cordova Houses in America, another Islamic Cordova House at ground zero is opposed by 70 per cent of the people. Describing America as "an accessory to the crime" of the 9/11 attacks and creating the Cordova House near Ground Zero, a place of mass murder in the name of Islam, to create harmony among people of different faiths, appears to be inconsistent and incompatible with peace and patriotism. However, President Obama, strong on Islam and soft on Islamic terrorism, backs the Islamic Center, the Cordova House, near the 9/11 site. Thousands of people assembled near Ground Zero on August 22, 2010 to oppose its construction there.

> As spokesmen from various Brotherhood front groups (notably, the Council on American Islamic Relations, the Muslim American Society and the Muslim Public Affairs Council) have been vociferously demanding that the construction of a mega-mosque is a test of our religious tolerance, more and more of us are realizing that this is what is known in Shariah as *taqiyya*—lying for the faith.[3]

Professor Mark Helprin writes:

> Mosques have commemoratively been established upon the ruins or in shells of the sacred buildings of other religions—most notably but not exclusively in Cordova, Jerusalem, Istanbul, and India. When sited in this fashion they are monuments to victory, and the chief objection to this one is not to its existence but that it would be near the site of atrocities—not just one—closely associated with mosques because they were planned and at times celebrated in them . . . That is not moderate. It is aggressively militant.

It is "in the interest of defeating terrorism, that we make clear that we view most Muslims as our allies in a common struggle against extremists," but "the terrorists might celebrate its presence as a twisted victory over our society's freedoms."[4]

Some lecture America on "recognition of the rights of others, tolerance and freedom of worship," but they cannot deliver the same message to certain Muslim countries where minorities do not have freedom of worship. Peace does not come from the provocations of either burning the Quran or erecting a mosque at the graveyard of three thousand people killed by radicals. On the erection of the mosque at ground zero, the King College's President Dinesh D'Souza comments:

> Undoubtedly radical Muslims around the world will view the mosque as a kind of triumphal monument. There is historical precedent for this. Muslims have a long tradition of building monuments to commemorate triumphs over their adversaries, as when they built the Dome of the Rock on the site of Solomon's Temple, or when Mehmet the Conqueror rode his horse into the Byzantine church Hagia Sophia and declared that it would be turned into a mosque.[5]

It is alleged that Babri Masjid was built by Emperor Babur in the sixteenth century on the ruins of Hindu God Rama's birthplace. Arab-Muslim invaders have destroyed other people's religious shrines and have built their mosques and minarets on the ruins.

As reported in the Toronto Sun,

> The Ottawa men charged with being part of a homegrown terrorist cell were plotting to bomb Parliament Hill, alleged a former counter-terrorism agent Friday. . . . Alleged ringleader Hiva Mohammad Alizadeh, 30, was about to leave the country. . . . Police had reason to believe the suspects were raising money to funnel to terrorist groups in Afghanistan to purchase improvised electronic devices to kill Canadian and coalition troops in Afghanistan. Alizadeh had travelled to Pakistan and Afghanistan before to receive training from al-Qaida-linked terrorist groups, said (Michael) Juneau-Katsuya.[6]

The jihadi networks—AQ, MB, ASG, JeM, JI, LeT, and others (Appendix 5)—remain a global terrorist threat. However, Islam, which is based on the Quran—the spiritual thoughts and noble deeds of the Prophet Mohammed—is not a threat as a religion, Islamic culture, which encompasses literature, music, painting, science, cuisine, sculpture, and the confluence of many cultures including Persian, Turkic, Mongol, Indian, Malay, Berber, Cordoba, and Indonesian, is also not a threat. The world is enriched by both.

Interestingly, Islamists do not consider Christianity or Judaism as threats. They did not target Saint Peter's basilica in Rome or the King Solomon temple in Jerusalem. It was not religiosity that was driving them; instead, their movement was political. The British compartmentalized Islamic religion and culture to repel the rebellion and resentment in South Asia and

Africa and to sustain the colonial empire. Americans also used Islamists to build their strategic empire. But the Soviets diffused them with the no-religion fervor of Marxism.

Islamists are resurgent in South Asia, Central Asia, South East Asia, Europe, Turkey, and the Middle East, particularly in Iraq where a secular government was toppled. There is an unholy alliance among jihadists, left-ists, and extremists in Saudi Arabia, Britain, France, Pakistan, and the United States, and since 1998, jihadists have been attacking their host countries, including Britain, Saudi Arabia, and Pakistan.

Almost ten years after 9/11, on March 29, 2010, terrorist savagery returned to Russia, with an act of terror reminiscent of the attack carried out in Beslan by the Black Widows in September 2004. At two subway stations in Moscow, two female suicide bombers conducted brazen attacks that killed thirty-nine people and injured seventy, and stirred fears of a terrorism re-vival in the country's population centers. Then, two days later, on March 31, two suicide bombers, including one wearing a police uniform, killed at least a dozen people, injuring twenty three, in Dagestan, the province east of Chechnya. On April 13 that same year, Muslim militants disguised as policemen and soldiers detonated bombs and opened fire in a series of coor-dinated attacks in a southern Philippine city, triggering clashes that killed at least twelve people. About twenty five Abu Sayyaf militants were involved in the attacks in Isabela City on the island province of Basilan, one of the most daring operations by the al-Qaida-linked group, according to regional military commander Lieutenant General Benjamin Dolorfino.[7] Although ter-rorist operations are unpredictable, an April 2006 report issued by the Na-tional Intelligence Estimate (NIE) has listed some trends: (a) jihadists are increasing in numbers and in locations worldwide, with increasing numbers of terrorist attacks against the United States and its interests everywhere, (b) jihadi groups will continue to seek WMDs, (c) terrorists will rely on the Internet and other new technologies to spread their messages, (d) Europe will remain an important venue for recruitments and staging attacks, and (e) a rise of radical ideologies based on an anti-Western and anti-globalization agenda. It is also noted that terrorists' use of electromagnetic terrorism has increased. This includes the intentional use of powerful electromagnetic (EM) pulse emitting devices or high-voltage pulse generators, with the aim of disrupting the normal operations of a country's electronic systems. Tar-geted operations include aircraft takeoff and landing control instrumenta-tion, telecommunication systems, electric devices used in managing nuclear power plant operations, electric generation, transmission and distribution, and equipment used in protecting environmentally hazardous facilities (see Chapters 5 and 6).

OBL endorsed the failed attempt to blow up a U.S. airliner on Christmas Day, 2009. He also threatened new attacks against the United States in an audio message in which he implied that he maintained some direct command over AQ-inspired offshoots.[8] AQ leaders assert, from their hide-out, that democracy is the very essence of heresy and polytheism, and that they want global Islamism, Sharia, and jihad in the land of the *kefirs* (infidels), *dar-al-harb* (the house of war). (Osama bin Laden [OBL] was killed on May 2, 2011 by U.S. forces at Abbottabad, Pakistan.) The radical Islamism in Europe emanates from multiculturalism and the emphasis on national identity. Francis Fukuyama has written about the sources of radicalism: "First, rapid transition to modernity has long spawned radicalization. Further, radical Islamism is as much a product of modernization and globalization as it is a religious phenomenon."[9] The EU Council's 2002 framework on combating terrorism is similar to America's. They differ from America with respect to counter-terrorism (as outlined in America's Patriot Act)[10] and the war on terror/war on AQ. In 1997, the United States established a list of thirty terrorist groups. In 2001 the UK listed twenty-one.[11] The conviction of terrorists in Europe is far less harsh than that of terrorists in America and there is no death penalty in Europe. Most European countries treat Islamist terrorists as criminals whereas America treats them as enemies of the West. Some coordinated counter terrorist measures (see Chapter 6) have been taken up by Australia, Canada, France, Germany, Greece, Italy, Norway, Spain, Sweden, and the United States. The UN has twelve protocols on terrorism.[12] European-born terrorists, who are neither oppressed, uneducated, nor unemployed, nor facing racism, economic deprivation, and discrimination, are enjoying Western rights, legal systems, diversity, tolerance, and freedom. Yet they may be found blowing themselves up in Tel Aviv cafés, plotting mayhem in South Asia, or planting bombs in subways in London or Madrid. With their visa-free passage to America as citizens of Europe, they are enabled in their intent to blow up strategically important American infrastructures. In the aftermath of the terrorist attacks in Madrid, Spanish Interior Minister Alfredo Perez Rubalcaba said the detainees in Spain were Islamists belonging to a well-organized group that had gone a step beyond radicalization. A Muslim leader in Barcelona, Spain, was quoted in certain media reports as saying the fourteen suspects—twelve Pakistanis, an Indian, and a Bangladeshi—were members of a "Pakistani-based group called Tablighi Jamaat."[13] The Tablighi Jamaat (TJ) has come up before in connection with terrorism plots. These included: the October 2002 Portland Seven and the September 2002 Lackawanna Six cases in the United States; the August 2006 plot to bomb airliners en route from London to the United States; the July 7, 2005, London Underground bombings; and the July 2007 attempted bombings in Glasgow, Scotland and in London. This group has been indoctrinated by radical imams to radicalize, to assert their Islamic identity, and to achieve caliphate in the world by jihad, taking advantage of the liberal secularism and multiculturalism of Europe while rejecting integration into Western society. Most of these terrorists do not consider their country of birth as their true country. Turkish–German author Necla Kelek, the author of *Die fremde Braut* (The Foreign Bride) states:

> Politicians and religious scholars of all faiths are right in pointing out that there are many varieties of Islam, that Islamism and Islam should not be confused, that there is no line in the Quran that would justify murder. But the assertion that radical Islamic fundamentalism and Islam have nothing to do with each other is like asserting that there was no link between Stalinism and Communism.

Michael Radu opines:

> It should seem obvious that the "root cause" is an ideology coming from and aiming at great goals beyond the boundaries of Europe. Yet that is precisely what most European politicians and intellectuals and many of their American colleagues avoid talking about, because of a pervasive fear of offending Muslim sensitivities.[14]

London and other cities in Britain are home to some of the most radical groups, including MB, Palestine's Hamas, Algerian Islamists, and branches of the Asian Jemaah Islamiya groups. Iranian parliament speaker Hashemi Rafsanjani, on May 1989, had openly called on Palestinians to kill Americans, Britons and other Westerners wherever they could find them. David Selbourne has provided an outline of the West's views of Islam after the 9/11 attacks[15]:

- *Daily Telegraph*—Islam was an "essentially peaceful faith"
- *The Times*—Islam was a "religion of compassion"
- *The Guardian*—Islam's message was one of "peace"
- President Bush—A faith committed to morality, Islam's teachings were "peaceful," "a religion of liberty and tolerance"

Compare with: Libyan leader Muammar Gaddafi has turned up the heat in his country's dispute with Switzerland, calling for jihad against it over a ban on the construction of minarets. "It is against unbelieving and apostate Switzerland that jihad (holy war) ought to be proclaimed by all means," Gaddafi said in a speech in the Mediterranean coastal city of Bengazi to mark the birthday of the Muslim Prophet Mohammed. "Jihad against Switzerland, against Zionism, against foreign aggression is not terrorism," Gaddafi said. "Any Muslim around the world who has dealings with Switzerland is an infidel (and is) against Islam, against Mohammed, against God, against the Koran," the leader told a crowd of thousands in a speech broadcast live on television.16 Jihadi terrorism has many identities, based on space and time, and the victims are not just Westerners, but also Russians, Indians, and Chinese. Or, in the words of [Indian-born Muslim author] Salman Rushdie in November 2001, "Let's start calling a spade a spade. Of course this is 'about Islam.'" President George W. Bush focused special attention on state supporters of terrorism with records of using (or pursuing) chemical, biological and nuclear weapons. However, it was a selective policy since it ignored some states that have sponsored more terrorists or developed more nuclear weapons than Iraq. But he was clear that the war on terror was against jihadists, the Gaddafi calls for jihad against Switzerland over minaret ban holy warriors, not against Islamists or the Islamic religion. A former senior Pentagon official of the Bush Administration, Douglas Feith, writes: "This is not a war against Islam. America is good to its Muslim citizens. U.S. military forces have fought on behalf of Muslims in the Gulf war, Somalia, Bosnia, and Afghanistan, all in the last dozen years."17 On January 30, 2010, it was reported from the Somalia capital, Mogadishu, that militants from the rebel group al Shabaab, (an affiliate of AQ), and an allied group, Hizb ul Islam, had assaulted "the strongholds of the enemies of Allah," causing more that twelve civilian deaths by suicide bombing. The Associated Press reports that a suicide bomber and gunmen wearing military uniforms attacked a hotel near Somalia's presidential palace on August 24, 2010, sparking a running gun battle with security forces. The attack on the Hotel Muna raised the two-day toll to at least 70. The multi-pronged assault came less than 24 hours after the country's most dangerous militant group—al-Shabaab—threatened a "massive" war against what it labeled as invaders, a reference to the 6,000 African Union troops in Mogadishu. They control much of southern Somalia and may take over Somalia soon. Terrorists, fleeing from South Asia, are also finding a near perfect haven in Yemen. The jihadists, who take pride in massacring people in marketplaces, suicide bombing religious processions, cutting the throats of journalists and broadcasting the videotapes, or cutting women into two halves after raping them—to cite only a few unholy acts—are not just a threat to democracy and to the Western world, but to Muslim regimes in Iran, Sudan, Afghanistan, Algeria, Pakistan, the Philippines, Saudi Arabia, and Uzbekistan, among other places.

Douglas Feith continues in his book, *War and Decision,*

> To discuss this murderous enemy in terms of networks and ideologies may
> sound abstract, but the network of Islamist extremists is a bloody, down-
> to-earth reality that has pervasive, practical effects on our lives—on our
> physical safety, civil liberties, and personal privacy.

State terrorism is commonly understood to refer to acts of violence, sponsored by states or outsourced to non-state actors inside the state, that target
civilians in the pursuit of political and ideological aims, territorial gain, or
strategic interest. As Professor Bobbitt noted that State cannot be protected
by the Westphalia sovereignty in view of the threat to international security
and stability to create a Sharia-based state (stoning, polygamy, under age
marriage, honor killing, female genital mutilation, FGM, beating wives
correctly in Islamic way, and others) to restore caliphate and also for that
failed, fragile, or failing states are a serious danger because they cannot
exercise sovereign control over their territory, unwilling, by neglect, or by
providing sanctuary to hostile terrorists in which terrorists plan and export
suicide bombing or the WMD and their insidious hatred to the world and
writes:

> A war against terror makes sense, as an idea, because terrorism has be-
> come more warlike, and war is becoming indistinguishable from counter-
> insurgency and counterterrorism operations; the war aim of the U.S and
> the U.K. is to preserve states of consent by protecting civilians, and this
> means that the Wars against terror will pursue three intertwined objec-
> tives; to pre-empt twenty-first century market state terrorism, to prevent
> WMD proliferation when these weapons would be used for compellance
> rather than deterrence, and to prevent or mitigate genocide, ethnic cleans-
> ing, and the human rights consequences of civilian catastrophes.[18]

The two current wars in Afghanistan and Iraq have been conducted to drive
out terrorists, or to eradicate future threats from the soil of those two nations. Despite these efforts and others, including deterrence, defense, strategic preparedness and alliances, the interrogation of several hundred
jihadists, and America's rushing of billions of dollars to both countries for
reconstruction and development, a future terrorist attack against the West
or South Asia has not been ruled out. The jihadists are looking for vulnerabilities.

The threat to Islam comes from the totalitarianism, fascism, and obscurantism of Wahhabi ideology, not from secularism, capitalism, globalization or free market economies. The "Dubai effect" (Dubai being The United

Arab Emirates' most prosperous city-state) emphasizes the new dimension of modern Islam. The threat of terror has increased, not subsided, bringing with it the news that Britain raised its terror level threat to "severe." Former Prime Minister Gordon Brown commented: "Britain and other nations face a sharply growing threat from al-Qaida-affiliated terrorists based in Yemen and an area of north Africa that includes nations such as Somalia, Nigeria, and Ethiopia."[19] The threat from WMDs has not diminished since 1998, when Osama bin Laden called on each of the faithful to acquire and use them, as part of every Muslim's Islamic duty towards the jihadist agenda. As Rolf Mowatt-Larssen reported:

> He has never given up the goal; indeed, in a 2007 video, he repeated his promise to use massive weapons to upend the global status quo, destroy the capitalist hegemony, and help create an Islamic caliphate. . . . AQ has been far more sophisticated in its pursuit of weapons of mass destruction than is commonly believed, pursuing parallel paths to acquiring weapons and forging alliances with groups that can offer resources and expertise.[20]

In commenting upon the recent thinking of intellectuals on Islam and Islamists, at the Literary Festival in India, The Wall Street Journal columnist Sadananda Dhume[21] observes: "Ms. Hirsi Ali described the faith she was born into as 'a dangerous, totalitarian ideology masquerading as a religion.' She argued against the moral relativism that has prevented Western intellectuals from scrutinizing Islam as they do in Christianity and Judaism. She asked why it seemed impossible to have a sober discussion about the Quran and the sayings of the Prophet Muhammad without riling Muslim sentiment, and made the case for bringing the Enlightenment to the blighted lands of the Middle East and South Asia. Tunku Varadarajan (an adjunct professor at Columbia University's Graduate School of Journalism) of the Daily Beast website talked of Arab-Muslim societies as 'terrible rulers and terrible oppositions, squeezed between despots and fanatical Islamists.' Max Rodenbeck[22] of the *Economist* described Lebanon as 'fragmented according to which conspiracy theory you subscribe to.' Lawrence Wright, a writer for the *New Yorker* and author of *The Looming Tower*, a widely read book on AQ, answered an often-asked question about American aggression by pointing out that 'Islam is under attack from the West in part because it attacked the West.'

Steve Coll[23] narrates that the genesis of global jihadism in what has come to be called AfPak and on Saudi Arabia's second most famous family are among the definitive works on either subject—calmly and carefully untangled a web linking zealous Saudi royals, Pakistani intelligence agents and tribal warlords in Afghanistan.

It is reported that a terror plot was foiled on October 27, 2010, when two cargo packages containing PETN (pentaerythritol trinitrate), a highly explosive organic compound, sent from Yemen and addressed to synagogues in Chicago, were intercepted in Britain and Dubai. This is alleged to have been done by Al Qaeda of the Arab Peninsula. The plot was the second to be broken up that week and followed the arrest of a Pakistani-born Northern Virginia man, Farooque Ahmed, who was alleged to have been planning to bomb Washington's Metro system. He was arrested by the FBI on October 27, 2010, on suspicion of taking part in what he thought to be plans for a simultaneous al Qaeda attack next year on multiple Northern Virginia Metrorail stations. Three suicide bombers, associated with Al Qaeda, launched an attack on the Chechen parliament on October 19, 2010, killing at least three people. PETN was allegedly one of the components of the bomb concealed by Umar Farouk Abdul Mutallab, the Nigerian man accused of trying to set off an explosion aboard Northwest Airlines Flight 253 as it approached Detroit, Michigan, on December 25. Abdul Mutallab is alleged to have been carrying 80 grams of PETN in that botched attack— also believed to have been the workings of al Qaeda in the Arabian Peninsula.[24] Islam as practiced or propagated by the Taliban and AQ is not accepted by devout Muslims such as Abdul Ghaffar Khan of the KP in Pakistan. (see chapter 4) The distinguished Pakistani Professor Ishtiaq Ahmed writes:

> Abdul Ghaffar Khan derived his inspiration from the Holy Prophet (PBUH) and Islam. He particularly emphasized the formative period in Makkah when the Prophet (PBUH) and his devoted followers had to face persecution but did not hit back at their oppressors . . . that all religious scriptures are amenable to a variety of interpretations; hence also the Quran and indeed the life of the Prophet (PBUH). Therefore it depends on the enquirer what support he seeks from the sacred sources. For those who are convinced that violence is the way forward for Muslims, they can select those portions of the sacred sources that seem to sanction violence. On the other hand, those who believe in peaceful and civilized ways of conducting their affairs can find plenty of material in the same sources that confirm their standpoint as well. Abdul Ghaffar Khan was a man of peace. He approached Islam in the hope of finding a complementary message to (Mahatma) Gandhi's interpretation of Hinduism as Ram Raj and *ahimsa* (non-violence) and he found it. The Taliban, Hamas, and AQ arbitrarily emphasize the wars fought during the lifetime of the Prophet and indeed allusions to the use of violence against non-Muslims in the Quran.[25]

The Jihadist movement is opposed by other Islamic intellectuals including Qatar based scholar Yusuf al Qaradawi, author of 50 books, and the Damascus-born, German-based political scientist Professor Bassam Tibi.[26]

Tibis is the founder of Islamology, a social-scientific study of Islam and conflict resolution. His views on secular Turkey, the only secular Muslim country among fifty-seven Muslim countries in the world, are expressed in the following passage:

> The only difference, however, between moderate and jihadist Islamists is the use of the ballot box instead of violence to come to power. It may be important to include Islamists in democracy but certainly not with the Western naive notion that inclusion will tame Islamism. While many moderate Muslims seek to Europeanize Islam, the Islamism practiced by the AKP (Turkey's Justice and Development Party—Adalet ve Kalkýnma Partisi) is an ideology of cultural divide, tension, and conflict, despite all of the pro-Europe rhetoric in which Islamists in Turkey engage in their pursuit to exploit the European Union for their agenda of Islamization.

Amazingly, moderate Muslims are not concerned with the corruption in, and abuses, of mosques, gender inequality and inheritance, domestic violence, forced marriages, honor killing, incest, drug abuse, cruel aspects of Sharia, and low rates of educational attainment. In Tibi's books,[27] the terms political Islam, Islamism, and Islamic fundamentalism are used interchangeably. However, the classic treatise on Islamic "international law" by the Muslim legal scholar Najib Armanazi acknowledges that international order, as established by the treaty of Westphalia [1648]—in which relations among states are organized on the basis of the mutual recognition of each other's sovereignty—is contradicted by the intention of the Arab conquerors to impose their rule everywhere. Political Islam is the best recipe for a new world disorder, which it claims is a new order, but it is restricted to delivering disorders. If contemporary Muslims continue to denounce modernization as a conspiracy of '*al-Taghrib*/Westernization' that is believed to be an instrument for weakening the Umma-Islamic community, then there is no hope for a better future. Aside from Turkey, there is no lasting democratic Muslim country. Muslims enjoy rights and privileges in democratic and secular countries that they do not get in Muslim countries. It is a myth that plurality, democracy, and diversity exist in Islam (see Chapters 1 and 3). The Qatari based Egyptian scholar

> Qaradawi, calls for a historical reading of some traditions—for instance those that could be read as denying women any role in public life—he fails to accept equality of the sexes and equal rights. The "moderation" of Qaradawi's positions on women's rights thus does not react a search for justice, but a pragmatist reading of the traditions in the interest of the umma.[28]

Even in secular Turkey, which was founded by Kemal Ataturk in 1924 after the collapse of the Caliphate in 1922, Islamic fundamentalism is on the rise. Most of the time, fundamentalism ushers in strong religion with purity in belief and practice and is associated with extremist violence and religious intolerance. Although fundamentalism is pervasive in most parts of the world, educated Muslim youths are unfortunately going back to Sharia, rejecting secularism, democracy, and reason for the faith.

Many Muslim elites make the accusatory claim that Dante's *Inferno*,[29] written in the fourteenth century, spurred the beginnings of Islamophobia— the fear, hatred, hostility, and intolerance of Islam. Yet for the "crime" of reproaching Islam, several noted novelists, including Michael Houellebecq and Robert Redeker have gone into hiding in their own country, France.[30] On the other hand, Omar Bakri, a Syrian born Lebanese national, Abu Qatada of Jordan, and Osama Nasser of Milan are not reprimanded for speaking freely; rather, "all three want the benefits of the (governments) they despise: they want the financial aid, the security, the (rule of) law, the justice, and the freedom of expression afforded by this government" (Abd al-Rahman al-Rashid, Al Arabiyya TV Network).[31] Afghanistan's author Abdul Zaeef is upset that America seems to be following in the footsteps of Russia: "The criminals from the Communist regimes and those selfish looters who called themselves 'mujahedeen' are responsible for much of the destruction and tragedies of the past."[32] He is still more bitter about America's frontline ally Pakistan. and continue in his book:

> They deceive the Arabs under the guise of Islamic nuclear power, saying that they are defending Islam and Islamic countries. They milk America and the European alliance against terrorism and they have been deceiving Pakistan and other Muslims around the world in the name of Kashmiri jihad. But behind the curtain, they have been betraying everyone.

The separation of religious Muslims from the militant, radical Muslim jihadists, is crucial to eradicate terrorism. The Afghanistan scholar Zaeef believes that in refusing to differentiate between AQ and more moderate groups in their societies and in denying the peoples of the region the tools of democracy and self government that the West extols, the United States and the West have helped spread the jihad.

It is not possible to know whether the majority of Muslims believe in holy jihad or in unholy jihad, or in other words, in following the doctrine in a militant rather than a spiritual sense. Middle East historian Bernard Lewis argues that "the overwhelming majority of classical theologians, jurists, and traditionalists (i.e., specialists in the hadith)understood the obligation of jihad in a military sense."[33] The scholar David Cook writes:

In reading Muslim literature—both contemporary and classical—one can see that the evidence for the primacy of spiritual jihad is negligible. Today it is certain that no Muslim, writing in a non-Western language (such as Arabic, Persian, and Urdu), would ever make claims that jihad is primarily nonviolent or has been superseded by the spiritual jihad. Such claims are made solely by Western scholars, primarily those who study Sufism and/or work in interfaith dialogue, and by Muslim apologists who are trying to present Islam in the most innocuous manner possible. The most charitable among them would like to see Islam transform itself from a religion rooted in and emphasizing domination and violence to the more peaceful and tolerant style of internal jihad. Other religions such as Judaism and Christianity have violent pasts and have gradually been transformed, reinterpreted or repudiated. This has yet to be accomplished in Islam. If and when this change happens, it will probably include a definition of jihad that will exclude violence and embrace true religious diversity and tolerance, and it may very well start with emphasizing the spiritual jihad. However, this redirection of jihad would require a complete separation between militant and spiritual jihad that is not present as yet in contemporary Islam.[34]

On the 9/11 attacks in America, Shiite Muslim author Reza Aslan[35] writes:

> Whatever else may have been at stake, whatever social or political motivations may have been behind their abominable act, there can be no doubt that these nineteen men believed they were acting in the service of God. They are engaged in a metaphysical conflict, not between armies or nations but between the angels of light and demons of darkness. They are fighting a cosmic war, not against the American imperium but against the eternal forces of evil. The Muslim world does have reason to feel under attack by a "crusading" West. Most of all, it will deny Jihadist ideologues their principal argument that the War on Terror is, in fact, a war against Islam. Because in the end, there is only one way to win a cosmic war: refuse to fight in it.[36]

The principle of al-wala wal bara provides jihadists to believe that offensive jihad against civilians and fellow Muslims as enemies is justified and an injustice to any Muslim in the world is perceived as an injustice to all Muslims. But this leads to an abject surrender to "cosmic warriors," "puppets in the hand of God" and to the savagery of suicide bombing. These cosmic warriors are mass murderers, not just in America, but in Spain, Britain and South Asia. Conversely, the Middle East expert Efraim Karsh[37] believes:

> Only when the political elites of the Middle East and the Muslim world reconcile themselves to the reality of state nationalism, forswear pan-Arab

and pan-Islamic imperialistic dreams, and make Islam a matter of private
faith rather than a tool of political ambition will the inhabitants of these
regions at last be able to look forward to a better future free of would-be-
Saladins (Saladin, 1138–1193, ruled over major African countries and
recaptured Palestine from the Kingdom of Jerusalem, defeating the
crusaders).

The Muslim scholar Reza Aslan denotes that Islam has had a long commitment to religious pluralism. Islam is and has always been a religion of
diversity. God may be One, but Islam most definitely is not. When, how,
and where is this true? However, the works of Ahmad Biruni and Mohsen
Madani are well known. It is widely known that Sh'ism and Sufism as well
as dhimmis and Ahmadiyyas, are not considered Muslims by Sunnis.
Dhimmis are treated as second class citizens. Ahmadiyyas, Baha'is, and
others are persecuted and murdered, and Shias are killed in the neighboring
country of Iran during the Moharam Ashura procession. Thousands of kefirs
were slaughtered in Africa, in Europe and in India, and their civilizations
were savagely destroyed and plundered whenever and wherever misruled
by the Caliphs, kings and sultans of history's greatest Islamic civilization.
There is no plurality, democracy, tolerance or diversity in Islam, and Sharia
has no place for these ideologies (see Chapters 1 and 3). Nevertheless, Al-
Jama'a al-Islamiya (the Egyptian Islamic Group, EIG), the largest jihadist
organization in the Arab world, and the Islamic Salvation Front (FIS) in
Algeria now favor democratization. Along with Sheikh Yusuf Qaradawi, an
Egyptian Sunni Muslim scholar and Islamist preacher best known for his al
Jazeera program, *ash-Shariah wal-Hayat* ("Shariah and Life") and Sheikh
Sayyed Tantawi, the Grand Imam of Al-Azahar in Cairo, the oldest reli-
gious institution in the Muslim world, the EIG leaders Essam Derbala and
Abdullah Ibrahim dismissed OBL's credentials, and A.Q. Derbala declared:
"Some claim that there is a crusader war led by America against Islam.
However, the majority of Muslims reject the existence of crusader wars."[38]
On civilization and monotheism[39] two Muslim scholars[40] observed:

(i) It must be mentioned that there are other religions which are also monotheistic: Persian polyglot Ahmad Biruni (973–1048), the first Muslim
scholar to study India and the tradition, and the founder of Indology during his 20 years stay in India, argued that "the Hindus, no less than the
Greeks, have philosophers who are believers in monotheism." Biruni argued that Hinduism was a monotheistic faith like Islam, and in order to
justify this assertion, he quotes Hindu texts and argues that the worship of
idols is "exclusively a characteristic of the common people, with which
the educated have nothing to do." He writes: "The educated among the

Hindus abhor anthropomorphisms of this kind, but the crowd and the members of the single sects use them most extensively." The Hindus believe with regard to God that he is one, eternal, without beginning and end, acting by free-will, almighty, all-wise, living, giving life, ruling, preserving; one who in his sovereignty is unique, beyond all likeness and unlikeness, and that he does not resemble anything nor does anything resemble him.

(ii) Mohsen Saeidi Madani[41] quotes Yaquibi (895 A.D.): "The Hindus are superior to all others in intelligence and thoughtfulness. They are more exact in astrology and astronomy than any other people. The Brahma Sidhanta is a good proof of their intellectual powers; by this book, the Greeks and Persian have also profited."

The 9/11 attacks united all schisms within Islam and brought the Muslim world a sense of joy and pride, because they damaged the superpower's two powerful institutions: its financial hub, the World Trade Center, and its defense center, the Pentagon. According to the political scientist Yossef Bodansky,[42]: "For the vast majority of Muslims—irrespective of their position in society or their views of Islamism—the desperate heroism of the perpetrators, their embrace of martyrdom, brought a sense of pride." Only after the 9/11 attacks did Americans purchase the Quran and Islamic books in huge numbers, host several sympathetic authors, apologists, and experts on Islam and terrorism on TV talk shows and documentaries, and publish Islamist books that have become bestsellers. Additionally, after 9/11, mosques and Islamic schools have grown large numbers, more aid has been provided to improve America's image in Muslim countries, and politicians, the media, and intellectuals are going out of their way to promote Islam as a great religion of peace—even though the attack was celebrated with irrational exuberance in almost all Muslim countries. Previously, the American embassy had been burnt twice in Islamabad, in 1979 and in 1989, for alleged American involvement in bombing of Masjid al-Haram, Islam's holy site at Mecca, and for the publication of Salman Rushdie's book, *The Satanic Verses*. To many Muslims, America remains *al-Adou al-Baeed*, the far enemy.

When in Peshawar/Islamabad, two Sikhs who were kidnapped for ransom were beheaded by the Pakistani Taliban on February 21, 2010, it was neither news, nor a problem for the *umma*. But if a Muslim teenager is killed accidentally in a mass protest by jihadists in Kashmir, it is an assault on the *umma*. Since 2009, militant activity has been on the increase in the Kashmir region, as fallout from the Afghanistan wars, from 1979 to the present. The four groups, LeT, JeM, HM, and HuM continue to try and wrest Kashmir from India. Starting with Nehru, India would not give an inch of Kashmir to Pakistan or allow any joint control of Kashmir (see Chapter 4). These are not India's homegrown terrorists.

There is a growing homegrown terrorist threat in America and Europe. The BBC News reports that on March 9, 2007, police in Ireland arrested seven people over an alleged plot to kill Swedish cartoonist Lars Vilks, whom Britain's Press Association news agency had identified as the target who depicted the Prophet Muhammad with the body of a dog. A Pennsylvania woman who called herself Jihad Jane[43] (Collene LaRose, a Muslim convert) was tied in October 2009 to an alleged assassination plot against a Swedish cartoonist Vilks. The indictment says LaRose recruited other people on the Internet to wage or support jihadist attacks. Yemeni authorities said this week that an American, Sharif Mobley, 26, who had worked for six years as a laborer at nuclear plants in New Jersey, had been arrested last week in Sana, the Yemeni capital, in a sweep of militants tied to the Yemeni branch of AQ and the Somali movement Al Shabaab. Taken to a hospital for medical treatment, Mr. Mobley was said to have grabbed a security guard's gun and shot two guards, one of them fatally, before being subdued. As an American citizen whose appearance allowed her to blend into Western society, LaRose[44] represents one of the worst fears of intelligence and FBI analysts focused on identifying terrorist threats. The Pakistani newspaper, *the Dawn* reported:

> Five Pakistani men linked to a terror plot in Britain similar to the attacks on the London transport system in 2005 were arrested days before they planned to strike, a hearing was told. A British intelligence officer, identified only as ZR, told an immigration panel that the group had been planning to stage an atrocity in April last year, but were seized in raids in northwest England.[45]

Terrorists think they can establish worldwide Sharia while America is engaged in two wars, and in view of a decline of the American empire. But they cannot realize this goal, partly because of the millennium-old cleft between Arab Muslims and non Arab Muslims, Sunnis and Shiites, except where the cause of Palestine is concerned. Professor Ishtiaq Ahmed[46] writes about the death of two Sikhs, focusing on Islamic communal prejudice:

> The barbaric, appalling beheading of Jaspal Singh—one of the three Sikhs who were taken hostage by the Taliban—has shocked decent, peace-loving people all over the world. . . . Beheadings and stoning to death are a regular occurrence in Saudi Arabia, in fact every Friday, I am told. Those given such savage treatment are Muslims from poor countries such as

Pakistan, Bangladesh, Somalia or non-Muslim workers from anywhere from Asia or Africa. Raping female servants, confiscating the papers of servants, paying them little or no wages are practices common to the larger Arab world of rich Emirates. . . . Yet, the devotion of Mawali, non-Arab Muslims, to the Muslim holy land is such that nobody dares say a word in criticism. The same is true of Iran. The Iranian mullahs established their hold over a civilized and ancient people by terrorizing them through the imposition of stoning to death and beheadings. Iran also allows *muta* or temporary marriage. I have never met any Shia who would allow his sister or daughter to contract temporary marriage. Obviously such a "freedom" is only for poor women who must sell their body to make a living. I have yet to meet a Pakistani Shia—even a communist—who is critical of what goes on in Iran.

Ultimately it is savage treatment, orthodox systems, and religious bigotry that are causing the terrorism. Mankind's future is fraught with peril, thanks to the Pakistani nukes that may be taken over by militants at any time. Pakistan is "vulnerable to an Iranian-style revolution that Islamists would exploit," as well as the spread of Salafist *jihadi* movements.[47] Saudis are exporting Salafi-Wahhabism, even while the world is importing Saudi oil. While, Saudi Arabia, which constitutes only 1 per cent of the world Muslim population, is supporting of the expenses of the entire Islamic faith, over-riding other sectarian Islam.

The path of peace must be pursued and preserved in a diverse society. This has been a surrender to the power of global terrorism, in India in particular, but a way to avoid Armageddon. It is believed that destroying OBL's AQ cult will destroy terrorism. AQ is not a cult, however, and it cannot be isolated from Islam. AQ senior leadership and their new Pakistani forces are reforming in the sanctuary of western Pakistan. Aligned with both the Afghan and Pakistani Taliban, AQ is gaining political allies in hopes of destabilizing that nation and working with its allies to secure nuclear weapons. It is also argued that Islam is not accountable for the bad acts of a few Muslims, just as all of Christianity is not responsible for Hitler, who was a Christian. The fact is that jihadism did not start with OBL or with a few Muslims. Most Muslim authors dismiss violence in the name of Islam. Moderate Muslims embrace the Mecca period of morality of Islam, whereas militant Muslims espouse the militancy of the Medina period of Islam. "Know that Paradise is under the shade of swords" (Book of Jihad, Sahih al Bukhari). There are now hundreds of jihad sleeper cells, AQ or not, in almost in all countries, some of which existed prior to OBL. Professor Dipak Gupta deals with other terrorist groups like the Tamil Tigers in Sri Lanka, the FARC (Revolutionary Armed Forces of Columbia) in Columbia, and the

IRA (Irish Republic Army) in Ireland are confined to their respective territories, with no universal religious agenda and no interest in the outside world.

They do not go to fight in Chechen, Xinjiang, Palestine, Iraq, Afghanistan, the Philippines, Thailand, Bosnia, or Kashmir. Congressman Gary Ackerman[48] said before a Congressional hearing:

> In the wake of the (26/11) Mumbai attack, investigators uncovered in controller records and e-mail accounts a list of 320 locations worldwide deemed by the LeT as possible targets for attack. Only 20 of the targets were located within India.

> LeT has been attacking U.S. forces in Afghanistan almost from day one and their forces are present throughout Afghanistan. The LeT has been slaughtering Indians by the score for decades. The LeT has put the world on notice that they intend to escalate the carnage and spread it worldwide,

said he. The LeT commander of the 2008 Mumbai attack, Zakiur Rehman Lakhvi, directs LeT operations from his detention center. In their trips to Pakistan, the CIA Director and the National Security Advisor have urged Pakistan to do more about the safe havens used by AQ, the Quetta Shura, the Haqqani network and LeT. According to veteran journalist Bob Woodward:

> If (Gen. James) Jones had the job as the new commandeer, he knew exactly what he would say to Obama after making an assessment: "Mr. President, I think the strategy is correct. But it was predicated on the fact that Pakistan would be coerced into moving more than they have been, particularly with regard to the Haqqani network and Quetta Shura. The Taliban war in Afghanistan was being run from these safe havens. And hundreds, if not thousands, of fighters were pouring across the border. The Taliban was taking full advantage of the safe havens to rest and train fighters before rotating them into Afghanistan for combat. In these circumstances, you cannot win. You can't do counterinsurgency. It is a cancer in the plan."[49]

Jihadists, supported by state apparatus, global facilitators, and unholy alliances with leftist liberals, seek a global hegemony. Moderate Muslims are weak and unwilling to confront them. The demands of jihadists are not negotiable. The resurgence of militant Islamists who wish to spread Sharia across the globe is galvanized by thousands of radical madrassas (see in Chapter 2) and mosques. Brent Stephen[50] writes on the proliferation of madrassas—in 1947, there were 300 madrassas, in 1990, 3,000 and in 2011,

40,000. Political Islam is embedded in Islamic religion as *Islam din wa-dawla* (Islam is religion and state).

It is not epistemological or metaphysical in any sense, except as per the philosopher Abu Nasr al-Farabi, who has built upon Plato's and Aristotle's writings on epistemology in Islam and on rightful governance. Islam has crossed many cultures and ethnicities, yet it is not an ethical and humanistic or an universal religion as *Kefirs, Takfirs, murtadd*, apostates, Dhimmis, Muslim women, and even Shias, are treated as second class. It is not just hostile to Abrahamic religion, it is even more hostile to Dharmic religions like Hinduism, Budhism, Jainism and Siikhism, among others. Radical Islam or jihadist terrorism is a grave concern to the world,[51] while the greater jihad, spiritual jihad, is noble. The presence of Islam in non-Muslim states with secular, democratic, and multicultural environments has become a national problem in each country where Muslims reside. If jihad means spiritual struggle, then why are Hindus not included as believers? Hindus are believers in the unification of the soul with God (Yoga), as the soul is never destroyed, only transmuted. Hinduism is also monotheistic, as its many Gods only have different names and appear in different incarnations. For Hindus, God exists nowhere and everywhere. Killing is not sanctioned by the creator of the soul, and Brahmins do not even touch butchers. Hindus are the greatest victims of Islamic jihad because of the perception that they are committing *shirk*, the Islamic sin of idolatry. The onslaught of Islamic jihad (imperialism) in the Indian subcontinent is far more egregious than British or European onslaught in the colonies, far worse than the Cambodian massacre or Mao Tse Tung's mass murders. Muslims' rendition of jihad is a direct affront to the Creator of the soul. Life could be easier for Muslims (and all others), as Professor Jalal writes,[52] if they try to repay their debt to the Creator by respecting the rights and dignity of fellow human beings irrespective of their ideological or religious denominations. This is not a contest between terrorists' imposition of Islam by killing and coercion and the human values of love and harmonious existence. It is not "equating jihad with violence and terror," or saying that it is at odds with the diametrically opposite doctrines of tolerance and peace. It is not "an ineffectual attempt to disguise their political bias against Islam," undermining jihadi threats and the universal values of tolerance, equality and dignity. She reiterates:

> The popular notion that although not all Muslims are terrorists, all terrorists are Muslims has vitiated the debate and become the single biggest obstacle to restoring some semblance of perspective on the much aligned concept of jihad.

Jihadists are criminals, have no regard for human life, and are responsible for the suffering of thousands of Muslims and non Muslims. According to the Bush doctrine, terrorists *have* no human rights. Every country, in self defense, can attack them in accordance with international law, superseding the sovereignty of the states sheltering them. Half of the Muslim population (1.3 billion) supports the Islamic movement. Twenty-five per cent of the population prefers to live in Islamic governments (Sharia), and twenty per cent support jihadists. Based on this study, over 90 million Muslims are in favor of jihadists while 52 million are hard core jihadists. Ninety million radical Islamists are no "fringe" and can wreak havoc in the world, a globalized menace. They assert that terrorist organizations are part of the foreign policy instruments of some governments and part of their power structures. The organizations have sympathizers among all strata of society including government officials, clergy, army, police, and even wealthy businessmen. Some states are incapable of controlling terrorists. Pakistan is an example.

> The sheer rate of acceleration of violence in Pakistan is an index of the enveloping loss of control. In the year 2003, the total fatalities in terrorism-related violence amounted to 189, but it has escalated dramatically thereafter to the unprecedented minimum of 6,715 in 2008 and 11,529 in 2009.[53]

It is categorically unacceptable and indiscreet that the popular Muslim view that waging jihad through terrorism is a religiously or socially justifiable activity. The Global Jihad became the new mission of the jihad due to personalities including Abu Qadata of Jordan, Abu Hamza al-Masri of London's Finsbury Park mosque, Abdullah Azzam, Qutb, Maududi, OBL, Ayman al-Zawahiri(AAZ), Hassan Nasrallah of Hezbollah, and others who believe they are following the Quran (2.216, 5.33, 8.39, 9.29, 9.5, 9.123, Appendix 4). AAZ writes that the epoch has begun; now Muslims must hasten to defend the honor of Islam. His is a call to further jihad. The voice of OBL is one of the most powerful voices of global jihad. In his view, there are three choices in Islam: either willing submission to the authority of Islam or payment of the *jizya*, thereby accepting physical submission to the authority of Islam or the Sword—for it is not right to let him (an infidel) live.[54] The jihadists want to recover all lands once occupied by Muslims from the glorious days of Islam and crush the rise of Western power, hegemony, civilization, and culture. In the eighteenth century, Arab jihadist Shah Waliullah (see Chapter 4) wanted an armed jihad against non-Muslims in South Asia when he saw the decline of Muslim power and the rise of Maratha, Sikhs, and Jats in India. However, in a tremendous tribute to Waliullah, the Mary Richardson Professor of History and the Director of the Center for South Asian and Indian Ocean Studies at Tufts University, Professor Ayesha Jalal, writes:

> It was because of the jihad carried out by the Prophet and his companions that Muslims conquered territories and established the Islamic way of life as the only logical course for humanity. This proved that jihad as armed struggle was vital for the political glory of the community. . . . To subject such sinners to compulsion, so that faith finds into their hearts and minds is an act of divine mercy. But for the compulsion to work, those causing the greatest harm have to be killed, their power broken and their riches captured, so that they pose no further threats.[55]

This sounds egregious and illogical, and it is an abysmal insult to the decency and civility of human beings. Jihadi terror in the name of Islam or Allah (God) is a rugged road to the stone age of tribalism and evil. The lesser jihad cannot be denied, abrogated, changed or denounced and cannot be applied for submission, subversion or conquering the world. Praying five times a day facing Mecca, spending Fridays at mosques, and fasting, feasting and moon-sighting during the Ramadan cannot herald greater jihad if the ultimate goal is subjugating or coercing mankind to live under Sharia. A large number of people do not want to live under seventh-century rules and consider the above ritual as idolatry. We are all apostates to some religious taboo. The world is shrinking. There is now less religion, more equality, less government, more liberty, less ethnicity, more plurality, less censorship, more communication, less martyrdom, more reconciliation, less world conquest, more world markets, and more interracial, color-blind, globalized villages. There would have been no need for drone attacks had the affected countries cleaned up the terrorist camps that were sending insurgents to neighboring states and beyond.

The British, French, Dutch, Spanish and others cannot get back occupied lands, nor can the Ottoman Empire be restored. Immigrants cannot be thrown back to their old countries, nor can they claim their law in adopted countries. The roads to Mecca, Medina, Jerusalem, Rome, or Amarnath should be accessible to all. There is an enormous gulf between the holy path of Muslim faith and the unholy political ideology of violent Muslim extremists, like the Fort Hood shooter, the Christmas Day bomber, the Times Square attacker and other American jihadists. The ideological differences among jihadists, Islamists, and violent Islamic terrorism are negligible within the prism of this common denominator: propagandize, proselytize, terrorize, and kill. As discussed in previous chapters, radical Islamists and their grievances did not arise from poverty, illiteracy or deprivation.

The Islamic resurgence cannot be heralded with the annihilation of human laws, due to some imaginary divine laws of absurdity. People should not be bombed by suicide attacks for visiting Data Ganj Baksh Sufi shrines to commemorate their saints or for praying in the Ahmadiyya's mosques at Lahore, Pakistan. (Both Sufis and Ahmadiyyas are considered heretical by Sunnis.) *Fatwa* are not issued for these criminals in the tradition of Ibn Taymiyyah on Mongols for their barbarity. But, religious authorities in the United Arab Emirates have issued a *fatwa* (legal opinion) on the children's card-collecting game Pokémon[TM], considered idolatrous. Along with Salman Rushdie and Taslima Nasrin, the Nigerian journalist Isioma Daniel was given *fatwa* for comments suggesting that the Prophet Muhammad might have chosen a wife from one of the contestants of the Miss World contest. Islamic fundamentalists are not all terrorists, but violent Islamic Islamists are terrorists.

Richard Haass, president, Council on Foreign Relations, believes:

> Alas, neither would terrorism fade if Israelis and Palestinians finally ended their conflict. AQ was initially motivated by a desire to rid the Arabian Peninsula of infidels. Its larger goal is to spread Islam in a form that closely resembles its pure, seventh-century character. It is being reported that "Islam is under siege." It is not possible. It is not just frightening to siege. Islam as no country or any organization wants to be a killing field. Besides, Muslim countries have the finest Islamic Public Relations organizations in the UK and the USA who defend Islam and Islamists.[56]

Many have protested the fact that any criticism of Islam is termed Islamophobia. In the words of former Labor Prime Minister Tony Blair of Britain: "It is not just your methods that are wrong, your ideas are absurd. Nobody is oppressing you. Your sense of grievance isn't justified."[57] Totalitarianism by jihadists may be correctly termed Islamofacism, as jihadists want Islam to control every part of the lives of human beings, not just religion, but customs, culture, society, governance, civil law, marriage, divorce, inheritance, education, economy, banking, international relations, domestic transactions, the press, entertainment, dress, language—almost everything in the world, including how women are treated. "Nothing, but nothing, could be further from McCain's (John McCain, the Republican Presidential candidate of 2008) belief that Islamofascism, or (in the terminology he favors) "radical Islamic extremism," is the "transcendent issue of the 21st century" and that "we engaged in a titanic struggle against it." Modern Muslims believe in *ijtihad*, an independent judgment—a rational interpretation of the Quran and *Sunnah*. There are also denials by most Muslims.

Ijtihad is associated with the Shia Muslims of the Jafari School and is not practiced by Sunni Muslims; a person who is qualified by extensive training to devise Ijtihad is called a *Mujtahid*. Yet there is not much difference between *Mujtahidists* and *Wahhabists*—Islamic fundamentalists. For most people, religion is a private matter, yet religion has been framed as a political matter from the earliest times. This may manifest as protests, resentment or resistance, sometime driven by militancy, and forceful rejection of existing systems; separation or secession for new nation-states; revolts against inequality (as when Untouchables in India converted to Islam); insurgence against repressive governments; and racial hatred (as when African-Americans embrace Islam in opposition to white Christians). Over the last sixty years, political Islam has turned into virulent, violent Islamic extremism whose sole aim is bloodshed that serves the cause of Islam. The rise of violent Islamism has been abetted by the fall of the Western powers, Communism, and dictators. As Sigmund Freud wrote to Albert Einstein in 1933: "People are like animals. They solve their problems through use of force." The holy aspects of Islam—spirituality, piety, and humanity—have been hijacked by global jihadists[58] with unholy acts of indiscriminate savagery. We all are victims of their unholy pursuits. From the ancient time, there have been fights between the divine, benevolent God and demonic, Satanic forces, between holy deeds of spirituality, peace, love, generosity, truth, enlightenment and unholy deeds of cruelty, barbarism, hypocrisy, falsehood, aggrandizement. The time has come for the first of these to prevail. However, moderate Muslim scholar Tariq Ramadan[59] has a different perspective on terror. He writes:

> The death of Osama bin Laden, as an icon and symbol of terrorism, is all but a non-event for the world's Muslims. His vision and actions were neither widely emulated nor respected, as numerous surveys by Western governments and anti-terrorism experts have confirmed. We are dealing, above all, with a primarily American, and more broadly European, event . . . But we must go well beyond the flurry of exuberance that saw people celebrating in the streets of New York. What lies ahead for the Middle East, as it contemplates two contradictory realities? On the one hand, there are the massively popular peaceful revolutions taking place in the Arab world. And on the other is the death of the symbol of violent extremism, of a leader of tiny marginal and marginalized groups.

The 2001 war in Afghanistan in 2001 (also known as the war on terror) was not won because of flawed strategic calculus and priorities. David Sanger writes: "And (President) Bush's reliance on (President) Musharraf to wage the war for him turned out to be one of the biggest misjudgments of the war on terror." But President Bush understood it as Sanger continues:

> With Pakistan, it revealed a misunderstanding of Musharraf and the games he was playing. Until the last eighteen months of his presidency, Bush appeared to believe what he said publicly about Musharraf, when he would walk him out to reporters at Camp David and pump him up as a man committed to democracy and a stalwart fighter against terrorism. He was neither.[60]

In addition, Bush's aligning with the wrong parties in Iraq and his war in Iraq in 2003 produced al Qaeda terrorists and radical Islamists in Iraq and elsewhere. And in the 1990s, President Reagan's support of the terrorist groups in Pakistan and Afghanistan, during the Soviet invasion of Afghanistan, only multiplied radical Islamists. But, despite the anti-war policies of France, Belgium and Spain, they are victims of the terrorists' attacks. Non Muslim immigrants, unlike Muslims, to Europe from Africa, Caribbean and Asia do not become radicalized terrorists. Lashkar-e-Taiba (LeT), allegedly aided and harbored by Pakistan's ISI, is now considered more dangerous than al Qaeda terrorists. As long as Pakistan provides sanctuary and support to the Taliban, LeT, and al Qaeda, the war in Afghanistan will not end.

Notwithstanding Sayyid Qutb' s worries of spiritual decline, sexual permissiveness, and moral decadence of the West, Qutb, a radical Islamist, wanted the restoration of Islamic values by violence and bloodshed. An ardent supporter of Qutb, Hasan al-Banna and his grandson Tariq Ramadan, an Islamist, do not want any change in Quran or Sharia, but Ayyan Hirsi Ali is for reform in Islamic doctrine, adopting enlightenment values of tolerance, pluralism, freedom, liberty, equality for women, and democracy. Islamists must abdicate deceit, deception, denial, and duplicity, *Taqiyya*, for a harmonious humanity. Radical Islamists, seeking worldwide caliphate, martyrdom, and mythical Paradise, renounce secular nationalism and enlightenment paradigms. Ian Buruma writes:

> Enlightenment values are often interpreted as Western values, not only by their erstwhile critics but by their current defenders. The main enemy is not just Islam, or Islamism, but the West by their promotion of moral relativism and multiculturalism.[61]

Let us hope, like Dutch philosopher Baruch Spinoza, French thinkers Alexi de Tocqueville, Francois Marie Arouet-Voltaire, and others, that enlightenment values prevail.

Notes

1. Dower, 2010, 303, 438, Judith Miller, Terror Target, *Wall Street Journal,* June 25, 2010; Lieberman, Joseph, Who's the Enemy in the War on Terror? *Wall Street Journal,* June 15, 2010.

2. Charles Krauthammer, *Terror—and candor in describing the Islamist ideology behind it*, *Washington Post*, July 2, 2010. Charles Krauthammer, Sacrilege at Ground Zero, *Washington Post,* August 13. 2010., Karen Hughes: Move the New York City mosque, as a sign of unity, *Washington Post,* August 22, 2010., Feisal Abdul Rauf, Building on Faith, *New York Times,* September 7, 2010,

3. Frank Gaffney, The end of the beginning for Shariah, *Washington Times,* August 26, 2010.

4. Mark Helprin, *The World Trade Center Mosque and the Constitution*, The Wall Street Journal, August 30, 2010.

5. D'Souza, Dinesh, 2010, 203, Anne Barnard, For Mosque Sponsors, *New York Times*, August 10, 2010.Rich Lowry, The Ground Zero Mosque: Not the Place, *The National Review,* August 10, 2010.Obama Strongly Backs Islam Center Near 9/11 Site, *New York Times*, August 14, 2010;Ross Douthat, Islam in Two Americas, *New York Times*, August 16, 2010.The Mosque of Misunderstanding, Opinion, *Wall Street Journal,* August 15, 2010. Niall Ferguson, America, the fragile empire Here today, gone tomorrow—could the United States fall that fast? *Los Angeles Times,* February 28, 2010; The Encyclopedia Britannica volume 1, 1985. 15th edition, has this to say about Ayodhya:"There are few monuments of any antiquity. Rama's birthplace is marked by a mosque, erected by the Moghul emperor Babur in 1528 on the site of an earlier temple."

6. Plot to bomb Parliament Hill alleged, by Kenneth Jackson, Toronto Sun, August 28, 2010

7. Clashes kill 12 in Philippines, April 14, 2010|Associated Press, http://articles.boston.com/2010-04-14/news/29285907_1_abu-sayyaf-muslim-militants-clashes; 11 dead as Muslim militants attack Philippine city, The Hindu, Manila, April 13, 2010, http://www.thehindu.com/news/international/article396241.ece

8. In audio message, bin Laden says he endorsed Dec. 25 airline bomb plot, by Jason Keyser, Washington Post, January 25, 2010.

9. Francis Fukuyama, A Year of Living Dangerously, Remember Theo van Gogh, and shudder for the future, *Wall Street Journal,* November 2, 2005.

10. USA PATRIOT ACT of 2001: This law, whose full title is "Uniting and Strengthening America by Providing Appropriate Tools Required to Intercept and Obstruct Terrorism" is the major legal response to the attacks of September 2001.

It broadens surveillance and other intelligence-gathering powers and provides additional legal weapons to prosecutors as well.

11. Radu, 2009, 510. Re: the ubiquitous claim that Islam is a "religion of peace." This idea is absurd on its face.

12. Status in the OSCE area of the Universal Anti-terrorism Conventions and Protocols as well as other international and regional legal instruments related to terrorism or cooperation in criminal matters, Action against Terrorism Unit Office of the Secretary General Organization for Security and Co-operation in Europe Wallnerstrasse, 6 A-1010 Vienna atu@osce.org, http://www.un.org/en/sc/ctc/specialmeetings/2011/docs/osce/2011-01-status-uati-legalinst.pdf (see Appendix 2).

13. Tablighi Jamaat: An Indirect Line to Terrorism, January 23, 2008 By Fred Burton and Scott Stewart, Stratford Global Intelligence, http://www.stratfor.com/weekly/tablighi_jamaat_indirect_line_terrorism.

14. Radu, 2009, 342, 471

15. Selbourne, 2005, 40, 86, 399; The Knickerbocker: Or, New-York Monthly Magazine, Volume 8 by Lewis Gaylord Clark, Kinahan Cornwallis, John Holmes Agnew, 2010, 413.

16. Gaddafi calls for jihad against Switzerland over minaret ban. The Sydney Morning Herald, February 26, 2010, http://www.smh.com.au/world/gaddafi-calls-for-jihad-against-switzerland-over-minaret-ban-20100226-p692.html.

17. Feith, *War and Decision*, 2008, 59, 168, 505.

18. Bobbitt, 2008, 236.

19. UK lifts Threat level, by Sylvia Hui, The Herald Sun, July 14, 2011, Christopher, Boucek, Yemen is a Near-Perfect Haven for Terrorists from South Asia, *The Independent,* December 31, 2009.

20. Rolf Mowatt-Larssen, AQ's Pursuit of Weapons of Mass Destruction, *Foreign Policy Magazine,* January 25, 2010, www.foreignpolicy.com/articles/2010/01/25/al_qaedas_pursuit_of_weapons_of_mass_destruction. Rolf Mowatt-Larssen, AQ Weapons of Mass Destruction Threat: Hype or Reality? Foreword by Graham Allison, Belfer Center for Science and International Affairs John. F. Kennedy School of Government, Harvard University, January 2010, http://belfercenter.ksg.harvard.edu/files/AQ-wmd-threat.pdf; M. Joby Warrick, Al Qaeda aims to hit U.S. with WMDs, Huge attack is top strategic goal, not "empty rhetoric," ex-CIA official says, NBC News/*Washington Post,* January 25, 2010.

21. Sadanand Dhume, *India's Group think on Islam: Wall Street Journal,* January 27, 2010.

22. Sadanand Dhume, *India's Group think on Islam: Wall Street Journal,* January 27, 2010.

23. Sadanand Dhume, *India's Group think on Islam: Wall Street Journal,* January 27, 2010.

24. Trial Date Set For Underwear Bomb Suspect, January 25, 2011 2:57 PM, CBS Detroit, http://detroit.cbslocal.com/2011/01/25/trial-date-set-for-underwear-bomb-suspect/.

25. Ishtiaq Ahmed, Abdul Ghaffar Khan, Islam and non-violence, *The Daily Times,* January26, 2010.

26. Bassam Tibi, Turkey's Islamist Danger. Islamists Approach Europe, *Middle East Quarterly,* Vol. 16, 1 (Winter 2009), pp. 47–54; Bassam Tibi, War and Peace in Islam, in: Andrew Bostom (Ed.), *The Legacy of Jihad* Prometheus Books, Amherst, New York, 2008. In contrast, the classic treatise on Islamic "international law" by the Muslim legal scholar Najib Armanazi acknowledges that international order, as established by the treaty of Westphalia [1648]—in which relations among states are organized on the basis of the mutual recognition of each other's sovereignty—is contradicted by the intention of the Arab conquerors to impose their rule everywhere (337); Bassam Tibi, Turkey's Islamist Danger. Islamists Approach Europe, *Middle East Quarterly,* Vol. 16, 1 (Winter 2009), pp. 47–54.

27. Bassam Tibi, War and Peace in Islam, in: Andrew Bostom (Ed.), *The Legacy of Jihadd* Prometheus Books, Amherst, New York, 2008, 337. Tibi (2008), Tibi (2009),

28. Graf, Bettina Graf, (ed), *The Global Mufti: The Phenomenon of Yusuf al-Qaradawi* (Columbia/Hurst), 2009, 207.

29. Dante Alighieri, *Dante's Inferno*, edited and with an introduction by Harold Bloom, Chelsea Publishers, Philadelphia, 2004 (Inferno XXVIII, pp. 19-42. See Image archive http://zombietime.com/mohammed_image_archive/dantes_inferno/ ; *The Divine Comedy,* translated by Allen Mandelbaum (New York: Bantam, 1982).

30. Elaine Sciolino, The teacher, Robert Redeker, 52, wrote in the center-right daily *Le Figaro* on that Muhammad was "a merciless warlord, a looter, a mass-murderer of Jews and a polygamist," and called the Quran "a book of incredible violence" (*New York Times*, September 30, 2006); Alan Riding: "To judge by the French press, Michel Houellebecq is the only writer who counts. And that was before the public had even read his latest novel, *The Possibility of an Island.* Then come the scandals surrounding Mr. Houellebecq's second and third novels, including the lawsuit that followed his published remark that 'Islam is the most stupid religion'" (New York Times, September 10, 2005).

31. Radu, 2009, 471

32. Abdul Salam Zaeef, 2010, 211, 235

33. Gabriel, 2008, 148

34. Cook, 2005, 165, 166

35. Reza Aslan, *No God but God,* Random House, New York, 2005, 262-263

36. Reza Aslan, *How to Win Cosmic War,* Random House, New York, 2009, 4-5, 11, 151

37. Karsh, 2006, 234; Yossef Bodansky, *Osama bin Laden: The Man Who Declared War on America*, Forum, New York, 2001. 503, *The High Cost of Peace: How Washington's Middle East Policy Left America Vulnerable to Terrorism,* Forum, New York, 2002., Jared Cohen, 2007.

38. Fawaz A. Gerges, *Journey of the Jihadists*, New York, N.Y: Harcourt Books, 2006, 203, 216; Farwaz A.Gerges, The Rise and Fall of Al Qaeda, Oxford, UK, Oxford University Press, 2011, 99.

39. S. Radhakrishnan, and Charles Moore (Eds), Indian Philosophy, 1957, 5, 16, 25, 630; *Advaita Vedanta: A Philosophical Reconstruction,* Eliot Deutsch, University of Hawaii Press, 1980. *Eight Upanisads, Vol 1 and 2,* Advaita Ashram,

Calcutta, 1998, 2000; *The Complete Works of Swami Vivekananda,* Vol. 1-8, Advaita Ashram, Calcutta, 1990. Biruni and the study of non-Islamic Religions, indefatigable traveler, www.robertnowlan.com/pdfs/al-Biruni, percent20Muhammad.pdf; *The Bhagavad Gita,* translated by Winthrop Sargeant, Albany, New York: State University of New York Press, 1984.

40. Ahmad Biruni(Ed.), *India,* Al Biruni, National Book Trust, 2005.

41. Mohsen Saeidi Madani, *Impact of Hindu Culture on Muslims,* M.D. Publications, New Delhi, 1993, 100.

42. Bodansky, Youssef, *Osama bin Laden:* New York, Forum.2001., 503

43. Jihad Jane, an American woman, faces terrorism charges *by Carrie Johnson, Washington Post,* March 10, 2010

44. Colleen LaRose: all-American neighbour or terrorist Jihad Jane? Arrest of 'cat lady', Ed Pilkington in New York, guardian.co.uk, 10 March 2010; Uriya Shavit and Frederic Wiesenbach, Muslim Strategies to Convert Western Christians, *Middle East Quarterly,* Spring 2009, 3-14.

45. Men seized days before planned attack in Britain, The Dawn, March 10. 2010

46. Ishtiaq Ahmed, *A time to humanise Islam, The Daily Times,* March 2, 2010.

47. Remarks by Selig S. Harrison, Director, Asia Program, Center for International Policy, Delivered at the Baluchistan International Conference, Washington, D.C., November 21, 2009, www.thebaluch.com/112109_SeligHarrison.php; The QDR in Perspective (Quadrennial Defense Review Independent Panel): Salafist *jihadi* movements, wedded to the use of violence and employing terror as their primary strategy, will remain both an international threat to the global system and a specific threat to America and its interests abroad. July 29, 2010, http://armedservices.house.gov/pdfs/FC072910/QDRIndependentPanelReport072910.pdf

48. Ackerman Statement from Hearing Entitled "Bad Company: Lashkar e-Tayyiba and the Growing Ambition of Islamist Militancy in Pakistan," March 11, 2010, http://ackerman.house.gov/index.cfm?sectionid=194&itemid=967.

49. Bob Woodward, *Obama's Wars,* Simon &Schuster, New York, NY, 2010, 379; Ross Douthat, *One Way Out, New York Times,* June 27, 2010.

50. Brent Stephen, The Face of Pakistan's Courage, The Wall Street Journal, July 12, 2011.

51. Sageman, 2008, 125-147, Stephen Kurczy, Top Ten American Jihadists, *Christian Science Monitor,* March 10, 2010., Rudolph Peters, in *The Legacy of Jihad* Prometheus Books, Amherst, New York, 2008. Andrew Bostom, (Ed. 2008), pp. 304, 321, 324, 325; Robert Wright, The Myth of Modern Jihad, *New York Times,* June 29, 2010.

52. Jalal, 2008. 304

53. Sanaullah Baloch: Pakistan's Other Fault Lines, *Daily Times,* March 28, 2010; David Ignatius, *To Pakistan, almost with love, The Washington Post,* March 4, 2010; Arif Nizami, *The Way the World Sees Us, The News,* Pakistan, June 26, 2010, http://www.thenews.com.pk/editorial_detail.asp?id=247198

54. Falk, and Morgenstern, 2009, 36

55. Jalal, 2008, 45, 48-49

56. Blair launches stinging attack on 'absurd' British Islamists, Nicholas Watt, political editor, The Observer, Sunday 1 July 2007, http://www.guardian.co.uk/politics/2007/jul/01/uk.terrorism; Podhoretz, 2008, 227.

57. Muhammad Abd al Salam (Abu Umamah, Ed.), *Jihad: The Absent Obligation* Birmingham, UK: Maktabah Al Ansaar, 2000, pp. 16, 79, www.islamistwatch.org/texts//obligation/oblig.html; Omar Nasiri, 2006; *164 Jihad Verses in the Quran,* Compiled by Yoel Natan, www.answering-islam.org/Quran/Themes/jihad_passages.html; David M. Haugen, S. Musser, and K. Lovelace (Eds.), 2009, 71.

58. Muhammad Abd al Salam (Abu Umamah, Ed.), *Jihad: The Absent Obligation* Birmingham, UK: Maktabah Al Ansaar, 2000, pp. 16, 79, www.islamistwatch.org/texts//obligation/oblig.html, Omar Nasiri, 2006; 164 *Jihad* Verses in the *Quran,* Compiled by Yoel Natan, www.answering-islam.org/Quran/Themes/jihad_passages.html; David M. Haugen, S. Musser, and K. Lovelace (Eds.), 2009, 71; Omar Abdel Rahman, Egyptian scholar on jihad: "If God . . . says, 'Do Jihad,' it means do jihad with the word, with the cannon, with the grenades, and with missiles. This is jihad."

59. Tariq Ramadan: Osama bin Laden is dead, but will West revive ties with Muslims?, Christian Science Monitor, May 6, 2011;Jonathan Laurence, The Prophet of Moderation: Tariq Ramadan's Quest to Reclaim Islam, *Foreign Affairs,* May--June 2007; Ian Buruma, Tariq Ramadan Has an Identity Issue, *New York Times,* February 4, 2007; Professor Ramadan and others had created a 'linguist lexicon' in which words such as 'Islamic terrorism', 'Jihad', and 'War on Terror' were banned from the use by officials (The European Commission); Walid Phares, *The Confrontation*, New York:Palgrave Macmillan, 2008, 177.

60. David Singer, *The Inheritance*, New York: Harmony Books, 2009, 122, 261;

61. Ian Buruma, Taming the Gods, Princeton, NJ: Princeton University Press, 2010, 94; Robert Audi, The Cambridge Dictionary of Philosophy, Cambridge, UK: Cambridge University Press, 1999.

Appendix 1

Terrorist Attacks and Organizations

I. Terrorist Attacks Since 2000

Compiled by William Robert Johnston and others, December 3, 2008, www.johnstonsarchive.net/terrorism/terrisrael.html (Number of deaths shown in parentheses)

Aug 2001:	attack on train south of Luanda, Angola (152)
11 Sep 2001:	crashing of hijacked planes into World Trade Center, New York City, Pentagon in Alexandria, Virginia, and site in Pennsylvania, USA (2819)
12 Oct 2002:	car bombing in Kuta, Indonesia (202)
26 Oct 2002:	hostage taking in theater in Moscow, Russia (170)
29 Aug 2003:	car bombing outside mosque in Najaf, Iraq (125)
1 Feb 2004:	two suicide bombings in Irbil, Iraq (109)
21 Feb 2004:	armed attack and arson at refugee camp, Uganda (239)
27 Feb 2004:	bombing and fire on ferry near Manila, Philippines (118)
2 Mar 2004:	multiple suicide bombings at shrines in Kadhimiya and Karbala, Iraq (188)
11 Mar 2004:	bombings of four trains in Madrid, Spain (191)
24 Jun 2004:	multiple bombings in several cities in Iraq (103)
1–3 Sep 2004:	hostage taking at school in Beslan, Russia (366)
28 Feb 2005:	car bombing outside medical clinic in Hilla, Iraq (135)
14 Sep 2005:	multiple suicide bombings and shooting attacks in Baghdad, Iraq (182)
5 Jan 2006:	bombings in Karbala, Ramadi, and Baghdad, Iraq (124)
11 Jul 2006:	multiple bombings on commuter trains in Mumbai, India (200)

16 Oct 2006:	truck bombing of military convoy near Habarana, Sri Lanka (103)
23 Nov 2006:	multiple car bombings in Baghdad, Iraq (202)
22 Jan 2007:	multiple bombings in Baghdad area, Iraq (101)
3 Feb 2007:	truck bombing in marketplace in Baghdad, Iraq (137)
6 Mar 2007:	two bombings and other attacks on pilgrims, Hilla, Iraq (137)
27 Mar 2007:	two truck bombings in Tal Afar, Iraq (152)
18 Apr 2007:	bombings in Baghdad, Iraq (193)
3–10 Jul 2007:	hostage taking and subsequent storming of mosque in Islamabad, Pakistan (102)
7 Jul 2007:	bombings in Baghdad and Armili, Iraq (182)
14 Aug 2007:	multiple truck bombings in Al-Qataniyah and Al-Adnaniyah, Iraq (520)
18 Oct 2007:	bombing of motorcade in Karachi, Pakistan (137)
17 Feb 2008:	bombing at Kandahar, Afghanistan (105)
26–29 Nov '08:	multiple gun and grenade attacks in Mumbai, India (174)

National Counterterrorism Center: Terrorist Attacks, Report 30 April 2008: http://wits.nctc.gov/reports/crot2007nctcannexfinal.PDF;

In 2010, there were 11,500 terrorists attacks in 72 countries resulting 50,000 victims, including 13,200 deaths. More than 75% terrorists attacks and deaths were in South Asia and East Asia. (http://www.nctc.gov/witsbanner/docs/2010_report_on_terrorism.pdf)

II. Organizations

Abu Nidal Organization (ANO), Abu Sayyaf Group (ASG)—The Philippines

Al-Aqsa Martyrs Brigade, Al-Muhajirourn (UK based), Ansar al-Islam Armed Islamic Group (GIA), Asbat al-Ansar, Aum Shinrikyo of Japan, Basque Fatherland and Liberty (ETA)

Communist Party of the Philippines/New People's Army (CPP/NPA), Continuity Irish Republican Army, Egyptian Islamic Jihad (EIJ), Gama'at al-Islamiyya (Islamic Group), Hamas (Islamic Resistance Movement)—Palestine, Harakat ul-Mujahidin (HuM)

Harakat-ul Jihad al-Islami/Bangladesh (HuJI-B)/Hizb ut-Tahrir (HuT, the party of liberation)

Hizb ul-Mujahidden (HuM, the party of holy warriors, the militant wing of the Jamaat-e-Islami (JeI), an Islamist organization

HuJI-B has connections to the Pakistani militant groups Harakat ul-Jihad-Islami (HuJI) and Harakat ul-Mujahedin (HuM), as well as LeT in Pakistan, Jammu, and Kashmir. The leaders of HuJI-B signed the February 1998 *fatwa* sponsored by OBL that declared American civilians legitimate targets for attack.

Hizballah/Hezbollah (Party of God)—Lebanon

Hizb-ut-Tahrir/Hizb-at-Tahrir al-Islami (HT/HuT); started in 1953 in Jerusalem by Taqiuaddin al-Nabhani, has branches in 40 countries (www.socialcohesion.co.uk/files/1257159197_1.pdf)

Indian Mujahideen (IM), Irish Republican Army (IRA), Islam4UK (UK-based), Islamic Jihad Group—Syria, Islamic Movement of Uzbekistan (IMU) /Islamic Jihad Union (IJU)

Jama'at-ud-Da'wah (JuD, launched in Lahore, Pakistan in 1985 as *Markaz Da''a wal Irshad*)

Jaish-e-Mohammed (JeM, Army of Mohammed), Jamiat-ul-Ulema-e-Islam (JUI), al-Jihad (Egyptian Islamic Jihad), Kahane Chai (Kach)

Jemaah Islamiah (JI)

Kongra-Gel (KGK, formerly Kurdistan Workers' Party, PKK, KADEK)

Kosovo Liberation Army (KLA), Lashkar-e Taiba (LeT) (Army of the Righteous)—South Asia

Lashkar i Jhangvi, Liberation Tigers of Tamil Eelam (LTTE)

Libyan Islamic Fighting Group (LIFG)

Moroccan Islamic Combatant Group (GICM)

Mujahedin-e Khalq Organization (MEK)

Muslim Brotherhood (MB)

National Liberation Army (ELN)

National Salvation Front (FSN)

Palestine Liberation Front (PLF)

Palestinian Islamic Jihad (PIJ)

Popular Front for the Liberation of Palestine (PFLP)

PFLP-General Command (PFLP-GC)

Tanzim Qa'idat al-Jihad fi Bilad al-Rafidayn (QJBR) (al-Qaida in Iraq; formerly Jama'at al-Tawhid wa'al-Jihad, JTJ, al-Zarqawi Network)

al-Qaida (AQ), AQ in the Islamic Maghreb (AQIM, formerly GSPC), AQ in Iraq (AQI), AQ in the Arab Pennisula (AQAP)

Revolutionary Armed Forces of Colombia (FARC), Revolutionary Nuclei (formerly ELA)

Revolutionary Organization 17 November

Revolutionary People's Liberation Party/Front (DHKP/C)

Sandanista National Liberation Front (FSLN), Shining Path (Sendero Luminoso, SL) of Peru

Sopha-e-Sahaba Pakistan (SSP), Students Islamic Movement of India (SIMI)
The Kurdish Workers Party (PKK) of Turkey/ Iraq
The Liberation Tigers of Tamil Elam of Sri Lanka
The Mahdi Army (Mukta Sadr) of Iraq (The Mahdi Army, also known as the Mahdi Militia or Jaish al Mahdi, is an Iraqi paramilitary force created by the Iraqi Shi'ite cleric Muqtada al-Sadr in June 2003)
Tehrik-i-Taliban of Pakistan (TTP). In December 2007, about thirteen disparate militant groups coalesced under the umbrella of Tehrik-i-Taliban Pakistan (TTP), also known as the Pakistani Taliban\United Jihad Council, United Self-Defense Forces of Colombia (AUC)
World Islamic Front

1. Abu Nidal Organization (ANO), founded by Abu Nidal (1937–2002), born Sabri Khalil al-Banna, who was also the founder of Fatah—The Revolutionary Council, a militant Palestinian group.
2. Popular Front for the Liberation of Palestine (PFLP), founded by George Habash in 1967 as a Marxist organization advocating multinational Arab revolution.
3. Popular Front for the Liberation of Palestine—General Command (PFLP-GC), which split from PFLP under the leadership of Ahmid Jibril in 1968.
4. Palestine Liberation Front, which split from PFLP in 1975.
5. Democratic Front for the Liberation of Palestine, formed from PFLP in 1969.
6. Islamic Resistance Movement or Hamas ("zeal"). Sheikh Ahmad Yassin founded Hamas in 1987, as an Islamic fundamentalist organization with ties to Egypt's Muslim Brotherhood. Since June 2007, after winning a large majority in the Palestinian Parliament and defeating rival Palestinian party Fatah in a series of violent clashes, Hamas has governed the Gaza portion of the Palestinian Territories.
7. Palestine Islamic Jihad, which aims to pursue jihad to form a Palestinian state.
8. Palestine Liberation Organization (PLO), which was led by Arafat. The PLO, an Arab-Palestinian terror group, was the most important member of the international terrorist network providing training, money, intelligence and weaponry for terrorist movements in Ireland, Spain, France, Germany, Japan, Italy, and Latin America.
9. Fatah, the largest faction of the PLO, which lost its majority in the Palestinian parliament to Hamas in January, 2006.

10. Hezbollah, an Iranian Shia group in Lebanon that maintains strong support among Lebanon's Shia population, and gained a surge of support from Lebanon's broader population (Sunni, Christian, Druze) immediately following the 2006 Lebanon war. www.nefafoundation.org/miscellaneous/FeaturedDocs/nefap akcamps0708.PDF)CRS Report for Congress, February 6, 2004, by A.K. Cronin, H. Aden, A. Frost and B. Jones

www.fas.org/irp/crs/RL32223.pdf

www.publicsafety.ohio.gov/links/terrorist_exclusion_list.pdf

www.nefafoundation.org/miscellaneous/FeaturedDocs/nefapakcamps 0708.pdf—Country Reports on Terrorism, August 2010, www.state.gov/ s/ct/rls/crt/2009/index.htm

www.humansecuritygateway.com/documents/USGOV_CountryReports OnTerrorism2009.pdf

Evan Kohmann, The Jihadists of Pakistan, www.nefafoundation.org/mis-cellaneous/pakistanjihad0806.pdf

Appendix 2

The UN Resolutions on Human Rights and Sovereignty

(i) The UN Action to Counter Terrorism

> The passing of the resolution on the United Nations Global Counter-Terrorism Strategy with its annexed Plan of Action by 192 Member States represents a common testament that we, the United Nations, will face terrorism head on and that terrorism in all its forms and manifestations, committed by whomever, wherever and for whatever purposes, must be condemned and shall not be tolerated.
>
> *—Sheikha Haya Rashed Al Khalifa,*
> *President of the 61st session of the*
> *General Assembly Launching the UN*
> *Global Counter-Terrorism Strategy*
> *on 19 September 2006.*

Sixteen universal instruments (thirteen instruments and three amendments) against international terrorism have been elaborated within the framework of the United Nations system relating to specific terrorist activities. Member States through the General Assembly have been increasingly coordinating their counter-terrorism efforts and continuing their legal norm-setting work. The Security Council has also been active in countering terrorism through resolutions and by establishing several subsidiary bodies. At the same time a number of programmes, offices and agencies of the United Nations system have been engaged in specific activities against terrorism, further assisting Member States in their counter-terrorism efforts.

To consolidate and enhance these activities, Member States in September 2006 embarked upon a new phase in their counter-terrorism efforts by agreeing on a global strategy to counter terrorism. The Strategy marks the first time that all Member States of the United Nations have agreed to a common strategic and operational framework to fight terrorism. The Strategy forms a basis for a concrete plan of action: to address the conditions conducive to the spread of terrorism; to prevent and combat terrorism; to take measures to build state capacity to fight terrorism; to strengthen the role of the United Nations in combating terrorism; and to ensure the respect of human rights while countering terrorism. The Strategy builds on the unique consensus achieved by world leaders at their 2005 September Summit to condemn terrorism in all its forms and manifestations.

Updates

The General Assembly held its first review of the implementation of the Strategy on 4–5 September 2008 and adopted a resolution reaffirming its commitment to the Strategy and its implementation. As one of the inputs to this process, the Secretary-General has compiled a report on activities of the UN system in implementing the Strategy.

(ii) UN Security Council Resolution 1373 (2001)

September 28, 2001
The Security Council,
Reaffirming its resolutions 1269 (1999) of 19 October 1999 and 1368 (2001) of 12 September 2001,

Reaffirming also its unequivocal condemnation of the terrorist attacks which took place in New York, Washington, D.C., and Pennsylvania on 11 September 2001, and expressing its determination to prevent all such acts,

Reaffirming further that such acts, like any act of international terrorism, constitute a threat to international peace and security,

Reaffirming the inherent right of individual or collective self-defence as recognized by the Charter of the United Nations as reiterated in resolution 1368 (2001),

Reaffirming the need to combat by all means, in accordance with the Charter of the United Nations, threats to international peace and security caused by terrorist acts,

Deeply concerned by the increase, in various regions of the world, of acts of terrorism motivated by intolerance or extremism,

Calling on States to work together urgently to prevent and suppress terrorist acts, including through increased cooperation and full implementation of the relevant international conventions relating to terrorism,

Recognizing the need for States to complement international cooperation by taking additional measures to prevent and suppress, in their territories through all lawful means, the financing and preparation of any acts of terrorism,

Reaffirming the principle established by the General Assembly in its declaration of October 1970 (resolution 2625 (XXV)) and reiterated by the Security Council in its resolution 1189 (1998) of 13 August 1998, namely that every State has the duty to refrain from organizing, instigating, assisting or participating in terrorist acts in another State or acquiescing in organized activities within its territory directed towards the commission of such acts,

Acting under Chapter VII of the Charter of the United Nations,

1. *Decides* that all States shall:
   (a) Prevent and suppress the financing of terrorist acts;
   (b) Criminalize the willful provision or collection, by any means, directly or indirectly, of funds by their nationals or in their territories with the intention that the funds should be used, or in the knowledge that they are to be used, in order to carry out terrorist acts;
   (c) Freeze without delay funds and other financial assets or economic resources of persons who commit, or attempt to commit, terrorist acts or participate in or facilitate the commission of terrorist acts; of entities owned or controlled directly or indirectly by such persons; and of persons and entities acting on behalf of, or at the direction of such persons and entities, including funds derived or generated from property owned or controlled directly or indirectly by such persons and associated persons and entities;
   (d) Prohibit their nationals or any persons and entities within their territories from making any funds, financial assets or economic resources or financial or other related services available, directly or indirectly, for the benefit of persons who commit or attempt to commit or facilitate or participate in the commission

of terrorist acts, of entities owned or controlled, directly or indirectly, by such persons and of persons and entities acting on behalf of or at the direction of such persons;

2. *Decides also* that all States shall:
   (a) Refrain from providing any form of support, active or passive, to entities or persons involved in terrorist acts, including by suppressing recruitment of members of terrorist groups and eliminating the supply of weapons to terrorists;
   (b) Take the necessary steps to prevent the commission of terrorist acts, including by provision of early warning to other States by exchange of information;
   (c) Deny safe haven to those who finance, plan, support, or commit terrorist acts, or provide safe havens;
   (d) Prevent those who finance, plan, facilitate or commit terrorist acts from using their respective territories for those purposes against other States or their citizens;
   (e) Ensure that any person who participates in the financing, planning, preparation or perpetration of terrorist acts or in supporting terrorist acts is brought to justice and ensure that, in addition to any other measures against them, such terrorist acts are established as serious criminal offences in domestic laws and regulations and that the punishment duly reflects the seriousness of such terrorist acts;
   (f) Afford one another the greatest measure of assistance in connection with criminal investigations or criminal proceedings relating to the financing or support of terrorist acts, including assistance in obtaining evidence in their possession necessary for the proceedings;
   (g) Prevent the movement of terrorists or terrorist groups by effective border controls and controls on issuance of identity papers and travel documents, and through measures for preventing counterfeiting, forgery or fraudulent use of identity papers and travel documents;

3. *Calls upon* all States to:
   (a) Find ways of intensifying and accelerating the exchange of operational information, especially regarding actions or movements of terrorist persons or networks; forged or falsified travel documents; traffic in arms, explosives or sensitive materials;

use of communications technologies by terrorist groups; and the threat posed by the possession of weapons of mass destruction by terrorist groups;

(b) Exchange information in accordance with international and domestic law and cooperate on administrative and judicial matters to prevent the commission of terrorist acts;

(c) Cooperate, particularly through bilateral and multilateral arrangements and agreements, to prevent and suppress terrorist attacks and take action against perpetrators of such acts;

(d) Become parties as soon as possible to the relevant international conventions and protocols relating to terrorism, including the International Convention for the Suppression of the Financing of Terrorism of 9 December 1999;

(e) Increase cooperation and fully implement the relevant international conventions and protocols relating to terrorism and Security Council resolutions 1269 (1999) and 1368 (2001);

(f) Take appropriate measures in conformity with the relevant provisions of national and international law, including international standards of human rights, before granting refugee status, for the purpose of ensuring that the asylum seeker has not planned, facilitated or participated in the commission of terrorist acts;

(g) Ensure, in conformity with international law, that refugee status is not abused by the perpetrators, organizers or facilitators of terrorist acts, and that claims of political motivation are not recognized as grounds for refusing requests for the extradition of alleged terrorists.

4. *Notes* with concern the close connection between international terrorism and transnational organized crime, illicit drugs, money-laundering, illegal arms-trafficking, and illegal movement of nuclear, chemical, biological and other potentially deadly materials, and in this regard emphasizes the need to enhance coordination of efforts on national, sub regional, regional and international levels in order to strengthen a global response to this serious challenge and threat to international security;

5. *Declares* that acts, methods, and practices of terrorism are contrary to the purposes and principles of the United Nations and that knowingly financing, planning and inciting terrorist acts are also contrary to the purposes and principles of the United Nations;

6. *Decides* to establish, in accordance with rule 28 of its provisional rules of procedure, a Committee of the Security Council, consisting of all the members of the Council, to monitor implementation of this resolution, with the assistance of appropriate expertise, and calls upon all States to report to the Committee, no later than 90 days from the date of adoption of this resolution and thereafter according to a timetable to be proposed by the Committee, on the steps they have taken to implement this resolution;

7. *Directs* the Committee to delineate its tasks, submit a work programme within 30 days of the adoption of this resolution, and to consider the support it requires, in consultation with the Secretary-General;

8. *Expresses* its determination to take all necessary steps in order to ensure the full implementation of this resolution, in accordance with its responsibilities under the Charter;

9. *Decides* to remain seized of this matter. (Courtesy of the UNO)

(iii) The Universal Declaration of Human Rights

On 10 December 1948, the General Assembly of the United Nations adopted and proclaimed the Universal Declaration of Human Rights, the full text of which appears in the following. Following this historic act, the Assembly called upon all Member countries to publicize the text of the Declaration and "to cause it to be disseminated, displayed, read and expounded principally in schools and other educational institutions, without distinction based on the political status of countries or territories."

PREAMBLE
Whereas recognition of the inherent dignity and of the equal and inalienable rights of all members of the human family is the foundation of freedom, justice and peace in the world,

Whereas disregard and contempt for human rights have resulted in barbarous acts which have outraged the conscience of mankind, and the advent of a world in which human beings shall enjoy freedom of speech and belief and freedom from fear and want has been proclaimed as the highest aspiration of the common people,

Whereas it is essential, if man is not to be compelled to have recourse, as a last resort, to rebellion against tyranny and oppression, that human rights should be protected by the rule of law,

Whereas it is essential to promote the development of friendly relations between nations,

Whereas the peoples of the United Nations have in the Charter reaffirmed their faith in fundamental human rights, in the dignity and worth of the human person and in the equal rights of men and women and have determined to promote social progress and better standards of life in larger freedom,

Whereas Member States have pledged themselves to achieve, in co-operation with the United Nations, the promotion of universal respect for and observance of human rights and fundamental freedoms,

Whereas a common understanding of these rights and freedoms is of the greatest importance for the full realization of this pledge, Now, Therefore THE GENERAL ASSEMBLY proclaims THIS UNIVERSAL DECLARATION OF HUMAN RIGHTS as a common standard of achievement for all peoples and all nations, to the end that every individual and every organ of society, keeping this Declaration constantly in mind, shall strive by teaching and education to promote respect for these rights and freedoms and by progressive measures, national and international, to secure their universal and effective recognition and observance, both among the peoples of Member States themselves and among the peoples of territories under their jurisdiction.

Article 1. *All human beings are born free and equal in dignity and rights. They are endowed with reason and conscience and should act towards one another in a spirit of brotherhood.*

Article 2. Everyone is entitled to all the rights and freedoms set forth in this Declaration, without distinction of any kind, such as race, colour, sex, language, religion, political or other opinion, national or social origin, property, birth or other status. Furthermore, no distinction shall be made on the basis of the political, jurisdictional or international status of the country or territory to which a person belongs, whether it be independent, trust, non-self-governing or under any other limitation of sovereignty.

Article 3. Everyone has the right to life, liberty and security of person.

Article 4. No one shall be held in slavery or servitude; slavery and the slave trade shall be prohibited in all their forms.

Article 5. No one shall be subjected to torture or to cruel, inhumane or degrading treatment or punishment.

Article 6. Everyone has the right to recognition everywhere as a person before the law.

Article 7. All are equal before the law and are entitled without any discrimination to equal protection of the law. All are entitled to equal protection against any discrimination in violation of this Declaration and against any incitement to such discrimination.

Article 8. Everyone has the right to an effective remedy by the competent national tribunals for acts violating the fundamental rights granted him by the constitution or by law.

Article 9. No one shall be subjected to arbitrary arrest, detention or exile.

Article 10. Everyone is entitled in full equality to a fair and public hearing by an independent and impartial tribunal, in the determination of his rights and obligations and of any criminal charge against him.

Article 11.
  (1) Everyone charged with a penal offence has the right to be presumed innocent until proved guilty according to law in a public trial at which he has had all the guarantees necessary for his defense.
  (2) No one shall be held guilty of any penal offence on account of any act or omission which did not constitute a penal offence, under national or international law, at the time when it was committed. Nor shall a heavier penalty be imposed than the one that was applicable at the time the penal offence was committed.

Article 12. No one shall be subjected to arbitrary interference with his privacy, family, home or correspondence, nor to attacks upon his honour and reputation. Everyone has the right to the protection of the law against such interference or attacks.

Article 13. (1) Everyone has the right to freedom of movement and residence within the borders of each state. (2) Everyone has the right to leave any country, including his own, and to return to his country.

Article 14. (1) Everyone has the right to seek and to enjoy in other countries asylum from persecution. (2) This right may not be invoked in the case of prosecutions genuinely arising from non-political crimes or from acts contrary to the purposes and principles of the United Nations.

Article 15. (1) Everyone has the right to a nationality. (2) No one shall be arbitrarily deprived of his nationality nor denied the right to change his nationality.

Article 16. (1) Men and women of full age, without any limitation due to race, nationality or religion, have the right to marry and to found a family. They are entitled to equal rights as to marriage, during marriage and at its dissolution. (2) Marriage shall be entered into only with the free and full consent of the intending spouses. (3) The family is the natural and fundamental group unit of society and is entitled to protection by society and the State.

Article 17. (1) Everyone has the right to own property alone as well as in association with others. (2) No one shall be arbitrarily deprived of his property.

Article 18. Everyone has the right to freedom of thought, conscience and religion; this right includes freedom to change his religion or belief, and freedom, either alone or in community with others and in public or private, to manifest his religion or belief in teaching, practice, worship and observance.

Article 19. Everyone has the right to freedom of opinion and expression; this right includes freedom to hold opinions without interference and to seek, receive and impart information and ideas through any media and regardless of frontiers.

(iv) UN Convention and Protocols on Terrorism

There are twelve UN Convention and Protocols on Terrorism: The major multilateral Conventions and Protocols related to states' responsibilities for combating terrorism. They are:

1. Offences and Certain Other Acts Committed on Board Aircraft;
2. Suppression of Unlawful Seizure of Aircraft;
3. uppression of Unlawful Acts Against the Safety of Civil Aviation;
4. Prevention and Punishment of Crimes Against Internationally Protected Persons;
5. International Convention Against the Taking of Hostages;
6. Physical Protection of Nuclear Material;
7. Suppression of Unlawful Acts of Violence at Airports Serving International Civil Aviation,
8. Suppression of Unlawful Acts Against the Safety of Civil Aviation;
9. Suppression of Unlawful Acts Against the Safety of Maritime Navigation;
10. Suppression of Unlawful Acts Against the Safety of Fixed Platforms Located on The Continental Shelf;
11. Marking of Plastic Explosives for the Purpose of Detection;
12. International Convention for the Suppression of the Financing of Terrorism.

(Courtesy of the UNO)

Appendix 3

Glossary

Adab	culture; social manner
Ahmadiyyas	minority Muslim sects in South Asia
Allah	God of Islam
Allahu Akbar	God is great
Al Qaeda	"the base," a terrorist group
Al Rahim	the merciful
Al-wala' wal-bara'	love and hate for Allah's sake
Aman	peace, protection
Amir (Emir)	leader
Aqidah	creed
Ayatollah	high-ranking Shia (Shiites)
Azaadi	freedom
Azaan (Adaan)	Call to prayer from masjids, or mosques
Backbone	Coast-to-coast trunk cables of fiber optics lines and other channels
Badla	revenge
Bid'ah	apostasy, heresy
Bismillah	in the name of God
Botnet	operates or controls network on commands from unauthorized users (a collection of software agents, or robots, that run autonomously and automatically). A network of computers using distributed computing software. It refers to a group of computers infected with the malicious kind of robot software (the bots), which damages computers with computer viruses.
Burqa	head-to-toe cover for Muslim women
Caliph	successors of Muhammad

Dar ul-Aman	abode of peace
Dar al-Harb	house of war, enemy territory
Dar al-Islam	the house of Islam—entire Islamic Community
Darul Ulam	abode of Islamic learning
Dawa(h) (Da'wa)	call to Islam, propagation of faith, Islamic proselytism
Dhimmi	Non-Muslims under Islamic sovereignty
Din	religion
Emir	Prince, military commanders
Encryption	codes that makes messages and data secret
Fasiq	liar, evil person
Fatwa	religious edict (the third source of Islamic law, the Quran and *Hadith* being the first and the second)
Fedayeen (fidayeen)	Suicide squads, suicide bombers
Fiqh	observance of rituals and morals; law
Fitna	disagreement, division
Ghazi	Warrior
Hacker	an unauthorized user who changes or damages software, or who attempts to gain unauthorized access to proprietary computer systems
Hadith	tradition, the life of the Prophet Mohammed, sayings of the Prophet
Hafiz	Who has memorized the Quran
Halal	Muslim way of ritually slaughtering animals
Harakat ul Mujahedeen (HuM)	Pakistani terrorist group
Haram	forbidden
Harb	warfare
Hartal	public strike to halt transportation, close business and shops
Hezbollah	Lebanon-based terrorist group
Hijab	head scarf
Hijra	emigration
Hisbah	public vigilance
Ibadat	worship
Id al-Fitr	the feast of breaking the Ramadan fast
Iddah	the waiting period of a widowed or divorced woman

Ijma	consensus
Ijtihad	the use of reason to arrive at knowledge of truth in religious matters
Imam	prayer leader, title for a religious leader
Iman	faith
Internet	A worldwide seamless connected telephone, computer connection links to provide access to billions of users at the same time. The systems consists of millions of private, public, academic, business, and government networks, of local to global scope, that are linked by a broad array of electronic, satellite, and optical networking technologies. It is an infrastructure of worldwide information systems.
Internet Service Provider (ISP)	provides wired or wireless connectivity of users to the Internet
Intifada	shaking off, fighting for freedom, uprising
Insallah	God willing
Insaniyat	humanity
Ishq	love
Islam	submission to Allah
Jahiliyyah	ignorance, arrogance, violent and explosive irascibility
Jihad	striving, struggling for the cause of Islam or the Prophet, holy war
Jihad al Akbar	the greater jihad
Jihad al-asghar	the lesser jihad
Jizya	tax on non-Muslims, nonbelievers, or infidels
Kafir (kefir, kaffar, kafer)	infidel, unbeliever
Kalifa	the caliph, the successor of Mohammed
Kalima	words or phrases to affirm faith, used when someone converts to Islam
Khalifa	The vice-regency of man on earth or succession to the Prophet
Kuffar	plural of Kafir, unbelievers, infidels
Kufr	Insolence
Lashkar-e-Taiba (LeT)	Pakistan-based terrorist group
Logic bomb	software to damage or destroy data

Madrassas (madrassah; madrasi, plural of madras)	religious seminaries
Maghfira	forgiveness
Mahdi/Mehdi	Twelfth Imam—the Guided One
Malware	malicious software that changes the original software; includes logic bombs, worms, and viruses
Masjid	mosque, a place of worship for Muslims
Maulana/Mawlana	Muslim scholar; master, learned person
Maulvi	religious teacher
Mawali	non-Arab Muslims
Mohajir	refugee
Mohammed/ Muhammad	founder of Islam, the Prophet
Mufti	a person authorized to issue a *fatwa*
Mujahedeen/ Mujahidin (*mujaheddîn*)	holy warriors, Islamic guerillas
Mujahid	one who practices jihad, holy warrior, Islamic guerilla
Muharram	Shia festival
Mullah	Islamic religious teacher
Munkar	reprehensible deed
Murtadd	apostate, one who has abandoned Islam
Namaz	prayer
Nifaq	hypocrisy
Pir	spiritual guide
Protocol	set of mutually agreed-on rules governing the format of messages that are exchanged between computers
Qawawali	devotional music
Qazi/Quadi	judge
Quami Madrassas	radical religious schools
Quran/Qur'an	the Muslim holy book, Koran
Qu'idat al-Jihad	Global Jihad
Ramadan/Ramazan	the ninth month of the Islamic calendar, the month of fasting, in which Muslims refrain from eating, drinking, and smoking from dawn until sunset. The Qur'an was first revealed to Prophet Muhammad during the month of Ramadan.
Saheed	martyr

Salaam Aleikum	Muslim greeting: peace be with you
Salat	the ritual of worship five times a day
Server	a computer or network system providing access to multiple users, serving web pages, e-mail, etc. It makes services such as access to data files, programs, and peripheral devices available to workstations on a network.
Shah	title of Iranian kings
Shahda	the Muslim faith: There is no God but God
Shahadat	martyrdom
Shaheed	martyr, anyone who is killed while fighting pagans, or rebels,
Sharia/Shariah/ Shari'ah	the way, Islamic law based on the Quran and sunna; a comprehensive laws governing Islamic society.
Shia/Shi'a/Shiites	followers of caliph Ali, fourth successor of the Prophet Muhammad
Shira	biographies of Prophet Mohammed
Shirk	(sin of) idolatry
Shura	consultation/council
Sunna(h)	custom, the example or way of life of the Prophet, embracing what he said, did, or agreed to; habit; The words, habits, and practices of Mohammed, as transmitted by reliable witnesses and recorded in the hadith and the Quran
Sunni	believers of the first four caliphs, successors of the Prophet Muhammad
Sura (h)	chapter, Council
Syed	chief of a clan or tribe
Tablegh (tabligh)	preaching
Tajdid	renewal
Takfir	Muslim apostate (Muslims who are not fundamentalists)
Takfiri	apostasy, impure, to be excommunicated (kafir infidel)
Takiyya	concealing feeling (sanctioned deception to protect or promote Islam)
Taklif	legal charge
Taliban	Islamic religious student
Tanzeem	group

Tawhid	unity of God
TCP/IP	the format used for transmission and reception of data over telephone wires to the Internet
Trapdoor	unauthorized software that is sent to let unauthorized users access the network
Trojan Horse	a computer program is designed to have destructive effects on computer operations
Ulema	priestly class of Muslims, Muslim scholars
Umma (ummah)	the Islamic community
Waqf	endowment of property for religious purposes
Worm	computer code planted illegally to destroy data in any system
Zakaht	tax on wealth, one of the five pillars of Islam obligatory on Muslims
Zakat	alms
Zimmi	protected non-Muslims
Zina	adultery

Appendix 4

The Quranic Verses and Islamic Sects

(a) Selected Quranic Verses

2:39: but those that deny and reject Our revelations shall be the heirs of Hell and they shall abide forever.

2:89: The curse of Allah is on the unbelievers.

2:223: Your women are a tilth for you (to cultivate). So go to your tilth as ye will.

4:12: A male shall inherit twice as much as a female.

4:15: If any one of your women is guilty of lewdness . . . confine them until death claims them.

4:16: If two men among you commit indecency (sodomy) punish them both. If they repent and mend their ways, let them be. Allah is forgiving and merciful.

4:34: Men are in charge of women, because Allah hath made the one of them to excel the other. As for those from whom ye fear rebellion, admonish them and banish them to beds apart, and scourge them.

4:144: O ye who believe! Choose not disbelievers for (your) friends in place of believers. Would you give Allah a clear warrant against you?

5:10: As for those who disbelieve and deny Our revelations, they are the heirs of Hell.

5:32: For that cause We decreed for the children of Israel that whosoever killeth a human being for other than manslaughter or corruption in the earth, it shall be as if he had killed all mankind, and whose saveth the life of one, it shall be as if he had saved the life of all mankind. Our messengers came unto them of old with clear proofs (of Allah's sovereignty), but afterwards lo! Many of them became prodigals in the earth.

5:33:   The only reward of those who make war upon Allah and His messenger and strive after corruption in the land will be that they will be killed or crucified, or have their hands and feet and on alternate sides cut off, or will be expelled out of the land. Such will be their degradation in the world, and in the Hereafter theirs will be an awful doom. . . .

5:51:   Believers, take neither Jews nor Christians for your friends. They are friends with one another. Whoever of you seeks their friendship shall become one of their numbers. Allah does not guide the wrong-doers.

5:57:   Believers, do not seek the friendship of the infidels and those who were given the Book before you, who have made your religion a jest and a pastime. . .

5:64:   The Jews say: "God's hand is chained." May their own hands be chained! May they be cursed for what they say!

8:12:   When thy Lord inspired the angels (saying:) I am with you. So make those who believe stand firm. I will throw fear into the hearts of those who disbelieve. Then smite the necks and smite of them each finger.

9:5:   Then when the sacred months have passed, slay the idolaters wherever ye find them, and take them (captive), and besiege them, and prepare for them each ambush. But if they repent and establish worship and pay the poor-due, then leave their way free. Lo! Allah is Forgiving, Merciful.

9:73:   Oh Prophet! Strive against the disbelievers and the hypocrites! Be harsh with them. Their ultimate abode is hell, a hapless journey's end.

22:19:   These twains (the believers and the disbelievers) are two opponents who contend concerning their Lord. But as for those who disbelieve, garments of fire will be cut out for them; boiling fluid will be poured down on their heads.

47:4:   When you meet the unbelievers in the battlefield strike off their heads and, when you have laid them low, bind your captives firmly. Then grant them their freedom or take ransom from them, until War shall lay down her burdens.

73:12:   We have in store for them (unbelievers) heavy fetters and a blazing fire, choking food and harrowing torment: on the day when the earth shall quiver with all its mountains and the mountains crumble into heaps of shifting sand.

76:1-5:   For the unbelievers we have prepared chains and fetters and a blazing Fire.

77:39: Woe on that day to the disbelievers! Begone to the Hell which you deny! Depart into the shadow that will rise high in three columns, giving neither shade nor shelter from the flames, and throwing up sparks as huge as towers, as bright as yellow camels.

98:7:   The unbelievers among the People of the Book and the pagans shall burn forever in the fire of Hell. They are the vilest of all creatures.

Sources:

1. Dawood, 1990.
2. Pickthall, 1996.

Below are some quotations from the Quran: Sami Alrabaa (2010), which appeared in *Europe News*, September 7, 2008.

Literally, the Quran says the following about the Jews, Christians, and other "unbelievers."

And the Jews say: Uzair is the son of Allah; and the Christians say: The Messiah is the son of Allah; these are the words of their mouths; they imitate the saying of those who disbelieved before; may Allah destroy them; how they are turned away! (9:30)

And the Jews will not be pleased with thee, nor will the Christians, till thou follow their creed. Say: Lo! the guidance of Allah (Himself) is Guidance. And if thou shouldst follow their desires after the knowledge which hath come unto thee, then wouldst thou have from Allah no protecting friend nor helper. (2:120)

And slay them (the unbelievers) wherever ye find them, and drive them out of places whence they drove you out, for prosecution is worse than slaughter (Idolatry is worse than carnage). And fight not with them at the inviolable place of worship until they first attack you there, but if they attack (there), and then slay them. Such is the reward of disbelievers. (2:191)

Let not the believers take the unbelievers for friends rather than believers; and whoever does this, he shall have nothing of (the guardianship of) Allah, but you should guard yourselves against them, guarding carefully; and Allah makes you cautious of (retribution from) Himself; and to Allah is the eventual coming. (3:28)

And guard yourselves against the fire which has been prepared for the unbelievers. (3:131)

And when ye go forth in the land, it is no sin for you to curtail (your) worship if ye fear that those who disbelieve may attack you. In truth the disbelievers are your open enemy to you. (4:101)

O you who believe! Fight those of the unbelievers who are near to you and let them find in you hardness; and know that Allah is with those who guard (against evil). (9:123)

Surely we have prepared for the unbelievers chains and shackles and a burning fire. (76:4)

O you who believe! if you obey a party from among those who have been given the Book, they will turn you back as unbelievers after you have believed. (3:100)

And of their taking usury (interest on money) when they were forbidden it, and of their devouring people's wealth by false pretences. We have prepared for those of them who disbelieve a painful doom. (4:161)

Lo! Allah has cursed the unbelievers and has prepared for them a burning fire. (33:64)

Does Allah discriminate?

You are the best of the nations raised up for (the benefit of) men; you enjoin what is right and forbid the wrong and believe in Allah; and if the followers of the Book had believed it would have been better for them; of them (some) are believers and most of them are transgressors. (3:110)

Therefore, what does the Quran say about those who turn their back to Islam and commit apostasy?

They long that ye should disbelieve even as they disbelieve, that ye may be upon a level (with them). So choose not friends from among them till they forsake their homes in the way of Allah; if they turn back (to enmity) then take them and kill them wherever ye find them, and choose no friend nor helper from among them. (4:89)

O you who believe! when you deal with each other in contracting a debt for a fixed time then call in to witness from among your men two witnesses; but if there are not two men, then one man and two women from among those whom you choose to be witnesses, so that if one of the two errs, the second of the two may remind the other. (2:282)

Women, according to the Quran, are, in general, unclean creatures.

O you who believe! do not go near prayer until you have washed yourselves; and if you have touched women, and you cannot find water, betake yourselves to pure earth, then wipe your faces and your hands; surely Allah is Pardoning, Forgiving. (4:43)

In case of inheritance, a woman inherits half of the portion a man inherits.

They ask you for a decision of the law. Say: Allah gives you a decision concerning the person who has neither parents nor offspring; if a man dies (and) he has no son and he has a sister, she shall have half of what he leaves, and he shall be her heir if she has no son; but if there be two (sisters), they shall have two-thirds of what he leaves; and if there are brethren, men and women, then the male shall have the like of the portion of two females; Allah makes clear to you, lest you err; and Allah knows all things. (4:176)

King Abdullah, the absolute monarch of Saudi Arabia, said in a televised speech broadcast on August 27, 2008, "We do not need democracy, we do not need political parties, we do not need Western human rights, we do not need their freedom of speech. What we need is the Quran. It regulates our life perfectly. It is the best legislation in the history of mankind; it is the word of Allah. There is nothing better than Allah's law."

The "Hadeeth," a collection of statements and comments that Prophet Mohammed allegedly made during his lifetime, is also full of atrocities. Here is a sample:

"A woman came to the Prophet and admitted that she had committed adultery and thereafter became pregnant. The Prophet summoned her husband and all people of Median (in Saudi Arabia). He said, 'This woman committed adultery. Therefore, after she delivers her innocent baby, all of you are going to stone her to death. This is Allah's verdict.' After she delivered her baby she was stoned to death in the center of the town." (Narrated by Muslim, a close contemporary follower of Mohammed, cited by Khoury, in *The Quran,* p. 550.)

On disabled people:

"The meanest beasts in God's sight are those that are deaf, dumb, and devoid of reason. Had God perceived any virtue in them, He would surely endowed them with hearing. But even if He made them hear, they would have turned away and refused to listen." (8:22-23, Dawood, 1990.)

(b) Islamic Sects

1. Sunnites (Sunni): Those who follow the tradition of the prophet are called Sunnites. They compose 90 percent of all Muslims. Since Mohammad left no clear instructions concerning his successor, Sunnites decided their Islamic leader should be nominated by representatives of the community. The "ulama" Sunnite religious scholars have less authority than the Imams and are considered to be teachers and wise sages. Sunnites accept the line of successions as passing through the four caliphs: Abu Bakr, Omar, Othman, and Ali.

2. Shiites (Shia): Their name means "partisans." They believe that only descendants of Mohammad's family are the rightful heirs to spiritual leadership. Found mainly in Iran, Yemen, Algeria, and Iraq, Shi'ites tend to revere the Shari'a (though not as fervently as the Wahhabi). About ten percent of all Muslims belong to this branch of Islam. Their leaders, Imams, wield dogmatic spiritual authority, as in the case of the Ayatollah Khomeini of Iran. Some Shi'ites believe that a twelfth Imam who disappeared in A.D. 882 will return someday as a messiah, the Madhi (guided one), to establish a kingdom on earth. The sub-sect *Ismailis* believes that an Imam of sinless perfection with the power to perform miracles always dwells on earth. They are firmly entrenched today as a merchant class in India and East Africa. The Aga Khan is their Imam.

3. Wahhabi/Wahabi/Salafi: This group tends to be the most strict and "puritanical." Mohammed Ibn Abd al-Wahhab founded the sect in the eighteenth century by preaching strict adherence to the Qur'an. Saudi Arabia's moralistic, authoritarian rule is an

example of Wahhabi devotion.

4. Druze: A secretive Islamic breakaway group concentrated in Lebanon around Mt. Harmon and in the mountains near Beirut and Sidon. They refer to themselves as the Mowahhidoon. Most Muslims consider the sect blasphemous since it declared that God was manifested in human form as the Egyptian caliph al Hakim Bi-amr Allah 1,000 years ago. They number at least 250,000. The Druze does not accept new members, virtually never discuss their faith and often pose as members of the dominant religion where they live.

5. Alawi: A small branch of Islam that broke away from the Shiite in the ninth century under the leadership of Ibn Nucair Namin Abdi. Almost exclusively found on the Syrian coast plains, the Alawi have 1.5 million members including Syrian President Hafez Assad.

6. Ismali: A Shiite sect that believes the succession of spiritual leadership should have continued through the sons of Muhammad Ibn Isma'il. The Ismali believe that Islam has never been without a living Imam, even though clearly recognized spiritual authority became increasingly rare.

7. Ahmadiyya: It was founded in Qadian, India, by Mirza Ghulam Ahmad, who died in 1908. Ahmadiyyas believe their founder was a renovator of Islam, a position some Muslims consider to be heretical. Ahmadiyyas believe the Prophet came as Krisna, the Hindu God. He said the Prophet will appear as Buddha sometime. Mirza Ghulam claimed towards the end of the nineteenth century to be the Mahdi of the latter days as awaited by the Muslims as well as the Promised Messiah (the spiritual second coming of Jesus). Ahmadiyya define their motto as "love for all and hatred for none." They treat Christians, Hindus, and Buddhists as believers.

8. Sufi: These are the mystics within the Muslim faith, a religious order that follows mystical interpretations of Islamic doctrines and practices. In South Asia, some Hindus believe that Sufism is a path to attain God, rejecting the worldliness prevalent in

Islamic Sultanates. After the fall of Muslim orthodoxy from power at the centre of India, the Sufi became free from the control of the Muslim orthodoxy and consorted with Hindu saints, who influenced them to an amazing extent. The Sufi adopted sacred devotion from the Vaishnava Vedantic School and Bhakti and Yogic practices of Hinduism. Some Muslims think Sufism is heretic, because they respect saints.

9. Barelvi Islam: Another Sect of Islam that gives more importance to Hadith. Deobandis and Barelvis are the two major groups of Muslims in the Subcontinent apart from the Shia. Barelvi Hanafis deem Deobandis to be kefir. Those hostile to the Barelvis deprecated them as the shrine-worshipping, the grave-worshiping, ignorant Barelvis. Much smaller sects in Pakistan include the Ahl-e-Hadees and Ahl-e-Tashee. The non-Pashtun population of Pakistan is predominantly Barelvi. The stronghold of Barelvism remains Punjab, the largest province of Pakistan. By one estimate, in Pakistan, the Shias are 18 percent, Ismailis 2 percent, Ahmediyas (Ahmadiyya) 2 percent, Barelvis 50 percent, Deobandis 20 percent, Ahle Hadith 4 percent, and other minorities 4 percent. The Ahle-e-Hadith is a small group of Sunni Muslims in India who do not consider themselves bound by any particular school of law and rely directly on the Prophet's Sunnah (the Quran and Hadith). By another estimate some 15 per cent of Pakistan's Sunni Muslims would consider themselves Deobandi, and some 60 per cent are in the Barelvi tradition based mostly in the province of Punjab. But some 64 per cent of the total seminaries are run by Deobandis, 25 per cent by the Barelvis, 6 percent by the Ahle Hadith and 3 percent by various Shiite organizations. The Barelvis, Shias, Ismalis (Pakistani Muhammed Jinnah's religion), and Ahmadiyyas joined the Pakistan movement, while the Deobandis opposed the formation of Pakistan, since they wanted to Islamize all of India. But the Deobandis in Pakistan owed their allegiance to Shabbir Ahmed Usmani, who organized the Deobandi ulema who were in favor of Pakistan into the Jamiat Ulema-i-Islam.

10. Baha'is: It is a monotheistic religion founded by Baha'u'llah in 1840 in Iran. There are an estimated five to six million Baha'is

around the world in more than 200 countries and territories. It has roots in Shia. Baha'i teachings emphasize the underlying unity of the major world religions. Religious history is seen to have unfolded through a series of divine messengers, each of whom established a religion. These messengers have included Abraham (Jew), Krishna (Hindu), Buddha (Buddhist), Jesus (Christian), Muhammed (Islam) and others, including most recently Baha'u'llah. The Islamic Republic of Iran did not recognize the Baha'is as a religious minority, and the sect has been officially persecuted.

11. Hanafi: Among the four established Sunni schools (the other three being Shafi, Maliki, and Hanbali) of legal thought (madhabs) in Islam, the Hanafi school is the oldest. It assimilates local customs and culture and is tolerant of other religious views, emphasizing the role of reason. The Hanafi School has the most followers in the Muslim world, predominantly among the Sunnis of Central Asia, South Asia, Iraq, Mauritius, Syria, Turkey, and Europe.

12: Kharaijits (also called Khawarijs): The earliest extremist sect in Islam were the Kharijites, the original heretics, who declared jihad against the unbelievers and the apostates: Muslims who refused to follow what they considered the "true path" of Islam. The sect, followers Ali bin Abi Talib, grandson of the Prophet, who became the fourth caliph in 657, started the first Islamic civil war in the late seventh century AD, concentrated in today's southern Iraq. They were very violent and committed political assassination in order to advance their cause, including the fourth Caliph Ali, the cousin of the Prophet Muhammad, in 661. The Kharijites believed that the act of sinning is analogous to Kefir (disbelief) and that every grave sinner was regarded as a *Kefir* (unbeliever). There are several groups influenced by Kharijite beliefs, including Takfir wal Hijra in Egypt, the Armed Islamic Group (GIA) in Algeria, and Palestinian Islamic Jihad and AQ. The sect appears to have influenced Muhammad Abdul Wahhab during the latter part of the eighteenth century.

13: Qaramatis: Like the Kharaijits, the Qaramatis (also called

Qaramitans, Carramathians) were followers of Hamdan al-Qaramat, another Muslim extremist who lived from 906 to 929. Qarmat started the first Ismailia movement in the later part of the ninth century. The Qaramitis were plundering and killing hajj pilgrims. According to them, the hajj had developed into *shirk* (idolatry) by Muslim Hajjis, because they were worshiping at the Kaaba and the black stone inside. In 930, they desecrated the holiest place Mecca, seizing the Kaaba and stealing this black meteorite.

(Adapted from: http://forum09.faithfreedom.org/viewtopic.php?f=30 &t=1188, www.familybible.org/Teaching/Religions/Islam/MajorSectsOf Islam.htm)

Appendix 5

Abbreviations

AAZ	Ayman al-Zawahiri
AHPC	All Parties Hurriyat Conference
AIML	All India Muslim Leagues
AJK	Azad Jammu and Kashmir
AQ	Al-Qaeda, al-Qaeda, al-Qa'ida
AQAP	AQ in the Arab Peninsula
AQIM	AQ in the Islamic Maghreb
BGP	Border Gateway Protocol
BJP	Bharatiya Janata Party
CIA	Central Intelligence Agency
CNCI	Comprehensive National Cybersecurity Initiative
DARPA	Defense Advanced Research Projects Agency
DDOS	Distributed Denial of Service
DHS	Department of Homeland Security
FATA	Federally Administered Tribal Agency in Pakistan
FBI	Federal Bureau of Investigation
HT/HeT	Hizb-e-Tahir—Central Asia Terrorist Organization
HuM	Harakat-ul Mujahideen/Hizb-ul-Mujahidden
IED	Improvised Explosive Device
IJU	Islamic Jihad Union
IMT	Islamic movement in Turkmenistan
IMU	Islamic Movement of Uzbekistan
INC	Indian National Congress
ISI	Inter-Service Intelligence Agency (Pakistan)
ISP	Internet Service Provider

JeM	Jaish-e-Mohammad
J&K	Jammu and Kashmir
JI	Jamaat-e-Islami/Jemaah Islamiah
JKLF	Jammu and Kashmir Liberation Front
JUD/JuD	Jama'at-ud-Da'wah Pakistan
JUI	Jamiat Ulema-e-Islam
JUM	Jamiat Ulema-e-Islam
KLA	Kosovo Liberation Army
KP	Khyber Pakhtunkhwa (formerly NWFP)
LAT	*The Los Angeles Times*
LeJ	Lashkar-e-Jhangvi
LeT	Lashkar-e-Taiba/Lashkar-e-Tayyeba
LOC	Line of Control
LTTE	Liberation of Tiger of Tamil Eelam
MB	Muslim Brotherhood
MC	Muslim Conference
MUF	Muslim United Front
NC	National Conference
NSA	National Security Agency
NYT	*The New York Times*
OBL	Osama bin Laden
OIC	Organization of Islamic Countries
PDP	Peoples Democratic Party
PLO	Palestinian Liberation Organization
SIMI	Students of Islamic Movements of India
SSP	Sipah-e-Sahaba Pakistan (SSP)
TCP/IP	Transmission Control Protocol/Internet Protocol— data for routing in the Internet
TNSM	Tehreek-e-Nafaz-e-Mohammadi
UJC	United Jihad Council
UNO	The United Nations Organization
VHP	Viswa Hindu Parishad
WMD	Weapons of mass destruction
WP	*The Washington Post*
WSJ	*The Wall Street Journal*
WT	*The Washington Times*

References

(NOTE: CUP: Columbia University Press, GHP: Green Haven Press, HUP: Harvard University Press, OUP: Oxford University Press, YUP: Yale University Press)

Abuza, Zachary, *Militant Islam in Southeast Asia,* Boulder, CO: Lynne Reiner Publishers, Inc. 2003.

Ahmed, Akbar, *Jinnah, Pakistan, and Islamic Identity, The Search for Saladin*, New York: Routledge. 1997.

Ahmed, Ishtiaq, *The Demand for Pakistan and Islam,* Daily Times, June 8, 2010.

Ajami, Fouad, *Autocracy and the Decline of the Arabs*, WSJ, August 6, 2009.

——, *Pakistan's Struggle for Modernity*, WSJ, May 26, 2010.

Akbar, M.J, *The Shade of Swords*, New York: Routledge, 2002.

Alexander, Mathew, *How to Break a Terrorist,* New York, NY: Free Press, 2008.

Alexander, Yonah and Milton Hoeing (Ed.), *Super Terrorism, Biological, Chemical, and Nuclear,* Ardsley: Transnational Publishers, Inc. 2001.

Ali, Ayaan Hirsi, *Infidel*, New York, NY: Free Press, 2007.

Ali, Tariq, *The Clash of Fundamentalists,* London: Verso. 2002.

Allawi, Ali A., *The Crisis of Islamic Civilization,* New Haven: YUP, 2009.

Allison, Graham, Nuclear Disorder, *Foreign Affairs,* January/February, pp. 74–85, 2010.

——, *Nuclear Terrorism,* New York: Times Books, Henry Holt. 2004.

Almond, G.R., S. Appleby, and E. Sivan, *Strong Religion,* Chicago: University of Chicago Press, 2003.

Amis, Martin, *The Second Plane,* New York: Alfred A. Knopf, 2008.

Angelis, Gina, *Cyber Crimes*, Philadelphia: Chelsea House Publishers, 2000.

An-Na'im, Abdullahi, *Islam and the Secular State,* Cambridge, MA: HUP, 2008.

Ansary, Tamim, *Destiny Disrupted,* New York: Public Affairs Books. Steerforth Press, 2009.

Armstrong, David and J. Trento, *America and the Islamic Bomb,* New York: Steerforth, 2007.

Armstrong, Karen, *Islam,* Waterville, [STATE?]: Thorndike Press, 2002.

———, *Muhammad,* New York: Harper One, Harper Collin Publishers, 2006.

Atwan, Abdel, *The Secret History of al Qaeda*, Berkley, CA: University of California, 2006.

Audi, Robert (Ed.), *The Cambridge Dictionary of Philosophy*, Cambridge, UK: Cambridge University Press, 1995.

Balkin, Karen, *The War on Terrorism,* Farmington Hills, MI: GHP, 2005.

Barber, Benjamin, *Jihad vs. MacWorld*, New York: Ballantine Books, Random House, 1995.

Barre, Elizabeth, *The Shaykh Al Islam, The Legacy of Ibn Taymiyya in 20th Century Political Islam,* Islamic Tradition, December 2004.

Basham, A.L, *The Origins and Development of Classical Hinduism,* Edited and Annotated by Kenneth Zysk, Boston: Beacon Press, 1989.

———, *The Wonder That Was India*, 3rd Revised Edition, London, MacMillan Publishers, Rupa, New Delhi, 2001.

Bashir, Halima, *Tears of the Desert*, New York: One World Ballantine Books, 2008.

Bawer, Bruce, *Surrender*, New York, Doubleday, 2009.

Benjamin, Daniel, *Will Terrorists Go Nuclear?* Amherst, NY: Prometheus Books, 2008.

———, *Strategic Counterterrorism*, Foreign Policy Paper, Number 7, Brookings Institution, Washington, D.C., October 2008.

Benjamin, D. and S. Simon, *The Age of Sacred Terror, Radical Islam's War Against America,* New York: Random House, 2003.

———, *The Next Attack*, New York: Times Books, 2005.

Benjamin, Daniel and Gabriel Weimann, What the Terrorists Have in Mind, *The New York Times,* October 27, 2004.

Bergen, Peter, *Holy War, Inc.* New York, NY: The Free Press, 2001.

——— and Thomas Luckmann, *The Social Construction of Reality,* New York, NY: Anchor Publishers/Random House, 1996.

Berkowitz, B., *Strategic Advantage,* Washington, D.C.: Georgetown University Press, 2008.

Berman, Eli, *Radical, Religious, and Violent: The New Economics of Terrorism*, Cambridge, MA: The MIT Press, 2009.

Berman, Paul, *Terror and Liberalism*, New York, W.W. Norton Company, 2003.

——, *The Flight of Intellectuals,* Hoboken, NJ: Melville House, 2010.

Blackburn, S., *The Oxford Dictionary of Philosophy,* New York: OUP, 1994.

Bloom, Mia, *Dying to kill,* New York: CUP, 2005.

Bobbitt, Philip, *Terror and Consent,* New York: Alfred A. Knopf, 2008.

Bodansky, Yossef, *Chechen Jihad,* New York: Harper Collins, 2007.

Bonner, Michael, *Jihad in Islamic History,* Princeton: Princeton University Press, 2006.

Boot, Max, "Pirates, Terrorism and Failed States," *WSJ,* December 9, 2008.

Bose, Sugata and Ayesha Jalal, *Modern South Asia,* New York: Routledge, 2004.

Bose, Sumantra, *Kashmir,* Cambridge, UK: Cambridge University Press, 2003.

Bostom, Andrew (Ed.), *The Legacy of Jihad:* Amherst, NY: Prometheus Books, 2008.

Brendon, Piers, *Decline and Fall of the British Empire,* NewYork: Alfred A. Knopf, 2009.

Brown, Stuart, D. Collinson, and R. Wilkinson (Eds.), *One Hundred Twentieth Century Philosophers*, New York: Routledge, 1998.

Brumberg, Daniel, "Islam Is Not the Solution (or the Problem)," *The Washington Quarterly* 29:1 pp. 97–116, 2005-06 97, 1997.

Buchanan, Patrick J., *Day of Reckoning,* New York: Thomas Dunne Books, St. Martin Press, 2007.

Bukay, David, *From Muhammad to Osama bin Laden*, New Brunswick, NJ: Transaction Publishers, 2008.

Burke, Jason, *Al-Qaeda,* New York: I.B. Taurus Co., 2003.

Burleigh, Michael, *Sacred Causes,* New York: Harper Collin Publishers, 2007.

——, *Blood and Rage*: New York: Harper Collin Publishers, 2009.

Burton, Fred, *Ghost,* New York, NY: Random House, 2008.

Buruma, Ian, *Murder in Amsterdam,* New York, NY: The Penguin Press, 2006.

Byman, Daniel, *The Five Front War*, Hoboken, N.J: John Wiley & Sons, Inc, 2008.

Caldwell, Christopher, *Reflections on the Revolution in Europe,* New York: Doubleday, 2009.

Chaliand, G. and A. Blin (Ed.), *The History of Terror,* Berkley, CA: University of California, 2007.

Chellaney, Brahma, "Insider threat to Pakistan's 'crown jewels,'" *The Hindu,* May 25, 2009.

Chomsky, Noam, *9-11,* New York: Seven Stories Press, 2001.

Chopra, Deepak, *Muhammed,* New York, Harper Collins Publishing, 2010.

Cigar, Norman (Tr.), *Al Qaeda's Doctrine for Insurgency, 'Abd Al Aziz Al-Murqrin's A Practical Course for Guerrilla War,* Washington, D.C.: Potomac Books, Inc, 2009.

Clark, W and P. Levin, Securing the Information Highway, *Foreign Affairs,* November/December 2009.

Clarke, David (Ed.), *Technology and Terrorism,* New Brunswick: Transaction Publishers, 2004.

Clarke, Richard, *Against All Enemies*, New York: Free Press, 2004.

———, Ten Years Later, *Atlantic Monthly,* Jan/Feb.2009.

———, *Your Government Failed You,* New York: Harper Collins Publishers, 2008.

——— and R. Knake, *Cyber War,* New York: Harper Collins Publishers, 2010.

Cohen, Jared, *Children of Jihad*, New York: Penguin Books, 2007.

Cohen, Stephen, "The Nation and the State of Pakistan," *The Washington Quarterly,* 25:3, pp. 109–122, 2002.

Cole, Dave, and Jules Lobel, *Less Safe, Less Free,* New York: The New Press, 2007.

Cole, Juan, *The Taliban, Women, and The Private Sphere in The Taliban and Crisis of Afghanistan,* Ed. by Robert Crews and Amin Tarzi, Cambridge, MA: HUP, 2008.

———, *Engaging Muslim World,* New York: Palgrave MacMillan/St. Martin Press, 2009.

Cole, Leonard, *The Eleventh Plague,* New York: W.H. Freeman, 1997.

Coll, Steve, *Ghost Wars,* New York: Penguin Books, 2003.

———, *The Osama bin Ladens,* New York: Penguin Books, 2009.

Cook, David, *Understanding Jihad,* Berkley: University of California Press, 2005.

Costigan, Sean and David Gold (Ed.), *Terrornomics,* Burlington: Ashgate, 2007.

Coughlin, Con, *Khomeini's Ghost,* New York: HarperCollins, 2009.

Crews, Robert and Amin Tarzi (Eds.), *The Taliban and the Crisis of Afghanistan*, Cambridge, MA: HUP, 2008.

Cruickshank, Paul and M. Ali, *Abu Musab Al Suri: Architect of the New Al Qaeda,* Studies in Conflict & Terrorism, 30:1–14, 2007.

Cutis, Lisa, After Mumbai: Time to Strengthen US-India Counterterrorism Cooperation, Heritage Foundation *Backgrounder #* 2217, December 9, 2008.

Dadwood, N.J., *The Quran, 5th Edition,* London: *Penguin* Books, 1990.

Darwish, Nonie, *Now They Call me Infidel*, New York: Penguin Books, 2006.

Dasgupta, C., *War and Diplomacy in Kashmir,* Thousand Oaks, CA: Sage Publications, 2002.

Davis, Paul and Kim Cragin (Ed.), *Social Science for Counter Terrorism*, Santa Monica: Rand National Defense Research Institute, 2009.

Delong-Bas, Natana, *Wahhabi Islam—From Revival and Reform to Global Jihad*, New York: OUP, 2004.

Dershowitz, Alan, *Why Terrorism Works,* New Haven, CT: YUP, 2002.

———, *Preemption: A Knife that Cuts Both Ways,* New York: W.W. Norton, 2006.

———, *Blasphemy*, Hoboken, NJ: John Wiley & Sons, 2007.

Dobbins, James, *After the Taliban*, Washington, D.C.: Potomac Books, Inc, 2008.

Docherty, Paddy, *The Khyber Pass, A History of Empire and Invasion*, New York: Union Square Press, an Imprint of Sterling Publishing Co. Inc., NY, 2008.

Dower, John, *Cultures of War*, New York: W.W. Norton /The New Press, 2010.

D'Souza, Dinesh, *The Root of Obama's Rage*, Washington, D.C.: Regnery Publishing, 2010.

Dudley, William, *India and Pakistan: Opposing View Points,* Farmington Hills, MI: GHP, 2003.

Durant, Will, *Our Oriental Heritage, The Story of Civilization, Vol. 1,* New York: Simon and Schuster, 1935.

Egdendorf, Laura (Ed.), *Terrorism,* Farmington Hills, MI: GHP, 2004.

Elshtain, Jean, *Just War Against Terror*, New York: Basic Books, 2003.

El -Fadl, Khalid Abou, *The Place of Tolerance*, Boston: Beacon Books, 2002.

Emerson, Steven, *Jihad Incorporated*, Amherst, NY: Prometheus Books, 2006.

Engel, Richard, *War Journal, My five years in Iraq,* New York: Simon and Schuster, 2008.

Esposito, John, Ed, *Political Islam, Revolution, Radicalism or Reform*, Boulder: Lynne Reiner Publishers, 1997.

———, Ed. *The Oxford History of Islam*, New York: OUP, 1999.

———, *The Unholy War*, *Terror in Name of Islam*, Oxford: OUP, 2002.

———, (Editor-in-Chief), *Islamic World; Past and Present*, New York: OUP, 2004.

Fair, C. Christine, "Pakistan's Partial War on Terror: The deadly result of cooperation with terrorists," *WSJ*, October 2009.

——, From Strategy to Implementation, Testimony presented before the House Foreign Affairs Committee, May 5, 2009.

——, "Time for Sober Relations," *The Washington Quarterly*, April 2009.

——, A Better Bargain for Aid to Pakistan, *WP*, May 30, 2009.

——, and Sumit Ganguly (Ed.), *Treading on Hallowed Ground,* New York, NY: OUP, 2008.

Falk, Ophir and Henry Morgenstern (Ed.), *Suicide Terror, Understanding and Confronting The Threat,* Hoboken, NJ: Wiley, 2009.

Fallaci, Oriana, *The Force of Reason,* New York: Rizzoli International, 2006.

Farah, Caesar, *Islam,* Hauppauge, NY: Barron's Educational Series, 2000.

Farmer, John, *The Ground Truth*, New York: Riverhead Books/Penguin Books, 2009.

Faruqui, N.A, *Ahmadiyyat in the Service of Islam, Ahmediayyaa Ish'at,* Newark, California: Lahore, Inc., 1983.

Feifer, Gregory, *The Great Gambit,* New York: Harper Collins Publishers, 2009.

Feith, Douglas, *War and Decision;* New York: Harper, 2008.

Feldman, Noah, *Fall and Rise of the Islamic State*, Princeton, NJ: Princeton University Press, 2008.

——, "Why Shariah?" *New York Times,* March 16, 2008.

Ferguson, Niall, *The War of the World,* New York, NY: The Penguin Press, 2006.

Fernea, Elizabeth and Robert Fernea, *The Arab World, Forty Years of Change*, New York, Anchor Books, Doubleday, 1985.

Filkins, Dexter, *The Forever War*, New York: Alfred A. Knopf, 2008.

Fischer, Eric, *Changing a National Framework for Cybersecurity*, New York, Nova Science Publishers, Inc, 2009.

Fischer, Louis, *Essentials of Gandhi,* New York: Vintage Books, 1962.

Fitzerald, Paul and Elizabeth Gould, *Invisible History*, San Francisco: City Lights Books, 2009.

Frantz, Douglas and Catherine Collins, *The Nuclear Jihad*, New York: Twelve Publishers/Hachette Books Group, 2008.

Freedman, Lawrence, *A Choice of Enemies—America Confronts the Middle East,* New York: Public Affairs, 2008.

Fregosi, Paul, *Jihad in the West*, Amherst, NY: Prometheus Books, 1998.

Friedman, Lauri (Ed.), *Weapons of Mass Destruction*, Farmington Hills, MI: GHP, 2007.

——, *Terrorism,* Farmington Hills, MI: GUP, 2005.

——, *What Motivates Suicide Bombers?* Farmington Hills, MI: GHP, 2005.

Friedman, Thomas, *The World Is Flat,* New York: Farrar, Straus and Giroux, 2005.

Frum, David and Richard Perle, *An End To Evil,* New York: Random House, 2003.

Fukuyama, Francis, A Year of Living Dangerously, *WSJ,* November 2, 2005.

Fuller, Graham, *A World without Islam*, Foreign Policy, January/February 2008.

———, *Invitation to Terror,* London: Continuum, 2003.

Furedi, Frank, *Why Education is not Educating* London: Continuum 2009.

———, *Invitation to Terror: The Expanding Empire of the Unknown*, London: Continuum, 2007.

Gabriel, Brigitte, *They Must Be Stopped*, New York, St. Martin's Press, 2009.

Galbraith, Peter, *Unintended Consequences*, New York: Simon & Schuster, 2008.

Gandhi, Mohandas, *Autobiography,* New York: Dover Publications, Inc., 1983.

Ganguly, Sumit, "Breaking America's Silence on Pakistan," *WSJ,* November 3, 2009.

———, "Pakistan's Fickle Ally Washington Must Stick by Islamabad," *Newsweek*, October 9, 2009.

———, and David Fidler (Ed.), *India and Counterinsurgency,* New York, NY: Routledge, 2009.

———, and David Hagerty, *Fearful Symmetry,* Seattle, WA: University of Washington Press, 2006.

——— and S.P. Kapur, (Ed.), *Nuclear Proliferation in South Asia,* New York: Routledge, 2009.

Gannon, Kathy, *I is for Infidel.* New York: Public Affairs Books, 2005.

———, Pakistan's Double Cross, *Newsweek,* September 18, 2008.

Gaubatz, P. David and P. Sperry, *Pakistan's Muslim Mafia: Inside the Secret Underworld That's Conspiring to Islamize America,* Los Angeles: WND Books, 2009.

Gerdes, Louise (Ed.), *Cyber Crime,* Detroit: Dale Carnegie Learning, 2009.

Ghosh, Tusar, et al. (Eds.), *Science and Technology of Terrorism and Counterterrorism*, New York: Marcel Dekker, Inc, 2002.

Glasstone, Samuel and Philip Dolan, *The Effects of Nuclear Weapons (Third Edition)*, U.S. Government Printing Office, 1977.

Gleave, Robert and E. Kermeli (Ed.), *Islamic Law*, London: I.B. Tauris, 2001.

Gul, Imtiaz, *The Most Dangerous Place: Pakistan's Lawless Frontier*, New York: Viking, 2010.

Gunaratna, Rohan, *Inside Al Qaeda,* New York: CUP, 2002.

Gupta, Dipak, *Who Are the Terrorists?* New York: Chelsea House, 2006.

Haass, Richard, *War of Necessity—War of Choice*, New York: Simon & Schuster, 2009.

Habeck, Mary, *Knowing the Enemy*, New Haven, CT: YUP, 2006.

Habibullah, Wajahat, *My Kashmir,* Washington, D.C.: United States Institute of Peace, 2008.

Hammes, Thomas, *The Sling and the Stone,* St. Paul: Zenith Press, 2004.

Hanson, Stephanie, Al-Shabaab, *Backgrounder,* Council on Foreign Relations, February 27, 2009.

Haqqani, Husain, *Pakistan, Between Mosque and Military,* Washington, D.C., Carnegie Endowment for International Peace, 2005.

——, Islam's Medieval Outpost, *Foreign Policy,* 2002.

——, Resolving America's Islamist Dilemma: New York, The Century Foundation, 2002.

Hardy, Justine, *In the Valley of Mist, Kashmir,* New York: Free Press, 2007.

Harrison, Selig, "Pakistan's Ethnic Fault Line," *Washington Post*, May 11, 2009.

——, *Pakistan: The State of the Union*, Special Report, Washington D.C. Center for International Policy, April, 2009.

Hartz, Paula, *Religion and Education*, Farmington Hills, MI: GHP, 2002.

Haugen, David, S. Musser and K. Lovelace (Ed.), *Islam,* Farmington Hills, MI: GHP, 2009.

Hazleton, Lesley, *After the Prophet,* New York: Doubleday, 2009.

Head, Tom (Ed.), *Religion and Education*, Farmington Hills, MI: GHP, 2005.

Heck, Paul L., "Jihad Revisited," *Journal of Religious Ethics* 32, no. 1: 95–128, 2004.

Hefner, Robert, Introduction: Islamism and U.S. Policy in South and Southeast Asia, NBR—The National Bureau of Asian Research Analysis, vol. 19, #4, August 2008.

Herman, Arthur, *Gandhi and Churchill,* New York: Bantam Books, Random House, 2008.

——, *War Without End: The Rise of Islamist Terrorism and Global Response*, New York, Routledge, 2002.

Hersh, Seymour, Defending the Arsenal, *The New Yorker*, November 16, 2009.

Hiro, Dilip, *Inside Central* Asia, New York: Overlook Duckworth, 2009.

Hodson, H. V, *Great Divide; Britain–India–Pakistan.* New York: OUP/ Athenaeum New York, 1971.

Hoffman, Bruce, The Myth of Grass-Roots Terrorism, *Foreign Affairs,* May/ June, pp. 133–139, 2008.

———, The Use of the Internet By Islamic Extremists, CT-262-1, Rand Report, presented to the House Permanent Select Committee on Intelligence, May 4, 2004.

———, *Inside Terrorism,* New York: CUP, 2006.

———, The Logic of Suicide Terrorism, *Atlantic Monthly,* June 2003.

———, *The Holy Terror,* Rand Report, Santa Monica: Rand Report, 1993.

Horowitz, David, *Unholy Alliance,* Washington, D.C.: Regnery Publishing, Inc., 2004.

———, *Left Illusions*, Dallas, Texas: Spence Publishing, 2003.

Hourani, Albert, *A History of the Arab Peoples*, Cambridge, MA: HUP, 1991.

Huntington, Samuel, *The Clash of Civilizations*, New York: Simon & Schuster, 1997.

Ibrahim, Raymond, *The Al Qaeda Reader*, New York: Doubleday, 2007.

Innes, Brian, *International Terrorism*, Broomall, PA: Mason Crest Publishers, 2003.

Israeli, Raphael, *The Spread of Islamikaze Terrorism in Europe,* Portland, OR Vallentine Mitchell, 2008.

Jalal, Ayesha, Transcript before the United States Commission on International Religious Freedom, March 17, 2009, Washington, D.C.: Federal News Service, 2009.

———, *Partisans of Allah*, Cambridge, MA: HUP, 2008.

———, *The Sole Spokesman–Jinnah,* New York: Cambridge University Press, 1985.

Jamal, Arif, *Shadow War,* Brooklyn, NY: Melville House, 2009.

Jansen, Johannes J.G., *The Dual Nature of Islamic Fundamentalism.* Ithaca, NY: Cornell University Press, 1997.

Jones, Seth G., "South Asia's Taliban Problem," *New York Times,* April 14, 2009.

———, *In the Graveyard of Empires,* New York: W.W. Norton and Company, 2009.

Jenkins, Brian, Going Jihad, The Fort Hood Slayings and Home-Grown Terrorism, CT-336: Testimony presented before the Senate Homeland Security and Governmental Affairs Committee, November 19, 2009.

Jenkins, B., J. Gilmore, and G. Hart, *Will Terrorists Go Nuclear?* Amherst, NY: Prometheus Books, 2008.

——, Countering Al Qaeda, *Rand Report,* Santa Monica: Rand Report, 2002.

Johnson, Paul, Relentlessly and Thoroughly, *National Review,* October 15, 2001.

——, "The Biggest Threat We Face," *National Review,* August 24, 2006.

Jones, Seth G., "South Asia's Taliban Problem," *New York Times,* April 14, 2009.

——, *In the Graveyard of Empires,* New York: W.W. Norton and Company, 2009.

Juergensmeyer, Mark, *Terror in the Mind of God: The Global Rise of Religious Violence*, Berkley CA: University of California Press, 2003.

Kagan, R., *The Return of History and the End of Dreams*, New York, Alfred A. Knopf, 2008.

Kaplan, Robert, Pakistan's Fatal Shore, *The Atlantic,* May 2009.

Karsh, Efraim, *Islamic Imperialism,* New Haven, CT: YUP, 2006.

Kean, Tomas and Lee Hamilton, Are We Safer Today? *WP,* September 9, 2007.

Kelsay, John, *Arguing the Just War in Islam,* Cambridge: CUP, 2007.

Kepel, Gilles, *Jihad: The Trail of Political Islam,* Cambridge, MA: HUP, 2002.

——, *The War for Muslim Minds*, Cambridge, MA: HUP, 2004.

Kepel, Gilles and J.P. Milelli (Ed.), *Al Qaeda in its Own Words*, Translated by Pascale Ghazale, Cambridge, MA: HUP, 2008.

Kessler, Ronald, *The Terrorist Watch*, New York: Crown Publishing, 2007.

Khan, Yasmin, *The Great Partition,* New Haven, CT: YUP, 2007.

Khan, Wali, *Facts are Facts, The Untold Story of India's Partition,* Awami National Party, 2004.

Khosrokhavar, Farhad, *Inside Jihadism: Understanding Jihadi Movements Worldwide,* Boulder, CO: Paradigm Publishers, 2009.

Kilcullen, David, *The Accidental Guerrilla,* New York: OUP, 2009.

Kissinger, Henry, "America needs an Afghan strategy, not an alibi," *WP,* June 25, 2010.

Klein, Joseph, *Surrendering to Islam,* FrontPageMagazine.com, November 14, 2007.

Kraemer, Joel, *Maimonides, The Life and World of One of Civilization's Greatest Minds,* New York: Doubleday, 2008.

Kramer, Franklin, Stuart Starr and Larry Wentz (Eds.), *Cyberpower and National Security*, Washington, D.C.: Potomac Books, 2009.

Kronenwetter, Michael, *Terrorism,* Westport, CT: Greenwood Press, 2004.

Krueger, Alan, *What Makes a Terrorist?* Princeton, NJ: Princeton University Press, 2007.

Kung, Hans, *Islam: Past, Present and Future*, Oxford, UK: Oneworld, 2007.

Kux, Dennis, *Pakistan: Flawed not Failed State*, New York: Foreign Policy Association, No. 322, Summer 2001.

Langman, Lauren and Douglas Morris, Islamic *Terrorism: From Retrenchment to Ressentiment and Beyond, in Essential Readings in Political Terrorism*, Harvey Kushner Ed. New York: Gordian Knot Press (University of Nebraska) 2002.

——, Richard Altschuler (Ed.), New York: Gordian Knot Books, 2002.

Langwith, Jacqueline, *Bioterrorism*, Farmington Hills, MI: GHP, 2008.

Lapidus, Ira, Conversation with Ira Lapidus, *Islamic Societies*, January 14, 2003.

——, *A History of Islamic Studies*, Cambridge, UK, Cambridge University Press, 2002.

Laqueur, Walter, *The Changing Face of Anti-Semitism*, New York: OUP, 2006.

——, *No End to Terror*, New York: Continuum, 2003.

Levy, Adrian and Catherine Scott-Clark, *Deception: Pakistan, the United States, and the Secret Trade in Nuclear Weapons*, New York: Walker, 2007.

Levy, Bernard-Henri, *Left in Dark Times*, New York: Random House, 2008.

——, *Who Killed Daniel Pearl?* Hoboken, NJ: Melville House, 2003

Lewis, Bernard, The Arab World in the Twenty-first Century, *Foreign Affairs*, March/April 2009.

——, *From Babel to Dragomans*, New York: OUP, 2004.

——, *The Crisis of Islam*, New York: Random House, 2004.

——, *Islam in History*, Chicago: OPEN Court, 2001.

——, "License to Kill: Usama bin Ladin's Declaration of Jihad," *Foreign Affairs*, November/December 1998.

——, *Islam and the West*, New York: OUP, 1993.

——, *The Political Language of Islam*, Chicago, IL: University of Chicago Press, 1988.

Lewis, Bernard and Buntzie Churchill, *Islam: the religion and the people*, Upper Saddle River, NJ: Wharton Publishing, 2009.

Lewis, David, *God's Crucible*, New York: W.W. Norton, 2008.

Lewis, Franklin, *Rumi, Past and Present, East and West*, Oxford, UK: Oneworld, 2003.

Lia, Brynjar, *Architect of Global Jihad*, New York: CUP/Hurst 2007.

Lieberman, Joseph, Who's the Enemy in the War on Terror? *WSJ*, June 15, 2010.

Lieven, Anatol, The Pressure on Pakistan, *Foreign Affairs,* January/February 2002.

Lilla, Mark, *The Stillborn God.* New York: Knopf, 2007.

Lincoln, Bruce, *Holy Terrors Talking about Religion after September 11,* Chicago, IL: The University of Chicago Press, 2003.

Logan, Michael (Ed.), *Weapons of Mass Destruction,* Farmington Hill, MI: GHP, 2006.

Luce, Edward, *In Spite of the Gods—The Rise of Modern India*, New York: Anchor Books/Random House, 2007.

Ludeman, Lonnie, *Random Process: Filtering, Estimation, and Detection*, Hoboken, NJ: John Wiley & Sons, 2003.

Luttwak, Edward, MIA in Mumbai, *LAT,* December, 2008.

——, Dead End: Counterinsurgency Warfare as Military Malpractice, *Harper's Magazine,* February 2007.

Mamdani, Mahmood, *Good Muslim, Bad Muslim, America, Cold War, and the Roots of Terror,* New York: Pantheon Books, 2004.

Manji, Irshad, *The Trouble with Islam: A Muslim Call for Reform,* New York: St. Martin's Press, 2004.

Mansfield, Peter, *A History of the Middle East*, England, Penguin Books, 2004.

Margulies, Philip, *The Rise of Islamic Fundamentalism*, Farmington Hills, MI: GHP, 2006.

Markey, Daniel, *AfPak to PakAf*, New York, NY: Council on Foreign Relations, April 2009.

——, *Securing Pakistan's Tribal Belt*, New York, NY: Council on Foreign Relations No. 36, August 2008.

Marston, Daniel, and Carter Malikasian (Ed.), *Counterinsurgency in Modern Warfare.* New York: Osprey Publishing Ltd./Random House, 2008.

Martin, Gus, *Essentials of Terrorism*, Thousand Oaks, CA: Sage Publication, 2008.

——, *Understanding Terrorism*, Thousand Oaks, CA: Sage Publication, 2006.

McCarthy, Andrew, *Willful Blindness: A Memoir of the Jihad*, New York: Encounter Books, 2008.

Mearsheimer, John, *The Tragedy of Great Power Politics*, New York: W.W. Norton, 2001.

Miller, Debra A., *Terrorism,* Farmington Hills, MI: Dale Carnegie Learning, 2008.

——, *Espionage and Intelligence,* Farmington Hills, MI: GHP, 2007å.

Miller, John, Jr., *The Unmaking of Americans,* New York: The Free Press, 1998.

Moghadam, Assaf, *The Roots of Terrorism*, New York: Chelsea House, 2006.

Mohanty, Nirode, Secularism and Minorities, *India Post*, May 21, 1999.

——, Babur, Baburnama and Babri Masjid, *India Post*, June 1998.

——, An Unprecedented Struggle to Achieve Liberty, *News India-Times*, New York, August 15, 1997.

——, Gandhi, Guest Column, *News India- Times*, NY, February 7, 1997.

——, UN Passage of Comprehensive Test Ban Treaty, Op-Ed, *News India-Times*, New York, 1996.

——, *Signal Processing*, New York: Van Nostrand Reinhold, 1987.

——, *Random Process*, New York: Van Nostrand Reinhold, 1986.

——, *Space Communication and Nuclear Scintillation*, New York: Van Nostrand Reinhold, 1991.

——, "A Memorable Excursion: A Review of In Light of India by Octavia Paz," San Francisco, *India Currents*, June 1998.

Moisi, Dominique, *The Geopolitics of Emotion—How a Culture of Fears, Humiliation, and Hope is Reshaping the World*, New York: Doubleday, 2009.

Mueller, John, *Overblown*, New York: Free Press, 2006.

Murawiec, Laurent, *The Mind of Jihad*, New York: Cambridge University Press, 2008.

Muthuswamy, Moorthy, *Defeating Political Islam*, Amherst, NY: Prometheus, 2009.

Naipaul, V.S, *Beyond Belief*, New York, Random House, 1998.

——, *India, A Million Mutinies Now*, New York: Viking, Penguin, 1991.

——, *Among The Believers*, New York: Vintage Books/Random House, 1982.

Nance, Malcome, *An End to Al-Qaeda: Destroying Bin Laden's Jihad and Restoring America's Honor*, St. Marten Press, New York, NY, 2010.

Napoleoni, Loretta, *Modern Jihad*, London/Sterling, Virginia: Pluto Press, 2003.

——, Terror Incorporated, New York: Seven Stories Press, 2005.

Nasiri, Omar, *Inside the Jihad*, New York: Basic Books, 2006.

Nasr, Vali, "Sects and Violence," *NYT*, Opinion, February 23, 2006.

National Geographic, "Islam's Fault Line," September 2007.

Naumkin, Vitaly, *Radical Islam in Central Asia, Between Pen and Rifle*, Lanham, MD: Rowman & Littlefield Publishers, Inc. NY, 2005.

Nawaz, Shuja, *Crossed Swords*, New York: OUP, 2008.

Newsweek International, "Pakistan: The Most Dangerous?" October 29, 2007.

Nye, Joseph S. Jr., *The Paradox of American Power*, Oxford: OUP, 2002.

Orens, Geoffrey (Ed.), *The Muslim World*, New York: The H.W. Wilson Company, 2003.

Pagden, Anthony, *Worlds at War*, New York, NY: Random House, 2008.

Pape, Robert, *Dying to Win, The Strategic Logic of Suicide,* New York, Random House, 2005.

Parthasarathy, G., Great Game Unfolds, *The Pioneer,* June 25, 2010.

Patai, Raphae, *The Arab Mind,* New York, NY: Hatherleigh Press, 2002.

Paz, Octavio, *In Light of India*, New York, NY: Harcourt Brace & Co., 1995.

Pelton, Robert, *Licensed to Kill: Hired Guns in the War on Terror*, New York: Three Rivers Press, 2006.

Perliger, Arie, *Middle Eastern Terrorism*, New York, NY: Chelsea House, 2006.

Pfaff, William, *The Irony of Manifest Destiny*, New York: Walker & Company, 2010.

Phares, Walid, *Future of Jihad,* New York, NY: Palgrave/Macmillan, 2005.

Phillips, Melanie, *Londonistan,* New York: Encounter Books, 2006.

Pipes, Daniel, *Militant Islam Reaches America*, New York, W.W. Norton & Company, 2002.

Podhoretz, Norman, *World War IV, The Long Struggle Against Islamofascism.* New York: Vintage Books, 2008.

Posner, Richard, *Countering Terrorism,* Lanham, MD: Rowman & Littlefield Inc., 2007.

Post, Jerrold, *The Mind of Terrorists*, New York: Palgrave Macmillan, 2007.

Power, Jonathan, "India is key to Pak, Afghan stability," *Arab News,* February 26, 2009.

Quineley, Kevin and D. Schmidt, *Business at Risk*, Cincinnati, Ohio: The National Underwriter Company, 2002.

Radhakrishnan, Sarvepalli, *The Principal Upanishads,* New Delhi: *INDUS,* An Imprint of Harper Collins, 1995.

—— and Charles Moore (Ed.), *Indian Philosophy*, Princeton, NJ: Princeton University Press, 1957.

Radu, Michael, *Europe's Ghost*, New York: Encounter Books, 2009.

Rahman, Fazlur, *Islam,* Chicago, IL: The University of Chicago Press, 1979.

——, *Islam and Modernity: Transformation and Intellectual Tradition*, Chicago: The University of Chicago Press, 1982.

——, *Revival and Reform in Islam,* Oxford, UK: Oneworld Books, 2000.

Ramadan, Tariq, *In the Footsteps of the Prophet: Lessons from the Life of Muhammad,* New York: OUP, 2007.

———, Europe's Islam Question, *The Guardian,* December 4, 2004.

Rashid, Ahmed, *Descent into Chaos,* New York. Viking, Penguin Books, 2008.

———, *Jihad, The Rise of Militant Islam,* New Haven, CT: YUP, 2002.

———, *Taliban: Militant Islam,* New Haven, CT: YUP, 2001.

Reich, Walter, Using the Holocaust to Attack the Jews, *WP,* February 1, 2009.

———, *Origins of Terror: Psychologies, Ideologies, Theologies, Status of Mind,* Washington, D.C.: The Woodrow Wilson Press, 1998.

Reilly, Robert, *The Closing of the Muslim Mind,* Wilmington, DE: ISI books, 2010.

Rhodes, Richard, *Arsenals of Folly,* New York Knopf/ Random House, 2007.

Richardson, Louise, *What Terrorists Want,* New York: Random House, 2006.

Riedel, Bruce, Pakistan and the Bomb, *WSJ,* May 30, 2009.

———, *The Search for Al Qaeda,* Washington, D.C.: Brookings Institution Press, 2008.

———, AQ Strikes Back, *Foreign Affairs,* May/June 2007.

Rinehart, James, *Apocalyptic Faith and Political Violence,* New York: Palgrave, 2006.

Roberts, J.M., *History of the World,* New York: OUP, 1993.

Robinson, Francis (Ed.), *The Cambridge Illustrated History of the Islamic World,* London: Cambridge University Press, 1996.

Roy, Olivier, *Secularism Confronts Islam,* translated by George Holoch Jr., New York: CUP, 2007.

———, *Globalized Islam, The Search for a New Ummah,* New York: CUP, 2004.

———, *Failure of Political Islam,* Cambridge, MA: HUP, 1996.

Rubin, Barnett and Ahmed Rashid, "Pakistan, Afghanistan and the West," *Foreign Affairs,* November/ December 2008.

Russell, Bertrand, *The Problems of Philosophy,* New York: Home University Library/OUP, 1912.

Ruthven, Malise, *A Fury for God, The Islamist Attack on America,* London: Granta Books, 2002.

———, *Islam in the World,* New York, OUP, 1984.

Sageman, Marc, *Leaderless Jihad—Terror Network in the Twenty-first Century,* Philadelphia, PA: University of Pennsylvania Press, 2008.

Said, Edward, The Last Interview by Peter Bradshaw, *The Guardian,* June 11, 2004.

———, *From Oslo to Iraq and the Road Map*, Amherst, NY: Pantheon Books, 2004.

———, War on Terrorism, *Observer,* September 16, 2001.

———, *Orientalism,* New York: Vintage/Anchor Books, 1979.

Santhanam, K. et al., *Jihadist in Jammu and Kashmir*, Thousand Oaks, CA: Sage Publications, 2003.

Sarila, Narendra, *The Shadow of Great Game*, New York: Carroll & Graf Publishers, 2006.

Schell, Jonathan, *The Unconquerable World*, New York: Metropolitan Books/ Henry Holt, 2003.

Scheuer, Michael, *Marching Toward Hell, America and Islam after Iraq*, New York: Free Press/Simon & Schuster, Inc 2008.

Schlesinger, Arthur M., Jr., *The Disuniting of America*: *Reflection on a Multicultural Society*, Knoxville, TN: Whittle Books, 1991.

Schofield, Victoria, *Kashmir in the Crossfire*, London: I.B. Tauris Publishers, 1996.

Schultheis, Rob, *Hunting Osama bin Laden,* New York: Skyhorse Publishing, Inc. 2008.

Schultz, Jr., Richard and Andrea Dew, *Insurgents, Terrorists and Militias,* New York: CUP, 2006.

Sciutto, Jim, *Against Us: The New Face of America's Enemies in the Muslim World*, New York: Random House, 2008.

Scott, Peter, *The Road to 9/11,* Berkley, CA: University of California Press, 2007.

Segal, Ronald, *Islam's Black Slaves*, New York: Farrar, Straus & Giroux, 2001.

Selbourne, David, *The Losing Battle with Islam,* Amherst, NY: Prometheus Books, 2005.

Sen, Amartaya, *The Argumentative Indian*, New York: Farrar, Straus and Giroux, 2005.

Shapiro, Jeremy and Benedict Suzan, "The French Experience of Counterterrorism," *Survival,* Vol. 45. No, 1, The International Institute for Strategic Studies, Spring 2003.

Sheehan, Michael, *Crush The Cell,* New York: Crown Publishers, 2008.

Silvers, Robert and Barbara Epstein (Ed.), *Striking Terror,* New York: Review Books, 2002.

Sisson, Richard and Leo Rose, *War and Secession, Pakistan, India and the Creation of Bangladesh*, Berkley, CA: University of California, 1990.

Spencer, Robert, *Stealth Jihad*, Washington, D.C.: Regnery Publishing, 2008.

———, *The Truth About Muhammad,* Washington, D.C.: Regnery Publishing, 2006.

———, *Islam Unveiled*, San Francisco, CA: Encounter Books, 2002.

Springer, David, J. Regens, and D. Edger, *Islamic Radicalism and Global Jihad*, Washington, D.C.: Georgetown University Press, 2009.

Spurlock, M., *Where In The World Is Osama bin Laden*, New York: Random House, 2008.

Steffen, Lloyd, *Holy War, Just War: Exploring the Moral Meaning of Religious Violence*, Lanham, MD: Rowman & Littlefield Publishers, 2007.

Stern, Jessica, Mind Over Martyr, *Foreign Affairs,* January/February, 2010.

———, "Five Myths about Terrorists—Who Becomes Terrorists," *WP,* January 1, 2010.

———, *Terror in the Name of God,* New York: Harper Collins, 2003.

———, *The Ultimate Terrorists*, Cambridge, MA: HUP, 1999.

Steven, G. and R. Gunaratna, *Counterterrorism*, Santa Barbara, CA: ABC-CLIO, Inc., 2004.

Steyn, Mark, *America Alone,* Washington, D.C.: Regnery Publishing, Inc, 2008.

———, The *One Percent Doctrine*, New York: Simon & Schuster, 2006.

Suskind, Ron, *The Way of the World*, New York: Harper Collins Publishers, 2008.

Swami, Praveen, *India, Pakistan and The Secret Jihad*, New York: Routledge, 2007.

Taheri, Amir, The Sunni–Shiite Network, *WSJ,* March 29, 2008.

Taylor, Charles, *Secular Age*, Cambridge, MA: The Belknap Press of HUP Cambridge, 2007.

Telhami, Shibley, "Why Suicide Terrorism Takes Root," *NYT,* April 14, 2002.

Tellis, Ashley, Pakistan's Record on Terrorism: Conflicted Goals, Compromised Performance, *The Washington Quarterly,* Spring 2008.

———, U.S.-India Atomic Energy Cooperation: Strategic and Nonproliferation Implications, Senior Associate, Carnegie Endowment for International Peace to the Senate Foreign Relations Committee, April 26, 2006.

Tenet, George, *At the Center of the Storm;* New York: Harper Collins Publishers, 2007.

Thakur, Ramesh and Oddny Wiggin (Ed.), *South Asia in the World*, United Nations University Press, New York, 2004.

Thiessen, Marc, *Courting Disaster,* Washington, D.C.: Regnery Publishing, 2010.

Tibi, Bassam, *The Challenge of Fundamentalism: Political Islam and the New World Order, New York:* Routledge, New York, 2008.

——, *Islam's Predicament with Cultural Modernity,* New York: Routledge, 2009.

Torr, James, *Weapons of Mass Destruction,* Farmington Hills, MI: GHP, 2005.

Toynbee, Arnold, *War and Civilization,* New York, OUP, 1950.

Treverton, G., *Intelligence for an Age of Terror,* New York: Cambridge University Press, 2009.

Tucker, David, "Terrorism, Networks, Strategy: Why the Conventional Wisdom is Wrong," *Homeland Security Affairs,* Vol. IV, No. 2, June 2008.

Tunzelmann, Alex, *Indian Summer, The Secret History of the End of An Empire,* New York: Henry Holt and Company, 2007.

U.S. Muslim Engagement Project, *A New Direction for U.S. Relations with The Muslim World, 2nd Printing,* Washington, D.C., February 2009.

USA TODAY, "The harder part of Af-Pak," March 30, 2009.

Vaughan, Bruce, Islamist Extremism in Bangladesh, CRS Report for Congress, Order Code RS22591, January 31, 2007.

Verghese, B.G., *A J&K Primer,* New Delhi: India Research Press, Center for Policy Research, 2007.

Vertigans, Stephen, *Militant Islam, Sociology of characteristics, causes and consequences,* London: Routledge, 2009.

Verton, Dan, *Black Ice, The Invisible Threat of Cyber-Terrorism, New York,* McGraw-Hill/Osborne, 2003.

Vidino, Lorenzo, *Al Qaeda in Europe,* Amherst, NY: Prometheus Books, 2006.

Vriens, Lauren, *Governing Under Sharia,* Council on Foreign Relations, March 23, 2009.

Warlad, Jean and Pravin Varaiya, *High Performance Communication Networks,* New York: Morgan Kaufman Publishers, 2000.

Warraq, Ibn, *Why I am not a Muslim,* Amherst, NY: Prometheus Books, 2003.

——, *What the Quran Really Says*, Amherst, NY: Prometheus Books, 2002.

——, (Ed.), *The Quest of the Historical Muhammad*, Amherst, Prometheus Books, 2000.

Weaver, Mary., *Pakistan: In the Shadow of Jihad and Afghanistan,* New York, Farrar, Straus, and Giroux, 2002.

Weinberg, Leonard and W. Eubank, *What is Terrorism?* New York: Chelsea House, 2006.

Weimann, Gabriel, *Terror in the Internet, The New Arena, the New Challenges,* Washington, D.C.: United State Institute of Peace Press, 2006.

Weismann, Steve and H. Krosney, *The Islamic Bomb,* New York: Random House, 1982.

Wheatcroft, Andrew, *Infidels,* New York: Random House, 2004.

Whittaker, David, *Terrorism,* Upper Saddle River, NJ: Longman, 2007.

Wiener, Norbert, *Cybernetics,* Cambridge, MA: MIT Press, 1961.

Wikipedia, The Free Encyclopedia.

Wiktorowicz, Quintan, (Ed.), *Islamic Activism, A Social Movement Theory Approach,* Bloomington: Indiana University Press, 2004.

Wilson, Mike, *Terrorism,* Farmington Hills, GHU, 2007.

Wolpert, Stanley, *A New History of India*, 7th edition, New York, OUP, 2004.

Woodward, Bob, *Obama's Wars*, New York: Simon & Schuster, 2010.

———, *Plan of Attack*, New York: Simon and Schuster, 2004.

———, *Bush at War*, New York: Simon and Schuster, 2002.

Wright, Lawrence, The Rebellion Within, *The New Yorker,* June 2, 2008.

———, *The Looming Tower*, New York: Alfred A. Knopf /Random House, 2006.

Wright, Robin, "Who Created Major Hasan?" *NYT,* November 21, 2009.

———, *Dreams and Shadows*, New York: The Penguin Press, 2008.

———, *Sacred Rage: The Wrath of Militant Islam*, New York: Simon and Schuster, 2001.

Young, Mitchell, *Culture Wars (Opposing Viewpoints),* Farmington Hills, MI: GHP, 2008.

———, *Terrorist Leaders*, Farmington Hills, MI: GHP, 2005.

Zaeef, Abdul, *My Life with the Taliban*, New York, NY: CUP, 2010.

Zakaria, Fareed, Learning to Live with Radical Islam, *Newsweek*, February 28, 2009.

———, *The Post-American World,* New York: W.W Norton & Company, 2008.

Zeskind, Leonard, *Blood and Politics,* New York: Farrar, Straus & Giroux, 2009.

Zissis, Carin, Council on Foreign Relations, Terror Groups in India, *Washington Post ,* December 1, 2008.

Index

Throughout this index, an *f* indicates a figure and *t* indicates a table on that page.

About the Author

Nirode Mohanty has taught and consulted on terrorism, surveillance; secure, satellite, and survival communications; GPS navigation, network architecture, nuclear scintillation and signal processing over forty years. He has taught communications systems, information theory, coding, computer networks, satellite communications, sensor fusion, anti-jam communications, wireless technology, radar, and signal processing at State University of New York, Buffalo, the University of California, Riverside, and California State University, Long Beach. Dr. Mohanty has directed research at various aerospace companies as a senior scientist, manager, and vice president and as a consultant. He has received the Excellence in Creativity Award from Rockwell International and various commendations. For his contribution to secure and survival communications systems, he has been elected an IEEE Fellow and is serving as an Associate Editor of the *International Journal on Telecommunication and Networking*. He has published three books: *Random Signals Estimation and Identifiation: Analysis and Applications*, *Signal Processing: Signals, Filtering and Detection*, and *Space Communications and Nuclear Scintillations*, published by Van Nostrand Reinhold, New York. He has received an M.S., M.S.E.E., and Ph.D. in Electrical Engineering from the University of Southern California.